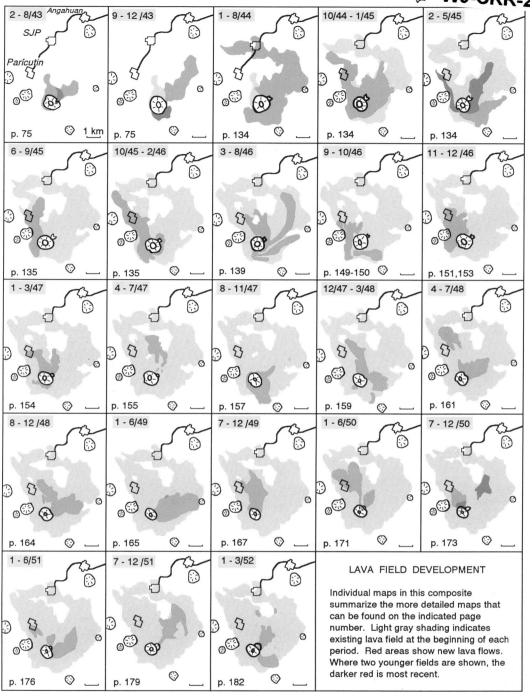

2 - 8/43 *Angahuan* *SJP* *Paricutin* p. 75	9 - 12 /43 p. 75	1 - 8/44 p. 134	10/44 - 1/45 p. 134	2 - 5/45 p. 134
6 - 9/45 p. 135	10/45 - 2/46 p. 135	3 - 8/46 p. 139	9 - 10/46 p. 149-150	11 - 12 /46 p. 151,153
1 - 3/47 p. 154	4 - 7/47 p. 155	8 - 11/47 p. 157	12/47 - 3/48 p. 159	4 - 7/48 p. 161
8 - 12 /48 p. 164	1 - 6/49 p. 165	7 - 12 /49 p. 167	1 - 6/50 p. 171	7 - 12 /50 p. 173
1 - 6/51 p. 176	7 - 12 /51 p. 179	1 - 3/52 p. 182		

1 km

LAVA FIELD DEVELOPMENT

Individual maps in this composite
summarize the more detailed maps that
can be found on the indicated page
number. Light gray shading indicates
existing lava field at the beginning of each
period. Red areas show new lava flows.
Where two younger fields are shown, the
darker red is most recent.

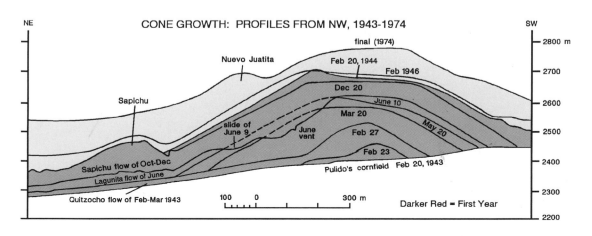

CONE GROWTH: PROFILES FROM NW, 1943-1974

NE   SW

final (1974)
Nuevo Juatita
Feb 20, 1944
Feb 1946
Dec 20
June 10
Sapichu
Mar 20
slide of June 9
June vent
Feb 27
May 20
Feb 23
Sapichu flow of Oct-Dec
Pulido's cornfield Feb 20, 1943
Lagunita flow of June
Quitzocho flow of Feb-Mar 1943

100   0   300 m

Darker Red = First Year

2800 m
2700
2600
2500
2400
2300
2200

PARÍCUTIN

PARÍCUTIN

The Volcano Born in a Mexican Cornfield

James F. Luhr and Tom Simkin, editors

with the collaboration of Margaret Cuasay

GEOSCIENCE PRESS, INC.
Phoenix, Arizona

Published in association with the Smithsonian Institution

Copyright © 1993 by the Smithsonian Institution
Library of Congress Catalog Card number 93-077812

No part of this book may be reproduced by any mechanical, photographic, or electronic process, or in the form of a phonographic
recording, nor may it be stored in a retrieval system, transmitted,
or otherwise copied for public or private use, without written permission from the publisher.

No claim is made for original government source material.

First published by Geoscience Press in 1993.

Publisher's Cataloging in Publication
(Prepared by Quality Books, Inc.)

Luhr, James F.
    Paricutin: the volcano born in a Mexican cornfield/James F.
Luhr, Tom Simkin.
    p. cm.
    ISBN 0-945005-11-3 (pbk.)
    ISBN 0-945005-14-8 (hard.)

    1. Paricutin (Volcano) 2. Volcanoes—Mexico.   I. Simkin, Tom.
II. Title.
QE523.P37L84 1993   551.2'1'0972
                           QBI93-656

Published by Geoscience Press
12629 N. Tatum Boulevard
Suite 201
Phoenix, Arizona 85032
(602) 953-2330

Manufactured in the United States of America

Contents

He who sees things grow from the beginning
will have the best view of them

Aristotle

I. Preface

Volcanology, more than most sciences, depends upon history. The range of volcanic activity, both in type and in magnitude, is huge, and volcano lifetimes are normally long, making the documented eruptions of the past particularly important in understanding the present and preparing for the future. Post-mortem investigations of an eruption's products can provide much valuable data, but the historical record is essential for understanding rates, sequences, interplay of processes, and the role of events that leave little or no trace of their passing.

New volcanoes are distinctly rare in the short history of volcanology, and the quality of Parícutin's documentation adds enormously to its unique value. As is common for well-studied events, though, many investigations were not completed until decades after the close of the eruption, and their publications are both widely scattered and often hard to obtain. Therefore we set out to gather these studies together into a single, cross-referenced and indexed volume to commemorate the 50th anniversary of this important event.

We felt a particular attraction to this project, because the Smithsonian's National Museum of Natural History has a special connection to Parícutin. That connection began with William Foshag, curator of mineralogy, who was in México (studying ore deposits) when the new volcano was born. He and his Mexican colleague Jenaro González-Reyna arrived at the volcano about 1 month later and, in what was an abrupt career change for both, devoted themselves to documenting the first 2½ years of its life. One of their greatest contributions to understanding the eruption was interviewing all important eye-witnesses to the volcano's earliest hours. These were first published in the Smithsonian Annual Report for 1946 and reprinted 10 years later in their major work (see p. 38-43 and 47-130). That article completed the classic 4-paper set on the Parícutin eruption, published as U.S. Geological Survey Bulletin 965.

Foshag was an avid photographer. During Parícutin's early years he took 16-mm color motion pictures of the eruption as well as many hundreds of still photographs. He also obtained copies of Parícutin photographs from many others and built what is probably the world's most extensive collection covering the early Parícutin years. These photographs, which number several thousand, are part of the Foshag Collections of the Smithsonian Archives. In 1951, Foshag took 151 of the finest Parícutin photographs in his collection and placed them, along with their negatives, in the U.S. National Archives. The ready availability of these photographic resources was an important reason for undertaking this book.

Another connecting link is that Foshag's detailed reporting on Parícutin can be viewed as a forerunner of later and continuing efforts at the National Museum of Natural History to report on active volcanism around the world. Such reporting has been conducted at the Smithsonian for more than 25 years. It began in 1968 with establishment of the Center for Short-Lived Phenomena. In 1975 the Center was succeeded by the Scientific Event Alert Network, which since 1990, has been known as the Global Volcanism Network. Each month we publish the *Global Volcanism Network Bulletin*, which includes 20-40 separate reports on active volcanoes incorporating information from a world-wide network of volcano watchers. The *Bulletin* is distributed to this network of about 1,500 correspondents, and others obtain the *Bulletin* by subscription through the American Geophysical Union. Thousands more are reached through summary reports prepared separately each month for scientific journals and electronic bulletin boards.

We were further encouraged to undertake this project by the favorable response to another volcano anniversary book, *Krakatau 1883: The Volcanic Eruption and Its Effects*, written by Simkin and our colleague Richard Fiske in the great eruption's centennial year.

Other significant Parícutin resources at the Smithsonian that further a special connection to the eruption are our collections of motion pictures and rock specimens. Building on the foundation of Foshag's 16-mm film, we have added important contributions from Frederick Pough and other sources to assemble a collection of more than 3 hours of high-quality color eruption footage. The museum has 408 specimens of volcanic rocks, granitic xenoliths, and fumarolic minerals from all stages of the Parícutin eruption. These include not only the extensive collections of Foshag, but also those of Ray Wilcox (U.S.G.S), who assembled the classic petrologic suite for Parícutin (see p. 324-346).

New Contributions

Although the book mainly consists of reprintings from published works on Parícutin, it contains many new elements as well. We have written brief biographies for key scientists, new introductory sections on the *Geological Setting* (p. 29-30, 243-245), and much linking text. Other new features are:

- The *Chronology of Events* on p. 10-28 provides a handy reference and time index for the years 1941-65, keyed to appropriate text passages, photos, and drawings.

- Three different air photographs of the Parícutin area prior to the eruption are given in Figs. 11-13, along with a pre-eruption topographic map of the immediate vent area.

- Many previously unpublished photographs are included, both in the 8 color plates and throughout the text. Among the black-and-white photographs are many portraits of people important to the Parícutin story.

- Mary Lee and Sid Nolan have written an epilogue to her 1979 study, updating that fascinating treatment of the eruption's human impact.

- As a means of demonstrating the "aging" of a cinder cone and associated lava field over time, we present in Figs. 150-158 stereographic air-photo pairs for Parícutin, Jorullo (1759-1774) and five other dated cones ranging over 40,000 years in age. These images convey a wealth of morphological information and repay well the effort required to view them in stereo.

- Lastly, we have assembled both a 342-reference bibliography of Parícutin literature and an 11-page index of subjects and names helping to tie together the many elements of this book.

Conventions

Different styles and sizes of type are used to distinguish different varieties of text. Except for this *Preface* and the first three chapters of the *Introduction*, all text written by us is designated by italicized 10-point News Serif typeface. Biographical treatments of reprinted authors are given as italicized 10-point text surrounded by a box. Starting on p. 31, reprinted text appears in the upright 10-point News Serif typeface used here. Reprinted quotations are set in smaller type (9 point) with an uneven right margin. We have attempted to preserve the original words in most reprinted articles, but have made minor changes for clarity and consistency with usage elsewhere in the book. Brackets identify new words, translations, or short editorial comments.

All units have been converted to metric equivalents, and units have been consistently abbreviated as follows:

$$km = kilometer = 0.621 \; miles$$
$$m = meter = 3.281 \; feet = 1.09 \; yards$$
$$cm = centimeter = 0.394 \; inches$$
$$mm = millimeter = 0.039 \; inches$$
$$kg = kilogram = 2.2 \; pounds$$
$$g = gram = 0.035 \; ounces$$
$$ha = hectare = 0.01 \; km^2 = 2.47 \; acres$$

All numbers followed by units have been converted to numerical form (except where they start a sentence). The four principal compass directions are spelled out, and all intermediate directions (NE, SSW) are abbreviated.

Ellipsis points (strings of periods) are used to represent material that we have omitted, with three points . . . marking words omitted from within a sentence, and four points indicating that we have omitted the remainder of the sentence . . . . Five points centered on a separate line

. . . . .

indicate that one or more paragraphs have been omitted. Although we have tried to be consistent in the use of ellipsis points, for stylistic reasons we have eliminated them after titles, at the start of a sentence or paragraph, and if the points ran over from one line of our text to the next. Readers who are interested in the exact wording of the reprinted text should consult the original articles.

In an effort to make the book more readable, all original footnotes, references, and editorial comments have been placed in a single section at the back of the book titled *Text Notes*. These notes are referenced by superscripted numbers within the text. Another back section, titled *Notes on Figures, Tables, and Plates*, lists sources and all other information that is not included in the captions.

Original articles about the Parícutin eruption used a variety of spellings for some local features. We have standardized all spellings in this book. Four features had particularly inconsistent spellings; our preferred names, followed by other spellings in parentheses are Sapichu (Zapichu), Canicjuata (Canijuata), Capatzun (Capatzin), and Corucjuata (Corujuata).

All important place names can be located on maps inside the front and back covers and on Fig. 130 (p. 191). To aid in location, geographic names throughout the text are followed by bracketed distance and direction from the new volcano.

Pronunciation Guide

We attempted to find a balance between maintaining authentic Spanish spellings and making the book accessible for non-Spanish speakers. Important Spanish words have been placed in italics, followed by bracketed or endnoted translations. Many of the local geographic names are blends of Tarascan and Spanish words. To non-Spanish speakers some of these names will seem unapproachable. We urge readers, though, to leap this cultural hurdle; to help lower the hurdle, we provide a pronunciation guide to 20 of the most important place names in the book. In Spanish, accented letters mark the emphasized syllable of a word. Thus, the word Parícutin is accented on the second syllable as explained below. For most unaccented words, the emphasis is placed on the second-to-last syllable.

Ahuán (ah-HWAN) is the name of a lava vent at the SSW foot of Parícutin volcano that became active in mid-November 1944.

Angahuan (an-GA-wahn) is an almost pure Tarascan village located 7 km NNE of the new volcano.

Caltzontzin (kahl-TZON-tzin) is the resettlement community for people from Parícutin village, located 5½ km E of Uruapan and 27 km ESE of the volcano.

Canicjuata (kan-ik-HUAT-a), or Cerro de Canicjuata, is an older cinder cone located about 1 km NW of the Parícutin vent. A scientific observatory located about 400 m NE of the base of this older cone was given the name Casita Canicjuata (*casita* means little house).

Cocjarao (coke-har-A-o), or Cerro de Cocjarao, is another older volcanic ridge located about 1 km SW of the new volcano. A triangulation station on Cerro de Cocjarao was referred to as the SW Station.

Cuezeño (koo-e-ZANE-yo) is the name of a field about 1 km NE of the village San Juan Parangaricutiro and 5½ km north of Parícutin volcano. This was the site of the main scientific observatory, called either Cuezeño Station or the Lower Casita.

Cuiyúsuru (koo-ee-YOO-soo-roo) is the name of the field, owned by Dionisio Pulido, in which the new volcano was born.

Itzícuaro (eat-ZEE-kware-o) is the name of the major river that drains the Parícutin region, also called the Itzícuaro Valley. The river flows westward from the north end of the lava field, and feeds into the mighty Río Balsas, which flows to the Pacific.

Jarátiro (har-AH-teer-o), or more commonly Cerro de Jarátiro, is the name of an older volcanic ridge with three prominent craters that lay about 1 km north of the Parícutin vent. The first scientific and tourist observatories were built on Cerro de Jarátiro, but the shelters had to be repeatedly moved as the lavas progressively covered the ridge and filled the craters. All but the highest point was ultimately buried (see Fig. 108).

Jorullo (hoar-OO-yo), which means "paradise" in the Tarascan Indian language, is the only other "new" volcano in the Parícutin area. This cinder cone was born in a ravine in 1759, and its eruption lasted for 15 years. Jorullo is located 81 km SE of Parícutin. See p. 364-371 and Plate 8B.

Michoacán (meech-o-ah-CAN) is the name of the Mexican state in which the new volcano was born.

Miguel Silva (MEE-gell SILL-va) is the name of a resettlement community for people from the villages of Zirosto and San Juan Parangaricutiro. It is located 65 km SE of the new volcano and 40 km SE of Caltzontzin, where the residents of Parícutin village were resettled.

Parícutin (par-EE-koo-teen) was the name of a village located 3 km NW of the new volcano, which was named in its honor. The village was quickly covered with ash and evacuated 4 months after the start of the eruption. The village site was later completely buried by lava.

Quitzocho (keet-ZO-cho) is the name of the field north of Cuiyúsuru field where the volcano was born. The first lava flow to the north of the developing cone was named the Quitzocho flow, and an uplifted ridge to the north of the new cone also bears its name (see Fig. 36).

San Juan Parangaricutiro (sahn wahn par-an-gar-ee-koo-TEER-o) was the name of a village located 4½ km north of the new volcano. Most of the village was buried by lava in 1944.

Sapichu (sah-PEE-chew) is the name of a vent that formed at the NE foot of Parícutin's main cone on October 18, 1943, and was active for 2½ months.

Tancítaro (tahn-SEE-tar-o), or Cerros de Tancítaro, is the name of a large extinct volcano, the highest in the region (3,842 m), whose summit lies 11 km SW of the new volcano. Tancítaro is also the name of a village on its SW flank, and 25 km SW of Parícutin volcano.

Taquí (tah-KEY) is the name of a lava vent at the SW foot of the Parícutin cone that became active in January 1944.

Uruapan (oor-oo-WOP-an) is a major city located 21½ km SE of the new volcano.

Zirosto (zeer-O-stow), a town located 8½ km NW of the new volcano, was severely affected by the eruption. In 1953 a majority of its residents moved to a new settlement, 2 km to the NW, which was named Zirosto Nuevo.

Acknowledgements

It would have been impossible to bring this photographically rich book to the reader at a relatively low price without support from the Seidell Fund, a bequest left to the Smithsonian Institution by Dr. Atherton Seidell upon his death in 1961. Dr. Seidell was a chemist and author of the standard reference work *Seidell's Solubility Tables*. In compiling those tables he gained a great appreciation for the difficulty of finding material that is out of print or otherwise difficult to obtain. His bequest was specifically designed to aid in the reprinting of such materials, by underwriting the publication costs and thereby lowering the price to the reader.

Fifty years is a good vantage point from which to look back at an important event. Major scientific studies have been completed, some historical perspective is possible, and many participants are still available to provide both flavor and insight. We particularly treasure the opportunity to have talked with so many who lived through the experience and its aftermath. Taped and filmed interviews with Jesús Anguiano, Frederick Bullard, Celedonio Gutiérrez-Acosta, Jesús Martínez-Bribiesca, Jesús Saldaña, the late Kenneth Segerstrom, and Ray Wilcox, provided us with a personal perspective on the eruption that we could never have obtained from popular or scientific articles.

For permission to republish copyrighted material we thank: Academic Press, American Geophysical Union, Cambridge University Press, Carnegie Institution of Washington, Defense Intelligence Agency, Ecological Society of America, Elsevier Science Publishers, Geofísica Internacional, Oxford University Press, Pergamon Press Incorporated, Plenum Publishing Corporation, Springer-Verlag, Texas A & M University, University of Chicago Press, University of Michigan Museum of Zoology, University of Texas Press, and individual authors. Credit information is listed together in the back section titled *Credits*.

Many individuals kindly loaned photographs and documents for use in the book or provided advice and encouragement: Jamie Allan, Jorge Aranda-Gómez, Gerardo Aguirre-Díaz, Margaret and the late Richard Barthelemy, Frederick Bullard, Charles Connor, Charles and Madeline Conrad, Winston Crausaz,

Zoltan de Cserna, William Foshag Jr., Luis García-Gutiérrez, Peggy Gennaro, Celedonio Gutiérrez-Acosta, Toshiaki Hasenaka, Karla Huff, Berlinda Kerkhof, Raymond and Elizabeth Krafft, Konrad Krauskopf, Verónica Loera y Chávez, Jesús Martínez-Bribiesca, Alexander McBirney, Tad Nichols, Mary and Sid Nolan, Fernando Ortega-Gutiérrez, Anna María Ortíz-Hernández, Dorothy Palmer, Frederick Pough, Karen Prestegaard, John Rees, Robert Ridky, Jesús Saldaña, Mildred and the late Kenneth Segerstrom, Claus Siebe, Richard Stoiber, Robert Tilling, Paul Wallace, and Ray Wilcox.

Mary and Sid Nolan wrote an epilogue to her 1979 anthropological study, specifically for inclusion in this book (p. 207-214). Izumi Yokoyama generously provided us with an unpublished list of earthquakes in the Parícutin region during the 9-year eruption period. Many of these events are incorporated into the *Chronology of Events* on p. 10-28. Jorge Aranda-Gómez and Gerardo Aguirre-Díaz accompanied Luhr to the Parícutin area on several occasions, providing essential assistance in finding and interviewing local people. Tricia Gabany aided us in arranging a meeting with the elders (*cabildo*) of San Juan Nuevo. *Cabildo* members spent a long evening session helping identify now-buried local fields and other geographic features on a pre-eruption topographic map. In particular we thank Tomás Anducho-Chávez, Matías Cuarao-Ruíz, Rafael Echeverria-Campoverde, Narciso Guerrero-Baltazár, Celedonio Gutiérrez-Acosta, and Jesús Huitron-Gutiérrez.

We received a great deal of technical assistance from colleagues at the Smithsonian. Production of the book fell on the shoulders of three individuals. Margaret Cuasay carried the project from the beginning almost to the end. She typed most of the original text into the computer and was the main person responsible for laying out camera-ready copy. This book could not have happened without her efforts. Jonathan Goldberg electronically redrafted many of the drawings in the book, maintaining a calm enthusiasm throughout numerous iterations on each. Athene Cua also played a major part in layout work and in proofreading.

In addition, we want to thank other Smithsonian colleagues: Victoria Avery, Lee Siebert, and Mary Ulbricht for proofreading, Shelly Borden for word processing, William Deiss and Ashley Wyant for their assistance during many trips to the Foshag Collections of the Smithsonian Archives, Richard Fiske for advice, Ben Fornshell for computer drafting, Tim Gooding and Tim Rose for preparation of polished thin sections, Leslie Hale for collections assistance, Victor Krantz for photography, Julia Lewis for photography and proofreading, Roland Pool and Ed Venzke for help with computer mysteries, and Ellen Thurnau and Dan Appleman for solving a variety of problems as they arose.

The overall layout of the book was designed by Harrison Shaffer of Whitewing Press, Tucson, Arizona, who provided us with a steady stream of professional advice.

All of these individuals helped to make the project enjoyable and memorable for us; we sincerely appreciate their assistance and generosity.

'This Volcano Owned and Operated by Dionisio Pulido'

URUAPAN, Mexico, March 8.—The United States may have its atom bomb, but all Mexico is still aghast at its spectacular new volcano, Paracutin, which again started a series of eruptions this week.

This district now has become a mecca for thousands of tourists daily, but they maintain a respectful distance from the crater with its flames and corroding gases.

Dionisio Pulido, father of 13 children, was on his corn patch with two oxen and his dog, Chauffeur, on Feb. 20, 1943, when the phenomenon which occurs perhaps once in 10,000 years—the birth of a volcano—started before his eyes.

Before fleeing forever from his 9-acre patch, he put up a wooden sign reading:

"This volcano owned and operated by Dionisio Pulido."

But Paracutin far surpassed the limits of his little farm, and many other homeless Mexicans may claim ownership, too. As for Pulido, he and his family migrated to the United States for jobs and a home.

Paracutin today is a blood-red mountain with gases that shoot 1,000 feet up while thousands of red-hot rocks spread destruction in all directions.

An atom bomb has nothing on Mexico's new volcano!

Today's Best INP AP Pictures TODAY

VOLCANO IN HIS CORNFIELD!

by Dr. Clyde Fisher
Honorary Curator, Hayden Planetarium

Imagine the shock to Dionisio Pulido, Mexican farmer! And imagine the glee of scientists, who have the treat of studying a volcano from its very birth!

Dionisio: His farm is ruined for 1,000 years

YOU can imagine Dionisio Pulido's amazement. A simple Indian farmer, he was plowing his cornfield, down there in Mexico, as he had done every year for most of a lifetime. And suddenly, out in the middle of the field, a column of smoke began to rise right out of the earth.

Dionisio ran over, and saw that the smoke was coming out of a little hole. He dropped a stone on the hole, but the smoke pushed right out around it. He hurried in alarm to his wife, and together they legged it to the village to get the wondering padre, priest. By the time they got back with the priest, the hole was 30 feet deep, and smoke was pouring out in dense clouds.

A volcano had been born — the first volcano in our lifetime known to have started from scratch. In a week it had built a cone 550 feet high; in 10 weeks it was 1,100 feet high. A few months later, when I got there, it was more than 1,500 feet high. And it is still growing.

It was just about a year ago that the volcano, a-borning, drove Dionisio out of what used to be his cornfield. Since then scientists have had, for the first time, a chance to observe a volcano from its earliest stages on. Only a few from this country have been able to make the pilgrimage.

MEXICO'S PET VOLCANO

Tourists pay out a pretty peso to see Paricutin make a terrible uproar without hurting anybody

Active volcanoes are often dreadful nuisances and should be given ample elbow room. This is not the case, however, with Paricutin, a lively 9-year-old volcano in Michoacan state, Mexico. True, as a baby, Paricutin did swallow up a village, ruin nearly six square miles of cornfields and build a mountain of lava. But it made up for this bumptiousness by never killing anybody and by obediently stopping its lava flow short of crosses planted by Catholic pilgrims. Even better, Paricutin permits visitors within 1,300

VOLCANO

PARICUTIN IS SAMPLE OF EARTH'S INTERIOR HELL

Here spouting dust and flame is Paricutin, world's youngest volcano. Where it stands today, on the high plains of Mexico 200 miles west of Mexico City there was a flat cornfield only 14 months ago. Paricutin, in its stormy infancy, has piled up a cone of rubble and giant boulders 1,200 ft. high. Its dust column sifting earthward has buried a village and blighted and depopulated several hundred square miles of once productive farmland.

Paricutin is of more than local interest, however, because it is the first volcano to come under scientific observation almost from the moment of its birth. The volcanoes are our single direct contact with the inside of the earth. Up through the 30-mile outer crust of the earth which insulates the life on the surface from the molten hell of the interior, volcanoes bring awful samples of the incalculable forces of nature which have reared up our mountains and designed our continents.

PARICUTIN'S DUST COLUMN MOUNTS 20,000 FEET INTO THE SKY. EASTWARD ON PREVAILING WINDS THE DUST PARTICLES TRAVEL AS FAR AS MEXICO CITY, 200 MILES AWAY

NEW YORK HERAL[D]

Mexicans Flee Volcano As Lava Stream Widens

URUAPAN, Mexico, Feb. 2 (UP).—Many residents fled from the area surrounding the Paricutin volcano today as the fiery mountain, which grew out of a corn field nine year ago, increased its activity.

Window panes in this town about fifteen miles from Paricutin were broken by the jar of the explosions and earthquakes. Residents said this year's activity is the most severe since the volcano was born Feb. 19, 1943.

Celedonio Gutierrez, Mexican geologist, said the lava stream is about 200 yards wide and from three to five feet deep. He said it was the first time he had seen the crater full of molten lava. By day, the crimson summit can be seen from the town of Charapengo,

New [

(Continu

tax on ho' 500,000 fro overnight streets.

Windsh sold by ' of $60, plan, to by motorists in uncongested idential.

The securitie fer tax, announ part of the cit variation on a year to ease troubles. Last y the state to do transactions revenue to th

This year right to imp

Newest Volcano Filmed in Color

United Artists has acquired world-wide distribution rights to the screen production "The Angry God," a tale of ancient Mexico filmed with the authentic background of the world's newest volcano, Paricutin.

"The Angry God" is the first feature-length film to be made in the new Fullcolor process. Sequences of erupting lava were filmed across several years by an expedition of the American Museum of Natural History, encamped near the emerge cano on Michoacan, Mexico. The musical score was con by Vernon Duke. The stor taken from a Good Houseke novel by Emma-Lindsay Squi

For Sale—Volcano

MEXICO CITY. — Want 't buy a volcano cheap? Dionisi Pulido, the only man in the world to own a volcano, wants to sell it. Pulido, on whose farm the Paricutin volcano sprung up in February, 1942, is now picking oranges at Puente, San Gabriel valley, Calif. He wrote to the newspaper Excelsior here: "Of course I am proud to be the only volcano owner in the world, but I can't farm on it and farming is the only thing I can do."

The Eruption and
Its Importance

The birth of a genuinely new volcano is an extraordinarily rare event. Although volcanic eruptions are common—on the order of 20 taking place at any given time and countless more passing unobserved on the sea floor—nearly all are helping to build older volcanoes that have been under construction for thousands of years. Great importance therefore attaches to the very first awakening of a new volcano, particularly when it is well observed and documented throughout its ensuing life. Such an event took place 50 years ago in a Mexican cornfield (Figs. 1 and 2), and this book attempts to tell its story in the words of eyewitnesses and the many who have studied both the eruption and its widespread effects . . . on people, agriculture, and the environment.

The responses of the local people to the eruption, and the threat posed to both their communities and their livelihoods, are major parts of the Parícutin story. Local folklore blames the eruption on the destruction of a holy cross that had been erected by priests as a symbol of peace between two neighboring communities engaged in a boundary dispute. A local plague of locusts in February 1942 was interpreted as the first sign of divine displeasure, with the culminating punishment coming one year later in the form of the new volcano.

The birth of Parícutin was preceded by 45 days of enhanced regional seismicity. Earthquakes large enough to be felt increased in number and intensity, reaching 300 on the day before the outbreak. The volcano's birth was witnessed by at least four Tarascan Indians who provided a rich record of its beginning. Particularly significant is the testimony of Dionisio Pulido (Fig. 3), the owner of the field. After hearing a thunderous noise, he noticed a new fissure:

"Here is something new and strange, thought I, and I searched on the ground for marks to see whether or not it had opened in the night, but could find none; and I saw that it was a kind of fissure that had a depth of only half a meter. I then felt a thunder, the trees trembled, and it was then I saw how, in the hole, the ground swelled and raised itself 2 or 2½ meters high, and a kind of smoke or fine dust—gray, like ashes—began to rise up in a portion of the crack . . . . Immediately more smoke began to rise, with a hiss or whistle, loud and continuous; and there was a smell of sulfur. I then became greatly frightened and tried to help unyoke one of the ox teams."

A group of local men approached the vent site when the eruption was about 1½ hours old, providing a sketch and other valuable observations. Another witness on the second night noted explosions of bombs, with:

". . . stones that rose to a height of 500 m. They flew through the air to fall 300-400 m from the vent. It is a great memory for me to have seen how the first stones fell on the plowed fields where I used to watch the cattle of my grandfather."

The first of many geologists arrived the next night. They were to keep the volcano under nearly constant observation for the next 9 years. New lava flows were regularly mapped and growth of the cone was carefully documented (see inside-front-cover maps and profiles). New features and processes were recorded before they were destroyed or buried by later phases of the eruption. At the end, the cone towered 424 m above the site of Pulido's cornfield.

Fig. 1 - Conceptual sketch depicting the birth of Parícutin, by Dr. Atl, one of the great learned men of México. "In the field of Quitzocho, near the village of Parícutin, in Michoacán, on February 20, 1943, a little before 5 in the afternoon, were seen the first manifestations of the birth of the volcano that was given the name of the village: Parícutin." See also paintings by Dr. Atl in Plate 7.

Fig. 2 - Parícutin volcano from 2½ km NNE at Cerro de Equijuata in March, 1944. The extinct parasitic cone Sapichu at the NE foot of the main cone. Rugged lava flows of June in the middle distance.

Fig. 3 - Dionisio Pulido, a Tarascan Indian farmer who lived in Parícutin village and owned the Cuiyúsuru field in which the new volcano was born as he watched.

"In the afternoon I joined my wife and son, who were watching the sheep, and inquired if anything new had occurred, since for 2 weeks we had felt strong tremors in the region. Paula replied, yes, that she had heard noise and thunder underground. Scarcely had she finished speaking when I, myself, heard a noise, like thunder during a rainstorm, but I could not explain it, for the sky above was clear and the day was so peaceful, as it is in February.

At 4 p.m. I left my wife to set fire to a pile of branches when I noticed that a *cueva* [cave or grotto], which was situated on one of the knolls of my farm, had opened . . . and I saw that it was a kind of fissure that had a depth of only half a meter. I set about to ignite the branches again when I felt a thunder, the trees trembled, and I turned to speak to Paula; and it was then I saw how, in the hole, the ground swelled and raised itself 2 or 2½ m high, and a kind of smoke or fine dust — gray, like ashes — began to rise up in a portion of the crack that I had not previously seen . . . . Immediately more smoke began to rise, with a hiss or whistle, loud and continuous; and there was a smell of sulfur. I then became greatly frightened."

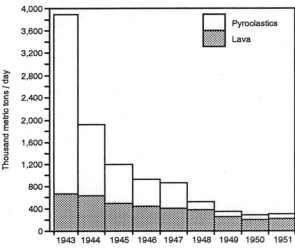

Fig. 4 - Average daily weights of pyroclastic material and lava erupted at Parícutin, by years, 1943-1951.

The central explosive vent of Parícutin produced virtually all of the bombs and ashes that rained from the air, but almost none of the lava flows. Instead, the lava issued from two vent complexes at the NE and SW bases of the main cone. Over time, the eruption became progressively less explosive, with lava dominating in the later years (Fig. 4). By the end of the eruption some 24.8 km² of land had been buried in lava, and an (overlapping) 300 km² covered with at least 15 cm of ash, the thickness above which vegetation failed to recover. The total amount of magma erupted during the nine years is estimated as 1.1 km³.

The eruption of Parícutin had a profound impact on the human, animal, and botanical life in the vicinity. The effects of the eruption were particularly severe for the five nearest communities (see inside-front-cover map). The people in all of these towns suffered great discomfort from ashfalls, which were particularly severe from the eruption's second to fifth month. The village that gave the volcano its name, only 3 km to its NW, was soon buried by ash and ultimately covered by lava. The town's 733 residents were compelled to evacuate 4 months after the eruption began, and the federal government provided new lands 27 km to the SE (in Caltzontzin, see inside-front-cover map). The larger village of San Juan Parangaricutiro (4-km north) underwent a more drawn-out and complex evacuation. The town's church possessed an ancient and revered crucifix, named *El Señor de Los Milagros* (The Lord of the Miracles), that the people hoped would protect them. In the eruption's 18th month, however, lava reached the town's outskirts. After an emotional last mass, celebrated in the unfinished church of San Juan, the townspeople followed the bishop in procession as he carried *El Señor* to their new home of San Juan Nuevo, 15 km to the SE. Most of San Juan was ultimately buried by Parícutin's lavas, but the church towers still project above the lava field as an enduring symbol of the eruption (Fig. 5).

Fig. 5 - The towers of the San Juan Parangaricutiro church (left tower unfinished), surrounded by 1944 San Juan lava flow from Parícutin volcano, which is seen erupting in the background.

An estimated 4,500 cattle and 550 horses died during the early heavy ashfalls as a result of breathing fine ash. These losses were devastating to the local people who depended upon animals for food, plowing, and transportation. As ashfall destroyed vegetation, it also destroyed the food supply and protective cover for local animals. Thus animal life was practically non-existent in the 300 km^2 area surrounding the cone where ash was deeper than 15 cm. Small mice survived closer to the cone along horse trails and near observatory cabins, and tracks of foxes were seen within 800 m of the active volcano. Crows came even closer, commonly visiting the cone during rains of ash and bombs to feed on wind-blown insects.

Insect loss affected local agriculture as well. Ashfall killed the natural predator of a cane-boring insect, resulting in a devastating 80-90% loss of the sugar cane harvest, but it also killed a particularly destructive fruit fly, resulting in a bumper crop of fruit. Small quantities of ash acted as a moisture-retaining mulch, and excellent crops of wheat and barley were harvested where ash thicknesses were less than 3 cm. Fine ash entered avocado flowers, though, preventing pollination and causing crop loss of over $300,000 U.S.

Successful agriculture depended upon a strategy to mix the older, nitrogen-rich soil with new ashes, and plowing the two layers together worked well where the ash was thin enough. An innovative experiment in lava reclamation was performed in 1957: Floodwaters that skirted the edge of the lava field, carrying both new ash and old soil in suspension, were diverted by farmers using a rock dam and forced to flow onto the barren new lava field. This diversion accumulated up to 3 m of new "soil", and the land was successfully cultivated just two years later.

Blanketing of the landscape with ash greatly increased runoff during the summer rains, and ash carried by the runoff added to its erosional power. Economically ruinous floods in 1943 carried large quantities of ash westward along the Río de Itzícuaro, reaching levels 7.5 m above the river bed and flow rates of 950 m^3/min. These ash-laden flood waters destroyed dams and silted over agricultural lands. In 1944, however, lava flows blocked roughly 40% of the ash-covered areas that formerly drained to the west, and the flooding was never again so severe. Parícutin infiltration studies revealed the significance of thin, fine-grained, low permeability layers that promoted runoff and erosion by acting as barriers to the downward migration of rainwater. Although vegetation generally helped retard erosion, standing dead tree trunks commonly acted to accelerate it by concentrating rainwater and thereby initiating gullies on their downhill sides. The lava field was found to act like a giant sponge; many streams and temporary lakes were completely drained into the porous, vesicular lavas. And erosion was not restricted to new ash. Deposition of fine Parícutin ash on nearby, older cinder cones caused deep, steep-sided gullies to develop that quickly eroded below the original ground level.

The region surrounding Parícutin is unusual within volcanic belts in containing no large active volcanoes. Instead it is dotted by approximately 1,000 small cinder cones similar to the new volcano. The presence of cinder cones without larger volcanoes is thought to reflect a relatively low eruption rate for the field as a whole. Geological studies show that activity has migrated southward in the field during about the last million years, a shift that is reflected in the chemistry of the volcanic rocks. The positions of cones in the field show statistically defined alignments and clusters that can be used to interpret the stress field orientation at the time of the eruptions. In the younger, southern part of the field, alignments have a NE-SW orientation. This parallels the subduction direction of the Cocos Plate beneath the southern edge of the North American Plate, the process that is thought to have produced all eruptions in the Mexican Volcanic Belt.

Igneous petrology, the study of volcanic rocks and their origin, has particularly benefited from the unusual circumstances of Parícutin. Specimens of lavas and bombs were collected throughout the 9-year eruption. The complete life history of the volcano can be traced to a single, subsurface magma chamber, and study of its successive products can yield important information on the changes and processes that took place there. In his classic study of the "blood relationship" between successive lavas, Ray Wilcox proved that melting and digestion of granitic crustal rocks must have accompanied the subsurface crystallization of the Parícutin magmas in order to explain the chemical and mineralogical evolution of the volcanic rocks appearing at the surface. Subsequent computer-based modeling studies of Wilcox's data and later analysis of the same samples both for trace-element abundances and for strontium and oxygen isotopic ratios have validated Wilcox's model.

Although Parícutin is the best-studied of history's "new" volcanoes, it is not alone, and for comparative purposes we have included accounts of Jorullo (México), Monte Nuovo (Italy), and Waiowa (New Guinea). Each of these volcano births was preceded by months to years of enhanced seismicity, and was followed by the building of a modest cone. Eruption durations varied from a week (Monte Nuevo, 1538), through a year (Waiowa, 1943-44), to 15 years (Jorullo 1759-75). The most interesting parallels to Parícutin are found with Jorullo, born in a ravine only 80 km SE of Parícutin. Its vents were also aligned NE-SW, its size was similar (9 km^2 lava field and 1-2 km^3 magma volume), and its magmas also became systematically richer in silica, and thus less fluid, as the eruption progressed. The outer margins of both the Parícutin and Jorullo lava fields, consequently, were defined by the early fluid magmas, while later, more viscous lavas tended to pile up closer to the vent. Both Waiowa and Monte Nuovo built cones less than 150 m high and neither produced lava flows; the former grew virtually without witnesses and the latter was born in a Pleistocene caldera (thereby barring it from true "new" volcano status).

Another new cone in an older volcanic setting is the Nicaraguan cinder cone Cerro Negro, born in 1850 on the flanks of the larger volcano Las Pilas. Its significance, though, is that it has erupted five times since its birth (most recently in 1992), showing that some cinder cones have been formed by more than one eruptive episode. Such examples are receiving special attention in this 50th anniversary year of the Parícutin eruption, as U.S. volcanologists ponder a young cinder cone located 20 km SSW of the proposed nuclear waste facility at Yucca Mountain, Nevada. Intensely serious consideration is being given to the possibility of renewed volcanism at this site, reminding us of the societal importance of understanding volcanism.

Parícutin has contributed much to this understanding, both in the studies described above and in the many lessons to be learned from studies reprinted in the remainder of this book. Among them are:

- Cone growth was most striking in the early days. Its height reached 30 m in the first 24 hours, doubled by the third day, and doubled again by the sixth. At the end of the first month it stood 148 m high and it reached 336 m at the end of the first year. From then on the growth was very slow, with 8 more years adding only the final 21% to reach 424 m in 1952.

- Lava flows began on the second day and continued, nearly unbroken, to the last. Continuous scientific observation documented not only complex overlapping flow sequences, but also dramatic changes to individual flows. One flow was later revived by intrusion of new magma that raised its upper surface (complete with cover of layered ash) over 100 m above its base. Conversely, another lava flow surface dropped to form a graben-like depression when the lava from its interior was suddenly drained into a deep crater encountered at the flow front.

- A hazard connected to lava-flow durations is illustrated by the San Juan flow, the eruption's largest. After 3 months of steady advance (avg. 2-3 m/hr) in early 1944, the flow front stopped 5 km north of the cone. Only its front had stopped, however, for after several weeks of apparent quiescence lava burst from the flow top and advanced at velocities as high as 180 m/hr to reach the outskirts of San Juan within weeks.

- Although most lava flows moved slowly—by over-riding debris that had just tumbled down the steep flow front—more fluid flows developed the smooth, platey surfaces that are typical of Hawaiian lavas. One remarkable flow was described as bulldozing soil ahead of itself during the eruption's 7th day.

- Continuous observation also demonstrated repeated shifting of explosive vents and many ephemeral features of ash deposition that would be difficult or impossible to decipher after the fact. In general, fluctuations in explosivity bore little apparent relationship to lava production, but raised ash columns above 6 km altitudes and dusted México City, 320 km to the east.

- Major slumps of the NE and SW sectors of the cone accompanied renewed outbreaks of lava from vents at the cone base. During strong explosive phases ashfalls would fill these breaches within days to weeks, restoring the cone's symmetry. These events led to complex geometric field relationships that might be mistaken in ancient deposits as evidence for a long or recurrent (polycyclic) eruption history.

- Eruptive products, both solid and gaseous, were strikingly different between the central and flank vents. The main crater primarily emitted ash and bombs along with gases rich in water and sulfur. The flank vents produced lava with little ash or bombs, and the gases were rich in hydrogen chloride. Measurement of gas compositions from only one of the vents would give a misleading picture of the total volatile budget.

- The combined rates of lava and ash emission declined steadily through the course of the eruption. These trends were reversed, however, during the final 6 months of Parícutin's life, when activity was characterized by frequent and violent explosions. The eruption ended abruptly on March 4, 1952. Earthquakes, rarely felt during the previous years, then resumed.

- Ashfall in the first year killed nearly all plant life within 5-8 km of the cone. No local famine resulted, though, because the eruption began just 60 days after the annual *maize* harvest.

- The cinder cone and lava field remain virtually barren of vegetation today, but pioneer species rapidly colonized both environments. Lichens and angiosperms were present on the cone rim within 5 years of the eruption's end, growing near warm acidic fumaroles that may have supplied nitrogen to the plants. By 1960, 33 species had invaded the lava field, including 2 pines. There vegetation depended upon moisture-retaining crevices and wind-blown sources of nitrogen.

- Four resettlement communities were established; the first only 4 months after the eruption's start and the last 10 years later, after it had ceased. The successes of these communities varied widely, with a major factor being the extent to which inhabitants were involved in planning their own new community.

- Although no humans were killed by ash or lava, 3 were killed by lightning believed to have been caused by the eruption. However, indirect causes took an estimated 100 lives at one resettlement center alone, by sickness, loss of will to live, and actions of hostile local people.

- Many sociological hazards developed only after the eruption had ended. Land disputes became more intense as the devastated zone regained agricultural value. These conflicts were heightened by the fact that the eruption had destroyed landmarks traditionally used as boundaries between properties. As recently as 1990 a man was killed and others injured in land disputes near the volcano.

Chronology of Events

Year	Date	Time	Remarks
1941			

weak tremors felt in region (see p. 49)

land disputes between residents of Parícutin and San Juan Parangaricutiro lead to death of Nicolás Toral (of Parícutin) near site of future eruption. Cross is placed high on flank of Cerros de Tancítaro by churchmen seeking peace. Cross is destroyed within days, increasing enmity (see p. 47)

1942

February — plague of locusts (see p. 48)

August — depression forms in Dionisio Pulido's field, around pre-existing pit 5 m in diameter and 1½ m deep (see p. 39)

Dec. 8 — oblique air photo of region (Fig. 11)

1943

Jan. 7 — 17:40 — first known Parícutin earthquake (M_s 4.4) recorded at Tacubaya station (320 km east of Parícutin in a México City suburb: Fig. 16: earthquake No. 1). All earthquake data below, to the start of the eruption, are based on records from this station. Only events of $M \geq 3.0$ were detected at this distance

January — Celedonio Gutiérrez learns of tremors and subterranean noises from residents a few kilometers south of volcano site (see p. 49)

Jan. 20-22 — 20:08 — $M_s = 3.9$ earthquake. (Another, also M_s 3.9, at 23:40 on Jan. 22) (Fig. 16: Nos. 2 and 3)

Jan. 28 — 19:33 — $M_s = 4.2$ earthquake (Fig. 16: No. 4)

Jan. 31 — World War II battle for Stalingrad ends with record 2.1 million fatalities

Year	Date	Time	Remarks
1943			

Feb. 5   noon   first felt seismicity at San Juan Parangaricutiro. Continues daily until eruption. Subterranean noise precedes tremor, and is proportional to earthquake intensity. Tremors increase in number and intensity, and are centered on Pulido's farm. [Felipe Cuara-Amezcua and Ruperto Torres support this date, but José Caballero gives Feb. 7 for first felt events in San Juan Parangaricutiro (see p. 49)]

Feb. 8   04:55 M_s = 4.3 earthquake felt as far as 120 km SW (largest of 3; others M_s 3.8 at 03:25 and M_s 3.6 at 19:57) (Fig. 16: Nos. 5-7)

Feb. 10   11:03 M_s = 3.7 earthquake (first of 3; others M_s 3.7 at 11:47 and M_s 3.3 at 12:12) (Fig. 16: Nos. 8-10)

Feb. 11   12:47 M_s = 4.0 earthquake (Fig. 16: No. 11). Newspaper reports 25-30 felt at San Juan Parangaricutiro on this day (see p. 51). Number increases through next 9 days

Feb. 13   05:17 M_s = 3.3 earthquake (Fig. 16: No. 12)

Feb. 14   03:48 M_s = 4.5 earthquake (largest of 5; others M_s 4.4 at 03:31, 3.6 at 04:02, 4.1 at 13:05, and 3.2 at 18:22) (Fig. 16: Nos. 13-17)

Feb. 15   17:00   tremors at San Juan Parangaricutiro reach alarming intensities but none have M_s >3.0 (see p. 49)

Feb. 16   01:36 M_s = 3.6 earthquake (Fig. 16: No. 18)

Feb. 17   17:40 M_s = 4.2 earthquake (Fig. 16: No. 19). Intensities of 3-4 (M-M scale) begin to be felt in area, increasing to Feb. 20

Feb. 18   18:39 M_s = 4.5 earthquake (Fig. 16: No. 20)

Feb. 19   23:19 M_s = 4.0 earthquake (Fig. 16: No. 21). About 300 earthquakes reported by residents of San Juan Parangaricutiro (see p. 51)

Feb. 20   07:15 M_s = 3.9 earthquake (Fig. 16: No. 22)

          10:00   subterranean noises heard and oscillatory tremors felt at San Juan Parangaricutiro [Jesús Anguiano said 14 hours before eruption, or about 2:30 a.m. (see p. 60)]. Village authorities send messenger to Uruapan for advice (see p. 49)

          ~16:00   Dionisio Pulido hears thunderous noise and soon notices newly opened fissure (30 m east-west) through knoll with central depression. Ground rises 2-2½ m in hole and ash begins to be ejected from fissure. Whistling noise accompanies increased ash emission. Paula Pulido sees dust column following the new fissure, then the opening of a 30 cm hole, a stronger ash cloud, and burning of nearby vegetation. Dionisio Pulido rides to Parícutin village, then to San Juan Parangaricutiro, alerting authorities (see p. 56). Celedonio Gutiérrez and official report of San Juan Parangaricutiro give eruption start time as 16:30. Aurora Cuara sees fissure form at this time (Fig. 22) and describes earth rising like a wall 1 m high, 10 m long, and 2 m wide, with small ash

Year	Date	Time	Remarks

1943 --

Feb. 20 (cont.) ~16:00   column and "sparks" at same time (16:30) that Gutiérrez sees column from San Juan Parangaricutiro (see p. 60)

~17:00   first photos, from near San Juan Parangaricutiro (Fig. 18)

17:20   light earthquakes, subterranean noises, and distant detonations reported at San Juan Parangaricutiro. Local tremors reported to cease with eruption's start (until next morning) (see p. 60)

17:35   Luis Ortíz Solorio, at San Juan Parangaricutiro, sees thin column of smoke. San Juan Parangaricutiro group sends investigating team, or "posse", arriving around 6 p.m. (see p. 58-59)

18:00   San Juan Parangaricutiro team sees trench-like fissure, hole, and projectiles to 5 m height; low mounds of fine ash along trench (Fig. 23) and "boiling sand" in vent itself. They witness opening of new fissure, widening orifice to 2 m diameter and increasing size of eruptive column (see p. 59). Rock and ash specimens collected by Jesús Anguiano

Dolores Pulido reaches site about this same time: sees smoke from hole and low mounds of ash, with "stones" falling up to 8 m from vent (see p. 57)

18:08 M_s = 6.0 earthquake located 530 km SE of Parícutin along the Middle America Trench (see p. 51)

20:00+   Gutiérrez sees "tongues of flame" rising 800 m after dusk, and lightning illuminating dense black cloud extending to south (see p. 60-61)

22:00   Aurora Cuara, from San Juan Parangaricutiro, sees incandescent projectiles and notes increased violence in hour before midnight (louder roars and lightning illuminating column) (see p. 58)

24:00   cone is estimated as 6 m high; first thunderous roars heard in San Juan Parangaricutiro; Quitzocho Period begins (see p. 66)

Feb. 21   04:00   cone is estimated as 8 m high (see p. 66)

08:00   Dionisio Pulido returns to cone; height estimated as 10-12 m, and "hurling out rocks with great violence" (see p. 66)

morning   strong earthquake, unrecorded at Tacubaya (M <3?), further alarms villagers, many of whom abandon homes (see p. 60). San Juan Parangaricutiro municipal government meets (see p. 61-62)

10:00   cone is estimated as 25 m high (see p. 66)

11:00   Aurora Cuara observes small growing cone, with what is probably lava flowing from it, the start of the Quitzocho flow (see p. 66). Cone has horseshoe shape, with east side kept open by flowing lava

Year 1943	Date	Time	Remarks

Feb. 21 (cont.)		13:00	cone is estimated as 30 m high, with a base 70 m in diameter (see p. 66; Figs. 25-26)
		14:00	noises particularly strong, having increased as vapors decreased earlier in day (see p. 61)
		afternoon	cone height estimated as 50 m (see p. 66)
		night	bombs rise to 500 m height, and fall 300-400 m from vent (see p. 61)
Feb. 22		03:21	M_s = 7.7 earthquake recorded at Tacubaya station and located 235 km SSE of Parícutin along the coast at a depth of 16 km (see p. 52). Described by Gutiérrez as 7-8 minute "agony" for local people (see p. 61)
		early morning	Byron Valle, flying over the volcano, sees second vent at base of cone with lava flowing to the north. Later photo (Fig. 27) shows cone breached to east by lava flowing rapidly to NE from central vent (see p. 68-69)
		night	Ezequiel Ordóñez is the first geologist to arrive at Parícutin. Estimates cone height that night as 40 m, and lava flow length as 800 m to north (see p. 64)
Feb. 23			Ordóñez estimates cone height as 60 m and Quitzocho lava flow rate as 6-12 m/hr to the NE (see p. 69; Fig. 28). Instituto de Geología scientists estimate cone height as 44 m. This and following cone-height estimates attributed to Instituto de Geología are from Plate E of the appendix to *El Parícutin: Estado de Michoacán*, T. Flores (editor). These values are typically lower than other estimates. Some of the discrepancy in cone-height estimates is undoubtedly related to differing assumptions about the original elevation of Pulido's field, although other discrepancies, such as those for Feb. 26-27 (below), appear to be inexplicably large. In this book we use 2,385 m as the pre-eruption elevation (see topographic map of Fig. 13)
		15:36	First Parícutin earthquake to be recorded at Tacubaya since start of eruption (M_s 3.4). A smaller event (M_s 3) follows in 2 hours, then 1-2/day every day or two through end of March[1]
Feb. 25			Photographs of Quitzocho lava flow moving north to cover cornfields (Plate 1A and B)
Feb. 26			Robles-Ramos gives cone height as 167 m, basal diameter as 730 m, and north-south crater diameter as 90 m. Flow speed down to 1-2 m/hr, ending first surge of Quitzocho flow (see p. 69-71). "Flashing arcs" first observed (see p. 69)
Feb. 27			Instituto de Geología scientists estimate cone height as 106 m
Feb. 28			Second surge of Quitzocho flow (see p. 71) clears breach and continues until March 20 (see p. 73)
Mar. 5			air photo showing cone with lava flowing to north (Fig. 34)

Year Date	Remarks
1943	
Mar. 5-9	seismograph 1.1 km from cone records tremor (see p. 50)
Mar. 18	heavy bomb stage ceases and heavy cineritic phase begins. This is the heaviest ash fall of the eruption and lasts until June 9 (see p. 76-78; Fig. 40). Pastoriu flow to SW from vent at south base of cone, beginning about 20:00 (see p. 78)
Mar. 20	Quitzocho flow from central vent ceases, and cone begins to heal breach on NE flank (see p. 76; Fig. 37). Flow continues to spread, however, extending 1.5 km NNW to the west slope of Cerro de Jarátiro ridge by end of March. Thickness there was about 15 m (see p. 73)
	Instituto de Geología scientists estimate cone height as 148 m
Mar. 25-26	William Foshag first arrives at Parícutin
April	typically windiest month. Prevailing west wind commonly creates dust storms from 9-10 a.m to 4-5 p.m. (see p. 285)
Apr. 9	fine ashfall of 112 g/m^2 in Morelia (125 km ENE) and 0.136 g/m^2 in México City (320 km east) (see p. 289). Local ashfall heavy from Mar. 19 to Apr. 17 (see p. 289). México City ashfall noted Apr. 8-10 (Bullard, 1984)
Apr. 17	Mesa del Corral flow issues to SW from (Pastoriu) vent at south base of cone, after explosive activity briefly ceases (see p. 78)
Apr. 19	Earthquake at 18:44 (M_S 4.6) starts largest seismic energy release of eruption. Another M_S 4.6 follows 89 minutes later and an M_S 4.2 80 minutes after that. Through the next 7 years, up to four Parícutin earthquakes are recorded at Tacubaya each month: all are in M_S 3-4.6 range and few ≥4.0[1]
May	Red Cross station established in San Juan Parangaricutiro (see p. 191)
May 20	Instituto de Geología scientists estimate cone height as 190 m
May 30	rainy season typically starts at end of May and continues to end of October. Showers nearly every afternoon and easterly winds deposit ash west of cone (see p. 289)
June 9	heaviest and most-destructive pyroclastic falls cease briefly from 3-9 p.m. Explosivity becomes intermittent (see p. 78-80)
	Instituto de Geología scientists estimate cone height as 198 m
June 10	major slump on north flank of cone (see p. 80; Figs. 42, 43, 46); Quitzocho ridge (to NNW) begins to rise by shallow intrusion (see p. 80; Figs. 44, 47, 48). Flows to 30 m/hr, but explosive activity drops to lowest level since start of eruption (see p. 80)
June 12	Parícutin lava flow advances NNW down Parícutin Arroyo toward Parícutin village. Flow rate measured as 25 m/hr on June 13 (see p. 83)

Year	Date	Remarks

1943 --

June 12 (cont.)   flood at Río de Itzícuaro hydroelectric plant 21 km WNW of cone reaches 5.2 m above river bed (see p. 296)

June 13   scientists recommend that Parícutin village be abandoned (see p. 83; Fig. 45), authorities agree in mid-June. Villagers resettle in Caltzontzin, 5½ km east of Uruapan, 27 km ESE of the new volcano, and 750 m lower in elevation than Parícutin village (see p. 190)

June 14   La Lagunita flow begins: flows east and north from vent high on north flank (within slump of June 10) (see p. 83; Fig. 46)

early July   cessation of lava flows from slump in north flank allows tephra fall to fill slump zone and restore symmetry of cone (see p. 87; Figs. 49-50)

July 3   large flood reported at San Pedro hydroelectric plant near Uruapan, 22 km SE of the cone, with peak discharge of 150 m^3/sec compared to normal discharge of 9 m^3/sec (see p. 296)

July 19   La Lagunita flow ceases 800 m north of vent (see p. 87)

July 24   major slump on north flank of cone; growth of Quitzocho ridge is accelerated (see p. 87-89; Fig. 57)

July 27   Parícutin lava flow nearly ceases 2 km NW of main cone, but village is depopulated and many homes destroyed by ashfall (see p. 87; Fig 51)

July 31   "flashing arc" first observed by Foshag and González-Reyna (see p. 89-93: but first noticed by others Feb. 26, see p. 69). Break of north flank from July 24 is now largely repaired (see p. 89; Fig. 58)

Aug. 2   third major slump on north flank of cone (see p. 94-95; Fig. 61); new movement on Quitzocho ridge at 150 m/day. Lava flow to NW in August (see p. 95)

Aug. 11   second major flood at Río de Itzícuaro hydroelectric plant reaches 5.8 m above river bed (see p. 296)

Aug. 26   small, short-lived vent at SW base of cone. Taquí vents later (Jan. 8, 1944) form at same place (see p. 95, 103). August 26 also marked the last major intrusion into Quitzocho ridge, lifting ridgetop more than 100 m above former land surface (see p. 87; Figs. 55 and 63)

Aug. 29   third major flood along Río de Itzícuaro reaches 7.5 m above river bed. Hydroelectric plant closed until Sept. 5 (see p. 296). Ken Segerstrom calculated peak discharge of 950 m^3/sec and peak velocity of 36 km/hr (see p. 296)

Sept. 6   Río de Itzícuaro hydroelectric plant regrets reopening: fourth major flood reaches 6.1 m above river bed. Plant closed until Sept. 28 (see p. 296)

Year Date	Remarks
1943	
Sept. 14	last fiesta of *El Señor de los Milagros* held in San Juan Parangaricutiro (see p. 191-192)
Sept. 18	new lava vent opens on SW flank, 60 m above base. Lava front moves to south and SE at about 130 m/day (see p. 96)
	another large flood reported at San Pedro hydroelectric plant near Uruapan, 22 km SE of the cone, again with peak discharge of 150 m^3/sec, ~17 times normal. Annual number of floods increases to 1944, but flood sizes decrease (see p. 296)
	Another "new" volcano is born - first explosive eruptions of Waiowa volcano in Goropu Mountains of New Guinea, SW Pacific (see Text Note 296, p. 406)
Oct. 6	Miguel Silva, a former *hacienda*, is selected as a second location for refugees (from Zirosto and San Juan Parangaricutiro) (see inside-front-cover map and p. 192). It is 5 km SSW of Ario de Rosales, 65 km ESE of the new cone, and 755 m lower in elevation than San Juan Parangaricutiro.
Oct. 17	lands are listed for settlement in Miguel Silva, and 1,000-1,200 refugees arrive by spring of 1944 (see p. 192)
Oct. 18	Quitzocho period ends at 23:00, with outbreak of Sapichu vent at NE cone base. Sapichu activity continues for 2½ months (see p. 96-103; Figs. 2, 64-69, 96; Plate 3B). Main crater activity drops (see p. 99)
Oct. 19	Foshag and González-Reyna estimate cone height as 365 m (see p. 66)
Nov. 3	Arnaldo Pfeiffer makes first ascent to the rim of the main cone (see p. 102)
Dec. 4	Pfeiffer again climbs cone, with Sgt. José Rosales of the Mexican Army (see p. 102)
Dec. 19	Abraham Camacho and Celedonio Gutiérrez climb cone and estimate height as 345 m (see p. 102)
Dec. 20	Instituto de Geología scientists estimate cone height as 299 m
Dec. 27	large explosive eruption at Waiowa, the "new" volcano in New Guinea, sends an eruption plume to 4½ km height (see Sept. 18 remark and p. 375)
Dec. 28	in Japan, an earthquake starts sequence of events building a new dome named Showa Shinzan at Usu volcano. In next 6 months, Fukaba village and nearby surroundings are uplifted about 50 m by subsurface intrusion of magma
1944	
date unknown	large-scale lumbering and commercial milling introduced to exploit supply of timber devastated by ash (see p. 227)

Year Date	Remarks
1944	

Jan. to May 1945 — plague of cane-boring insects, after ashfall exterminated their natural predator, destroys 80-90% of sugarcane crop around Los Reyes (see p. 216)

early 1944 — Bracero Program is established and men from region affected by Parícutin eruption are urged to enlist as contract laborers in the United States (see p. 194)

At Miguel Silva, more refugees arrive than the designated land can support. Violence escalates, and local rancheros kill secular leaders of the refugee settlement. Fighting then breaks out among refugees, compounding their health and agricultural problems (see p. 192)

Jan. 8 — Sapichu period ends with lava flows having reached 4 km north of cone. Taquí period begins from opposite (SW) foot of main cone. Explosivity of main cone resumes (see p. 103; Fig. 71-72, 74)

Jan. 10 — distant earthquakes felt at 14:10 - 14:35, but no effects noted on volcano (see p. 105)

Feb. 6 — Taquí flows, which ceased on Jan. 12 after 4 days of activity, resume. Flows cover much of south and east foot of main cone, and hornitos form on surfaces (see p. 106). In the next half year, this northward-moving lava, later known as the San Juan flow, will cover by far the largest area of any lavas in the 9-year eruption, defining the northern boundary of the lava field and partially burying San Juan Parangaricutiro (see inside-front-cover maps)

February — seismometer is installed near San Juan Parangaricutiro by Teodoro Flores and colleagues of the Instituto de Geología (see p. 192)

Feb. 10 — the Taquí vent area is observed to be buried under accumulated lava (see p. 106)

Feb. 13 — another explosive eruption is observed at Waiowa, the "new" volcano in New Guinea (see Dec. 27, 1943 remark and p. 376)

Feb. 20 — Instituto de Geología scientists estimate height of 1-year-old cone as 336 m

March — people in San Juan Parangaricutiro agree to stay until lava reaches the cemetery (see p. 192)

Mar. 6 — Fred Pough and others observe spectacular lava fountains at Mesa de Los Hornitos (see p. 108-109)

early April — movement at flow front of Taquí/San Juan lava has virtually ceased

Apr. 14 — following 2 weeks of near stagnation, lava bursts from top of Taquí/San Juan flow (see p. 115, Text Note 49, and p. 192-193)

Apr. 23-24 — unusual luminous phenomena are seen in the eruption plume at night (see p. 111)

Year Date	Remarks
1944	
Apr. 24	lava that had previously emerged from the top of the Taquí/San Juan flow reaches the San Juan-Uruapan road and is now 600 m from the outskirts of San Juan Parangaricutiro (see p. 115). Lava flows from the vent at rates up to 180 m/hr, the highest recorded for the eruption. Water lines are moved, and the new road from San Juan to Angahuan (and Uruapan) is rapidly completed (see p. 193)
early May	lava reaches San Juan Parangaricutiro cemetery, 4½ km north of the vents, and temporarily halts (see p. 115, 193)
May	founding of third refugee settlement at Rancho de Los Conejos (later San Juan Nuevo), the site previously selected by villagers of San Juan Parangaricutiro. It is located 15 km SE of the new volcano and only 380 m lower in elevation than the old town (see p. 192-194).
May 8	bishop, having arrived from Zamora the previous day, celebrates final mass in unfinished church of San Juan Parangaricutiro (see p. 193)
May 9	bishop lifts *El Señor de Los Milagros* from altar in San Juan Parangaricutiro church and leads evacuation procession to Angahuan. Procession reaches Uruapan next day and Rancho de Los Conejos resettlement village on May 11 (see p. 193-194; Fig. 131)
May 24	William Foshag, Jenaro González-Reyna, and others observe development of volcancitos and hornitos on Mesa de Los Hornitos at WSW base of cone (see p. 106, 114; Figs. 75 and 76, Plate 3A)
June 17	San Juan lava flow, after resuming northward movement, enters town itself (see p. 115-121; Figs. 83-84, 88-92; Plate 6A and B)
June 23	a column of smoke rises from another cornfield, this one near Fukaba village, Japan (see Dec 28, 1943 remark). Phreatic explosions and continued uplift build dome-shaped mountain, Showa-Shinzan, 140-170 m high in next 4 months
July	William H. Burt finds wildlife population "practically non-existant" throughout zone of >300 km^2 where ash thickness exceeds 15 cm. Returns in summers of 1945 and 1947 to document return of vertebrates (see p. 235-238)
July 8	San Juan lava flow front now 2 km beyond San Juan Parangaricutiro. All but a few outlying squares of the town covered by mid-July (see p. 118)
July 9	settlement name formally changed from Rancho de los Conejos to San Juan Nuevo Parangaricutiro (see p. 194)
July 23	another explosive eruption is observed at at Waiowa, the "new" volcano in New Guinea; eventually builds cone 150 m high (see Feb. 13 remark; p. 377; Text Note 298 on p. 406)

Year Date	Remarks
1944	
late July-early Aug.	Campamento tongue of the Taquí flow begins to spread over previous flows around base of main cone. These flows circled the main cone on the east and spread west past Sapichu (see p. 122)
early August	San Juan lava flow stops after reaching Llano de Huirambosta, 2 km west of San Juan Parangaricutiro (see p. 122; Fig. 86)
by Aug. 15	Campamento tongue begins to flow into 2nd Jarátiro crater, 1½ km north of new volcano. By August 17 it fills the old crater almost to the lower eastern rim (see p. 122; Figs. 93 and 108)
Aug. 31	last reported eruption from Waiowa, New Guinea (see July 23 remark and p. 377)
Sept. 27	lava from Taquí vents starts flowing directly north, on west side of cone, covering village of Parícutin (see p. 122)
October	refugee population at Miguel Silva, which reached 1,000-1,200 in spring, down to about 300 within a year of its settlement (see p. 192)
Oct. 20	after 3 weeks of northward travel, flow from west side of main cone meets the older and longer eastern lobe at its terminus, 2 km west of San Juan Parangaricutiro (see p. 122)
early Nov.	Incandescent lava finally appears at Showa-Shinzan (Japan - see June 23 remark above). Slow, viscous extrusion over next 11 months builds summit dome nearly 300 m above its 1943 base, but this new mountain is a subsidiary feature of Usu volcano, rather than a "new" volcano like Parícutin and Waiowa
mid November	Ahuán vent opens at SSW base of cone (see p. 123-126; Figs. 94-96)
Nov. 26	Foshag and González-Reyna climb cone and use aneroid barometer to record highest elevation on eastern rim as 2,740 m (see p. 122), 355 m above Pulido's cornfield
Dec. 2	Ahuán lava circles south and east sides of cone and reaches Sapichu (see p. 124)
Dec. 9	tongues of lava break out from the Ahuán lava front near Sapichu. Lava pours into the deepest and last-remaining crater of Cerro de Jarátiro and threatens the Instituto de Geología observatory cabin, which is hastily dismantled and moved to a higher point on Cerro de Jarátiro (see p. 124-125; Fig. 108)
Dec. 31	54% of Parícutin's 9-year output (⅔ of tephra and ⅓ of lava totals) has erupted by end of 1944 (see Fig. 4, Table 23)

Year Date	Remarks
1945	--
Feb. 4	new lava vent opens on SW flank, about 400 m WNW of the Ahuán vent (see p. 132)
Feb. 20	end of second year: "the period of high drama was over" (see p. 194). Main outline of lava field established by Dec. 1944, and later flows piled on top of earlier ones or buried remaining patches of uncovered ground within the field (see inside-front-cover maps)
March 7	village of Parícutin is almost completely buried by lava that moved north from the Feb. 4 vent (see p. 132)
late March	two new vents open between the Feb. 4 vent and the Ahuán vents (see p. 132)
early April	six new vents form briefly at Mesa de Los Hornitos, on the WSW flank, as main cone explosivity decreases (see p. 132)
early May	strong explosive activity from the main cone is renewed (see p. 132)
May 7	Germany surrenders
mid May	continuous observations halted until October (see p. 134)
May 26	vertical airphotos taken of Parícutin cone and lava field (see Figs. 150 and 151)
late June	lava emission shifts back from the Ahuán vent (SSW base) to the area of the Taquí vents (SW base) (see p. 128)
July 4	lava field around Ahuán vent almost completely inactive. Activity shifts back to Taquí vent area (see p. 128)
Aug. 6	last day of fieldwork at Parícutin for William Foshag and Jenaro González-Reyna; 2½ years of observations completed (Foshag and González-Reyna, 1956: p. 359)
Aug. 14	V-J day - Japan surrenders September 2, ending World War II
end September	lava flows north from Mesa de Los Hornitos have all ceased, as have flows on SE and east sides of main cone (see p. 136)
late October	continuous observations resume. New flows from Mesa de Los Hornitos (see p. 136)
Nov. 16	3 weeks of quiet begin at main cone, between 3-week periods of moderate activity (see p. 136)

Year Date	Remarks
1946	
Jan. 20	another 3-week period of quiet broken by variable explosions. NE-SW "furrow" of main vent cored out to form wide and deep inner crater (see p. 136)
Jan. 22	new lava flow from crack near Mesa de Los Hornitos soon covers older flow from same area (see p. 136)
Jan. 28	last remnants of Parícutin village covered around this time. Unusually explosive activity begins; continuing through February (see p. 136)
February	crater diameter is 400 m, the largest of the 9-year eruption
Mar. 3	new *boca* opens near south base of cone. Flows over Parícutin village had ceased by end of February (see p. 138)
mid March	strong eruptive activity from the main crater begins again, and lasts until Apr. 18 (see p. 136)
Mar. 17	south side of cone slumps as a new *boca* opens in area of Ahuán vents. Main lava flow lobe reaches Sapichu by Apr. 3 and stops at base of Cerro de Jarátiro by June 12; another lobe continues NE at 2 m/hr (see p. 136, 143)
Apr. 27-29	heavy ash column rivals those of 1943 (see p. 137). Weak activity, then strong steam emission May 3-5 (see p. 140)
May 6	heavy pyroclastics again, followed by repeat of above cycle (see p. 140)
May 20	another pyroclastic phase adds 20 m to SE rim height (see p. 140)
June 11	another pyroclastic cycle starts, followed by yet another on July 2 (see p. 140-141)
June 20	another new Ahuán flow moves rapidly east and north; flow front is 2 km north of Sapichu by end of August (see p. 143, 149)
June 22	Mar. 17 flow finally stops about 1 km SE of San Juan Parangaricutiro (see p. 143)
July 12	new lava flow from Ahuán vent, at SSW base, reaches 3½ km NE before halting Aug. 7 (see p. 143)
July 18	Ken Segerstrom records most intense rainfall of year for Cuezeño station (5½ km north of cone): 46 mm in 2 hours (see p. 284)
July 27	Segerstrom and Gutiérrez climb the cone and make a topographic map of crater and summit (see p. 141; Fig. 107)
July-August	large spring dries up at San Juan Nuevo (15 km SE of new volcano); eruption causes many other changes in springs (see p. 286-287, 307)
Aug. 4-5	night eruption starts long pyroclastic phase, culminating in ash to 3 km height on Aug. 13 and continuing through Aug. 25 (see p. 142)

Year Date	Remarks
1946	
Aug. 8	another flow from south of cone starts west, then doubles back to east (see p. 143)
Aug. 20	government gives 1,425,000 pesos (about $300,000 in 1946 U.S.) to Los Reyes cane producers after loss of crop (see Jan. 1944 - May 1945 remark and p. 286).
Sept. 1 and 15	additional pyroclastic phases begin cycles (see p. 142)
Sept. 16	Segerstrom measures elevation for highest point of cone as 2,750.9 m (see p. 142)
Sept. 18	Ray Wilcox arrives as the "permanent observer" and starts quantitative graph of daily eruptive characteristics (see p. 131, 146; Fig 110)
Sept. 20	storm erodes a new gully 7-8 m wide and 5.8 m deep, 850 m NW of cone base. Enlarged to 20 m wide and 12.4 m deep in next 3 weeks (see p. 295 and Fig. 171)
October	Segerstrom maps tephra, calculating volume as 0.65 km^3 within 1 mm isopach (50% of total 9-year eruption) (see p. 289, Table 22, and inside-front-cover isopach map)
Oct. 13-15	strong lava fountaining at Mesa de Los Hornitos vent with complementary decrease in activity at main cone (see p. 149)
Oct. 18	Ahuán vent ceases activity after declining through late September (see p. 149)
November	lava flow overrides and destroys Canicjuata observatory, 1½ km NW of cone (see p. 149)
Nov. 5-8	strong lava production at the Mesa de Los Hornitos vent (see p. 149)
Nov. 24, 27, 29	earthquakes felt at Cuezeño (5½ km north of cone) and (Nov. 29) Angahuan (see p. 149). Tacubaya station in México City (320 km east) records 6 Parícutin earthquakes during month, including 3 on Nov. 24 and 1 on Nov. 27[1]. This is the highest monthly total since March 1943 (see Fig. 17 bottom)
Nov. 28	Wilcox measures highest rim elevation as 2,758.9 m by triangulation, for a cone height of 374 m (see p. 147)
Dec. 1-20	relatively strong lava effusion (see p. 152)
Dec. 10	exceptionally strong explosions (see p. 152)
Dec. 16	heavy pyroclastic eruptions resume and continue until Feb. 14, 1947 (see p. 152)
December	Cocjarao observatory is built 800 m SW of the cone base (completed January) (see p. 152)

Year	Date	Remarks
1947		

	January	Upper Casita observatory cabins on Cerro de Jarátiro are threatened by the Dec. 1946 lavas and are moved and rebuilt 300 m west of Jarátiro triangulation station (see p. 152)
	Jan. 13	NE flank slumps (see p. 152-153)
	Jan. 14 or 15	SW flank of cone slumps as a new Puertecito lava vent opens on SW base, about 100 m NNW of Ahuán vent (see p. 152)
	Jan. 19	lava emission ceases on SW side at the Mesa de Los Hornitos vents and the "new Sapichu" (or "Nuevo Juatita") vent forms at the base of the NE-flank slump of January 13 (see p. 153). First vent (Nuevo Juatita) on NE side of main cone in 3 years, will remain active until close of eruption in 1952 (see p. 172, 175, 178, 183; Plate 6C)
	Jan. 22 - Feb. 25	another period of strong lava effusion (see p. 152)
	Feb. 15	heavy pyroclastic eruptions cease abruptly (see p.152)
	Feb. 20	Carl Fries Jr. and Celedonio Gutiérrez estimate height of 4-year-old cone by alidade as 360 m (see Table 4)
	Mar. 2	lava effusion at SW (Puertecito) vent stops as that at NE (Nuevo Juatita) vent increases (see p. 153)
	Mar. 15-28	heavy pyroclastic activity resumes without precursors (see p. 152)
	Apr. 9	last sampled lava with relatively constant basaltic andesite composition. All subsequent lavas have <5.3 wt.% MgO, and become increasingly richer in SiO_2 and alkalies to the end of the eruption (see Tables 25 and 26, Figs. 191 and 200)
	Apr. 13	gigantic fountaining at NE cone base (see p. 154)
	June 10	first lava with >0.1 vol.% orthopyroxene phenocrysts (see Table 25, Fig. 188)
	July	highest number of recorded earthquakes (6, tying Nov. 1946) since March 1943, followed by 2 months without any (see Fig. 17 bottom)[1]
	Aug. 10-11	extraordinarily intense explosions; vegetation blighted 10 km away (see p. 156)
	Aug. 14-19	flow from SW vent spreads to north, around west side of cone (see p. 157)
	Sept. 1	Ahuán vent reopens and becomes the main lava producer (see p. 156-157)
	Sept. 5	first lava with <2 vol.% olivine phenocrysts (see Table 25, Fig. 188)
	Oct. 9	lava production ceases at the (Nuevo Juatita) vents on NE flank (see p. 157)

Year	Date	Remarks

1947 --

	Oct. 20	inner rim of cone, building for months, passes outer rim and cone height increases rapidly (see p. 156). Outward form of cone remains about the same from end of October through end of eruption in 1952 (see profiles inside front cover)
	early November	temporary pyroclastic vent opens near the top of the SW slump segment and remains active until Nov. 15 (see p. 156)
	December	last remnants of Sapichu cone, on NE flank, are finally buried by lava from SW vents (see p. 101). Bullard (1984), however, states that Sapichu was buried in the summer of 1946
	Dec. 30	last sample containing olivine microphenocrysts - all earlier samples had them (see Table 25, Fig. 188)

1948 --

	Feb. 7	Nuevo Juatita vents at the NE base reopen. By Feb. 12 the Ahuán vents (SSW base) are quiet and Nuevo Juatita becomes the main lava producer until the close of the eruption in 1952. Explosive activity at main cone declines, and bomb-eroded rills (formed on its flanks in December-January) start to degrade (see p. 158-159)
	early-mid April	collapse of the inactive (SW) Puertecito vent area and slump of the adjacent SW flank of the main cone (see p. 160)
	May 25	explosion throws bombs 1 km NW of crater vent. Lava flow moves NE from Nuevo Juatita vents (NE flank), reaching 2 km distance by end of July (see p. 161)
	June 4-5	temporary lull in otherwise strong lava production at Nuevo Juatita vents (NE-flank) clogs outlet channel (see p. 160)
	late June	lava flow from Nuevo Juatita vents, which started Feb. 7, finally stops 4.1 km to NNW (see p. 161)
	July 31	Ray Wilcox departs and Celedonio Gutiérrez is designated as "resident observer" at Parícutin. With Carl Fries as supervisor he continues daily record keeping until the end of the eruption in 1952 (see p. 131, 162)
	late October	lava flows from Nuevo Juatita that began in July, stop 2½ km to the NNW. New lava flows move toward NE and east (see p. 165)

1949 --

	date unknown	Dionisio Pulido dies in Caltzontzin (see p. 195, and Text Note 32 on p. 401)
	Jan. 4-9	tremendous explosions heard 200 km away; earth tremors common (see p. 163)
	Jan. 27	Fries and Gutiérrez climb cone and observe only one active central vent, in contrast to two or more in recent years (see p. 163)

Year Date	Remarks

early February	lava flow rate, moderate to great since August, drops notably and remains low until end of June (see p. 165)
June 13	explosion throws blocks 1 km from cone. Similar explosions on Apr. 2 and 5, May 13, and June 11 (see p. 163)
end June	lava, moving east from Nuevo Juatita vents (NE flank) since October, stops about 1.7 km to east (see p. 168, Fig. 123)
July 3-4	Nuevo Juatita vents at NE base are briefly stopped up and the old Puertecito vent at the SW base reopens, accompanied by slumping of the SW flank (see·p. 166-168)
July 5	lava flow starts moving north from Nuevo Juatita vents; flow is constant for next 6 months (see p. 167)
July 30	old Puertecito vent area on SW flank ceases erupting (see p. 168)
Aug. 27 and 31	gas bubble eruptions from Nuevo Juatita vents on NE flank. Similar activity on Oct. 12 and 20, Nov. 1 and 29 (see p. 168)
October	last column height >3 km for next 4 months. Ash production continues to decline (see p. 165-166)
Nov. 21 and 28	major explosions (also Aug. 5 and Dec. 24) follow brief periods of inactivity and throw fragments 2 km from volcano; accompanied by increase in flow of lava (see p. 166)

1950 --

month unknown	publication of Dr. Atl's richly illustrated book on the eruption: *¿Como nace y crece un volcán?: El Parícutin* (see Fig. 1 and Plate 7)
Feb. 8	Ezequiel Ordóñez dies in México City at age 83 (see p. 63)
Feb. 16	eruptive column to 4 km above summit. Strong explosivity in January and February, declining in later months. Ashfall also declining (see p. 169)
Feb. 21	Fries and Gutiérrez use alidade to measure highest elevation for west peak of 2,795.1 m, which they convert to a cone height of 397 m (see Table 3). In this book we use 2,385 m as the pre-eruption elevation of Pulido's field (see topographic map of Fig. 13), and thus calculate a cone height of 410 m
Apr. 2	vent blows open at mid-slope on NE flank (see p. 169)
Apr. 28	Fries and Gutiérrez measure highest elevation for west peak as 2,796.6 m (see Table 3); thus cone height is 412 m
July 7	Fries and Gutiérrez repeat alidade measurement of west peak elevation and again record 2,796.6 m (see Table 3); cone height remains 412 m

Year	Date	Remarks
1950		
	August	lava flows NNW of cone, advancing from Nuevo Juatita vents on NE flank since mid 1949, finally cease. Flow fronts to >20 m high (see p. 170)
	Oct. 12	breakthrough at Nuevo Juatita vents on NE flank beheads ongoing lava flows to NNW, halting them with flow fronts nearly 3 km from vents and launching new flows farther to NW (see p. 172)
1951		
	Jan. 21	Mount Lamington erupts in New Guinea; pyroclastic flows kill 2,942 people
	early March	lava flows to NW that began last October end in area of buried Parícutin village (see p. 175)
	May 12	"No. 1" vent blows open on lower NE flank and erupts with declining force, feeding a small amount of lava for 1 week and dying at end of June (see p. 174-175)
	May 18	NE saddle and NE crater rim begin to slump (see p. 174)
	May 25	Fries climbs cone, finding radically changed crater (see p. 174)
	June 9	"No. 2" vent blows open higher on the NE flank and erupts strongly, with probably more material ejected than from the main crater. Rivals main crater in diameter by end of June (see p. 174-175)
	Aug. 27	"No. 2" vent, which had been migrating toward the SW, coalesces with the main crater (see p. 178)
	end October	lava flow that started at Nuevo Juatita vents on NE flank in March ends 4.5 km to north (see p. 178-179)
1952		
	Jan. 1	new vents at SE base of Nuevo Juatita vent mound feed lava flow that reaches 1½ km ESE in early February (see p. 183)
	Jan. - Feb.	eruptive column heights over 3 km and increased ashfall. Explosive events exceed total in preceding 6 months. Lava production also increases - to triple rate of July 1950 - June 1951 (see p. 180, 184)
	Feb. 8	new lava flows from Nuevo Juatita head NE, ultimately reaching 1.8 km NNE at eruption's end (see p. 183-184)
	Feb. 25	lava emission and strong explosions cease after final spasm; activity declines to intermittent, noiseless explosive puffs (see p. 179-181)
	Mar. 4	all eruptive activity ends after small burst at 09:15 (see p. 181)

Year	Date	Remarks
1952		
	Mar. 27-28	earthquakes, seldom felt in recent years, are common after eruptions cease. Several per month felt in Cuezeño (5½ km north of volcano) through September (see p. 183). Three earthquakes with magnitudes ≥3.0 in April after 7 months without any at this magnitude[1] (see Fig. 17)
	Apr. 4	M_S 4.0 earthquake is first (of any magnitude) recorded from Parícutin in last 10 months at Tacubaya in México City (320 km east), and the first of this size in nearly 2 years. An M_S 4.3 is recorded on Apr. 11, and 3 M_S 3.9-4.2 events are recorded on Apr. 23[1]
	Apr. 29	photos of cone and crater from the air taken by Fries[118]
	May 1	Fries and Gutiérrez use alidade to measure final elevation for west peak of 2,808.6 m, (see Table 7), yielding a final cone height of 424 m above Pulido's field
	August	best harvests since birth of volcano (see p. 195)
	Oct. 3	Gutiérrez hears "loud subterranean noise" but sees no perceptible change in volcano (see p. 183)
1953		
		fourth resettlement community: majority of Zirosto population moves to "New Zirosto", 2 km farther NW, in major social disruption (see p. 195)
1954		
		commercial timber production ended by excessive cutting (see 1944 remark). Government withdraws timber-cutting permission, but opens contracts with turpentine industry (see p. 227-228)
1956		
	May 21	William Foshag dies at age 62, 2 months after publication of his important study, co-authored with Jenaro González-Reyna, *Birth and Development of Parícutin Volcano* (see p. 37-43, 47-130)
1957		
	February	Segerstrom returns after 10 years to continue erosion studies. Other field studies in Dec. 1960 and June 1965 (see p. 303-311)
		cone rim colonized by lichens and 2 angiosperms after 5 years. Fourteen species, including pine, found in 1958 (see p. 222)

Year Date	Remarks
<u>1957</u>	---
	incidents of aggression as people move back into volcanic zone. These were particularly strong between former residents from Caltzontzin (original Parícutin) and Nuevo San Juan (original San Juan Parangaricutiro). Escalation in 1965 led to livestock killing and burning of 128 houses in volcanic zone. Surveyors settle boundary disputes in 1969 (see p. 196)
	first cultivation of 9 hectares of land on top of 1944 lava flows NE of cone. Soil ~3 m thick formed by man-made diversion of drainage along east side of lava field (see p. 309)
<u>1960</u>	---
	lavas already supporting 33 species of plants: trees to 4 m height in 1978 (see p. 222)
summer	Willis Eggler compares cone plants with those found in 1957 (see p. 231-232)
<u>1964</u>	---
Aug. 15	Dr. Atl dies in Cuernavaca, México, at age 89 (see p. 382)
<u>1965</u>	---
June 11	Segerstrom returns to cone for description of its stability. No rock slides and very similar to 1960 visit (see p. 307)
July 11	Carl Fries dies in México at age 54 (see p. 162)

Local time = Greenwich Mean Time — 6 hours

Geological Setting

The following brief discussion of the geologic setting of Parícutin volcano is intended for general readers. A more detailed treatment of this topic is presented in a later chapter (p. 243-245).

Most of México's active volcanoes, including Parícutin, are concentrated in a band that runs from east to west for over 1,200 km across the southern part of the country. This band is referred to as the Mexican Volcanic Belt, and it has been the site of volcanic activity for more than 10 million years (Fig. 6). Over that time, a thick pile of volcanic rocks has accumulated to an average elevation of 2,000 m above sea level. Moisture-laden winds blow from the Pacific Ocean and as they rise northward over this high volcanic plateau they produce abundant rains during the summer months of June, July, and August. Coupled with the fertile volcanic soil, these dependable rains make the Mexican Volcanic Belt a rich agricultural region and, therefore, home to the majority of Mexican people. Three of the four largest cities in México are located here: México City, Guadalajara, and Puebla. As a consequence, the lives of México's people and the activity of its volcanoes are intimately linked.

Like all active volcanic regions forming the Ring of Fire that encircles most of the Pacific Ocean, the Mexican Volcanic Belt is a product of subduction. According to modern concepts of Plate Tectonics, the earth's surface is broken into about a dozen large plates and many small ones. These plates form the rigid outer shell of our planet. Their motions relative to one another, which can exceed 10 cm per year, re-flect churnings of the hot, yet solid interior as the earth tries to rid itself of heat in the same way that a pot of soup boils. Most earthquakes and volcanic eruptions take place near these dynamic plate boundaries, which can be grouped into three types depending on the specific nature of the plate motions: spreading centers where two plates separate, subduction zones where two plates move toward one another, and San Andreas-type strike-slip fault zones where two plates move sideways.

The Mexican Volcanic Belt is a continental subduction zone, similar to those in the Andes, the Cascades, Kamchatka, and Japan, which form other portions of the Pacific Ring of Fire. Parícutin volcano, however, lies in an unusual portion of the Mexican Volcanic Belt that includes parts of the states Michoacán and Guanajuato. Instead of containing a few large volcanic centers that erupt intermittently for tens of thousands of years, the Michoacán-Guanajuato Volcanic Field is dominated by about 1,000 widely scattered, small volcanic centers, most of which formed during a single eruption and then became extinct. Only two have formed in historical time: Jorullo, which erupted for 15 years beginning in 1759, and Parícutin, which erupted for 9 years beginning in 1943. This anomalous style of volcanic activity has produced a high, rolling, forested countryside that is one of the most beautiful in all of México. It is no wonder that the people of the area were reluctant to leave when Parícutin volcano came abruptly into their lives on Feb. 20, 1943.

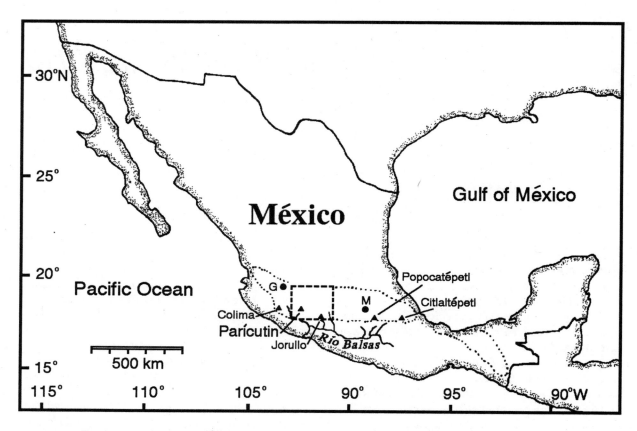

Fig. 6. Location map of México showing the position of Parícutin and Jorullo volcanoes within the Michoacán-Guanajuato Volcanic Field (dashed rectangle) and three large active volcanoes along the southern boundary of the Mexican Volcanic Belt (dotted fields): Colima, Popocatépetl, and Citlaltépetl.

The Area Prior to the Eruption

People and Communities

Nolan (1979)

In this section we reprint only those portions of Nolan (1979) that describe the people and communities prior to the eruption. Portions that treat the effects of the eruption and human responses are reprinted on p. 189-207.

Community Life Before the Volcano

In folk mythology the time before the volcano was a golden age when the region was beautiful and prosperous. Folk songs describe the flowers and singing birds, the rains of summer, and the green fields—a time when all was pleasure and happiness. The region lay along the northern foot of the Cerros de Tancítaro [3,842 m], an old strato-volcano that loomed above a landscape dotted with hundreds of younger and smaller volcanic forms. These were interlaced with a network of valleys that lay at an elevation of about 2,100 m. The valleys and gentle slopes around the villages were cultivated, or allowed to grow in pastures that supported locally owned livestock. The ancient cinder cones and the rocky badlands of old lava flows were covered with forests of pine and oak (p. 217-218, 229-231). These forests provided cover for the region's wild fauna, which primarily consisted of deer, rabbits, many species of birds, and wild bees valued for their honey.

The life of the region's people was not so idyllic as the folk songs suggest, but it was not a bad life. The very lack of abundant resources and transportation networks had left it a place where village farmers, many of whom spoke the Tarascan language, still followed traditional patterns as subsistence tillers of the soil. Most of the valley lands were in private ownership but, according to custom in most commu-

Mary Lee Nolan received her Ph.D. in anthropology at Texas A&M University in 1972. Her dissertation, titled "The towns of the volcano: A study of the human consequences of the eruption of Parícutin volcano"[2], was based on written records and oral histories collected largely from persons who had witnessed the eruptions. This article was published 7 years later and builds on her dissertation work to tell the story of five communities that were affected by the eruption in different ways. Roughly 80% of the local political center, San Juan Parangaricutiro, was buried by lava from the eruption, and the nearby village of Parícutin was first deeply blanketed by ash and then covered with lava. The farming villages of Angahuan, Zacán, and Zirosto were also severely affected by ash (see map inside front cover). Nolan emphasizes that each community responded in different ways that were largely dictated by the social make-up and organization of the town. The article follows these five communities from the time before the eruption through the early 1970s, and stresses the relationship between community responses and the larger socioeconomic forces at work in México during this period. Nolan also discusses these responses to the eruption in the light of more generalized responses to any environmental hazard.

Mary Nolan now teaches in the Geosciences Department of Oregon State University.

nities, were not supposed to be sold to outsiders without the consent of community elders who had paid their dues to society by sponsoring religious fiestas [in a social structure known as the *mayordomía*]. Forest lands were generally in community ownership. They were utilized for timber, with which village homes were built, and for resin sold to nearby turpentine distilleries. Each village had its own craft traditions, as was the custom in the Sierra Tarasca, and goods were exchanged in nearby market towns and during the fairs held in association with local fiestas. One *hacienda* had been established in the region, but its sphere of influence affected only the Zacán community. In many ways, life before the volcano followed the socio-economic model laid down by the Spanish bishop Vasco de Quiroga some four centuries earlier in the wake of the Spanish conquest.

In a general way, the communities to be affected by the volcano were similar. All were designated as *pueblos*, a term that can mean either a village or town. Populations were small, ranging from 733 in Parícutin village to 1,895 in San Juan Parangaricutiro (hereafter referred to as San Juan)[3]. All had been founded as Tarascan Indian settlements. In 1940 some

Fig. 7. Replica of *El Señor de Los Milagros* that is used in processions from San Juan Nuevo to the old church in San Juan Parangaricutiro (see Plate 8A).

people in each of the communities spoke the Tarascan language, although the number varied from 100% in Angahuan to only 20% in Zirosto, indicating that the communities lay along the margin of a shrinking Tarascan culture area[4]. The settlements looked much alike. All were laid out in grid patterns centered on churches. Styles of architecture were much the same, although some communities had a higher proportion of stone and adobe houses than others[4]. Most dwelling lots contained a wooden *troje*, or family ceremonial structure, and a *cocina*, or kitchen structure where the family cooked, ate and slept[5]. The primary resource base for these small communities was composed of the village fields, pastures, and forests. They were relatively isolated physically. The bus trip from San Juan to Uruapan [a major city 22 km to the SE] took 3 hours over an extremely bad road[3], and the region's only telephone had been installed in San Juan only a year or so before the eruptions. San Juan was also the only town with electricity, produced by a small generator that powered lighting for the church and government offices.

Despite their similarities, these communities were distinctive in numerous ways, including orientations toward the larger Mexican society. Some of the communities were, in a sense, preadapted to take advantage of new opportunities, whereas others were either ill prepared for, or particularly resistant to, massive socio-economic changes. The differences rather than the similarities best explain the unique adaptation made by each community in the wake of an abrupt convergence of physical and social forces for change.

San Juan Parangaricutiro

San Juan, the largest, most important town of the region, was *cabecera* [governmental center] of the *municipio* [a political subdivision corresponding roughly to an American township] that contained all but one of the communities. *Mestizo* or Spanish-speaking families were present in the town by the late eighteenth century. Gradually, the percentage of Spanish speakers increased, so that by 1940 they constituted a majority of the population of 1,895. However, the Tarascan-speaking 32% numbered 725 persons and constituted a community within a community. San Juan was the only town described as having two distinct ethnic groups[2,6]. This ethnic division between Indians and *mestizos* was, however, mitigated by San Juan's possession of an extremely powerful icon in the form of a crucifix called the Lord of the Miracles [*El Señor de los Milagros*] (Fig. 7). The image was revered by Indian and *mestizo* alike and both groups valued the profits and status that resulted from being a major regional pilgrimage shrine. Meeting religious obligations was still important to the local achievement of secular power. In 1945, San Juan was a *mestizo* town with a significant Tarascan minority and a traditional local symbol capable of serving to rally both groups in an effort to preserve the community.

Zirosto

The 1,314 people of Zirosto had been oriented toward *mestizo* culture for several generations. The process began with the rise of mule driving, mule-string ownership, and moneylending in the late eighteenth century. By the early twentieth century there was a marked difference between rich and poor families in terms of access to resources and styles of living, although Spanish did not replace Tarascan as the local language until the second decade of the twentieth century. The 20% of the population that claimed to speak Tarascan in 1940 included men from the mule-driving families who used the language for trade in the Sierra, as well as older people and some women. All who discussed Zirosto claimed that there had been no ethnic difference between those who could speak Tarascan in 1940 and those who could not, although genealogical research indicates that there were a few poor and conservative families with Tarascan surnames who were more Indian in orientation than the majority of Zirosto's citizens.

Meanwhile, Zirosto had suffered economic decline as the importance of mule trade was undercut by railroads and highways. The traditional [*mayordomía*] system for sponsoring fiestas was given up in the 1930s when members of the wealthy families refused to accept the burdens, and there had been an exodus of the younger members of these families. When the volcano erupted, Zirosto faced catastrophe with a nineteenth-century *mestizo* orientation.... Compared with the other communities, Zirosto seems to have lacked community solidarity prior to the eruptions.

Angahuan

Angahuan was the most Indian of the villages. All of its 1,098 people spoke Tarascan, and many were monolinguals. Their version of Tarascan was notably different from that spoken in other places[5,7]. The people of Angahuan generally kept to themselves, and few men had ventured far from the boundaries of the community lands prior to 1943. The rule of endogamy [choosing partners from within the community] was strong, although the village contained a few women who had married in from other communities. Two of these women, who had come to Angahuan prior to 1910, were still known locally as "the old lady from San Juan" and the "old lady from Paracho." Community lands were not sold to outsiders and people from other places were not allowed to live permanently in Angahuan. It is said that school teachers sent by the government during the 1930s usually did not remain long, largely because of local hostility.

Before the volcano, Angahuan . . . restricted its social and economic interactions with other communities to an extent that seems to have been unusual for Sierra Tarascan towns in the early 1940s.

Parícutin

The 733 people of Parícutin village were also Tarascan speakers but were considerably more open to the outside world than the people of Angahuan. This greater receptivity to new people and ideas was indicated by fairly frequent exogamous marriages [choosing partners from outside the community], a desire for education, willingness to accept school teachers in the community, and an active agrarian movement. Fifteen percent of the population claimed not to speak Tarascan in 1940, although they probably did, because the Indian tongue was the language of street and household. In spite of these portents of change, the *mayordomía* system was still in effect. Relationships with San Juan were poor because of a longstanding land feud with the neighboring community. As a result of actions by Parícutin's "agrarianists" that were seen as hostile and sacriligious, much of the blame for the volcanic eruption was eventually placed on this small community.

Zacán

Zacán's 876 people were transitional. The half who claimed to speak Tarascan were mostly older people. Men of the village had worked in other parts of the nation since the eighteenth century and some had worked in the United States in the early twentieth century. Apparently, these travelers had been welcomed back into the community, and the tales of their adventures were a part of the community life. The community decision to acculturate toward the norms of the larger society was made before the volcano. The transition from old to new orientations was symbolized in 1941 when the *mayordomía* system of sponsoring local fiestas was abandoned on the advice of a priest and the locally born head of the school, who had traveled widely and had also achieved traditional status in the community by serving as *mayordomo* for the Saint's Day fiesta.

The traditional system demanded hard work and self-sacrifice because the *mayordomo* of a village fiesta had to serve in expensive lesser positions of ceremonial responsibility before he could hope to expend his life savings to pay most of the costs of a major fiesta. The reward was local status and a strong voice in decisions affecting the community[8,9]. Thus, in Zacán the focus of community service changed from the sponsoring of fiestas toward the goal of producing educated children "for México." This transition had just begun when Parícutin devastated the village lands and forced adjustments, which included a period of life in Mexican towns and cities for many families. There men and women had firsthand experience with the benefits of education, and they were to bring this message back to the village.

Other portions of Nolan (1979) concerning the effects of the Parícutin eruption on these five communities are reprinted on p. 189-207. Mary and Sid Nolan have also written a new epilogue for this book (p. 207-214), which extends her study of the "towns of the volcano" for the years since 1971.

Landscape, Vegetation, and Land Use

Rees (1979)

> *John D. Rees received a Master's degree in geography from UCLA in 1961 for his thesis "Changes in Tarascan settlement and economy related to the eruption of Parícutin"[10], and a Ph.D. from the same department in 1971 for his dissertation "Forest utilization by Tarascan agriculturists in Michoacán, México"[11]. In this article, Rees discusses the local economy, natural vegetation, agricultural practices, and settlement patterns in the Parícutin region, and how these were affected by the eruption.*
>
> *John Rees now teaches in the Department of Geography and Urban Analysis at California State University, Los Angeles.*

Sections of his article that describe the situation prior to the eruption are reprinted here. On p. 215- *228 we reprint portions that treat the effects of the eruption.*

Introduction

The cone of Parícutin volcano is situated on the northern flank of Tancítaro, in the upper watershed of the westward-trending Itzícuaro Valley [see inside-front- and back-cover maps]. Parícutin is the most recent of the more than 150 cinder cones that are identified within an area of approximately 1,600 km^2 around it [see p. 245-254]. The majority of the cones are composed of semi-consolidated bedded ash, lapilli, and volcanic bombs; lava flows make up a small area of the surface of most cinder cones. Two types of cone shapes are common: (a) those that are conical with a flat-floored crater, and (b) those that have been breached by volcanic explosions or lava flows and subsequently eroded, leaving one or more sides removed. Flat-floored craters are sometimes cleared of timber and utilized as sites for long-fallow, short-cropping *maize* cultivation. Long fallow is a result of the less fertile and more droughty soils of crater floors.

Although volcanoes and cinder cones are the most imposing landforms, lava flows cover large areas of the Itzícuaro Valley. The lower slopes of Parícutin and many older cones are buried by extensive lava fields. In some cases, the lava flows are narrow on the higher slopes and fan out on lower ones. Flows from Tancítaro and from cinder cones have produced a bench-and-cliff topography. The majority of the ancient flows have undergone considerable weathering and possess a true soil surface that is forested or is in long-fallow, short-cropping plow agriculture. The more recent flows, however, are lava badlands with an extremely rough, blocky rubble of vesicular basalt [*malpais*[12]] that is difficult to cross on foot and usually prevents entry by cattle and other hoofed animals. Although not used for crops or grazing, these lava badlands produce timber that is exploited by Tarascan Indian woodsmen, who are forced to backpack timber products to sites from which pack animals can operate.

Examination of air photos taken in 1934 for the Departmento Agrario [see airphoto composite in Fig. 12] shows that the bottom of the Itzícuaro Valley prior to the eruption of Parícutin was composed of older lava benches and other depositional surfaces. These depositional surfaces were initially produced by airborne ash and lapilli, later augmented by alluvial deposits from nearby slopes. Before the Parícutin eruption, older lava benches and depositional areas made up the cultivable land, whereas the steep bench cliffs, recent flows, cinder cone slopes, and upper slopes of Tancítaro . . . were heavily wooded[13].

Pre-Eruption Settlement and Economy

The villages of the Itzícuaro Valley are located on the valley flatlands at sites not too distant from seeps or springs to serve for domestic use and stock watering. Most villages were founded in the sixteenth century by Spanish monks who resettled the Tarascan Indians from their mountain hamlets to sites on valley flatlands better suited for plow agriculture and close supervision.

The modern Tarascan culture is a mixture of pre-Columbian, colonial, and modern Mexican traits. Pre-Columbian characteristics predominate in the Tarascan language, in major food crops, in the diet and food preparation, and in ceremonial use of certain wild plants. Colonial Spanish influence survives in a conservative form of Roman Catholicism, and in the social structure with its dual political and religious hierarchy and obligatory rituals and feasts that form the prime basis for social prestige. Many of the economic and material aspects of the Tarascan lifestyle also date to colonial times. Examples include the village grid plan, the house types, the land tenure system, sixteenth-century Mediterranean agricultural technology, the presence of some European orchard and field crops, and the cottage production of handicrafts[4].

Villages whose residents consisted of Tarascan Indians or their Spanish-speaking descendants, and who were later disrupted by the Parícutin eruption, included San Juan Parangaricutiro, Zirosto, Angahuan, Zacán, and Parícutin [see inside-front-cover map]. At the time of the eruption these villages were in communication with other areas of México. Their main contacts were through Uruapan and Los Reyes, the regional market towns where the villages sold their small-crop surpluses and forestry and crafts products, and where they purchased factory-made goods in return. Contacts beyond the immediate region were made by traders and those who did harvest labor beyond the Tarascan-language region. These outside contacts, and the government primary school present in each village, helped to expand the use of the Spanish language and accelerated the partial integration of the Tarascans into the national Mexican culture. Use of the Tarascan language had noticeably declined by the time of the 1940 census in two of the settlements affected by Parícutin: Zirosto and San Juan Parangaricutiro[4].

Until the late nineteenth century all lands in the Upper Itzícuaro Valley were communal, with title deeded to individual villages. The village community held title to all land, and village residents inherited or purchased use rights to village house lots, to parcels on the open fields, and to parcels in the forests. After the beginning of the twentieth century, individuals were allowed to register their individual usufruct lands [owned individually but available to other community members for non-damaging use]; thus, conversion of village land to deeded private property took place. This was called to a halt when the Agrarian Code was enforced in the 1940s. In the 1940s, however, the bulk of the cropland was not registered, and few of the registered parcels were sold to outsiders.

At the time of the eruption, two types of traditional land ownership, communal and private, existed in the villages. A third type, the *ejido*, had been introduced by the federal government at Zacán prior to the eruption. (The large Mexican private estate, the *hacienda*, existed only in non-Tarascan areas beyond the Upper Itzícuaro Valley.) The *ejido* is a type of communal land tenure in which the federal government holds the title, and the use rights are held by individuals belonging to the village *ejido* organization. This new type of land tenure was later introduced at the resettlement village of Zirosto Nuevo, 2 km NW of Zirosto, and at resettlement villages beyond the Itzícuaro Valley.

At the time of the eruption, as is still the case today, most village families practiced subsistence agriculture supplemented by forestry and grazing. Crop production methods were traditional, involving manual labor and use of the wooden plow pulled by two oxen [Fig. 8]. Improved hybrid *maize* varieties and chemical fertilizers were not accepted by most families. *Maize* was produced, often intercropped with beans and squash, on unfenced plots on the open fields, on fenced plots on nearby slopes, and on shifting cultivation sites within the forest. Most open field plots and fenced plots on adjoining slopes were fallowed every other year. The use of the digging stick and the hoe was limited to house-lot gardens and steep shifting cultivation sites. The shifting cultivation sites usually required longer fallow periods, and the less fertile plots often were allowed to return to forest. On the open fields the ground was prepared by plowing under the weed growth of the previous fallow during late summer or early fall, and then cross-plowed before seeding took place in late April or early May. The *maize* was plowed at least once to ensure good drainage for the seedlings and to sup-

Fig. 8. Oxen used to pull a wooden plow in the Parícutin region.

little significance. Hunting and gathering existed but were of minor importance.

In the forest, women of the village gathered edible greens, mushrooms, and various other edible and medicinal plants for family use and for sale in Uruapan. At Christmas time, decorative plants and foliage were gathered for sale to Uruapan residents for making Nativity scenes. In the forest, too, most of the cattle grazed, as did poor-quality sheep kept for their meat and wool. Almost all the families in the village owned a burro, a dog, some pigs, and several chickens. Horses and mules were not common because of their high initial cost and the need for higher quality pasturage. Most farming families owned or had access to a pair of oxen; cattle were highly valued as animals for plowing and as capital investment.

Dead time in the agricultural cycle had always been taken up by forestry activities. Pine beams were hand-hewed, and pine and fir shingles were hand-split. Lumber was hand-sawed or hand-hewed into planks or boards. Pine resin was collected most commonly from *Pinus oocarpa*, *Pinus leiophylla*, *Pinus michoacana*, and *Pinus montezumae*, and was shipped to turpentine distilleries in Uruapan. Oak charcoal was produced exclusively for non-Tarascan market towns. All these originated from timber growing on pure communal lands or on forest parcels controlled by individual use rights. Villagers lacking use rights to croplands often depended entirely on forestry for subsistence.

At the time of the eruption, government policy limited the scale of timber production. Existing forestry regulations and new laws enforced in March 1943 required written governmental approval for the cutting of timber to be sold, taxes to be paid on timber sold, and documents accompanying each shipment. The individual Tarascan cutting only an occasional pine found the regulations difficult to comply with, and lacking documentation, his burro-loads of timber products became contraband. The federal government, not wanting to provoke violence, permitted small-scale illegal production and sale, but prohibited larger shipment of timber to other areas of Mexico.

press weeds; a second weeding cultivation was sometimes carried out. The *maize* and bean harvest, generally in late December, was done by the entire family and some hired labor from a nearby village. Upon the agreed date at the end of harvest, the outside fences of the open fields were let down and grazing animals soon removed all signs of cultivated plant life, except for the furrows.

The presence of human and animal refuse on house-lot gardens permitted intensive cultivation of horticulture. The women of the family attended to several vegetables, which included roasting ear and ceremonial *maize*, European cabbage, squash, broad beans, chayote (*Sechium edule*), and husk tomato (*Physalis angulata*). Medicinal and culinary herbs and ornamental flowers were grown. Deciduous fruit trees such as peach, pear, apple, *tejocote* (Mexican crab apple—*Crataegus mexicana*), and *capulín*, a native cherry (*Prunus capuli*), grew unattended. Fruit was the only house-lot garden crop sold outside the village but was usually undersized, and the larger varieties were commonly hail-damaged.

Subsistence agriculture provided the principal, though not the only, source of income for the villagers. Forestry was important as a supplementary source for most agriculturalists, and the primary source of income for the landless. The production of handicrafts in the villages occupied a few full-time specialists but was the part-time occupation of many who were engaged in the other economic activities; the total output for sale outside the village was of

Local Geography

Foshag and González-Reyna (1956)

William Foshag (Figs. 9, 101, and 220)[14] began his career at the Smithsonian Institution's National Museum of Natural History in 1919 and became a curator in 1929. His research was primarily focused on the mineral and mining localities of México and the United States. Foshag first visited Parícutin volcano on March 25, 1943, about one month after the start of the eruption. Through August of 1945 he spent over 120 days in the field at Parícutin, in the company of his colleague Jenaro González-Reyna (Fig. 10), from the Instituto de Geología of the Mexican National University, and other scientists. Of their many contributions to the understanding of Parícutin volcano, Foshag and González-Reyna are probably best remembered for their important oral history of the eyewitnesses to the birth of the volcano, which we have reprinted in its entirety below (p. 54-62). Foshag and González-Reyna also presented a detailed description of the development of the Parícutin eruption during the first 2½ years, accompanied by sketches, maps, and 71 exquisite photographs, many of which we have reproduced.

Foshag played an important role in the U.S. National Committee for the Study of Parícutin Volcano, sponsored by the National Research Council[15]. In cooperation with a similar committee of Mexican scientists, it coordinated research activity at Parícutin and kept the volcano under almost constant observation during the 9 years of its life. The U.S. committee concluded its work in 1951 when 151 of the finest black and white photographs were sent to the U.S. National Archives, along with captions and negatives. Several thousand other photographs of Parícutin were acquired by Foshag and are now part of the Foshag Collection in the Smithsonian Archives. We have made extensive use of both these important photographic resources for the Parícutin eruption.

Foshag received the Roebling Medal of the Mineralogical Society of America in 1954[16]. He was engaged in studies of the fumarolic gases and minerals from Parícutin when he died on May 21, 1956, at the age of 62, two months after the publication of this article. Additional details of Foshag's life and career can be found in memorials written by Ross[17] and Shaller[18].

Jenaro González-Reyna[19], like Parícutin volcano, was born in the state of Michoacán. González-Reyna was a distinguished mining geologist who published scientific studies of many specific ore deposits in México and inventories of the industrial minerals in the states of Zacatecas and Chihuahua. He was a geologist for the state of Querétaro, director of the Mining Department of the Secretary of the Economy, director of the Metallic Minerals Section for the National Institute of Geology, chief of geologists and engineers in the National Institute for the Investigation of Mineral Resources, and in 1956, the Secretary General of the 20th International Geological Congress celebrated in México City. González-Reyna died in México City in 1967.

Fig. 9. William F. Foshag during his studies at Parícutin volcano.

Fig. 10. Jenaro González-Reyna (far right) at Parícutin volcano in the company of Ezequiel Ordonez, Ivan Wilson, and Guillermo Svoboda (right to left).

Here we reprint those portions of Foshag and González-Reyna (1956) that concern the local geographic setting of the Parícutin area prior to the eruption. Many of the features described in this section can be seen on Figs. 12 and 13, composites of air photographs taken in 1936, and on the inside-cover maps.

Local Geography

Before the advent of Parícutin volcano, the principal town of the region was San Juan Parangaricutiro. As is the custom in naming towns in southern México, the designations frequently combine the Spanish name of the town (San Juan) with its indigenous name (Parangaricutiro) . . . . San Juan Parangaricutiro was also the commercial center of the region . . . . The beautiful 18th century church of the town housed the famous Señor de los Milagros [Fig. 7], the figure of a saint venerated throughout the region. An annual celebration and fair was held in honor of this saint on each 14th day of September.

Two kilometers south of San Juan Parangaricutiro was the village of Parícutin, consisting of about 150 Tarascan families. Parícutin was famous for its fruit, particularly pears. West of San Juan Parangaricutiro is Zirosto, also a Tarascan village. About 2 km NE of San Juan Parangaricutiro is the village of Angahuan, a pure Tarascan town, and now, since the destruction of San Juan Parangaricutiro, the largest town of the *municipio*. A beautiful ancient Franciscan chapel faces the main plaza of the town. Zacán is a Tarascan village to the north of San Juan Parangaricutiro and at a higher elevation.

About these villages lie their cultivated fields devoted chiefly to the growing of corn, except on the higher elevations where wheat prospers. Surrounding the fields are wooded old volcanic cones or ridges formed by old lava flows. Rich cornfields occupy the craters of many of these old volcanoes, and oak and pine forests, which are a source of timber and turpentine, cover the volcanic slopes.

Three kilometers south of San Juan Parangaricutiro and 2 km SE of Parícutin lay a small valley, bordered on almost all sides by pine-clad volcanic hills. On the north was Cerro de Jarátiro, with three ancient but well-preserved craters; to the SE was the conical wooded mass of the extinct volcano Cerro Prieto, with several alluvium-filled craters; to the south Cerro de Camiro, Cerro del Cebo, and the lower slopes of Cerros de Tancítaro, with its incumbent later cones; and to the west the steep front of the volcanic Mesa de Cocjarao and the eroded cone of Cerro de Canicjuata [Figs. 12 and 13].

Among the parcels of the land within this valley were two adjoining ones: Llano de Quitzocho and Llano de Cuiyúsuru[20], both belonging to Parícutin. They were separated by a stone wall and were considered valuable for their forest lands and cultivated fields. Barbarino Gutiérrez owned Quitzocho, and Dionisio Pulido owned Cuiyúsuru. A large rock, called Piedra del Sol because it caught the early morning rays of the sun, was a nearby boundary marker. Lava flows now completely fill this small valley, and it is difficult for one who did not know it before the lavas came to picture its original charm. It had a diameter from north to south of 2¼ km, and from east to west, 1½ km. The south end of the valley was occupied by several old lava flows, whose steep fronts formed wooded scarps and crests bore cultivated fields. From these volcanic terraces the ground sloped gently north toward Cerro de Jarátiro. The lowest point in the valley at the foot of Cerro de Jarátiro had an altitude (by aneroid) of 2,375 m . . . The valley was drained by Parícutin Arroyo, whose principal headwaters were between the old volcanic cone of Cerro de Canicjuata and the high lava terrace of the Mesa de Cocjarao. Near its headwaters was the spring that supplied Parícutin village with its potable water. Parícutin Arroyo carried a flow of water only during the rainy season. A small tributary, usually dry, passed through the cultivated lands of Cuiyúsuru. Parícutin Arroyo left the valley through a narrow gap between the lower slopes of Cerro de Canicjuata and Cerro de Jarátiro [Figs. 12 and 13] near the parcel Titizu, where it was a steep-walled gully about 4 m deep. It then passed the east edge of Parícutin village, turned west, and joined the Arroyo Principal of San Juan Parangaricutiro in the fields of Huirambosta.

At the eastern foot of Cerro do Jarátiro was the parcel of land La Lagunita, a small depressed area sometimes occupied by an ephemeral pond. Drainage to the NE was not well defined; a few shallow *arroyos* joined the Arroyo Principal above San Juan Parangaricutiro, along the San Juan Parangaricutiro-Uruapan road.

Except for trees along Parícutin Arroyo and its tributaries and a few small copses of pines, the valley land was cultivated. No permanent dwellings were in the valley, but stone walls or fences separated one parcel of land from another. The little used Uruapan-Parícutin road followed the foot of Cerro de Jarátiro, and wood roads and horse trails passed through the forest lands. The road to Camiro, Teruto, San Nicolás, and other points skirted the valley on the east.

One of the minor features of the valley that attracted some attention was a small hole in the farm Cuiyúsuru. Dionisio Pulido, owner of the farm, described it as having a diameter of 5 m and a depth of 1½ m. Sra. Severiana Murillo, now an old lady, recalled how, as a child more than 50 years ago, she played about the pit. She remembers it well because her father warned her to avoid the spot, because, he said, it was the entrance to an old spanish mine (although no mining activity has been recorded in the region) and because one frequently heard subterranean noises near the hole, as if made by falling rocks. The children amused themselves about this hole because it emitted a pleasant warmth, and they probed it with sticks without touching a bottom.

Robles-Ramos[21] quotes Vicente Mediano as relating that he noted a depression that had formed in the field as early as the month of August 1942, and that a kind of mist was emitted from it during a period of rains, but he attached little importance to it. Dionisio Pulido sometimes referred to this pit as a *resumidero*, a hole in a closed basin through which storm waters escaped during the rainy season.

As is usual in these regions of Michoacán, the tillable lands are privately owned, but the forest lands belong, in large part, to the villages. The forests, being sources of lumber and turpentine, are an important asset to the community. The owners of the *parcelas*, or farms, live in the villages, and the workers travel each day with their oxen and tools from the village to their fields or to the forest, returning in the evening to their homes.

39

Fig. 11. Oblique airphoto view of Parícutin region from the NE taken in Dec. 1942, 2 months before the start of the eruption. Interpretive sketch below.

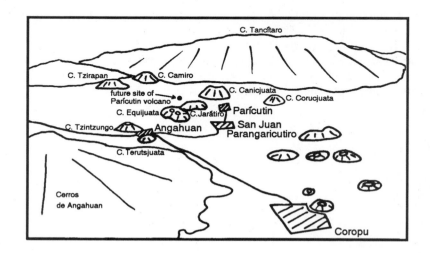

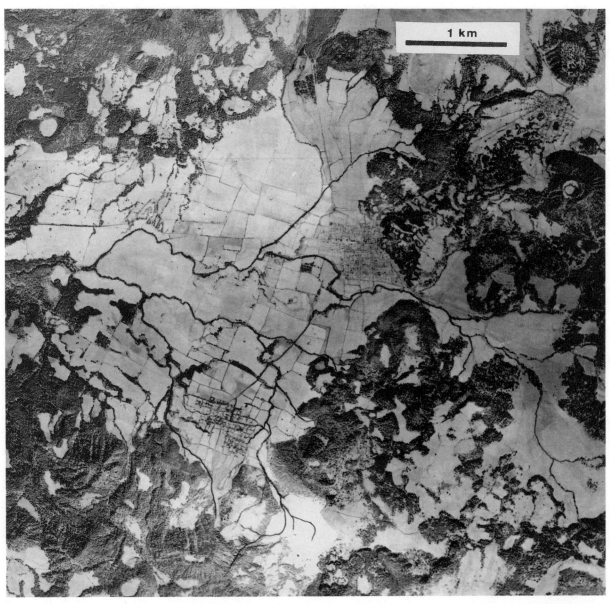

Fig. 12. Airphoto composite of the Parícutin region taken in 1936, 7 years before the start of the eruption. Interpretive sketch (lower right) shows site of eruption (triangle) as well as final outline of the lava field.

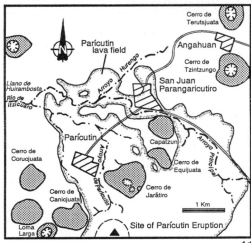

41

Fig. 13. Airphoto composite of the area immediately surrounding the future site of Parícutin volcano, probably also taken in 1936. Facing page shows topography and geography of the same area.

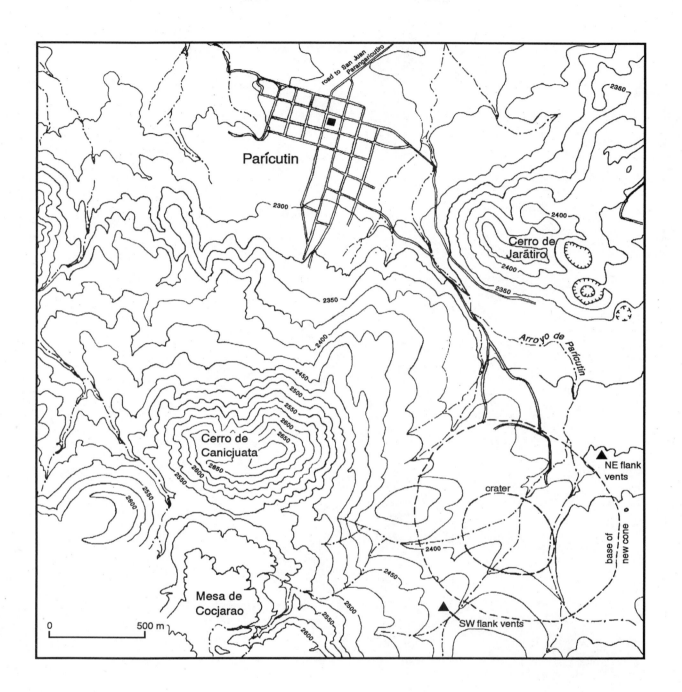

Birth and Development of Parícutin Volcano Mexico

By WILLIAM F. FOSHAG *and* JENARO GONZÁLEZ R.

GEOLOGIC INVESTIGATIONS IN THE PARÍCUTIN AREA, MEXICO

GEOLOGICAL SURVEY BULLETIN 965-D

Prepared in cooperation with the Comisión Impulsora y Coordinadora de la Investigación Científica de México, under the auspices of the Interdepartmental Committee on Scientific and Cultural Cooperation, Department of State

the VOLCANO that grows in a cornfield

1 "About every sixty seconds, day and night, Paricutin volcano has been erupting since its birth five years ago," writes Gene Rossi, a friend of Canadian Club visiting in Mexico. "In a farmer's quiet cornfield, at three o'clock in the afternoon of February 20, 1943, the earth started to smoke. Then, with a thunderous roar and an earthquake, Paricutin announced its own birth.

III. Birth and Eruption History

NEW YORK WORLD-TELEGRAM, WEDNESDAY, APRIL 28, 1943.

New Nature Marvel
Below Rio Grande

TRAVEL and RESORTS

America
at Folk

'Volcano Hurled Piano-Sized Rocks — We Ducked'

U. S. Colonel Tells of Mexican Visit

(This account of a trip to Mexico's volcano was contained in a letter written last month by Col. Alexander Macnab to a friend in New York. Colonel Macnab is author of the infantry rifle manual which has been in use since World War I.)

The new volcano in Michoacan state is the sight of the century. No words could describe the grandeur of the thing. At night it is a breath-taking object of wonder. In the dark the mountain itself (it is now more than 1200 feet high, having started five weeks ago in a level field) is a blood-red color, as are all of the rocks thrown out by it. Most of them are semimolten with the heat.

The flaming gases shoot up about 1000 feet, and then thousands of rocks of all sizes go shooting on upward and upward until some of them get mixed with the stars. We timed some of them on their downward flight, and a great many were up more than 3000 feet.

There were red-hot rocks in the air all of the time, some going up and others coming down. Most of these fall on the sides of the volcano or back into the crater—but many land out on the __ yond the ___

Tossing tons of rock, lava and sand heavenward with its growing pains, Mexico's new volcano, Paricutin, is impressive by day.

From photographs of M. S. Valladares.

has been improvised and the land has been made federal property. Plans for setting up an observatory at some nearby safe spot are being discussed.

In the meantime the lava is pouring out, particularly on the northeast side. One Mexican scientist reports:

"The intensity of the heat has destroyed all vegetation and the lava river, which advances about seven feet per hour, has reached a depth of from 45 to 100 feet, according to the depressions of the soil.

"As it advances, the lava pushes up the ground and grass as if it were an immense rake cleaning the surface to facilitate its smooth running. These lava waves threaten the whole valley."

The government has moved neighboring families out of danger.　　　—G. H.

Early Vacation Offer.

Special to the World-Telegram.

KIAMESH__

Watch__

Dr. D__
sort of __
bottom __
most no__
favorite __
day and __
ning.

The occ__
which can __
be avoided __
one side af__
the probab__
burning sto__
ones would __
down. Keep__
for these vis__
this stiff nec__

Del Rio wa__
picture of h__
rocks. Which __
because he c__
watching the __
swooshing app__
would have to__
into the camer__
fused to be a __
foolishness.

We took a com__
with food, wate__
We had a coupl__
tarpaulins which __
handy in constr__
over the kitchen a__
area to protect ou__
volcanic sands an__

Birthday of a VOLCANO . . .

Tad Nichols found acid-fumes of three-year-old Paricutin ruined lenses of his cameras

WHEN TAD NICHOLS, the Arizona geologist-photographer, whirled away in an Army helicopter to get some fresh pictures of Paricutin, he made one interesting—but tragic—photographic discovery. Nichols, who makes his home base at Tucson, Arizona—Paricutin will celebrate its third birthday February 20—as most proud fathers have made of their baby sons.

Using a 3¼ x 4¼ news type camera loaded with color film, Nichols and his pilot whirled up as close as he could get to the rim of the evil-looking crater without getting caught in the explosive rain of ash and boulders, and obtained some of the most successful shots yet taken of the crater. Then the helicopter fluttered down the slope, which was streaming with crashing rocks and boulders, and Nichols landed to photograph steam vents and fumaroles (holes from which smoke issued) in the __ At this point he was using a 35mm. camera. "With__ it," he said, "the gases were condensing__ the apparent fog on the __ ___ piece of tissue."

of his photographer-friends. Nichols consulted chemists who told him that the presence of hydrofluoric acid in the gases coming from the volcano had probably been the cause. "Whatever it was," he says, "our lenses will have to be re-ground and polished. It was interesting to note that only the exterior of the front element was affected although the presence of hydrochloric acid corroded all metal surfaces of my camera and tripod which were not chromium plated. The fumes, fortunately did not penetrate the camera itself. Strangely, the acid does not act on ordinary glass of viewfinders, nor always on haze filters, and hence, if I visit the volcano again I shall use clear glass filters over all my camera lenses."

Paricutin not only is dangerous, as Nichols found, to unprotected lenses, but in general is not an easy photographic subject, as increasing numbers of tourists-photographers will find out. Nichols used Panatomic-X film with K2 and G filters. Exposures for the pictures shown on these pages were made by light meter, and it was found that a tremendous range in light values existed between the sky and the black, almost non-reflective lava and ash. A basic exposure of 1/50th of a second at f/6.3, with K2 filter, resulted in overexposure of the sky which had to be given considerable correction when making the prints. The weather was very variable, and bad, with much cloud and rain."

Nichols' pictures have recorded the interesting difference in the types of lava which have pushed out from Paricutin's base (not over the crater's rim as might be thought). The flow which covered the Tarascan Indian town of San Juan consists of gigantic, rough blocks, but the newer flow of last summer broke into small crumbling rocks which advanced in clouds of dust.

Toward evening, red-hot "bombs" present the world's greatest display of fireworks, thrown 1,000 feet into the air. Some of these volcanic bombs are boulders two or three feet across. Some fall back into the mouth of the crater. Others land on the sides and go rushing down ___ to the accompaniment of inner rumbling__

Precursors to the Eruption

Following the birth of Parícutin volcano on Feb. 20, 1943, three different phenomena were said to have foretold the pending eruption. Among these precursors, two are allegorical in nature: the destruction of a cross placed upon Tancítaro volcano in 1941, and a plague of locusts that affected the region in February of 1942. The third precursor is more firmly based in science: a sequence of earthquakes that built in intensity during the two weeks preceding the eruption.

Destruction of the Cross on Tancítaro Volcano

Foshag and González-Reyna (1956)

The tragedy of the people of the region about Parícutin began, according to their beliefs, many years ago. Then San Juan Parangaricutiro, the town that became the important center of the area, the greatest in influence, and the governing head of the *municipio*, bought lands from other villages to add to its municipal domain. Parícutin, too, sold lands to San Juan Parangaricutiro; but San Juan Parangaricutiro, according to those of Parícutin, took to itself more than it had purchased. Parícutin offered to settle for *"4 cargas más cuartillos de pesos,"* in accordance with an ancient manner of payment; but no accord or compromise could be agreed upon. This situation led to constant and acrimonious disputes, until there developed such a deep feeling of enmity that those of one village hardly dared pass upon the lands of the other. This animosity led to frequent altercations on the disputed lands, during one of which Nicolás Toral, of Parícutin, lost his life, almost on the spot where the new volcano was to break forth.

The ecclesiastical authorities of the parish, desiring that the dispute should cease and the two villages live in harmony, placed upon Peña del Horno, a huge rock high on the flanks of Cerros de Tancítaro [see inside-front-cover map], a large wooden cross with an inscribed plaque of silver, facing the part of the valley that included the disputed lands. To inaugurate this anticipated happy period, the parish priest, in the presence of a large assemblage of people, held a solemn mass and blessed the sacred symbol.

Some days passed in peace, until it was discovered that the cross had been cut down and had disappeared, an act of sacrilege committed perhaps under the misapprehension that the cross was intended to fix the disputed boundary line. The finger of suspicion pointed to a poor stutterer, Padilla of Parícutin, who henceforth lived in some anxiety and danger.

The Tarascan *tharepeti*, a council of patriarchs that met periodically to deliberate matters of communal interest and to augur the signs of the future, considered this event with dark forebodings and prognosticated a punishment without equal, a punishment that would cause their misery and ruin. Sra. Justina Sánchez, of Parícutin, no doubt influenced by the prediction of the *tharepeti*, saw in her dreams a fire issue from the earth and consume everything. This incident, which the outbreak of the volcano seemed later so strikingly to confirm, profoundly impressed many of the people.

While the sacrilege of the cross was generally considered the major sin that brought the destruction to the region, there were persons who believed that their personal slight sins were a contributory factor.

In spite of these beliefs as to its ultimate cause, the people recognized the volcano as a natural phenomenon and readily connected the growing cone and the flowing lava with similar features of the region with which they had an everyday familiarity—the wooded cones, the cultivated valleys and benches, and the rugged *malpais*[12].

Plague of Locusts

Gutiérrez (1972)

The following story of Celedonio Gutiérrez was extracted, with minor modifications, from the introduction to this article, written by Mary Lee Nolan.

Celedonio Gutiérrez-Acosta (Figs. 14 and 120) was born the son of a peasant farmer in San Juan Parangaricutiro in 1908. He had three or four years of schooling as a child and later two years of night school. He lived an ordinary life for a resident of San Juan Parangaricutiro, where he had assumed minor positions in the administration. After the birth of Parícutin, Gutiérrez was appointed by the president of San Juan to receive and assist the scientists who came to study the volcano. He was a major source of information for the historical studies of Foshag and González-Reyna, and assisted in the field studies of Segerstrom, Wilcox, Fries, and others. Throughout the eruption of Parícutin, Gutiérrez kept diaries of events and his impressions. This article is based on those diaries. His account is particularly important because he appears to have been the only resident of San Juan Parangaricutiro to have committed impressions to paper as events were happening. Gutiérrez was instructed by Wilcox in keeping scientific records of the eruptive activity. He ultimately was designated the "resident observer" at Parícutin for the joint monitoring efforts of the U.S. Geological Survey and the Mexican Instituto Nacional de Investigación Científica, and performed this task, with supervision by Carl Fries, continuously from 1948 until the end of the eruption in 1952. The results of this monitoring effort were published in a series of co-authored reports, reproduced on p. 162-184.

Gutiérrez lives in San Juan Nuevo, where he presides over the Parícutin Museum in his home.

We reprint here only a short section of Gutiérrez (1972) that deals with the locust plague of 1942.

In the following year of 1942, precisely in the same month of February, there appeared a plague of locusts so thick that they almost obscured the sun throughout the region from the towns of Zirosto, Zacán, and Parícutin to San Juan and Angahuan. Everyone thought that this plague would finish all the corn, since in 15 days the locusts had already eaten most of the leaves of the trees and the whiskers of the pines. The insects were so glutted that all the trees hung with them, and branches fell from the weight. On the ground there was not an inch where one could step, and the air was so filled that one could not see. The government first sent pastes to poison the plague, but instead cattle were poisoned and died in the fields. Then the government sent a truck with gasoline and gave 10 machines for burning the insects. For more than a month the battle raged day and night. Hundreds and hundreds of insects fell flat on the ground, but even this did not lessen their numbers. Then everyone decided to scare off the pests by making noises with bands of music, fireworks, drums, tin vessels, and other things, and thus the locusts were forced to retreat. Here you see the first punishment of this region, which was to be continued in February of the following year of 1943 with the eruption of the volcano.

Earthquakes

The next few paragraphs from Foshag and González-Reyna (1956) summarize various anecdotal accounts of the earthquakes that preceded the outbreak of Parícutin volcano. This is followed by reprinting of major portions of Yokoyama and De la Cruz-Reyna (1990), who discuss the seismographs in operation at the time of the eruption and interpret the instrumental record.

Foshag and González-Reyna (1956)

Early February is the season when the villagers are in the fields, cleaning the land or otherwise occupied in preparing for the first plowing of the year. It was then that the first premonitive tremors were felt and the first subterranean noises heard.

Celedonio Gutiérrez has given us some account of the few weeks preceding the outbreak of the volcano, a translation of which is given here:

The year 1943 began. When I visited a friend on a ranch called Titzicato, some few kilometers south of where the new volcano broke forth, he told me that some tremors had already begun in these places and they heard many noises in the center of the earth. These tremors began to be felt in San Juan Parangaricutiro the following month, the 5th of February, at midday, and every day until the 20th. During these 15 days of tremors there were some stronger than others; when we heard the subterranean noises we awaited the tremor. According to the noise the movement of the earth was strong or weak. They followed each other almost every minute. If they were delayed, the noise or the tremor was stronger.

The people could not feel secure nor have confidence to remain in their houses to sleep. They knelt down frequently to pray to God that the earth would not sink, such was the movement during so many days of earthquakes. They brought forth the Image of the Santo Cristo Milagroso, of this village, in procession and the earthquakes ceased. I write this because I have seen it and not because it was told to me.

The priest Sr. José Caballero, then parish priest of San Juan Parangaricutiro, related that light earth tremors began to be felt on February 7, 1943. On the 15th, at 5 p.m., they reached an alarming intensity. At 10 a.m. on the 20th subterranean noises were heard in San Juan Parangaricutiro; and the tremors were then, without exception, oscillatory. Sr. Caballero recalled that when he first came to San Juan Parangaricutiro and Parícutin as parish priest in 1933, the walls of the churches of both villages were fissured to a notable extent, suggesting to him that tremors were already active at that early date.

Professor Ruperto Torres L., editor of a newspaper at Uruapan and a resident of that town for many years, related that some 2 years before the outbreak of Parícutin volcano, rather weak tremors were felt in the region. No particular significance was ascribed to them, since they were generally considered to be tectonic tremors with an origin in the Pacific Ocean, a not infrequent occurrence in the littoral of Colima, Michoacán, and Guerrero. According to Professor Torres, tremors were again felt on the 5th of February 1943, but no importance was attached to them. By February 10 the tremors were more frequent and of greater intensity but were still considered to have a distant origin. On the 20th a messenger from San Juan Parangaricutiro arrived in Uruapan with word from the *presidente*, Sr. Felipe Cuara-Amezcua, to the *presidente* of Uruapan, reporting in alarming terms that the region of San Juan Parangaricutiro and

Fig. 14. Celedonio Gutiérrez (right), Dionisio Pulido (center) and Ariel Hernández-Velasco (left) in Los Reyes, taken in June 1946.

Parícutin was experiencing such strong and frequent tremors that neither the municipal nor church authorities, nor the people, knew what to do. On the same evening a second messenger arrived with word that the tremors had ceased but that a volcano had broken out between the fields of Cuiyúsuru and Quitzocho. An urgent plea for help was then dispatched to the Governor of the State at Morelia.

According to Sr. Felipe Cuara-Amezcua, earth tremors began to be noticeable on February 5, 1943, increasing in number and intensity until more than 200 were experienced in a day. The tremors became so frequent and strong that it was feared that the church at San Juan Parangaricutiro, with its massive masonry walls, would collapse. The parish priest, José Caballero, had the image of the saint *El Señor de los Milagros* removed to the plaza, facing, by a strange coincidence, the point where the new volcano would break out. These tremors were accompanied by subterranean noises. Both the tremors and noises seemed to center in Cuiyúsuru, which led him to believe that Cerro Prieto, an ancient cone that lay immediately adjacent to the farm, would break its age-long rest and erupt.

According to Robles-Ramos[21] the earthquakes varied between intensities 3 and 4, Mercalli's scale.

Yokoyama and De la Cruz-Reyna (1990)

Previous Work

Many reports on geological and geophysical observations of the activity of Parícutin volcano from its birth to development are available. However, reports on its seismic activity are scarce.

Flores-Covarrubias[22] descriptively discussed the earthquakes observed by the Mexican Seismological Network before and after the outburst of the volcano, mainly from the viewpoint of seismometry. These earthquakes include the precursory ones of the Parícutin eruption and tectonic ones occurring along the Pacific coast.

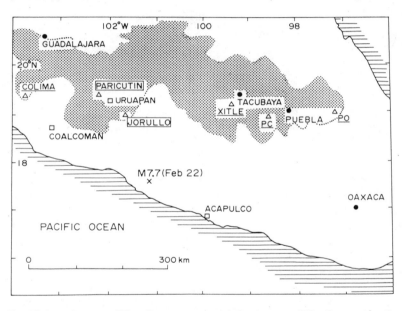

Fig. 15. Location map. Triangles represent active volcanoes (PC = Popocatépetl; PO = Pico de Orizaba [Citlaltépetl]) and solid circles the seismological stations in the 1940s. Stippling indicates most of the Trans-Mexican Volcanic Belt.

Flores-Covarrubias[23] observed volcanic tremor recorded on a vertical seismograph of Mintrop-Wiechert type (natural period 0.9 s) at a point about 1.1 km distant from the volcano during March 5 to 9, 1943. He reported that the predominant periods of the tremors were grouped into two bands, 0.1 ~ 0.2 s and 0.35 ~ 0.60 s. Comparative discussion of spectra of volcanic tremors at various volcanoes (e.g. Shimozuru[24], Fig. 9) shows that the above predominant periods seem to be rather short considering the volcano was effusing basalt-andesitic lavas (the Quitzocho flow) during the observation. However, it should be pointed out that these predominant periods were confined to a particular stage of the activity and a particular observation point.

Available Data and Limits of the Discussions

During the 1940s, the Mexican Seismological Network was under operation using mainly seismographs of the Weichert type. The closest stations to Parícutin were about 180 km to the NW in Guadalajara, Tacubaya in México City, located about 320 km east of the volcano, Puebla, about 430 km to the east, and Oaxaca, 650 km to the SE (Fig. 15). The seismograms were recorded on smoked paper. The recording speed was not always uniform, about 60 mm min^{-1}, which resulted in small errors in estimating (S-P) durations. Guadalajara, Puebla, and Oaxaca had similar systems and low magnifications. Tacubaya had a higher magnification and registered more Parícutin earthquakes than any of the others.

The seismograms containing the earthquakes reported in *Catalogue of Earthquakes of the Mexican Seismological Network* are preserved at the Tacubaya station. These were reexamined by the authors. Some earthquakes originating in the Parícutin area were also registered at the Guadalajara station, and their seismograms were also examined.

Limitations of the data include confinement of our reexamination of seismograms to events registered in the *Catalogue*. The seismograms of the Tacubaya station for December 1942 do not exist because the seismographs were then under repair. Therefore, we cannot determine the seismic activity of Parícutin volcano before January 1943 at the same level of instrumental magnification. However, seismograms for the Guadalajara station do not show any earthquakes of M > 3.6 during December 1942 that appear to have originated from the Parícutin area.

Due to the low magnification of the seismographs . . . and the seismic noise level at the Tacubaya station, detection capability is limited to earthquakes of trace amplitude of 1 mm and larger. This translates into a magnitude of 3.0 for earthquakes (as will be seen later) occurring in the Parícutin area. Actually we could use only the seismograms from the Tacubaya station, because the magnifications of the seismographs of the Guadalajara station were lower and unable to detect Parícutin earthquakes of M < 3.6. The lack of readings from the closer Guadalajara station added to the problem of determining hypocenters precisely.

Besides seismological data, visual determination of eruption rates, and topographic changes, we cannot find any quantitative deformation or barometric pressure data[25] during the eruption of Parícutin volcano.

Identification of the Parícutin Earthquakes

Precursory Earthquakes Observed at Tacubaya

A discussion follows concerning the methods used to distinguish Parícutin earthquakes from tectonic events along the Middle America Trench. With greatly improved coverage of seismological stations, earthquake location is much easier today, but as discussed above, many of the relatively low-magnitude events that preceded and followed the birth of Parícutin in the 1940s were only recorded by the Tacubaya station. The authors first screened the set of possible earthquakes for those having appropriate distances from Tacubaya (300-340 km) as determined from the difference in arrival times of S and P waves. They then analyzed the spectra of the P and S waves and found it possible to distinguish in this way Parícutin-related events from earthquakes along the trench.

. . . . .

In total, twenty-two precursory earthquakes were identified with the 1943 eruption of Parícutin . . . . In the present paper all the events are in local time (GMT - 6 hours), in order to simplify correlation with local earthquake intensity information and reported visual phenomena. The first detected precursory earthquake exceeding magnitude 3.0 occurred on January 7, 1943, 45 days before the outbreak of the volcano. It is difficult to find any changes in (S-P) durations and in dominant frequency as functions of time.

According to Flores[26], in mid-February 1943, the Central Seismological Station (Tacubaya) reported that a series of microearthquakes were registered starting on February 7, and that their epicenters were located at San Juan Parangaricutiro, about 5 km distance from the present Parícutin volcano. However, in the *Catalogue of Earthquakes* published by the Central Station, one finds only two probable Parícutin earthquakes around February 7: one occurred at 03:25 February 8, and the other at 04:55 February 8 . . . . The latter was reported to have been felt at Coalcoman, at about 120 km distance SW from Parícutin (Fig. 15).

Volcanic Earthquakes Felt Around Parícutin Before Its Outbreak

According to Foshag and González-Reyna (see p. 49), the priest José Caballero recalled that when he first came to San Juan Parangaricutiro and Parícutin in 1933, the walls of the churches of both villages were fissured to a notable extent, suggesting to him that tremors already occurred at that early date. Considering that this area is not very far from the seismically active zone of the Pacific trench, these fissures noticed 10 years before the outbreak, may not necessarily be attributed to activity of Parícutin volcano. Again according to Foshag and Gonzalez-Reyna (see p. 49), one of the villagers, Celedonio Gutiérrez, felt the first premonitory tremors in San Juan Parangaricutiro at midday of February 5. These tremors must have been rather local because we did not find any instrumental reports about the events in the Catalogue of Earthquakes.

According to Trask[27], a newspaper dated February 12, 1943 reported that 25 to 30 earthquakes were felt at San Juan Parangaricutiro on the previous day. Subsequent reports indicated that the activity rapidly increased day by day, reaching about 300 earthquakes on February 19. There were no descriptions of continuing activity on February 20. The early report may include earthquake No. 11 (M 4.0), and the latter account may be related to earthquake No. 20 (M 4.5) [Fig. 16].

According to Robles-Ramos[21], countless small local shocks occurred around Parícutin after 13:00 of February 7 and until February 14. Seismic movements of intensity 3-4 on the Mercalli Scale began 3 days before the outbreak, some of which were accompanied by ground noises. It is notable that small precursory earthquakes that were felt, rapidly increased in number toward the outbreak, while the Tacubaya seismographs recorded only the larger ones of M ≥ 3.0. Closely before the outbreak of Parícutin volcano, several moderate tectonic earthquakes occurred at the Pacific coast. These occurred at 18:35 and 20:07 February 16 (M 4.9 and 4.5, respectively), and 23:16 February 19 (M 3.7). After the onset of eruption, an earthquake of M 6.0 occurred at 15°53'N, 98°56'W at 18:08 February 20. Two days after the outbreak, at 03:21 February 22, an earthquake of magnitude 7.7 [28] occurred near the Pacific coast at 17.6°N, 101.2°W, and depth 16 km (Fig. 15). It is natural to suspect some relationship between such large tectonic earthquakes and the eruption of Parícutin volcano. Earthquake movements acting at a volcano possibly may trigger its activity if it is under critical condition, and this effect may be exemplified by other correlations, such as the 1960 Chilean earthquake (M 8.5), and 48 hours later eruption of Puyehue volcano, which was about 300 km distance from the earthquake epicenter. The reverse cases may be probable if a volcano is located near the epicentral area. The 1914 eruption of Sakurajima volcano was believed to have triggered the earthquake of M 7.1 nearby. Parícutin volcano is about 220 km from the epicenter of the February 22 earthquake, and it seems too far to have triggered the earthquake.

As mentioned above, the Tacubaya station could only detect earthquakes in the Parícutin area, 320 km away, with magnitudes equal or greater than 3.0. Considering location errors, only events occurring in the distance range 300 to 340 km are considered. This may represent a good sample of earthquakes that actually originated in the Parícutin region. The largest earthquakes of each month ($4.0 \leq M < 4.6$) during the period are plotted in Fig. 17 (middle). In 1941 and 1942, before the outbreak, the Tacubaya station recorded some earthquakes of $M \leq 4.0$. It is difficult to determine whether these were directly associated with the activity of Parícutin volcano or were tectonic earthquakes occurring in the above distance range, because identification by means of spectral analysis can not be applied to such small earthquakes. This is a limit of accuracy in the present discussion. The seismic activity was rather high in March 1943, after the outbreak, and the activity, including earthquakes of magnitude larger than 4.0, continued with highs and lows until 1950. Thereafter, until 1953, following the end of the eruption on March 4, 1952, the seismicity was as low as it was in 1941 and 1942. In April 1952 the seismicity renewed slightly. This may have been due to readjustment of stresses around the volcano. [The chronology of the eruption (see p. 10-28) includes all earthquakes in the Parícutin area during the 9 years of the eruption, from an unpublished list kindly provided by Yokoyama.]

According to Wilcox (see p. 338, Fig. 191), the lavas notably increased in SiO_2 content in 1947. This caused an increase in viscosity of the lavas, and may have influenced the eruption rate: a stepwise decrease superimposed on an exponential decrease is noticeable in Fig. 17 (top), which is reproduced from Fries (see Fig. 4 and p. 313-314). Scandone[28] interpreted the declining rate in the last four years as due to the absorption of energy by the process of differentiation, and roughly speaking, the seismic activity shows a decreasing tendency after 1947 (Fig. 17).

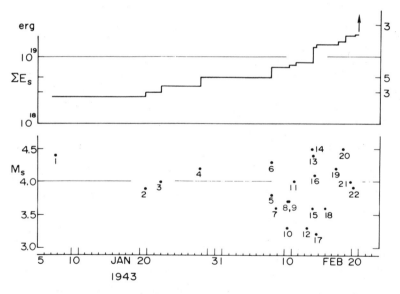

Fig. 16. Magnitudes M_s of precursory volcanic earthquakes (bottom) and their cumulative seismic energy releases E_s (top) . . . . The upward arrow shows the outbreak of Parícutin volcano. [Numerals show the events in sequence].

Earthquake Activity of Parícutin Volcano During 1941 to 1953

In order to identify the volcanogenetic earthquakes in this region, seismic activity during the period 1941 to 1953 including that directly related with the Parícutin eruption was examined: monthly numbers of the earthquakes reported in the *Catalogue* are shown in Fig. 17 (bottom).

Seismic Energy Release by the Precursory Earthquakes

The procedure is explained by which the authors determined earthquake magnitudes and seismic energy release.

The magnitudes of precursory earthquakes are thus determined as shown in Fig. 16 (bottom), where two earthquakes are of magnitude 4.5 and another two have magnitude 4.4. Except for the first earthquake on January 7, which was one of the largest, the maximum earthquake magnitudes increased with time towards the outbreak.

Volcanological Significance

Threshold of Cumulative Seismic Energy Released by Precursory Earthquakes

Beneath active volcanoes, energy is supplied from depth by the ascent of magmas, release of gases, and conduction of heat, and is then stored in various forms: elastic, thermal, and others. Some of these forms of energy are released during the opening of paths for magma ascent towards the vents. As the paths are fractured, part of the energy is radiated as seismic waves and frictional heat. The outbreaks of volcanic eruptions are triggered by fractures reaching the surface. The cumulative release of seismic energy is a measure of the fracturing. One may correlate the precursory earthquakes with opening of the magma paths to the earth's surface. We may assume that the magma-filled cracks would be closed by lithostatic pressure with time after eruptions.

Statistically there is a certain threshold of cumulative precursory seismic energy release after which volcanic eruptions start. Yokoyama[29] estimated this threshold as $10^{17\text{-}18}$ ergs for polygenetic andesitic or dacitic volcanoes erupting after a period of long quiescence, say more than 10 years.

In the case of monogenetic eruptions, the magma-filled cracks must be opened in a presumably less fractured crust, and may need more energy than polygenetic eruptions even considering that their magmas are basaltic or andesitic.

The cumulative seismic energy released by precursory earthquakes of Parícutin volcano is shown in Fig. 16 (top). The curve increases exponentially toward the outbreak and totals 2×10^{19} ergs, corresponding to the energy release from a single earthquake of M 5.0. Considering that the Parícutin lavas are basaltic andesite, the volcano released a fairly large amount of seismic energy in opening magma paths. This must be one of the characteristics of monogenetic eruptions. It is reported that the 1759 eruption of Jorullo volcano was preceded by violent earthquake swarms and its activity continued for 15 years[30]. In these two examples of historical activity of monogenetic volcanoes, the eruptions lasted for rather long periods (9 and 15 years); this may be another characteristic of monogenetic eruptions.

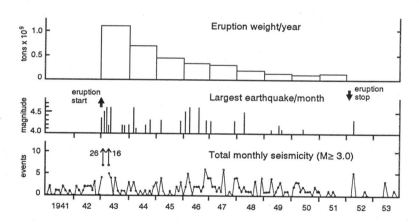

Fig. 17. Seismicity summary 1941 to 1953. The lower plot shows monthly numbers (n) of earthquakes probably occurring in the Parícutin area; they have magnitudes ≥3 and epicentral distances from the Tacubaya station of 300 to 340 km. The middle plot shows the largest earthquake (M ≥ 4) for each month, with arrows marking the beginning and end of the eruption. The top plot shows the annual eruption rate of Parícutin volcano in tons after Fries (1953).

The paper concludes with a discussion of the magma feeding system beneath Parícutin volcano and a theoretical treatment of magma ascent, which are not reproduced here.

Birth (The First Hours)

Foshag and González-Reyna (1956)

Sources of Information

For about a week or more before the initial outbreak of Parícutin volcano, accounts appeared in México City newspapers mentioning the recurrent earth tremors in the Uruapan region. In one of these accounts the *presidente municipal* of San Juan Parangaricutiro, Sr. Felipe Cuara-Amezcua, predicted a new volcanic outbreak. In spite of this warning, available geologists were unprepared for the event that followed. Fortunately, the manifestation was witnessed by several inhabitants of the area, Tarascan Indians, whose keen perception and innate knowledge of natural phenomena are responsible for the first adequate account of the birth of a new volcano.

Among the actual eyewitnesses to this unusual event, we were able to interview Sr. Dionisio Pulido, owner of Cuiyúsuru, the farm that brought forth the volcano; Sra. Paula Cervantes Rangel de Pulido, his wife; Sr. Dolores Pulido, his brother; all of Parícutin; and Sra. Aurora Cuara of San Juan Parangaricutiro.

Demetrio Toral, a laborer from Parícutin employed by Pulido as helper, was plowing land at Cuiyúsuru. He had just completed a furrow and was about to turn his plow when the first outbreak of the volcano occurred almost in the exact furrow he had just drawn. This remarkable circumstance has led some people into the brief that Toral "plowed up the volcano." Toral, a deaf mute, died soon after in Caltzontzin.

It has been reported that José María Isidro was also present at the outbreak of the volcano, but we have been unable to locate him.

A lad of San Juan Parangaricutiro [Luís Mora-Garcia], hearing the accounts of the outbreak being discussed by the townspeople in the plaza, went to Ticuiro, a field near the edge of town, and took photographs (Fig. 18) of the event. The time was about 5 p.m.

Immediately after the outbreak of the volcano, the *presidente municipal* of San Juan Parangaricutiro sent a group to the spot to investigate the event. Of the group members we succeeded in finding Jesús Anguiano[31], Jesús Martínez, and Luis Ortíz Solorio and obtaining from them an account of the events that occurred an hour or so after the initial outbreak.

Among the officials of the *municipio* who contributed accounts were the *presidente municipal* Sr. Felipe Cuara-Amezcua and the parish priest, Sr. José Caballero. Sr. Celedonio Gutiérrez, of San Juan Parangaricutiro, has maintained a diary since the beginning of the volcano's activity and has given us access to a copy of this valuable document. Finally, the event is succinctly described in the official records of the *municipio* of San Juan Parangaricutiro, a certified copy of which Sr. Cuara-Amezcua prepared for us.

Dionisio Pulido

Dionisio Pulido (Figs. 3, 14 and 19) was a resident of the village of Parícutin. For 31 years he was owner of Cuiyúsuru farm. He is now a resident of Caltzontzin[32], near Uruapan, a village organized to accommodate the former inhabitants of Parícutin. His farm was divided into three parts: one which he worked himself, one which he shared with his brother Dolores, and one which he rented on shares to others. Upon his land was a small hole (mentioned by Sra. Murillo) with an

Fig. 18. First photographs of Parícutin volcano, taken just after the start of the eruption on Feb. 20, 1943 by a boy from San Juan Parangaricutiro. [Celedonio Gutiérrez informed us that the boy was named Luís Mora-Garcia and was about 14 years old]. The photos were taken from slightly different angles near Ticuiro, 5 km NNW of the volcano and about 2 km west of San Juan Parangaricutiro. The upper photo was taken at about 5:00 p.m., 30 minutes after the start of the eruption. The lower photo was taken at about 6:00 p.m. In the lower photo, Cerro de Jarátiro is on the left, Cerro de Camiro is in the far center, and Cerro de Canicjuata is on the right. Parícutin village lies near the foot of Canicjuata. The fields of San Juan Parangaricutiro are in the foreground.

Fig. 19. Dionisio Pulido, who witnessed the birth of Parícutin.

apparent depth of 1½ m. Year after year he and Dolores cast dirt and debris into this hole without succeeding in filling it. Frequently Pulido hid his ox yoke and plow in it to spare the trouble of bringing them to Parícutin. Before January 1943 nothing unusual about his farm attracted his attention. Its picturesque and peaceful environment pleased his Tarascan nature. Never, not even on the day of the initial volcanic outbreak on Cuiyúsuru, did he note any unusual warmth in the ground, as has been so frequently stated in popular accounts of the event.

On February 20, 1943, Pulido left his village, going to his farm to prepare the fields for the spring sowing. He was accompanied by his wife, Paula, his small son, who would watch the sheep, and Demetrio Toral, his helper, to begin the plowing. The day was calm, and the sky was clear. Pulido's account, as he related it to us, follows:

In the afternoon I joined my wife and son, who were watching the sheep, and inquired if anything new had occurred, since for 2 weeks we had felt strong tremors in the region. Paula replied, yes, that she had heard noise and thunder underground. Scarcely had she finished speaking when I, myself, heard a noise, like thunder during a rainstorm, but I could not explain it, for the sky above was clear and the day was so peaceful, as it is in February.

At 4 p.m. I left my wife to set fire to a pile of branches that Demetrio and I and another, whose name I cannot remember, had gathered. I went to burn the branches when I noticed that a *cueva*[33] [cave or grotto], which was situated on one of the knolls of my farm, had opened[34], and I noticed that this fissure, as I followed it with my eye, was long and passed from where I stood, through the hole, and continued in the direction of Cerro de Canicjuata, where Canicjuata joins Mesa de Cocjarao [about 1 km due west]. Here is something new and strange, thought I, and I searched on the ground for marks to see whether or not it had opened in the night, but could find none; and I saw that it was a kind of fissure that had a depth of only half a meter. I set about to ignite the branches again when I felt a thunder, the trees trembled, and I turned to speak to Paula; and it was then I saw how, in the hole, the ground swelled and raised itself 2 or 2½ m high, and a kind of smoke or fine dust—gray, like ashes—began to rise up in a portion of the crack that I had not previously seen near the *resumidero*[33] [hole or crevice]. Immediately more smoke began to rise, with a hiss or whistle, loud and continuous; and there was a smell of sulfur. I then became greatly frightened and tried to help unyoke one of the ox teams. I hardly knew what to do, so stunned was I before this, not knowing what to think or what to do and not able to find my wife or my son or my animals. Finally my wits returned and I recalled the sacred *Señor de los Milagros*, which was in the church in San Juan Parangaricutiro and in a loud voice I cried, "*Santo Señor de los Milagros*, you brought me into this world—now save me from the dangers in which I am about to die"; and I looked toward the fissure whence rose the smoke; and my fear for the first time disappeared. I ran to see if I could save my family and my companions and my oxen, but I did not see them and thought that they had taken the oxen to the spring for water. I saw that there was no longer any water in the spring, for it was near the fissure, and I thought the water was lost because of the fissure. Then, very frightened, I mounted my mare and galloped to Parícutin, where I found my wife and son and friends awaiting, fearing that I might be dead and that they would never see me again. On the road to Parícutin I thought of my little animals, the yoke oxen, that were going to die in that flame and smoke, but upon arriving at my house I was happy to see that they were there.

Upon his arrival at Parícutin, Pulido reported the event to the Chief of the Parícutin subdivision, Sr. C. Agustín Sánchez, who then accompanied him to San Juan Parangaricutiro to report to the *presidente* of the *municipio*, Sr. Felipe Cuara-Amezcua.

On the following day Pulido drove his oxen to the forest to graze and then went to his farm to see what had occurred. When he arrived there at 8 a.m. he saw a hill, which he estimated to be 10 m high, had formed and that this mound emitted smoke and hurled out rocks with great violence.

Alfonso De la O Carreño[35] states that a light seism accompanied by subterranean noises and followed by a distant detonation was perceived at San Juan Parangaricutiro on Saturday, the 20th, at 5:20 p.m. Pulido reported to him that, at 4 p.m. and before, he walked about his farm hearing noises like those of a heavy freshet, that the sky was cloudless, and that he looked in all directions to localize the noise. Then suddenly he saw a large column of black smoke arise from a depression, and a fissure, 5 cm wide, open in the soil; and he was able to follow the eastward-trending fissure with his eye for 30 m.

Paula Pulido

Paula Cervantes Rangel de Pulido (Fig. 20), wife of Dionisio Pulido, accompained her husband to watch the sheep. She is Tarascan; and although she understands Spanish, she does not speak it. Dolores Pulido acted as our interpreter. Sra. Pulido also related her account to Sra. Amalia Vargas de Ortíz, of San Juan Parangaricutiro, who in turn told it to us. According to Sra. Ortíz, Paula Pulido spent part of the day in the shade of an oak, watching the sheep grazing on the sparse herbage. As the sheep moved on she changed her position to another nearby tree, and it was from there that she saw a small whirling dust column (*remolinito*) follow a small fissure in the soil, moving from a point called Quijata to Cuiyúsuru, a distance of about a kilometer. A kind of fissure 5 cm wide and 30 cm deep opened as the dust column moved toward Cuiyúsuru depositing a pale-gray dust. The column stopped near the oak tree she had left a short time before, and a hole 30 cm wide opened, and a smoke began to rise. Her first reaction was one of surprise and delight in watching the "pretty *remolinito*" as it traveled along, fissuring the soil.

Her account to us, through Dolores Pulido, follows:

About 4:00 p.m., after talking to my husband, I heard a kind of loud whistle, like the noise of water falling on live coals or hot embers. This noise was completely distinct from the underground noise I had been hearing, and the trees swayed strongly and continuously. I was about 100 m from the place where these things took place, when I saw, issuing from a crevice that had formed, a little cloud of gray and I smelled an odor like sulfur, and I noticed that some pines about 30 m from the

Fig. 20. Paula Cervantes Rangel de Pulido, wife of Dionisio Pulido, who witnessed the birth of Parícutin.

orifice began to burn. I called to my husband. Then the ground rose in the form of a confused cake above the open fissure and then disappeared, but I cannot say whether it blew out or fell back—I believe it swallowed itself. I was sure the earth was on fire and it would consume itself. From the fissure arose a gray column of smoke, without force, depositing a fine gray dust.

Now very much frightened, Paula Pulido fled to Parícutin and there awaited with great anxiety some word of the fate of her husband.

Dolores Pulido

On the afternoon of February 20, Dolores Pulido was working in the forest on Cerro de Janánboro [4½ km WNW of the new volcano]. He saw a column of smoke arising from Cuiyúsuru; and since he was part owner of land there, he went to see what was taking place. He reached the spot about 6 p.m. and saw smoke issuing from a hole in the ground. About this vent were low mounds of fine gray ash. He was unable to approach closer than 8 m because of falling stones. He then took fright and fled. He returned to

Fig. 21. Aurora Cuara, who witnessed the birth of Parícutin.

the place the next morning and found a gentle rain of "sand" falling about the spot.

Aurora Cuara

All during the day of February 20, while Gregorio Cuara and his family were at their farm at San Nicolás about 20 km from San Juan Parangaricutiro, they felt strong tremors and heard subterranean noises resembling the noise of a motor or a stone rolling down a rocky slope. The trail from San Nicolás to San Juan Parangaricutiro passes Quitzocho and almost at the foot of Piedra del Sol ["Rock of the Sun" was 900 m ENE of the new vent]. Sra. Aurora Cuara [Fig. 21], a Tarascan women of unusual intelligence and perception, and one of her children were returning to San Juan Parangaricutiro by this path and had reached Piedra del Sol about 4:30 p.m. There Sra. Cuara saw

Pulido gathering branches and weeds into a pile and saw his helper, Toral, complete a furrow in his plowing, passing over the precise point where the earth was to open a moment later. As the helper was about to make the turn to commence a new furrow, a fissure split the earth in a direction toward Cerro de Canicjuata. The earth rose as a wall 10 m long and 2 m wide to a height of about a meter, and a gray smoke of a very fine gray dust ascended. Although greatly frightened, Sra. Cuara climbed Piedra del Sol, in order to observe better this unusual event. The fissure was no more than 50 m away. In addition to the small dust column, she also saw "sparks" thrown out. She watched Pulido try to help unyoke the oxen; and when he fled in fright she, too, lost courage and, with her child, ran toward the town. A drawing from a sketch by Sra. Cuara (Fig. 22) shows the position of various features and eyewitnesses as she saw them.

At 10 o'clock at night she could clearly see from San Juan Parangaricutiro, between the pine trees of the forest, incandescent bombs thrown into the air. Sometime between 11 and 12 p.m., the new volcano began to roar, incandescent stones were hurled up with great force, and a column of smoke, illuminated by lightning flashes, arose.

The following day, about 11 a.m., Sra. Cuara returned by the same path to see what had happened to her husband in San Nicolás. A small hill of stones of various sizes and of sand had formed about the vent where the smoke had first found exit. Some of the rocks hurled from the vent were very large and exploded in the air. She described the little hill as round in form, and she could clearly see a fire, which she afterward learned was lava, issue slowly from the bottom of it.

Luis Ortíz Solorio

Luis Ortíz Solorio was standing on the street corner near his house in San Juan Parangaricutiro talking to his neighbor the shoemaker. It was a quarter past 5 in the afternoon. Ten minutes later, looking toward Quitzocho, he saw a thin column of smoke arising. He went to the plaza, where many people were gathered in front of the church, for news had come that the earth had opened and smoke was issuing from a crack in the ground on Cuiyúsuru. The parish priest, Sr. José Caballero, with the permission of the *presidente*, Sr. Felipe Cuara-Amezcua, decided to send a group of men to the spot to see what had taken place. Solorio offered to go and was joined by Jesús Anguiano[31], Jesús Martínez, Epitacio Murillo, Hilario Anguiano, Epitacio Clasope, Justiniano Cirícuti,

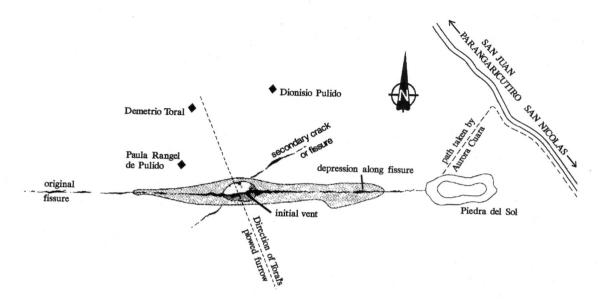

Fig. 22. Parícutin volcano at the time of its initial outbreak, showing the positions of the various features and eyewitnesses as seen by Sra. Aurora Cuara. Distances are schematic.

Antonio Escalera, Miguel Campoverde and some others whose names Solorio has now forgotten.

The priest gave them his blessing, and they went on horseback, riding rapidly, and arrived at the spot about 6 p.m. In the soil of Cuiyúsuru they saw a sort of fissure, at the SW end of which was a hole about half a meter in diameter from which smoke issued and some hot rocks were hurled not very high in the air. Jesús Anguiano and Jesús Martínez, in order to obtain a nearer view, approached close to the hole. Solorio then saw a fracture forming about 6 m from the center of the vent and called to Anguiano and Martínez to come back. Hardly had they leapt back when the wall fell in, widening the orifice to 2 m and increasing the size of the smoke column.

When they returned to San Juan Parangaricutiro, they related what they had seen, how the earth had opened and how smoke and small stones, like incandescent marbles and oranges were being cast out from a vent that continued growing bigger. The priest then consulted a book on Vesuvius in the church library, and they were convinced that they had seen a volcano.

Anguiano and Martínez

Jesús Anguiano[31] and Jesús Martínez, both about 22 years old and of San Juan Parangaricutiro, were the first of the group leaving the plaza to arrive at Cuiyúsuru. They found the soil fissured in the form of a trench and saw a hole from whence smoke issued. Around the hole was a slumped area about 20 m long and 12 m wide, bounded by a crack along which were low mounds, ½ m high, of very fine hot dust. This dust was gray, like ashes or cement; and Anguiano, wrapping a handkerchief about his hand, collected a sample of it to show in the village. From the vent itself fine dust, "sparks", and stones were thrown out. Anguiano and Martínez approached within a few meters of the vent, where a choking odor pervaded and the ground shook violently, "jumping up and down, not with the swaying motion we felt in Parangaricutiro." In the vent the sand "boiled" vigorously like the bubbling sand in a rising spring, with a noise like a large jug of water boiling violently, or boulders dragged along a steam bed by a river in flood. Small stones were cast up to height of 5 m. Anguiano collected two and found them very hot[36].

The fissure in the soil extended in a direction toward the setting sun, that is, toward the point where Cerro de Canicjuata joins Mesa de Cocjarao [1 km west], and the spring that supplied water to Parícutin. Anguiano modeled the appearance of the vent and its surroundings in the soil for us, a sketch of which is shown in Fig. 23. In the plan, he indicated a small cross fissure, passing southwestward through the vent.

In the plaza of San Juan Parangaricutiro the townspeople awaited their return with great anxiety. They related what they had seen, and Anguiano delivered the ashes and two bombs to the priest. The stones, being still hot, were placed in a dish; and the priest exorcised them, imploring Heaven to cease this

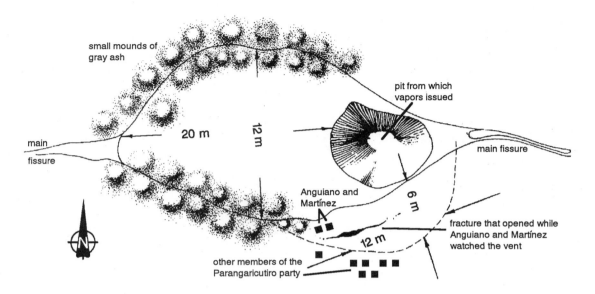

Fig. 23. Parícutin volcano at 6 p.m., February 20, 1943, showing the appearance of the vent and its surroundings as seen by Jesús Anguiano[31].

terrible apparition, as a benediction and grace to the inhabitants of the region.

Anguiano added that for 14 hours before the outbreak of the volcano frequent tremors shook San Juan Parangaricutiro and the subterranean noises that accompanied these tremors seemed to come from Cerro de Jarátiro [1.5 km north of the new volcano].

Celedonio Gutiérrez

Celedonio Gutiérrez [Fig. 14], of San Juan Parangaricutiro, was not an actual witness to the initial outbreak of the volcano, but was in the town when the event occurred. Being an unusually keen and competent observer, his account of the first few days has more than ordinary value. Gutiérrez wrote for us the following account:

When I returned from my work in the fields, I saw a gray column of smoke arise from the place where the parcels of Quitzocho and Cuiyúsuru were located and that this column spread little by little. It was 4:30 o'clock in the afternoon of the 20th of February 1943. When I reached the church, I saw the *presidente municipal*, the parish priest, and many people gathered in the plaza. Quickly they ordered that a group of men go to investigate what it was that was burning. After a time the men returned saying that the earth had opened in Cuiyúsuru, splitting it in the form of a crevice running from east to west, and that there, and from a hole that had also opened, fine sand and very hot stones issued,

collecting in small mounds on both sides of the crevice, and that they made a terrifying noise as they were ejected.

With the outbreak of the volcano, the earth tremors ceased, much to the relief of the populace. The priest and *presidente* allayed their fears somewhat, but on the morning of the 21st a strong earthquake threw them into panic, and they abandoned their homes; those from Parícutin fleeing to San Juan Parangaricutiro, those from Parangaricutiro to Angahuan or Uruapan, and those from Angahuan to the mountains.

The volcano broke out on Saturday, February 20, at about half past 4 in the afternoon. What a great surprise for my village and for the world! The earth was burned, and there began to ascend a small simple column that grew little by little; a vapor of strange gray rising silently toward the SE. A little later many people came from Parícutin, which was nearest to the volcano. The *presidente municipal*, Don Felipe Cuara-Amezcua, prepared to move the people from the place and had already asked, by means of telegraph, for trucks to transport all the people. But the people despaired and began to leave on foot, on horse, or on burro, or however they were able.

In the afternoon, when night began to fall, one could hear more noises. These we called *rezaques*[37]. Some tongues of flame began to appear, as of fire, that rose about 800 m into the air, and others even higher that loosened a rain, as of artificial golden fire. At 8 or 9 at night, some flashes of lightning shot from the vent into the column of vapor. The column was now very dense and black and extended toward the south. It covered the grand mountain of Tancítaro, for the first sand and ashes were in this direction and cast the first cold shadow of the volcano over this area. From this hour the rays of the sun that warmed the mountains and the beautiful green fields ceased, and the green leaves of the smaller plants that nourished the cattle died from the ashes that now began to appear. How strange and rare to see the clouds form, the first clouds of the volcano. Only a short time before the sky was blue, for the dry season had already begun. So, then, we passed the first night, contemplating and admiring this new event.

On the following day, Sunday the 21st, the dense vapors ceased. When the vapors diminished, the noise increased; and at 2 in the afternoon they were very strong. With each blast, white vapors accompanied by blue flames arose; the vapors appeared as if one shook a white sheet in the air.

After the first night, it threw up some tongues of fire, which were almost of pure sand. On the following night one noted that they were explosions of bombs and that the stones rose to a height of 500 m. They flew through the air to fall 300-400 m from the vent. It is a great memory for me to have seen, during these first days, how the first stones fell on the plowed fields of Quitzocho, where I used to watch the cattle of my grandfather.

At 3 o'clock on the morning of Monday, the 22nd, there were earthquakes like we never had before. The earth shook for 7 or 8 minutes, with intervals of a few seconds. The people imagined that this was the ultimate agony of a great region. Who could check the great movement of an entire region?[38] Only the omnipotent God, in his great power, with his divine omnipotence, thought of us. It was He who saved us.

The first lava that the volcano gave forth, to the east of the little cone, flowed 3 m per hour, according to the data of Sr. Geologist don Ezequiel Ordóñez, who was sent by the Comisión Impulsora y Coordinadora de la Investigación Científica, México, D. F., to observe this important novelty. This gentleman, 78 years of age, through his studies and experience, convinced us that there was no danger to our village and counseled that the people return to their homes. Now this same gentleman showed us the first lava flow, moving like dough, from which fell incandescent rocks from one side or another, such rocks as we knew before, without knowing how they formed. We also saw the *malpais*[12], which we knew before, without an idea of its origin. Without doubt, this answers not only how the *malpais* formed but also the tillable land and the mountains that I knew. We saw the lava as it covered the *cruza* [second plowing] made by the yokes of oxen from Parícutin and which needed only

8 days for sowing. Now one sees an admirable flow of fire, covering the last traces of our footsteps and of the works of man that he made during the life that God permitted him.

Record of San Juan Parangaricutiro

Sr. Felipe Cuara-Amezcua, *presidente* of the *municipio* of San Juan Parangaricutiro, has provided us with a certified copy of the record of the meeting of the municipal council signed by the council members, which is, as far as the municipal records are concerned, the official history of this unusual event. A translation of this document follows:

In the village of San Juan Parangaricutiro, seat of the municipality of the same name, State of Michoacán de Ocampo, at 10 o'clock of the 21st day of the month of February 1943, gathered in the public hall of the municipal government, under urgent summons, the councilmen: Felipe Cuara-Amezcua, municipal mayor; Félix Anducho, trustee; Rafael Ortíz-Enriques; Ambrosio Soto; and Rutilio Sandoval; as well as Agustín Sánchez, resident of said place. The Regidor, Felipe Cuara-Amezcua, President, declared the session opened, stating that yesterday at about 6 p.m., Messrs. Sánchez and Pulido presented themselves, telling, greatly excited, of the appearance of a strange conflagration that occurred at 5 p.m. yesterday in the valley called Cuiyúsuru, to the east of the village of Parícutin. They asked that they be taken immediately to the place of the happening that one could see for oneself the truth of their assertion; at the time Dionisio Pulido, owner of the above-mentioned property, gave information that early on the day of the event, he left his village [Parícutin] to tend his sheep in company with his wife Paula Rangel de Pulido and to visit his properties situated in the said valley; that in the afternoon, at an early hour, he left the place, asking his wife to watch the sheep until he returned; that about 4 p.m. he returned to the place and asked Demetrio Torres [Toral] who worked in the fields, to unyoke the oxen and take them to water, after which he returned to his wife suggesting that she return to the village, going then to examine the work done in the fields, arriving at the slope of the nearby hill to the east; that there, about 5 p.m., he felt a strong tremor and din in the earth, to which he paid little attention, since seisms had been frequent for more than 8 days, but he continued hearing loud subterranean noises accompanying the tremors, and then, thoroughly frightened, he turned his gaze to the west, that is, toward his village, observing with surprise that down there in a depression long tongues of fire arose, with a great deal of smoke and noises never heard before. A terrible panic seized him, and he fled toward Parícutin, where he arrived out of breath, immediately recounting to C. Agustín Sánchez, chief of the Parícutin subdivision, what had occurred. That Señor Sánchez, convincing himself of the truth of what Pulido had told him, went with him to the municipal president of Parangaricutiro where, totally alarmed, they gave the facts to C. Felipe Cuara-Amezcua, who with the haste the case merited, went with the informants to the place where the phenomenon had appeared, and later they learned that it was a volcano. Returning to Parangaricutiro, the municipal president summoned the members of the council to attend the present extraordinary session and consider this matter, now that the fear has extended to all the nearby villages, and solicit, for this reason, ample powers from the council to act; he gave as important in the case that now the volcano grew with real fury and, with it, the panic of the inhabitants of the region who abandoned their homes and possessions. It was conceded at once to C. Felipe Cuara-Amezcua, who immediately began action to solve the problem in the best manner, soliciting by telephone and telegraph the help of General of Division, don Manuel Avila Camacho, Constitutional President of the Republic; General of Division, don Lázaro Cárdenas, Secretary of National Defense; of General Félix Ireta Vivieros, Governor of the State; the Department of Agriculture and Government; municipal authorities of Uruapan; and other official agencies. Upon the proposal of some residents of this place and of Parícutin, the correct name that the mentioned volcano should bear was discussed, and after ample deliberation, in which was taken into account the history, traditions, and desires of the people, it was unanimously denominated "Volcán de Parícutin."

Summary of Accounts

After a fortnight of subterranean noises and local earthquakes that appeared to center between Cerro de Jarátiro and Cerro Prieto, lying to the SE of Parícutin village [see inside-cover maps], and which continually increased in number and intensity, a small fissure appeared in the soil of the cultivated lands of Cuiyúsuru farm. This fissure, beginning near Piedra del Sol, extended westward toward a point where Cerro de Canicjuata joins Mesa de Cocjarao and passed through a small cave or sink on Cuiyúsuru farm. The fissure had an observed length of about 50 m, a width of 5 cm, and an apparent depth of only ½ m. A small subsidiary fissure having a SW direction also formed. The evidence suggests that the fissure opened during the afternoon of February 20, probably about 4 o'clock, or half an hour before the initial outbreak of the volcano. At about 4:30 p.m. at a point on the fissure sulfurous gases and steam were emitted with a pop, followed by a whistling noise; and a small eruptive column arose from the newly formed vent.

The vent was originally of small size, about 30 cm in diameter, according to Paula Pulido; and the eruptive column consisted of fine dust and small incandescent stones. The vent gradually widened by slumping of its walls, and the eruptive column gradually increased in size (Fig. 18). Ejected stones collected during this period consisted of fragments of basalt different in character from Parícutin lava, and probably represent the walls of the fissure . . . .[39]

Some time between 11 and 12 p.m. the activity of the new volcano became violent; incandescent rocks were violently ejected in great numbers, and a large eruptive column, accompanied by frequent lightning flashes and a tremendous roaring sound, arose from the newly formed vent. This change in activity suggests that the advancing gases of the initial phase were followed by the rising lava column and that it reached the surface at this time.

Ordóñez (1947)

Ezequiel Ordóñez (Fig. 10 and 24) was born on Hacienda San Nicolás Peralta, near Lerma in the state of México, on April 10, 1867. He was to become the most famous geologist in the history of México. Ordóñez attended the National Engineering School, collaborated on the Geologic Map of the Mexican Republic (1888), and three years later joined the National Geological Institute, where he served as sub-director from 1895-1906. Along with the director of the Institute, José Guadalupe Aguilera, Ordóñez organized the 10th International Geological Congress in México City (1906), and served as the general secretary.

Ordóñez left the Geological Institute in 1906 for oil exploration work with private companies that took him from México to Tierra del Fuego. As in most things, he was spectacularly successful in these endeavors. In 1915 he discovered Cerro Azúl No. 4, perhaps the most famous Mexican oil well, which was the second largest producer in the world. Ordóñez is considered the father of the Mexican oil industry. In later years he taught at the National School of Engineering and had two brief periods as director of the Geological Institute.

Ordóñez wrote prodigeously during his long career, covering a broad array of geologic topics, including many important publications concerning the volcanoes of México. He was nearly 76 years old in 1943 when Parícutin volcano was born. Ordóñez immediately traveled to Michoacán and was the first geologist to observe the new volcano, arriving on its third day of activity. Over the next 4 years, he authored 10 richly illustrated articles about the first half of the eruption, and his photographs were used in the publications of many other scientists. Ezequiel Ordóñez died on February 8, 1950 in México City, about 2 years before the end of the Parícutin eruption. Further details on the life of Ordóñez can be found in the Enciclopedia de México and in biographies by Castillo-Tejero and Martínez-Portillo[40].

Fig. 24. Ezequiel Ordóñez and his assistant Abram González at the front of a lava flow from Parícutin volcano.

Here we reprint a short section concerning the earliest days of the eruption. This material overlaps in time with the preceeding section from Foshag and Gonzalez-Reyna (1956), but gives a somewhat different perspective.

The Birth of Parícutin

Until early in 1943 nothing disturbed the quiet and relatively happy life of the people of San Juan Parangaricutiro and surrounding small settlements; their time was devoted to the cultivation of corn and various fruits, lumbering, and the extraction of resin in the beautiful pine forests that covered the slopes of the surrounding mountains and hills between the flat cultivated valley lands.

The story of the birth of Parícutin volcano has been told somewhat differently by several people who claimed to have witnessed the beginning of the eruption, and it is now difficult to evaluate the truth of these different versions, although none differ fundamentally, except perhaps in small details and in the exact hour of he beginning of the phenomenon.

Whether Dionisio Pulido, the owner of the parcel of land from which the volcano burst forth, really saw it or whether others were the actual observers is now a disputed fact, but I favor the story as told to me, not only by Pulido but also by Señor Felipe Cuara, the Mayor of San Juan Parangaricutiro, to whom I talked early on the morning of the 23rd of February 1943, three days after the eruption began. I had spent the previous night close to the extraordinary scene of the birth of the new mountain, and upon arriving in San Juan early the following morning I found that practically all the townspeople had abandoned their homes. Greatly excited, Cuara told me that morning of the earthquakes and frequent tremors that had been felt in San Juan, Parícutin, Zirosto, Corupo, Los Reyes, etc., since the 5th of February. The tremors and strong quakes occurred with great irregularity; on certain days few or none were felt, while at other times the ground tremors were strong enough to damage the walls of the church in San Juan. This large and beautifully decorated church was so greatly beloved by the inhabitants of the area, that they had placed in it for worship their most sacred and adored image "El Santo Cristo de los Milagros". Later on in July 1944 this image was moved to the new village of "Los Conejos" where the people of San Juan were removed a few days before their church and town were destroyed by a lava flow.

My first idea was to interview those who claimed to have actually witnessed the beginning of the phenomenon; and therefore I induced Sr. Pulido to relate to me what he had seen on his land on Saturday, the 20th of February. He had gone there early that morning with his wife to pasture his few sheep, in spite of the frequent earthquakes, strange noises, and rumblings that had been felt and heard.

According to his version, at about noon that day the quakes and underground noises increased to such an extent that he became greatly alarmed. He then noticed that from a small depression on his land as well as from a narrow crack that crossed it, thin columns of white vapor began to rise, and that about four o'clock in the afternoon these vapors appeared as dark smoke seeming to contain flames and accompanied by very loud noises and ground tremors. Badly frightened, he hurriedly abandoned the area with his wife in order to advise people of Parícutin and the authorities of San Juan Parangaricutiro of what he had seen. Still later the subterranean rumblings, strange noises and ground tremors became even more intense, and the townspeople could distinguish a thick column of dark smoke and incandescent rocks shooting upward. Some men who approached the scene that night noticed that a small mound had already formed around the place where the phenomenon originated.

Somewhat skeptical I arrived at the scene of the eruption on the night of the 22nd of February, but was soon convinced that I was witnessing a sight that few other humans had ever seen, the initial stages of the growth of a new volcano. Tremendous explosions were heard, ground tremors were felt frequently, and a thick high column of vapors with a great many incandescent rocks could be seen rising almost continuously from the center of a small conical mound then estimated to be 40 m high. On the same night I noticed a red glow on the slope of the mound and large incandescent rocks rolled down a low rocky incline with a distinctly peculiar tinkling noise. Upon approaching this low scarp as closely as possible, it was found to be the front of a large lava flow moving from the north side of the base of the mound over a flat cornfield that extended for nearly 800 m from the small prominence.

In order to obtain an idea of the topographical aspect of the site where the small new cone was rapidly growing, I circled the mound as closely as the numerous large falling bombs would permit. I then observed that the narrow elongated cornfield called Cuiyúsuru, was really a low, gently inclined terrace that was bounded on the south by the low ridges that connect with the spurs of the high Tancítaro group of mountains. To the north, this terrace-like bench covered with trees here and there and crossed by several stone fences that served as boundaries between the parcels of land of different owners, sloped gently to join the flat called Quitzocho, over which the lava was moving rapidly. Still farther to the north of this cornfield there rises a group of high hills, among which the one nearest the new cone called Cerro de Jarátiro (Figs. 12 and 13) afforded an excellent observation post to view the new volcano. The first observatory cabin was built on this hill and later had to be moved several times to successively higher ground because of the invasion by new lava flows [positions of cabins are shown on the map of Fig. 108, p. 144].

A prominent feature of the SE slope of Cerro de Jarátiro was the existence of three old craters situated very close to each other and averaging 300 m in diameter and from 30 to 60 m in depth, and as the eruption of the volcano progressed they had been filled by the new lava at different times [see Fig. 108].

As one may easily understand, during the initial stages of the eruption of Parícutin, much of the material thrown out came from the soil, subsoil, and fragments derived from the walls of the conduit through which the eruption was taking place, as proved by fragments of andesite that collected around the cone during the first days of the eruption. The blowing out of material that was essentially derived from the surface rocks and soil seems to have lasted only a short time and was soon followed by the first lava flow through the crater of the new volcano and by the eruption of pyroclastic material composed of sand, ash, small pieces of scoria, and basaltic bombs of all sizes.

From the first night spent at the volcano I noticed that the lava moving rapidly away from the eastern side of the growing cone came directly from the center of the incipient crater, which was breached on the eastern side. From the top of a hill situated about 450 m from the cone opposite the breach it was possible to see the interior of the crater and I noticed the lava was flowing from 3 vents aligned from east to west and located precisely in the center of the crater. The lava from these *bocas* rose in pulsations or large bubbles and spouted much like a fountain. Great chunks of plastic material rose high into the air accompanied by a dense column of vapors and tremendous explosions, and at times a "chugging" noise like that of a starting locomotive was heard. During the evenings the red flow of half molten rock from the vents was magnificent as it illuminated the high inner slopes of the crater. Farther along its course the lava moved between two narrow ridges terminating on the Quitzocho flat in a scarped front.

Studies by Foshag and González-Reyna (1943-1945)

Foshag and González-Reyna (1956)

Development of Parícutin Volcano

After the initial outbreak of Parícutin volcano, 2½ years were to pass before it became apparent that the new volcano had acquired a definite pattern of activity and could be considered a well-established, mature volcanic edifice. This interval of development may be divided into three periods, depending primarily on the vent with which the principal activity was associated. These we propose to call the Quitzocho, Sapichu, and Taquí periods.

The Quitzocho period lasted 8 months, from the birth until October 18, 1943. The activity was centered exclusively in the original Cuiyúsuru vent, about which the volcano built its cone. The important feature during this period was the growing cone and the accidents that befell it. At the end of this period the cone had almost reached its full height, or about 365 m, and had acquired a considerable degree of stability. The Quitzocho period terminated suddenly with the outbreak of new vents, the Sapichu vents, at the NE foot of the cone.

The Sapichu period lasted only 2½ months, until January 8, 1944. A small adventitious horseshoe-shaped edifice, called Sapichu, was built about one of the vents, but the principal feature was the almost constant emission of lava to form a broad flow. During the Sapichu period, activity in the main crater was greatly reduced, and no significant changes took place in the main cone.

With the cessation of lava emission from Sapichu, activity shifted to two vents, the Taquí and Ahuán, on the SW and SSW sides of the cone, respectively. A period of almost continuous lava emission set in, during which the cone showed erratic and variable activity but no significant change in configuration. This period we have called the Taquí period.

Quitzocho Period

Early Explosive Phase

February 21.—One may consider the Quitzocho period as beginning at midnight, February 20. The vent now had 7 hours of development, and the growing cone was 6 m high and elongate in form, with its long axis east and west[21]. About this time the first thunderous roars were heard in San Juan Parangaricutiro, 4½ km north. The earth tremors that were felt during the past fortnight now ceased and were not felt again. At 4 a.m., February 21, the cone was estimated as being 8 m high. Dionisio Pulido visited his farm at 8 a.m. and reported the cone as 10 to 12 m high. Mauricio Duarte estimated the height as 25 m at 10 a.m. and that the column rose higher than Cerros de Tancítaro [3,842 m elevation, about 1,460 m higher than Pulido's field (~2,385 m: Fig. 13)]. Jorge Treviño described the volcano as a low cone with an oval crater at 11 a.m., from which arose a black eruptive column accompanied by strong explosive blasts. Sra. Aurora Cuara, who passed the volcano at 11 a.m., described it as a small round hill of stones, from which rocks were hurled into the air. From the bottom of this hill a "fire" [lava?] slowly issued. Between 12 a.m. and 1 p.m. the volcano began again to eject many bombs, the bursts spreading in the form of a fan and dropping bombs in a wide east-west zone [paralleling the initial fissure]. At 1 p.m. the cone was estimated as 30 m high, with a base 70 m in diameter. Jorge Treviño estimated that on this afternoon the cone was 50 m high. Celedonio Gutiérrez reported that the eruptive column diminished in size during the early part of the day and that the ejectamenta changed from ash to bombs accompanied by white vapors and blue flames. These bombs were hurled to a height of 500 m, some falling 300 to 400 m from the cone.

Fig. 25. February 21, 1943. The new cone, about 30 m high, appears above the treetops at about 1 p.m. Taken from the NE.

Fig. 26. February 21, 1943. The new cone, with a height of 30-50 m, and the cultivated fields upon which it grew. Many of the same field markings and trees can be seen in Fig. 28, taken two days later as lava was moving toward the NE.

Photographs of the volcano by Salvador Ceja (Fig. 25) and Dr. J. Trinidad (Fig. 26) and motion pictures by Jorge Treviño show the cone as a low dome, with slope angles of 32° toward the west but more gently inclined toward the east. This asymmetry of the cone indicates that it had already been breached and that lava had already flowed toward the east. The eruptive column, as shown by motion pictures, rose rather lazily without well-defined volutes or cauliflowers. Large tatters of lava up to a meter across were ejected in abundance. According to Celedonio Gutiérrez, these had imitative shapes, resembling birds and objects, indicating that they were still plastic. At least two neighboring vents were present in the crater. The western vent appeared more active and its column more heavily laden with ash; the eastern vent was erratic in its action and appeared to be somewhat smaller than the western vent.

The eruptive activity of February 21 is described by Celedonio Gutiérrez (personal communication) as follows:

On this day, which was Sunday, between one o'clock in the morning and until 12 o'clock, the eruption of the volcano did not vary much from that of late yesterday. The eruptive column was like that previously observed, rising towards the heavens in large agitated cauliflowers, which left the crater with great force, and from which fell much ash and many bombs. The only difference noted was that now one saw no electrical discharges.

Between 12 and 13 o'clock the volume of ejected material began to diminish and ash ceased to fall. Bombs continued to be thrown out but in less quantity, and there were deep, heavy, thunderous noises, increasing in intensity.

Between 13 and 15 o'clock the explosions increased in both force and frequency; the amount of material, however, diminished each time, but the fear of the people of San Juan Parangaricutiro increased. One could see with each explosion in the volcanic vent small white clouds of smoke arise with great force, like from the mouth of a cannon. The explosions were extraordinarily violent, greater than cannonading.

From 15 o'clock until 3 o'clock [February 22] the form and type of the explosions showed no change.

Other observers described the cone as having a horseshoe form, open toward the NE. The dark-gray eruptive column rose to a great height and was accompanied by many bombs, some of them of great size, and a sort of coarse sand. The eruption seemed to issue from a long opening, in the form of a fissure, westward toward Mesa de Cocjarao. From the ground it was impossible to determine accurately the number of eruptive throats, but it appeared to have but one,

Fig. 27. February 22, 1943. The new cone viewed from the NE. Great quantities of ejected bombs and lapilli caused the new cone to grow rapidly. Cone height on this day probably 50-60 m. Vapors from the (Quitzocho) lava flow are around the base of the cone. Cerros de Tancítaro in the right background.

large and somewhat elongated. These inconsistent descriptions of the cone and its activity suggest that the eruption was quite variable.

It is likely the lava first issued from the surface vents sometime during this day. Sra. Cuara apparently saw lava at 11 o'clock. The great quantity of viscous bombs indicates that the rising lava column had already reached the surface, and the horseshoe shape of the cone suggests that the weak cone had been breached by flowing lava. Perhaps the rising lava column first reached the surface at midnight of February 20, when the first thunderous roars were heard in San Juan Parangaricutiro and incandescent rocks were hurled up with great force.

February 22.—Mr. C. Byron Valle, who flew over the volcano on the early morning of this day, reported that he distinctly saw two vents in the crater. A smaller one at the base of the cone, did not have much explosive force; and lava appeared to issue from it. A larger vent showed only explosive activity. At the altitude of the plane, a distinct sulfurous odor was apparent, which Mr. Valle characterized as an odor similar to that about a smelter.

Celedonio Gutiérrez reported that at 3 a.m. a strong earthquake, stronger than any yet felt, shook the region intermittently for 7 or 8 minutes. This earthquake was felt over a wide area in México, and its epicenter was determined to lie 370 km SE of Parícutin, off the coast near Acapulco, a spot of frequent strong earthquakes [see p. 52]. It therefore had no direct connection with Parícutin volcano.

Celedonio Gutiérrez in his diary described the activity for this day as follows:

Between 2 and 3 o'clock, after a terrible night occasioned by the tremendous noise of the volcano, strong earthquake shocks were felt, much greater than those felt before the birth of the volcano, which lasted for 8 seconds. After the earthquake the terrible explosions of the volcano began to diminish little by little, but did not cease. Although the thunderous noises were now not so strong, the eruption could not by any means be called silent. Ash fell in moderate quantity but, in contrast, bombs were ejected in great quantities and arose to an elevation of about 400-500 m. The eruptive column from the crater was not very large but it rose to an elevation of about 1,500 m.

Photographs by Rufus C. Morrow (Fig. 27) taken on this day show an irregularly shaped cone open to the east, indicating breaching by flowing lava. The eruptive column was larger and denser than on the preceding day and contained a great quantity of large bombs.

The already well advanced lava flow formed an irregular tongue that moved northeastward, emitting abundant white vapors from scattered fumaroles along an advancing flow front 6-8 m high. At no later time did this or any other lava flow show such an abundance of vaporous emissions. The first lava flow we have called the Quitzocho flow. The shape and character of the eruptive column suggest numerous and violent explosions in the crater. Celedonio Gutiérrez reported explosions each 10-12 seconds and that the ejected bombs assumed odd shapes, such as heads, hands, and feet, indicating that they were tatters of viscous lava.

February 23.—Eruptive activity continued with the abundant emission of bombs but with little ash. Ordóñez reported the cone had a height of about 60 m (Fig. 28) and that the lava advanced at a rate of 6-12 m/hr.

February 24.—The activity of the crater continued in a regular fashion, with many bombs ejected but little ash deposited on the fields [Fig. 29]. The lava flowed as a broad sheet, 700 m long[41] and advanced 5 m/hr. A blanket of fragments and scoriae covered the lava surface. The emission of vapors from the flow appeared greatly diminished and localized in fumaroles along the border of the flow.

February 25.—The activity from the crater continued strongly but with somewhat better defined cauliflowers and a thicker eruptive column [Fig. 30], indicating somewhat increased activity. According to Waitz[41] and Robles-Ramos[21], the explosive bursts averaged 16 per minute. These Robles-Ramos classified as 6 blasts, 9 explosions, and 1 lightning discharge per minute. De la O Carreño[35] noted 20 explosions per minute and Teodoro Flores, 17 explosions per minute, 3 strong, 5 medium, 9 weak. Waitz reported that the breach, which had been kept clear by the constant flow of lava, now showed some signs of building up, indicating a cessation of flow from the vent, and that the advance of the lava was reduced to 3 m/hr.

February 26.—On this day the height of the cone was measured by Robles-Ramos[21] as being 167 m, with the diameter of the base 730 m and the diameter of the crater 90 m across in a north-south direction [Fig. 31].

With the cessation of the lava flow the day before, the explosive activity in the crater had increased. A medium-sized black eruptive column rose majestically

to a height of about 5,000 m and terminated in a broad, white cumulus cloud. Some strong explosive bursts ejected heavily laden clouds, the ash raining down upon the cone. At 2 p.m. a wet ash fell, the moisture probably due to the condensation of water vapor in the eruptive column. De la O Carreño[35] reported that on many occasions the granules of ash were coated with a thin film of water.

Waitz[41], Robles-Ramos[21], and De la O Carreño[35] distinguished three types of explosions: (1) blasts, (2) gaseous explosions, and (3) electrical discharges. The blasts were dull prolonged roars, like a jet produced by a piston in a steam engine, and yielded a vertical column of vapors heavily laden with ash, and carrying few bombs. The duration of these blasts varied, sometimes continuing for 6 minutes. When these blasts were numerous and prolonged, the explosive activity was cineritic. [This uncommon term is used by Foshag and González-Reyna to describe eruptions that produced abundant cinders and heavy ashfalls in the surrounding region.] The gaseous explosions were violent expulsions of gas, with strong detonations, giving rise to cauliflowers. They were accompanied by innumerable quantities of bombs, hurled as high as 750 m and thrown as far as 900 m from the cone. The electrical discharges were vigorous detonations without eruptive phenomena. The visible flashes were short zigzag or arborescent bolts of lightning in the cineritic eruptive column [Fig. 32].

Observers noted rapidly moving arcs of light in the eruptive column, followed by extremely heavy explosions. The arcs were described by De la O Carreño[35] as an intensely luminous yellow band and by Robles-Ramos[21] as whitish yellow. Waitz[41] identified these flashes as the "flashing arcs" of Perret[42]. These arcs were plainly visible in daylight.

By this day the lava flow had spread over a considerable area and formed a mass of irregular outline, the narrowest part 464 m wide. It had a steep front, 5-11 m high, and an irregular surface covered with a jumble of scoriaceous blocks of irregular shape. The lava front was loose rubble with sporadic exposures of torn and twisted lava. During the day, red incandescence could be seen in the crevasses of the lava front, and at night patches of bright incandescence marked the slowly advancing lobes of viscous lava. The rate of advance was now reduced to 1-2 m/hr. As the flow advanced it frequently piled up a bank of soil along its foot. De la O Carreño[35] gave the following statistics for the cone on this day: Elevation of the cone 167 m, diameter of the base of the cone 615 m, diameter across the crater 150 m, slope of the cone 33° 10', approximate volume of the

Fig. 28. February 23, 1943. Heavy emission of bombs with moderate eruptive column. Cone is about 60 m high. Llano de Quitzocho in the foreground. Quitzocho lava flow with abundant fumaroles in the middle ground. View from the NE. Compare with Fig. 26, taken from about the same place two days earlier.

Fig. 29. February 24, 1943. Vaporous eruptive column with little ash. Cone height is 60-100 m. Same view from NE as Fig. 18 (bottom), with Cerro de Canicjuata on right.

Fig. 30. February 25, 1943. The cone is horseshoe shaped and open to the east, feeding the Quitzocho lava flow, which is visible in the lower left. The trees near the base of the cone are denuded by falling bombs. Cone height is probably about 100 m. Taken from the NE.

cone 19.5 million m³, daily increment (5.9 days) 3.33 million m³, explosions per minute 17, increment of growth per explosion 136 m³, volume of the lava flow 7 million m³.

. . . . .

Many visitors came to the volcano during this period, attracted by the awesome spectacle of its explosive activity. At night the appearance of the volcano was particularly impressive. Innumerable incandescent bombs formed an almost continuously rising column of "fire" that ascended to 750 m and then rained down upon the cone and the surrounding terrain. This incandescent column illuminated the area with a weird light, brighter than the moonlight. The thunderous roars and rushing blasts, punctuated by the sharp crack of explosions, the thud of the bombs upon the flanks of the cone, the lightning discharges, the strong vibrations of the air and ground, held the spectator in awed fascination.

The first day of the new volcano saw the first surge of lava [see Plate 1A and B], which spread rapidly at first but gradually diminished its rate of advance until the seventh day when it stopped, and showed a tendency for the cone to heal its breach. On February 28, however, a second lava surge began, which cleared the breach. From the east the crater had the appearance of a low amphitheatre with three active vents plainly visible. The lowest and easternmost was the smallest, and the westernmost was the largest and highest; all were separated from each other by narrow septa joined to the inner crater walls. Usually these vents acted independently of each other, although they were sometimes active simultaneously.

The lava flowed from the amphitheater toward the east; but upon clearing the flanking wall of the cone, it turned north and moved down the slope as a scoria-covered flow, covering the lands of Quitzocho.

The activity on February 28 has been described by Trask[43]. The ejectamenta consisted of viscous lava bombs and coarse ash. The smoke column was relatively thin, consisting of isolated cauliflower bursts, strung together in a vertical column. The explosive bursts had the appearance of originating at the throat of the vent, or only a very short distance below. Explosions occurred at fairly regular intervals of about 4 seconds; sometimes explosions came in rapid succession, sometimes at intervals of 6 to 8 seconds . . . . The greater part of the material ejected at this stage consisted of bombs rather than of ash or sand. Each explosion threw bombs 600-900 m into the air. Most of them fell upon the cone. The greatest distance from the cone that bombs were found was 1,000 m from the center of the volcano. The bombs rose so high that many of them took 12 to 15 seconds

Fig. 31. February 26, 1943. The horseshoe-shaped cone is 167 m high. Quitzocho lava flow with fumaroles is in the middle ground. Taken from the NE. Compare the earlier photos shown in Figs. 26 and 28, which were taken from about the same point, and on which many field markings and other features can be identified.

to fall back to the crater rim, 500-1,000 m below. They were roughly spherical, and their size ranged from that of "a nut to that of a house", but most of them ranged from 1 to 2 m in diameter. The largest block Trask saw was 15 m in diameter and was hurled 90 m above the summit of the crater . . . . Almost all the bombs were entirely solid when they fell, for they did not change their form upon impact. The lava flowed at a rate of .1 m/hr toward the west and spread laterally at a rate of ⅓ m/hr.

Explosions continued during the early days of March, sometimes so strongly that windows in San Juan Parangaricutiro rattled and doors swung open and shut with each explosion. Not only were the explosions heard in the town, but the blasts were distinctly felt. The eruptive activity continued to increase each day, but with rare brief intervals when the crater was silent. Activity and the shape of the cone remained essentially unchanged until March 18.

The first advance of the Quitzocho flow, which began sometime during February 21, must have been rapid for it had already covered an extensive area when it was first recognized as a lava flow by Ordóñez. It soon slackened its pace, however, the moving fronts advancing at rates varying from 1 to 2 m/hr during its first week, later slowing to a rate of only several meters per day. At least two surges were recognizable, one terminating on February 26, the second beginning on February 28 and continuing until March 20.

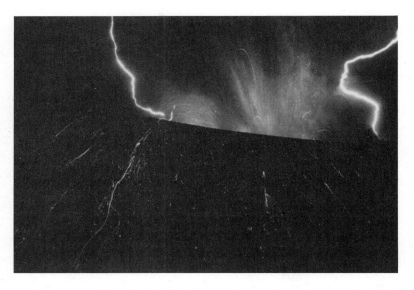

Fig. 32. May 25, 1943. Lightning flashes were frequent in the dense, swiftly rising eruptive column.

Fig. 33. March 2, 1943. Heavy bomb and lapilli emission. The horseshoe shape of the cone is apparent. Quitzocho lava flow in middle ground. Note the sparse cover of ash in the cultivated fields. Taken from the NE.

The Quitzocho flow spread out in a great sheet with a steep rubbly front ranging from 6 to 15 m high. The front advanced slowly, but little flowing lava was discernible. The surface of the flow, after it came to complete rest, was undulating and very hummocky, sloping at about 5° from the foot of the cone to the north (Fig. 33). One of the features that distinguished the Quitzocho from later flows was the apparently high content of volatile constituents, as manifested by its abundant fumaroles. These fumaroles, however, were not generally distributed through the flow but localized along its periphery (Fig. 34), usually along the front face, at the crest of the front, or in a zone less than 50 m back from the crest. A few weak fumaroles at the summits of conical knolls were situated on the lava mesa itself. The Quitzocho flow issued directly from the explosive vent of the crater (Fig. 35). By the end of March it had spread over the entire Llano de Quitzocho to the western slope of Cerro de Jarátiro ridge [Fig. 36].

Fig. 34. March 5, 1943. Oblique air view of the cone from the NE. Quitzocho flow in the foreground with fumaroles around its periphery; Cuiyúsuru, right; Teruto, middle ground. Small trees in bottom center of photo can be clearly seen on the earlier photos of Figs. 26 and 28.

Fig. 35. March 10, 1943. Breached eastern side of cone showing the crater and hummocky, bomb-covered surface of Quitzocho lava flow. In the foreground are the remains of a forest destroyed by bomb and lapilli falls.

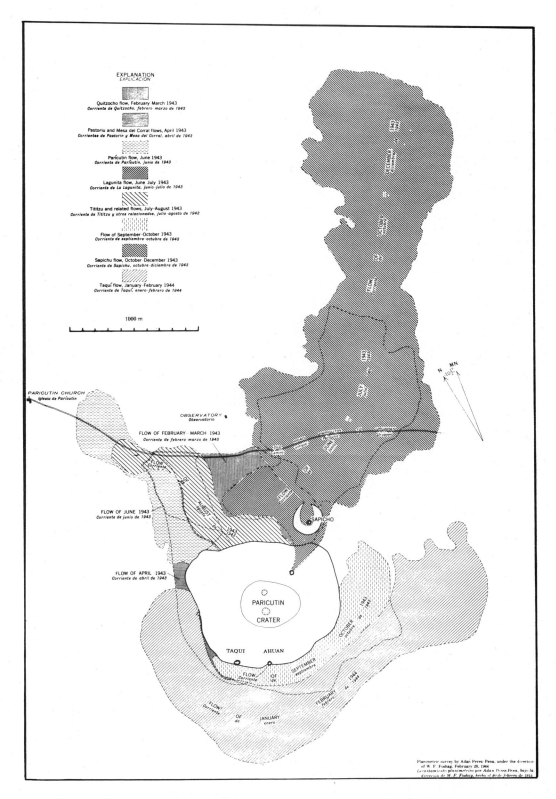

Fig. 36. Map of Parícutin volcano showing the lava flows of the first year. Planimetric survey by Adan Perez-Peña under the direction of W.F. Foshag, Feburary 20, 1944.

On March 20 the cone began to heal its breach, indicating that feeding of the Quitzocho flow had ceased; the flow front, however, continued to spread in all directions (Fig. 37).

During the period of the Quitzocho flow the explosive activity was, in general, moderate compared with later activity. Nonetheless, the accompanying noises were terrific. The ejected material consisted principally of bombs that were largely semi-fluid in character, indicating that the explosions took place at or near the surface in a rising column of liquid magma. The cone grew rapidly, but the spread of ash over the surrounding terrain was comparatively slight.

The cone frequently changed its configuration during this period, owing in part to the varying activity or shifting of the three vents, but owing

Fig. 37. March 20, 1943. The Quitzocho lava flow has almost reached its maximum extent at the foot of Cerro the Jarátiro. The cone is still asymmetrical owing to repeated breaching. Taken from the eastern foot of Cerro de Jarátiro.

chiefly to the erratic flow of the lava. During pauses in the emission of lava, the wall of the volcano was built up by the accumulation of ejected bombs, only to be breached again by a new lava surge. The volcano showed alternately a conical form or a horseshoe shape. The original small mound, roughly conical, changed to a horseshoe shape with the first flow of lava. From February 21 to 25 it remained in this form, becoming cone shaped again for a brief period, February 26 to 27, only to be breached again on February 28. This breach was finally restored on March 20. The cone, thereafter, attained such proportions that lava flows were no longer able to breach the cone completely.

Heavy Cineritic Phase

On March 18 the heavy bomb stage ceased; the crater passed into a very heavy cineritic phase that continued with some variation until early June. It was during this period that the greatest ash damage to the surrounding countryside was done. A huge column of ash and vapors boiled violently from the volcano in turbulent cauliflowers. Frequently they completely filled the crater from rim to rim, rising as a majestic eruptive column to a height of 6 km or more [Fig. 38].

The cineritic phase began on March 18 and continued all day with gradually increasing intensity until, in the night, the activity changed to a dense, billowing black eruptive column, and great "flames" or fountains of incandescent bombs rose to a considerable height. The number of heavy explosions increased; a deep roar seemed to come from the depths of the earth, and the ground shook under apparently ceaseless shocks. The fury of this night exceeded anything hitherto experienced at Parícutin and filled the observers with alarm, but by morning the violence diminished, and the noise changed to a continuous low rumble. The crater of the cone now appeared considerably enlarged, and a dense black, heavily ash-laden column rose in majestic volutes high into the atmosphere (Fig. 39). The winds, which at this season prevail from the west and SW, carried the fine ash far to the east. Some ash had previously fallen on the region, but its distribution was very local; even in the immediate environs of the cone it was not more than a few centimeters thick. From March 18 to June 9, however, the ash fall was by far the heaviest experienced in the history of Parícutin. The ash cloud hung like a black pall over the region to the east and NE so that the day was like dusk. A smoky haze dimmed the light of the sun as far east as Toluca [265 km east], and fine ash fell on the rooftops and streets of Zacapu [70 km NE], Pátzcuaro [75 km east], and Morelia [125 km ENE]. [Hernández-Velasco[210] made repeated ash-fall measurements in México City during the period March 29 to July 30, 1943. Maximum values of about 300 mg/m^2 were recorded for March 29 and April 12.] The Charapán-Uruapan highway was covered with a thin mantle of ash, which swirled

Fig. 38. March 24, 1943. Tremendous cineritic activity, with eruptive column 6 km high. Front of the Mesa del Corral lava flow in the middle ground. Taken [northward] from Tititzu, 3 km away.

Fig. 39. April 22, 1943. The breached cone, now partly restored, and the inner cone or "ombligo" [navel], seen as the curved inner crater rim. Very heavy cineritic activity. Taken from the south.

about and drifted into small windrows like dry snow. The fields and forests took on a dusty dark hue. Nearer the volcano the ash sifted through the trees of the forest with a gentle rustle like falling hail and blocked the Uruapan-Parícutin road. Figures passing but a few yards away appeared eerie and ghost-like in the ashy haze. Even at a distance of several kilometers, vesicular fragments as much as a few centimeters across drifted down. On March 27, 15 cm of ash fell at a point 6 km to the east of the cone. During early May the ash fall at Uruapan became so heavy that it was necessary to clear the roofs of the houses; it filled the patios to a depth of a few centimeters and all but halted motorcar traffic in the streets. With the coming of the June rains, much of this ash was washed from the slopes of the hills, almost completely filling some of the small steep-walled *arroyos*, and in time the ash blanket over the fields and in the forest became so completely blended with the soil that it was no longer apparent over much of the area originally covered.

During April (Fig. 39), May (Fig. 40), and early June (Fig. 41), the eruption continued as a magnificent vertical column rising in volutes to a tremendous height. Based on angle measurements taken from Uruapan, we calculated its altitude as 6 km above the crater . . . .

During this period the surface winds were from the west, but the higher winds carried the ash curtain toward the south. Bombs of the larger sizes fell upon the cone or on the fields and in the forests for a radius of about 1 km about the cone. Bombs found in the woods some distance from the cone were frequently as much as a meter or more in diameter. They fell in such numbers that it was impossible to approach the base of the volcano. The temperature of the air was distinctly cooler in the falling ash or lapilli beyond the zone of bombs than outside an ash fall. Small lapilli were distinctly cold to the touch. It was not until the falling lapilli reached about 3 cm in size that they showed perceptible warmth.

At about 8 p.m., March 18, the noises of the crater began to diminish; at the same time the eruptive column increased and became heavily laden with ash. The cone was now so silent that the inhabitants of the region believed that the volcano would cease or change to some new activity. Not a visible bomb rose about the crater rim. Now a second vent opened on the south side of the cone, and lava flowed in two streams toward the SW [Fig. 36]. The area lying between the cone and the lowest slopes of Cerros de Tancítaro had many *cañadas*, small basins, and small mesas; and the new flow filled some of the larger basins. The flow was short and was soon covered and hidden by heavy ash falls. Its lava differed from that of the Quitzocho flow in being more blocky and more heavily oxidized, red or cinnamon. Unfortunately, no record was made of its particular characteristics nor the extent of its fumarole emissions. This flow we have called the Pastoriu flow.

During most of April 17 the heavy ash column continued as previously, but at 3:30 p.m. activity again ceased, and the eruptive column died down completely. About a quarter of an hour later eruptive activity resumed, but with much less ash and many bombs, accompanied by deep grating roars. With this change in explosive activity, a second lava flow broke out from the same vent from which the Pastoriu flow had issued; the new flow carried with it a large portion of the south side of the cone, which formed a ridge, 60 or more meters high, moving slowly toward the SW . . . . This flow was typical block lava. We have called it the Mesa del Corral flow [Fig. 36].

With the outbreak of the Mesa del Corral flow, the crater resumed its heavy cineritic stage. The heavy ash falls of this period soon repaired the break of the cone and covered the flow, but its effect was evident for some months afterward as a high halfdome-like hump on the SW flank of the cone. After a few days of cineritic activity an inner or "daughter" cone, called the *ombligo* (navel) by the natives, showed itself above the crater rim, eventually rising to an elevation of about 30 m above the old crater edge. This inner cone continued to grow and finally merged with the main cone, the last perceptible trace of which was a narrow bench that marked the old crater rim (Fig. 39).

Recurring Flows

In early June, Parícutin entered into a new and violent phase of activity, characterized by intermittent but very violent explosive activity from the crater, by various lava flows, and by the rafting of the north side of the cone on three occasions. From early June into August the volcano showed its most varied and spectacular activity. The variety is described from notes taken during our stay from June 9 to 19.

June 9.—Upon approaching San Juan Parangaricutiro at 2 p.m., we could see through a gap in the encircling hills the cone of Parícutin and its huge billowing column of ash. At 3 p.m., while we were awaiting our horses and mules, a casual glance toward the volcano showed a remarkable change, a rather sudden and marked decrease of the smoke to a thin languid column that shrunk perceptibly as we watched, as if a valve had been closed and the volcano was subsiding to rest. A half hour later there

Fig. 40. May 24, 1943. Heavy cineritic activity, accompanied by abundant bombs. Taken from Cerro de Jarátiro.

Fig. 41. June 9, 1943. Eruptive column from the Uruapan highway. Plume of drifting ash to the south and clouds forming beneath it. Extinct volcanic cones in the middle distance. Taken from the east.

remained but a thin wisp of pale vapor and an occasional quiet burst of large bombs with little ash; and an unnatural calm settled over the cone. The change was so unexpected and so unusual that we all thought the volcano was dying and many of us gathered with the *presidente municipal* for a celebration.

We arrived at the camp on Cerro de Jarátiro about 4 p.m. The Quitzocho flow was now completely covered with ash, except for the peaks and crags that projected above the surface or faced the edge of the flow, and the numerous fumaroles along the lava front lazily gave off their usual white or bluish fumes.

The bursts from the crater threw out a scattering of large viscous bombs, without ash or much visible vapors, accompanied by a deep throaty rumble. This rather tranquil state did not last long. Soon the activity began to increase, gradually, almost imperceptibly, until at 9 p.m. the bursts followed each other in rapid succession. Strong explosive bursts now came each ½ - 4 seconds, hurling large blocks, some to a height of more than 600 m (12 seconds to fall). These bombs showed many irregular and changing shapes; rods, clubs, and mace-like projectiles, some like boomerangs or T's and a surprising number like birds soaring through the air, all indicative of the viscous state of the bombs. Upon falling on the slopes of the cone, these bombs broke into cascading fragments or rolled down the slope like pinwheels, casting incandescent fragments in leaping arcs before them. The noise of the large explosions was tremendous, and one could feel the blast of air at the camp 1½ km away . . . .

Early in the evening I noticed a slight offset in the summit line of the cone, as if a segment had slumped slightly. By midnight this straight displacement became a distinct sag (Fig. 42).

June 10.—The indescribable noise and confusion continued until 2 a.m. At 2:10 the tremendous roar suddenly ceased . . . .

Daylight revealed a huge break in the cone (Fig. 43). A segment embracing about one-quarter of its perimeter had moved out (carried out by lava we learned later). The side walls of the break were steep, and the slumped portion lay in two long terraces at the base of the cone. The volcano was now very quiet, with only rare bursts of bombs, but with a heavy, slowly rising eruptive column.

The summit of the lower of the two main terraces sloped down from the east end of the break at a 5° angle to the west end, and its front showed a regular wall with slopes at the angle of repose (about 32°). This lower terrace advanced very slowly toward the

north, its movement dislocating rocks on the lower slope, which rolled down raising a fine pinkish dust.

The western extremity of this lower terrace had a reddish oxidized color, and the frequent falls of rock raised plumes of pinkish ash. At 11 a.m. incandescent moving lava appeared at this point. For the first time in the life of the volcano, the eruptive activity of the crater had so diminished that one could reach the base of the cone with reasonable safety, and we were able to watch the lava at close hand. The lava front, although incandescent in the crevices and gashes and in the blocks that spalled off, showed no liquid lava. It advanced at a rate of 30 m/hr as an apparently solid wall of rock and rubble. Huge incandescent masses were dislodged and rolled to the foot of the flow, and there was a continuous disintegration and streaming of incandescent pebble-like fragments or sand down the seamy lava front. Blocks on the lava front disintegrated with a continuous crackle, to which was added the tinkle of sliding scoriae. The hottest incandescent lava was orange red. No visible fumes were given off, and there was no perceptible odor. The flow carried a cover of ash, the surface of which was wet from the rains and steamed from the heat below.

All during the day the crater was quiet with only rare explosive bursts that yielded a huge eruptive column rising silently to a height of about 5 km.

At about 7:40 p.m. a thin white column of vapors suddenly appeared near the NW base of the cone. This column was larger than the fumaroles and located within the main part of the Quitzocho flow where no fumaroles were situated. Within a minute or two the base of the vapor column became suffused a deep pink, indicating a reflection from incandescent lava, which rapidly increased in intensity. We hastened to the spot, crossing over a newly formed ridge of ash, furrowed and seamed by small crevasses (Fig. 44). This ridge, which ultimately extended NNW from the base of the cone and was later to show striking changes, we have called the Quitzocho ridge. Beyond we found a new low cliff of lava, with incandescent patches, slowly advancing and disintegrating. Huge incandescent blocks broke from the front and rolled to the foot; and small incandescent fragments, hardly distinguishable from liquid lava, streamed down its face.

About 15 minutes after our arrival, a spot on the lava front became more incandescent (orange yellow) and began to work like slowly rising dough. In one-half a minute the lava at this spot began to flow and spread, and within 5 minutes a front 5 m across flowed down the slope like molasses. This flow,

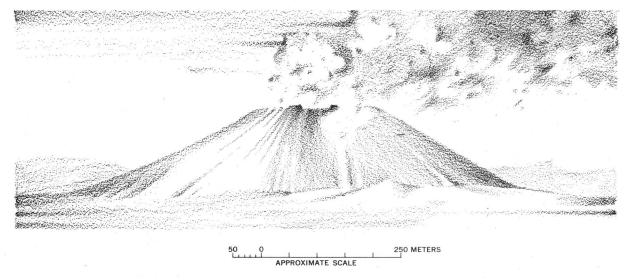

50   0   250 METERS
APPROXIMATE SCALE

Fig. 42. Parícutin volcano on June 9, 1943, at 9 p.m., showing the cone, complete except for a slight slump in the north crater rim. Ash-covered Quitzocho flow in the foreground.

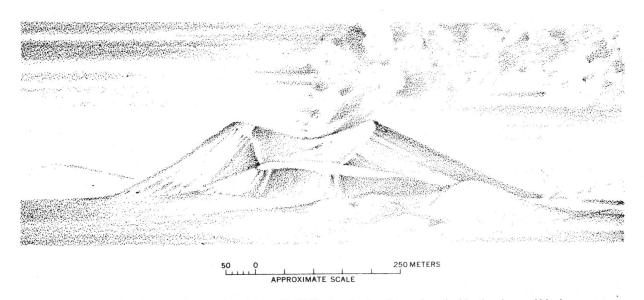

50   0   250 METERS
APPROXIMATE SCALE

Fig. 43. The cone on the morning of June 10, 1943, showing the slumped north side, the slumped block as a high sloping terrace, and the lava flow to the right. The knoll to the right indicates the beginning of the Quitzocho ridge.

Fig. 44. June 10, 1943. Early stage in the growth of Quitzocho ridge by injection of lava below the ash.

moving between the newly formed ash ridge and a knoll upon which we had taken stance, moved so rapidly that we feared we might be cut off . . . .

Upon returning toward our camp we found the newly formed ridge of ash higher and more deeply furrowed. With considerable trepidation we climbed an eminence and saw at our feet the apparent source of the lava, an incandescent stream, perhaps 20 m wide, moving noiselessly along, dappled with moving blocks of congealed black lava. Its apparent source was the foot of the collapsed terrace, from which it appeared to flow quietly and without disturbance.

June 12.—The morning was heavily overcast, and rain drizzled down. From a station NE of the cone, two eruptive columns were distinguishable—one from the western part of the crater gave off dense gray smoke; the second, near the NE rim, yielded some bombs and less ash.

At 2:30 p.m. the rain ceased somewhat; and when we went out to place some collecting tubes in the fumaroles, we found the new ridge now increased to about 30 m in height and, beyond the ridge, new lava flowing down the Parícutin Arroyo in the direction of

Parícutin village [see pre-eruption airphotos and maps of Figs. 12 and 13]. This already well-advanced lava flow had its apparent source beneath the ash near the vent of yesterday's flow. It issued from the south end of the ridge near the base of the cone and flowed toward the north over the old ash-covered lavas. As the flow moved to the edge of Parícutin Arroyo, its front became steeper until it was entirely free of the congealed clinkers with which most flows are covered, exposing the actual moving incandescent lava below. Its advance took place as slowly bulging lobes, which gave the entire moving front a gross botryoidal appearance [like a bunch of grapes], bulging and cracking with an ever-changing surface. Such clinkers as formed rolled down this front to the *arroyo* below. As the bulges reached a certain degree of protuberance, they tore off and rolled down the *arroyo* slope as viscous masses. Most prominent was a basal bulge, slowly turning under and incorporating within itself the accumulated clinkers at the base of the flow. Sparse bluish fumes arose from the lava, but the only sound was the tinkle of moving clinkers. The advancing front was 4-5 m high. This flow we have called the Parícutin flow [Fig. 36].

Fig. 45. June 13, 1943. Parícutin lava flow approaching Parícutin village, with crosses erected in hopes of stopping the lava, which advances as a moving wall of rubble.

June 13.—The day was cloudy and rainy when we awoke at daybreak to a tremendous grating roar that continued without interruption, except for very rare periods of one-half minute of complete silence . . . . Don Felipe Cuara-Amezcua [*presidente municipal* of San Juan Parangaricutiro] came on horseback in some agitation to tell us that Parícutin village was threatened by lava (the Parícutin flow)[Fig. 45]. On arriving there, we found the lava of yesterday had advanced well beyond the limits of the Mesa del Corral flow and was moving forward at a rate of 25 m/hr but spreading laterally at only 2½ m/hr. With Parícutin village located on a low ridge, we concluded that the lateral push of the lava would not be sufficient to cover more than perhaps a few of the lower houses. We counselled, however, the people to evacuate the town, because their fields were already beyond use from the heavy cover of ash and there seemed no surcease from the continuing ash falls. The Mexican Government had offered them facilities to evacuate their village and to settle on new lands in unaffected areas. This was sad advice to a people so deeply attached to their soil, and many were loath to accept it.

June 14.—During the morning hours a variety of noises came from the crater. Sometimes the sounds were roars, and occasionally a tremendous explosive burst, sometimes a sound like the sigh of a high wind in the pine trees. The noises came chiefly from the south vent, but there were erratic bursts from the north crater.

In the early morning a new lava flow burst out on the upper slopes of the cone above the upper terrace, between a resistant pyramidal remnant of the cone and the eastern wall of the break. Its point of origin was about 75 m below the lower lip of the north crater, and the lava flowed as a cascade down the terraced slopes to the NE base of the cone and beyond (Fig. 46). This flow we have called the Lagunita flow, because it invaded and covered the lands of La Lagunita. The lava emitted bluish fumes, sometimes tinged a brownish yellow. The flow advanced at a rate of 15 m/hr into the dead pine forest.

Fig. 46. June 19, 1943. View of Parícutin volcano from the north, on Cerro de Jarátiro, showing the break in the north slope of the cone, and the north crater vent. Below it is the lava vent behind a slumped block, which feeds the Lagunita lava flow toward the left. Vapors are also being emitted from the south crater vent, which lies beyond the ridge behind the north vent. Broken terraces are in the middle distance and the smooth domes of the Quitzocho ridge to the right; the ash-covered Quitzocho lava in the foreground.

We went to Parícutin village at 4 p.m. and found the lava still advancing. The front progressed at a rate of 21 m/hr and its lateral push had carried it within 80 m of the first house of the village. Many houses were being dismantled, and trucks had already arrived to evacuate the people.

June 15.—In the morning we went to Parícutin village. The lava flow had slowed to a low speed, greater toward the NW in the direction of San Juan Parangaricutiro, much less laterally. The west side of the flow was then about 20 m from the first house in the village, and the inhabitants had placed an additional cross before the dwelling to ward off the danger of its destruction. A few weak fumaroles had already formed in the flow, indicating that it was now practically at rest; and the fumaroles were beginning to yield thin white, yellow, or orange sublimates.

In the afternoon we went to the Lagunita flow, which moved down the terraces from the upper vent.

This had spread in a sheet between the Quitzocho flow and the low hills bordering the eastern edge of the valley [Fig. 36]. The Lagunita flow was thicker than the Parícutin flow and advanced more slowly, 5-10 m/hr. It was viscous, bulging here and there as the moving lava broke through the front of advancing rubble. There was no odor, few fumes, and little noise, except for the tinkle of sliding clinkers. The flow followed the general slope of the terrain but moved over low slopes of hummocky ground and low knolls.

At night the volcano offered a magnificent sight—a bright incandescent eruptive column showered bombs upon the cone, and the two brilliant rivers of orange lava cascaded from the vent to the base of the cone and flowed to the lava field in the valley, where myriad lights looked like a city viewed from a distant hill.

. . . . .

June 19.—The north slope was now a smooth concave swale, with lava flowing from a mound-like vent about two-thirds up the cone and rising some 10-15 m above the upper terrace level. From this vent thin blue vapors arose. Some 15 m above this was a small vent perhaps 4 m across from which ejected material rushed as if from a blowtorch, yielding a small column of vapors and ash. The saddle-shaped crater rim, with a black resistant comb, formed a low scarp to the east. The lava flowed quietly down the terrace toward the east and spread over the lands of La Lagunita.

This period beginning on June 9 and continuing for about 1 month was one of the most active and violent in the life of the volcano, surpassed only by the tremendous eruptions in late July. The striking changes that took place in the configuration of the broken cone, the kaleidoscopic variations in the eruptive activity, the rapid shifting of the lava vents, and the tremendous surges of viscous lava set this period apart from any other period in the history of the volcano. The alignment of the shifting lava vents in a northeasterly direction suggests a lava source from a fissure striking in this direction . . . .

Quitzocho Ridge

One of the conspicuous features of the volcano, until covered by the lavas of 1947, was the high ridge that extended from the NW base of the cone to Cerro de Jarátiro. This ridge had its inception during the night of June 10, at the time of the break in the north side of the cone. [Here the authors backtrack, chronologically, to describe the origin of this feature.] Just how the ridge began cannot exactly be told, for during the day our attention was attracted by the phenomena of the advancing terraces and the outbreak of lava.

The original ridge formed a line of low hummocks extending from the base of the volcano to the edge of the Mesa del Corral flow at the foot of Cerro de Jarátiro (Fig. 44). By June 12 this ridge was about 10 m above the old ash-covered surface of the Mesa del Corral flow, and the ash showed much evidence of oxidation by intruded lava. [Geologists generally think of intrusion by "magma", the name for partially molten rock existing below the earth's surface. Only when "magma" reaches the surface and begins to flow is it called "lava". The authors are correct in describing intrusion by "lava" here, however, because this magma had already flowed on the surface as lava before intruding beneath the Quitzocho ridge.] On this day, too, the Parícutin flow issued from the south end of the ridge near the base of the cone and flowed toward the north.

The ridge grew almost imperceptibly, or at least we paid little attention to it, for at first it was little different from the usual hummocky aspect of the heavily ash-covered Quitzocho and Mesa del Corral flows, and the numerous outbreaks of lava from the cone attracted our attention. The smooth ash cover was elevated and domed, broken by numerous cracks, with patches of pushed or slumped ash (Figs. 47 and 48). The top of the ridge showed deep fissures in the ash and displaced or raised blocks of ash. A few patches of reddish oxidized lava were exposed in the flanks of the ridge. The ash was obviously being slowly raised into a domed ridge by the injection of lava beneath, perhaps by additions of fluid lava to the underlying old lava flow from a source at the NW edge of the lower terrace.

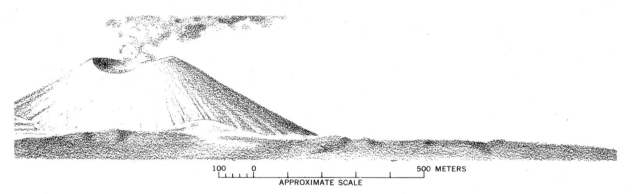

Fig. 47. Quitzocho ridge in early June, showing the smooth ash-covered Quitzocho and Mesa del Corral lava flows.

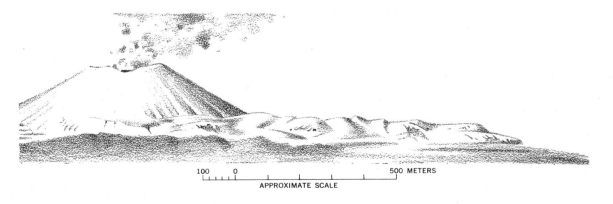

Fig. 48. Quitzocho ridge after the flow of June 9, 1943, showing the smooth ash raised by injection of lava below.

Activity of July-August: Two N-Flank
Slumps and Growth of Quitzocho Ridge

The Lagunita lava (Fig. 49) on the NE side flowed intermittently until July 19, when its movement down the slope was very slow, about 1 m in 5 minutes. In the evening of the 19th the last weak surge of lava from its vent was observed. The break in the NE slope of the cone was now reduced to a wedge-shaped segment that formed a sag in the upper line of the crater. At the inverted apex of the triangular break about half way up the slope of the cone was the lava vent. The lava flowed down two trench-like channels, spreading over the fields of La Lagunita and Turímbiro. This flow was similar to other flows, a blocky lava, its surface covered by a mantle of blocks and clinkers. The last lava of this flow moved as a tongue over the ash-covered Quitzocho lava between the eastern end of Cerro de Jarátiro and the base of the cone.

With the diminution of the lava flow from the vents, the break in the cone began to fill with ejectamenta from the crater. With each new surge of lava, now at intervals of 2 days or more and then of short duration, ash slides occurred in the break; but with the total cessation of lava flows, the cone very soon returned to its normal even slope.

The last stage of this interesting period of lava flows was the brief outburst of chimney-like vents on the slopes of the cone (Fig. 50), these vents coinciding as nearly as can be determined with the lava vents of this period[44].

On July 27 we returned to Parícutin after a day's visit to Uruapan and found striking changes taking place. In traveling from Uruapan to San Juan Parangaricutiro, we were struck with the large quantity of pinkish and reddish dust that arose from somewhere near the north base of the cone. This dust obscured the cone, so that we could not clearly perceive its state, although it was apparent that some significant change was taking place.

From San Juan Parangaricutiro we passed through the now entirely depopulated village of Parícutin, where many of the houses had collapsed from the weight of ash [Fig. 51]. The Parícutin lava flow that threatened to engulf the village had now practically ceased its advance, although an occasional creaking noise indicated that there remained some slight movement in the mass. Scattered weak fumaroles had formed, spotting the lava with thin patches of white and yellow salts.

Seen from the Parícutin Arroyo, now completely filled with lava, it was strikingly evident that the Quitzocho ridge had greatly increased in size and that

the north slope of the cone had suffered another slump such as we had observed in June. According to our informants, this new break in the cone and the changes in the topography of the Quitzocho ridge took place at 2 p.m., during our absence, without preliminary warning (Fig. 52).

The cone showed a wide concave break on its north front, now partly restored by the fall of bombs and ash. The north side was a rather flat facet of the cone, at the foot of which was a rubble terrace, or rather a ridge, for a shallow valley separated the terrace from the cone. This terrace, oriented towards the north, joined the Quitzocho ridge to the cone. Between the terrace and the Quitzocho ridge was a saddle, which we frequently traversed later in going to and from the opposite side of the cone. The south end of the Quitzocho ridge rose about 130 m above the original surface and was crowned by several large irregular masses of rock. These rock masses, we were later to discover, were congealed lava and the remnants of the lava vent from which the June lavas issued. They had moved several hundred meters toward the north, carried out upon the surface of lava flowing below. For many months the incandescent fissures in these rocks served us as guides at night, and the rocks we called Los Faroles ["the lanterns": Fig. 52].

The Quitzocho ridge had changed from a relatively low ridge (Fig. 44) with smooth slopes of velvety-appearing ash to a mesa capped by bedded ash (Figs. 53 and 54) with steep slopes of pinkish and reddish oxidized ash and rubble. As the sides slowly expanded, blocks of lava and streams of clinkers rolled down the slope, raising a pinkish or reddish dust that settled over the wet, black ash that covered the old Quitzocho and Mesa del Corral lava flows.

But the most striking change was shown by the ridge front, facing the slopes of Cerro de Jarátiro. This front, now about 100 m high, was a steep, rugged and broken scarp, turreted with huge masses of lava. This scarp was ever changing in its features. The huge exposures of congealed lava were in a constant state of disintegration to small rubble or fine sand, which streamed down the seamed face of the ridge like small flows (Fig. 55). A viscous lava frequently bulged from beneath the huge blocks; and the whole front, although apparently congealed, was slowly advancing. At times huge blocks of rock many meters across slowly tilted forward, then rolled to the foot of the face with an earth-shaking thud. Although many masses were lost from the front by disintegration or fall, new ones formed by crevassing of the front. One of the results of this action was an accumulation of debris at the foot of the slope made

Fig. 49. June 28, 1943. The broken cone, viewed from the ENE on Cerro de Curupichu after the break of June 10, is now partly restored. Lava issues from a vent high on the flank of the cone (the Lagunita flow) and spreads out in the valley below.

up of angular fragments ranging from 5 m in diameter to fine sand and dust. During this disintegration pink dust rose in copious quantities. At night we observed what appeared to be short tongues of flame playing over some of the crevices in the congealed masses.

Within the next few days several flows broke out laterally . . . from the Quitzocho ridge. Very near the north scarp of the ridge nearly a kilometer from the cone, the first, a short flow, issued from an orifice on the west slope and encircled the nose of the ridge. A second broke out from a point near the first and flowed a short distance toward the NW, yielding a scarp of jumbled blocks and clinkers (Fig. 56). A third flow breached the ridge about 100 m back from its nose and poured out in a brilliant flood of incandescent lava, carrying with it huge blocks riding majestically down the incandescent stream. This sheet flowed quietly but rapidly at its orifice, but the front soon slowed to a speed of about 40 m/hr. This flow, moving on top of the Parícutin flow, reached about one-half the distance of the Parícutin flow and there halted, forming a terrace upon the older flow. This second flow toward Parícutin village we have called the Tititzu flow, because its front coincides generally with the lands of Tititzu [Fig. 36].

Since the break of the cone on the morning of July 24, the crater was in intense activity (Figs. 57), yielding a dense and heavy eruptive column with heavy cauliflower heads. The amount of material ejected was great enough to heal the break in the cone and restore it to almost complete symmetry. [Figs. 57 and 58 show the dramatic changes that occurred over five days in late July]. Heavy ash clouds drifted to the SW raining ash upon the pine forests of Cerros de Tancítaro. On July 31, at 11 a.m., a distinct change in the activity in the crater took place, similar to the change that preceded the break of June 10. The noise increased, and the eruptive column diminished until the activity was

Fig. 50. Early July, 1943. Chimney on the north flank of the cone at the site of one of the June eruptive vents, after the cone had been restored by uninterrupted ash fall. Lava of June on ash-covered lavas of the Quitzocho flow. View from Cerro de Jarátiro.

Fig. 51. July 30, 1943. House covered with ash in the village of Parícutin.

reduced to a thin spasmodic column of tenuous vapors (Fig. 58), or even to no visible vapors at all. Larger ejectamenta increased, and large viscous masses were hurled high in the air. One could frequently discern their shapes and how they changed in their flight through the air. The explosions, coming 4 to 15 seconds apart, gave off a deep throaty reverberating roar, and the trepidations were distinctly perceptible at camp. Shortly after 6 p.m. the first remarkable "flashing arc" occurred. An arc of yellow light shot

Fig. 52. July 10, 1943. A later break in the cone. The rocky peaks in the center of the photo, "Los Faroles", once a part of the cone, are now part of Quitzocho ridge. Taken from Cerro de Jarátiro.

Fig. 53. September 1943. Portion of Quitzocho ridge showing elevated stratified ash on top and the intruded and now disintegrated lava below. [In the stratified section, fresh black ash is interlayered with pinkish ash derived from collapse of oxidized blocks from the intruding lava.]

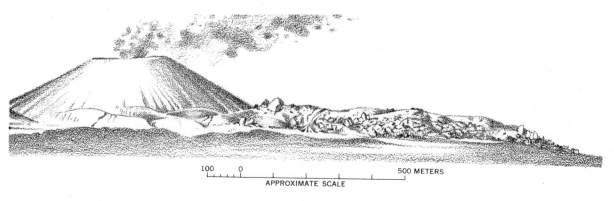

100   0   500 METERS
APPROXIMATE SCALE

Fig. 54. Quitzocho ridge after the injection of lava in July-August 1943. Disintegrated lava appears from below the ash. The protuberant blocks are cores of disintegrating lava.

Fig. 55. August 25, 1943. Late stage in the growth of Quitzocho ridge. The large blocks at the ridge terminus are of disintegrating lava. The dust, left center, is from boulders displaced by the elevation of the ridge. The foot of Cerro de Jarátiro is to the left.

Fig. 56. July 31, 1944. Typical block lava front of a small flow from Quitzocho ridge.

Fig. 57. July 26, 1943. Cone viewed from Cerro de Jarátiro after the break in late July. Tremendous explosion from the north crater vent and heavy emission from south vent. Quitzocho ridge in the middle ground; ash-covered Quitzocho lava with salt-incrusted fumaroles in foreground.

Fig. 58. July 31, 1943. Heavy explosions with large bombs and moderate vaporous eruptive column. Viewed from the same place on Cerro de Jarátiro, this photo shows that the late-July break of the cone is now largely repaired, only 5 days after the photo above (Fig. 57). An old crater of Cerro de Jarátiro in the foreground.

Fig. 59. August 1, 1943. Tremendous bursts of huge lava bubbles in crater, accompanied by flashing arcs, yielding huge tatters of viscous lava. Taken from Cerro de Jarátiro.

Fig. 60. August 1, 1943. Bursting of huge lava bubbles; time exposure about 15 seconds. Ejected masses of viscous lava flow down the slopes of the cone. Dark area in upper center is a weak eruptive column. Taken from Cerro de Jarátiro.

from the crater with great speed, flashed into the sky, and disappeared. This was immediately followed by a tremendous burst of immense masses of viscous incandescent lava which, upon falling on the flanks of the cone, flowed slowly down the slope. Six seconds later, the time for the sound to travel from the crater to the camp, a tremendous blast of noise shook the camp. This awesome and startling spectacle brought involuntary bursts of applause from the tourists gathered near the camp, as if the spectacle were a part of a great theatrical production.

Other similar bursts took place during the night at intervals of 15 minutes to an hour. With darkness the explosions were even more awesome than in the dusk of twilight. Tongues of lava repeatedly rose high above the crater rim, there to burst into shreds (Fig. 59). We estimate some to have risen 100 m above the rim. They appeared like huge bubbles, botryoidal on the surface and presumably filled with gases. When they burst, huge glowing masses of viscous lava were flung over the cone, some so far as to clear the slopes and fall on the surrounding ash field. Sometimes a second tongue, overtaking an earlier one, would tear it into huge shreds.

The heaviest explosions, however, took place within the crater, and it was with these that the flashing arcs occurred. The first signal of an approaching arc was a bright and widespread suffusion of deep pink above the crater, a reflection of the incandescent lava in the crater upon the rising vapors and the low hanging clouds above. This was followed immediately by the rapidly expanding arc of yellow light, seemingly rising with lightning speed into the sky. Quickly thereafter came the burst of huge incandescent orange lava masses (Fig. 60) and a blast of warm air distinctly perceptible 1½ km away. Lastly came the deafening roar of the explosion.

In the morning when we visited the base of the cone, we found huge bombs scattered about. Many were spindle bombs, some 1½ m in diameter and somewhat more in length. Large masses of congealed lava were plastered upon the other bombs at the base. All the bombs were forms characteristic of molten but rather viscous lava. One huge fish-shaped bomb measuring 7 m long fell several hundred meters from the foot of the cone. This was the only time that we observed characteristic spindle bombs among the ejecta of the volcano.

Fig. 61. August 2, 1943. The break in the cone in early afternoon. Huge jets of black ash play from the broken segment of the cone. The rocks, "Los Faroles", that crown the ridge are beginning to move to the left. In the foreground is one of the craters of Cerro de Jarátiro, the ridge on which the photograph was taken.

The character of the activity and the nature of the bombs led us to believe that a lake of lava had arisen in the crater and that huge bubbles of gas rising through the conduit had brought on the terrifying explosions of the night before.

During the morning of August 2, heavy explosive activity continued with the ejection of large bombs but modest eruptive columns. In late morning, explosive activity increased and at 12:30 p.m. had reached such violence that we looked for some new event to occur. At 1 p.m. the north slope collapsed with startling noiseless suddenness. A great section, about one-quarter of the periphery of the cone, slid out amidst a tremendous confusion of ash (Fig. 61). Soon great jets of dense black ash shot up from the edges of the break: first on the east about two-thirds of the way up the break, then several lower down, and then from the west side of the break—each persisted for several minutes and then died down, only for new ones to break out some other place. A huge ash jet, ascending to a great height, arose from the middle of the break. The sudden apparition of these startling ash jets and the kaleidoscopic confusion of dust and fog made it impossible to obtain a clear sequence of the events that

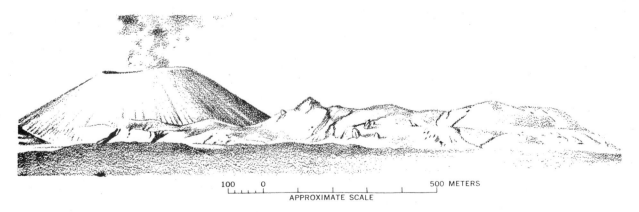

100   0   500 METERS
APPROXIMATE SCALE

Fig. 62. Quitzocho ridge in late 1944. This is the final development of the ridge, with its asperities smoothed by ash.

were taking place in the break. After an indeterminate period during which we watched this startling play of forces, the action subsided; and we could discern a sheet of lava moving down the slope from a vent not distinguishable to us, flowing down a valley formed by the terrace of the collapsed cone segment and the broken slope of the cone.

The Quitzocho ridge now took on new movement. By sighting from a point at the camp to a landmark on the slopes of Cerros de Tancítaro opposite, one could follow the perceptible movement of the rocks (Los Faroles) that crowned the ridge. It was estimated from rough angular measurements that the ridge moved northward almost 150 m during 24 hours. After this first day's advance, the movement ceased but resumed several days later for an additional advance of about 75 to 100 m.

. . . . .

The lava flow from the break moved toward the NW and spread out in a broad sheet at the foot of Cerro de Canicjuata, eventually meeting the old lavas of the first Parícutin flow [Fig. 36].

Following the events of late July and early August, the volcano settled into a state of irregular activity, the eruptive column varying from a lazy emission of pure-white vapors to dense, heavily ash-charged columns, from periods of almost silent eruptions to heavy roars, and from a few ejected bombs to splendid night pyrotechnics. During this erratic and variable period, the summit of the cone showed frequent changes in its configuration, losing its even and level outline. This was due to the shifting explosive vents in the crater and to collapse and slides within the crater itself. During the previous 6 or 7 months any irregularity in the configuration of the cone was transitory, and the contour of the cone was rapidly restored to its normal form by the heavy falls of bombs and ash. In fact, it was surprising with what rapidity a serious break in the cone could be restored. During this period of erratic but moderate activity, no lava flowed from any vent.

On August 25 the crater, as it had in early June and late July, showed a diminution in activity followed by intense explosions. At first the eruptive column was greatly reduced and even ceased at times, but heavy explosions in the crater increased in strength during the night and the following day, reaching an intensity equaling the explosions of early August[45], causing some alarm to the observers in the camp at Cerro de Jarátiro. During this tremendous activity, some instantaneous earth shocks of medium intensity were felt, and intense rumbles were heard from the depths of the earth. Six or seven times during these days sudden explosions of unusual intensity occurred. From the camp one could see vapors of a tenuous yellow arise with each explosion from the center of the crater. At the same time, bluish fumes arose from a vent to the east. With each strong explosion a huge halo (flashing arc) shot up with extraordinary rapidity, momentarily lighting up the top of the cone and even the blue sky and the clouds . . . . In this period of heavy explosions, lava broke out from the SW base of the cone, yielding a small flow that moved along the south base. Another broke out of Quitzocho ridge about 600 m from the base of the cone, and the Quitzocho ridge (Fig. 62) itself showed evidence of new movement or growth. The ridge not only increased in elevation, but huge blocks, even larger in size than those of early August and semi-fluid in character, rolled down the high front facing Cerro de Jarátiro, raising clouds of pinkish dust.

Activity of September-October:
Decreased Explosivity

From late August to September 18, the crater showed variable activity (Fig. 63), frequently erratic, weak, and much reduced in explosivity. The bursts came at irregular intervals of from 3 to 20 seconds, often sending up no more than a single sharp finger of ash and bombs into the air.

Since the beginning of the volcano, whirlwinds charged with volcanic dust were common on the ash-covered lava flows where the cool air from the surrounding hills, meeting the hot air arising from the lava, caused atmospheric turbulence. Sharply defined whirlwinds, often rising to great heights, added a majestic new element to the landscape. Sometimes as many as a dozen could be seen; some almost fixed in position, others moving leisurely over the lava, all rotating with considerable speed. Where they

Fig. 63. September 17, 1943. Lazy emission of ash-laden eruptive column. On the right is part of the Quitzocho ridge with "Los Faroles" at the right. Old crater of Cerro de Jarátiro in foreground. Taken from Cerro de Jarátiro.

encountered trees, they had the force to tear off large limbs and hurl them into the air.

On September 18 we saw many well-formed whirlwinds of striking distinctness, which formed on the slopes of the cone. A black, heavily ash-ladened eruptive column rose lazily from the crater and drifted at a low altitude toward the west. Dust from the falling bombs was slowly drawn along the slope of the cone toward the summit where it met the ash cloud from the eruptive column drifting downward. Here they began to whirl, growing upward until they

met the low overhanging dark pall of the eruptive column. Some were thick and swirled languidly; others were thin, sharply defined, and rotated rapidly. Some were estimated to be a kilometer long, extending from the slope of the cone to the pall of the eruptive column. Some changed their positions very slowly; others moved down the slope of the cone and across the ash fields toward Cerro de Canicjuata before breaking up.

On September 18 the eruptive column began again to subside, and heavy throaty explosions again took place indicating another probable outburst of lava which, indeed, occurred on the afternoon of this day from the SW base of the cone. The lava advanced along the south and SE bases of the cone, moving over the lava of August 25-26. According to Ordóñez[45] the very fluid lava formed a low continuous fountain on the flank of the cone some 60 m above the older lavas and flowed down the slopes between two levees. It spread out at the base of the cone as a low dome, which expanded to a flow, advancing over a width of 100 to 300 m for a distance of 400 m in 3 days and spreading over the basin formed by the cone and the slopes of Cerros de Tancítaro to the south.

After this period of lava activity, the cone again passed into a relatively quiet stage, with the eruptive column reduced in size but without the heavy explosions that presaged the advent of new lava flows. The eruptive column frequently carried little ash and rose in lazy cottony volutes and apparently consisted largely of steam. Activity continued in this erratic manner until October 15, when a new phase of activity was about to set in.

Sapichu Period

Sapichu Vents

The 7-month Quitzocho period, from March 18 to October 17, was followed by a 2½-month period in which the principal activity shifted to a subsidiary vent that broke out near the NE base of the cone and much reduced the eruptive activity of the main crater. A small cone, built up about this subsidiary vent, was named Sapichu by the Tarascan inhabitants of the area, from the Tarascan word meaning little or small.

This period of activity we shall call the Sapichu period. The continuous eruptions of Sapichu yielded one of the most spectacular sights to be seen during the history of Parícutin.

On the 17th of October, earth tremors, which were frequent although weak during the preceding phase, greatly increased both in number and intensity until they became almost continuous; and the dishes in the refreshment stands on Cerro de Jarátiro rattled almost constantly. These trepidations continued until the night of October 18. According to our informant, Sra. Aurora Cuara [Fig. 21], at 11 p.m. a series of vents suddenly opened, aligned in a northeasterly direction.

Fig. 64. October 20, 1943. Outbreak of Sapichu viewed from the east on its 2nd day. A series of vents extending from base of main cone 300 m to NE broke out in the old Lagunita flow. One persisted to form Sapichu.

This new outbreak began with a heavy explosion; bombs and lava fragments were hurled into the air from the new vents to a height somewhat greater than the main cone. According to Manuel de la Vega, Mexican alpinist, the explosion was immediately preceded by a strong earth shock and followed by subterranean noises. At the same time, a fissure several hundred meters in length formed in the Quitzocho and the incumbent Lagunita flows, and five or more vents opened up, spouting incandescent lava many meters into the air (Fig. 64). Sra. Cuara estimated that the line of vents extended for 300 m. From these vents, "flames" of bluish yellow and orange arose. The accompanying noise was like that of a starting railway locomotive, a noise we had come to associate with escaping gases from a rising lava column, usually at the initiation of a new flow or lava surge. Meanwhile the crater of the cone ceased ejecting bombs, and the eruptive column changed to a dense black ash column, with, she said, "flames (incandescent ash) that covered all the horizon."

According to Sr. Arno Brehme, the vents followed the crest of a low domed ridge fissured parallel to its axis, suggesting that the lava of the Lagunita flow had first been elevated by injection. De la Vega reported 5 vents. Brehme also reported 5; but Sra. Cuara, who from the vantage point of Cerro de Jarátiro had an excellent view, saw 7. Three of these, in the lava field NE of the base of the cone, yielded steam, a few small bombs, and no ash. An orifice on the flank of the cone was more active, ejecting viscous lava in small quantity to form a small mound. But the principal vent, which was to persist and build a cone, was in the lava field near the base of the cone and ejected numerous viscous lava bombs, and a wide lava flow issued from the vent. Ordóñez[45] reported that three vents remained in activity on the second day. One was active only at long intervals. A second, more active, with a low cone half open toward the north, was situated on the flank of the cone. The third vent, lying directly NE of the second vent, was the largest and was partially inclosed in a horseshoe-shaped "cone". This third vent showed explosive bursts at intervals about a second apart and threw up a column of viscous lava bombs to a height of 120 m, accompanied by moderate to formidable explosive noises.

On October 21 the main new vent was in full eruption, with explosions following one another in rapid succession at a rate of 65 per minute (Fig. 65). The ejected material was stretched viscous masses of lava that were torn into several discrete bombs during flight. A cone had begun to form by the accumulation of ejected material about the vent, but at this stage inclosed only an arc of about one-sixth of the circle to the SW of the vent. This wall was steep and about 15 m high. A second orifice, about 50 m from the main vent, erupted at intervals of 5-30 minutes with a sound like a locomotive starting. With each period of activity it emitted a few puffs of yellowish-brown fumes, or dust, and then subsided. About 20 m SW of the main vent was a slit-like orifice, aligned and sloping toward the main vent, which erupted every 4 or 5 minutes, throwing out viscous lumps of lava that plopped onto the ground. A white steaming crack extended from the crater rim to about two-thirds of the way down the slope of the cone[46].

Fig. 65. October 21, 1943. The new adventitious cone, Sapichu, at the NE base of Parícutin on its 3ʳᵈ day. A continuous fountain of viscous bombs without visible eruptive column. Taken from the east.

At the end of 4 days of activity the small upper vent on the flank of the cone ceased its explosive activity, but its locus remained evident for many days afterwards as a small ash-covered knoll, stained yellow and white with fumarole products and from which arose a gentle curl of vapor.

The remaining vent, now christened Sapichu, continued to eject viscous bombs without cease and to build its cone. Great quantities of lava continued to pour from its throat in surges that were sporadic but continuous enough to maintain an open breach on the NE side of the new cone. At no time in its 2½-month history did Sapichu assume a completely conical shape. From the very beginning to its last day of existence, it was always a lune-shaped "cone". During Sapichu's first days its crest was of irregular and changing outline, depending on the vagaries of explosion and slumping. On October 23 it had a low, semi-circular form with a ragged crater rim. This rim was somewhat lower at the head of the cone where the ejected bombs from the vent scoured the walls. This sag was flanked by two small ear-like peaks. As the cone grew and gained stability, it assumed a more regular form, eventually becoming a smooth horse-shoe. A series of parallel steaming cracks formed on the main cone above this vent.

Ordóñez[47] states that on the morning of October 23 (8:05 a.m. October 22, according to David Gallagher[46] and Storm[48]) a new vent opened on the outside flank of the main cone, about 50 m below the NE rim of the crater (Fig. 66). From it, dense black ash arose in small cauliflowers, with a noise like the escape of air under high pressure. The actual vent had a diameter of about 6-10 m. Its eruptive column rose 80 m and mingled with the vapors from the main crater. Gallagher describes the eruptions as exploding about 60 times per minute, yielding huge volumes of dark-gray ash, and the column as rising in cauliflower volutes. The outbreak continued, with a few pauses of variable intervals, until early afternoon. Gallagher places this vent on the line of the steaming crack observed 2 days earlier on the slope of the cone above Sapichu.

The area around this new vent, or chimney, and the cracks below it later developed by subsidence into a smooth-sloped swale of hot and muddy ash, spotted with patches of white, yellow, and greenish salts.

Eruptive Activity of Sapichu

From the first day until Sapichu began to show some diminution in its explosive activity in late December, eruptive activity was notably constant and regular. The lava flow, although showing some variability, was continuous. Explosions from the vent occurred at fairly regular intervals, almost one each second, hurling viscous lava to a maximum height of 300 m. These bombs appeared incandescent even during daylight. This fountain of incandescent bombs illuminated the environs of the cone at night and presented a magnificent spectacle. With rare exceptions the ejected bombs were all of one type, an inflated vesicular sponge that was

Fig. 66. October 22, 1943. Eruptive chimney and steaming cracks on the NE slope of Parícutin, and the new cone of Sapichu at the base of the cone. Taken from NW.

shiny black inside and dull, dark olive brown outside. The larger bombs were sufficiently viscous to flatten somewhat upon impact with the ground, and coins could be forced into them to yield souvenir pieces. This type of bomb was so characteristic of Sapichu that we referred to them and other similar ejecta as Sapichu type. A very rare and curious type of bomb, not observed at any other time, was a dense nodular mass without gas cavities. They showed small olivine phenocrysts in an aphanitic groundmass.

The characteristic ash of Sapichu was dark brown, very spongy in texture, and frequently of a dendritic structure. Fine filaments of glass were common in this ash. Bombs of xenolithic material were more common in the ejectamenta of Sapichu than in that from the main cone and showed a greater degree of fusion. Ordóñez[47] reports that on November 20 the amount of this ash was so great that the ground around Sapichu was covered with a light-colored mantle resembling snow, but we were unable to find such a layer by digging a pit in the ash. These erratic bombs are evidently fused masses of diorite from the underlying basement rocks. The smaller fused fragments were very vesicular and snow white. They usually showed unfused quartz grains within the vesicular masses. Larger fragments were similarly fused, although some of the larger bombs were only partially so.

In remarkable contrast to the activity of the main cone, Sapichu showed no visible eruptive column, other than the ejected bombs. Bluish-white vapors, or rarely rusty-brown fumes (or dust), rose from the vent but were soon dissipated into the atmosphere. If at-

mospheric conditions were propitious, the emitted vapors condensed some hundred meters above the cone, forming a "tail" that widened upward into a white cumulus cloud (Fig. 67). It was evident from the volume of these clouds, some of which covered a large part of the visible horizon, that a great quantity of condensable vapors was being discharged from the eruptive vent. The rare times when one observed ash in the rising column were short intervals following a brief quiescence, usually no longer than 10 seconds, during which a thin brownish or dense black column arose to a height of a few hundred meters. During these brief and rare periods a vesicular red or black coke-like ash fell sparingly. No lightning discharges were observed in the emissions from Sapichu.

During Sapichu's period of eruption the crater of the main cone showed very reduced activity (Fig. 68), and there were times when no visible vapors arose from its crater. Two vents were still apparent: a central one, which sometimes showed mild explosive activity, and one near the NE rim, from which only languid white clouds arose. Few incandescent bombs could be seen during the nights. Such bombs as fell outside the crater were an assorted lot: irregular aphanitic fragments, scoriaceous lumps, welded masses of small agglomeratic fragments, and a few round concretion-like bombs of aphanitic lava, suggesting that in spite of its reduced activity, viscous lava was still present in the throat of the vent. The noises from the crater, too, were much diminished, the only sound audible at the camp being a subdued thundering rumble.

Fig. 67. December 6, 1943. The vaporous emission from Sapichu sometimes condensed as a huge cloud above the volcano. Cumulus clouds in background. Taken from Angahuan, 7 km NNE.

Fig. 68. November 28, 1943. During eruption of Sapichu, seen in the lower left, activity in the Parícutin crater was reduced to a lazy emission of vapor. A depressed boggy swale extended from the summit toward Sapichu, and the north slope was crusted with salts. Taken from Cerro de Jarátiro.

Crater of Sapichu

On January 8 we entered the crater of Sapichu for the first time and approached within 30 m of the vent itself. The orifice was about 1 m across and located upon the summit of a low lava mound. Sparse bluish-white vapors arose from the orifice, and occasionally a sudden belch of gas threw out a few small incandescent fragments of lava.

On January 10 activity in the crater of Sapichu was completely extinct, and we were able to examine the whole apparatus in detail [Fig. 69]. The vent, about 1 m in diameter, was at the base of the south inside wall of the cone, which was about 50 m high. Peering into this vent to a depth of about 2½ m, we could see tenuous fumes issuing from incandescent crevasses, but there was no distinct odor about the orifice. The lava of the vent seemed distinctly massive.

The walls of the crater were made up of semi-compacted bombs and had slopes up to 60°, but rocks were almost constantly sloughing off to form a talus fan at the base. Above the eruptive throat and to the right was a low cave-like overhang. This cave and the walls immediately above the orifice were veneered with smooth massive lava for a distance of about 15 m above the vent. Above this were steeply dipping lenses of massive rock 15 to 25 cm thick, evidently huge masses of viscous lava thrown against the walls during violent explosive bursts. There were also steeply inclined slickensides where slabs of viscous lava slid off the walls, as we had observed on December 5. At the horseshoe ends of the cone, the walls were made up of loosely compacted broken bombs. The bomb material was coarsely stratified with the beds dipping toward the axis of the horseshoe. The eastern limb of the horseshoe was broken into blocks and separated by crevasses where the flowing lava had begun to carry away blocks of the walls.

The lava in the crater consisted of twisted slabs of semi-vesicular rock, covered by scoriaceous and slaggy bombs. Several terraces were discernible, evidence of several distinct lava surges.

With the cessation of the eruption, activity in Sapichu completely ceased and was never resumed.

Fig. 69. January 1944. View into the extinct, horseshoe-shaped crater of Sapichu, with the main cone of Parícutin behind. Ash-covered Sapichu lava in foreground. Sapichu became extinct on January 8, 1944, and is now buried under lava. Taken from the NE.

Not even fumarolic vapor arose from the vent. In time the sloughing of the walls reduced the crater to a semi-funnel, with walls of about 35°. In November and December 1947, lava flows from the Taquí vents covered the last remaining traces of the Sapichu cone [see Plate 3B].

The lava flow of Sapichu greatly exceeded any of the previous lava flows; in fact, exceeded all the previous flows combined. It covered an area of 3¼ km² [Fig. 36] and had an estimated mass of 38.5 million metric tons. It completely covered the Lagunita flow (June-July 1943) and a part of the Quitzocho flow (February-March 1943) as well as the lands of Corúnguaro, Turímbaro, Jarátiro, Titítziro, Churingo, Terúpicua, Tipacuaro, Cheraquijando, Piedra del Sol, Nitzicátaro, Chorétiro, La Lomita, and El Pajarito, extending to and in places crossing the San Juan Parangaricutiro-Uruapan road (Figs. 36 and 70).

The lavas showed the same characteristics as previous flows, both in type of material and in their advance as a steep-walled rubbly front. The surface of the lava flow was the usual confused jumble of dark-gray blocks, profusely mottled with oxidized patches of brick red. Spires or towers of breccia-like material rose here and there above the general level of the flow, and irregular ridges of twisted lava could be seen. Only a few persistent fumaroles developed in the Sapichu flow. Most of these were localized along a scarp where the Sapichu flow poured over the old front of the Lagunita flow onto the ash-covered fields of La Lagunita.

The ultimate front, at the San Juan Parangaricutiro-Uruapan road, about 3 km NE of its vent, formed a scarp about 10 m high (Fig. 70) made up of blocks of disintegrated lava and scoriaceous clinkers of all sizes. The largest block observed had a volume of about 300 m³. Crags of solid lava protruded from the rubble but showed no flow surfaces.

With the cessation of activity at Sapichu, the main crater resumed its normal explosive activity; the eruptive column rose in successive cauliflowers with the ejection of considerable ash and bombs and the usual noises.

Fig. 70. March 23, 1944. The rubble front of the Sapichu lava flow at the San Juan Parangaricutiro-Uruapan road. A common type of lava at Parícutin.

Crater of the Main Cone

During the reduced activity of the main crater, the cone was ascended for the first time, by Sr. Arnaldo Pfeiffer, veteran alpinist of Morelia, on November 3; and Sr. Pfeiffer, accompanied by Sgt. José Rosales of the Mexican Army, stationed at San Juan Parangaricutiro, made another ascent on December 4. Pfeiffer reported that the area below the low northeastern rim was very muddy, hot, and steamy. The crater rim was very narrow, not more than a meter wide; but he was unable to see into the depths of the crater because of the copious vapor clouds that filled it.

On December 19 an ascent was made by Srs. Abraham Camacho and Celedonio Gutiérrez, who reported that the crater was funnel shaped and its steep walls were covered with small and large black rocks. In the bottom of the crater were three small funnel-shaped vents, oriented east-west. Vapors issued from these vents, sometimes simultaneously, sometimes alternately. A large fumarole, located on the eastern wall of the crater, emitted abundant vapors. About this fumarole the walls were encrusted with white and yellow sublimates. At that time the cone had an elevation of 345 m above the level of Quitzocho[47].

Luís Aguilar and Sgt. José Rosales ascended the cone on January 5, 1944. At that time the crater had the form of a shallow dish. The crater contained five funnel-shaped vents, the principal one near the SW edge of the crater. A very strong odor, described by Aguilar as similar to the odor of the *hornito* gases (hydrochloric acid), pervaded the crater; and there were abundant yellow sublimates within the crater. During their stay on the rim the volcano began to thunder and give off puffs of black smoke; whereupon they came down very quickly.

Summary of Sapichu Period

Sapichu and its accessory vents broke out along the line of the small fissure that appeared at Llano de Cuiyúsuru during the birth of the volcano on February 20 [Fig. 22]. This apparent line of weakness includes, besides Sapichu and its accompanying vents, the main crater vents and the vents of the Mesa del Corral flows on the opposite side of the cone. This last vent, became an important locus of later lava flows. This line was also a marked tremor zone. Sapichu, therefore, evidently occupied a position on one of the important fissures of Parícutin volcano.

Sapichu throughout its entire life showed only a strombolian type of activity, because the explosive activity took place at the summit of a continuously rising lava column where it was unimpeded by any overburden in the throat. In many respects Sapichu showed the characteristics of the main volcano during its early stage, but with these important differences: its explosive activity was less violent but more regular and its lava flow much larger and more regular. The greater explosive capacity of the original vent and the greater abundance of fumaroles in the Quitzocho flow suggest that the gaseous content of the Sapichu lava had decreased from that of the earlier flows. The quantity of ejected diorite blocks was much greater from Sapichu than from the main cone, and the blocks showed a greater degree of fusion.

Although there may have been some pauses in the emission of lava from the Sapichu vent, they were not directly observable, the flow of lava being essentially continuous. This is in contrast to the Quitzocho period when lava flowed from the main vent in frequent surges and even in individual flows. Because of this continuous flow of lava from Sapichu, its "cone" was never complete and always maintained a horseshoe shape; for the flowing lava stream continuously carried away the accumulating bombs from its NE side. Masses of these bombs were later found a kilometer or more from the cone, where they had been carried by the lava stream. In the Michoacán basalt province, there are a number of such cones, some of which undoubtedly had a history similar to that of Sapichu [see Figs. 157-158].

This horseshoe shape allowed clear observation of the character of the explosions in the vent. These explosions took place at the top of the rising lava column or at depths of no more than a few meters below the surface. The explosive activity also clearly showed that a vent free of accumulated debris or of slumping from the sides of a funnel-shaped crater yielded an eruptive column free of dense ash or triturated material [powder]. The ejectamenta from the freely rising lava column consisted of vesicular spongy bombs or shredded ash. The eruptive column yielded by such a rising lava is tenuous, consisting largely of invisible water vapor that, when atmospheric conditions are appropriate, condenses as cumulus-like clouds far above the vent.

One of the more remarkable features of Sapichu was the relatively small diameter of the vent. The lava vents in later flows were not large, but in none was it so small as at Sapichu. Its vent, hardly more than 1 m in diameter, was capable of supplying a lava front more than a kilometer across and about 5 m high and maintaining this front in a state of continuous, if slow, advance.

This lava flow was of the same nature as the previous flows. The total area covered by the Sapichu lavas was found, upon measurement, to be 3¼ km². The lava differed very little, chemically, from the lava of the previous period.

Although it was evident that Sapichu occupied a position on a fissure, it showed no apparent change of location or movement along this line and remained fixed throughout its life. The fact that its cone showed no appreciable change, other than those incident to its growth, tends to confirm this observation.

During the 2½-month life of Sapichu, activity in the main crater was considerably reduced, yielding a light-gray eruptive column from a central vent and white vapors from a vent near the NE rim. For a day during the early period of Sapichu, a vent on the NE slope, corresponding to the lava vent of the Lagunita flow, sent up an intermittent eruptive column.

Taquí Period

Taquí Vents

With the cessation of eruptions at Sapichu, the locus of active lava vents changed to the SW base of the cone, and the eruptive activity of the main crater greatly increased. By January 8, when the last dying gasp of Sapichu was observed, the main crater was again in full activity, with a billowing eruptive column rising in well-formed cauliflowers to considerable heights. Ash began to fall again in perceptible amounts in the form of brownish corky grains, coke-like fragments, or as small flaky spalls. Bombs, too, again fell on the cone in abundance. These consisted of dense, rounded congealed masses, semi-scoriaceous platy masses, or irregular blocks of agglomerate of partially welded fragments. Explosive activity appeared to be localized in the SW, or main vent of the crater. Explosive noises were rare, the sounds accompanying the activity being the surf-like noise characteristic of heavy bomb activity.

About midnight on January 7 a bright-pink reflection appeared over the SW base of the cone, indicating the presence of incandescent lava in that vicinity. The next morning revealed 2 new lava vents from which 2 active flows issued (Fig. 71). These vents were, as near as we could determine, at the locus of the small and short-lived vent of August 26, 1943. They were destined to be the most persistently active of any of the lava vents and to yield the greatest of Parícutin's lava flows. The 2 vents were about 25 m apart and separated by a crevassed and bomb-spattered septum of congealed lava. The north orifice occupied the head of the narrow steep-walled

Fig. 71. January 8, 1944. First day of the Taquí lava flow. Three vents yielded a continuous flow of lava. View from NW with lower flank of Cerro de Canicjuata in foreground and steaming lower slopes of the main cone to the upper left.

trench formed by levees of congealed lava. This vent was surrounded by an aureole of spatter bombs. The lava in the vent was in a state of continuous ebullition, the incandescent lava spattering up to a height of 10 m or more; and incandescent lava coursed rapidly, at an estimated rate of 1 m/sec, down the levee-bordered trench. The second, or south, lava vent, also at the head of a narrow trench, was more erratic in its behavior, sometimes spattering violently and sometimes flowing quietly but copiously down its self-made channel. There was an apparent connection between these two vents. When the south vent entered a state of violent ebullition, the activity of the north vent diminished or was even reduced to a quiet flow. From both vents and the flowing lava, bluish fumes arose, sometimes tinged with brown; and a strong odor of hydrochloric acid was evident about the vents. These vents we called the Taquí vents; and the flow that issued from them, the Taquí flow [Fig. 36].

Above the lava vents was a bulge in the slope of the cone, surmounted by a narrow terrace about one-third way up the cone. This smooth bulge of ash was traversed by a series of small cracks from which white steam issued continuously; and the whole bulge was moist with condensed steam, contrasting with the dry ash slopes surrounding it. In the ash on the terrace

directly above the south lava vent was an orifice, about 3 m in diameter and of unknown depth, from which issued dense white steam clouds.

The lava as it flowed from the vents changed rapidly from bright incandescence to a black stream dappled with glowing spots [Fig. 71]. Overlapping tongues of different stages of incandescence suggested that the emission of lava was not entirely regular and occurred in surges that followed one another in rapid succession.

By the next day, January 9, the lava vents had changed some. The north orifice remained in constant ebullition, but the south vent flowed quietly, without spatter. The south orifice and a third vent observed behind it were separated by the lava septum. This vent may have been present on January 8 but not sufficiently active to have attracted attention. It was very erratic in its activity, spattering lava at rare intervals. The steam orifice above the vents showed increased activity, giving off an occasional short burst of ash-laden steam, and in mid-afternoon showed an almost continuous activity, emitting a small ash-laden eruptive column and ejecting some small bombs (Fig. 72).

On the lower slopes of the cone, immediately south of the vents, the ash showed crevasses from which steam with a strong hydrochloric acid odor issued. The ash about these crevasses was stained with yellow alteration products. The north lava vent made little noise other than a faint "shu-uh shu-uh," and the south vent was quiet except for a rare low "chu-chu-chu." These sounds we had learned to associate with a rising lava column.

The lava from the two vents flowed rapidly down the low slope into the small valley formed by the cone and the east slope of the Mesa de Cocjarao. Although the general land slope was toward the north, a low ridge blocked the flow of lava in this direction, diverting the stream to the south and along the SW base of the cone. The lava flowed freely from the vents and had a crude ropy surface, rather distinct in structure from any of the previous lavas, but the advancing front presented the characteristic jumble of clinkers and lava blocks shown by the previous flows.

Directly opposite the vents, on the lowest slopes of the Mesa de Cocjarao in lava-free terrain, we found a fissured and displaced ash zone about 200 m long and 100 m wide, extending from the lateral slope of the lava to the foot of the Mesa itself (Fig. 73). This zone had a strike of N50°E. Vertical displacements in the fissures of this zone did not exceed 30 cm. This unusual development of fissures in original, tree-covered terrain was unique in our experience at Parícutin. Later we were able to discover that this belt was also a zone of distinct tremors or, as we called it, a tremor zone (Fig. 74). This zone corresponded, as near as we could determine, with the direction of one of the original fissures that appeared on February 20, 1943 [Fig. 22].

On January 10 two distinct earthquake shocks were felt, one at 2:10 p.m. and another at 2:35 p.m. Later inquiry showed that these shocks were felt and re-

Fig. 72. January 9, 1944. Area of the Taquí vents, which are on the lower slope, an eruptive chimney upon an upper knoll. Taquí lava flow on the lower left; slopes of Mesa de Cocjarao lower right.

Fig. 73. January 8, 1944. Fissures and displacement in ash along a "tremor zone" at the foot of Mesa de Cocjarao, SW of the cone.

corded in México City and that their epicenter was in the State of Guerrero and therefore had no close connection with Parícutin volcano. These shocks induced no evident change in the activity in the crater or in the lava vents.

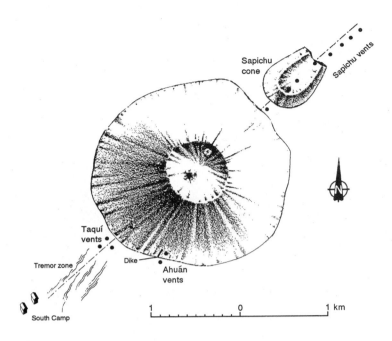

Fig. 74. Parícutin volcano, showing the vents of 1943-44.

Taquí Lava Flow

According to reports, the first flow of lava from the Taquí vents continued until January 12. On February 6 these vents reopened and again poured out lava. By February 10 when we again visited the spot, we found it greatly changed from its condition of a month before. Many of these changes were evidently due to the accumulation of lava, which was now great enough to submerge the vents of Taquí, so that lava no longer issued freely at the surface. The lava continued to issue from its original vents but flowed beneath a thick crust of congealed lava, following irregular and wandering channels, to appear eventually at the surface several hundred meters from the Taquí vents.

During the month that had elapsed since the outbreak of lava at Taquí, the lava stream had advanced around the south and east sides of the base of the cone, filling the valley formed by the cone and the lower northern flanks of Cerros de Tancítaro [Fig. 36]. The lava front, about a kilometer long and 3 m high, reached a point near Sapichu where it debouched onto rolling pine-covered terrain and ignited the trees in its advance through the forest. This lava advanced much like previous flows, with bulging lobes of viscous lava near the base and clinkers and blocks rolling down the front, stirring up small plumes of pinkish dust. Although the terrain over which the flow moved was of low smooth ridges

and shallow *arroyos*, the advance of the front was rather uniform, its continuity broken only in three places, where tongues of lava showed a more rapid advance down some small *arroyos*.

. . . . .

This point marks the end of the first year of Parícutin's activity, the important stages of which are illustrated in Fig. 36 and cone profiles inside the front cover.

On March 1 when we again visited Parícutin, we found the lava field about Taquí vent greatly changed. The lava now completely filled the basin lying between the cone and the lower slopes of Mesa de Cocjarao and had surmounted the saddle that connected the two; but except for a short cold tongue of lava toward the north, the lava still continued its old course along the south base of the cone. In place of the active flowing vents, which were now deeply buried under the accumulation of flows, we found three steeply conical peaks with vertical shaft-like craters, which Ordóñez[45] called *volcancitos* (Fig. 75), and a great number of low irregular pinnacles of vesicular lava, or *hornitos* [Figs. 76 and 77], upon the congealed surface of the lava. Bluish vapors arose from summit vents of the *volcancito*, the irregular openings in the *hornitos*, and the fissures in the lava, and a strong odor of hydrochloric acid pervaded the vicinity. A wide area was brilliantly colored by an orange-yellow incrustation, imparting a weird, colorful beauty to this otherwise bleak and depressing landscape. A loud hissing, like the escape of steam from a number of vents, could be heard from some distance away.

At or about the locus of the original Taquí vent was a tall, slender *volcancito*, and nearby to the west was another rough dome-shaped one, with a wide incandescent throat in its western flank. Still farther to the west was a steep conical *volcancito* with a glowing open mouth near its summit, and adjoining this was a smaller one, crusted on its southern side by a small rough tongue of lava. Nearby was an open cave-like throat in a low dome-like eminence, which showed a number of incandescent crevasses and hissed particularly loudly. About this line of *volcancitos* was a zone of fresh rough clinkery lava that had evidently only recently flowed over the older

Fig. 75. May 24, 1944. A *volcancito* on the surface of the Taquí lava flow. Such edifices ejected small bombs and emitted burning gases and bluish fumes from their summit vents. They were situated above the area of the Taquí vents and were due to a flow of gas-charged lava through cracks in the lava crust.

Fig. 76. May 24, 1944. Surface of the Taquí lava flow showing part of the *hornito* fields. Abundant yellow and orange salts colored the area, named Mesa de Los Hornitos. Taken from the NE.

Fig. 77. March 22, 1944. Burning gases from the orifices of the *hornito* "Soplete". These flames were pale blue and only visible at dusk and night. The vents were lined with fused lava. Time exposure at night. [See Plate 4A].

yielding flames and that the strong hissing, so apparent in the area, was due to the escape of gases associated with these flames. The flames appeared pale violet in the light of dusk, but at darkness appeared pale blue and tinged at their edges with yellow [see Plate 3A]. Above the large flames arose bluish-white fumes, or vapors. The flames from the *volcancitos* rose continuously in waving tongues, the larger ones rising to a height of 2 m above the orifice. In the spacious orifice of the largest *volcancito*, the flames burst forth spasmodically at frequent intervals, like a flash or ball of pale fire. From the *hornitos* and low excrescences, the flames shot out with a continuous hissing like small blowtorch flames. The small vents from which the flames issued were lined with a thin coating of fused but viscous lava, which suggested a refusion of the lava by the heat generated by the burning gases.

· · · · ·

From the air, no flowing lava could be observed about the Taquí vent; but about ½ km downstream, a ribbon of red glowing lava apparently issued from beneath a lava crust. This stream showed continuous incandescence for about 300 m, where it changed to a winding black river, moving over older gray lava.

The lava flow itself had not only advanced considerably since February but had also increased in thickness. The main front moved slowly, but at frequent intervals tongues of lava broke out from the rubble-covered face, forming outliers of twisted and crevassed black lava quite distinct from the more characteristic blocky form of the main mass. These tongues appeared to be essentially solid but yet showed some slight creaking advance.

On the evening of March 6 occurred a most spectacular outbreak of lava fountains on Mesa de Los Hornitos, above the buried Taquí lava vents. Dr. Frederick H. Pough has given us an account of this event:

· · · · ·

Te Ata, Luís, and I went around to the far side of the volcano (west) to photograph the blue flames at close range. We crossed the older lava dotted with *hornitos* and came close to the foot of the cone. At this spot a ridge

ash-covered flow. Beyond the *volcancitos* the zone of *hornitos* followed the course of the lava stream. Here were dozens of these remarkable *hornitos*, but the abundant strong and choking fumes prevented an examination of them at close hand. Later we were able to study them in detail and even had the opportunity to see one grow. In addition to these pinnacle-like *hornitos*, one could observe numerous small warty excrescences of lava, usually less than 2 m across, upon the old lava surface. Like the larger *hornitos* they showed small incandescent orifices, and they were, undoubtedly, low forms of the more conspicuous *hornitos*.

On March 3 we first observed flames from both the *volcancitos* and the *hornitos*. At dusk a faint-violet flame was perceptible, waving like a tenuous banner above the orifice of one of the *volcancitos*. Then similar flames were observed above the wide orifice of the largest *volcancito* and finally flames from orifices in the lava crust. Occasionaly small incandescent stones were ejected from these vents. Within the area of the *volcancitos*, one could see that each incandescent orifice of the *hornitos* was likewise

30 m high and with two humps each about 10 m high extended toward the west . . . . Beyond the ridge were several *hornitos* and *volcancitos* . . . .

That evening we found the volcano in only moderate activity with an occasional small bomb rolling down the slope. Since it was still light we dawdled around the base of the cone until it began to get dark. No particular or unusual activity was seen in any of the *volcancitos*, nothing to attract any special attention.

Shortly before seven, as it began to darken, we surmounted the ridge and saw that the *volcancito* we had selected for photographs had become very active and was emitting lava. A pool of lava had filled the throat and was beginning to overflow to the NE. Gas was still coming out with force, making huge bursting bubbles, splashing fragments almost a meter in the air . . . .

The noise that accompanied this eruption was much like that of the plopping of a mud volcano, plus a hissing of the escaping gas. While we were watching this spectacular display we noted an increase in activity in the isolated *volcancito* behind us, which began to throw out a few gobs of molten matter.

The activity from the first vent continued, with occasional bursts from the nearer vent, but most of the eruption was concealed behind the ridge. It was not possible or safe to go onto the recent flow, so the only alternative seemed to be to climb on the main cone. As we started our climb we noted that minor activity was showing in several other vents, all throwing out rocks and casting a glow on the escaping vapors suggesting that incandescent lava was in the throats, and that the gas output had increased. The plan of going along the slope was revised when the small fumarole in the saddle began to throw out a few rocks. In a few minutes this vent became increasingly violent and soon lava welled up in its throat and began to spill over. Meanwhile the whole series of *volcancitos* that made up the complex of the ridge was repeating this overture, with lava spilling from several of them. In about ten minutes—it was now completely dark—a thrilling spectacle developed. The lava seemed to enlarge the vents and to expand them into considerable-sized openings. Gas rushed out and breaking bubbles threw liquid fragments high in the air, probably 45-60 m. The solid fountains of the lava were about 5-10 m high, and above them the air was filled with flying fragments. The fountains cascaded down to form a flow, not very fluid but advancing in big ropy curds in a stream about 60 cm thick, ferrying cooler bits on its surface. Activity kept increasing and, although we were standing about 30 m from the vent, the lava fragments soon began falling unpleasantly close. We decided then upon another retreat; salvaged our instruments from where they had

been placed less than a meter in front of the advancing tongue and went farther back on the old flow.

From this spot about 100 yards from the vents we had a magnificent view of seven simultaneously operating lava fountains, with the flowing lava merged into a single front advancing toward us over the older partially ash-coated lava. The sounds were still the same, the noises of a dozen mud volcanoes, with a plopping and a hissing and a little crackling from the cooling lava surfaces all merging into one amazing concert. Not all of the gas vents were producing lava. In some places holes were blown in the flowing lava by gas vents that were being covered as the liquid advanced. They looked dark, but were probably dark in the sense that sunspots look dark on the disc of the sun.

Gradually the eruption began to die down, the fountains diminished, and the fragments were no longer tossed so high in the sky. By 8:00 all but the vent in the saddle had ceased producing fountains. The whole spectacle lasted little more than an hour.

On March 21 the area about the Taquí vents, now called Mesa de Los Hornitos, showed still further changes. Most conspicuous changes were in the *volcancitos*. The largest *volcancito*, which presented a wide open mouth on its south flank, was now a symmetrical cone about 15 m high, with a deep chimney-like opening at its summit . . . . The neighboring *volcancito*, from which previously the biggest flames arose, was collapsed on its south slope. On the floor of this old *volcancito*, a tall, slender *hornito* had formed rising slightly above the old rim. This *hornito*, which we called the "Soplete", or blowtorch, because of its action, could be observed readily from a distance of less than a meter at a station on the old *volcancito* rim. From its summit orifice, gases rushed with a hissing. Stones tossed into this orifice were immediately ejected by the rush of gases. At night one could see a blowtorch-like flame of pale blue issue from its summit vent (Fig. 77). Sticks held in this flame were readily ignited. We succeeded in breaking off the tip of the Soplete and found it lined with brilliant spangles of hematite and delicate arborescent groups of magnetite.

Immediately west . . . was a new feature, a "window" in the congealed crust where the flowing lava could be observed. David Gallagher (personal communication) had already observed this window on March 8. The window was about 3 m wide, 12 m long, and bordered at its head and lateral sides by a levee of scoriaceous lava, presumably built up by spatter from the flowing lava stream. The lava issued

Fig. 78. March 21, 1944. Area of the buried Taquí vents, then called Mesa de Los Hornitos. Pahoehoe lava from *volcancito* to the left. Taken from the north.

quietly from beneath the crust and flowed calmly, except for a low heaving motion, to disappear again beneath the crust at the lower end of the window. Its rate of flow was estimated at about 20 cm/sec. Bluish vapors with a strong acid odor arose copiously from the flow.

A considerable area north of the *volcancitos* was covered by a fresh flow of pahoehoe lava (Fig. 78), a lava form rarely observed at Parícutin. Ropy structure was not well shown; instead, the lava showed a flat, hummocky surface with a slaggy skin covered with fern-like streaks of stretched vesicles. The source of this pahoehoe lava could not be exactly determined but appeared to be the large cone-shaped *volcancito*.

Tremor Zone

Shortly after the outbreak of the Taquí vent, the Tarascans moved their refreshment stands from Cerro de Jarátiro on the north side of the volcano to a broad terrace at the foot of Cocjarao Mesa on the SW side, directly opposite Mesa de Los Hornitos, for the spectacle for the tourists was now the ever-changing lava activity of the Taquí vents. This campsite became known as Campamento de Aurora. A few hundred meters to the south was the zone of fissures mentioned on p. 105 in the section entitled "Taquí Vents" [Figs. 73 and 74]. On March 22 we discovered quite by accident that this belt was also a "tremor zone". It was noticed that in the belt of the old fissure

zone, the ground was in a state of varying but continuous trepidation, which, however, was not perceptible 100 m to one side or the other. The zone could be delimited by sitting at various points in the area or, as we found later, more easily by observing the tremor of the branches on dead pine trees. A plumb bob suspended from a log partially buried in the ash clearly demonstrated the variations in the trepidations. This zone of tremors had a direction, as near as could be determined, of N70°E and coincided, as nearly as our information allowed, with the direction of the original fissure of February 20, 1943 [Fig. 22]. The line of the *volcancitos* had a direction of N75°E. We have no evidence, however, that this apparent coincidence had any real significance.

A striking relationship between the variation in the intensity of the tremor and the explosive activity in the main crater was readily apparent. Although in general the trepidations were gentle and only apparent when one was seated somewhere along the zone, there were frequent intervals when the tremors suddenly increased and were relatively strong for an interval of less than a second. Three and a half to 4 seconds after these sharper shocks, an eruptive burst occurred in the crater. The estimated distance from Campamento de Aurora to the crater vent was about 1 km. It was repeatedly noted after an unusual lapse of time without explosions that the next tremor would be relatively strong. Two months later, on May 22, the tremor zone showed weaker but still distinct trepidations.

Crater Activity

During March the eruptive activity in the crater was quite variable, ranging from a weak eruptive column with a deep rumbling to huge wooly cauliflowers rising in continuous succession but with little sound (Figs. 2 and 79). The active vent appeared to be very close to the SW crater rim, which was lower than the north rim, presumably owing to the proximity of the eruption. The activity of the volcano continued with little appreciable change, except perhaps for a diminution of ash in the eruptive column. From this period on, the majestically rising eruptive column was frequently very pale, or even pure white, indicating a minimum amount of included ash [see Plate 5A]. Sometimes the column rose, without visible vapors, as a tenuous cloud of pale-brown ash, accompanied by a deep, throaty rumble. A pale-brown shredded ash, like that of Sapichu, fell sparingly during such an eruption. This suggests that the eruptive throat was open and not choked and that the rushing vapors abraded the open throat of its fused lining . . . .

Luminous Phenomena

On April 24 we observed a curious luminescent phenomenon above the cone. This luminescence was first called to our attention by Ezequiel Ordóñez, who had seen it strikingly displayed the previous night and described it as "searchlights playing out of the crater". It appears that this unusual occurrence owed its origin, or at least its visibility, to a special disposition of centers of activity in the crater. A thin erect eruptive column rose continuously and without apparent force from a vent very close to the NE edge of the crater. The night was still, without wind, but the upper currents of air carried the eruptive column lazily toward the east, and one could see sparkling stars in the clear, cloudless sky in the area above the crater. A second vent near the center of the crater gave off single lazy bursts at intervals of one-half to an hour or more. The dust of the explosions from this second vent drifted slowly toward the west. In the region where this dust cloud eventually disappeared, a dancing luminescence appeared, usually at a height estimated at 200 - 1,000 m above the crater and extending well westward toward Cerro de Canicjuata. This luminescence differed from the ordinary pink reflection of incandescent lava upon clouds or rising vapor by its bluish-white color, by the fact that it persisted long after the ash cloud had dissipated entirely from view, and because stars were distinctly visible through it. Its appearance reminded one, in its

movement and color, of the aurora borealis. It appeared most distinctly some time after an eruptive burst from the central vent and remained clearly visible until the next explosion occurred, alternately expanding toward Cerro de Canicjuata and then retracting toward the crater. We watched this spectacle for several hours, seeking some simple explanation for it. Less striking, but still well defined, was a shaft of light of similar appearance that followed the inner, or crater, side of the eruption column. From Ordóñez' description, it appears that the phenomenon showed itself even more strikingly the preceding evening.

The Crater

After the long period in which the crater showed persistent explosive activity, the volcano became somewhat more erratic in its action, and there were brief periods of consistently reduced activity when it was feasible to climb the cone to the crater rim. On May 22, activity in the crater was still normal; a full eruptive column rose majestically in full voluting cauliflowers . . . [Fig. 80]. But on the 23rd, activity was reduced to a lazy, weak column, charged with a pale shredded ash, which on the 24th was still further reduced to a tenuous dust column with little visible vapor. On May 25 visible emissions had almost ceased, although a deep, low growl from the crater indicated that gaseous emissions were still being given off. Advantage was taken of this condition to make our first ascent of the cone and to perceive its shape and observe the character of its activity [Fig. 81].

The crater was eccentrically funnel shaped, the SW wall being steeper than the other slopes and the SW rim lower. The western slope showed a narrow bench from the crater rim to a precipitous slope of semi-consolidated tuff, the bench being the remnant of an older inner slope when the crater floor was at a higher level. Except for the gentle slope from the rim to this residual bench, the crater rim was very sharp. The inner slope of the crater, made up of loose or only slightly consolidated lapilli, with very few bombs, sloped directly to a small basin appearing to be no more than 2 or 3 m in diameter (Fig. 82). At times this basin showed incandescent lava and even produced a few weak gas bubbles that spattered some lava about a meter into the air. Usually, however, the basin floor was covered with ash that slid down from the nearby slopes. Occasionally this vent showed some mild and sporadic activity, during which a brownish dust arose in a thin, weak, and tenuous column. Somewhat higher than this lower vent was a

Fig. 79. March 22, 1944. Parícutin volcano from Mesa de Cocjarao, 1 km SW. The lowered south rim is due to scouring by the eruptive column of the south crater vent. Eruptive column is pale buff and largely vaporous.

Fig. 80. May 22, 1944. Eruptive column from north crater vent, viewed from Cerro de Jarátiro.

Fig. 81. May 25, 1944. Foshag, Gallagher, and González-Reyna at the crater rim. At this time the crater was a steep inverted cone.

circularly depressed area in the side wall of the crater [Fig. 82]. This saucer-shaped depression was about 8 m in diameter and bounded by an almost continuous circular crack. In the bottom of this saucer were two small irregular vents, and around them was a halo-like zone of thin sublimate products. Steam issued from these two vents almost continuously with a tremendous grating roar. For much of the time, the vapors issuing from the vents were invisible, their presence attested only by the deep roar from the orifices and the condensation of the vapors into

Fig. 82. May 25, 1944. The interior of the crater as viewed from the west rim. A small vent in the bottom (just out of view in the lower left center) emitted a small column of brownish dust; a saucer-shaped depression in the lower south flank (lower right) jetted invisible vapors with a grating roar. Eruptive activity on this day very much reduced.

irregular rising clouds above the crater rim. At other times, however, the vapors rushed out of the vents as visible jets of steam, as if escaping from a nozzle at high velocities. No distinct odor was apparent on the crater rim. Except for the emission of vapors, which condensed in tatters of clouds above the crater rim, there was little else given off by the crater vents, and the crater activity can be said to have been in a greatly reduced state.

During this rather erratic and reduced state of activity, there appeared little movement of lava in the flows. Issuing from a secondary vent in the Taquí lava front, a subsidiary tongue of torn and twisted lava was advancing slowly over a portion of the lands of La Lagunita. Activity at the *hornitos*, however, indicated that the lava still flowed beneath the congealed crust at Mesa de Los Hornitos.

Hornitos and Volcancitos

Late in the afternoon of May 24, several interesting events took place that throw some light on the formation of *hornitos* and *volcancitos*. At the "cave"—a collapsed *volcancito* that was a prominent feature of Mesa de Los Hornitos for the last few months—a small lava flow suddenly broke out, issuing from a small area of jumbled rock, locus of the original *volcancito* vent. This pasty lava flowed slowly from the vent, and the throat soon became a bubbling mass of viscous lava from which doughy bombs were thrown out to the height of about a meter. These congealed to irregular shining black masses. Two narrow open fissures in the congealed crust of the lava of Mesa de Los Hornitos connected the cave with a large rough hornito that occupied the former site of the lava window. These crevasses were lined with a thin film of sublimates, fine spangles of hematite, and a chocolate-colored dust. From a point on the larger fissure, there suddenly issued a rush of gas with a loud hissing and a small column of fine brown dust, followed by a very vesicular froth of viscous lava that grew within a quarter of an hour into an hornito about a meter high. The rapid rush of gases from the orifices blew small irregular fragments from the vents and even loosened larger slaggy masses from the growing hornito. In this manner a hornito originates and grows—a froth of gas-laden lava spewing from a crevice upon the crust of the flow. We were unable, unfortunately, to continue our observations on this hornito during its complete life.

At the same time, a large conical *volcancito*, lying between the cave and the base of the cone, began to pour out a thin viscous tongue of lava from its summit orifice. Flowing down the steep side of the cone to its base, this lava tongue congealed as a small rough flow, demonstrating the manner in which a *volcancito* grows in size.

Parangaricutiro Lava Tongue

From its outbreak on January 8 along the SW base of the cone until early April, the Taquí lava flow had advanced to the east base of Cerro de Equijuata, 2½ NNE of the crater, filling the valley of Tipacuaro from Cerro de Equijuata on the west to Lomas de Capánguito on the east. Its advance had now practically ceased, only a few weak lobes moving slowly and erratically forward. By April 24[49], however, lava burst out of the summit of the Taquí flow and covered the lands of Turímbiro near the east base of Cerro de Equijuata and reached the San Juan Parangaricutiro-Uruapan road, advancing in two tongues and threatening the waterline to the town. Its front was now but 600 m from the outskirts of the town. A lava stream about 10 m wide flowed quietly from its vent at a rate of about 180 m/hr.

The east approach to San Juan Parangaricutiro [Fig. 83] was through the short narrow valley of Juanantacua, connecting the arable fields of Rancho Tipacuaro with the town. To the south of this valley rose the steep wooded slopes of Cerro de Capatzun; and to the north, the slopes of the mesa-like fields and woods of Nicorroso that lie between San Juan Parangaricutiro and Angahuan. Through this narrow valley passed the road from Uruapan to San Juan Parangaricutiro. During the month of May, the lava flows that broke out of the lava front at Turímbiro and were actively advancing in April completely filled this small valley and came to rest in the cemetery at the edge of the town. The main lava front extending across the valley for a distance of 150 m was about 10 m high and had the usual appearance of a mass of block lava, rubble, and clinkers. At this time we were not impressed with any essential difference beteeen this flow front and others we had witnessed, but photographs suggest that this form was more clinkery and less blocky than previous flows. A narrow tongue of torn and twisted lava had advanced several hundred meters down the narrow but steep-walled Arroyo Principal, which passed the eastern edge of town [Fig. 12]. Such torn and twisted lava, although observed previously as short ephemeral lobes in the earlier flows, was, as we shall later see, the characteristic lava of the late stage of the Taquí flow.

After a brief (ca. 1 month) period of repose, the lava front at the edge of San Juan Parangaricutiro again resumed its advance, and on June 17 began to invade the town itself (Fig. 84). The flow followed Arroyo Principal at the eastern edge of the town but, spreading laterally when the *arroyo* was filled, soon reached the first street. The new advance of lava showed distinct differences both in character of movement and in structure from previous flows. The advance of the lava down Arroyo Principal was rather rapid; the lateral spread was at a rate of 1 to 2 m/hr. But instead of advancing as a moving front of rubble, the lava moved as distinct and independent lobes. At intervals along and usually halfway up the lava face, viscous lava broke out in tongues. The movement of the lobes persisted for less than a day, when they congealed; and the intervening sectors put out other lobes. These lobes sometimes issued from distinct orifices, yielding rough tongues suggesting toothpaste squeezed from a tube.

Fig. 83. January 1944. San Juan Parangaricutiro and the new volcano, 5 months prior to the arrival of lava. Cerro de Jarátiro lies behind the town to the lower right of the volcano, and Cerro de Canicjuata is to the upper left of the church. Taken from the north.

At the same time, the main body of lava continued its advance, yielding not so much the clinkery blocky surface of the earlier flows but huge torn and slaggy masses (Fig. 85). Torn and striated blocks rose above the ground level of the lava, frequently showing a grooved, or harsh surface. The creaking of the moving blocks was frequently heard. The lower portion of the Taquí flow, beginning at the cemetery and extending to its ultimate advance at Huirambosta, we have called the Parangaricutiro tongue.

Fig. 84. June 17, 1944. San Juan Parangaricutiro in the foreground, the Parangaricutiro lava tongue beyond; Parícutin lava flow (right center) steaming from recent rain. Cerro de Canicjuata on right; Cerro de Jarátiro in center, in front of Parícutin volcano. Taken from Cerro de La Capilla, just north of town.

The advancing tongue, as it flowed down the steep and narrow Arroyo Principal, frequently showed remarkable fluidity. At a point about a kilometer below the town, the flow advanced down the *arroyo* as a steep front at a rate of about 40 m/hr. Almost the entire front, confined by the steep high walls of the *arroyo*, was incandescent and flowed like soft tar in bulging lobes. This rapid and incandescent advance compared in rate of movement and apparent liquidity to other lava flows near their source. If one considers that this lava had presumably left the Taquí vent 6 months before and had already traveled 8 km, with several pauses, the retention of its heat and power to advance seems remarkable. A few days later a number of distinct lava streams broke forth from the summit of the lava flow near its farthest advance, moved rapidly down the flanks in radial incandescent streams, and then spread out into a fan-shaped mass (Fig. 86), covering 350,000 m^2 of terrain in a single night.

During this period (June and July) the rainy season was already well advanced, and the high humidity of the atmosphere was conducive to the condensation of vapors emitted by the lava, so that these vapors frequently became distinctly visible, particularly over the lava at the cemetery where it had accumulated in considerable thickness in the narrow stretch between Cerro de Capatzun and Cerro de Calvario. Banks or clouds of vapor formed several hundred meters above the lava flow, with moving pendulous stringers, or "tails" of vapor hanging below them and indicating that the lava, although now more than 6 km from its vent, still contained and emitted considerable vapors.

The eruptive activity in the crater during the summer was considerably reduced and more erratic than previously (Fig. 87). Frequently the pure-white eruptive column contained only ashless vapors that

Fig. 85. July 1, 1944. Torn structure of the Parangaricutiro tongue of the Taquí flows, which is peculiar to this tongue.

Fig. 86. December 2, 1944. Aerial view, end of the Parangaricutiro lava flow at Llano de Huirambosta, 5 km NW of the new cone. Individual lava emissions from the top of the lava flow are shown, a feature peculiar to this tongue.

rose languidly, sometimes to a great height. At other times invisible vapors issued from the crater and condensed as white cumulus clouds above the volcano. It was often difficult to distinguish these eruptive vapors from the normal clouds brought on by the rainy season. At other times the column consisted of a tenuous brownish dust without visible vapors.

Fig. 87. August 16, 1944. Characteristic eruptive column during this period. Quitzocho ridge to the right. Campamento tongue of the Taquí flow behind the houses. Taken from Cerro de Jarátiro.

Destruction of San Juan Parangaricutiro

The steady and inexorable advance of the lava finally convinced the remaining inhabitants of San Juan Parangaricutiro that they must evacuate their town (Figs. 88 and 89) . . . . Because of their deep attachment to the soil, many remained until the lava covered the last small corner of their land, then sadly departed by the trucks their government had placed at their disposal. With the destruction of the church, the strongest tie that bound them to the place was broken. [As described on p. 193-194, the revered crucifix *El Señor de Los Milagros* was removed from the church on May 9.] By mid-July all but a few outlying squares at the western edge of the town were covered by lava. Of the church only the 23-m-high tower, and its unfinished twin projected above the torn lava surface (Figs. 5, 90, and 91; Plates 6A and B), and the apse with its altar nestled within a basin of jumbled lava blocks. Curiously enough, a small kipuka[50] within the middle of the flow lay uncovered a short distance to the NE of the church.

The following described July days may be considered as typical of the events during this period:

July 6, 1944—As we entered San Juan Parangaricutiro at about 7 p.m., the cone showed two well-defined and separate eruptive columns: one from the central portion of the crater rather weak and very pale gray; and one from the south vent, more voluminous and grayer—both rose languidly without cauliflowers. No noise was audible in San Juan Parangaricutiro, and there were no incandescent ejecta until about midnight when bursts of glowing ash appeared intermittently in a column of increased size and a few bombs fell on the west slope of the cone.

We found that the lava had spread considerably toward the west, across the northern part of the town and less toward the SW in the direction of the church, from which it was now only 25 m distant. As before, the lava advanced as spreading tongues, or lobes, moving toward the west at a rate of about 2 m/hr and toward the south about 1 m/hr. The north and faster-moving lava front was lower (3 m high) than the slower south front (5-8 m high).

During the night the eruptive column rose majestically to a height of 1½ km and was then carried abruptly toward the SW by the upper air currents.

July 7, 1944—The lava continued its normal advance. The people of the town[51] busily removed the last of the houses and dismantled the interior of the church [Fig. 92]. The men removed the heavy beams, while the women and children carried away the cupboard doors and the flower stands. On this day they removed the pulpit, confessional booths, and the carved stone baptismal font. The padre believed that the church would have remained secure, had they not removed the sacred image of *El Señor de Los Milagros*. Only a few old people remained, and they feverishly dismantled their houses by day and disconsolately watched the advance of the lava by night—there remained but one street free of lava in the town.

We made a tour of the lava front in the late afternoon and evening. The west, or lateral, lobe had decreased its rate of advance; and behind the church it no longer showed apparent motion, having stopped 20 m from the apse [Fig. 91]; but a new tongue was advancing from the NE toward the parish wing. The flow down Arroyo Principal showed renewed activity after a period of almost complete quiescence; tongues of viscous lava broke out laterally at many points. At Hidalgo Street three caves with domed roofs had formed in the lava, presumably by the arching of the surface crusts. The main flow had increased in height to about 15 m above the ground level, making its total thickness from the *arroyo* bottom about 20 m. Some lateral tongues broke out near the crest of the main flow and moved viscously down the lava front. We watched a fine lateral tongue issue from a cave-like orifice near the crest of the main stream, flowing

Fig. 88. June 19, 1944. Evacuation of San Juan Parangaricutiro.

Fig. 89. June 20, 1944. Parangaricutiro lava tongue advancing slowly through the town.

Fig. 90. June 30, 1944. Parangaricutiro lava tongue covering the town.

Fig. 91. July 7, 1944. Parangaricutiro lava tongue approaching church of San Juan Parangaricutiro.

like soft tar down the torn and jumbled lava face and finally spreading fanwise at the base of the flow. Near the terminus of the main lava tongue a number of flows broke out from the top of the lava and moved in radial streams from their source (Fig. 86). The main lava flow at this time was 1⅓ km beyond the outskirts of the town.

. . . . .

July 8, 1944—The lava tongue behind the church showed no apparent movement, but the new lobe advancing from the NE approached slowly and was only 20 m from the parish wing of the church.

We went to Zirosto village, 8 km west of San Juan Parangaricutiro, following the length of the flow. The lava tongue had now reached the Llano de Huirambosta, almost 2 km beyond San Juan Parangaricutiro. The activity of the lateral tongues, so strikingly active last night, had now diminished or completely ceased. The summit flows of last night had spread fanwise over the fields to cover a large area of land but were now completely motionless.

The forest along the Zirosto road was badly damaged, with broken limbs and many dead trees. The fields of Zirosto were covered with a heavy mantle of ash, for the heaviest falls of last year drifted largely in this direction. About one-half of the inhabitants had deserted the town. One of the inhabitants reported the depth of the ash to be about a meter. Attempts to raise corn in the ash failed; for although the seeds sprouted, the shoots soon withered and died.

. . . . .

By early August the lava tongue of San Juan Parangaricutiro had entirely ceased its movement, its

Fig. 92. July 7, 1944. Dismantling the church, San Juan Parangaricutiro.

ultimate advance reaching Llano de Huirambosta, where the *arroyos* of Parícutin and San Juan Parangaricutiro joined [Fig. 12]. The Taquí flow, following its mean course, had a length of 10 km with a maximum spread, over the lands of Quitzocho, La Lagunita, and Huaririo, of 2½ km.

A stereopair of airphotographs in Fig. 151 (p. 263) shows the Parangaricutiro lava flow surrounding the church and covering much of San Juan Parangaricutiro. Plate 6A shows the church from the air.

Later Stage of Taquí Flow

The Taquí vent continued to yield abundant lava, which sometime during late July or early August, instead of finding its way by sub-surface flow to the lava tongue of Parangaricutiro, advanced as a sheet from an undetermined point overriding the previous flows around the base of the cone. This secondary vent fed a front of lava that spread from the cone across the valley to Curínguaro, advancing as an irregular wall toward the north. A narrow tongue turned westward and passed the base of Sapichu and flowed between the old ash-covered Quitzocho flow and the flanks of Cerro de Jarátiro, its ultimate narrow and torn tip forming a sliver of lava between the Quitzocho ridge and Cerro de Jarátiro. This tongue, called the Campamento tongue, had by August 15 built a wall of rubble rising above the level of the second Cerro de Jarátiro crater [Fig. 93: probably the middle crater, shown, on Figs. 13 and 108]. A thin stream of lava, flowing between low-bounding levees of rubble, reached the bottom of the old crater where it formed a low fan-like delta. On the 17th, liquid lava broke out of the front above the old Cerro de Jarátiro crater rim along a front of about 30 m and poured into this ancient crater. Within 6 hours the flow filled the old crater almost to its lower eastern lip. The effect of this outbreak was to drain fluid lava from the main body of the Campamento tongue and to form a graben-like depression traversed by rubbly parallel ridges extending toward Sapichu. Soon after, new incandescent tongues issued from secondary vents in the neighborhood of Sapichu, which appeared, in the obscurity of the night, to come from points near the head of the subsided or graben-like area . . . .

On September 27[52], lava from the Taquí vents, after having flowed for more than 8 months around the south and east sides of the base of the cone, began flowing directly north on the cone's west side, following Arroyo de Parícutin and filling the valley between the first Parícutin flow and Cerro de Canicjuata. This new flow issued from a "graben" in Mesa de Los Hornitos. Upon reaching the flatter terrain about Parícutin village, it spread laterally and covered the site of that unfortunate ash-buried town. Continuing along Arroyo de Parícutin, it invaded Llano de Huirambosta and on October 20 finally joined the Parangaricutiro tongue near the end of its course. This later Parícutin flow showed the normal characteristics of Parícutin's lava, a high steep front, mantled with broken blocks and clinkers, and partial discoloration by gaseous emanations. The contact of these two lava flows formed an interesting contrast of lava types. A few weak fumaroles developed in the lower part of the flow but did not persist.

The Crater on November 26, 1944

A second ascent of Parícutin volcano was made on the morning of November 26. The general configuration of the crater was somewhat changed from what we saw on May 25. The rim of the crater was now rounded and not sharp as on the previous ascent, and one could walk along the broad crater edge with ease. The highest point on the crater rim was the eastern edge, where the aneroid barometer read 2,740 m. The western edge was somewhat lower, 2,710 m and the north lip 2,690 m. The south lip was the lowest, but a regular shower of bombs in that direction precluded a complete circuit of the cone. The inner north slope of the crater was occupied by a bomb-littered bench, the remnant of a previously higher floor. The inner edge of this bench, which rose slightly from a low trough, had an altitude of 2,675 m. From the rim of the crater and the bench, the sides sloped down to both a central and a south vent. The central vent was a deep, narrow funnel and showed but little activity. Small clouds of white vapors rose lazily from the orifice, occasionally increasing in volume until they filled the bottom of the crater.

The south vent was a saucer-shaped depression in the bottom of which were 5 or 6 main orifices, with perhaps some smaller ones.

Fig. 93. August 17, 1944. Lava flows about to pass into old crater (lower right). Instituto de Geología observatory cabin on southern crater rim.

This vent showed violent but erratic steam activity; jets of vapor rushed from the orifices with great velocity, abrading the adjoining crater wall. The individual jets of vapor coalesced somewhat below the crater rim into a medium-sized light-colored eruptive column. Activity in the individual orifices was not steady but irregular and erratic. The largest orifice was an irregular opening, perhaps 4 m across, which blew off at frequent intervals tearing incandescent lava from its throat and carrying bombs well above the crater rim. Orifice number 2 was small, less than a meter across, and almost continually blew off white steam. This orifice had a cone mouth, like a miniature volcano, about 75 cm high. Orifice number 3, not clearly visible, gave off copious white vapors directed toward the SW. Orifice number 4 appeared to be a double vent that blew off at intervals of ½ to 3 minutes toward the west and carried some ash. Other vents could not be clearly distinguished in the vaporous confusion in the crater pit.

The vapor column carried with it bombs torn from the throat of the vents. One could sometimes observe a large bomb torn from the orifice. The vents also discharged finer material. In addition, the eruptive column scoured ash from the nearby wall. Occasionally material slumped from the crater walls into the vent and was blown out in ashy volutes by the rushing vapors.

The noise of the vents, particularly from orifice number 1, as heard from the crater rim, was almost deafening. Numerous shocks swayed the upper part of the cone, particularly near the lower south rim, where the tremors were so strong and frequent as to induce in one a feeling of dizziness. Frequently the activity in the orifices of the south vent increased after a heavy tremor, but no regular relationship was observed.

Ahuán Flow

Sometime in mid-November, exact date not known, lava broke out at the SSW base of the cone, below the south vent in the crater (Fig. 94). Accompanying this flow was a slump in the south slope of the cone, forming a triangular segment, reaching about one-half the way up the slope of the cone. At the eastern end

of this break the crater slope showed a steep, half-funnel-like slide at the base of which issued the lava stream [Fig. 95]. As near as can be judged, this point coincided with the vent of the September 1943 flow [Fig. 36] and occupied a position on a line through the main crater and the Sapichu vents [Fig. 74]. A small lava dike was exposed in the wall of the cone a short distance above the lava vent. This dike, 50 cm wide, had a N-S strike and a dip of 65°E. On the opposite side of the lava stream, or to the east, was a small pyramidal hill of fume-oxidized ash, evidently a section of the main triangular slump, which was broken off, twisted, and carried about 100 m by the

Fig. 94. Mid November, 1944. The Ahuán break and beginning of the Ahuán flows, viewed from the south. In the foreground lava of the Taquí flows. Fresh lava appears black.

outbreak of the lava. At the south base of this small hill stood a contorted slab of lava, a part of the dike exposed in the cone's wall. This slab had a remarkable resemblance to a seated rabbit, and for this reason we named the vent Ahuán ("auani" is Tarascan for rabbit). The lava issued quietly from the base of the funnel-shaped slope, passed under a low lava bridge where congealed crust had already begun to form, flowed eastward with a faint tinkling, and emitted choking bluish fumes. The flow showed a bright-orange incandescence dappled with abundant dark scoriaceous clinkers.

Fig. 95. November 27, 1944. The Ahuán vent from the air. The Ahuán flow covers the Taquí flow. Taken from the west.

On December 2 we were able to cross the rough clinkery surface to the edge of the moving lava stream. By this time the apparent vent had moved downstream by about 10 m owing to the congelation of the surface over the upper part of the flow. At the head of the flow was a low horseshoe-shaped levee about 2 m across. Between this levee and the moving lava were several incandescent crevasses from which hissing invisible vapors issued. Lava issued quietly from the narrow vent. About 50 m below the vent the stream was 6 m wide. It showed an orange incandescence dappled black by congealed lava and did not break up into clinkers in the upper part of the flow. The flow moved quietly with an occasional heaving of the surface. On rare occasions these heaving spots swelled to large blisters, some of which burst with a hiss and scattered incandescent masses of viscous lava. This flow we have called the Ahuán flow.

. . . . .

On the crusted head of the flow between the apparent lava vent and the base of the cone was an hornito, about 1½ m through the base and 1½ m high. It contained many incandescent orifices, particularly on its summit. These vents carried delicate growths of hematite and magnetite crystals. Gases issued from these vents with a continuous hissing. The maximum temperature measured in the incandescent orifices of this hornito was 1,080°C. Measurements in the crevasses surrounding the head of the lava flow were 1,020°C [see p. 317-320].

By December 2 the Ahuán flow had encircled the south and east sides of the cone and moved over the older ash-covered Sapichu and the Taquí flows (Fig. 96). The lava front extended from Sapichu south-

eastward across the older lava fields. The lava front reached a height of 15 m; and from this front of rubble, tongues of rough lava extended at intervals in advance of the main flow. The subsidiary tongues sometimes reached a length of 300 m. The whole front advanced slowly and erratically except at its NW corner near Sapichu, where the lava front was broken by subsidiary lava tongues . . . .

Late in the evening a strong steady glow over the western portion of the old and apparently congealed Campamento tongue suggested the reappearance of incandescent lava. A wide and deep gash had developed and cut diagonally across the lava, almost to the pushing Ahuán lava, a distance of about 150 or 200 m. Apparently this new channel had opened very recently, for lava had only now begun to pour from the mouth of the gash . . . . This curious action of the apparently congealed Campamento tongue suggests that the flow contained a still fluid core, surrounded by a shell of congealed lava, and that the pressure exerted upon this body of still-molten material by the push of the Ahuán lava caused the rupture of the shell and the escape of the contained molten material.

Meanwhile, new tongues of lava, breaking out from the Ahuán lava front near Sapichu, moved rapidly but erratically northward, and on December 8 reached our camp, threatening to destroy the cabins. These cabins [Figs. 80 and 87], built along the edge of one of the old craters [probably the SE rim of the northern crater seen in Figs. 13 (p. 42-43) and 108 (p. 144)], were about 50 m above Quitzocho, or the fields at the foot of Cerro de Jarátiro. The great change in the topographic appearance of the vicinity can well be imagined, for it was no longer necessary to descend a high hill to reach the lava level; a glance from the cabin window revealed a high and rubbly lava front overlooking the cabin itself. A long rapidly advancing tongue moved past the doorway, spilled into the remaining uncovered portion of the parcel of La Lagunita, and spreading rapidly the next day, poured into the deepest and last remaining old crater of Cerro de Jarátiro.

The cabin was hurriedly dismantled and moved to [a higher point farther west on] Cerro de Jarátiro, about 100 m above Quitzocho; it seemingly was inconceivable that the lava would ever reach this elevation on the summit of a high ridge, but the cabin

Fig. 96. November 29, 1944. The main cone and crater and the Ahuán flow viewed from the SSE. Sapichu (upper right) lies at the NE base of the cone.

was again moved in December 1946 to escape a higher lava flow.

With the outbreak of the Ahuán vent, activity at Mesa de Los Hornitos greatly subsided, owing probably to a diminution, if not entire cessation, of lava from the now deeply buried Taquí vent. Mesa de Los Hornitos was greatly disturbed and traversed by deep crevasses. An ash mantle covered the lava and smoothed its surface. The *volcancitos* were so modified that they were no longer recognizable, while the *hornitos* were mere hummocks of ash, from the summits of which protruded slaggy lava, frequently tinted by sublimates of alteration products.

Some of the crevasses in the lava crust were the reopenings of older cracks and frequently showed bright alteration colors, owing to the passage of gases through these older crevices. Some of the crevasses, too, reopened old cracks along which the froth of the *hornitos* had passed, and exposed their channelways

to view. The features of the *hornitos* thus exposed confirmed the previous observation that they are a froth of gas-charged lava that arose along cracks in the congealed crust of the flow. Dissection of some recently extinct *hornitos* showed them to have a spongy open structure. Sometimes small quantities of steam still issued from these dissected *hornitos*, and a sharp odor suggesting hydrochloric and sulfurous acids was frequently detectable. The condensed steam wet the surface of the cracks and cavities and had a biting acid taste. The cavity walls of the *hornitos* showed considerable rock alteration. Flesh-pink to minium-red or pale-gray coatings colored the surfaces, and there were frequently nests of needle-like sulfur crystals, golden-yellow stalactites of chloraluminite, small pearly laths of gypsum, and other less well defined products.

During the period of early Ahuán activity, the crater showed a more than usual heavy eruptive column, although only lightly charged with ash. The activity, however, was extremely variable, changing from periods of no visible vaporous emissions to heavy wooly cauliflowers with frequent lightning. From the configuration of the crater as seen on November 26 and the level of the lava vent for the Ahuán flow, it was quite evident that the throat of the crater vent and the base of the eruptive column were not more than a few meters above the top of the rising lava column in the lava conduit.

. . . . .

The calm and continuous flow of lava from the vent, unaffected by the wide and sometimes sudden changes in the crater's activity, was frequently and widely commented upon.

Fig. 97. January 23, 1945. Interior of the crater, with one eruptive vent and a medium-sized eruptive column charged with ash.

In the course of the next few months the apparent source of the Ahuán flow moved progressively downstream, owing to the accumulation of congealed lava over the upper reaches of the flow. This frozen roof became a jumble of blocks and scattered low *hornitos*, brilliantly colored with efflorescences of yellow, orange, and buff sublimates. By mid-January 1945 the flowing lava issued from a low-domed tunnel, about 150 m from its original source. Here the open orifice was about 3 m wide, and the lava moved at a rate of about 45 m/hr. This small secondary vent fed a large lava front moving along the south and east sides of the base of the cone, passing Sapichu and spreading out over the surface of the older flows. The main flow then divided into two irregular tongues:

one, now rather sluggish in movement, flowed toward the west as far as Quitzocho ridge and the camp; a second, actively advancing as a sinuous irregular tongue, moved toward Cerro de Pantzingo, 5.5 km east of the new cone near the NE edge of the lava field.

The Crater on January 22, 1945

An ascent was made to the crater rim during the late afternoon of January 22. In the morning a thin eruptive column arose, accompanied by a tenuous gritty ash and a roar like a heavy surf; the column became heavier during the afternoon and rose in volutes. The north rim had an altitude, by aneroid, of 2,685 m. At this time the crater had a single throat, about the locus of the south vent (Fig. 97). The south inner wall sloped directly to this vent at the angle of repose, but the north wall showed a well-defined bench and the remnants of two others.

The eruptive crater vent itself appeared to be a chimney with a throat about 3 m in diameter, but it could not be clearly seen because of its position below the old terrace. Violent explosions in the vent induced a strong swaying motion to the summit of the cone. The explosion interval was erratic. Explosions averaged about 10 per minute. The eruptive column was blasted violently from the vent, but a few meters above the throat it expanded into its first volute and then rose more languidly. Frequently the eruptive column drifted slowly around the crater with a spiraling motion. When such a drifting column engulfed us on the crater rim, a slight odor of hydrogen sulfide was perceptible; and a frothy, semi-pumiceous ash fell in irregular fragments up to 10 cm in size. Bombs were ejected from the vent; those a meter or so across seldom rose higher than 50 m. The bombs appeared to be semi-molten, as they seemed to change shape in their flight.

The effect after dark was fearsome. The incandescent bombs left the crater throat with great speed to form a fan of fire. The larger, slow-moving bombs could be discerned easily, but the innumerable smaller bombs and lapilli were but streaks of light to the eye.

Both in daylight and after dark, compression waves in the eruptive column frequently followed the explosive bursts. When the noise was a rumbling roar, many thin compression rings followed one another in rapid succession. In spite of the tremendous explosions the noise at the crater rim could not compare to that of November 26.

. . . . .

The Crater on May 27, 1945

On May 27, 1945, the crater was entered by W.F. Foshag, John V.N. Dorr, Carl Fries, and Celedonio Gutiérrez, and again to the crater rim on that night by Dorr and Fries. During the day a pure-white steam column issued from the north vent of the crater with a loud rushing noise, carrying bombs that fell on the eastern rim and slope of the cone (Fig. 98). At rare intervals the south vent gave off a single burst of dense black ash and many bombs. These heavy bursts from the south vent yielded a majestic eruptive column that frequently filled the entire crater and rose rapidly to a height of about a kilometer.

The two vents, as seen from the crater rim, did not seem to occupy the exact positions observed on previous ascents. The north vent was close to the NE edge of the crater, the steep interior walls of the crater sloping directly to a chimney-like orifice. The south vent occupied more nearly the center of the crater and was much deeper and separated from the north crater by a septal ridge. The walls sloped regularly from the rim to the bottom of the crater, which showed no open orifice.

The activity of the north crater consisted of an almost continuous jet of steam issuing from the open vent with a harsh grating roar. A few highly vesicular brown bombs, like those yielded by Sapichu, were ejected to a height of 150 to 250 m, rarely to 500 m, above the throat of the vent. The column was slightly inclined toward the east, consequently the greater number of bombs fell on the east slope of the crater and cone. There were but rare pauses of a few seconds in the emission of vapors, the column almost immediately issuing again. The remarkable feature of this vent was the almost constant emission of white vapors and the almost total absence of ash. A slight sulfurous odor pervaded the crater.

During the 3 hours spent in the crater, the south vent showed no signs of activity, although the bomb-littered terrace and inner slopes of the crater indicated that considerable ejectamenta were thrown out during the single explosive bursts to which it was subjected. In the evening, however, Fries and Dorr observed one of these terrifying explosions from the crater rim. The eruption began with a noise like the explosion of a small charge of powder in loose ground and was immediately followed by a rapidly rising but silent heavy eruptive column, which mushroomed out overhead into a dense black pall, from which showered dark (not incandescent) bombs and ash. Previous to this explosion there was no apparent

Fig. 98. May 27, 1945. Interior of crater with two vents; the north vent emits a continuous column of white vapors; the south vent, beyond the low medial ridge, erupts at irregular intervals. [Taken from the north rim.]

change in the crater itself to give warning of the impending blast, which occurred almost instantaneously. With this single burst, this vent resumed its inactive state.

In the upper part of the septal ridge separating the two main vents, on the slope of the larger but less active crater, were three incandescent orifices, the largest about 1½ m across. From these issued strong jets of vapor. They were undoubtedly connected with the north vent, for their activity increased and decreased in consonance with changes in activity at this vent.

Lightning was observed at night in the occasional heavy ash column, but none was seen in the steam column.

Late Stage of Taquí Flow

Some time during late June, lava activity shifted from the Ahuán vent back to the area of the Taquí vent. On July 4 the lava field about Ahuán was almost completely inactive; a broad flow of rough, clinkery lava, following the SW base of the cone, flowed toward the NW and still showed some slight movement. The large conical *volcancito*, which was a conspicuous feature of the Ahuán flow, was reduced to a pinnacled remnant surrounded by rough lava. Abundant bluish-white fumes issued from vents in the remnant of the *volcancito*. A line of gas vents and sublimate-incrusted cracks marked the last channel of the lava.

Lava now issued from a crevasse in a low dome near the locus of the old Taquí vents. This dome of lava had a precipitous SE front, suggesting a scarp,

Fig. 99. July 31, 1945. Interior of crater with one active vent. The bench is a remnant of a higher floor of the crater. Taken from the south.

perhaps owing to elevation of the crust by the injection of lava beneath. A crevasse almost bisected this low lava dome. Lava issued quietly from the lower part of this crevasse as a stream about a meter wide that widened rapidly down its course and split into three tongues. One could approach to within 3 m of the apparent vent and observe the movement of the lava. It did not appear to well up from any perceptible vent but flowed from its point of origin without disturbance. As the lava moved, the surface pulled apart like viscous tar to form a rough surface. Lower down the course of the flow, the surface was pulled

into loose congealed clinkers that rode along the surface of the flow.

Above the apparent lava vent, the dome showed incandescent crevasses from which choking bluish-white fumes hissed; the vents and the crevasses were colored gray or buff by deposited sublimates.

. . . . .

On July 31, our last visit to Mesa de Los Hornitos, the lava dome from which the flow issued remained relatively unchanged, although the lava now issued not only from the crevasse, as previously, but had also broken out on the opposite side of the dome and from the foot of the dome's scarp. A short flow was moving from the original vent and another from the vent at the base of the scarp, but the principal flow issued from the dome opposite the original vent and formed a long lava stream that extended to the north for more than 1½ km. The Ahuán area showed no apparent activity, but the area was colored with a large patch of yellowish sublimates.

. . . . .

In late July the crater showed a funnel-shaped form, surrounded on the west, north, and east by a broad terrace (Fig. 99). The single eruptive vent probably represented the more persistent south vent. During the brief interval when little ash issued from the crater, it could be seen that the bottom of this vent was occupied by three, or perhaps more, incandescent orifices, from which the vapors escaped with great force. For a brief period two small incandescent orifices, emitting small plumes of dirty vapor, appeared on the inner north slope of the crater, below the encircling terrace.

Summary of the Taquí Period

Although the SW flank of the cone showed a minor emission of lava on August 26, 1943, persistent activity did not begin in this area until January 7, 1944, with the outbreak of the Taquí vents. This outbreak immediately followed the complete cessation of activity in the Sapichu vent. The Taquí orifice became the most persistent and long lived of any Parícutin lava vent. Emission of lava from the Taquí vents alternated with lesser flows from the Ahuán vent, an orifice corresponding to the earlier Pastoriu and Mesa del Corral flows . . . . Because activity from the Taquí vents alternated with that from the Ahuán vent, we have included the Ahuán activity in the Taquí period.

Taquí's activity began with the surging of lava from three small vents at the SW base of the cone, which were soon, however, engulfed and covered by their own lava. Numerous flows and tongues of lava issued from these vents, most of which did not appear directly at the locus of the vents themselves but broke out on the surface some distance away after first flowing for variable distances beneath the congealed crust. The largest of these flows, which we have called the Taquí flow, had a total length of about 10 km and covered an area of arable land belonging to San Juan Parangaricutiro and Parícutin, including the two towns themselves. It is difficult to estimate the total ejectamenta and lava during the Taquí period, because the average thickness of the Taquí lavas is not well known. Over Llano de Quitzocho it reached a thickness of about 60 m. The area covered by the flows of this period, to July 1945, was $17\frac{3}{4}$ km^2. At the end of this period the cone had an elevation of about 340 m above the original terrain and a basal diameter of 1 km. The diameter of the crater was about 400 m.

The main crater showed greater activity during the Taquí period than the preceding Sapichu period, but considerably less than during the Quitzocho period. During the Taquí period, explosive activity was erratic, sometimes for very brief periods reaching a violence equal to activity during the Quitzocho period, but frequently being reduced to weak emissions, even less than that shown during the Sapichu period. Rarely was the eruptive column heavily charged with ash, and it frequently consisted of apparently pure steam. Bomb and ash types ejected were similar to those of the previous periods.

During the Taquí period, the cone showed little increase in elevation. Slight increases, owing to an increment of new ejecta, were offset by slides in the crater and by rainwash. These variations induced little change in the appearance of the cone. The crater line showed some notable changes, particularly the north and south crater rims, owing to scouring by the north and south crater vents, sometimes resulting in a marked saddle shape to the crater rim. The only notable changes in the exterior form of the cone were the minor slumps induced by the initiation of the Taquí and Ahuán flows.

The most striking feature of the Taquí period was the growth of *volcancitos* and *hornitos* on the surface of the Taquí flow and, to a much lesser extent, on the Ahuán flow. These owed their origin, perhaps, to the fortuitous circumstance that the actual lava vents became buried under their own flows, allowing the molten lava to move through channels beneath a crust, rather than as overriding tongues as in the previous flows. Emanations from the subcrustal lava were then forced to find their escape through various channels in the crust itself. These emissions contained combustible gases, as demonstrated by the striking flames that were frequently observed over both the *volcancitos* and *hornitos*. The fountaining of gas-charged lava from crustal vents to form *volcancitos* presented a beautiful spectacle. The short flows that issued from the *volcancitos* yielded a smooth, hummocky, pahoehoe-like flow or an unusual "cordwood" form of lava.

The lavas of the Taquí and Ahuán vents showed no appreciable differences from those of previous flows, yielding the usual rubble and clinker-covered surface. The only striking difference was in the Parangaricutiro tongue [p. 115-117; Fig. 85], whose torn and jagged appearance is in marked contrast to other lavas. This may be due to its prolonged period of flow. Four and one-half months elapsed from the time the lava issued from the vent until it reached the outskirts of San Juan Parangaricutiro and changed its characteristic structure. Perhaps an essential difference between the Parangaricutiro tongue and other tongues and flows was its mode of advance, much of which took place, not as overriding tongues, but as subcrustal flow. During this time, the lava presumably underwent some crystallization and undoubtedly lost much of its volatile contents. After a pause and apparent quiescence of about 3 months, [in early April] the Parangaricutiro tongue broke out from beneath its cover of rubble and clinkers at Turímbiro, near the base of Cerro de Equijuata, or about 5 km from its original source.

It was during the Taquí period that there were occasional opportunities to ascend the cone and observe the configuration and activity of the crater. The presence of a persistent and permanent vent near the SW edge of the crater, so frequently apparent in the position of the eruptive column, was confirmed, as was also the lesser but still important NE vent. There were also ephemeral vents. The inner configuration of the crater depended largely upon the relative activity of these separate orifices as well as upon the intensity of the activity itself. The actual orifices of the vents were surprisingly small, considering the size of the emitted eruptive column. The character of the eruptive column was also conditioned by the inner configuration of the crater. When the eruptive orifices were open, a vapor column free of, or only slightly charged with ash resulted. If the eruptive orifice was choked with ash and debris, frequent ash slides took place into the vent, or the eruptive column scoured the adjacent wall, the eruptive column was charged with ash. When the eruptive vents were open, the small quantity of ash carried by the eruptive column consisted of brown shredded slag, scoured from the molten lining of the crater vent, and the eruptive column had a pale-brownish and "gritty" appearance. When the vents were choked, the ash consisted of a variety of forms including shredded slag, triturated material, and spalls, that is to say, such material as made up the cone itself.

During the 18 months that the Taquí period was under observation, it became evident that no further unusual change in the activity of the volcano was likely to take place, that the volcano had settled down to a comparatively regular routine, and that its formative period had drawn to a close. It was no longer an infant volcano but a mature, volcanic apparatus. Activity, although continuous, was considerably reduced in force; and the cone acquired such a degree of stability that it became difficult to change radically its configuration or size. Parícutin was now an established volcano. Its period of youth and development could be considered closed.

The Year Following World War II (1945-1946)

As the period of systematic observation by Foshag and González came to an end in August 1945, the United States Committee for the Study of Parícutin Volcano[15] worked to establish a system of continued monitoring. During the following year, three different teams of investigators were responsible for reporting on Parícutin's activity in sequential time periods (Krauskopf and Williams; Kennedy; Segerstrom and Gutiérrez). September 18, 1946, saw the arrival of Ray Wilcox, who was designated by the U.S. Geological Survey and the U.S. Parícutin Committee as the permanent observer at the volcano. Six reports by Wilcox and colleagues covered the activity until July 31, 1948. At that point, the responsibility of continued observations was placed in the hands of Celedonio Gutiérrez, who had been trained by Wilcox. Thereafter, Gutiérrez was designated as the resident observer and worked closely with Carl Fries, who was in charge of the U.S. Geological Survey's mission in México. Fries and Gutiérrez published seven additional reports that documented activity until the eruption ended on March 4, 1952. These 16 sequential reports were published in the _Transactions of the American Geophysical Union_, and are reproduced in large part below. Particularly valuable are maps showing the distribution of lava flows for each period. Modified versions of these maps arranged in time sequence are also shown in a composite map inside the front cover, to permit easy visualization of the pattern of lava movement throughout the eruption. The individual maps are also shown in large format on the following pages. Most of the 16 reports cover a 4-6 month period and follow a standard format of general overview followed by descriptions of the activity at the main vent, subsidiary vents, and then lava flows. Following the arrival of Wilcox, all reports contained one or more "diagrams of eruptive characteristics", a graphical record of eruptive noises, the height and width of the eruptive column, and quantities of ashfall, bombs, and lavas produced. We have only reproduced one of these diagrams, the first to be published, as Fig. 110. Information about rainfall and other aspects of weather, a part of most reports, is represented here only by the summary statements in the final report.

Parícutin During Its Third Year

Krauskopf and Williams (1946)

Among the large cast of scientists that made pilgrimage to Parícutin during the eruption years, Konrad Krauskopf[53] (Fig. 100) is notable both for his important contributions to understanding the workings of the volcano[54], and for his subsequent success during a long and diverse career. He has the unusual distinction of having earned two Ph.D. degrees: in Chemistry from the University of California in 1934 at the age of 24, and in Geology from Stanford in 1939. This combination of interests and talents prepared Krauskopf to play an important role in the blossoming field of geochemistry, including major contributions to the understanding of volcanic gases, ore deposits, the composition of seawater and marine sediments, and a widely used textbook: Introduction to Geochemistry. Krauskopf served as the president of the Geological Society of America (GSA), the Geochemical Society (GS), and the American Geological Institute, and received numerous awards including the Day Medal[55] (GSA: 1960) and the Goldschmidt Medal[56] (GS: 1982).

Here we reprint portions of Krauskopf and Williams' study of Parícutin's activity during its third year (Feb. 1945 - Feb. 1946). Later in the book we reprint several other studies by Krauskopf concerning the temperature and viscosity of Parícutin's lavas (see p. 319-320), and his model for the mechanisms of gas release and different eruptive styles (see p. 321-323).

Howel Williams[57] (Fig. 101) was one of the most influential volcanologists of the 20th century. He spent most of his career as a professor at the University of California. Williams was a skilled writer, with a command of the language that is rare to find in modern scientific literature. He was at the height of his career when Parícutin erupted in 1943. Two of his greatest works had been published in the preceding two years: Calderas and their Origin (1941) and The Geology of Crater Lake National Park, Oregon (1942). On p. 245-254 we reprint portions of Williams' major study of the older volcanoes of the Parícutin region.

During February and March, 1945, eruption of lava diminished while the explosive activity of the summit crater increased in intensity. The Ahuán vent, at the SSW base of the main cone, continued to discharge lava throughout this period. A long stream moved slowly around the south and east base of the cone and continued northward beyond the parasitic cone of Sapichu for more than 3 km, spreading across much of the great San Juan flow of 1944 and the older flow from Sapichu. In many places, the new lava was injected sill-like under these older flows, raising and arching them locally as much as 18 m. Another long flow issued from a vent that opened on February 4 about 400 m WNW of the Ahuán vent. By the second week of March, this flow had spread northward past Canicjuata as a narrow stream 3¼ km long and had buried most of the village of Parícutin not previously inundated by lava (Fig. 102).

During the closing days of March, two new lava vents opened close to the SW base of the cone, between those just mentioned. These continued to emit lava throughout April and the first half of May. Indeed, by early May, the flow from the eastern one,

close to the Ahuán vent, had moved eastward for more than 3 km, extending beyond the margins of the San Juan flow in the neighborhood of Mechicano.

Early in April, 6 other vents opened on the Mesa de Los Hornitos, adjacent to the [WSW] foot of the main cone, but their activity lasted only a few days and they merely discharged short tongues of lava. At about the same time, the old ash-covered lavas of the Mesa were repeatedly fissured and differentially upheaved, presumably by buried injections of lava.

The pronounced increase in discharge of lava during April coincided with a general diminution in explosive activity. In brief, the conditions were almost the reverse of those during March. There were times in April when little or no vapor rose from the summit crater for hours at a stretch, and one such quiet spell lasted almost a full day.

Strong explosive activity was renewed during the first two weeks of May. Indeed, on May 5, as if to celebrate the national holiday[58], the activity reached a violence that it had not attained previously in 1945. Bombs up to 60 cm in diameter were hurled almost 900 m above the crater rim, and the outer flanks of

Fig. 100. Konrad Krauskopf (left), Kenneth Segerstrom (center), and Luis García-Gutiérrez (right) near the entrance to the Parícutin crater in 1946.

Fig. 101. Howel Williams (left), Emmanuel Zies (center), and William Foshag (right) on Cerro de Jarátiro.

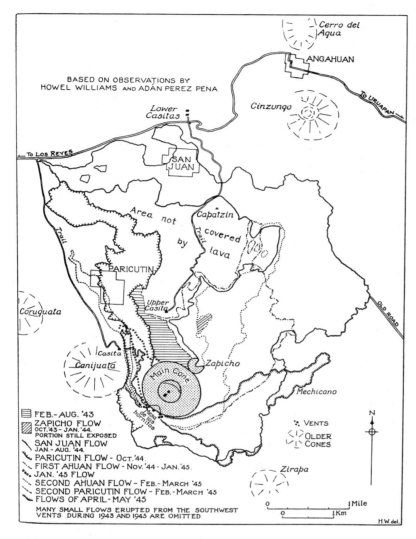

BASED ON OBSERVATIONS BY HOWEL WILLIAMS AND ADÁN PEREZ PEÑA

FEB.- AUG. '43
ZAPICHO FLOW OCT.'43 - JAN.'44. PORTION STILL EXPOSED
SAN JUAN FLOW JAN.- AUG. '44.
PARICUTIN FLOW - OCT.'44.
FIRST AHUAN FLOW - Nov.'44 - JAN.'45.
JAN. '45 FLOW
SECOND AHUAN FLOW - FEB.- MARCH '45
SECOND PARICUTIN FLOW - FEB.- MARCH '45
FLOWS OF APRIL- MAY '45
MANY SMALL FLOWS ERUPTED FROM THE SOUTHWEST VENTS DURING 1943 AND 1945 ARE OMITTED

Fig. 102. Areas covered by Parícutin lava flows to May, 1945 (Williams and Perez Peña).

the cone were drenched with incandescent ejecta. Several small outbreaks of lava were also observed during the first half of May on the Mesa de Los Hornitos, and one tongue pushed northward beyond the Casita on the slopes of Canicjuata [*casita*, the spanish word for "little house", was used by the scientists to indicate their various observatory cabins surrounding the new volcano. As shown on Fig. 102, three *Casitas* were in use at this time. This one, named simply "Casita", was located at the NE foot of Cerro de Canicjuata, about 1¼ km NW of the main vent. "Upper Casita" refers to the observatory on Cerro de Jarátiro, 1½ km north of the vent, and "Lower Casitas" indicates the observatory about 1 km north of San Juan Parangaricutiro and 5½ north of the vent (also called Cuezeño station)].

There was little change in the form of the summit crater of Parícutin between February and the middle of May, 1945 [see descriptions by Foshag and González-Reyna on p. 126-127]. During most of that period the crater was marked by a broad crescentic bench on the NE side, a short distance below the rim. On the opposite side, there was a deep, funnel-shaped pit close to the bottom of which were two small *bocas* ["boca" is spanish for mouth, and is used to refer to small vents]. These lay almost in line with Sapichu and the vent cluster at the SW base of the cone. Usually only the southwestern of the two *bocas* was active, but occasionally both were active in unison. Although the diameters of the *bocas* varied somewhat from time to time, they were seldom more than a few meters across. And yet it was from these surprisingly small pipes that all of the great ash- and bomb-showers were erupted. Noteworthy also was the fact that the mouths of the pipes stood only a little higher than the lava vents at the SW base of the cone, where explosive activity was very rare and slight.

No correlation was detected between the emission of lava by the outer vents and the explosive intensity of the summit crater. No matter whether the latter lay quiet or behaved with violence, the lava flowed uniformly from the outside vents.

The thickness of the ash-mantle over the region surrounding Parícutin, up to the middle of May, is indicated in Fig. 103.

From May until the end of October, 1945, the volcano was not under continuous observation. Reports of occasional visitors indicate that activity of the crater was much the same as during March and April—in general fairly quiet, with brief periods of stronger activity when the eruption cloud was thick and bomb-showers were frequent. The total amount of ash erupted during this period must have been small, since the lavas of May and later had scarcely a trace of ash-cover until early 1946. Lava continued to flow from vents on the Mesa de Los Hornitos. The three principal flows (Fig. 104) were: (1) A flow along the

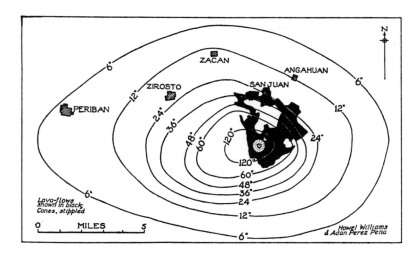

Fig. 103. Thickness of Parícutin ash to May, 1945.

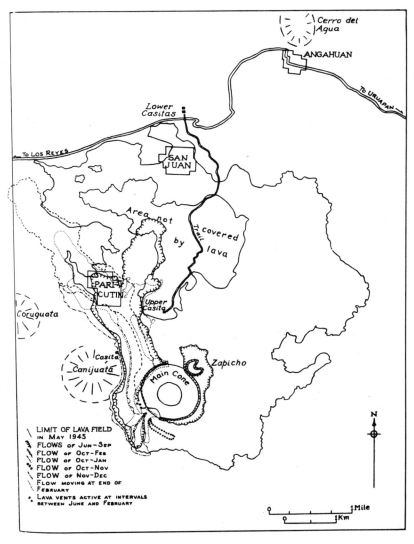

Fig. 104. Areas covered by Parícutin lava flows, June, 1945 to February, 1946.

SE and east base of the cone, which split on the small cone of Sapichu and reunited north of it; (2) a flow, or perhaps more than one flow, which moved along the NW base of the cone and then turned north along the east edge of the lava field, reaching land not previously covered just south of San Juan Parangaricutiro; (3) a flow on the west side of the lava field, whose tip barely reached new ground in the village of Parícutin. These flows had all ceased to move by the end of September.

In late October, when continuous observation was resumed, two new flows had started, practically superposed on the upper courses of the second and third flows just mentioned. These new flows had their origin in two prominent fissures on the Mesa de Los Hornitos, one parallel to the base of the cone and the other approximately radial to it (Fig. 105). The two streams continued to move at an apparently uniform rate until mid-December, when the western one (from the radial crack) gradually died. Thereafter, until at least the end of February, only a single major flow remained in motion—at first the one from the crack parallel to the edge of the cone, then after January 22 a new flow from the radial crack. The long-lived flow from the parallel crack covered the last vestiges of the village of Parícutin and moved on down the valley to a point nearly 800 m farther west than the limit of previous lavas. The new flow from the radial crack was superposed on this flow in its lower course, and by the end of February 1946 its tip was already over 800 m NW of Parícutin. Several other short-lived flows were limited to the Mesa de Los Hornitos. After September there was no movement of lava on the SE or east sides of the cone.

Up to January 20, 1946, eruptive activity from the crater alternated between periods of feeble emission of gas and periods of mild eruption characterized by fairly thick eruption clouds and frequent small bomb showers. Each period lasted about three weeks: (1) between late October and mid November activity was moderate, although for one interval of over a day (November 6 to 7) the volcano was completely quiet; (2) from November 16 to December 7 practically nothing but gas was emitted from the crater, generally without much noise; (3) between December 8 and January 2 moderate activity was resumed; (4) from January 2 to 20 the eruption again consisted chiefly of gas emission but was somewhat noisier than in the earlier "quiet" period. January 20, 1946, marked the apparent beginning of another active period; but this time the pattern was varied, for on January 28 the eruption cloud rather suddenly became wide and dense, showering the landscape with abundant sand

and dust. All through February the volcano continued to be unusually active, with a thick dark cloud, almost continuous showers of bombs, and periods of loud explosions. At times, according to natives, the eruption reached an intensity comparable with the much greater activity of the volcano in its early days.

The form of the crater changed markedly with the kind of eruption. During the first "active" period in early November only a single vent was present, which built around itself a small cone of fragmental material. In the ensuing "quiet" period the cone was destroyed and a steep-walled inner crater with two vents was formed, the vents lying roughly on a line between Sapichu and the Mesa de Los Hornitos. A striking pattern of roughly concentric steam cracks and small faults surrounded the inner crater, suggesting slumping toward the interior of the crater. During the next "active" period the pattern of cracks was destroyed and the NE part of the inner crater was filled by the formation of a new cone around the more active of the two vents. In early January this cone in turn disappeared, the inner crater became a NE-SW furrow, and the pattern of concentric cracks was reformed. The exceptional activity of late January and February was marked by an enormous increase in the size of the inner crater, to a diameter over half that of the entire crater and a depth of at least 85 m, bringing the vent down to practically the level of the lava vent on the Mesa de Los Hornitos.

Little correlation was observed between activity of the lava flows and activity of the crater, except for the odd fact that the beginning of the active period in late January was marked by a sudden shift in the place of origin of the moving lava from the fissure parallel to the base of the cone to the radial fissure.

On its third birthday, February 20, 1946, Parícutin was still putting on a good performance, belying the many predictions that its days of active eruption are almost over. [Further details of the activity at the SW vents during the period November 1945 to February 1946 can be found in articles by Krauskopf [54].

April 12 to May 3, 1946

Kennedy (1946)

The activity of Parícutin varied greatly during the period April 12 to May 3. The strong eruptive activity that began in mid-March, marked on March 17 by the formation of a new *boca* with a short-lived *volcancito* and by external changes in the form of the cone, continued until April 18. The period April 12-18 was marked by bomb-showers and explosive blasts at the rate of 10-15/min, mostly from the south vent of the double crater. Most of the bombs fell into the north crater and on the north flank of the cone. From April 19 to 26 the activity was, in general, very weak, and little ash and few bombs were projected beyond the rim of the cone. Explosions were very rare, and the weak vapor column from the volcano was accompanied by a dull surf-like roar. Most of the vapor emerged from a small vent near the center of the divide between the two coalescing craters. A heavy ash column, at times approaching in intensity that of 1943, emerged from the volcano from April 27 to 29. The ash was erupted from both the north and south vents of the crater, though the south vent is believed to have contributed the most. From April 30 to May 3 the activity was again very weak, and only a feeble column rose above the cone.

Form of the Crater

The crater was examined on April 13, 14, 20, and 30. During the first two ascents, extremely heavy bomb-showers shot northward from the south vent of the large double coalescing crater, making a thorough examination impossible. At that time the heavy bomb-showers that occurred at the rate 10-15/min, were erupting from a fissure-like opening, approximately 2 m wide and 15 m long in a WNW direction, in the bottom of the 80-m deep funnel-shaped south crater. A small vent estimated to be 1 m in diameter, located nearly in the center of the divide between the two craters, was emitting a steady jet of steam at high velocity. The north crater intermittently erupted thick clouds of ash, but no glowing material was seen within the ash.

Few changes took place between April 13 and 20. On the last date, the fissure at the bottom of the south crater was considerably larger, and material from above had begun to cave actively into it. There were then four vents located in a row along the divide between the two craters, and a separate steam jet was coming from each one. Steam was emerging from several small fissures on the broad rim adjacent to the crater.

Considerably greater changes had taken place by April 30. Caving of the south crater walls had progressed much further, and these walls were lined with numerous vertical scarps from 1-2 m high that were actively caving headward. These scarps did not represent faults, but were the upward moving fronts along which the caving was taking place. Enlargement of the crater was accompanied by shifting toward the

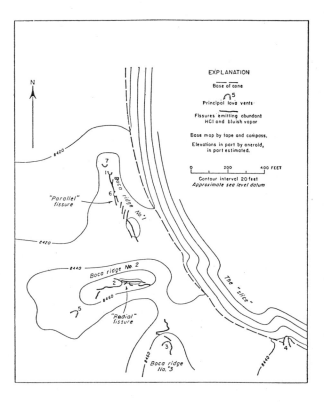

Fig. 105. Sketch map of SW flank vents in November, 1945.

north of the divide between the two craters; the steam vents, earlier on this divide, were now well within the south crater. The fissures on the rim, which earlier had been emitting steam, were at this time emitting heavy sulfur fumes, and they were lined with large quantities of arborescent sulfur crystals. The north crater could be examined at this time, and although found to be considerably larger than the south crater, it was not as deep and was not being enlarged by caving. It was completely stopped up by material that had dropped into it from the eruptions in the south crater, the nearly flat central part being red hot in an area of about 15 m in diameter, but no visible gases were emerging through this material. There was no apparent correlation between the activity in the several vents in the craters.

Activity of the Bocas

Most of the following notes on *boca* activity are taken from observations made by Rafael Molina-Berbeyer.

On March 3, a new *boca* developed on the south side of the cone, not far from its base [near the position of the old no. 4 *boca* (Fig. 105)]. This new *boca* was accompanied by the formation of a spatter cone, named Volcancito Quiquichio by the observers at the time, presumably Celedonio Gutiérrez and

Rafael Molina-Berbeyer [equivalent to the Ahuán vent of others]. Most of the spatter cone was soon destroyed and carried out in the moving lava.

At the time of my first visit, on April 13, the lava was quietly flowing out from the side of the cone in a quantity estimated to be about equal to that from the active *bocas* in the past year. Development of the *boca* was accompanied by considerable slumping of the cone in its vicinity; some segments slid out more than 50 m. The old no. 1 *boca* (Fig. 105), which was supplying lava at the time of the Quiquichio *boca* development, abruptly declined when this new *boca* formed, and its activity ceased entirely on April 4.

. . . . .

Lava Flows

The extensive flows that were moving over the buried village of Parícutin in mid-February ceased to flow at about the end of that month, and their position as shown on (Fig. 104) is about the same at present. Early in March a side tongue of lava pushed northeastward from no. 1 *boca*, around the west side of the cone and over the ash-covered flows of 1943. This flow had ceased to issue from its *boca* by March 18, and early in April the movement of the lower part of this lava, which covered the September flow south of the Casita, had also ceased.

Lava from the Quiquichio *boca* [Ahuán vent] flowed as a narrow tongue at a rate of about 300 m/day for the first five days after its start. This tongue encircled the eastern side of the cone and had by April[59] 3 almost reached Sapichu, where it was obstructed by higher ground. During the remainder of March the lava spread in several tongues laterally away from the cone toward the north and NW. During April three main tongues of this flow spread northward over the 1944 flows, and by mid-April one of these had advanced over the high ground between Sapichu and the remnant of the Sapichu flow still exposed, moving rapidly over the low ground SE and south of the Upper Casita [final extent as of June 12 shown on Fig. 106]. By May 2 this flow was only a few hundred meters east of a line projected south from the Upper Casita, though well below the level of the ridge occupied by the cabin.

Measurements of Lava Flow Rates

On April 17, the flow moving around the north side of Sapichu was about 300 m wide, had a front 10 m high, a slope of 3-5°, and a speed of 28 m/day. During April 19-28, the front of the same flow was advancing an average of 20 m/day.

On April 17, the lava flow emerging from the *boca* had a slope of 4°, was 15 m wide, and flowed 2 m/min. On April 18, the stream 30 m from its *boca* had a slope of 4°, was 10 m wide, and moved 5 m/min; 300 m from the *boca* the lava stream sloped 10°; it was 20 m wide, and flowed 2 m/min.

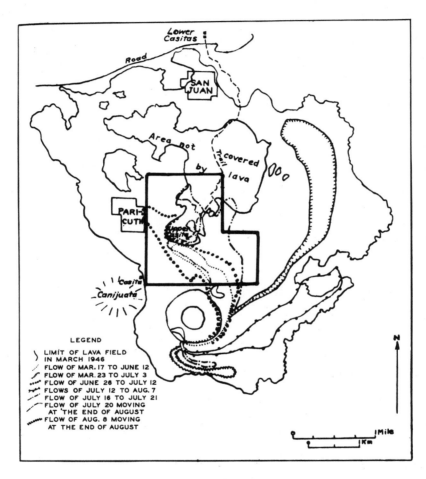

Fig. 106. Areas covered by Parícutin lava flows, March 17 to August 31, 1946. This map is based on Fig. 104. A small flow on the west side, which ceased at its *boca* on March 18 and at its front on April 4, is omitted.

May 4 To September 8, 1946

Segerstrom and Gutiérrez (1947)

Kenneth Segerstrom[60] received his B.A. degree from the University of Denver, where he majored in Mathematics and Chemistry and minored in Spanish. While in college he found summer employment with the U.S. Geological Survey as a rodman, and the geologists that he worked for taught him how to use the alidade and how to make topographic maps. His knowledge of Spanish and topographic methods opened the doors of opportunity for him that ultimately led to his important studies of erosion at Parícutin, which we reprint in large part on p. 283-311. After the bombing of Pearl Harbor in 1941, Segerstrom was sent to Zacatecas, México, to prepare a base map for studies of mercury deposits conducted by Dave Gallagher under a cooperative U.S.-México program for strategic minerals. Gallagher, once a professor at Yale, had a strong influence on Segerstrom, introduced him to geology, and convinced the topographer to return to school for formal training. Segerstrom spent 1942 at Pomona College with A.L. Woodford, and took 31 hours of geology classes in two semesters. Shortly after his return to Zacatecas, Parícutin was born. Segerstrom first visited the volcano in April of 1943. He was ultimately assigned to Parícutin, in order to prepare topographic maps of the area and isopach maps of the ash-fall blanket.

Segerstrom and Gutiérrez covered the last interval of observation prior to the arrival of Wilcox at Parícutin. A biography of Celedonio Gutiérrez is given on p. 48.

The eruptive activity of Parícutin volcano has been classified by Ordóñez and Hernández-Velasco into three phases, each seeming to follow the other in succession: (1) the "tubular eruption", consisting of explosive reports as if from tube-like cannons, synchronized with puffs of vapor and forming a column charged with much pyroclastic material; (2) the "silent eruption", varying from rolling, thunder-like explosions, deep and subdued, through periods of complete silence, to rare noises like the faint beating of the surf, accompanied by the emission of considerable pyroclastic material; and (3) the "gaseous eruption", characterized by a steady noise like that of escaping steam, during which white vapors are emitted, at times stained yellow with traces of ash. Kennedy [see p. 137] described the activity as having been very weak from April 30 to May 3, following an earlier period of strong eruption. On the afternoon of May 3, the third phase of the above succession started with a steady steam-escape roar accompanied by the emission of light vapors or none at all. This continued through May 5.

On May 6, phase 1 began again, with a tubular eruption characterized by a black column that was full of ejecta as in March, 1943. On the next day there was virtual silence, but some pyroclastic material was erupted. On May 8 this turned into another gaseous phase, which lasted until noon of May 13, when a renewal of strong activity was heralded by puffs of vapor and deep explosions. This tubular phase lasted until May 20, and the emission of pyroclastic material was so great that a part of the SE rim of the crater rose about 20 m in height, nearly attaining the altitude of the east peak. The silent eruption that followed continued nearly to the end of the month, gradually giving way to a gaseous eruption with its characteristic emission of white vapors. Of the three vents in the crater described by Kennedy, the SW one contributed most of the ejecta during the May 13-20 eruption, whereas the gaseous activity at the end of May came from the small central vent, causing it to become larger at the expense of its neighbors, both of which were quickly stopped up and covered. During the first days of June the east peak became incrusted with white salts. The SW vent blew open again, emitting vapors that were generally more yellowish than those from the central vent. Some 15 m SW of the central vent and about 5 m lower, a small, new vent opened and emitted puffs of reddish vapor . . . Another cycle began on June 11, starting with a tubular eruption marked by typical periodic explosions and accompanied by a fall of ash, scoriae, and bombs, becoming silent on June 18; occasional puffs of vapor occurred with weak, rolling explosions. Then on June 21 the gaseous stage reappeared. On the next day periodic explosive reports were noted, and with the strongest ones, some rocks were thrown out. The tubular activity increased in strength, except for an unnatural calm from June 27 to 30, until it culminated on the night of July 2 in bomb-throwing comparable to the earlier, more active years. This phase was actually a multiple one, for the central and SW vents were frequently active together, the former emitting white vapors with a roar of escaping steam and the latter sending forth yellowish, grayish, or reddish vapors colored by ash and scoriae.

The comparatively silent eruption that observers have grown to expect as a transition between the tubular and gaseous phases lasted only through July 4. From July 5 to 31 occurred an unusually long period of gaseous activity. The white vapors, accompanied by a steady steam-escape sound that usually marks this phase, rose invisibly to some hundreds of meters above the crater, where they then condensed to form a cumulus cloud. Only when the relative humidity of the atmosphere was high, as in the afternoons and especially at dawn, was the vapor visible all the way down to the crater. The SW vent and the long-dormant NE vent remained inactive.

During July the relatively quiet SW vent exposed to view its vertical-walled throat of agglomerate. The NE vent remained closed under a thickening pile of red talus, and faults with as much as 2 m of displacement developed among the fissures that encircled it. The central vent had opened to about 10 m in diameter, exhibiting the agglomerate-walled throat from which the gaseous eruption emerged. At moments of diminished sound, a few ejecta were hurled out. At the end of July increasing amounts of yellow and white sublimates were noted around the concentric fissures spaced 2-3 m apart that lined the inside of the crater. From these cracks rose a colorless gas with an odor mostly of SO_2, rarely of H_2S. On the map of the crater (Fig. 107) made on July 27, the two open vents, B and C, are shown by small concentric rings. A is the talus-covered site of the NE vent, which formed a slight depression; D is the site of the short-lived explosive vent seen early in June; E is the saddle in the NE inner rim; and F is the saddle in the SW

rim. F was an inner-rim site until the slump of March 17, which destroyed the SW outer rim that had earlier occupied approximately the position G-H. Points E, S, and 2,738 rose during April and May, but T, the saddle in the NE outer rim, rose scarcely at all. The largest fault fissure on the inner north rim of the crater is shown on the map, but many other fissures that lined the inner crater walls at that time are not shown.

The renewed activity of the crater during August was in striking contrast to the comparative quiescence during July. The steady steam-escape noise from the eruption grew more erratic on August 2. The whiteness of the vapors became dirtied by a thin veil of ash, and at night there was more incandescence than had been seen for a month. A transition period from gaseous to tubular eruption occurred during the

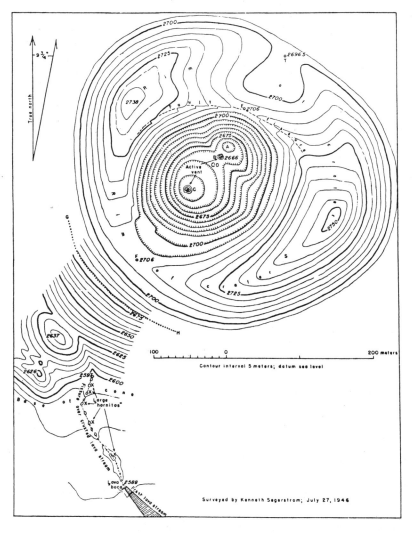

Fig. 107. Map of the crater, Parícutin volcano on July 27, 1946.

night of August 4-5, ushering a tall incandescent column bearing large quantities of ash and bombs, but accompanied only briefly by the usual loud tubular reports. Periods of silence were noted on August 5, but a heavy emission of pyroclastics continued, mostly accompanied by rolling explosions but featuring, on August 6, loud pounding noises like those of a switch locomotive. On August 6 and 7 compression waves made pulsating flashes that could be seen over the top of the crater for great distances. During an absence of the writers, Ariel Hernández-Velasco reported that the tubular eruption continued from August 9 to 13, with an ash-and-bomb-charged column that on August 13 lifted ash as high as 3 km, and with reports that on August 11 and 12 were heard as far away as the city of Uruapan.

The phase of strong activity lasted through August 25, but of varying nature, featuring characteristics of both the tubular and silent eruptions. It ranged from long periods of silence, as on August 14 and 15, through brief but earth-shaking reports at irregular intervals of several minutes, as on August 22, to rolling thunderous explosions lasting four to five seconds and closely spaced, as on August 25. All the eruptive variations during this period produced great amounts of ash. East winds, typical of the rainy season, carried almost all the ash westward and northwestward from the cone. On August 24 the column of vapors was dropping appreciable loads of dust as far as 50 km to the NW. New ash was deposited every day at the Lower Casitas, 1 km north of San Juan Parangaricutiro, making turbid the rain water that was collected from the roof. Rain gages at both Jarátiro and San Juan frequently showed several millimeters of ash from one observation to the next.

August 26 dawned with a gaseous explosion. The steam-escape sound was continuous but variable in intensity throughout the rest of the month, as was the usually thin white vapor column, which varied from brief periods of invisibility to an occasional thick yellowish column. On rare occasions a double column was noted, and observations from the top of the cone on August 28 showed that the respective roles of the two eruptive vents seemed to have been reversed since the month before, the more yellowish vapors now coming from the central vent instead of from the SW one.

On August 28 the west base of the cone was seen to be deeply littered with fragments averaging 10 cm in diameter, from the August bomb showers. Slightly up the slopes were broad talus cones of lapilli, uniformly about 1 cm in diameter. From the summit rim of the cone the central vent was seen to have broadened, but the SW and NE vents had not changed during the month. Only ephemeral white vapors issued from the SW vent and none, of course, from the buried NE vent, but the central one discharged yellowish vapors, composed mostly of water but bearing some ash and lapilli, accompanied by the usual gaseous roar. The strong August eruption had built up the inner north rim about 16 m, leaving the outer edge not noticeably changed.

On September 1 another cycle of activity was entered into, beginning with the renewal of a sometimes tubular-like, sometimes silent eruption, often featuring low, deep rumbling explosions with much emission of bombs, which on September 6 soared obliquely to the north and landed far down the sides of the cone. A short-lived gaseous eruption on September 7 turned the next day into a new, equally brief tubular phase, consisting of very deep, intermittent explosions. During the night of September 8, a nearly inaudible fountain of incandescent material rose and fell for hours, not once dying down completely. The next morning enormous bombs showered the west side of the crater, one of which, 2 m in diameter, was observed to land at the west base. The silent phase this time continued until September 15, accompanied by appreciable amounts of new ash, which was deposited to the west, and by a sound varying from that of beating surf, on September 12, to complete silence on the two succeeding days.

On the afternoon of September 15, the loud continuous roar so well known by now began again. By September 18, the characteristic whitish vapors were tinged with yellow again, and short cessations of the roaring noise were accompanied by showers of small bombs. The following altitude determinations of the crater made on September 16 should be compared with those of Fig. 107: east peak 2,750.9 m, west peak 2,747.6 m, north inner rim 2,726.3 m.

A visit to the cone on September 18 revealed that the west base had been blanketed with 10 cm of new ash in the previous three weeks, covering bomb fragments and the adjacent lava. The central explosive vent, which originally occupied a ridge-top position between the broader NE and SW vents had grown very broad and deep. The depression marking the defunct NE vent had disappeared altogether, as had the ridge between it and the SW vent. However, three eruptive throats were still in evidence. On a narrow shelf part way up the side of the great central throat, thin slow-moving white vapors drifted up from the nearly destroyed old SW vent, and on a yet narrower bench across the central throat to the NE, a lusty new vent was shooting out a strong jet of steam. The latter, with a diameter of 2 m, was much smaller and situated much lower than the old NE vent. A vertical wall of agglomerate 20 m high descended from the new vent to the floor of the central throat, 80 m below the average of the crater rim. The inner south rim showed a great broadening inward toward the center. The growing west peak had attained a knife-edge profile, dropping steeply on both sides and built of loose, very fine ash. Some development of a new bench on the east side of the inner crater was noted. Abundant yellow and orange sublimates had formed on the east peak, and from very narrow fissures whitish vapors smelling of SO_2 streamed out.

Of the two branches of lava flow that emerged from the rejuvenated Ahuán *boca* on March 17, one was 4 km NE of the cone by May 6, and the other had almost reached the base of the hill of the Upper Casita [Cerro de Jarátiro]. The lava stream at and near its source had by May 14 sunk into a trench 2-4 m deep and 15 m wide, along the south base of the cone. Five days later a collapse of the walls buried the still-alive flow for the first 100 m from its source.

By May 26 part of the lava was emerging 50 m south of the original exit, and 100 m to the east, as described above. Between the foot of the cone and the south exit, a row of four *hornitos* emitting a steady roar had developed. By May 31 the southernmost exit of lava was 100 m south of the cone, and new spatter cones occupied the intervening distance. At this time the speed of the flow at the *boca* was about 9 m/min, and the speed of the moving fronts of lava varied from ½ to 4 m/hr.

By June 12 the flow at the base of [Cerro de Jarátiro] had stopped, but the NE lava front was moving at 2 m/hr. Ten days later it had reached its point of greatest advance over the old San Juan flow, not far from where the trail from San Juan to the Upper Casita crossed it. On June 26 a new branch of the stream of lava moving at the east base of the cone started toward Sapichu, and two days later it had again surrounded this satellite cone, now nearly buried in the successive flows that had passed it. At its front the new stream had a speed of 15 m/hr on June 28, and 10 m/hr the next day. During June the line of puffing *hornitos* at Ahuán gradually became more quiet. The lava in the south Ahuán *boca* rose and fell rhythmically during periods of observation, while the *boca* area itself rose about 4 m above the adjacent lava field. The long NE flow, sapped by its vigorous Sapichu branch, had become completely inactive by July 3, but the active branch stream had again reached the base of [Cerro de Jarátiro] by the next day, moving 5 m/hr at its front.

On July 12 a new tongue was observed to head eastward from the base of the cone, almost immediately sapping all the flow from the northern tongue of June 26. On about July 16 the lava emerging from the south end of the row of Ahuán *hornitos* stopped adding its stream to the more easterly, buried flow, and sent a new tongue southeastward for five days. On June 20 a new flow darted northward from the east side of the cone, repeating the route past Sapichu much traveled by earlier flows, draining away the source flow of the east tongue of July 12. By August 7 the latter came to a halt, after invading half the area of a small peninsula of virgin ground about 3 km east of the cone. By the end of July the southernmost exit of the Ahuán lava was 170 m from the base of the cone.

During August the flow north of Sapichu developed four distinct lobes in the vicinity of the Upper Casita. The topographic map of Cerro de Jarátiro (Fig. 108) shows the details of the lava inundation from March 6, 1943 onward. On about August 8 a new lava flow started from the Ahuán *hornitos* about 50 m nearer the volcano than the previous *boca*, or 120 m south of the base of the cone. Its course was westward for 125 m, where it doubled back to the south and SE in a great bow that seemed to touch the outer limits of previous flows in the vicinity. At the same time, short-lived flows emerged from each of the first three spatter cones south of the volcano, coalescing and congealing about 30 m on each side of the line of *hornitos*.

On about September 11 a new active lava *boca* opened in the old Mesa de Los Hornitos area, [WSW] of the cone. Since the spectacular slumping of the south side of the cone on March 17, and the re-issuing of lava from the Ahuán area, the only activity seen for months on Mesa de Los Hornitos had been the gradual forming of a hogback ridge rising up to 15 m above the surrounding cold lava field. In one week the new flow had reached the base of the hills SW of the outer limits of the earlier flows. The broad front sent lobes to the NW and SE along the margin of the lava field.

During the first two weeks in September only the southernmost one of the four lobes in the vicinity of Cerro de Jarátiro remained active. This lobe was fed by a stream about 5 m wide that originated near the base of a fumarole-topped hill between Cerro de Jarátiro and the volcano, and it followed the south and west base of Jarátiro. From the same source a newer, smaller lobe was seen on September 16 to be riding slowly over old lava a few hundred meters east of the Upper Casita.

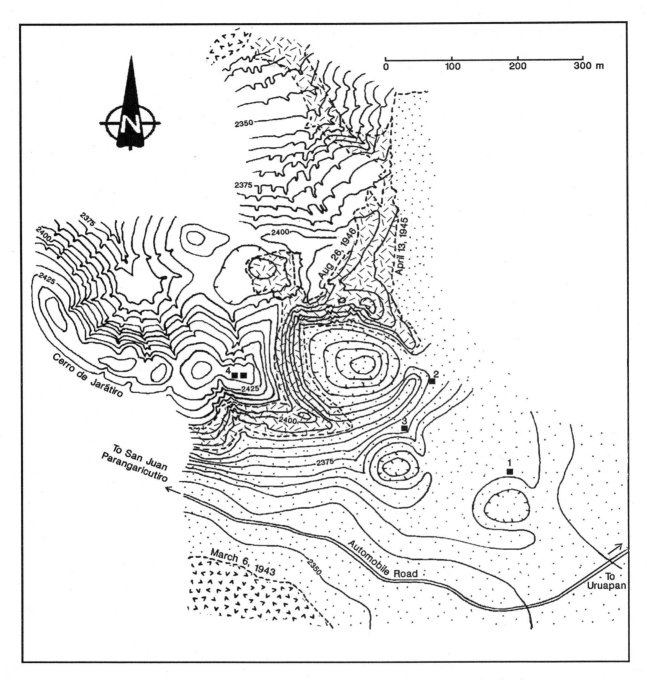

Fig. 108. Topographic map of Cerro de Jarátiro, 1½ km north of Parícutin volcano, showing the extent of the lava field on March 6, 1943, April 13, 1945, and August 26, 1946. Numbered squares indicate successive positions of observatory cabins. The No. 4 cabins were in turn moved 400 m farther west in January 1947.

A temporary resurgence of the lava near the east end of the flow of July 12 to August 7 was on September 18 sending out two short narrow lobes over old lava, toward the remaining uncovered part of a peninsula of virgin land. The *boca* of the flow south of Ahuán, which had commenced on August 8, had migrated by September 18 about 50 m south, and the still-moving lava front had advanced to a point approximately due south of the easternmost edge of the base of the cone.

Figure 106 shows the Parícutin lava flows from March 17 to August 31, 1946; it does not include the September flows described above.

Studies by Wilcox and Others (1946-48)

September 18 to November 30, 1946

Wilcox (1947a)

Ray Wilcox[61] (Fig. 109) entered the University of Wisconsin to major in mechanical engineering, but by the end of his sophomore year had become fascinated with geology and switched majors. After receiving his B.Sc. degree in geology in 1933, the lack of jobs in the midst of the depression convinced him to stay in school. He subsequently obtained a Masters degree in mineralogy and petrology from Wisconsin in 1937, and for his Ph.D. dissertation Wilcox investigated a mixed rhyolite-basalt complex in Yellowstone Park[62]. He studied under the famous mineralogist R.C. Emmons, receiving his Ph.D. in 1941. Wilcox spent the war years in the Army Signal Corps, stationed in Alaska. He was put in charge of Army studies at Okmok Volcano on Umnak Island when it erupted in 1943, which whetted his appetite for research at active volcanoes. Wilcox returned to Washington D.C. at the end of the war and was in the right place at the right time when the U.S. Geological Survey and the U.S. Committee for the Study of Parícutin Volcano decided to formalize observations at Parícutin; he was named as the "permanent observer" of Parícutin and arrived at the volcano on September 18, 1946. As mentioned earlier, Wilcox and colleagues wrote six reports, covering the evolution of the eruption until July 31, 1948. His wife and young son lived in Uruapan during those years, where Wilcox would join them on weekends. A daughter was born in México City in 1947. He moved to Denver after the Parícutin assignment in 1948 with many specimens that he had collected, and from these and donations by Foshag, Krauskopf, Fries, and others, he built the extensive suite of more than 125 specimens that formed the basis of his classic petrologic study, reprinted later in this book (p. 324-346).

This report consists primarily of the graph of eruptive characteristics (Fig. 110), and lava flow maps (Figs. 111-113). Since most of the generalities and details of the activity can be obtained by examination of these figures, the written portion of the report will deal only with points of special interest in the figures and with information not there represented.

Graph of eruptive characteristics
Figure 110 shows graphically the day-by-day variations in the activity of the volcano together with other possibly related phenomena. Although the time scale of Fig. 110 is quantitative, the values expressed on the vertical scales of those portions pertaining to the eruptive activity itself are necessarily qualitative. In setting up convenient vertical scales for the amounts of lava and pyroclastics, the expression "very great" was chosen to represent the same order of magnitude as that of the most intense eruption of Parícutin volcano in the past. The measure of this quantity was established by co-observation and discussion with several long-time observers of the

volcano, notably Ezequiel Ordóñez and Celedonio Gutiérrez.

The height of the eruptive column may be taken as a rough measure of the kinetic and thermal energy of the eruption from the cone, but at times this criterion fails completely because of strong winds and possibly other meteorological factors that do not allow the column to mature to its ideal height.

Noises accompanying the eruption from the cone are usually characteristic for each phase of eruption and are shown in Fig. 110 by letter symbols, explanations of which are shown in Table 1.

Since the beginning of his observations of the volcano, Ordóñez [see p. 63-65] has used a classification of eruptive activity originally based on the characteristic noise accompanying each phase. The noise types listed in Table 1 fit into the classification by Ordóñez about as follows: A and B, in the ideal case, accompany the silent phase; C, D, or E, and sometimes H, accompany the tubular phase, and F and G, or H accompany the gaseous phase.

Variations in tidal force and barometric pressure, phenomena that have been suggested as possible factors affecting volcanic activity, are shown above the eruptive characteristics of Fig. 110. Barometric pressures were plotted from hourly readings of a fixed aneroid barometer at the Lower Casitas, 5½ km north of the cone. Maximum and minimum values of tide-producing force, computed for the locality of Parícutin volcano by the U.S. Coast and Geodetic Survey, were plotted and the intervening values sketched. Although a thorough analysis of these data has not yet been made, preliminary study does not seem to show a consistent correlation of the activity of Parícutin volcano with either barometric pressure or tidal force during the period September 18 to November 30, 1946.

Activity of the Cone

During this period, as shown in Fig. 110, the eruption of pyroclastics from the cone was generally erratic, and the amount erupted changed abruptly many times from one extreme to the other. The emission of vapors was great, regardless of the amount of pyroclastics.

The character of the crater on September 18 has been described by Segerstrom and Gutiérrez (see p. 142-143). On October 22 the form of the crater was that of a simple inverted cone, 140 m deep, with three vents spaced within a radius of 20 m at the bottom. These vents emitted strong jets of yellowish-white vapors, accompanied by little ash and few bombs. On November 1 the crater was bowl-shaped and only

Fig. 109. Ray Wilcox and a tuna cactus in Valle de Santiago, Guanajuato, México, on October 7, 1948.

about 30 m in depth. By November 26 a conical crater had formed within the bowl-shaped crater and had extended the total depth to 100 m. At the bottom, multiple jets of vapor issued from incandescent perforations in a rock plug about 15 m in diameter.

The external form of the cone changed little during September 18 to November 30. All portions of the rim grew slightly, and the elevation of the highest point, the east rim, increased from 2,750.9 m above sea level on September 16 to 2,758.9 m on November 28 [all height estimates were based on triangulation surveys]. Sometime during the period November 26-29 occurred a limited collapse of a portion of the V-shaped notch between the cone proper and the SW segment of the cone that had been shoved outward in March, 1946. It is not known whether this collapse

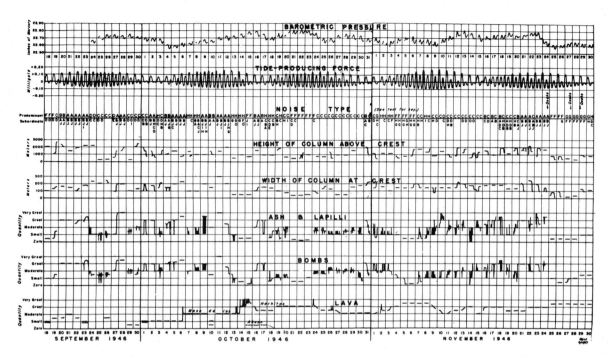

Fig. 110. Eruptive characteristics of Parícutin volcano from September 18 to November 30, 1946.

Table 1. Noise types of Fig. 110, diagram of eruptive characteristics.

Type	Description
A	Soft surging or swishing noise, barely audible at distances greater than 1 km
B	Loud and more profound surging noise than A, similar to heavy surf breaking on a shore
C	Thunder-like noise, rolling and reverberating, lasting 2-15 seconds, often initiated by heavier explosions
D	Noise like that of muffled heavy artillery fire
E	Noise like that of light artillery fire, sharper than D and often producing visible compression waves
F	A steady rushing roar, like the jet emission of steam under very high pressure, continuing uninterrupted for periods greater than 1 minute
G	Undulating noise of jet emission of steam under high pressure; this type often sounds like a distant, fast-moving railroad train, with the intensity and quality of the noise changing as the train passes irregularities in the terrain
H	Intermittent noise of jet emission of steam, usually harsher in quality than F or G; alternating periods of noise and silence range from 3-60 seconds in length, and at times are sufficiently regular in periodicity to resemble the slow chugging of a hard-pulling freight engine
I	Noise like that of a pistol shot, caused by discharge of electricity in the eruptive column
J	Flat slap noise, caused by falling volcanic bombs; with many bombs falling, the noise resembles the confused beat of horses' hoofs
O	Complete lack of noise for more than 5 minutes

and the associated collapse of the crest of the then defunct Ahuán vent were related to sharp earthquakes felt at Cuezeño [Lower Casitas, 5½ km north of cone] on November 24 and 27 and at Angahuan [7 km NNE of cone] on November 29. Erosional rills, an uncommon feature, were noted on the eastern flank of the cone November 11, and by November 29 many had attained a depth of 30 cm.

Activity of the Lava Vents

Figure 110 shows the relative rates of lava production from the vents. The Ahuán vent, at the SSW base of the cone, displayed declining activity during the latter part of September and finally ceased about October 18. The Mesa de Los Hornitos vent, 100 m from the WSW base of the cone, was the major producing vent during the period of this report. Its rate of lava production was only small to moderate until October 13. From October 13-15 a series of brilliant lava fountains occurred at this vent, building up an arc-shaped spatter cone 10 m in height. The conelet, however, was gradually destroyed in the ensuing weeks by the steady flow of lava from the vent area. The strong lava fountaining of October 13-15 coincided with a temporary decrease in the amount of pyroclastics erupted from the cone, and a period of strong lava production November 5-8 coincided with a similar decrease in pyroclastics from the cone.

Activity of the Lava Flows

The maps of Figs. 111-113 show the areas covered by lava during September, October, and November. In September (Fig. 111) the pincer-like flow that partially surrounded Cerro de Jarátiro was the continuation of an Ahuán vent flow of August that had circled the east base of the main cone and Sapichu. The small flow, 1 km NW of Curínguaro, was the dying movement of another Ahuán vent flow of August. During September three flows locally passed the previous limits of the lava field.

The flows of October (Fig. 112) were mainly from the Mesa de Los Hornitos vent, located on a divide WSW of the main cone. Because of this situation on the divide, the flows from the Mesa de Los Hornitos

Fig. 111. Areas covered by Parícutin lava flows, September, 1946.

vent took up various initial courses, depending upon which side of the vent mound they spilled over. Whereas the September flow had been southward, the October flows first went westward, and then northwestward and northward. One flow, following the western edge of the lava field, cut behind and isolated the abandoned Canicjuata Observatory [labeled "Casita"].

During November (Fig. 113) the still-active flows of October continued an additional 800 m northward across the site of the buried village of Parícutin. Another flow, following the western border of the lava field for a distance of 2 km in the vicinity of Cerro de Canicjuata, overrode and destroyed Canicjuata Observatory. During the latter part of November a strong flow followed the west base of the main cone, completely covering a previous flow of November, and at the end of the month was spreading actively northward from the cone.

Fig. 112. Areas covered by Parícutin lava flows, October, 1946.

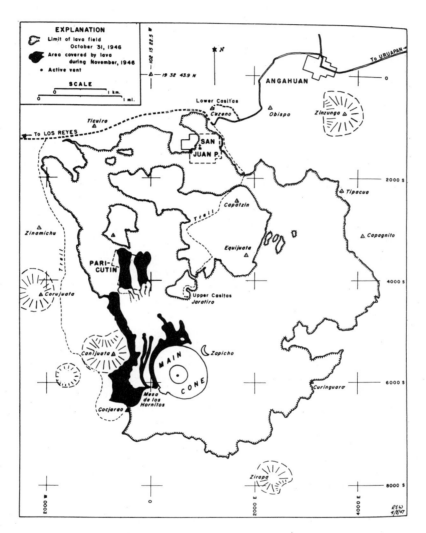

Fig. 113. Areas covered by Parícutin lava flows, November, 1946.

The surface structure of the flows from this period, September through November, consisted for the most part of rubble and jagged blocks of reddish-black basalt. This structure is typical of most of the previous flows of Parícutin volcano with the exception of the extensive San Juan flow of 1944 and local lobes of other flows, surfaces of which are made up of crags and large spines.

December 1, 1946 to March 31, 1947

Wilcox (1947b)

During this reporting interval . . . periods of predominantly heavy pyroclastic eruption occurred December 16 to February 14 and March 15 to 28, and periods of greater effusion of lava occurred December 1 to 20 and January 22 to February 25.

During January two segments of the cone slumped, one to the SW side and the other diametrically opposite on the NE side. A new lava vent was initiated at the base of each segment almost simultaneously with the slumping. The opening of the new vent at the NE base marked the first time since the death of the old Sapichu vent in January, 1944 that lava issued from that side of the cone.

Although a thorough analysis of the observational data has not yet been made, preliminary study does not seem to show a consistent correlation of the activity of Parícutin volcano with either barometric pressure or tide-producing force during the period December 1, 1946 to March 31, 1947. Complementary activity of the cone and the lava vents, while suggested at times, likewise does not appear to be consistent enough to form a basis for conclusions.

A provisional observatory was built in December and January at Cocjarao station, 800 m SW of the base of the cone [shown on Fig. 114 and later referred to as the "SW Casita"]. The Upper Casita at Jarátiro station, menaced by a December lava flow, were moved and rebuilt as one unit in January at a higher point about 300 m west of Jarátiro station.

Activity of the Cone

During the first half of December the activity was characterized by strong explosions with small to moderate amounts of ash and moderate to great amounts of bombs. On December 10, my companions and I, then at Jorullo volcano, 81 km SE of Parícutin,

could hear ponderous explosions apparently originating at Parícutin volcano. The data of Gutiérrez, examined later, indicated that the explosions of December 10 were of exceptional intensity.

A suggestion of periodic variation in the generally heavy eruption occurred during December 19-31, in which period a brief decrease in the quantity of pyroclastics occurred at intervals of 2-3 days, but this apparent periodicity was not carried on into January and February.

On February 15 the heavy eruption of pyroclastics ceased abruptly, and during March 1-10 the pyroclastic activity was the weakest that I had witnessed. On March 15 the heavy pyroclastic activity was suddenly resumed without preliminary symptoms and continued generally heavy through the end of the month.

Form of the Crater and Cone

The form of the crater on February 18 was that of a 40-m-deep bowl, in the bottom of which a steep cone-shaped inner crater extended down another 20 m. On the lower part of the SW wall of the inner crater was a group of closely spaced incandescent jets, from which dense vapors and some incandescent ash and bombs issued with great force. The NE and SW rims of the crater were sharp whereas the SE and NW rims were crescentic platforms. On February 24 the form of the crater had not changed except the vents were then capped by a perforated rock plug, through which the vapors issued with the same intensity as that of February 18. On March 13, Ariel Hernández-Velasco reported that the crater still had the form of a cone-within-a-bowl, and much vapor was issuing from cracks in the SW wall as well as from the vents proper.

The external form of the cone changed markedly during this 4-month period. On December 4 two sets of steam cracks converging downward were observed on the SW flank of the cone in the same positions as the borders of the segment of the cone that had been shoved outward in March, 1946. On January 14 or 15 the segment of the cone between the steam cracks slumped, leaving scarps about 2 m in height extending down the side of the cone, and at the same time the new "Puertecito" lava vent opened at the base of the slumped segment. Slight additional slumping and sagging of this segment occurred during ensuing weeks, depressing the SW rim an estimated total of 10 m below its original elevation.

Diametrically opposite, a segment of the NE flank of the cone slumped January 13, the bordering fractures first appearing at the top of the cone and extending farther down the flank from day to day. On January 19 a portion of the base of the slumped segment, exactly in line radially with the old Sapichu vent, was pushed and rotated outward to open the new "Sapichu" vent, (later named the "Noreste" or "Juatito" vent by the Mexican investigators). Additional slumping and sagging of the NE segment during January and February totaled about 7 m at the rim.

Activity of the Lava Vents

During December the only lava vents active were those of the Mesa de Los Hornitos area. By the end of January these vents had stagnated, together with the briefly rejuvenated Ahuán vent. The main bulk of the lava production was taken over by the Puertecito vent [Fig. 115] . . . . The new Sapichu vent . . . produced a steady but very small amount of lava during January and February. The areas of the Mesa de Los Hornitos and the Ahuán vents [Fig. 115], although producing no lava flows during February, increased in height an estimated 10 to 20 m during the early part of February, evidently due to slow extrusions and to intrusion below the surface. The main producer in February continued to be the Puertecito vent, but on March 2 it stagnated at the same time that strong activity was begun at the Juatito vent.

Thus the period January 13 to March 2 was one of reorientation of the lava activity at the volcano. Four vents were active simultaneously during the initial stages of slumping of the cone segments in January, and it is notable that the Juatito vent, 100 m lower in elevation than the Puertecito vent and therefore apparently more favorably situated, played a minor role in lava production for almost a month and a half before taking the lead.

Activity of the Lava Flows

The lava flows of December are shown in Fig. 114 and those of January through March are combined in Fig. 115. During December a flow

from the Mesa de Los Hornitos vents sent tongues on either side of Cerro de Jarátiro and only stopped just before reaching the Upper Casita. During February the persistent fumaroles on the ash-covered hills between Jarátiro and the cone, landmarks for three years, were buried by the flow from the Puertecito vent. By March 31 the still-moving Sapichu flow had exceeded the previous lava limit between Cerro de Jarátiro and Cerro de Equijuata and had cut the horse trail leading to the Upper Casita.

Structurally the flows from the Mesa de Los Hornitos, Ahuán, and Puertecito vents were similar to the majority of the previous Parícutin flows, having a surface of reddish-brown rubble and cinders. The surface of the slow-moving Sapichu flow of January and February, on the other hand, was composed of large dense blocks and extrusions, black in color. After this flow had gained speed in March, the

Fig. 114. Areas covered by Parícutin lava flows, December, 1946.

153

Fig. 115. Areas covered by Parícutin lava flows, January 1 to March 31, 1947.

changed from time to time, and occasionally one vent would be erupting pyroclastics while another would be discharging only vapors.

Form of the Cone and Crater

The only observation of the interior of the crater during the period of this report was made on June 9 by Samuel Shoup-Oropeza, who reported that the crater bottom was about 150 m below the west rim, with the saddle-like SW rim being especially sharp. Three vents about 2 m in diameter were situated somewhat SW of the geometrical center of the crater along a NE-SW line about 15 m in length. A fourth vent, 1 m in diameter, was offset about 8 m to the SE of the SW portion of this line.

. . . . .

The piling up of successive lava flows about the base of the cone has caused a marked decrease in relief of the cone during the last two years, in spite of the actual slow increase in altitude of the rim, as illustrated by the triangulation data in Table 2.

Activity of the Lava Vents

Only the Juatito vents, located along a fracture zone bearing slightly east of north from the NE base of the cone (see Fig. 116), produced lava during April 1 to July 31, and the rate of lava production was more erratic than usual. The amount of lava erupted during July was the smallest observed for any similar period since the present program of observation began in September 1946.

From April 1 to 13 the two lava vents closest to the cone on the fracture zone were active. On April 13 gigantic fountaining from the vent at the immediate NE base marked its temporary cessation of activity, and at the same time the vent situated about 150 m out from the base of the cone was opened with one single fountain surge, and this vent became the chief lava producer during the remainder of the period. The persistence of the location of the outermost vent, despite strong fluctuations in volume of flow, makes it probable that this is a true "primary" vent, as defined by Bullard[52], rather than simply the mouth of a crusted-over lava stream. Fumes issued strongly from the fracture zone connecting it with the base of

surface was composed of the more usual rubble and cinders.

April 1 to July 31, 1947

Wilcox (1948a)

Activity of the Cone

The eruption of pyroclastics . . . was very erratic in May, June, and July. Periods of intense eruption were seldom more than a few hours' duration, and the changes from weak to intense pyroclastic eruption and vice versa were usually sudden and without recognizable preliminary symptoms. The quantity and intensity of emission of vapors from the crater was generally great, regardless of the amounts of pyroclastics, except during July. The position and size of the individual discharge vents within the crater

Table 2. Changes in elevation of rim and base of cone from May 1945 to June 1947.

Location		Elevation		Increase
		May 1945	June 1947	
		m	m	m
Rim,	West peak	2730	2756	26
	NE saddle	2710	2737	27
	East peak	2740	2760	20
Base,	West base	2490	2584	94
	NE base	2460	2540	80
	SW base	2545	2638	93

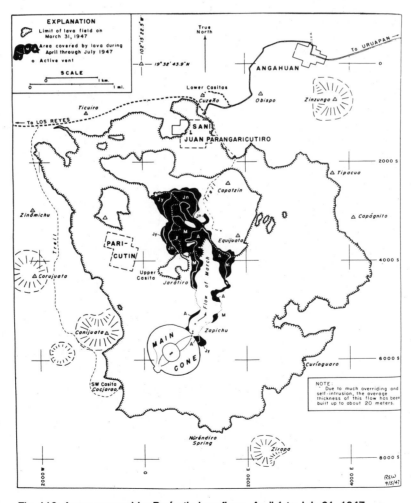

Fig. 116. Areas covered by Parícutin lava flows, April 1 to July 31, 1947.

the cone, and at intervals the minor vents situated along this fracture zone had brief periods of activity. The intermittent activity of the vent at the immediate NE base of the cone, notably the fountaining of lava on May 8 and 17, June 14, 18, and 22, July 8 and 11, built up the area until the section of cone pyroclastics that had been shoved outward with the original opening of the vent in January 1947 was almost buried.

Activity of the Lava Flows

The area covered by lava from April 1 to July 31, 1947 is shown on the map (Fig. 116). Except for the limited spreading of the lava around the vent at the NE base of the cone, the lava continued to flow northward in the channel established in March. The fronts of this main flow were extended, the lower reaches widened, and the thickness of the flow greatly increased by overriding and self-intrusion. During May the front split into four tongues that cascaded northward down the Jarátiro-Capatzun scarp, piling up and coalescing at the base. The spread of the flow eastward around Equijuata ceased in May. During June the main front spread westward and northward, augmenting its thickness over the areas already covered, and in July the rate of advance of the front greatly decreased. With the passage of the flow down the Jarátiro-Capatzun scarp, the trail to the Upper Casita at Cerro de Jarátiro was cut, and approach to the Upper Casita and the cone became more difficult.

August 1 to November 30, 1947

Wilcox and Shoup-Oropeza (1948)

Activity of the Cone

The erratic variations in the eruption of pyroclastics continued during August and November, with the periods of strong eruption of pyroclastics lengthening somewhat during October and November. At intervals, especially during August and September, several crater vents were active simultaneously, with differing amounts of pyroclastics and vapors issuing from the separate vents.

On August 10 and 11, extraordinarily intense explosions occurred, ejecting an ultra-fine buff-colored ash in addition to the normal pyroclastics. This ash, falling in the northern sector, blighted vegetation for a distance of 10 km from the volcano. It is possible that the blighting action was caused by the smothering of the plants by the ultra-fine ash. A sample of the still undisturbed ash was collected

August 15 and tested for chlorine, sulfurous and sulfuric ions, none of which was found to be present. It is possible that they might have escaped during the four days following the ashfall[63].

The explosions of August 10 and 11 were reported to have been of great strength, projecting bombs several hundred meters beyond the base of the cone. Frequent jumps of the barograph pen of 0.05 inches of mercury and greater were recorded as a result of the compression waves from the explosions. On September 26, a single gigantic explosion threw bombs as far as the base of Cerro de Canicjuata, a distance of 1 km from the center of the main cone.

A temporary pyroclastic vent was opened near the top of the SW slump segment early in November (Fig. 117). On November 6, copious white vapors were observed issuing from the site, and on November 7, one short burst of ash and bombs was erupted almost without noise, leaving a shallow crater from which white vapors issued intermittently. On November 15, another brief eruption of pyroclastics was observed. Subsequently no more than vapors were observed to be erupted.

Form of the Cone and Crater

An inner crater rim, which for some months had been building up within the main crater, passed the level of the outer rim about October 20. Thenceforth, with the continued growth of this inner rim, the altitude of the cone increased rapidly . . . . The diameter of the inner rim on November 30 was about 220 m, compared to the 300 m diameter of the outer rim, by then, almost obliterated.

A steep-walled pit, about 6 m in diameter and 8 m in depth, formed September 4 at the site of the similar pit of July 5 near the top of the NE slump segment, but was refilled with pyroclastics within three weeks. In an analogous position on the SW slump segment an intermittently active pyroclastic vent was initiated early in November (see above), forming a shallow crater never more than 4 m in depth when observed. By November 30 it had been filled with pyroclastics. The bordering fractures of the NE slump segment were renewed from time to time but no appreciable downward movement of the segment was observed.

Activity of the Lava Vents

On August 11 the NE vents increased their activity. On August 14 the Puertecito vent, at the base of the SW slump segment, became strongly active, but by August 28 had declined to only slight activity. On September 1 the Ahuán lava vent, about 100 m south of the Puertecito vent at the SSW base of the cone, opened and was thereafter the chief lava producer. The NE vents showed only slight activity during September and none at all after October 9.

The Ahuán lava vent steadily increased in height because of brief floodings of the vent mound. The altitude of the vent on November 7 was 2,654.2 m above sea level, 8.8 m higher than on August 28. The persistent channel leading south out of the vent mound was well exposed November 30 when the level of the lava stream had dropped greatly, revealing a channel 10 m in width and more than 7 m deep.

Activity of the Lava Flows

The long flow from March to July (Fig. 117), which had proceeded north from the NE lava vents, slowed to a virtual stop during August, although negligible movements continued during September. On August 16 a new flow started east from the outermost of the NE vents and continued to extend its front until the middle of September. A short flow pushed NW from the innermost vent during September[64].

The initial flow from the Puertecito vent, at the base of the SW slump segment, started August 14 and proceeded rapidly around the west base of the cone, following the drained channel of the flow from January to March. Its movement stopped August 19 while lava continued to spread south and SE from the vent during the remainder of August. The flow from the Ahuán vent started September 1 and spread with great rapidity on a wide front to the SE. Although the whole of the front remained active during October and November, the forward advance became subordinate to the process of building up the thickness of the flow. The movement of this flow, instead of being in a few selected channels, was radially from the base of the vent mound, forming a surface of large concentric waves.

Fig. 117. Areas covered by Parícutin lava flows, August 1 to November 30, 1947.

The front was usually 10-13 m in height and composed of blocky reddish lava. A noteworthy characteristic of the front was the continuous snapping and popping noise of small flakes spalling off the cooling blocks. On November 30 all of the front showed activity, and the most rapid movement was in the lobe spreading NE. The SE lobe had approached to within 30 m of Nuréndiro Spring [Fig. 117].

A new trail was built during November across the lava field to the Upper Casita at Cerro de Jarátiro. A deep gully formed during the wet season made it necessary to reach the SW Casita by crossing the lava between Cerro de Canicjuata and the main cone rather than circling behind Canicjuata.

December 1, 1947 to March 31, 1948

Wilcox (1948b)

Parícutin volcano . . . completed its fifth year of activity on February 20, 1948. During this fifth year the eruption was of the same order of intensity as that of the preceding year and consisted of almost constant lava outpouring with intermittent pyroclastic activity. No symptoms of an early termination of the activity were discernible.

. . . . .

Activity of the Cone

During December and January the pyroclastic activity of the cone was extremely erratic, and periods of strong activity rarely lasted more than a few hours. Frequent pyroclastic explosions took place, even during the periods of generally weak activity, and usually followed momentary complete cessations of activity. As in previous months, the variations in the eruption were too frequent to be adequately represented on the scale of the diagram of eruptive characteristics. Eruption was often from multiple vents in the crater, and on one occasion, January 8, the temporary pyroclastic vent on the SW flank [see p. 156] was active for several hours.

Soon after the opening of the new lava vent at the NE base of the cone, February 7, the pyroclastic activity of the cone became noticeably less erratic, and the ratio of bombs to ash decreased greatly. The nocturnal displays of bomb showers became less spectacular, and on many nights no glow could be seen reflected from the crater.

Form of the Cone and Crater

During December and January the interior of the crater was not observed. On February 16 the crater had the form of a shallow funnel about 60 m in depth, and portions of the crater had subsided slightly inside a rim fracture. The one active vent was somewhat SW of the geometrical center, erupting a small amount of ash and bombs at intervals. On February 20, according to Ivan Wilson [Fig. 10], the crater was perhaps 75 m in depth, with a sharp serrated rim and steep walls. Along a NE-SW line at the bottom were three vents, of which only the central one, about 5 m in diameter, was active during observation. On March 11 the crater was more than 100 m in depth, and engulfment of portions of the rim had developed an even more serrated lip. Just outside the west rim a narrow crack extended partway around the cone. Two crater vents were active, again

along a NE-SW line, the NE one emitting vapors and the SW one emitting ash.

Bomb-eroded rills on the cone flanks had been noted occasionally in the past, but they were not as outstanding as the regularly spaced gullies developed during December and January. About 15 of these gullies, as much as 3 m in depth, were gradually eroded in the steam-saturated portion of the upper NW flank, each starting about 10 m below the rim and extending ⅓ the distance down the flank. Coalescing depositional fans spread downward from the lower end of each gully. Although bomb showers were equally frequent on other flanks, no other gullies developed. With the decrease in quantity of bombs during February and March, the sharpness of relief of the NW gullies decreased.

. . . . .

The general increase of the cone's height that had continued for many months ended in February 1948 with the beginning of a phase of engulfment. Probably about 5 m of the decrease in elevation of the NE rim after January 31 can be accounted for by subsiding and sagging of the slump segment, while the remainder was caused by engulfment.

Activity of the Lava Vents

The Ahuán lava vent, on the SSW flank of the cone (Fig. 118), was in general strongly active up to the first part of February. Due to occasional surges of lava that flooded the vent mound, its height increased 27 m during the period August 28 to January 30 and finally reached an elevation of 2,672 m, only about 90 m less than that of the SW rim of the crater. During most of this time the lava cascaded southward out of the vent mound through a persistent channel, seen at times of low activity to have a cross section about 10 m wide by 7 m or more deep. The Puertecito lava vent, at the immediate SW base of the cone, was active only during the first few days in February, and the amount of lava produced was negligible. The site of the Mesa de Los Hornitos vent during January cracked and swelled slightly, and hot, relatively dry vapors were emitted. Contrary to expectations, however, it was not this vent, but the vent at the NE base of the cone that opened soon after.

The opening of the NE vent was preceded on February 6 by a renewal of subsidence between the bordering fractures of the NE slump segment. On the evening of February 7 a pinpoint glow was noted on the NE flank about 20 m above the site of the previous NE vent (January-September 1947). Within ½ hour the lava was cascading down the flank in large quantities but no fountaining occurred. This spot became the new lava's vent and after February 12 no activity was observed at the Ahuán vent. The NE vent increased in elevation from time to time due to flooding, and gradually developed as a protuberance at the base of the cone. By the end of March the vent had risen 21 m to an elevation of 2,584 m, or 174 m below the level of the NE rim. On March 10 a section of the north side of the vent mound was shoved out during strong fountaining and made an outlet channel down which lava cascaded for the remainder of the month.

Activity of the Lava Flows

As seen in Fig. 118, the flow from the Ahuán (SSW) vent, [active since Sept. 1] continued to spread widely in its NE lobe during December, January, and February, but no movement of its SE lobe took place after December. This flow was notable for its great thickness (about 18 m average) and its tendency to spread radially, leaving great concentric waves on its surface. The surface structure consisted of the blocky and cindery rubble normal to most Parícutin flows.

The flow from the NE vent, starting February 7, had reached the brink of the Jarátiro-Capatzun scarp by the end of February. By March 17 it had cut the newly built trail to the Upper Casita, and at the end of March its front was advancing into the "island" occupied by Parícutin triangulation station [Fig. 118]. The thickness of this

Fig. 118. Areas covered by Parícutin lava flows, December 1, 1947 to March 31, 1948.

flow was normal, averaging probably less than 9 m, and the surface structure was typical blocky rubble. The average rate of advance of the front was about 55 m/day, somewhat greater than normal for a Parícutin flow of this length and breadth.

April 1 to July 31, 1948

Wilcox and Gutiérrez (1948)

Activity of the Cone

The pyroclastic activity of the main cone during this period was generally weak. The only prolonged strong eruptions of pyroclastics occurred June 11-13, 29-30, and July 22-29. Vapors continued to be given off strongly, however, during much of the time when the pyroclastic eruptions were weak.

Occasionally there were periods characterized by puff-like eruptions of ash and bombs, too brief to be represented on [the diagram of eruptive characteristics: i.e. Table 1]; these occurred notably April 7, May 17-21, June 9, and July 1-2, 6-8, and 30. A single explosion of great intensity on May 25 threw bombs to a distance of more than 1 km in the NW quadrant from the crater vent. These puffs were similar to the frequent pyroclastic explosions of December 1947 and January 1948 [see p. 158], but were for the most part less intense. The normal sequence leading up to an explosion of this type was a gradual decrease in the quantity of ash for a period of 5-15 minutes, often followed by an apparent complete cessation of eruptions for a minute or two, and then a sudden grand burst of ash and bombs that might continue for 5 minutes or more before moderating.

On ascending the cone May 17, a single crater vent clogged with viscous lava was seen, which was periodically blown out in part and torn into shreds by the strong surges of vapors. The bombs so ejected were highly vesicular and, on landing, some were still plastic enough to flatten. This type of bomb, the surface of which is light brown, differs from the black, usually more dense and less plastic bombs that accompany heavy ash eruptions.

Form of the Cone

On May 17 the interior of the crater was a shallow bowl with a single vent set in a funnel-shaped depression about 30 m in greatest diameter. The NE and SW rims of the crater were low, and the NW and SE rims rose to a height of about 70 m above the bottom of the bowl.

During the period covered by this report only minor changes occurred in the external form of the cone, except for the slumping of a portion of the SW flank brought about by the collapse in April of the area around the Puertecito lava vent (see below). The bordering fractures of the NE slump segment of the cone were reopened from time to time, but those of the old SW slump segment were not observed to reappear. The bomb-eroded rills present on the NW flank in January (see p. 158) were still visible in May, although greatly subdued.

. . . . .

Activity of the Lava Vents

The lava vent at the NE base of the cone was the only active one during the period of this report, and its nearly continuous production varied generally from moderate to great . . . . With repeated overflowing of the vent and the outlet channels, the vent mound rose to form a separate conelet at the base of the main cone. The outlet channel to the north, which had persisted since May 10, clogged June 4-5 during a temporary lull in the flow of lava, and thereafter all the lava cascaded down the NE flank of the vent mound in a channel that had been carrying some lava since May 25. On July 10 the lava abandoned this latter channel and flowed down to the NW face of the mound. A fresh cascade down the north face began July 28, while the NW cascade continued.

Two strong explosions at the lava vent occurred May 16, tearing apart huge masses of viscous lava and scattering them for distances up to 60 m from the vent. These explosions, separated by an interval of 3 hours, were of an intensity much greater than any witnessed previously by us at the lava vent and took place during a period when the flow of lava had become abnormally sluggish.

During April 1 to July 31 no lava was observed to come from the vents at the SW base of the cone. A large collapse of the Puertecito vent, at the immediate SW base of the cone, occurred sometime before April 22. On May 17 the roughly circular border of this collapsed area was about 70 m in diameter, and the bottom was about 40 m below the level of the western edge. The walls, where not composed of rubble and talus, showed massive lava. The NE edge of the collapse had encroached on the cone proper and had drawn down a portion of the cone material. No fumarolic activity of appreciable magnitude was observed within the depression, although hot vapors issued from a fractured zone that extended along the base of the cone for a distance of about 40 m NW from the collapse.

The medial portion of the Ahuán lava vent, 100 m SSE of the Puertecito vent, likewise collapsed to form a depression about 30 m long. The Mesa de Los Hornitos lava vent [on the WSW flank] did not undergo any recognizable change in form during this period, although it continued to give off hot vapors.

Activity of the Lava Flows

The areas invaded by new lava are shown in solid black in Fig. 119. The flow of February and March continued to advance northwestward but in decreasing monthly increments until it ceased entirely the latter part of June. This flow, with a total length of about 4,100 m, is the longest flow in 2 years. A lobe started NE of the vent May 25, and by the end of July, when movement had virtually ceased, its length was about 2 km. With the change of the lava cascade to the NW flank of the vent mound July 10, a new lobe started northward over the February flow, and its active front had reached almost to the western base of Cerro de Jarátiro by the end of July. A narrow lobe (not differentiated on Fig. 119) fed by the newly opened north outlet channel started NNE July 28 and had advanced about 400 m by July 31.

The lava movement was sluggish, and as usual, the flows developed mantles of coarse red-brown rubble. On several occasions sharp gas discharges from the moving lava near the source threw fragments as much as 15 m into the air. Sharp pistol-like discharges frequently were heard from the lower reaches of the flow as a result of spalling and flaking of cool blocks.

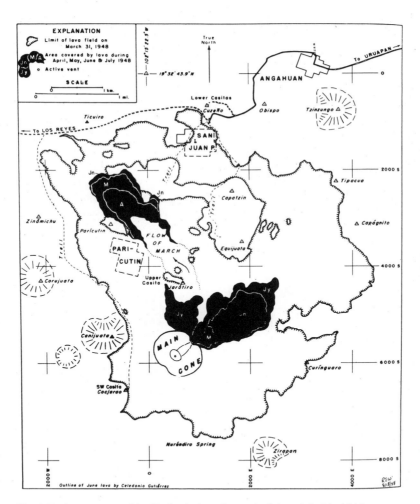

Fig. 119. Areas covered by Parícutin lava flows, April 1 to July 31, 1948.

Studies by Fries and Gutiérrez (1948-52)

August 1, 1948 to June 30, 1949

Fries and Gutiérrez (1950a)

Carl Fries, Jr.[65] (Fig. 120) studied geology at the University of Wisconsin in Madison, where he received his Bachelor's degree in geology in 1937 and a Master's degree in 1939, with a specialty in economic and structural geology. Fries joined the U.S. Geological Survey in 1939, and was involved in projects examining deposits of tin in New Mexico and Nevada and topaz in South Carolina. In February 1942 he joined a group of U.S. geologists working in México under a technical assistance program headed by William Foshag. Parícutin volcano erupted the following year. In 1945, Fries was named Chief of the Mexican office of the U.S. Geological Survey, a position that he held for the next 12 years. During those years, Fries developed a great love for both the land and the people of México. He was widely admired as a scientist, an administrator, and a good-will ambassador. He and the U.S. and Mexican geologists working with him produced many important studies concerning the minerals and geology of México. Fries became heavily involved in documenting the Parícutin eruption in August 1948, following the return of Ray Wilcox to the U.S. He maintained that involvement until the end of the eruption 3½ years later. Fries worked closely with Celedonio Gutiérrez (Figs. 14 and 120: biography on p. 48), the "resident observer" of those years, and the two men co-authored seven reports, reprinted below, that cover the last years of the eruption.

In 1957 Fries dropped to part-time status with the U.S. Geological Survey while he pursued a Ph.D. degree at the University of Arizona, awarded in 1959. He then took a research position at the Geology Institute of the Mexican National University, where he remained until his death on July 11, 1965. During those years he continued his studies of Mexican geology, and is credited with having established the first laboratory in México for the radiometric dating of rocks.

This brief biography was drawn from the memorial by Salas[66] and from Fries et al[66].

Activity of the Cone

During the period covered by this report, Parícutin passed its sixth birthday (February 20), continuing to perform on much the same scale as in the previous two years. On the whole, the quantity of ash erupted continued to decrease, as judged from the recorded ashfall . . . and the new lava from early 1948 onward is still nearly bare of ash, but eruption of vapors and bombs continued with roughly the same intensity as the year before. The eruptive column rose at times to heights of more than 3,000 m above the rim of the crater; periods of complete quiescence were few and lasted generally no more than a few minutes before eruptive activity resumed. The most heavily charged pyroclastic eruptions were accompanied by flashes of lightning within the column, as in former years, and occurred on 1-5 days of each month of the period covered.

Fig. 120. Carl Fries (right) on the seventh anniversary of the birth of Parícutin volcano (Feb. 20, 1950). Also present (from left to right) are Celedonio Gutiérrez, Ricardo Monges-López, Pedro Gutiérrez, Fredrick H. Pough, and Lazaro Victoriano. Parícutin volcano in upper left.

Eruptions came in large part from a single vent in the center of the crater, although two vents were seen when the cone was ascended on May 19, 1949 . . . . This condition contrasts with the almost constant presence, in former years, of two or more vents in the bottom of the crater.

In the period January 4-9, 1949, a series of tremendous explosions occurred that could be heard as far as 200 km from the volcano, and earth tremors were frequent in a radius of several kilometers from the cone. On April 2 and 5, 1949, other intense explosions could be heard as far as Pátzcuaro, 69 km east. Similar explosions that shook the earth occurred on May 13 and on June 11, 13, 20, and 28-30, 1949. The explosion of June 13 apparently tore out the center of the crater, for blocks 1-2 m in diameter, of reddish-brown slightly welded rubble, were hurled several hundred meters beyond the base of the cone in the west quadrant, and smaller blocks were found more than 1 km from the cone. Such explosions compare with the strongest eruptions of the first year of Parícutin's activity, though now they come singly and at widely spaced intervals.

Form of the Cone and Crater

The NE flank of the cone continued to slump intermittently during the period covered, possibly as a result of a simple erosion of the roof of the lava tube, or possibly by partial plugging of the lava vent and its forceful reopening by lava pushing through the flank of the cone. Minor slumps occurred on August 12, 1948, and again on October 14, 1948, and others appeared on November 28, 1948, and February 16, 1949, but from then until the end of June, no movement of consequence was noted. The deep depression at the SW base of the cone, formed by collapse of the lava-vent area in April 1948 (see p. 160), was gradually being filled with pyroclastic material erupted from the crater. The bomb-eroded rills on the NW flank of the cone, mentioned in the last report (see p. 160), were also filled in and have nearly disappeared. Lava flowing to the NW and SE buried a part of the base of the cone in the NE quadrant, so that the visible area covered by the cone was slightly smaller by the end of the period.

The crater, as usual, continued to show great variations in both form and depth. On the ascent of January 27, 1949, the eruptions were so violent that all of the crater could not be seen, but the central part appeared to be a single bowl about 40 m deep, situated in the center of the cone and surrounded by a broad terrace a few meters lower than the outer rim. There appeared to be a single wide throat. On March 30, 1949, the terrace was broader and the central bowl was shallower, probably not more than 25 m deep. The single throat consisted of a nearly vertical hole in the bottom of the bowl, with a diameter of about 5 m at the top and about 3 m at the point where it dropped out of sight. On the ascent of May 19, 1949, the terraces were still narrower and at nearly the same height as the outer rim of the cone . . . . The central part of the crater consisted of a double bowl aligned in a NE-SW direction and divided by a narrow, very low ridge. The bottom of the double bowl was about 20 m below the NE saddle and showed two small throats from 1 to 3 m in diameter, and several smaller openings. Eruptions from the two main throats were not of the same character; the SW throat erupted ash and bombs and the NE throat erupted only vapors. However, the two vents reacted nearly alike to changes in eruptive intensity. The SW throat was by far the stronger of the two, and the walls around it were caving actively. On the ascent of July 6, 1949, made soon enough after the end of the period covered by this report to indicate the form of the crater on June 30, 1949, the entire central part of the crater was

occupied by a conical mound and the lowest part of the interior of the crater was no more than 5 or 6 m below the saddles . . . . The single, nearly vertical throat was about 6 m across. A possibly similar process occurred in 1947 with the building up of an inner cone, the crater rim diameter of which, however, was about ⅔ that of the main outer rim (see p. 156). By October, 1947, the elevation of the inner rim surpassed that of the outer rim, and shortly thereafter the flanks of the inner cone coalesced with those of the main cone.

Activity of the Lava Vents

During the period covered by this report, lava continued to issue without interruption from the vent that formed at the NE base of the cone on February 7, 1948 (see p. 158-159), while the vent area at the SW base of the cone remained inactive. At the beginning of August this NE vent occupied the top of a low mound from which lava flowed in two cascades, toward the north and NW. By August 12, 1948, the NW cascade had ceased, but lava continued to flow toward the north until September 5, 1948, when it too ceased and a new east-flowing cascade formed. During the rest of the period, repeated surges flooded the vent area and caused changes in the direction of the cascade, but always within the NE quadrant (see Figs. 121 and 122). These floodings gradually built up the vent mound from an elevation of 2,622 m above sea level at the end of July, 1948 to about 2,643 m at the end of June, 1949 . . . at which time the vent was only 119 m below the NE saddle of the cone and about 30 m below the old vent area at the SW base of the cone. Any appreciable future rise in the elevation of the NE vent, or plugging up of this vent by lava freezing, may possibly force the reopening of the SW vents.

Eruptions of gases and some ash and bombs occurred from time to time at the lava vent almost every month during the period covered. Some of these eruptions were so heavily charged with ash, bombs, and vapors that they appeared like miniature atomic-bomb blasts, par-

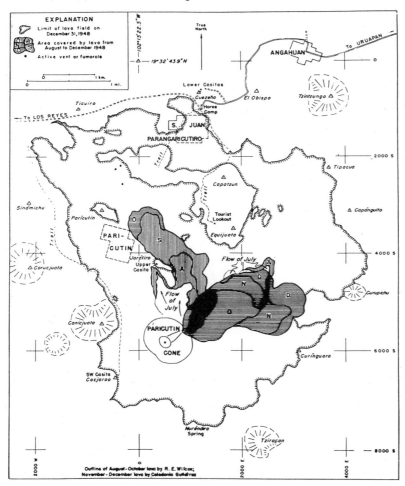

Fig. 121. Areas covered by Parícutin lava flows, August 1 to December 31, 1948.

ticularly as they always came in single puffs. These eruptions were much more frequent than in the earlier life of this vent. Other explosions at the lava vent were not accompanied by ash eruptions and resulted only in the hurling out of a scattering of pasty blobs of lava, or in puffs of blue vapors. On April 25, 1949, the only lava fountain observed during this period spurted to a height of several meters for about 5 minutes. At other times sudden surges caused the lava to spill over the top of the vent mound.

The depression at the SW base of the cone, where lava had formerly issued, was gradually being filled and the area showed almost no activity. At one place, however, gases rushed out of loose rubble at temperatures ranging probably as high as 500°C, for they ignited in a few seconds any combustible material placed in their path. Fumarolic activity in this area was moderately intense during the whole period, and some cracks appeared in the ash cover on the lava late in the spring. This indicates that some movement was probably occurring there, although it was not great enough to be measured by alidade from located stations.

Fig. 122. Areas covered by Parícutin lava flows, January 1 to June 30, 1949.

Activity of the Lava Flows

The rate of flow of lava at the vent from August, 1948 to January, 1949, was generally moderate to great, but early in February, 1949, the volume of lava decreased notably and remained smaller until the end of June. The NW-flowing lava stream continued to move at its front until late in October, 1948, although it had been cut off at its source nearly a month earlier, when an east-flowing cascade suddenly formed as a result of flooding. A small part of Cerro de Jarátiro and two islands of old ground to the north of Jarátiro were buried by the NW-flowing stream (see Fig. 121). From October to the end of June all the new lava moved toward the NE and east of the volcano, burying most of the peninsula of old ground that extended west from Curupichu (see Figs. 121 and 122). All the flows were of the normal type and were, as usual, mantled with angular reddish-brown rubble.

At their fronts they ranged from about 5 to 9 m in thickness. Slight movement occurred along the margins of some of the lobes as late as 3 months after the flows ceased to be fed from the vent.

July 1 to December 31, 1949

Fries and Gutiérrez (1950b)

Activity of the Cone

Eruptions from the crater continued, as in other years, to be extremely variable from hour to hour and from day to day . . . . Eruptive activity seemed, on the whole, to be slightly less intense than during the preceding half year. The eruptive column rose to heights of 3,000 m or more above the cone on only 8 days in July, 1 day in August, and 3 days in October, not reaching such heights during the rest of the period. Such strong eruptions were therefore less frequent than in former years, and periods of complete inactivity were moreover somewhat longer than usual. On November 28, for instance, eruptions ceased completely for 1 hour, and on December 23, the cone was inactive for 2 hours; periods of inactivity of less than 20 minutes were frequent. Emission of ash continued to decline, and only 1.8 mm fell at Cuezeño station [5½ km north], in constrast to 5.3 mm in the corresponding period of 1948. Heavily charged ash and bomb eruptions . . . were accompanied as usual by electric discharges within the column or from the column to the rim of the cone. Such discharges occurred on 2 days in July, 3 days in August, 3 days in September, 1 day in October, and 3 days in December, but they were less frequent than during the first half of 1949. At times the eruptive column was nearly invisible until it reached a height of 100 m or more above the cone, where it condensed into a thick whitish cloud of steam . . . a feature that has been noted at frequent times in former years. Eruptions seem to have issued from only one vent in the crater for the greater part of the period. Early in November, however, two distinct columns were visible, although when Gutiérrez ascended the cone on the 14th of that month, the NE vent was found to be stopped up. This vent was apparently blasted open again on the following day, for two eruptive columns reappeared and remained visible for several days thereafter.

Unusually strong explosions that shook the earth in a radius of several kilometers from the volcano and hurled large pyroclastic blocks out beyond the base of the cone occurred on August 5, November 21 and 28, and December 24. These tremendous explosions were usually preceded by short periods of almost complete inactivity, and some of them were so violent that fragments were blown nearly 2 km from the volcano. The largest single block noted after the November 28 explosion was 5.6 m long by 1.6 m wide. It consisted of dense lava and was found near the NW base of the cone. These eruptions seem to have come as a result of the crater vents being stopped up or the throat being reduced in size by pressure from the sides, and they were generally followed within 24 hours by a marked temporary increase in the flow of lava. The frequency of these explosions was much the same as in the preceding half year.

Form of the Cone and Crater

The outward form of the cone did not change greatly through the second half of 1949. The elevation of the east peak was unchanged . . . within the limits of accuracy of measurement, and it has in fact remained about the same since the end of October, 1947, when it was 2,774.2 m above sea level. The west peak, however, continued to be built up through accumulation of pyroclastic material. It reached a greater height by the end of December than at any former time, having risen nearly 17 m during the half year. The saddle, or low point of the NE rim also continued to rise and reached nearly the same altitude as the east peak. This rise was possible because that flank of the cone did not slump during this 6-month period as it had done in the previous year. The SW saddle appeared on inspection during ascents to the crater to have remained about the same, probably because of repeated slumping of the SW flank of the cone, which nullified the effect of filling by pyroclastic material.

In the first few days of July the SW flank of the cone slumped actively between two bordering faults about 120 m apart (see Fig. 123). This movement was accompanied by the re-opening of the lava vent on that side of the cone. On July 6, when we ascended the volcano from that side, the faults had vertical scarps more than 1 m high, and gases and steam were issuing lazily from place to place along the fault lines. On October 18 the scarps had been covered by pyroclastic material erupted from the crater, although that segment of the flank was still appreciably depressed. In the middle of November a second, minor slump took place, principally at the saddle, but this had been healed when the crater was visited on December 14, at which time the flank of the cone had nearly regained its normally rounded form. In the last few days of December, however, the SW rim and flank of the cone began to slump again, suggesting movement of lava concealed beneath that area. The depression that had formerly appeared at the SW base of the cone and that had been nearly filled with pyroclastic material by the end of the previous 6 months, was eradicated completely early in July by lava pushing up into the area and forming, instead, a low mound. On December 14 the slopes of the outer north, NW, and west flanks of the cone were measured and found to be uniformly 34°, which is 2° or 3° steeper than the slopes of these flanks in the summer of 1943.

The cone was ascended in order to inspect the crater on July 7, October 18, November 14 and 17, and December 14. The form of the crater on July 6 was described . . . in the previous report (see p. 164). The conical mound that occupied the center of the crater at that time was probably destroyed by the strong explosion of August 5, if not before; but at any rate, by October 18 the crater consisted of an oval-shaped bowl elongated in a NE direction and about 25 m deep. The rounded bottom of the bowl, which was lined with scoriae at dull-red heat, did not have any constant vents or openings. The eruptions, which at that time were so strong as to prevent more than a quick look and a rapid retreat, rent through different parts of this pasty false bottom every few seconds, tearing off huge chunks of soft lava and hurling them as high as 100 m into the air, accompanied by deafening thunder. However, the bottom did not in any sense resemble a lava lake. The position of the bowl corresponded more or less to that of the SW vent at those times when two vents have been present in the crater. A terrace with a maximum width of 100 m extended from the east peak to the lip of the central bowl, at about the same altitude; it narrowed at the NE saddle and west peak and disappeared at the SW saddle.

. . . . .

On November 14 the crater consisted of a double bowl with a very low divide. The bottom of the NE part was stopped up, although it had a circular fissure in the center and appeared to be ready to blow open at any time; the SW bowl was pierced by a vent about 10 m in diameter, through which the usual eruptions tore their way. On November 17 this double bowl was much the same, except that a vent 2 m in diameter appeared 15 m or so to the NW of the main SW vent, and a circular slumped area had formed near the SW saddle or rim of the crater. Gases and steam issued from cracks in this saddle during the entire period. On December 14 only one oval-shaped bowl was present, but, as the explosive activity was too intense to permit an approach to its lip, the bottom could not be seen. The eruptions appeared, however, to come from a single wide vent in the bottom of this bowl, which seemed to be no more than 20 m lower than the SW saddle. The terrace from the rim of the cone to the central bowl was even wider than earlier in the 6-month period.

Fig. 123. Areas covered by Parícutin lava flows, July 1 to December 31, 1949.

Activity of the Lava Vents

During the entire period, lava continued to issue without interruption from the vent at the NE base of the cone, named Nuevo Juatita by Ezequiel Ordóñez, and for a few days early in July the old Puertecito vent at the SW base of the cone was active (see Fig. 123). At the beginning of the period the NE Nuevo Juatita vent supplied a sluggish flow of lava that cascaded toward the SE, but on July 3 and 4 this lava became too stiff to move and came to a halt. On July 5 the pressure of the lava in the conduit forced up a large plug of solid material to a height of 4-5 m above the lava-vent mound, and during the afternoon this plug gradually parted into several pieces, permitting the fluid lava beneath to escape and, by evening, to flow in a cascade toward the north. In the following months this north cascade was constantly active and remained in the same position until the end of the 6-month period.

On August 27 and 31 large gas bubbles pushed through the lava conduit and tore off fragments of the pasty lava, hurling them forcibly some tens of meters from the vent. Such gas eruptions occurred also on October 12 and 20 and on November 1 and 29. Some of these bubbles were accompanied by lava surges and slight flooding of the vent mound, but not all extra surges of lava were accompanied by gas eruptions. No ash eruptions were seen at the lava-vent during these 6 months. The unusually strong explosions in the crater, which were mentioned in a preceding paragraph, were generally followed within 24 hours by an increase in lava flow, although other increases in flow occurred without any apparent relation to strong crater eruptions. The volume of lava issuing from the Nuevo Juatita vent was more nearly uniform during this period than in the previous year. Because of intermittent floodings of the vent area, the lava-vent mound rose about 7 m in height during the 6-month period . . . .

While the Nuevo Juatita vent was stopped up early in July, the old SW Puertecito vent was again forced open, probably on July 3 or 4. Lava apparently pushed through the side of the main cone, for the SW flank slumped markedly while the vent was being reopened. A large plug of solid lava was shoved out ahead of the fluid material, into the area that had formerly been occupied by a depression (see p. 160), the new lava then filling this depression and forming a low, roundish mound. The highest part of this mound consisted of two pyramids 10 or 15 m high, composed of the older, solid lava that had been pushed out while the vent was being reopened. The duration of the activity is not known exactly, but it was probably less than 2 weeks, for on July 30 the flow was found to have come to a halt 150 m from the vent and the area was completely quiet, except for fumaroles and gas escape such as have characterized this area for the past year and a half. On visits to the crater in October, November, and December the Puertecito vent area was found almost unchanged, the only visible evidence of activity being a slight cracking of the ash cover and the issue at several places of burning-hot gases. Unless these gases should cool appreciably as time goes on, further lava activity can probably be expected in this area.

Activity of the Lava Flows

The lava flowing to the SE and east from the Nuevo Juatita vent was cut off at its source in the first days of July and hence advanced only a few meters beyond its position at the end of June (see Fig. 123). The flow to the north and NW advanced steadily through the period, until it had reached a maximum distance of 3,100 m from the vent at the end of December, when it seemed to be advancing at about the same rate as in the preceding 6 months. One small island of original ground was covered by this flow, and four other islands were reduced in size. The island on which the Upper Casita was built and which formed the highest part of Cerro de Jarátiro was reduced in size but not entirely covered, although the lava now stands higher than the remaining old ground and hides the Upper Casita from view except from such high points as the top of Parícutin cone. The island to the north of the buried village of Parícutin was invaded by a tongue of lava late in December, and the large island between this village and San Juan Parangaricutiro was invaded by a second tongue. The lava fronts were generally from 10 to 12 m high.

At a point just below the Nuevo Juatita vent on October 14, the lava stream was about 10 m wide by probably 3 m deep and flowed at a rate of 4 m/min. This would amount to a flow of about 173,000 m³/day or, assuming a constant rate, a total volume of about 32,000,000 m³ for the 6 months. This volume is some 15% greater than the probable actual amount of lava extruded during this period, which may have been more nearly 25,000,000 m³, indicating that the average rate of flow was somewhat less than 4 m/min, for the estimated width and thickness of the lava stream do not seem to be too great.

The SW Puertecito lava flow was active probably less than 2 weeks. It divided into two tongues near the vent, one of which advanced about 150 m to the west and the other 150 m to the south before coming to a halt.

January 1 to June 30, 1950

Fries and Gutiérrez (1951a)

Eruptive Activity

Eruptions from the crater continued to be as erratic as in other years . . . . In general, however, the months of January and February were characterized by frequent, tremendously strong explosions . . . that hurled out great quantities of rock fragments and pasty lava, some as large as several tons, which fell at times as far as 2 km from the eruptive vent. These explosions were generally preceded by several minutes of complete inactivity. They occurred on more than 15 days during these 2 months and were accompanied by local earth tremors. March and April were characterized by moderately strong activity and frequent, though somewhat less intense and more heavily charged eruptions than those of the first 2 months. During May and June the strong explosions were infrequent and the eruptions consisted largely of whitish to yellowish gases with small quantities of rock fragments and very little ash. Electric discharges within the eruptive column accompanied the stronger eruptions during every month of the period described.

A new noise type, designated by the letter P, was first heard in March and was audible from time to time in the following months, and the diagrams of eruptive characteristics were modified to include it. The new type of noise sounds more nearly like type D than like any of the others [Table 1: p. 148], but differs in that the explosions are very short and are repeated rapidly at intervals of one to two seconds.

The eruptive column rose to a maximum height of about 4,000 m above the top of the cone on February 16, after a particularly strong explosion. On several other days it reached heights of 3,000 to 3,500 m, but in general it flattened out in the upper winds at a height of less than 2,500 m above the cone. Eruption of ash continued to decline gradually. At the more distant Cuezeño station [5½ km N of the vent] the total ashfall was only 5.2 mm . . . and at the closer Equijuata station [2½ km NE of the vent] it was 7.7 mm during the 6-month period. Measurements show a constant decrease in ashfall at Cuezeño for the 3 yearly periods from July 1947 to June 1950, during which precise records have been maintained. The total for this 3-year period was only 51.9 mm, whereas in the 3 years and 8 months from February 1943 to October 1946, at least 480 mm of ash fell at Cuezeño [see inside-front-cover map].

Form of the Cone and Crater

The outer form of the cone remained about the same throughout the first half of 1950. Periodic slumps of the NE flank in January, February, and April continued to keep that part somewhat depressed and to maintain the NE saddle in the crater rim. At 06:00 on April 2 a vent blew open suddenly at midslope on the NE flank, and from it were hurled out dense vapors, ash, and rock and lava fragments for 1½

hours. These eruptions were simultaneous with and nearly on the same scale as those from the main crater, indicating that the vents were probably connected within the cone itself, possibly along the top of the lava conduit leading to the lava-vent mound on the NE side. The SW flank has also remained depressed in part, because of small slumps caused by the strong explosions of January, February, and April, and in part because the increment of pyroclastic material has apparently not been great enough to eradicate the effect of the large slumps of that flank in the last half of 1949.

The elevation of points on the rim of the volcano (see Tables 3 and 4) did not change greatly in the first half of 1950. The NE saddle is several meters lower because of slumping over the lava conduit, which presumably passes under or through that flank.

Table 3. Elevation[a] above sea level of points on Parícutin volcano.

Date	West peak	Lowest point of northeast rim	Outer east peak[b]	Inner east peak[c]	Lava-vent mound
1950	m	m	m	m	m
February 21	2795.1	2770.8	2772.7	2783.5	2650.8
April 28	2796.6	2770.8	2774.2	2783.5	2655.1
July 7	2796.6	2766.3	2774.2	2780.5	2656.6

[a]Determined by alidade from Cuezeño station; estimated accuracy of ± 1.5 m.
[b]Point recorded in earlier published activity reports.
[c]Point on rim of inner crater; horizontal distance from Cuezeño station is 5240 m.

Table 4. Changes in height of Parícutin cone.

Date	Height of cone	Increase in height between dates shown		Period of time elapsed	
	m	m	m		
February 23, 1943	44[a]		44	3 days	
June 9, 1943	198	336	154	3 1/2 mo	1 yr
February 20, 1944	336		138	8 1/2 mo	
February 20, 1947	360		24	3 yr	
February 21, 1950	397	61	37	3 yr	6 yr

The outer east peak has risen a meter or so, and the inner east peak has apparently slumped somewhat into the crater, dropping about 3 m in height. The profile of the cone, viewed from the north, continues to show three points, which correspond to the outer east peak, the inner east peak (east rim of presently active crater), and the west peak. The maximum height of the cone above its original base was about 397 m on February 21, 1950 (see Table 4), in comparison with 360 m on the same day of 1947 and 336 m on that day of 1944. Hence, in the 3 years after the end of the first year of eruptive activity, the cone rose about 24 m, and in the following period of three years it rose 37 m. This suggests that in recent years coarse pyroclastic material erupted from the crater has not decreased as greatly in volume as has the finer ash, confirming visual estimates of those who have observed the activity over the past 7 years.

The part of the cone visible is somewhat smaller now than it was 3 years ago. By way of comparison, the maximum diameter of the base of the cone, from NW to SE, was 1,100 m in February 1946 and the minimum diameter was 950 m, whereas the present maximum, in the same direction, is 940 m and the minimum is 700 m. The maximum diameter of the rim in February 1946 was 400 m, whereas it is now only 280 m. The decrease at the base has been caused by the piling up of lava flows over the lower slopes; the decrease at the top has been due to a decline in the average intensity of the eruptions, which are now not strong enough to keep such a wide crater cleaned out.

The active part of the crater continued to show variations in depth, form, and the location of eruptive throats. In general, only one throat was active at any one time during most of the period. On several days in early and late June, however, simultaneously active throats were noted independently by Gutiérrez and Howel Williams. On ascents to the crater on April 28 and July 7, Fries found the crater to be about 20 to 25 m deep, in the form of a single bowl with an elongated bottom oriented in a NW-SE direction. This departure from the normal NE-SW elongation of the crater bottom, or alignment of the throats, had never been noted before, and it was apparently constant for several months. Eruptions came from the NW end of the elongated bottom in April, and from the SE end in July. At both times the bottom was red-hot and the actual throats were less than 3 m across. The throats blew open somewhat plastically with each eruption, but the activity was too strong and erratic to permit spending more than a few minutes on the top of the volcano for further observation. This crater seems to occupy the normal SW eruptive-throat area, and the normal NE throat area has apparently been completely covered over by pyroclastic material. The rim of the crater is a sharp ridge except around the eastern side, where there is a terrace between the inner and outer east peaks about 80 m in maximum width.

Activity of the Lava Vents

Lava issued only from the NE Nuevo Juatita vent during the first half of 1950 and had, by the end of June, been flowing continuously from this vent for 2 years and 5 months. The mound around the vent continued to rise as a result of periodic flooding and was about 9 m higher at the end of the period than at the beginning (see Table 3). This mound had risen 7 m in the preceding 6-month period and about 19 m in the year before that, making a total rise of 35 m in 2 years. At the end of June 1950, the vent mound was only 110 m below the NE saddle of the crater rim, about 85 m below the eruptive throat in the crater, and only 15 m lower than the old vent area at the SW base of the cone.

The lava continued to cascade toward the north until April 10, when the sluggish flow solidified sufficiently to force the lava to break through, flood the top of the mound, and form a second cascade toward the NE. These two cascades continued until the end of June, although the flow was not divided uniformly between the two and was carried mainly by one or the other at any given time. Bubbles of gas were erupted from the vent at several times during the period, and on January 17 one of these eruptions hurled pasty blobs of lava to a height of 60 to 80 m. Strong explosions in the main crater on March 23 were accompanied by a series of gas eruptions from the lava vent.

No lava activity was observed at the SW base of the cone, although the area continued to furnish very hot gases at several places. As the lava is piled up thickly in this area and has been blanketed by ash for several years, it seems to have held its heat longer than in other areas. As a result, the rains that drench the lava field during the wet summer season are in part returned as steam, giving the area an eerie aspect for several months . . . . This steam is nearly odorless, in contrast to the choking acid gases given off by the active flows.

Activity of the Lava Flows

The rate of flow down the lava cascades was as variable as usual. The cascade toward the north continued to supply the two lobes that were active to the NNW of the cone in December, 1949. The westerly lobe obliterated completely the island of old ground to the north of the old Parícutin village, and the other lobe covered a large part of the old ground to the SW of San Juan Parangaricutiro (see Fig. 124). The fronts of these lobes were much higher than any that had been observed in former years, being probably more than 20 m high in some places . . . . These fronts continued to move sluggishly at the end of the period. The flow from the NE cascade moved slowly over the older lavas and had nearly reached the edge of the lava field at the base of Cerro de Equijuata [2¾ km NNE of the cone] by the end of the period.

The area covered by the advancing lava from the north cascade amounted to about 1,656,000 m² during the 6-month period, and that covered by the lava from the NE cascade was about 604,000 m², for a total of 2,260,000 m². This compares with a total area of 2,640,000 m² covered during the second half of 1949. Assuming that the average thickness of this lava is 10 m, which seems to be a reasonable figure, the total volume extruded in the first half of 1950 would be about 23 million m³, in contrast to an estimated 25 million m³ in the preceding 6 months [see p. 168]. In view of the errors that certainly enter into these calculations, it is not clear whether there has been an actual decrease in the rate of flow, but if so, it must have been small.

The total area covered by Parícutin lava at the end of June amounted to about 24.2 km². [This represents an increase of just 10% since the end of 1946, when the area covered was estimated as 22 km²].

Three strong fumaroles continued to deposit NH₄Cl on the lava to the SW of San Juan Parangaricutiro (see Fig. 124) that came to rest in June 1948. Warm air still rises from some parts of the thin San Juan flow, which ceased moving more than 5 years ago.

July 1 to December 31, 1950

Fries and Gutiérrez (1951b)

Eruptive Activity

Eruptions from the crater were on the whole somewhat less strong than formerly, although short periods of intense activity continued to occur from time to time . . . .

The eruptive column reached a height of 3,000 m above the crater on one day each in July, September, and November, although it averaged little more than 1,500 m in height during the 6-month period. Electric discharges were observed in the column on four days in July, five days in September, six days in October,

Fig. 124. Areas covered by Parícutin lava flows, January 1 to June 30, 1950.

two days in November, and two days in December. Brief intervals of 2-4 minutes of complete quiescence, followed by tremendous explosions that blew out enormous tonnages of pyroclastic material, occurred on 2 or 3 days each in October and December. Such explosions were always accompanied by local earth tremors. Less violent explosions were observed on 1-4 days of every month. A strong regional earthquake, whose epicenter was in the State of Oaxaca some 600 km to the SE, shook the area on December 16 without causing any visible change in eruptive or lava activity on that or the following day.

The strongest eruptions hurled rocks to a height of 500-800 m above the crater, indicating that the "muzzle" velocity of these eruptions was 98-127 m/second. At the lower figure, a block of rock that has reached its highest point will fall for about 10 seconds before hitting the flank of the cone, in contrast to about 13 seconds for the higher figure. These velocities are comparable to those measured during the first year of the volcano's activity, when bombs were rarely observed to require more than 11 or 12 seconds to fall from the tops of their arcs. At present, however, the periods of such strong activity are short-lived and infrequent, whereas in the first year they were of long duration and were interrupted by only short intervals of moderate to weak activity. Moreover, the average diameter of the eruptive vent is now considerably less than in 1943, and hence the volume of material erupted by equally strong explosions is now smaller.

The average volume of pyroclastic material erupted from the volcano has apparently continued to decline. At Equijuata station [2½ km NE of the vent], only 3.9 mm of ash fell in the second half of 1950, as compared with 4.1 mm in the corresponding period of 1949. The ash fall at Cuezeño station [5½ km N of the vent] was only 2.1 mm, of which a small part may have consisted of wind-blown surface ash collected by the gage, particularly during the dry months of November and December when dust storms were frequent.

Form of the Cone and Crater

Parícutin cone had much the same exterior form at the end of December 1950 as in the preceding June. It continued to present a three-pointed profile as seen from the north, although the NE saddle was relatively less conspicuous and the inner east peak was nearly as high as the west peak. No change was noted on the SW side of the cone, except for a more rounded appearance due to the accumulation of pyroclastic material. On November 19 a vent blew open near the center of the saddle in the NE rim of the cone. Although this was sealed almost immediately, the NE flank continued to slump slowly during the next 2 weeks. New material erupted from the crater, however, had healed these wounds by the end of December.

The base of the cone was found to measure 940 m from NW to SE and 600 m from NE to SW. The latter dimension is even less than it was 6 months ago, as lava from the NE Nuevo Juatita vent has gradually been covering the lower flank on that side. The crater rim measured 220 m from NW to SE, between the west peak and the inner east peak, although the rim extended 50 m farther to the SE, out to the outer east peak. The crater diameter from NE to SW was only 140 m.

. . . . .

When Fries ascended the cone on July 7, the bottom of the crater was a bowl about 25 m deep, elongated in a NW-SE direction and pierced by eruptions near its SE end. Gutiérrez ascended the cone on July 18 and found the crater to be about 20 m deep, relative to the NE saddle. Eruptions came from a throat about 9 m in diameter located on the NW side of the bottom of the bowl. A second throat about 10 m to the SE was filled and glowing red. On another ascent on August 27, Gutiérrez found the crater to consist of a roundish bowl with a single eruptive throat in the center. The SE wall of the crater was fractured and appeared to be slumping.

On December 29 we found the crater bottom to be elongated in a NE-SW direction, or at right angles to the elongation of the past 7 or 8 months. Although the eruptions were intense and heavily laden with ash and bombs . . . the throat could be seen at times between explosions to consist of a fissure about 3 m wide and perhaps 20 m long. Eruptions issued from different parts of the fissure at different times, although occasionally they came from several parts of the fissure at the same time. The bottom was about 25 m below the NE saddle. The only terrace present late in December was between the outer and inner east peaks; it had a maximum width of 50 m and sloped from the crater lip toward the outer east peak. The SW saddle seemed to be a few meters higher than the NE saddle.

Activity of the Lava Vents

The only point of lava issue during the period was the Nuevo Juatita vent at the NE base of the cone. This vent has now been continuously active for nearly 3 years. Periodic floodings around the point of lava issue have built the cone higher by about 5 m in the past 6 months . . . or at a rate about equal to that of each of the last three 6-month periods. Lava flowed in two cascades, one to the NE and the other to the NW, until October 12, when strong flooding permitted it to break through a little farther to the west and at a lower level (see Fig. 125). This beheaded the flow to the NE, and all the lava then descended to the NW. Cutting off the feed to the NE cascade permitted the steep channel to be emptied and to show the characteristic, nearly vertical walls and the 5-7 m depth of such channels. Gas eruptions from the vent were noted only on July 27, and a small incipient fountain was observed for a few minutes on September 27. Lava emission was otherwise quiet and generally very sluggish. On December 29 the flow at the base of the NW cascade was so sluggish that one could walk out on the lava as far as 10 m from its edge . . . . The volume of fumes given off by the fresh lava is now considerably less than in former years, making observation correspondingly easier.

Activity of the Lava Flows

The flow from the NE cascade continued to move along the base of Equijuata until late in October, when it came to rest as a result of beheading. It had covered two small islands of old ground and a part of the base of Equijuata (see Fig. 125). The flow from the NW cascade continued to pile up at its front to the east of Sinámichu station [4 km NW of the vent: Fig. 125], advancing a little beyond its position in June. The outbreak of October 12 beheaded this flow also, and the route of the new lava was west of that of the previous flow, mainly over the older, ash-covered flows. The front of this new flow had advanced about 1,900 m by the end of December. No marked difference was noted in the character of these flows as compared with those of the past several years.

The area covered by new lava during the second half of 1950 amounted to about 2,080,000 m², as determined by measurements with a planimeter. The average thickness of this lava is estimated to be at least 8 m, ranging from perhaps 4 m near the base of the cascade to about 20 m at the NW front. The volume of lava extruded during the 6-month period was therefore about 17,000,000 m³. This was notably smaller than that of any earlier 6-month period on record, and the average daily volume was less than half that of 1948.

January 1 to June 30, 1951

Fries and Gutiérrez (1952a)

Eruptive Activity

No marked change was noted in the maximum intensity of eruptions, although the duration of strong eruptions seems, on the whole, to be less than in the second half of 1950, and periods of weak eruption were longer and more frequent than formerly. The height of the eruptive column exceeded 2,000 m on only 3-5 days of each month, and electric discharges were heard on only 1 or 2 days of each month—as usual, during the strongest ash eruptions.

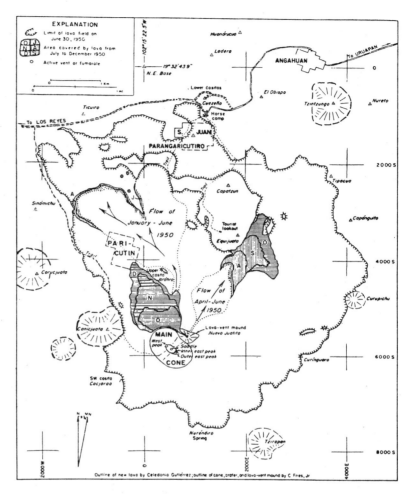

Fig. 125. Areas covered by Parícutin lava flows, July 1 to December 31, 1950.

The most notable difference in eruptive activity was a gradual increase in frequency of the periodic explosive type of eruption. These explosions were usually preceded by 1-5 minutes of complete quiescence and each was accompanied by a loud report, earth tremors, and a strong emission of ash and bombs. They were usually succeeded by a period of several minutes to more than 1 hour of the silent type of eruption, in which large quantities of ash were emitted without much noise. It is presumed that the normal eruptive activity was too weak to keep the crater throats continuously open. After sufficient pressure had been built up, great blasts suddenly blew out this accumulated material, the strongest blasts hurling bombs as far as 1 km from the base of the cone. The accompanying noise was comparable to that of several simultaneous thunder claps heard at close range, so intense that the needle of the continuous-recording barometer at Cuezeño station, 5½ km north of the volcano, was sent skidding across the record sheet. Such blasts occurred as often as 15-20 times during January and February, somewhat less frequently in March and April, and again with increased frequency during May and June . . . .

A vent that blew open in the lower NE flank of the cone on May 12 erupted much like the main crater for several days, while a small flow of lava oozed out of its bottom . . . . At times the eruptions from the vent and the crater were simultaneous, but at other times they were apparently unrelated to each other. By May 18 the eruptions from this vent, which we have named the No. 1 eruptive vent, had become less frequent and were noted only 3-5 times an hour. The frequency of eruptions continued to decrease during the rest of the month, although on some days as many as 6 blasts occcured in an hour. The blasts from the vent were generally followed by a series of weaker gas eruptions, which sounded much like the puffing of a slow-moving locomotive, a noise that has been characteristic of explosive vents filled with lava. By the end of June this No. 1 eruptive vent had become stopped up and was partly covered by pyroclastics.

A second vent that blew open higher in the NE flank of the cone on June 9 erupted also much like the main crater. In fact, eruptions from it were generally stronger than those from the main crater itself . . . . Occasionally the eruptions from the crater and No. 2 vent were simultaneous, but generally they were unrelated; at times the two vents and the main crater were in eruption simultaneously. With the formation of No. 2 vent, the activity of No. 1 vent declined markedly, and within 2 weeks the large volume of bombs and ash from No. 2 vent had nearly buried the lower No. 1 vent. By the end of June, No. 2 vent had settled down to a nearly constant rhythm of periodic eruptions heavily laden with ash and bombs . . . . These came every 5-20 minutes and were followed for 1-3 minutes by a continuous eruption of the silent type. On the whole, the volume of material erupted from this vent was probably greater than that from the main crater.

Ashfall has continued to decline in volume, only 1.1 mm having been recorded at Cuezeño station [5½ km N of the vent] and 5.2 mm at Equijuata station [2½ km NE of the vent] during the first half of 1951, in contrast to 5.1 and 7.7 mm at these stations during the first half of 1950. A continuous decline in ashfall over the past 5 years is evident in the data. In general, the ashfall in each year appears to have been only about half that of the preceding year. It is now so light that accurate records are difficult to obtain at distances of more than 3 km.

Form of the Cone and Crater

On February 20, the volcano's 8th birthday, the cone and crater were much like the description given in the last activity report (see p. 172) . . . . Gutiérrez ascended the cone on February 27 and found the crater to be about 30 m deep relative to the NE saddle, and to have a roundish bottom about 12 m in diameter bounded by a circular fracture. The bottom consisted of reddish, somewhat pasty material through which the eruptions pushed their way, but it could not be considered as representing a lava lake, for it did not have a flat surface. On March 10 a double eruptive column indicated that a second throat had formed in the crater, but it lasted only a day or so, apparently, for a single column was noted on the following day. On a second ascent to the crater on May 7, the Gutiérrez found the crater bottom to be about 50 m below the NE saddle and to contain a throat 12-14 m long and 8 m wide, oriented NE-SW.

On May 12 at 08:30 a depression began to form in the lower NE flank of the cone and soon became an eruptive vent (No. 1). A small flow of lava issued from this vent and kept the lower side open, much like the small cone of Sapichu in 1943. The bottom of this vent was only 11 m higher than the top of Nuevo Juatita lava-vent mound . . . . No open throat was ever noted, as lava occupied the bottom and the eruptions pushed their way through the lava. On May 18 the NE saddle of the crater rim began to break up and slump. On May 25, when Fries visited the cone and crater, eruptive activity in No. 1 vent had declined to the extent that the bottom could be seen. The main crater was found to be radically altered, as all the walls were broken up into segments that were gradually slumping into the bottom. The NE saddle was about 10 m lower than formerly, and a large slice of the inner east peak had slumped into the crater, causing the inner and outer east peaks to form a single east peak. The bottom of the crater was elongated NE-SW. A throat about 1 m in diameter, surrounded by material at red heat, occupied the SW side of the bottom. The NE side of the bottom showed a narrow vent about 8 m long oriented NE-SW. Strong eruptions came from this throat, whereas the small SW throat erupted mainly gases. The bottom of the crater was only about 30 m below the NE saddle.

On the morning of June 9 a second depression began to form in the NE flank of the cone, at a point some 20 m higher than No. 1 vent. This depression grew rapidly by frequent eruptions that blew out large volumes of the material forming the flank of the cone.

By the end of June this No. 2 eruptive vent rivaled the main crater in diameter and activity . . . . A high, firmly cemented pyroclastic ridge separated No. 2 vent from the main crater, in a position roughly equivalent to the former NE saddle. The lower rim of No. 2 vent was only 31 m higher than the top of Nuevo Juatita lava-vent mound. Material erupted from No. 2 vent had covered No. 1 vent and was rounding out the lower flank of the cone. If No. 2 vent should continue to coalesce with the main crater, the two together would have a nearly circular rim about 250 m in diameter. Even this dimension would be much less than the size of the crater in February 1946, when the maximum diameter was 400 m.

Activity of the Lava Vents

Lava flowed from No. 1 eruptive vent for only a week or so after the vent formed on May 12. Gas eruptions from this vent were vigorous and frequent for the first 2 weeks and then tapered off and ceased by the end of June. These eruptions were at first accompanied by large volumes of ash and bombs, but after 3 weeks very little ash was erupted and the material consisted mainly of pasty lava blown out of the vent by the force of the gas escape. At times the lava was lifted 4-5 m, appearing as a fountain. After June 9, when No. 2 eruptive vent formed, No. 1 vent ceased to erupt ash and bombs and gave off only sporadic belches of gas.

Nuevo Juatita vent, however, supplied lava during the entire 6-month period. The NW cascade, which had formed in October 1950, continued to be active until February 3, when freezing of the lava surface and a break-through initiated a second cascade to the NE. These two cascades were alternately active until March 9, either one or the other carrying the major part of the lava flowing from the vent. On that day, however, freezing of the lava at the vent caused a break-through at a somewhat lower level to the SE, with the consequent beheading of the NW and NE cascades. The SE cascade was continuously active until the end of June, when it still showed a normal rate of flow. Brief flooding at several times during the period caused overflows toward the main cone and also to the east, broadening and rounding out the vent mound. Weak gas eruptions from Nuevo Juatita were noted on at least 1 day each month.

Activity of the Lava Flows

The new lava moved over older flows to the NW until the early part of March, when it had reached the position of buried Parícutin village (see Fig. 126). A small flow from the NE cascade moved about 1,200 m north, also over older flows. The tiny flow from No. 1 eruptive vent formed a tongue about 20 m wide and 600 m long against the NE and east base of the main cone. The largest flow, from the SE cascade, had moved 2,500 m NE of the main cone by the end of June. The total area covered by these four flows was about 2,560,000 m², and the average thickness of the flows is estimated to have been about 7 m, which is less than it has been for the past 3 years because the flows were fairly near their source and had not yet piled up notably at their fronts. The total volume of lava for the first half of 1951 is thus estimated to have been about 18,000,000 m³, which is equivalent to an average daily volume of 99,000 m³. The total thickness of the lava field around the NE and north base of the main cone is now between 200 and 250 m and reaches a maximum of at least 275 m below the top of Nuevo Juatita vent mound.

Table 5 gives the volume of lava erupted at Parícutin at different periods since the birth of the volcano and shows the decline in lava volume over the past 3 years. The volume appears to have remained nearly constant at about 190,000 m³ daily, on the average, until the end of 1948. In the first 6 months of 1949 the average daily volume dropped to 133,000 m³ and held at nearly that level until the middle of 1950. In the second half of 1950, however, it dropped below 100,000 m³ for the first time, and in the first half of the present year it has continued to hold at about that level. Thus the average daily volume of lava issuing from Parícutin is now only about half the daily volume of the first 5 years of the volcano's existence. This small decline is in marked contrast to the great decline in explosive eruptive activity and volume of ashfall.

Although the lava volume of 1943 could not be determined from published maps and reports, the average daily volume is believed to have been roughly equal to that for the period 1944-1948. Assuming that this daily volume averaged 190,000 m³, the total volume for the period from the birth of the volcano to January 6, 1944, would be about 61,000,000 m³. The total volume of lava extruded at Parícutin up to the end of June 1951 was therefore about 500,000,000 m³, or 0.5 km³.

Table 5. Areas covered by, and estimated volumes of, Parícutin lava for different periods.

Period	Area covered by lava[a]	Estimated average thickness[b]	Estimated total volume for period	Estimated average daily volume for period
	sq m	m	cu m	cu m
Feb. 20, 1943-Jan. 8, 1944	?	?	61,000,000[c]	190,000[c]
Jan. 9, 1944-July 31, 1948	60,460,000	5.2	316,000,000[d]	189,000[d]
Aug. 1-Dec. 31, 1948	4,050,000	8	32,000,000	209,000
Jan. 1-June 30, 1949	2,440,000	10	24,000,000	133,000
July 1-Dec. 31, 1949	2,640,000	9.5	25,000,000	136,000
Jan. 1-June 30, 1950	2,260,000	10	23,000,000	127,000
July 1-Dec. 31, 1950	2,080,000	8	17,000,000	92,000
Jan. 1-June 30, 1951	2,560,000	7	18,000,000	99,000

[a]Determined by means of planimetric measurements on published maps.

[b]Estimated from personal observations or from published descriptions of lava flows; highest estimates correspond to periods when lava piled up near ends of long flows.

[c]Straight estimate; not based on actual measurements because no accurate maps were made to cover period.

[d]Compiled from planimetric measurements and lava-thickness estimates for 11 consecutive periods.

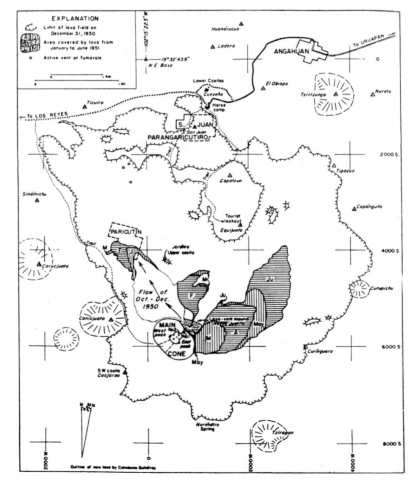

Fig. 126. Areas covered by Parícutin lava flows, January 1 to June 30, 1951.

July 1 to December 31, 1951

Fries and Gutiérrez (1952b)

In the second half of 1951 the volume of both pyroclastic material and new lava increased appreciably over that of the preceding 6-month period, thus interrupting the continuous decline in activity noted over the years since the birth of the volcano. The volumes of ash and lava, in fact, seem to have more or less recovered their general level of 1949. The period is notable also for the great increase in frequency and intensity of violent explosions or detonations in the crater. As many as 15-20 occurred on some days in late December, in contrast to about 45 explosions in the entire second half of 1950 . . . .

Activity of the Cone

Eruptions from the crater were probably stronger, on the average, than during any 6-month period since the middle of 1949. The eruptive column reached a maximum height of about 3,000 m in July and August, 2,500 m in September and October, and 2,800 m in November and December. The average height of the column was about 2,000 m in July and August, 1,500 m in September, 2,000 m in October, and 1,800 m in November and December. Electric discharges in the eruptive column during ash-laden eruptions were noted on 5 days in July, 8 days each in August, September, and October, and 1 day in November; none were heard in December.

The explosive type of eruption described in some detail in the previous activity report (see p. 173-174) has continued to increase in frequency and intensity. These explosions are possibly better called detonations, for they are much like the detonation of a charge of dynamite. Some of them seem to occur down in the throat of the volcano, and others seem to occur in the crater. They suggest the instantaneous rupture of a metal tank filled with gas under high pressure. The moderately strong explosions . . . peppered the top and base of Nuevo Juatita lava-vent mound with rocks and bombs, and the most intense explosions or detonations hurled rocks as far away as the top of Cerro de Canicjuata, nearly 2 km NW of the crater. Even in the first year of the volcano's history, rocks rarely reached the top of that hill.

The graphs from the continuously recording barograph in the observatory cabin at Cuezeño station [5½ km north of the vent] have provided a rough measure of the frequency of these strong blasts. In the second half of 1950, for example, about 45 of them were recorded, of which 3 were particularly intense.

In the first half in 1951 some 80 explosions were counted, of which 5 were extremely intense. During the second half of 1951, however, nearly 400 explosions were registered, and about 30 of these were particularly strong. In the latter period, the frequency of the explosions was greatest during August, September, October, and the last week in December. In the periods of greatest frequency, the shortest interval noted between explosions was about 15 minutes, although intervals of 2-6 hours were more common. The explosions were usually preceded by periods or weak gas and bomb eruptions with little ash, and were followed by periods of heavy ash eruptions. Our experience leads us to believe that the explosions are caused by pyroclastic material falling back into the crater and clogging one of the throats. In December the explosions arose from the SW crater throat, although some of the earlier ones came from the NE crater throat.

No. 1 eruptive vent, described in the previous activity report (see p. 174), had become inactive late in June, but on July 2 it again erupted gases intermittently and continued until about July 11, when it ceased to function and was quickly buried. No. 2 eruptive vent, also mentioned in that report (see p. 174), continued to be active and erupted more ash and bombs, on the whole, than the main crater vent. During the early part of the period, eruptions from No. 2 vent came every 5-10 minutes; later they slowed down to 1 every 5-20 minutes, although on some days they were more frequent than that. No constant relation was noted between the eruptions from the main crater and from No. 2 vent, either in timing or intensity. No. 2 vent became the NE crater throat before the end of the period, by coalescing with the main crater.

Ashfall in the second half of 1951 amounted to 4.7 mm at Cuezeño station and 9.9 mm at Equijuata station . . . . This was a sharp increase over the ashfall at those stations in the same periods of 1950 and 1949, although it did not equal that of the second half of 1948. The increase was due to the activity of No. 2 eruptive vent (NE crater vent), which supplied the major part of the ash erupted by the volcano in the second half of 1951. This 6-month period seems to be the first in the history of Parícutin to show an appreciable increase in ashfall over that of a corresponding 6-month period in an earlier year, and it is apparently the first time that the continuous decline in activity has been interrupted. In spite of the increased ashfall in the second half of the year, the total ash recorded at Cuezeño station for the year 1951 was less than the total for 1950 . . . owing to the very slight ashfall in the first 6 months of 1951, although at Equijuata station the total for the year was greater than in 1950.

Form of the Cone and Crater

At the beginning of the period, No. 2 eruptive vent was separated from the main crater by a steep, firmly cemented pyroclastic ridge, and on July 12 its NE rim was only 42 m higher than the top of Nuevo Juatita lava-vent mound . . . . No. 2 vent continued to migrate southwestward and to break down the pyroclastic ridge separating it from the main crater, until by August 27 it had coalesced with the main crater . . . . It then occupied the position of the former NE throat of the crater, before that throat was buried in 1950. By the end of December . . . the NE flank of the cone had become rounded out by pyroclastic material from the crater, and the lowest point on the NE rim of the crater had risen 34 m. The flank of the cone had encroached on the lava-vent mound and had covered the depression between the cone and the mound.

The crater side of the west peak was gradually eaten away by slumping and explosions . . . and the peak consequently dropped about 8 m in elevation during the period. The east peak rose about 7 m in altitude by accumulation of pyroclastic material, and at the end of the period it was about 3 m higher than the west peak. On December 29 the crater rim had a diameter of roughly 280 m from NW to SE, and 260 m from NE to SW. The latter dimension is more than twice that of March 1951.

Owing to the highly erratic occurrence of strong explosions, an attempt to climb the cone was not considered advisable during this period. It was felt that anyone caught on top of the cone at the time of such an explosion would have a slim chance of surviving, and the odds of being caught were not in one's favor during most of the period. There were intervals of a week or two at a time, of course, when the danger was not very great, but a method of predicting behavior has not yet been devised. Notwithstanding, it was learned early in January that Carlos García-Gutiérrez, of the Mexican Institute of Mineral Resources, and Eduardo Chávez, of the Tepalcatepec Commission, had made the ascent from the east on December 16. These men were not aware of the frequency and intensity of the strong explosions, and the barograph record shows that none had occurred for several days before their ascent. They report that the crater had two main throats aligned NE-SW, with a low ridge between. The NE throat was erupting ash and bombs almost continuously, but the SW throat was filled and showed only gas eruptions through small holes that pushed their way up through somewhat plastic material on one side of the rounded, filled bottom. This is the throat that was noted from the observatory cabin to produce the intense explosions and to expel only gases otherwise. The condition reported by García and Chávez concurs with our opinion that the explosions are due to the stopping up of a throat. Unless conditions should change, we recommend that visitors do not ascend the cone without first asking for advice at the observatory cabin.

Activity of the Lava Vents

No. 1 eruptive vent, described in the previous report (see p. 174), had supplied a small flow of lava in May and had become nearly inactive by the end of June. On July 2, however, gas eruptions again issued from this vent, at intervals of 5-10 minutes, and pasty lava was lifted several meters with each eruption. Activity decreased gradually in the following week, but a small flow of lava issued from the vent during July 9-11, after which the vent became stopped up and covered by pyroclastics from No. 2 vent.

The main, Nuevo Juatita lava vent at the NE base of the volcano supplied lava continuously through the 6-month period. The cascade to the SE, which had formed in March, continued to operate until the end of September, when an overflow caused a new cascade to descend to the east and NE. Several overflows occurred from time to time during the following months, but no other new cascade was formed until December 30, when a second NE cascade began to descend just west of the October-December cascade (see Fig. 127). The pyroclastic material from the crater gradually covered the SW side of the lava-vent mound and caused the point of lava issue to shift southeastward. Periodic overflows then built up the mound on that side, so that on December 30 the highest point of the mound was about 30 m farther from Cuezeño station than at the beginning of the period . . . . The height of the mound increased nearly 13 m during the period. Gas eruptions through this vent were not observed as in earlier periods, although very minor gas escapes could well have missed observation. The bright glow caused by the lava issuing from the vent at night suggested that the flow was somewhat more voluminous during this period than it had been for the past 12 months.

Activity of the Lava Flows

The flow that began in March had reached a point about 4.5 km from the vent when it came to rest at the end of October because of beheading at its source on October 1. The tip of this flow was only 260 m from the point where the horse trail crosses the San Juan lava at the north end of Cerro de Capatzun (see Fig. 127). This new flow covered three small islands of old terrain to the east of Equijuata and encroached on the east base of Cerro de Capatzun; the rest of it moved over older lava from Parícutin.

The flow that began on October 1 moved northeastward to the base of Equijuata, where it split into two tongues around this hill. In the first month the flow had advanced 2 km over older lava from Parícutin, but thereafter its fronts advanced more slowly. The lava invaded old terrain around the south base of Cerro de Equijuata and around the knoll on which the tourist lookout is located, cutting the trail to the lookout at one point and affording the tourists a close view of the moving front. At the end of December this flow had three tongues, one to the east of Cerro de Equijuata, another to its west, and a third to the east in the direction of Cerro de Curupichu, where it overrode the 1951 lava. It was not certain whether the new cascade that formed on December 30 would behead this flow or whether it would unite with the flow.

The area covered by new lava during the second half of 1951 was about 2,820,000 m^2 and was larger than that of any 6-month period since the second half of 1948. As the flows were relatively narrow and moved over inclined ground, the average thickness of the lava was not very great and is believed to have been about 7 m. On this assumption, then, the volume extruded in the second half of 1951 was about 20,000,000 m^3, or an average daily volume of 108,000 m^3. This represents an increase of about 9,000 m^3/day over the first half of 1951 and 16,000 m^3/day over the second half of 1950 (see Table 5, p. 176). The increased lava volume accords with observations of increased flow at the lava vent, and it is also in accord with the increased activity of the eruptive vents, as indicated by the greater ashfall. Taking into consideration these two factors, we feel justified in concluding that the continuous decline in

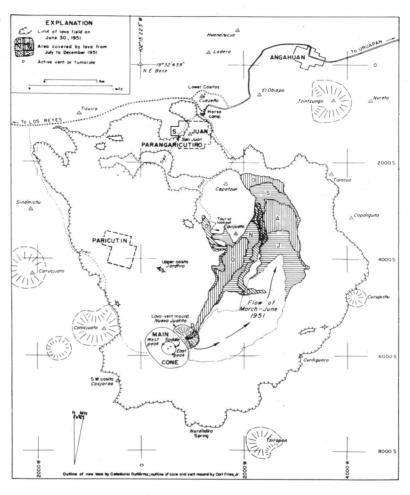

Fig. 127. Areas covered by Parícutin lava flows, July 1 to December 31, 1951.

the activity of Parícutin, witnessed up to the middle of 1951, has definitely been interrupted. Whether or not the interruption represents a final spurt in activity before the death of the volcano remains to be seen.

Activity in 1952:
The End of the Eruption
Fries and Gutiérrez (1954)

Lava emission at Parícutin volcano came to an abrupt end early on February 25, 1952, just 4½ days after the volcano's 9th anniversary. Explosive activity in the crater declined just as abruptly on the same day and continued only as intermittent, weak, noiseless puffs until March 4, when all activity came to a complete halt. In the 15 months between March, 1952, and June, 1953, when this paper was written, no further activity occurred either in the crater or at the lava vents; and in our opinion, renewed eruptions are unlikely.

During the volcano's brief final period of activity early in 1952, not only lava and ash eruption, but also explosive activity continued to increase notably over the period previously described (see p. 177-179). The trend toward increased activity had already been well established in the second half of 1951, when the earlier continuous decline in activity was first definitely interrupted. Rainfall for the year 1952 was also greater than that of the year before, although this increase had no close relationship to the activity of the volcano.

. . . . .

Activity of the Cone

The eruptive column reached a maximum height of 3,000 m in both January and February, and its average height was about 2,000 m, being thus greater, on the average, than during the preceding 6-month period. Electrical discharges within the ash column and from the ash column to the cone occurred, as usual, during heavy ash eruptions.

Ashfall continued to increase in volume over the second half of 1951 and during January and February, 1952 . . . was about five times that of the first 2 months of 1951. For example, the total ashfall for January and February, 1952, was 3.2 mm at Cuezeño station [5½ km north] and 10.7 mm at Equijuata station [2½ km NE], in comparison with 0.6 mm and 2.2 mm at those stations in January and February, 1951. A comparison of annual ashfall from 1947 to 1952 is presented in Table 6. The cessation of strong eruptions on February 25 corresponded with the cessation of the fall of newly erupted ash in the rain gages.

. . . . .

The strong detonations characteristic of the last 2 years or so of the volcano's eruptive history con-

Table 6. Annual rainfall and ashfall at Cuezeño and Equijuata stations, 1947 to 1952.

Period	Cuezeño station		Equijuata station	
	Rainfall (total)	Ashfall (total)	Rainfall (total)	Ashfall (total)
	mm	mm	mm	mm
1947[a]	1480.5	43.9	2411.4	129.2
1948[a]	1710.8	12.3	1893.2	45.6
1949[a]	1355.2	8.7	1593.9	16.8
1950[a]	1315.0	7.2	1761.5	11.6
1951[a]	1510.6	5.8[b]	1600.9	15.1[b]
1952	1708.5	3.2[b]	1781.6	12.7[b]

[a]FRIES and GUTIÉRREZ [1952b, Table 2].
[b]Ash was erupted only in January and February, 1952.

tinued to increase in frequency; some 280 detonations were marked by the continuous-recording barograph during January and about 305 between February 1 and 25, 1952, when the strong eruptions ceased abruptly. This frequency contrasts with a total of about 400 such detonations in the entire second half of 1951. Bombs a few centimeters in diameter rose to heights of 100-1,200 m above the cone during the strongest of these explosions, in contrast to heights of 500-600 m during periods of ordinarily strong eruptive activity. Coarse pyroclastic material expelled by these intense explosions was so abundant that its fall on the flanks of the cone and near the base raised dust clouds that obscured the cone from view for some minutes at a time. Blocks of lava weighing more than 100 tons each were hurled from the crater and fell beyond the base of the cone.

Beginning on January 1 both crater vents (see p. 177-178) were active and of nearly equal eruptive intensity. At times the eruptions were simultaneous in the two vents and at other times they showed no relationship from one vent to the other. On January 23 the eruptions alternated from white vapor to black ash-laden vapors, but at other times such an alternation was not observed. In addition to ordinary explosions every 5-15 seconds, intense detonations occurred at intervals of 15 minutes to 4 hours, without exhibiting any recognizable periodicity.

On February 24, the last day of strong continuous eruptive activity, the ash eruption was of the type that first began on March 18, 1943, and ash rained down over the countryside in large quantities, especially NE of the cone, where a gray curtain extended several kilometers from the volcano. This eruption was apparently the final spasm of activity, for during that same night continuous activity came to a halt. Except for a few intense explosions the following day, eruptions occurred only intermittently until March 4, when activity ceased entirely.

A description of the last day of strong but discontinuous eruptions (February 25), as translated from the notes of Gutiérrez, is as follows:

At dawn the crater of Parícutin volcano is wholly without eruption—without any noise and even without any vapor arising from it. It is very rare for such a drastic change to occur so shortly after such great activity, and for the volcano to be completely dead. At 13:00 a fantastically great volume of vapors again bursts forth in a cauliflower-like pillar from which great quantities of rock and ash are hurled, accompanied by the detonations of electrical discharges. At 13:30 the vapors cease and the crater becomes inactive. Five minutes later there appears another eruption, which lasts until 14:00. At 16:00 another eruption, with a weak, deep-seated detonation, appears and ceases within 5 minutes. At 16:15 another weak eruption arises in the form of an aborescent column of black vapors and ceases almost immediately. At 16:30 a further eruption appears very weakly. At 17:00 another weak eruption surges forth, and at 18:30 some vapors arise without force. Each of these intermittent eruptions of a few minutes' duration arises without force and without noise, or with very faint sounds like the sighing of a strong breeze through the pine trees. At 21:00 another weak eruption appears in the crater, which thereafter remains silent and without hurling out a single incandescent rock—all visible pyroclastic activity has ceased.

On February 26 only weak intermittent eruptions occurred, carrying the vapor column to only about 1,000 m above the cone. Activity ceased almost immediately after each eruption and the vapor cloud was carried away by the wind. Variable but small quantities of fine-grained pyroclastic material were hurled out. On February 27 the eruptions were similar to those of the preceding day, and the vapor cloud was dissipated in a few minutes. Periods of several hours passed without eruptions. On February 28 the eruptions came about once an hour, and only 3 out of 10 of them carried any observable pyroclastic material. The vapors, which were yellowish and whitish, disappeared at a height of about 500 m above the cone, although those from the strongest explosions rose to nearly 2,000 m. Similar conditions were observed on February 29. On March 1 small eruptions were observed at 06:30, 08:00, 09:00, 10:00, 12:00, 17:15, 18:00, and 19:25. On March 2 a small eruption occurred at 11:30, and on March 3 eruptions were recorded at 12:15, 17:05, and 17:30. On March 4 only two eruptions were seen, one at 06:50 and another at 09:15. This last eruption was apparently the final one, for not a single eruption was observed thereafter. None of the eruptions after February 25 was strong enough to be marked by the continuous-recording barograph.

Form of the Cone and Crater

The final two months of activity in the crater had little effect on the general outward appearance of the cone (see Fig. 128). The NE and SW saddles and flanks were somewhat filled in and rounded out, and both peaks were further built up, as shown in Table 7. The vertical changes were accompanied by small changes in the horizontal distances of the points reported. The highest point on the cone is the west peak, which is less than 1 m higher than the east peak and about 4 m lower than it was in August, 1951, owing probably to the frequent strong detonations during the last few months of the volcano's active life. The two peaks rise about 424 m above the level of the original surface of Pulido's cornfield [2,385 m], where eruption first began on February 20, 1943. The base of the cone is oval and has a diameter of about 650 m NE to SW and 900 m from the NW to the SE, but the crater rim is nearly round and has a diameter of some 280 m (see Fig. 128). The NE saddle is only 79 m higher than the top of the Nuevo Juatita lava-vent mound on the NE side of the cone, and the SW saddle is probably less than 70 m higher than the old lava-vent mound at the base of the cone on that side.

The two crater vents are aligned in the usual NE-SW direction .... The NE vent seems to have had somewhat less intense eruptions in the last few weeks than the SW vent, as its funnel is not as broad and its bottom is not quite as deep. The first ascent to the crater in 1952 was made by the Gutiérrez and Jesús Saldaña on March 8, four days after the last eruption. At that time the two vents were stopped up with blocks of reddish cemented rubble, which probably represented slumped material from the lower part of the interior of the crater. The bottoms were some 30 or 40 m below the NE and SW saddles. Steam rose lazily in small wisps from several concentric fissures around the south, SW, and west sectors of the crater rim. The SE and NW interior slopes of the crater were partly covered with white and pale-yellow sublimates, similar to the sublimates of ammonium chloride with variable small quantities of iron chloride common on the flanks of the cone for some years and on the ash around fumaroles issuing from the new lava flows. No new or unusual type of sublimate was noted.

On April 29 Fries chartered a small airplane in Uruapan and flew over the cone and lava fields in order to take pictures .... Fissures around the southwestern half of the crater rim were plainly visible ... and the sublimates appeared as remnants of snow. On the following days, we climbed to the top of the cone and Gutiérrez could verify the further slumping of the interior flanks of the southwestern half of the cone ....

On June 26 Gutiérrez climbed the cone again and found the fissures to be further widened and lengthened, extending even into the east and west peaks. The bottom of the SW vent had sunk and the interior flanks of the crater were slumping into it. The NE vent was further filled with slumped material from the inner walls of the crater. Another ascent was

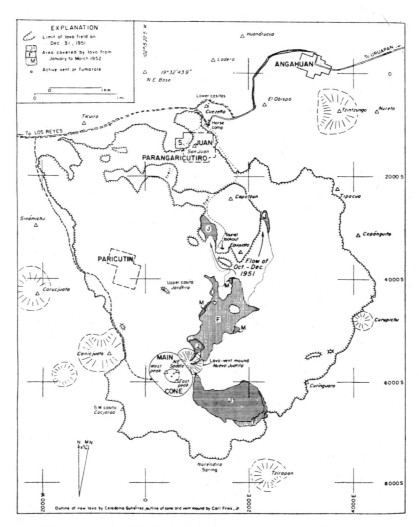

Fig. 128. Areas covered by Parícutin lava flows, January 1 to March 31, 1952.

Table 7. Horizontal distances[a] from Cuezeño station and elevations[b] above sea level, of points on Parícutin volcano.

Date	West peak		Lowest point on northeast rim		East peak		Lava-vent mound	
	Distance	Elevation	Distance	Elevation	Distance	Elevation	Distance	Elevation
	m	m	m	m	m	m	m	m
May 1, 1952	5230	2808.6	5170	2770.3	5370	2807.9	5000	2691.5

[a]Estimated accuracy of horizontal distances is within ten meters.
[b]Elevations determined by alidade from Cuezeño station; estimated accuracy of two meters.

182

made on August 14. The bottoms of the filled vents seemed to have continued to sink, and slumping of the inner flanks of the crater was further advanced. On November 5, Gutiérrez and Jesús Saldaña, accompanied by B. W. Wilson, geologist of the U.S. Geological Survey, visited the crater to note any changes since the ascent in August. The fissures had continued to widen and lengthen, the interior flanks of the crater had continued to slump, and the two vent fillings seemed to have sunk even further. This sinking of the vent fillings probably caused slumping of the inner walls of the crater and is responsible for maintaining a nearly constant difference of elevation between the bottom and the rim of the crater.

Reports of eruptions after March 4 occurred from time to time in local newspapers, but continuous observations by Gutiérrez and Saldaña, as well as repeated trips to the top of the cone, confirmed the absence of any eruption after March 4. At 15:15 on October 3, Gutiérrez heard a loud subterranean noise as if an explosion had occurred under the cone, but this disturbance produced no detectable change on the surface of the cone or in the crater.

Although earthquakes were seldom felt in the vicinity of Parícutin during the few years previous to the cessation of volcanic activity, many were felt in the months immediately after. Earthquakes were felt at Cuezeño on March 27 and 28, April 4, 5, and 11, May 18, 20, 21, 23, and 25, July 18, 21, and 26, September 18 and 25, and October 10. These were compared with the records at the Central Seismological Station in Tacubaya [320 km east of Parícutin] in the Federal District. Out of 33 shocks noted by Gutiérrez at Cuezeño station in March and April, only six were recorded at Tacubaya. Three of these six had their epicenters at distances of 285 and 322 km from Tacubaya, and as the distance from there to Parícutin is about 320 km, the shocks probably had their origin at the volcano. Tacubaya reported three quakes on May 25 and one on October 10. None of these had their origin near Parícutin, however, but they were felt over a large area that included Parícutin. Many of the shocks felt at Cuezeño station were not recorded at Tacubaya, an indication that these quakes were only of local origin and were related to the volcano. We thought that the strong local quakes in March and April might herald a renewal of eruptive activity, but, as the frequency of the quakes decreased later in the year, the danger was felt to be less imminent as time went on. The stronger shocks tumbled loose blocks on the surface of the flows and down the steep lava fronts, raising columns of dust. These shocks undoubtedly aggravated the slumping of the interior walls of the crater and possibly the sinking of the vent fillings. They did not, however, produce any major changes in the features of the cone and around the volcano.

Activity of the Lava Vents

Only the Nuevo Juatita vent was active in 1952. The cascade of lava that began to flow toward the NE on December 30, 1951, continued for only a few days (see Fig. 128), although on January 16 it again became active for a few days. On January 1 a new lava vent opened at the SE base of the lava-vent mound and continued to supply lava until the end of the month, when the NE cascade again became active. On February 8 a second NE cascade formed and lava continued to flow from it in large volume until on the 22nd of the month, the flow seemed to become sluggish on the surface. During the evening of February 24 the emission of lava declined abruptly, and on the morning of February 25 it ceased altogether, not to be resumed up to the time of writing this report (June, 1953). As noted above, the cessation of lava emission was accompanied by the cessation of continuous eruptions in the crater, but the lava-flow fronts continued to move, of course, for some days after the flow of lava ceased at the vents.

On March 8 the area of the NE lava vent was fissured and the reddish glow of hot basalt could be seen in the fissures, but there was no movement of the lava. After rainstorms in June, tenuous white vapors rose above the entire area of vents, fissures, and the final lava flows. Such vapors after rainstorms continued for the rest of the year and were often quite dense. They consisted principally of steam formed by the action of the underlying hot lava on rain water that seeped down through the cover of ash and cooled lava. At the end of the year, intense heat was still being emitted by the lava-vent areas on the NE and SW sides of the cone.

Activity of the Lava Flows

The flow that moved northward from the cone, around the base of Cerro de Equijuata, continued to advance early in January, although it was cut off at its source late in December, 1951. The tongue on the west side of Cerro de Equijuata moved over old terrain at the base of Cerro de Capatzun. The new flow that began to move SE on January 1 reached the edge of the Parícutin lava field early in February and covered a little of old terrain. On February 8, 1952, new lava cascaded northeastward over the flows of 1951. The front of this new flow continued to advance sluggishly for a few days in March, even though the cascade was beheaded on February 25.

The area covered by lava in the first two months of 1952 was 1,910,000 m². Assuming that the average thickness was 8 m, the total volume of lava extruded was 15,000,000 m³, or some 270,000 m³/day on the average. This was nearly three times the average daily volume of lava extruded during the second half of 1950 and the first half of 1951. We therefore see that both lava and ash emission increased notably in the last few months of the volcano's activity. The total area covered by the lava field, including the cone itself, is now 24.8 km², in comparison with 22 km² at the end of 1946 and 24.2 km² at the end of June, 1950 (see p. 171).

Weather Data

Total rainfall for the year at Cuezeño station [5½ km N of the vent] was 1,708.5 mm, an amount about equal to the 1948 total, but considerably greater than that of any other year from 1947 through 1951 (see Table 6). Certainly the effect of eruptions from Parícutin volcano on the rainfall at Cuezeño was not particularly great and was outweighed by other factors. Although the general pattern of annual rainfall at Equijuata station [2½ NE of the vent] was similar to that at Cuezeño station, the lack of relationship to eruptions is not so clear. Certainly some of the precipitated moisture near the cone was re-evaporated by the hot lava and returned to the atmosphere. This may have augmented the rainfall in the area, thereby causing the precipitation at Equijuata to be greater than at Cuezeño. The smaller excess of rainfall at Equijuata over that at Cuezeño in 1952 may be due in part to the cooling of the lavas and consequent decrease in re-evaporation near the cone.

Hot air and other gases continued to rise from the cone and the nearby lava fields in the months after cessation of eruption and on many days condensed over the cone before clouds formed elsewhere in the region. Usually the first clouds to form in the morning were almost directly above the cone, and later in the day the normal moisture clouds mingled with these to obliterate them as separate features. At times, people who saw these white clouds from a distance were certain that the volcano was in eruption and thus spread rumors to that effect. Even as late as November, 1952, puffy white clouds formed at several hundred meters above the cone and lingered there after other normal clouds had evaporated. This phenomenon suggests that some water vapor was still rising from the cone and lava fields. Possibly the heat from the latest flows carried moist air up to the level where it condensed. Drainage from the north slopes of the high Cerros de Tancítaro, south of the cone, almost in its entirety flows [around and seeps into the Parícutin lava field (see p. 303-306)], and the evaporation of this moisture probably accounts in large part for the puffy clouds above the cone.

. . . . .

As befitting closure, Celedonio Gutiérrez, a lifetime resident of the area, wrote the following commentary in his diary on March 20, 1952:

Our volcano of Parícutin is like a dream, in which we visualized the activity and fury of its eruptions for nine years and four days. That we actually saw it come into being, grow, and then die, seems to be completely unreal, but Parícutin's activity cannot be a dream, for the high mountain now present is an irrefutable witness before the world.

LAVA ENGULFS 2 MEXICO TOWNS, MENACES OTHERS

Advancing on 25-Mile Front From Paricutin Volcano — Refugees Throng Highways.

MEXICO CITY, July 19 (AP).— Millions of tons of molten lava pouring along a 25-mile front from Paricutin, Mexico's new volcano, have engulfed two towns and are threatening to wipe out three others.

Paricutin, the town from which the volcano takes its name, and Parangaricutiro, already are buried.

The lava is moving 200 yards a day toward Zacan, San Francisco Pariban and Zirosto, which have been partly evacuated. Residents are leaving other towns farther ahead.

Highways leading from the doomed region, 200 miles west of here, are crammed with caravans of Tarascan Indians swarming to higher ground with such belongings as they could scrape together.

Earthshaking explosions are heard at more or less regular intervals from the elevated center of the sea of lava. At each explosion a higher wave of melted stone pushes out from the volcano, born in February, 1948.

Nothing is now visible of the town of Paricutin—except the towers and roof of the church, which are expected to fall at any time.

The five-feet-thick walls of the famous church of Our Lord of Miracles in Parangaricutiro have been warped, melted or caved in by the lava, which has completely filled the church. The facade of the church still totters, but one of the two high towers has fallen and been swallowed up. Part of the high roof of the apse can barely be seen.

Dwellers of the region painted a gruesome picture of the lava pouring by night into the church of Our Lord of Miracles. The tombs on the inside were shattered, they said, and white skeletons together with sacred images floated on the tide pouring out of the sides of the church. Then all were reduced to ashes.

Travelers from Paricutin Valley described a violent electrical storm which occurred there several nights ago. Terrific claps of thunder vied with the explosions of the volcano and jagged lightning flashed over the sea of lava. The heavy rain, they said, had no effect on the lava flow, save to hide it for awhile under a blanket of white steam and increase the odor of sulphur in the air.

EXODO DEL PUEBLO DE PARANGARICUTIRO

Se cree que el río de lava en breve inundará éste.— Numerosas personas arriban a Uruapan cargando sus pobres bienes

Telegrama para EL UNIVERSAL

URUAPAN, Mich. 15 de junio de 1943.—El torrente de lava que arroja por su nuevo cráter el Paricutin, no avanza como han supuesto los alarmistas, hacia Uruapan. Hasta ahora, no obstante la rapidez de la invasión de la materia candente, sólo ha quedado cubierto en gran parte Paricutin, el poblado ya desierto y del que han salido los últimos habitantes que persistían en alojarse en los lugares más elevados y al parecer seguros.

El río de lava sí llegará en bre-

ve a Parangaricutiro y éste es desalojado rápidamente con ayuda de las autoridades municipales de esta ciudad, que han escuchado las llamadas de alarma de los habitantes de la zona invadida y que por medio del jefe de tránsito lo-

Sigue en la Página Dieciséis.

BARATAS

Vendo dos casas. Todos servicios. Oriente 85 Núm. 218, Col. Ixtacchuatl y Fundidora de Monterrey Núm. 306, Col. Industrial. SR. SIERRA. J-17-90. 13-12-49.

VENDEMOS

lancha remolcador de 30' de largo, casco de acero, motor "Lathrop" marino de 100 HP. STANDARD MACHINERY & SUPPLY CO., S. A.
ATENAS No. 31. Tel. Erie.

MANZANAS

Compramos siempre que sean sanas y maduras. Indíquenos precio puestas en México, D. F.

MUNDET

Calle Sabino 329. MEXICO, D. F.

BULBOS

Acabamos de recibir una pequeña partida con extenso surtido de números, precios baratos. ¡Solamente vendemos hasta dos bulbos a ca-

---

SUNDAY, DECEMBER 4, 1955.

PARACUTIN HOLDS A BLEAK THREAT

Mexican Farmlands Blighted by Land's Newest Volcano but Indians Fight Back

By PAUL P. KENNEDY

Special to The New York Times.

URUAPAN, Mexico, Nov. 29— Paracutin, one of the world's youngest volcanoes, has been dead for nearly four years but its imprint remains heavy and black on the countryside of Michoacán State near here.

Season after season since Paracutin quieted from its nine-year rampage in March, 1952, the patient Tarascan Indian farmers have gone about their bleak tasks of trying to reclaim their farmlands from the volcanic ashes. But it is the same story each year—pathetic half-formed cornstalks and stray wisps of brown grass.

The fight has not been wholly unsuccessful. Foot by foot the grim farmers are forcing the thin ashes on the periphery of the devastated area to yield a

flocking to the state of Michoacán.

Almost overnight their economy changed from farming to crafts, small industry and tourism. The villagers still are not content with this state of things, despite the fact they earn per capita much more than they did in farming.

The Indians patiently put in their crops but the results hardly vary from year to year. And after the crops come in—a failure—the farmers fall back on the villages, assisting in such things as box-making, weaving and the continuing trade in tourism.

The major effects of the volcano have shown themselves in the youth of the villages. The young men grew up with the young mountain and have adopted many of the customs and the language of the tourists they have been serving these many years.

Meanwhile the resettled natives of the villages now buried under tons of lava still have not become accustomed to their surroundings in the new village of Caltonztzing. It is only twenty miles from Paracutin, but no one has gone back to see the old places.

One resident said, "Why go back? There is nothing there but blackness."

LA ALDEA DE PARICUTIN BAJO LA LAVA DEL VOLCAN

En Plena Erupción

Gobelinos
SIGLOS XVI. y XVII
SOLO EN
GALERIAS ORDAZ
MADERO 17 TERCER PISO
MEXICO, D. F.

APERITAL DE LOR

El Aperitivo Mundial

EL UNIVERSAL
EL GRAN DIARIO DE MEXICO
SEGUNDA SECCION

Director:
PEDRO MALABEHAR PEÑA | NUMERO 9,665

AÑO XXVII.—TOMO CVI. | Presidente y Gerente: LIC. MIGUEL LANZ DURET | MEXICO, D. F.—MIERCOLES 16 DE JUNIO DE 1943

VICTIMAS DE UN DERRUMBE

TELE-VISIONES

Por TERENCIO.

RESPONSABILIDAD

El constructor y contratista del edificio de Miguel Abed, en la esquina de Isabel la Católica y Venustiano Carranza, es el señor M. Rebolledo, persona seria y de responsabilidad.

¿Por qué entonces, sin que se le exigiera las autoridades, no ha procurado proteger al público, y se ha constituido en creador de la "veredita tropical", y por lo menos, sancionado por su tolerancia, que los maestros de obras se complacen la mitad de la banqueta?

La ignoramos. Pero no hay un transeúnte que pase frente al Banco Nacional, que no reniegue cada vez que sobre su cabeza caen trozos de yeso, piedras, agua, etcétera. Y eso el mejor de los casos, porque en escasamente el arroyo, con riesgo de la vida.

Como el Jefe de Inspectores de Construcción se hace sordo, confiamos en que el señor Rebolledo atenderá los clamores del público, de los cuales no somos sino el vocero subordinado.

* * *

PROSA

Nos aseguran que don Noé de la Flor Casanova, Gobernador de Tabasco, es poeta.

Con un nombre tan perfumado y galante, encontramos lógico y...

EL ARTISTA QUE TOCA LA GUITARRA CON UNA SOLA MANO

LOS TECHOS SE LES CAYERON

Varios miembros de una familia resultaron heridos, al caerles los techos de la casa que habitaban. - Grandes trabajos para hacer el salvamento

Toda una familia, con excepción de dos de sus miembros, resultó víctima de un derrumbe en la casa que habitaban, en número 161 de la Calzada de Guadalupe, donde a la vez funciona la fábrica de Productos de Zinc, S. R. L. cuyo Gerente es el señor Jesús Goya. Al principio se creyó que se trataba de alguna explosión que había destruido la finca, pero más tarde se comprobó que solamente se originó, la caída de los techos de una manera intempestiva debido a su mal estado.

Se trata de una vieja casona que ocupa casi una manzana, pues tiene también salida por la calles de Riquelme 43. Parte de ella se compone de cuartos sin techar donde los operarios de la factoría realizaban algunos... otro lado no había pisos que ocupados, de 23 a la milla que era lo dar la casa.

Ayer, cerca de... a media manzana a... las habitacion... pantes estaban... darles tiempo... fnieron encima...

VISION APOCALIPTICA

...nuestra el nuevo cráter del Paricutín. En ella puede verse la visión apocalíptica.

Otra perspectiva del volcán, en plena erupción. Una enorme columna de humo se levanta del nuevo cráter hasta perderse en las altas regiones. El terrorífico espectáculo encierra, sin embargo, una belleza pasmosa.

EXODO DEL PUEBLO DE PARANGARICUTIRO

LAVA BURIES TOWNS

Mexico City, July 19 (A. P.).— Millions of tons of molten lava pouring along a twenty-five-mile front from Paricutin, Mexico's new-born volcano, have engulfed two towns and are threatening to wipe out three others. Paricutin, the town from which the volcano takes its name, and Parangaricutiro already are buried.

The lava is moving 200 yards a day toward Zacan, San Francisco, Pariban and Zirosto, which have been partly evacuated. Residents also are leaving other towns farther ahead. Highways leading from the doomed region are crammed with caravans of Tarascan Indians swarming to higher ground with such belongings— animals and household effects— as they could hastily scrape together.

Nothing is now visible of the town of Paricutin — Tarascan name for San Juan—except the towers and roof of the church, which are expected to fall at any time.

Human Communities
and Their Responses

Nolan (1979)

Earlier portions of this article, describing the "Towns of the Volcano" prior to the eruption, are reprinted on p. 31-34.

The Time of the Eruption

Convergence

The least studied aspect of the Parícutin eruption was the impact on the region's people. Nevertheless, the people affected by the volcano were the subject of considerable attention and were exposed to an unprecedented number of people from beyond the region. By 25 February, 1943, not only scientists, but tourists, reporters, curiosity seekers, and even peasants from other villages were arriving to witness the spectacle of Parícutin's eruption. Thus, from the very beginning of the physical catastrophe that destroyed their lands, the people affected by Parícutin volcano were also exposed to a radically changed social environment. As refugees, tourist guides, and even field research assistants, they came into contact with a great variety of people from beyond their region, especially North Americans and urban Mexicans. They became subjects of concern and planned social change for officials representing the rapidly modernizing Mexican nation. Within the first week, governmental agencies began a search for vacant lands where people from the eruption zone could be relocated[67].

Behavior patterns during the period of earthquakes and the early days of the eruptions were similar to those observed in connection with other catastrophic events that provide warning before direct impact. Curiosity leading to investigation and to remaining in the area to watch[68], exaggerated fantasies in an unfamiliar situation[69], and individual differences in choice of a time to leave the region or even to leave at all[68,70] are apparently common reactions. As is often found in disaster studies[71-73], the family was an important unit of action and members of the extended family residing outside the impact zone provided a source of aid.

Events of the Quitzocho Period

The period of volcanic activity that lasted from February until October 1943 began with explosive activity followed, after March 18, by a heavy fall of cinders and ashes. When the seasonal rains began in May, the "rain of sand" was replaced by a terrible "rain of mud." Both ruined attempts at farming over a wide area, and forests in the eruption zone began to die. The pyroclastic fall also created highly uncomfortable conditions for humans within a radius of about 25 km from the cinder cone (Fig. 129), but particularly within the five villages in the immediate area[6] [see p. 31-34, and inside-front-cover maps].

Many of the people who first fled the eruption zone in fear soon returned home; however, within the first 3 months after the volcanic outbreak, a more permanent exodus began. It was composed mostly of those who had kinsmen in other communities or skills allowing reasonable employment in other places and/or resources that could be liquidated to pay for relocation. In other words, it was generally the richer, better-educated, more exogamous [persons who choose marriage partners from outside their community], Spanish-speaking *mestizos* who first left their home communities. However, some of the richer families stayed because their wealth was in land and homes that could not be disposed of without sacrifice, and they felt they had too much to lose by leaving. A few of the early migrants were among the poor but

Fig. 129. Women of San Juan Parangaricutiro approaching the church on their knees to pray that the volcano might cease. February 27, 1943.

ambitious Spanish speakers who had already been thinking of leaving their villages to seek better opportunities elsewhere.

Hardly anyone left the Indian-oriented communities of Parícutin and Angahuan during this period, but by mid-June 1943, the situation in Parícutin village was desperate. Water sources had disappeared. Fields were buried to great depths under ash and, in some cases, lava. The heavy pyroclastic fall had destroyed the roof of the church and many of the homes [see p. 87, Fig. 51]. When lava began flowing down an *arroyo* in the direction of the village, government officials and geologists agreed that the town should be evacuated, even though the geologists were reasonably certain that it was not in immediate danger of inundation by lava [see p. 83].

As discussed by Rees[10], various agencies of the Mexican government were involved in evaluating privately owned haciendas, ejidos (see p. 35), and other lands as possible sites for resettlement. An hacienda at Caltzontzin (5½ km east of Uruapan and

27 km ESE of the new volcano: Fig. 130) was purchased in early May 1943. This purchase included 100 hectares (a hectare equals 2.47 acres or 0.01 km²) of arable land, 160 hectares of woodlands, and 5 hectares of avocado orchards. More than 200 hectares were also transferred from the neighboring ejido of San Francisco Uruapan, bringing the total lands of the Caltzontzin settlement to nearly 500 hectares. By July 10, all of the people of Parícutin village and their possessions had been moved to Caltzontzin. Construction of the new houses on the rectangular grid plan of a classic Mexican village was largely complete by September, and in March 1944 the communal ejido organization was formed and parcels of land were assigned.

Accounts of the evacuation of Parícutin village by the Mexican army range from stories of people forced into government trucks at gunpoint to dramatic accounts of a peasant population gladly following General Lázaro Cárdenas to a new land, a new destiny, and a better future. All the accounts apparently contain some truth, because many of Parícutin's younger citizens did welcome new opportunities, whereas many others, especially among the older people, "did not wish to leave and . . . preferred to die covered with lava rather than abandon their homes"[6]. Dying under the lava was not permitted either by nature or other men. Lava did not cover Parícutin village until more than a year after its evacuation [March, 1945], and then only slowly.

The new settlement of Caltzontzin . . . lay at an altitude of about 1,525 m, [about 750 m lower than Parícutin village]. There the formerly isolated highland Tarascans of Parícutin were given lands in *ejido*, new houses that they did not like, and new shoes that most were not accustomed to wearing. Many well-meant efforts were made to help them adjust to their new situation, but little attention was paid to some of their deepest, non-economic needs. It would have been a simple matter to change the name of the refugee settlement to Parícutin Nuevo, but this was not done and the loss of the community name was symbolic of many other losses in the continuity of life. Culture shock stemming from too much change too fast plagued the Caltzontzin refugee settlement for more than a generation[2,10].

The Volcanic Zone

Meanwhile, in the volcanic zone conditions worsened as the reserves from the 1942 harvest were consumed and it became obvious there would be no harvest in 1943. Resin collection was no longer possible and

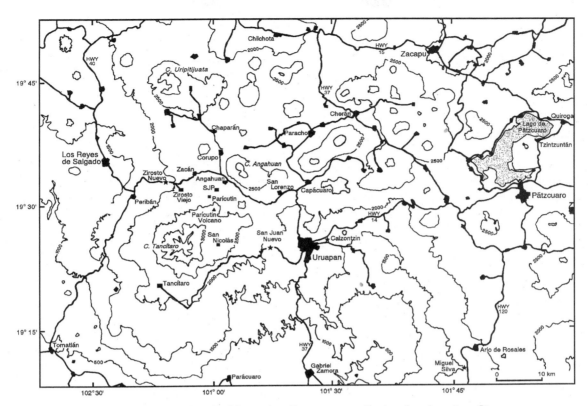

Fig. 130. Topographic map of the modern Tarascan area. Contour lines in meters. Stars show four refugee towns discussed in text.

more trees were dying. The livestock, their bellies full of pyroclastics from consumption of ash-covered vegetation, also began to die[6]. Wild fruits and berries, bees, and wild game disappeared from the landscape.

Families continued to leave the sierra. Some, especially from Zacán and San Juan Parangaricutiro, went to other Mexican towns and cities. Others, primarily from Zirosto, headed for lands in the Ario de Rosales *municipio* [a political subdivision corresponding roughly to an American township], where the government was reported to be planning a major refugee settlement. Salvaging the dead and dying forests, road building, and guiding tourists and scientists provided a meager subsistence for those who remained in the volcanic zone through the summer of 1943. In San Juan boys sold rocks from the volcano to visitors, and men and women established refreshment stands dangerously near the eruptions. A Red Cross station was established in San Juan in May 1943, and famine was averted through the donation of nearly 800,000 pesos [$165,000 U.S.] worth of food and other goods by various relief agencies.

The heaviest and most destructive period of pyroclastic fall in the volcano's short history ceased on 9 June 1943, but the sands did not remain where they had fallen. They were shifted and reshifted by wind and water, deeply eroding slopes and burying some former fields to great depths.

Numerous town meetings were held in San Juan Parangaricutiro to consider relocation but the remaining people "were not able to make the effort to uproot their hearts and take themselves to another place far away"[6]. General Cárdenas came in person to urge resettlement. Finally, the men of San Juan were given governmental permission to locate an acceptable site for a refugee settlement, but resistance to relocation continued. In spite of 6 months of "hell under the shadows of the vapors, black clouds, cold rains of sticky sand, cinders, and ashes"[6], the people of San Juan prepared a final September fiesta for the Lord of the Miracles [Fig. 7]. Pilgrims came by the thousands, from Michoacán and elsewhere in México, and even from other nations. Because they suspected that the great pilgrimage shrine was doomed and that 14 September 1943 marked the last year of fiesta in San Juan, "Men and women with tears in their eyes kissed the divine feet of Our Lord of the Miracles. With loud sobs they kissed the altars and the sacred face"[6].

The Sapichu Period

October 17, 1943 to 8 January 1944 has been termed the Sapichu period by geologists, after the name given to a small subsidiary cone on the NE base of the main cone. Eruptions from Sapichu provided a spectacle for tourists, but the main cone became so quiet that it was climbed several times during November and December 1943 (see p. 102).

The principal human event of the period was the founding of Miguel Silva, [a resettlement community located about 65 km SE of the new volcano and about 40 km SE of the Caltzontzin settlement, where the Parícutin villagers were moved: Fig. 130]. The search for a resettlement location in the *municipio* of Ario de Rosales . . . was initiated during the first week of the eruptions[67]. Several Zirosto families moved into the area on their own initiative during the summer of 1943. They settled near a *rancho* and attempted to farm vacant lands that had belonged to the Hacienda de las Animas prior to its expropriation in 1938. On 6 October 1943, the ex-*hacienda* was formally selected as a refugee location and the lands were listed for settlement on 17 October. Refugees from Zirosto and San Juan Parangaricutiro were offered 2,616 hectares [26.2 km^2], and from late 1943 through the spring of 1944, 1,000-1,200 refugees poured into the settlement. Government trucks provided transportation and the Banco Nacional de Credito Ejital issued loans, although no *ejido* grants had yet been made[67].

Secular leadership was composed of men from both communities. Probably 80% of Zirosto's population relocated, but the number was considerably smaller from San Juan. It is usually explained that the many Tarascan speakers of the latter community were the most resistant to resettlement, although Zirosto's fewer Tarascan speakers were represented.

Unfortunately, the *hacienda* lands had not been adequately surveyed, and when the survey was completed, it was found that only 350 hectares of the vast area was suitable for agriculture. By this time, 310 men, most with families, were already there[67]. Obviously, the major problem with the Miguel Silva settlement was that more refugees arrived than the land could support. In early 1944, the local rancheros killed the secular leaders of the refugee settlement and threatened the priest, who was recalled to another post. They also killed the surviving livestock and

otherwise waged war on the huge number of refugees who had descended upon them.

With local leadership gone, refugees from San Juan and Zirosto began to fight among themselves. The climate, although not excessively hot at an altitude of about 1,500 m, was unfamiliar to these highland people [San Juan Parangaricutiro elevation - 2,255 m, Zirosto elevation - 2,040 m]. Many of the seeds they brought failed to grow. In addition, the water was bad and most of the refugees were sick with intestinal disorders and malaria. As many as one-tenth of the refugees died, especially the older people, who are said to have lacked the will to live under such conditions.

Within a year, many of the survivors left Miguel Silva, and by 1946 the population had decreased to about 300[4]. Most of the San Juan refugees went to San Juan Nuevo after its founding in May 1944. Zirosto families either went to the United States or returned to the volcanic zone. The few from Zirosto who stayed cut themselves off emotionally from the mother community and came to view themselves as the pioneer founders of a new settlement on a difficult frontier. Many looked with disdain on those who returned to the Sierra "to eat the sands of the volcano."

The Taquí Period

In January 1944, two new lava vents opened on the SW base of the original cone (see p. 103-105). The flows from these Taquí vents began on 7 January and continued until the end of July 1945, when scientific observations were temporarily discontinued. The lava flows from these vents ultimately covered San Juan Parangaricutiro.

As the wall of molten lava slowly approached in March 1944, the people remaining in San Juan reached an agreement. Although the site of a new settlement had already been chosen at Rancho Los Conejos by the men of the community [7½ km W of Uruapan and 15 km SE of the new volcano: Fig. 130], it was decided that no one would leave the town until the lava flow reached the cemetery[6] . . . . Faith that the Lord of the Miracles would save San Juan Parangaricutiro was reinforced by the belief that science would bring salvation. The latter belief stemmed from the establishment of a seismographic station by Mexican geologists in February 1944[6]. However, both the clergy and the scientists were active in the attempt to reconcile the townsmen to the eventual necessity of relocation.

On 14 April 1944, the lava flow sprang from the tunnels that had hidden its progress. By 24 April, a burst of molten lava from the 9-m-high flow front reached the San Juan-Uruapan road, and the water lines to San Juan were endangered and moved. The road, which passed through a narrow valley, was as yet the only good access to San Juan Parangaricutiro for motorized traffic, and in a spurt of activity the road linking San Juan to Angahuan and thence to the Uruapan highway was completed[6].

The 9-m-high wall of the main lava front continued to move at a rate of 4-5 m/hr as tongues of lava surged forth more rapidly through the pass along the old road and the steep-walled *arroyo* that ran along the town's eastern edge. In early May, the lava flow reached the cemetery, where it slowed in its progression to a few centimeters per hour. Families came to the foot of the lava front, and there, kneeling on the graves of their ancestors, they prayed. In respect for the March agreement, few asked that the town be spared, but only for time to dismantle their church and their homes and take with them all they could of their beloved town. They "cried out to the Lord of the Miracles offering to go with Him, even to the place in which He would make us think we should remain"[6].

On 7 May, the bishop arrived from Zamora accompanied by several priests and other church officials. The next day, the bishop celebrated a solemn mass and confirmed the local children, and an old priest arose to address the people of San Juan Parangaricutiro. He was Father Luís Gómez, who had served in the community between 1895 and 1917, and it was under his guidance that the colonial church had been dismantled and a new church begun. He spoke of his sadness in seeing the still unfinished church threatened with destruction, but he added that "the Lord God who had allowed the temple to be built was now allowing it to vanish and we should not regret it so much because that loss was nothing compared to the loss of a human being, or worse of the inhabitants of an entire town"[6]. When Father Gómez finished speaking, "everyone wept, women and men, and perhaps these were the last sounds of voices to be heard in that place . . . . The sound of the echo filled the space and then vibrated for a long time inside the church, which soon would be destroyed by the lava"[6].

Even in this emotional moment, the San Juan community was divided because there were still a few who wanted to keep the image of the Lord of the Miracles in the church in hope of a miraculous salvation from the advancing lava. To counteract this belief, and avoid possible disaster, the bishop lifted the image of Christ from its place above the altar on 9 May. Accompanied by church officials and supportive townsmen, he held the image high in the beginning of a small procession. A few people threw themselves in the path of the procession, but their fellow townsmen pulled them aside and joined the march behind the most sacred symbol of their community [Fig. 131]. Soon all were following, and the people spent the night in Angahuan, where the Lord of the Miracles rested in the company of the image of Santiago, patron of that town.

On 10 May 1944, the procession continued toward Uruapan. All along the route groups of pilgrims met

Fig. 131. The ancient crucifix *El Señor de Los Milagros* [The Lord of the Miracles] carried in procession evacuating San Juan Parangaricutiro on May 9, 1944.

the people of San Juan. "They were weeping, seeing that the Holy Christ had left the town of San Juan and was being carried away without their knowledge of where He would be transferred"[6]. The viewers who lined the roads came out to kiss the image and give water to those who walked behind. When the refugees reached the Uruapan highway, they found great crowds of people who offered them food and water and walked beside the procession shooting off fireworks.

At the edge of Uruapan, the multitude was so great that people could hardly move as the priests of the city came out to meet the procession. "On seeing that people could no longer walk on the streets of the city, some men were asked to pass the word that no one was to move from the place he was occupying. Hundreds of men formed an arm chain in order to take Our Lord in between"[6]. The city was decorated as for fiesta and the people were shouting, "Long live Christ the King." Thus, along the route of procession, a feeling of hope built among the people of San Juan and they "felt a kind of comfort and were sure that we were traveling on a road along which Our Lord was guiding us"[6].

On the third day, the people of San Juan reached the valley they had chosen as their new home. Because of their insistence on choosing a new home, they received only a town site and no agricultural lands. They had lost their position as head town of *municipio*. Many of the richer and more prominent citizens had left the community early in the eruption period, and in the early days in the new settlement people had to do without things to which they had long been accustomed, such as schools, piped water, and electricity in the main plaza. For a time, many lived in tents, although a small chapel for the Lord of the Miracles was built immediately. [The villagers were given house lots of the same size and at the same relative location as they had in the former village.][11] The new place was called Rancho Los Conejos, "the little hamlet of the rabbits." People in Uruapan still make jokes about San Juan of the Rabbits, but government documents indicate that the men of San Juan had the name of the settlement formally changed to San Juan Nuevo Parangaricutiro on 9 July 1944[74]. By that time, old San Juan and its church had been buried under lava. People from San Juan who had previously left for Mexican cities or had attempted pioneering at Miguel Silva soon joined the San Juan Nuevo community.

The Bracero Program

By early 1944, a new economic opportunity emerged as men from communities affected by the volcano were urged to enlist as contract laborers in the United States. The importance of the *bracero* program as a stimulus for change is unquestioned. The *braceros* [Spanish for day laborers] experienced life in a very different cultural setting, and the opportunities for capital accumulation were enormous. It had been established that during the World War II years, *bracero* workers could make 15 to 20 times as much as they could have earned from the same labor in México[75]. In contrast with the situation in most other Mexican communities, where quotas were imposed and this opportunity was open only to a few men with good connections or a lucky lottery ticket, all able-bodied men from towns in the volcanic zone and the refugee settlements could enlist as *braceros*.

The communities varied in the extent to which opportunities for *bracero* work were accepted.

Although exact figures are not available, it is probable that a large majority of the men of San Juan Parangaricutiro and Caltzontzin [the resettlement community for Parícutin village] worked at least once as *braceros*. Many also went from Zacán, but there was a somewhat greater tendency for men of that community to seek wage labor in nearby Mexican cities and towns. A large number of those who had attempted to settle at Miguel Silva [refugees from Zirosto and San Juan Parangaricutiro] also enlisted as *braceros*, but few of those from Zirosto who had not gone first to Miguel Silva. Hardly any of Angahuan's men accepted the opportunity. This was partly due to a general reluctance to leave the community, and perhaps to some extent to the fact that Angahuan had inherited the traffic in scientists and tourists after the evacuation of San Juan Parangaricutiro. It is said locally that men could not become *braceros* because they could not speak much, if any, Spanish, but this is not a completely adequate reason, because numerous Tarascan monolinguals went as *braceros* from San Juan and Caltzontzin.

The Later Years of the Eruption

By the volcano's second anniversary, February 1945, the period of high drama was over. Never again were the Parícutin eruptions so catastrophic or, for very long, so spectacular. The lava field was outlined by December 1944, and later eruptions added depth and buried exposed areas within the field. People remaining in the volcanic zone tried various strategies of subsistence. They felled the forests, including areas that had not been damaged by the eruptions, and in Angahuan they guided tourists. Seed was planted in pure ash but did not survive. Ash shoveled off small plots by hand produced some crops in sheltered house lots but was not effective in the open fields because the sand drifted back over the clearings. Slopes blown or washed free from ash were put into cultivation, including high mountain lands where crops were subject to frost hazard[10,76].

By 1946, the wild bees were returning to the sierra and wild berries and crab apples near the grave of San Juan Parangaricutiro bore abundant fruits. Crops ripened in painstakingly uncovered soil on lands near Zacán and Zirosto, and some wheat ripened on the lands of Angahuan. Fighting broke out between the men of Zacán and the *rancho* of Las Palmas over lands that Zacán had claimed for generations but that had become particularly desirable because they lay away from the zone of devastation[77]. In Zirosto, men began taking the treasures of the ancient monastic church to sell in the cities.

Meanwhile, adjustments were underway in the refugee settlements. Caltzontzin's citizens began rebuilding their government-designed homes to fit their tastes[10]. Miguel Silva got a pure-water system and favorable government intervention in the feud with the local rancheros[67]. The population stabilized as the survivors began to think of themselves as pioneers rather than refugees. In San Juan Nuevo Parangaricutiro (or San Juan Nuevo), the ground was blessed for the consecration of a new church for the Lord of the Miracles . . . .

Life was resuming a more normal rhythm, which included the volcano's occasional periods of major activity . . . . Dionisio Pulido died in Caltzontzin in 1949[32], and the *ejido* grant to Miguel Silva was confirmed. Zacán found a new technique for waging war with Las Palmas by claiming that old boundaries had been obscured by the ash. In the same year a new species of grass not previously known in the region began invading areas of deep ash.

The year 1950 began with strong, fairly frequent explosions from Parícutin and a few earth tremors. Dust storms were severe during the dry spring and damaged vegetation that was moving back into the zone of devastation. Mosses, lichens, and ferns were found in moist places on the thinner lavas. The people of Angahuan were putting corn lands back into production, and as pasturage revived, the region's livestock population increased. Around Zacán, lands had been washed sufficiently free of ash to permit a return to nearly normal agriculture, although the land war with Las Palmas continued[77].

In 1951 it was dry in the spring as usual. In the summer it rained. The volcano erupted occasionally. Life had, indeed, returned to normal. For some geologists, as judged from their writings, the volcano became boring because nothing new happened. For others it became more interesting because it was repetitive and therefore predictable. For Celedonio Gutiérrez, "Every day for nine years the volcano was different. The earthquakes were recorded and the march of the lavas. All this, for me, was very interesting"[2]. Then, on 4 March 1952, Parícutin was dead. Spring brought damaging dust storms, but the following summer was unusually wet and many areas were washed clean of ash. The best harvests since the birth of the volcano were gathered in August 1952.

The Immediate Aftermath

For most people in the refugee towns, the end of the eruptions did not matter very much. They had long before come to terms with new destinies. Nor was it of much importance in Zacán, where agriculture was already nearly normal. Angahuan, however, had become dependent economically on tourists who came to see the eruptions. As word spread that the show was over, the tourist traffic virtually disappeared. Some men were finally forced to leave town as temporary laborers because the lands were still too unproductive to support a population that had increased slightly during the eruption years. Although a new generation of tourists eventually returned to see the volcano they had read about in school textbooks, Angahuan tourist guides still look wistfully at the conical black form of Parícutin. Most probably feel what one expressed: "It would be nice if the volcano would erupt again—just a little bit."

In Zirosto the last act of a social tragedy was played out when the community fragmented into the spatially discrete settlements of Zirosto Viejo and Zirosto Nuevo [Fig. 130]. Things had been going badly for a long time, and men had fought among themselves for the few available resources. In about 1949, the church of the once important colonial monastery burned, and the baptistry was fragmented into three pieces by a lightning bolt from the eruption column. When the eruptions ended, the Mexican government encouraged the Zirosto population to relocate [about 2 km NW] to the site of Rancho Barranco Seca, which was on the Uruapan-Los Reyes road. [An outside contractor established a lumber mill here in 1944 to exploit timber killed by the eruption.][11] In return for relocation, the people were promised an *ejido* grant, a 6-year school, bus service along the road, electricity, piped water, and street lights. [Barranca Seca later became known as Zirosto Nuevo when in 1952 the federal government transferred 317 hectares from another *ejido*, and purchased 184 additional hectares from private owners.][11]

A majority went to Zirosto Nuevo in 1953, but some adamantly refused to leave the old town. Brothers made different choices, placing strain on family relations and the solidarity of kinship networks. It is said in Zirosto Nuevo that the move would have been truly successful if all had gone together, taking with them the old bells that symbolized the community. In Old Zirosto, those who left are blamed. It is argued that if all had stayed, the Mexican government would eventually have rerouted the road, provided electricity, water, 6 years of school, and all the other benefits. In terms of social disruption Zirosto became, as is said locally, the town "most destroyed by the volcano[2]."

Community Life After the Eruption

As the years passed, plant and animal life continued its regeneration in the zone of early devastation. Slowly, plants invaded the lava fields and appeared in scattered, humble forms on the dead cinder cone. Although the lava field will remain agriculturally useless for centuries, areas of light ashfall were back in production before the eruptions ceased. Areas of heavy ashfall and places where ash had washed down on former fields, covering them to depths of several meters, remained useless for agriculture in the early 1970s[2,78]. However, urban entrepreneurs had discovered an economic value for pyroclastic deposits and some deep sand deposits were being mined for use in concrete manufacture.

As fertility returned to areas of medium ashfall, both naturally and through human efforts, the conditions generated by the eruptions continued to affect human life. Incidents of aggression and land wars with loss of human life became more intense in the region as formerly useless lands regained agricultural value. These conflicts were particularly difficult to settle because the eruptions had destroyed landmarks traditionally used as boundaries between one village or individual and another.

The longstanding struggle between Zacán and Rancho La Palma was resolved in 1957 when Zacán was allowed to annex the *rancho* and thus became politically responsible for it. Sporadic sniping continued for several more years[77].

The most serious later hostilities involved San Juan Nuevo, Caltzontzin, and the people of *ranchos* founded by both refugee settlements on community lands in the volcanic zone. Court battles were in process by the early 1950s and incidents of aggression were reported in 1959 and 1960. In 1965, the feud intensified and reports of hired gunmen, killings, and substantial property destruction were filed with government agencies by San Juan Nuevo and Caltzontzin. In 1969, representatives of the two communities agreed to let trained surveyors set the disputed boundaries. The exact toll in lives and property is impossible to estimate because the record consists largely of unsupported claim and counterclaim from the feuding communities. In April 1967, however, a government investigator documented destruction of harvest, killing of livestock, and the burning of 128 houses (*casas*) in small volcanic-zone settlements[77].

The San Juan-Caltzontzin land war clearly retarded the course of permanent resettlement in the volcanic zone. In 1971, both communities contained a number of families who had left the volcanic-zone *ranchos* during the height of the conflict.

The Towns of the Volcano in the Early 1970s

Although the eruptions ended in 1952, social pressures for change continued to affect the three eruption-zone settlements and the four refugee communities. In 1971, these seven communities were quite different in spite of their original similarities and their shared history of experience with a catastrophic natural event. To a considerable extent they represented a cross section of rural México under the pressures of a rapidly changing socio-economic order.

San Juan Nuevo symbolized the success story of the modernizing rural *cabecera*, or *municipio* head town, capable of retaining meaningful traditions in the course of change. It also provided a case study of one of México's numerous thriving pilgrimage centers. In contrast, Old Zirosto exemplified the community that declines even as others progress. Zirosto Nuevo was the community with insufficient roots and communal purpose. Miguel Silva could be compared with many pioneer settlements that have developed on newly opened lands in recent years. Caltzontzin had its counterparts in the numerous small communities that are being transformed into urban *barrios* as cities expand across the countryside. Zacán was the village that gave the best of its young to the growing urban middle class and declined in the process. Angahuan was the adamantly Indian town, greatly changed, yet clinging to outward expression of tradition, a condition complicated by the interests of tourists and folk-craft developers.

The general trend of change was toward greater interaction with the larger Mexican society accompanied by loss of Tarascan traditions. This generalization, however, obscures a multitude of complex variations in the nature of the new societal adjustments.

Except in Angahuan, where everyone still spoke the Indian language, use of Tarascan was declining. No exact figures are available, but only a few of the elderly spoke Tarascan in Zacán, Miguel Silva, and the Zirostos, although a few poets and songwriters in Zacán and Miguel Silva cultivated the language for artistic purposes. Tarascan was sometimes heard on the streets of San Juan Nuevo, but one of the local priests estimated that only about 20% of the population, mostly elderly, could use the language fluently. Tarascan was more frequently heard in Caltzontzin, and was deliberately retained as a household language by several relatively affluent

Table 8. Comparison of the study towns with other Michoacán communities. Towns ranked by number of facilities and services in 1940.

| Community | Population | Items[a] | | | | | | | | | | | | | |
		Autonomous and named	Elementary school	Plaza or square	Government organization	Bar or cantina	Bakery	Barber shop	Butcher shop	Resident priest	Hotel or inn	Pool hall	Resident doctor	Movie theater	Gas station
Quiroga	1940:3009	×	×	×	×	×	×	×	×	×	×	×	×	×	×
Quiroga	1970:7129	×	×	×	×	×	×	×	×	×	×	×	×	×	×
Old San Juan	1940:1895	×	×	×	×	×	×	×	×	×	×	×	×	—	—
New San Juan	1970:4689	×	×	×	×	×	×	×	×	×	×	×	×	×	—
Cherán	1940:3358	×	×	×	×	×	×	×	×	×	×	×	—	—	—
Cherán	1970:7793	×	×	×	×	×	×	×	×	×	×	×	×	×	×
Zirosto	1940:1314	×	×	×	×	?	×	×	×	×	×	×	f	—	—
Old Zirosto	1970: 434	×	×	×	—	—	—	—	—	—	—	—	—	—	—
New Zirosto	1970:1085	×	×	—	×	—	×	×	×	—	—	—	f	—	—
Miguel Silva	1970: 648	×	×	×	×	—	—	—	×	×	—	—	—	—	—
Tzintzuntzan	1940:1077	×	×	×	×	×	×	—	—	×	—	—	—	—	—
Tzintzuntzan	1970:2174	×	×	×	×	×	×	—	—	×	—	×	—	—	—
Zacán	1940: 876	×	×	×	×	—	—	—	—	—	—	—	—	—	—
Zacán	1970: 926	×	×	×	×	—	×	×	×	—	—	×	—	—	—
Parícutin	1940: 733	×	×	×	—	—	?	—	—	—	—	—	—	—	—
Caltzontzin	1970:1295	×	×	×	×	—	×	—	×	×	—	×	—	—	—
Angahuan	1940:1098	×	*	×	—	—	—	—	—	—	—	—	—	—	—
Angahuan	1970:1762	×	×	×	×	×	×	—	×	×	—	—	—	—	—

[a]The 1940s item list for Quiroga, Cherán, and Tzintzuntzan was compiled by Young and Fujimoto (1965) from ethnographic accounts. The second item count for these towns comes from the 1967 data collected by Graves et al. (1969). Items for the towns of the volcano reflect conditions in 1943 and 1971 (Nolan 1972).

× = item present
? = conflicting information
f = item had recently been present
* = item present off and on

families, but for the most part, Spanish was the first language of the younger generation.

In 1971, fiestas were celebrated in all the communities, but the traditional *mayordomía* system [see p. 32-33] survived only in San Juan Nuevo. There, the great fiesta for the Lord of the Miracles had long been sponsored by the community as a whole, but individual sponsorship of the fiesta of the town's patron saint remained a route to local power and prestige in the early 1970s. It was only one such route, however.

Traditional Tarascan dress, particularly for women, was common in Angahuan, not particularly unusual in San Juan Nuevo and Caltzontzin, and either rare or nonexistent in Zacán, the Zirostos, and Miguel Silva. As might be expected, traditional housing was most notable in Angahuan, Zacán, and old Zirosto, the three settlements that remained in place in the volcanic zone.

By 1971 all settlements but Old Zirosto had federally sponsored electric power, a piped supply of potable water, and a 6-year elementary school. Only Old Zirosto lacked a post office and bus service to the center of town. Comparison between the study towns and three other Michoacán communities along the lines of "institutional differentiation"[79] is presented in Table 8[80]. Data for the existence of these traits in the communities affected by the volcano in 1943 and 1971 were obtained through interviews with knowledgeable older citizens during the 1971 field season. The results of these interviews were checked by administering the same set of questions to at least two other people in each town. Probably because the volcano provided such an excellent time marker, there were few inconsistencies in response about what was present in 1943.

Comparison of communities in the 1940s indicates that Zacán, Parícutin, and Angahuan were relatively undeveloped. They also had the smallest populations. San Juan Parangaricutiro and Zirosto, in contrast, were well-developed towns for the region. Both compared favorably with the much larger community of Cherán [38 km NE of the new volcano: Fig. 130], which had recently won the advantage of location on a paved highway.

Table 9. Comparison of the study towns with other Mexican communities.

Number[a] of items	Selected Mexican towns as of 1967 (1960 population figures)	Study towns, 1943 (1940 population)	Study towns, 1971 (1970 population)
24	Quiroga, Michoacán (5336)		
23	Mitla, Oaxaca (3651)		San Juan (4698)
21	Cheran, Michoacán (5651)		
20		San Juan (1895)	
19	Cajititlan, Jalisco (1880)		
18	Aldama, Guanajuato (1919)		
17	Lagunillas, Michoacán (1981)		
16	Yalalag, Oaxaca (3117)	Zorosto (1314)	Caltzontzin (1295)
15	San Pedro, Tobasco (1500)		Zacan (926) and Angahuan (1762)
14	Tzintzuntzan, Michoacán (1840)		
13	Teotitlan, Oaxaca (2849)		
12	Amatenango, Chiapas (1832)		New Zirosto (1085) and Miguel Silva (648)
11	Santa Rosa, Guanajuato (632)		
9	Zangarro, Michoacán (327)		
8	Atzompa, Oaxaca (1726)		
7	Santa Cruz Etla, Oaxaca (613)		Old Zirosto (434)
6	San Feli Rigo, Puebla (701)	Zacan (876) and Parícutin (733)	
5	Chachalacas, Veracruz (208)		
4	Kikeil, Yucatan (230)	Angahuan (1098)	
2	Tatacuatitla, Hidalgo (153)		
1	Carmen, Sinaloa (221)		

[a]Items drawn from Graves et al. (1969) are elementary school, grocery store, mass once a year, church, square or plaza, government organization, government official, public transportation, bakery, butcher shop, shipping service, newspaper delivery, barber shop, resident priest, bar or cantina, telephone, billiard parlor, movie theater, resident doctor, filling station, restaurant, hotel or inn, secular organization, and secondary school. Only the number of traits present is considered in this table.

By 1971, the item list no longer "scaled" but still served as a useful measure of comparative change. San Juan Parangaricutiro was already close to the top of this scale in 1943, as were Quiroga, Cherán, and Zirosto. San Juan, which lost many of these facilities and services during the eruption years, had regained its high position by 1971. None of the fragments of Zirosto had reached the level of the mother community in the pre-volcanic period. Caltzontzin, Zacán, and Angahuan had acquired appreciably more new facilities and services during the time period involved than had Tzintzuntzan, an intensively studied *mestizo* community with a Tarascan heritage, located on the shores of Lake Pátzcuaro, [73 km ENE of the new volcano: Fig. 130].

Another comparative measure based on 24 facilities and services[79] allows comparison between the communities affected by Parícutin and a selection of other small Mexican towns and villages (Table 9). As in the first comparison, the most obvious features are the failure of any of the Zirosto-derived communities to reach the 1943 level of the mother community, and the major increases in services and facilities achieved by Caltzontzin, Zacán, and Angahuan. Pre-volcanic San Juan Parangaricutiro was too close to the top of the scale to show much change along this dimension. If such items as dry-goods stores, banking facilities, and farm-supply outlets were added, the amount of change in San Juan could be better evaluated.

In 1971, the towns were still predominantly agricultural communities (Fig. 132). According to the 1970 Mexican census[81], more than three-fourths of the work force in Angahuan, the Zirostos, and Miguel Silva was engaged in primary activities. Well over 60% of the workers in San Juan Nuevo and Caltzontzin labored in field and forest. In those towns, as in Angahuan, there was a substantial amount of small industry, mostly backyard enterprises, and in Caltzontzin's case, a plant in which hand-loomed textiles were produced. The largest percentage of the work force engaged in commerce and services was in Zacán, where slightly less than half of the population was employed in the primary sector of the economy. Since there was relatively little local development of commerce and services, it seems likely that these figures describe people who maintained the community as a home base but were employed in Uruapan and elsewhere. In keeping with an old Zacán tradition, some were musicians who primarily made a living by playing in urban nightspots during the weekends. Periods of work in the United States, often without permits, were common, especially among younger men from San Juan Nuevo and Zacán. Migrant labor of various kinds in other parts of México also resulted in contributions to the local economies.

There had been a general trend toward population growth, as was occurring all over México during the same time period. However, only the San Juan community had more than doubled in size, and none of the offshoots of Zirosto had reached the size of the pre-volcanic town. Comparative population figures are included in Table 8.

In a nation like México, where migration of the young from rural areas to the cities is a major means of adaptation to changing conditions and rural population pressures, the viability of the rural community is, to some degree, indicated by the out-migrants' ability to achieve positions of economic and social reward in the larger society. The custom of keeping track of professionals, common in many small Mexican communities, provides an indicator of achievement along these lines. Examination of Fig. 133 shows that Zacán and Caltzontzin were significantly more productive of offspring with careers in teaching, medicine, law, engineering, and other professions requiring educational certification than any of the other communities. For more than a generation, Caltzontzin young people had been located a short bus ride from Uruapan schools. In 1971, Zacán children still had to leave their home community for larger towns to continue their studies beyond the sixth grade, a fact that makes the Zacán achievement more remarkable than that of Caltzontzin.

Educational levels of local residents also showed differences that may well influence continued viability of adjustments. Three-fourths of the adults in San Juan Nuevo, Zacán, and Miguel Silva were literate, according to the 1970 census figures, whereas fewer than half the adults in old Zirosto could read and write. The other communities were intermediate. Miguel Silva had the highest percentage of children aged 6-14 in elementary school, followed closely by Zacán. The lowest percentage was represented by Old Zirosto, which only had three grades of school available locally. Twenty-nine percent of the Zacán adults held degrees from primary school, whereas only 4% of the adults in the Zirostos had graduated from a 6-year educational course.

Objective attempts to measure change and current circumstances convey only part of the complex reality that geographers sometimes refer to as the "personality" of places. The uniqueness of each town was reflected in some degree by the way people spoke of their community when first questioned. Comments collected from a diverse, although not systematically sampled, variety of people carried much the same message within a town, but differed appreciably from community to community. The consistency of initial statements about past community experience and future possibilities showed no particular variation with the individual's socio-economic status within the community, and was affected to only a slight degree by age and experience in the pre-volcanic community.

In-depth interviews with selected people resulted in more complex interpretations of community but were rarely completely inconsistent with initial statements. Examination of first-reaction statements recorded in field notes suggested that there were certain things that people in each community more or less automatically expressed to outsiders on initial acquaintance. Although the extent to which these statements reflected internalized perceptions of the community, its history, and its prospects is unknown, their very consistency within a town was certain to affect the perceptions of outsiders, some of whom might make decisions that affected the community. Further research along these lines should be undertaken, because if the differences in local perception of the community success in dealing with conditions created by the eruptions and present problems were as great as they seemed, the implications are important.

In general, people in San Juan Nuevo and Miguel Silva expressed the most positive views of community. In both cases, these views related to a perception of past success in meeting the challenges of the eruption years. In Zacán there was a strong

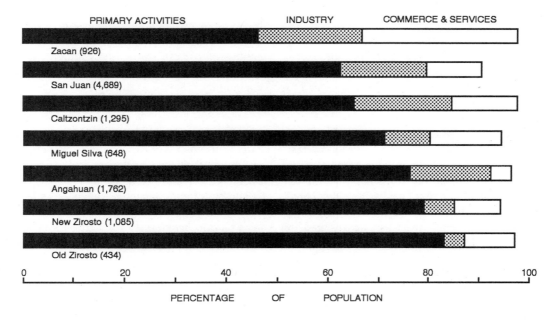

Fig. 132. Occupational categories in the communities as of 1970.

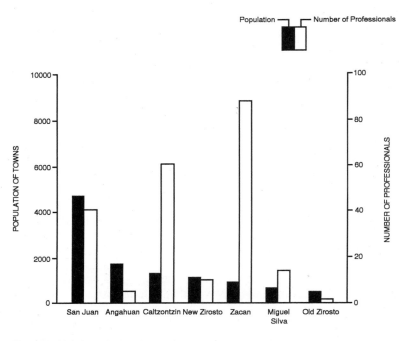

Fig. 133. Number of offspring with professional positions, 1971.

expression of community educational achievement, thought to have resulted from an opening of horizons during the volcanic years, but there was also concern about community future because few of the educated young could work in this small, still relatively remote community. The basic note was positive, perhaps best expressed in a local woman's statement that "we are giving our children to México." In both Zirosto Viejo and Zirosto Nuevo, emphasis was placed on the "death" of the old community, sometimes followed by a casting of blame on the other highland settlement. There was much ambivalence in Caltzontzin, but in spite of individual achievements and what seemed to be a new sense of hope and community spirit, there was a downbeat cast to many comments. Half the people spoken with almost immediately volunteered information that the town was poor, and in contrast to San Juan Nuevo and Miguel Silva, there was a tendency to state that the old town had been better than the new. The notion that "we had to come here" was often reflected, and the positive note, if there was one, might best be paraphrased as "we endured in spite of all the things that happened to us." In Angahuan, the constant refrain was, "We are indigenous. We are Tarascans." It prefaced and/or ended many other statements about community.

Comparisons

The two largest, richest, and most *mestizo* [mixed Spanish and Indian heritage] of the original communities were San Juan Parangaricutiro and Zirosto. In both cases, agricultural lands near the communities were destroyed, although the devastation of many San Juan fields by lava represents a more permanent loss of land. Both communities also had vast forest reserves, including stands of timber not badly damaged during the eruptions. The most significant difference in the experience of the two was that whereas San Juan had to be evacuated in the face of the lava flow, old Zirosto, though virtually buried in sand, was never threatened by lava; thus the choice of remaining in the home community stayed open. Accounts of growing social stress in San Juan prior to the evacuation indicate that the community may well have been saved by the lava that destroyed the town site[6].

In any event, the San Juan community survived and eventually prospered while Zirosto fragmented into small social units. None of these pieces of Zirosto had regained either the population or the importance of the pre-volcanic community. Zirosto Viejo and Zirosto Nuevo, which exist a few kilometers apart in the highlands, were not highly viable as communities, and there was bitterness between the two settlements. In contrast, those of Zirosto who endured the hardships of pioneering in Miguel Silva were proud of their new community. They had reinterpreted the old traditions and established new ones around their common frontier experience. They were also better educated and more open to new ideas than the people of either Zirosto Viejo or Zirosto Nuevo. However, their town was small, their land base poor, and the opportunities for growth severely limited.

The building of San Juan Nuevo was an epic story. This community of nearly 5,000 people was again the head town of *municipio*. The battle for lands in *ejido* was won in 1968, and the new lands connected the town site with community lands in the volcanic zone, thus creating a geographical unit. San Juan graduated its first class from secondary school in 1971. In 1973 the road to Uruapan was paved, reducing an hour's journey by bus or car to about 10 minutes. Possibly because the growing community offered local opportunity for ambitious young people, educational orientations stressed literacy but not advanced degrees. Perhaps most important symbolically, the people of San Juan had built a great brick church for the Lord of the Miracles. The community was again a major shrine visited by more pilgrims than ever before and from greater distances. Many came as before to ask for health or pay respects to the Lord of the Miracles, but increasing numbers came to witness the "Miracle of San Juan," interpreted as a miracle of achievement through faith and hard work in the face of heavy odds.

The former difference between Indian and *mestizo* had greatly diminished, and San Juan's traditions, old and new, were thriving and profitable. In San Juan Nuevo it was said, "We are the same town and the same people. Only the place is different." The people were exceptionally proud, resourceful, and confident of their ability to cope with new changes.

San Juan Nuevo can also be compared with Parícutin-Caltzontzin, the other group to be resettled near Uruapan. The Caltzontzin refugee settlement seemed like a perfect opportunity to make Mexicans out of Indians overnight, and little effort was spared in furthering this dream of Lázaro Cárdenas and other change agents. The people received much more government assistance than those of San Juan, and the *ejido* grant was the most generous received by any refugee settlement in terms of good farmlands relative to population. The new location on the outskirts of Uruapan provided proximity to jobs and schools. San Juan Nuevo was several kilometers more distant from the city, and the road, which ran over mountainous terrain, was extremely bad until 1973; thus San Juan's access to urban opportunities was more limited than Caltzontzin's. Nevertheless, Caltzontzin was not an especially happy community in 1971, and its people often referred to local poverty. Because the majority of Caltzontzin's citizens seemed reasonably well off for Mexican villagers, poverty seems to have meant being poorer than their urban neighbors. According to a 17-year-old girl whose father owned two brickyards, a truck, and a brick house, people in Caltzontzin were so impoverished that they could not afford lavish fifteenth-birthday parties for their daughters.

However, the true poverty that existed in Caltzontzin was more obvious than in the other communities. The obviously poor were ragged in dress, ill-housed, generally illiterate, and often unemployed, and they were particularly notable because they composed a relatively small minority of the population. The mark of poverty had little to do with retention of certain aspects of Tarascan traditionalism. Although some of the poor were among the most conservative inhabitants of the town, others had lost all roots in the Indian heritage, including the language. In contrast, some of the more prosperous families with the best-educated children spoke Tarascan at home and preferred houses modeled on the traditional style, although there was a widespread tendency to regard symbols of Tarascan-ness as obsolete.

Several lines of evidence suggested that this originally homogeneous community had developed a definite class structure within 28 years. It was marked by differences in dress, quality of housing, educational level, and patterns of mate selection. The symbols of class position were much like those evident in the nearby city. Uruapan people sometimes spoke of Caltzontzin as just another *barrio*, or district, of the city. The edge of Uruapan was growing ever nearer to Caltzontzin, and eventually the larger community would absorb the smaller physically as well as in social patterns.

In spite of numerous somewhat fatalistic comments about past and future community destiny, there were some strong positive notes in 1971. A new generation that had never known life in Parícutin village identified with the new town, and the period of massive culture shock that followed relocation had largely ended. A young priest who arrived in 1967 had worked diligently toward the creation of community pride and solidarity. He reinstituted an annual fiesta for the patron saint sponsored by the community at large. The celebrations stressed sports events rather than traditional dances. He raised money for a new church, but the men of the town told him they would rather have an enclosed basketball court, and he agreed. As he explained this decision, it was what the people needed. The church could be built later. Local men finished the basketball court in the summer of 1971 in time for the fiesta games. The name of the team, emblazoned on the shirts of the players, was "Parícutin".

As was the case in all the towns, Caltzontzin was plagued with too little land for its population and shortages of outside work. However, many families had encouraged their children to seek education. By 1971, 55 young people had taken advantage of scholarships and/or proximity to urban schools to win professional degrees. Most of these were school-teachers, but among those still in school there was an increasing trend toward university educations in engineering and other practical fields. The proximity of Uruapan meant that young people with good educations did not necessarily have to leave the home region to find employment, although many were established in more distant towns and cities.

Angahuan and Zacán also offered an interesting comparison. Both were small, isolated villages before the volcano. Zacán's agricultural lands were not as badly damaged as those of Angahuan, but the latter town was richer in forest resources. In addition, Angahuan had income from tourism during the volcanic period and afterwards, whereas Zacán did not. Both communities remained in their original locations, and they looked much alike because of the traditional nature of the housing. Angahuan was an hour by road from Uruapan, whereas it took an additional 15-20 minutes by car to reach Zacán. Each highland community had six grades of school available locally, and in 1971 there were no secondary schools within commuting distance. Both Angahuan and Zacán had faced the same geological ordeal and had much the same options for response. Therefore, the differences are astonishing unless one considers the very different social orientations of these two villages in the early 1940s.

During the most difficult years of the eruptions, many Zacán families moved to nearby towns and cities, and some of the men worked as *braceros*. Strong ties with the home community were, however, retained. The realization of a need to educate the children grew stronger. Within 20 years, this small, economically devastated community with six grades of school available locally, boasted 88 children with professional degrees. Many other offspring held white-collar and technical positions in Mexican cities. An organization of the professionals of Zacán, based in Uruapan, raised scholarship money for local children, and the kinsmen and friends who had established themselves in urban areas provided additional aid. Because of lack of local opportunity, most of Zacán's educated children did not return home permanently. The approximate 25% of the population that did not send children to local elementary school was inheriting the village. For others, the decline of Zacán was considered a tragedy offset by the belief that their educated children could contribute to the larger society and find good lives in the process. Zacán in 1971 appeared traditional in terms of material culture because the parents and grandparents of the educated offspring were using available funds to educate more children, rather than build new homes. It seemed likely that any family who attempted to display prosperity but refused to supply educational opportunities for offspring would meet the kinds of local sanctions that in the past induced the more affluent to sponsor fiestas.

Angahuan was considered different, closed and apart in 1943, and it retained this reputation in 1971. The Tarascans of Angahuan met the volcanic crisis with a staunch refusal to move, a decision made possible because the town was not reached by the lava field. Very few of its men accepted the opportunity to work as *braceros* and almost none of its people took up temporary residence elsewhere in México. When competition was eliminated by the evacuation of San Juan Parangaricutiro, Angahuan found economic salvation through catering to tourists.

An institution of tourist guiding had emerged by 1971. The guides were considered marginal by several local elders because their work did not involve traditions of obtaining sustenance from field and forest. Their primary function seemed to be a combination of allowing a flow of income into the community and ensuring the least possible contact between locals and outsiders. Tourist income primarily benefited hotelkeepers and restauranteurs in Uruapan because Angahuan had no such facilities. Even the direct sale of craft items was limited. It was mediated by the tourist guides, who carefully screened prospective buyers before taking them into homes where wares were displayed. Because crafts were not displayed on the streets, considerable revenue was probably lost to the community. Many tourists who passed through to see the volcano did not know that crafts were available locally. In 1971 one shop, owned by a local power figure, displayed the local goods, but it was tucked away on a corner off the main square. Craft entrepreneurs who sold to shop owners in Uruapan and other cities did not advertise the goods available within their house lots or display such goods in the little shops that some of them owned along the main tourist access into town. It seemed likely that powerful social sanctions were operating against an economic activity that would lead toward obvious differences in wealth, although it seemed equally likely that subjugation of craft sales to maintenance of "an image of limited good"[9] would not last much longer. Mechanized carpentry had already become important and was resulting in economic differentiation, although both the activity and the differences in prosperity deriving from it could be hidden behind the high walls of the house lots.

Perhaps most critical for the future of Angahuan was the increasing commercialization of visible aspects of the Indian heritage. The town's importance as a tourist attraction near Uruapan was based on its proximity to the scene of volcanic devastation and its importance as a staging point for guides and horses. However, by the late 1960s it was being viewed by urban entrepreneurs as a quaint Tarascan village and thus a tourist attraction in its own right. The national thrust to make Mexicans out of Indians, which had contributed to social-psychological traumas in Caltzontzin, was waning. A new theme emphasized respect for indigenous traditions. Undoubtedly good as a basic idea, this emphasis was potentially damaging for the community that found its new place in the larger society as an enclave of "professional Indians" needed to meet tourist expectations. There was reason to believe that Angahuan was in danger of falling into this category.

In spite of its outward appearance of traditionalism, Angahuan had changed drastically. As Celedonio Gutiérrez of San Juan Nuevo stated it, "They have changed far more than we have." The community was linked economically to the larger society to a far greater extent than before the volcano. The underlying roots of traditional life were greatly diminished, although the exterior manifestations of house type, dress, and fiesta dances remained. The population had grown substantially and was placing a strain on the resource base. Some community lands had been sold to outsiders, who had begun capital-intensive development of these lands with the aid of employees from the village. Such people were viewed by many as patrons in the traditional sense. Thus, the first line of the "corporate community's" defense against the world beyond had been broken[82].

Although literacy rates and percentages of young children in schools were about average for the communities affected by the volcano, there seemed to exist relatively little insight into the value of education except as a defense mechanism against the encroaching Spanish-speaking society. As one elderly local leader put it, there was no point in much education because schools did not teach the young how to work on the land. Yet, in another conversation, the same man said there was a need in México for more engineers and agricultural technicians. In contrast to those in Zacán, few parents in Angahuan seemed to have grasped the idea that their children could be engineers, teachers, and agricultural technicians of the future given a certain native ability, hard work, parental sacrifice, and good luck.

The Parícutin Eruption as a Hazard Event

Most geographical literature on human response to environmental hazards focuses on specific hazard conditions. Works such as that by Hewitt and Burton[83] that deal with all the hazards faced by a particular people in a given place are rare. Yet people in hazard zones do not respond exclusively to events labeled "floods", "earthquakes", or "volcanic eruptions", but to the perceived totality of their constantly changing life situations. Even during the impact period of a particular hazard event, the environment may be charged with other hazardous conditions, including social hazards. Convergence of hazard events is often a factor in major disasters, and volcanic eruptions are particularly complex because they generate a complex set of environmental problems.

As is the case during any volcanic eruption, the people affected by Parícutin dealt with a large variety of hazards during the eruption years. These included hazards such as tornado-like storms, which ordinarily affect the region; hazards such as lightning and earthquakes, which were intensified during the eruption period; and hazards associated uniquely with volcanic activity, such as pyroclastic falls and lava flows. Decisions to remain in the volcanic zone or relocate were made in the context of real and perceived social and biotic hazards outside the zone, not just in response to volcanic conditions. For some people, particularly those of Angahuan, the world beyond the familiar region was seen as more threatening than the volcano, and this perception affected human action[2]. The hazards of relocation in Miguel Silva were greater than those in the volcanic zone. Only three people, all struck by lightning thought to be associated with volcanic activity, were killed as a direct consequence of the eruptions[84]. In contrast, the colonization of Miguel Silva took an estimated 100 lives[78] from a combination of malarial conditions, polluted water supplies, loss of will to live—especially among the elderly sick—and the actions of hostile natives. The multi-hazard nature of the eruption period is summarized in Table 10, which is based on hazard lists presented by UNESCO[85], Burton and Kates[86], and Burton et al[87].

Early work in environmental hazard research that focused on the United States and other urban-industrial countries suggested that people in a hazard zone seldom recognize the full range of theoretically possible adjustments[88]. However, the people affected by Parícutin responded with an exceptionally wide

Table 10. Hazards faced by the affected people during the eruption period.

I. Volcanic eruption

II. Hazards directly or indirectly connected with the eruptions or the products of the eruptions plus other variables
  1. *Earthquakes* in addition to those to which the region is ordinarily subject
  2. *Air pollution* from pyroclastic fall
  3. *Shifting sands*, after pyroclastic fall
  4. *Sandstorms*, especially in windy spring months
  5. *Mineral deficiencies and excesses* in the pyroclastic materials covering formerly fertile fields
  6. *Landslides* and mudslides relating to the shifting of pyroclastics
  7. *Lightning* associated with the eruption column, in addition to that associated with thunderstorms in the region
  8. *Floods* due to topographic changes resulting from the eruptions
  9. *Drought*, including failure of the regular water supply because of covering of springs with pyroclastics and changes in groundwater levels and extremely droughty soils resulting from high concentrations of volcanic sands
  10. *Agricultural frost*, always a hazard at high elevations, but greatly intensified during the eruption period by more extensive plantings in high, relatively ash-free lands

III. Other physical environmental hazards common to the region but not associated with the eruptions
  1. *Tornadolike storms*, strong enough to fell trees and deroof homes
  2. *Hail*
  3. *Fog*, which may have been more intense during the eruptions, but which did not constitute a major hazard

IV. Biological hazards recorded in the region
  1. *Insect plague*, including locust plague, which damaged crops before the eruptions and was described as the "first punishment" for the sins that produced the volcano (Gutiérrez 1972:13)
  2. *Epidemic disease*, apparently not too serious since the major cholera years of the nineteenth century
  3. *Death of game and livestock* from ingestion of vegetation covered with pyroclastics directly related to the eruptions

V. Biological hazards in Miguel Silva
  1. *Polluted water*
  2. *Malaria*
  3. *Nonviability* of highland seed corn and other plants

VI. Sociocultural hazards related to the eruptions and relocations
  1. *Culture shock* and/or serious psychological breakdown including loss of will to live, especially among the elderly (Nolan 1972:179)
  2. *Perception of the world* beyond the region as alien, perhaps hostile
  3. *Low economic viability* outside the region due in some cases to lack of literacy often combined with little or no knowledge of Spanish, and lack of training in skills other than those of subsistence agriculture
  4. *Hostility* of local rancheros at Miguel Silva, leading to at least two murders
  5. *Land wars* in the volcanic zone during and after the eruptions, resulting in loss of life and property

range of adjustments. Results of a major collaborative research program focused on human response to a variety of hazards in many countries[89] have since indicated that peasant agriculturalists tend to show more adaptive ingenuity than the urbanites of more advanced societies. Burton et al.[87] have concluded that "the pattern of folk response is a larger number of adjustments and a high rate of adoptions among individuals and communities" as compared with the "favored adjustments" of modern industrial society, which tend to be "uniform in application, inflexible, and difficult to change." Thus, results of research in the Parícutin area that ran counter to accepted theoretical trends in the early 1970s[84] now fall into the category of what should be expected.

The difference in response between ethnically and economically similar communities affected by Parícutin has its parallel in a study of five Eskimo villages affected by the 1964 Alaska earthquake[90]. This study also supports the finding that an essentially religious response to catastrophe, combined with other actions, can be highly adaptive, especially during the recovery period. Old notions of peasant fatalism in the face of hazard and disaster such as those presented by Kendrick[91], Kingdon-Ward[92], and Sjoberg[93] probably need revision. One must always be careful, however, to avoid confusion of past and present. Evidence that modern peasants generally are not highly fatalistic does not prove that this orientation was not widespread in the past. It is only suggestive.

There may have been pre-historic episodes of volcanic activity that pitted man against nature in situations little influenced by outside social conditions, but this was obviously not the case during the Parícutin eruptions. The convergence of social pressures for change with a physically destructive environmental event make it impossible meaningfully to distinguish socio-cultural changes induced by the eruptions from changes resulting from response to the modernizing larger society. As has been found in other studies of disaster-impacted communities, the rate of change was accelerated, but the essential direction of change showed little variance from expected patterns[94].

For most of the affected communities, the changes were in the direction of greater integration with the modern Mexican socio-economic system and many would have occurred even had there been no volcano. New roads, the building of dams, penetration of a region by change agents such as schoolteachers, discovery of a place by promoters of tourism, or decisions concerning location of industrial plants can also be catalysts for social change in traditional communities. There was nothing unique about Parícutin as a volcano in its impact on the eruption-zone communities except for the fact that it abruptly destroyed their traditional means of livelihood at a time when the larger society could encourage both relocation and alternative ways to make a living.

It should be emphasized that not all change was in the direction of general societal trends. The remnant population of Old Zirosto was probably more isolated from Mexican life in 1971 than was the town's population in 1943, and neither Zirosto Nuevo nor Miguel Silva had regained the mother town's pre-volcanic position in terms of local facilities and services. This is not so unusual, however. Recent North American history is full of examples of communities that declined even as others progressed. Near ghost towns now stand where once-prosperous communities were bypassed by railroads and later highways. The abandoned buildings of crossroads farm-market towns attest to loss of function after the spread of the automobile carried the rural population to larger trade centers. Zirosto, with its prosperity tied to mule driving, was in a state of economic decline before the eruptions[2]. Had there been no volcano, the community would not have fragmented, and the decline might have been reversed. But there is no way to know exactly what would have happened in any of these communities if Parícutin volcano had not appeared when and where it did.

In examining change that coincides with a catastrophic event, a distinction should be made between the concepts of eventual result and direct cause. Many things happened as a result of the volcano, yet hardly anything other than the destruction of farmlands and two town sites was actually *caused* by the eruptions—that is, was an inevitable consequence. The distinction between result and causation can be illustrated with the story of Manuel, the Zirosto-born principal of a school in a medium-sized Michoacán town. According to Manuel, he would not be a schoolteacher today if Parícutin had not erupted. His family was poor and lived some distance from the center of Zirosto. He had no schooling until his family moved to Miguel Silva when he was 11 years old. There he began elementary school and because of societal attention focused on the children of refugees, he received scholarships that allowed him to complete normal school. This man and many others who were children in the volcanic zone during the eruption years believe with good reason that they are schoolteachers because of the volcano.

Thus, the volcano is an important part of the explanation for the course of individual lives, just as it is a critical episode in the history of seven Mexican communities. Many lives would have been different had there been no volcano, and the affected communities would have had a different history. Yet, as a man of San Juan Nuevo pointed out after listing the advantages of the new town site, "We would have had all those things anyway by now, in the old town. It really didn't make any difference".

Discussion and Conclusions

Adaptation in the Communities
The Parícutin eruptions severely damaged the traditional resource base of five farm communities. The changed physical environment forced new adaptations, which included migration and the acceptance of new ways of making a living in the volcanic zone and elsewhere. Those who continued as volcanic-zone agriculturalists developed strategies for dealing with ash-covered lands [see p. 223-228 and 285-286], and farmers in refugee settlements of Caltzontzin—and particularly Miguel Silva—were forced to adapt their traditional agricultural technology to lands of lower elevation. In two communities, one in the volcanic zone and the other in a relocation site near a city, advanced education for the younger generation was an important means of dealing with new conditions. However, even in these towns only a minority of the young achieved advanced degrees, and most of the highly educated left the community.

The fact that individuals and communities responded differently to similar physical and social forces for change suggests that neither the volcano nor the larger society determined the exact nature of the new adaptations. Change occurred because people adapted to a changed environment, but the variety of adaptation was too great to be discussed in terms of simple cause-and-effect relationships. However, the idea of pre-adaptation is useful. Some individuals and populations are better suited to certain kinds of environmental change than are others. When change occurs, they may prosper even as those best adapted to the former environmental conditions flounder in search of appropriate new responses. Within the framework of this case study, some communities were more receptive to the new opportunities offered by a modernizing México than were others[95].

Perhaps more important for the future is the community tradition of success or failure in controlling destiny. In this situation of forced response, some individuals and community units made deliberate choices. Others simply reacted, thus becoming pawns in the hands of nature and the larger society. At the individual level, choice reflected personality and family influence as well as the kaleidoscope of physical and social factors[96]. Communities chose or failed to choose in accordance with their traditions, the quality of local leadership, and agreed-upon perceptions of the total situation.

The people of communities with a tradition of choice and shared belief in the desirability of the outcome seemed to display a greater sense of potential control over future events than those of communities that had a tradition of simply coping with outside events perceived as uncontrollable.

San Juan and Caltzontzin exemplified the difference between choice and making the decision work, and lack of choice combined with continual coping. Although community differences in perception of control over destiny probably go back much earlier, the early eruption period proved a crucial testing point of local will. The lava flows represented a natural event that could not be controlled and that permitted no adaptation in place. Yet, although the flows covered the sites of two settlements, only the people of San Juan were truly forced to evacuate because of the lava. Some people of that community watched as the lava covered their house lots, then turned away to join their fellow citizens in a refugee settlement that they had insisted on choosing. When slow-moving lava eventually covered the site of Parícutin village more than a year after its evacuation, only a few scientists were present to record the event. The people of Parícutin had long before obeyed government orders to move to a strange place with an alien name, which they had not chosen. As a reward for their cooperativeness, the people of Parícutin-Caltzontzin received lands in *ejido* and much special attention. As a result of their stubbornness, the people of San Juan were initially given no *ejido* lands and much less special governmental attention.

Nearly 28 years later, people in Caltzontzin were explaining that they had to come to the new place, and some were complaining about past governmental unfairness and insufficiency of current aid. Even educating children was occasionally described as something that had to be done because the community had few resources. The ideal of educating offspring for a better way of life and as a contribution to the nation, frequently expressed in Zacán, was not very evident in Caltzontzin. As recognized by the priest and some local secular leaders, the community needed to build a more positive self-image.

In contrast, people in San Juan Nuevo pointed out the good features of the new place and often emphasized their communal wisdom in choosing it. Rather than complaining about lack of governmental

assistance, they boasted about their achievement in building the new town by themselves, although they were quick to explain how they had won concessions from larger, more powerful political entities.

It seemed that there was an important difference between the people of communities that had a tradition of control over destiny and those that had a tradition of coping, or, as in the case of the Zirostos, a history of failure to meet the challenge of the past. The greatest consideration of future community choices in the face of new problems was found in San Juan Nuevo, Zacán, and Miguel Silva, the communities with the greatest apparent sense of control over past events. The significance of these microcultural differences is supported by recent experimental studies with human subjects and animals indicating that even the illusion of control improves performance in several kinds of situations[97].

Archaeological Implications

The archaeologist must often deal with only remnants of material culture and evidence of past physical environmental conditions. Unless historical records are also available, extrapolations must be made from that base. Assuming that no historical documentation existed, future archaeological explorations in the Parícutin volcanic zone would show that two settlements had been overwhelmed by lava. With adequate funding for surveys, archaeologists could probably establish much the same zone of devastation defined by geologists in the 1940s. Because no human remains would be found in the volcanic layer, it could be assumed that people from the lava-covered settlements had relocated. Perhaps the sparsity of material remains around the stone churches, house foundations, and walls of those former settlements would suggest that the migrants took most of their possessions with them, which was the case.

Presumably, however, the few things left behind would indicate the general level of technology at the time of the eruptions. New settlements on layers of heavy ash, such as the *ranchos* established by people originally from the region as the lands became more productive, would show in their remains an increased level of technological sophistication. An observer viewing the remains of a *rancho* burned during the 1960s land wars commented on sadness over the loss of "hand-operated tortilla presses, transistor radios, sewing machines . . . national flags and sports equipment"[74]. It would be evident that major changes in material culture had occurred between the onset of the eruptions and the period of recolonization; however, more extensive investigations would show the same radios, sewing machines, and sports equipment appearing at about the same time in other sierra communities far beyond the eruption zone. Examination of only the volcanic zone could lead to speculations about migrations of new peoples, but a broader survey would suggest that the eruptions occurred during a period of rapid and extensive culture change.

This case study, based on written and oral accounts collected largely from individuals who witnessed the eruptions of Parícutin volcano, may provide insights that can help in the interpretation of material cultural evidence. As a general rule, the Parícutin case suggests that volcanic eruptions do cause change in patterns of human life and habitation, but that the eruption events do not determine what the changes will be. It may also be taken as a generalization that similar groups of people affected by the same physical event may adjust to changed conditions in quite different ways and that the perceived success or failure of choices made during times of crisis will affect future decisions and the ongoing course of community history.

EPILOGUE

Nolan and Nolan (1993)

As a valuable addition to this book, Mary Nolan and her husband Sid have written this epilogue to her 1979 study.

Introduction

In January, 1991, 20 years after completing field work in the communities affected by Parícutin volcano, we returned to the region to revisit the towns, renew old friendships, and inquire about changes that had taken place since the initial study in 1971. We had visited some of the towns briefly in 1972 and 1974, but had not been back to Michoacán since then. We had kept in touch with events in San Juan Nuevo through occasional correspondence with Celedonio Gutiérrez and administrators at the shrine of the Lord of the Miracles, and through conversations with anthropologists, geographers, and geologists who continued to study in the region.

We knew that San Juan Nuevo not only had continued to grow, but also had actively attempted to control its destiny as a community. We knew little of what had happened in the other communities. We wondered how their peoples had fared in a changing nation, and if community traditions of success or

failure in controlling destiny had made any difference in the long run.

Initial Impressions of Change

During our 1991 investigations, we visited each community and made extensive notes that form the basis for the following descriptions of the towns at that time.

San Juan Nuevo Parangaricutiro

In 1991, the road from Uruapan to San Juan Nuevo, which had been paved 18 years before, was well maintained and led to the town's paved main streets. The plaza was ringed with a variety of shops, inns, and restaurants and its center was filled with market stands offering locally made foods and handicrafts. A resin refinery, constructed by the Comunidad Indigena, had been dedicated in 1990, and a new park with a chapel, restaurant, and playground was situated on a hill overlooking the town. The park was accessible by a stepped path and a paved road, and we were told that it was intended as a terminus for a road to be constructed through San Juan lands to the old town site in the volcanic zone.

The exterior of the Church of the Lord of the Miracles was little changed, except for the addition of several new religious displays on the grounds, but the interior had been transformed from unadorned brick to bright white walls embellished with gold leaf ornamentation. Masses were well attended by visitors and pilgrims from other parts of México and from the United States. Indicative of the shrine's growing importance, we later were to encounter one of San Juan Nuevo's priests among some 250 clerics and scholars from all over the world who attended the First Vatican Conference on Pilgrimage held in Rome in February, 1992. With a population of more than 10,000, San Juan Nuevo continued to give the impression of a growing rural service community and pilgrimage center.

Caltzontzin

Twenty years before, the people of Caltzontzin had hoped for a paved road and incorporation into the Uruapan *municipio*. The highway was completed in about 1980. We followed it out of Uruapan as it paralleled the railroad tracks past a paper mill and a Pemex gasoline distribution depot. Between the mill and the depot, a large auto junk yard sprawled at the turnoff to a bumpy dirt road leading to the town. Across the main road from the intersection loomed the gray walls of a prison bristling with barbed wire and guard towers. It had been located there a decade before by an edict of the state government. Uruapan city buses plying back and forth along the highway announced the Caltzontzin-Penal route, firmly linking the town with the institution.

Little had changed along the rutted boulevard that led into the town, except for the addition of several more shops and a doctor's office. The plaza was surrounded by a wall, but the grounds were poorly maintained. In spite of some avocado and citrus trees along the streets, the town still had a dusty, barren look. New houses had been built up the hillsides above the town, but there were no formal streets leading to them. A modest church had been constructed adjacent to the covered basketball court, but the enthusiastic priest was gone. His successor, a somewhat discouraged older man from Zamora, lamented the lack of cooperation among the Caltzontzin populace, and he worried about the influences of the numerous relatives of prisoners who lived temporarily in the town while their husbands, fathers, or sons served time at the penitentiary. His list of perceived problems included a lack of adequate employment, drunkenness, and drug abuse, the latter aggravated by the demand for drugs within the prison. Apparently part of that demand was being met by a few Caltzontzin entrepreneurs.

"It is a poor town," commented one of the men working on the new altar in the church. The priest and a local doctor said that a few men worked at the paper mill, but that the prison had not provided many jobs for long-time Caltzontzin residents because the guards came from elsewhere, although some had settled in the town. The conflict between Caltzontzin and San Juan Nuevo over rights to lands in the volcanic zone has been resolved, and animosities had receded with time, but the priest said that San Juan Nuevo continued to be envied as more fortunate, largely because of outside income brought in by pilgrims to the shrine of the Lord of the Miracles.

It seems highly unlikely that the people of Caltzontzin could have prevented the building of the prison adjacent to their community, and there was little they could do to avoid the associations so clearly expressed on the landscape and labeled on the buses. Some families had left to re-establish themselves as farmers on Parícutin community lands in the volcanic zone. Others, especially among the well educated, had moved to other parts of Uruapan or to other cities. The rest persevered, adapting once again to a new set of circumstances imposed upon them by outside forces.

Angahuan

The drive from Uruapan to villages in the volcanic zone was much easier than in the past due to paving of the highway to Los Reyes in the late 1980s. In 1991, few signs of the eruption remained on the approach to Angahuan, until the first glimpse of the mountain between rows of tall cornstalks in the fields and flourishing fruit trees. Life had returned to the ash.

At the first turnoff to Angahuan, a sign on a small, wooden casita promised information to the passing tourist -- but the casita was closed. Just past the structure, a more familiar sight appeared as two hopeful guides jumped up from their resting places on the side of the road and tried to wave us to a stop. We proceeded to the town plaza where we negotiated for two horses and a guide to visit the San Juan church site.

With the guide on foot alongside, the horses proceeded out of the plaza area and through the town at a slow, walking gait. Some distance beyond the built up area, the horses turned from the ash-surfaced road and headed for a narrow path that led down through the pine-forested slopes to the lava fields. Just ahead, however, a small sign nailed to a pine proclaimed "Mirador". We would like to visit the Mirador, we told the guide. "It would be better on the way back", he responded. But, we insisted.

The Mirador, which we remembered merely as a view point, proved to be a well maintained tourist complex complete with overnight accommodations, rest rooms, a conference room, a recreation hall, a restaurant, and a terrace with a striking view of Parícutin volcano and the half-buried San Juan church. There were plans for a visitors center that would eventually house a museum and, possibly, a craft shop for the sale of locally produced items.

Other guides with horses awaited tourists who knew about the Mirador and drove through the village to reach it. From the direction of Uruapan, there had been no sign indicating the existence of the facility, nor did we see any information posted in the plaza. Later, however, we found a small, wooden sign visible to tourists approaching from Los Reyes and Zacán, or from Uruapan if they bypassed the first entrance to Angahuan. It simply said, "Albergo." Lack of tourist information not withstanding, the Mirador was popular, especially on Sundays. On one Sunday in January, two cabins were occupied by couples from the U.S. who were staying for several days. In addition several family groups of Mexican tourists were spending the weekend and were joined by day-trippers, mostly from Zamora. The young men of these families had brought off-road motorbikes with them and spent most of the day roaring around the edge of the lava field.

Constructed with government financing in 1982, the *Mirador* complex began as a community effort with various groups of Angahuanese taking turns running it. However, according to the current manager, this arrangement did not work, and the complex had fallen into a state of disrepair. In 1991, the facility was in good condition under the sole management of an Angahuan man who had completed secondary school and seemed knowledgeable about the demands of urban Mexican and international tourists. He lamented the lack of cooperation among the townspeople in their approach to the tourist business. No one, for example, would man the information booth that state tourism authorities had built at the entrance to the town. Rather, the guides preferred to continue their traditional approach of waving-down approaching tourists, or offering their services around the plaza or at the *Mirador*. The manager was also having trouble coordinating the crafts people to set up a shop at the tourism facility.

The *Mirador* facility marked a change in the tourism landscape of Angahuan, but the local orientation to the guide and craft businesses had changed little. Although more homes openly displayed weavings and woodcrafts for sale, there was no outdoor market, nor any sign of a central shop. However, the town had obviously grown, with *trojes* [traditional steep-roofed wooden houses] covering much of the formerly vacant area between the town and the highway. Several elegant new multi-story wooden houses, in the Tarascan style reminiscent of places such as Pátzcuaro, had been built near the center of town. Their presence indicated the lessening of any emphasis on economic equality among the town's residents, a characteristic often theorized to be inherent in indigenous Mexican communities.

Zacán

The paved road eased the once tedious journey from Angahuan to Zacán to a drive of only a few minutes. Zacán's colonial-period churches stood proudly in their places and the town had a prosperous, although much less traditional, appearance. Several new houses were under construction and older residences had been remodeled. Four large television satellite dishes adorned house lots along the highway that bisected the town.

As in the past, Zacán residents continued to express a sense of pride in their community and its achievements. Because the paved road greatly reduced the time necessary to travel to Uruapan or Los Reyes, it had recently become much more feasible to live in Zacán while studying or working in one or the other urban center.

Zirosto Viejo and Zirosto Nuevo

The paved road continued beyond Zacán through numerous avocado groves to the Zirosto Viejo turnoff. Little of the former ghost-town atmosphere remained in the original Zirosto settlement. Volcanic ash still blew down the unpaved main street, but there were street lights. The homes and the few small shops had electricity. The ruined colonial church had been reconstructed on a modest scale and reopened in 1987. The original bell, which had been a center of conflict with Zirosto Nuevo, remained there. The elementary school had been expanded to six grades, and was well attended by neatly dressed children. In addition, a government health clinic was under construction.

In Zirosto Nuevo, the highway broadened to 4 lanes through the town, but it remained the only paved thoroughfare. The plaza, which formerly was only an empty space, had been adorned with small shrubs and flowers, although weeds indicated casual maintenance. The church was finished, complete with a new tower, and was well-kept inside. Most houses had TV antennas, and there were several satellite dishes. A local merchant noted that nearly every family in town owned a car or truck, and new-house construction was in evidence.

Here, as in the original community, people said there were no problems between the two Zirostos. The avocado orchards had brought prosperity, and as life became better, the inter-related populations had renewed a sense of being essentially one community. Better roads and increased vehicle ownership aided in reaffirming the ties between the two settlements.

Miguel Silva

Increased prosperity was also benefiting former Zirosto families in the distant resettlement location of Miguel Silva near Ario de Rosales. The paved highway running through town was lined with stores, auto repair facilities, and eating establishments that catered to travelers and truckers as well as the local residents. A sizable new church had been built in a modernistic style and served as a district gathering center for celebration of the feast of Our Lady of

Guadalupe in December. A large, well-kept plaza centered on a statue of Lázaro Cárdenas. The elementary school had been expanded, and a local, fully staffed secondary school was attended by teenagers in neat uniforms.

A stroll through the back streets revealed many new houses, said to have been constructed with money from work in the United States. The newer homes and most of the older houses were plastered, sturdily built, and embellished with well-tended gardens. Several older couples had numerous children who lived in the United States. Some of the young people who had gone north had married Anglo-Americans, and a few of the elementary school children spoke English as a result of long stays in *El Norte*. As in the past, the people were exceptionally open, inquisitive, and very friendly.

Facilities and Services
In the 1971 study, selected facilities and services were used to compare the towns affected by the volcano with each other and with other Mexican communities (Tables 8 and 9). Our observations and questions about the same things in 1991 revealed almost as much about general directions of change in México as about the differences between the communities. Electronic video games, for example, were displacing billiard parlors as sources of amusement, and the presence of a movie theater was considered much less important than the availability of rental video tapes and games. One less community had a bakery in 1991 than in 1971, and the number of communities with barber shops had declined by one. Two other communities, previously without barber shops, had opened beauty shops, yet still had no barber shops. Perhaps these were "unisex" hair parlors, a possibility suggested by a sign in a Caltzontzin window. As roads and public transportation improve, as more rural people acquire their own vehicles, and as modern communication technology reaches remote areas, it is inevitable that some of the older measures of community development cease to have much meaning.

At the community level, however, some things are important if the town is truly viable. In 1991, all of the towns of the volcano had autonomous status, governmental organizations and officials, churches, regular masses, distinctly marked plazas, grocery stores, and butcher shops or regular butchering services. All were on or very near paved roads and had good access to public transportation, which presumes that they had access to shipping services. All had electricity, water systems, and local schooling

through at least the first six years. None had a formal gasoline station, although most had gasoline for sale somewhere in town and several had auto repair shops.

All of the seven communities had as many or more facilities and services as they had in 1971 and each of the three towns derived from the old Zirosto community had substantially more. Zirosto Viejo showed the greatest increase from 7 of 24 possible facilities and services in 1971 to 13 in 1991. Not surprisingly, San Juan Nuevo showed little change because in 1971 it was already near the top of the 24-item scale. There were changes in some of the kinds of facilities communities cared to support. Angahuan had lost its bakery, but gained a hotel and restaurant. Zacán's billiard parlor had closed and there was, as yet, no place to rent videos, but the town had gained a doctor. Caltzontzin had a place that rented video tapes as well as a photo-copy service. A bakery and barber shop had been added in Miguel Silva, and Zirosto Nuevo had gained a recognizable plaza and a resident priest. Zirosto Viejo had a local government organization and a regular butcher service, neither of which were present 20 years before. Perhaps more importantly, the community had acquired electricity and a government health clinic was under construction.

Resident doctors were the most frequent new additions among the towns. Only San Juan Nuevo had a local doctor in 1971, but 20 years later Caltzontzin, Miguel Silva, Zirosto Nuevo, and Zacán had their own physicians. In all four of these communities, the doctors were native sons or daughters who had returned to practice medicine in their home towns.

Demographic Changes
Some of the changes encountered in the towns after 20 years were predictable. Others were less expected, but fit into the general Mexican patterns of population growth, changing educational aspirations, shifts in viable occupations, and attitudes toward ethnic diversity.

Efforts to compare the demographics of the towns beyond 1970 were limited to the *municipio*-level 1990 census data available at the time of this writing. This confines statistical comparisons to San Juan Nuevo, and then only to the *municipio,* which includes the town and several rural *ranchos*. Nevertheless, some trends evident in the changes from 1970 to 1990 are interesting. All of the other towns are contained within much larger *municipios* than San Juan, thus limiting statistical comparisons. Observations and interviews allow tentative comparisons with the San Juan *municipio* data.

Plate 1

A. First lava flow from Parícutin, the Quitzocho flow, moving northward over cornfields prepared for planting; rock wall separates two fields. Photo taken by Instituto de Geología from the north on the eruption's fifth day (Feb. 25, 1943). Dark, ash-rich plume rises from the new volcano, whose flanks are obscured by fine dust and vapor. See p. 69.

B. Closer view of lava flow on same day as above. Cone height is probably about 100 m. Large volcanic bombs roll down the flanks of the cone.

Plate 2

A.   Time-exposure at night of incandescent trajectories from Parícutin volcano, 1943. Photo by Carl Fries.

B.   Time-exposure at night showing incandescent fountain with trails of blocks rolling down the
upper cone in 1948. Photo by Carl Fries.

Plate 3

A. Blue flames at the mouths of *hornitos* on Mesa de Los Hornitos at the WSW base of the main cone, March 1944. See p. 106-109, 114, and Fig. 76-77. Photo by Frederick Pough.

B. Sapichu, a horseshoe-shaped parasitic vent at the NE base of the main Parícutin cone, was a major lava producer during October 1943 - January 1944 (see p. 96-103). This photo, taken from the NE summit of the main cone in early 1945 shows Sapichu in the process of being buried by lava flows from vents on the SW flank. The highest point of Sapichu was finally buried in December 1947. Photo by Kenneth Segerstrom.

Plate 4

A. Incandescent lava
    moving in a channel,
    probably close to the
    SW-flank vents, with
    main cone in back-
    ground, January 1946.
    See Fig. 104 for map
    of lava flows at that
    time. Photo by Ken
    Segerstrom.

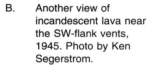

B. Another view of
    incandescent lava near
    the SW-flank vents,
    1945. Photo by Ken
    Segerstrom.

C. Incandescent block at base
    of advancing lava flow front.
    Lava flows moved slowly, like
    giant caterpiller tractor
    treads, with large blocks
    rolling down the flow front
    and often breaking open as
    they landed. Photo by Carl
    Fries.

Plate 5

A. White, ash-poor steam plume rising above the cone.

B. Dark, ash-rich plume rising from cone. The church tower in the newly buried town of San Juan Parangaricutiro is visible just to the left of the cone base. The wooden buildings in the foreground were on the NW outskirts of the town. Photo from the north in October, 1944.

C. Ash-rich eruption column seen from the first observatory cabin (1½ km to the north), with Celedonio Gutiérrez, 1944. Photo by Ken Segerstrom.

Plate 6

A.   View of the unfinished San Juan Parangaricutiro church and west margin of 1944 lava flows. Photo by Katia Krafft in 1981.

B.   The church and surrounding lava. Photo by Ray Wilcox in 1947.

C.   Post-eruption airplane view from the east shows the main cone and the NE-flank vent mound of Nuevo Juatita, which was the main source of lava during the last 5 years of the eruption (see p. 167-183). The summit of Nuevo Juatita is covered with white fumarolic sublimate minerals. The older cones Canicjuata and Corucjuata are visible in the upper left. Photo by Katia Krafft in 1981.

Plate 7

A. Painting by Dr. Atl: "During the first part of September 1943 it rained steadily and one could only see the sun at rare times. But on Sunday September 19 the atmosphere cleared completely and in the night, a great ring of clouds formed on the horizon leaving the celestial firmament clear and adorned with stars. Within the thin vapor from a silent eruption the stars resembled the cinders that the volcano hurled with fabulous force into the sky."

B. Another painting by Dr. Atl: "In the night the volcano emitted a shower of embers. Most time-exposure color photographs taken of this nocturnal spectacle are completely false, not only because of excessive chromatic intonation, but also because they present the embers as luminous parabolas, which gives a misleading view of the eruption's character."

C. Three Mexican postage stamps featuring the work of Dr. Atl: upper left - self-portrait of Dr. Atl painted in 1955; upper right - Parícutin volcano in eruption during 1943; lower - the new volcano in eruption with the church of San Juan Parangaricutiro.

Plate 8

A. Annual 17-km procession on *Viernes de Dolores* (Friday of Sorrows, one week before Good Friday) from San Juan Nuevo (15 km SE of the new volcano) to the church of the parent community San Juan Parangaricutiro (4½ km north of the volcano). Parícutin volcano is in the background. 1981 photo by Katia Krafft.

B. Jorullo, another "new" volcano, born in 1759, 81 km SE of Parícutin. In this view from the NW, the final black tongue of unvegetated lava that flowed north from the crater rim is visible on the center horizon. One of its four parasitic cones, Volcán del Norte, is near the photo's left margin. See discussion on p. 364-371.

Population Growth

Based on estimates given by knowledgeable residents, including priests, doctors, long-established merchants and school teachers, all but one of the seven towns increased substantially in population between 1970 and 1990. According to Mexican national census data, the population of the *municipio* of San Juan grew from 10,118 in 1980 to 13,264 in 1990, a 31% increase. This exceeds the 20% increase of the national population of México over the decade. Residential construction evident in the town itself supports local estimates of a doubling of the 1970 population to about 10,000.

Caltzontzin also grew in the 1980s, largely due to an influx of people who came to work in the prison or to reside temporarily in the community while family members were incarcerated. There was also some growth among long-term Caltzontzin families, according to a local doctor. The 1990 population probably exceeded 2,000 relatively permanent residents, or about double that of 1970. There was no important increase in the land base during the same period.

Angahuan was visibly larger in 1991. What had mainly been open space in 1971 between the main road and the town plaza approximately 1 km away, had largely filled with house lots. Local people estimated that the town had grown to about 5,000 residents, nearly triple the 1970 figure. Knowledgeable people in nearby towns attributed this growth to the continuation of the custom in Angahuan of marrying when very young and producing large numbers of children, in contrast with trends elsewhere in the region toward later marriage and smaller families. The larger population was intensifying pressures on the town's agricultural resources, although this was alleviated somewhat as the fertility of Angahuan lands damaged by volcanic ash fall had increased over time. Some local people expressed concerns that communal forests were being seriously depleted by overcutting.

Population growth, although not as dramatic as in Angahuan, was also noticeable in both Zirostos. In the case of Zirosto Viejo, this was a reversal of a trend since the eruption that seemed in 1971 to have doomed the town to perpetual unimportance, if not extinction. Its 1991 population was estimated to be nearly 1,000, while that of Zirosto Nuevo had exceeded 2,000. The lowland settlement at Miguel Silva had grown to nearly 1,500. Thus, all three populations with roots in pre-eruption Zirosto had approximately doubled in size between 1970 and 1990. Part of this growth reflected the return of

retired people, and in some cases entire families, from decades of work in the United States.

Zacán was an exception among the seven towns with an apparently stable population of about 1,000 compared with a census count of 926 in 1970. The retired director of the local primary school and a life-long resident, observed that about as many people left Zacán or died as were born or moved there each year. Most of the out-migration was among young people, so the net result was an aging population. This was reinforced by the return of some former residents who had spent their working lives elsewhere in México or in the United States. Changes in this trend were anticipated, however, because the paved highway made it more practical for people to live in Zacán and commute to jobs in larger settlements.

Education

Emphasis on education had increased generally in all of the towns by 1991, but to varying degrees. Part of this may be attributable to the institution of the *tele-secundaria* programs, which provide high-school-level televised instruction under the supervision of a minimum number of teachers. This service was available in Angahuan, Zacán, and in both Zirosto Viejo and Nuevo. San Juan Nuevo and Miguel Silva had regular, fully staffed, secondary schools. Caltzontzin students who went past the sixth grade still commuted to Uruapan.

Census data for the San Juan Nuevo *municipio* indicated a dramatic shift towards a more educated populace. In 1980, 31% of the *municipio* residents aged 6 years or older had no formal education. By 1990, this had declined to 17%. Even more dramatic was the change from only 7.6% of that population segment having gone beyond primary school instruction in 1980 to 18.7% in 1990. The establishment of a San Juan secondary school in 1971 had greatly increased opportunities for post-primary education and this, in turn, had increased the number of young people continuing for more advanced degrees. As an example, only the youngest of Celedonio Gutiérrez's several children had earned a professional degree as a teacher. However, several of the children of his older sons and daughters had acquired higher levels of education than their parents. In 1991, Celedonio was proud that he had a grandson and granddaughter who had become doctors and a granddaughter who is a dentist.

School attendance was said to be good in the Zirostos, Miguel Silva, and Zacán. Although informants in Zirosto Viejo knew of no sons or daughters of the town who had become professionals, they attributed this to the difficulty of going beyond primary school, and expected the situation to change with the recent installation of a *tele-secundaria*. People in Zirosto Nuevo recounted stories of several professionals from the town, and talked about one agricultural engineer who lived there. Similarly, teachers at the Miguel Silva primary school said that many of their students had gone on to professional training, although they had no record of their numbers.

Gross enrollment in Zacán's elementary school had declined, according to Eva Mendez, its retired director. She attributed this to the fact that many Zacán couples now limit their families to two or three children and estimated that at least 90% of school-age children attend regularly. The local *tele-secundaria*, which is staffed with one teacher for each class year, is popular. Zacán residents continued to place an emphasis on higher education. The community's new professionals since 1971 included Eva's two daughters, one a dentist and the other a nurse. The numerous professionals from the community who lived elsewhere still maintained active contact with the town and two of their urban-based organizations helped sponsor an annual cultural festival in October.

School attendance in Caltzontzin was said to be fairly good in 1991, although it was freely admitted that numerous local children do not complete primary school. The town continues to produce offspring with professional degrees, but in contrast to his enthusiastic predecessor, the new priest kept no record of them. He said that the community had a few resident doctors and lawyers who worked in Uruapan as well as some engineers and an anthropologist who was studying race relationships. One of the two local medical clinics was operated by a young female doctor from the town who also owned one of the pharmacies.

Education was apparently less valued in Angahuan. According to the *Mirador* manager and other residents, many children do not complete elementary school, and some never start. The *tele-secundaria* was said to be attended by only 4-5 students. Some families, however, did emphasize education, as evidenced by the manager's personal situation. He completed secondary school, his oldest daughter was attending a college preparatory school in another town, and all of his younger children were in primary school. Angahuan has produced relatively few offspring with professional degrees, although there have been some teachers.

In several towns, people expressed concern that young people leaving the villages for professional education and training were finding it difficult to get jobs appropriate to their degrees, and when they did, they often could not make enough money to live decently. This reflected a pessimism about the future that was in sharp contrast to the optimism generally prevalent in 1971. This problem was not unique to the "Towns of the Volcano", however, but a general one throughout México at the time.

Occupations

Agriculture remained important to the economies of the towns. In San Juan Nuevo, for example, the census data indicated a slight increase from 43% to 49% between 1980 and 1990 in the workers engaged in agriculture, animal husbandry, or forestry. This, however, reflected a sharp drop from 60% in 1970. During the past decade, there was a dramatic shift toward employment in the industrial sector—from 8.5% in 1980 to 20.4% in 1990.

Informants in Angahuan, Zacán, the Zirostos, and Miguel Silva named agriculture as the main occupation for the residents of their communities. As a result of population increases, actual numbers of people trying to make a living from the land had increased, even as percentages of farmers decreased. In the area around the Zirostos, avocado orchards, which were just beginning to be planted in the early 1970s, were doing well, but there was an ominous note for the future. People in both Zirosto Viejo and Nuevo complained that some of the best avocado lands had been acquired by absentee landlords who had no family ties to either community. To the extent that this was the case, some of the income from this profitable crop was being drained from the local economy.

In Caltzontzin, it was said that only the older people still worked in the fields, and the priest thought that younger people were neglecting the potential fertility of their house lots. Younger workers, including those who originally came from outside the community, were employed in the nearby paper mill, the prison, or commuted to jobs in Uruapan. Unemployment was a problem, but there were also more shops than in any other town but San Juan Nuevo. These included two pharmacies, a bicycle repair shop, an electric supplies store, several shoe stores and dry-good stores, a number of small groceries, at least four butcher shops, and a stand that sold fresh fish. As had been the case two decades earlier, Caltzontzin was much more urban in its perspectives than any of the other towns, but it had not reached the favorable position within the urban setting that had been the hope of some of its citizens.

Tourism and crafts continued to contribute to Angahuan's largely agrarian economy. In addition to the numerous guides who continue to offer their services and horses for trips to the volcano, there were more local crafts openly displayed for sale in 1991 than in 1971. The *Mirador* complex was staffed by local residents. There was talk of expanding these operations and instituting a craft shop. At one time there was a plan for a furniture factory, which would make more efficient use of wood from the communal forests than the packing crates that many Angahuan workshops produce, but nothing had come of it as of 1991.

All of the towns claimed residents who had worked, and were working at the time, in the United States. This merely continued an old pattern for most of the communities, but marked a substantial change for Angahuan, a town that exported relatively few workers in the years before 1971.

Ethnicity

The towns exhibited a general trend away from many aspects of the traditional Tarascan culture, but there were selected retentions. The San Juan census data reflected a decline in one very important measure of ethnicity between 1980 to 1990. In 1980, 9% of the *municipio* population of 5 years or older spoke Tarascan. One percent, or 75 individuals, spoke no Spanish. By 1990, the proportion of Tarascan speakers had dropped to 5%. Two people spoke no Spanish—a man and a woman—both over the age of 50.

San Juan continued to actively maintain aspects of the Tarascan culture, especially the fiesta *danzas*. These were performed during all fiestas, including that of the patron saint in summer, for the festival of the Lord of the Miracles in September, for the Virgin of Guadalupe in December, for the Day of The Three Kings in January, and for carnival. A few women strolled around the plaza or sold crafts in traditional Tarascan dress, especially on Sundays and festival days.

In contrast with 1971, most of the women observed in Caltzontzin wore modern clothes, although a few wore various parts of the traditional dress in modified form. Tarascan was still spoken by some families, but according to the local priest, most of the young people used the indigenous language only when talking with their elders. Traditional *danzas* were performed in December, but not during the town patron saint's fiesta in the summer. As in 1971, that occasion is marked by popular dances, sporting events, and a bullfight. Caltzontzin's history as a supposedly traditional Tarascan community before the volcano, the rapidity of social differentiation in the community after relocation, the local anthropologist's study of race relations, and the priest's contentions that some of the local people were under-employed because they did not really want to work, all combined to suggest a need for further socio-anthropological investigation of this complex community.

Zacán's link with its indigenous past was manifest mainly in the "cultural festival" held each October. Exhibitions of crafts, music, and *danzas* were a part of this celebration, which was initiated in 1972. Dramatic performances and poetry readings were given in both Spanish and Tarascan. Traditional *danzas* were also performed during the patron saint's day in the summer. Few people in Zacán use Tarascan on a daily basis. The town remained as it had been in 1971, a place where the people viewed themselves as Mexicans with an indigenous heritage that they proudly shared with fellow citizens.

There was little evidence of a strong sense of ethnicity in either of the Zirostos. A few older people still spoke Tarascan, but we saw no women in traditional dress during our 1991 visits. The same was the case for Miguel Silva. These towns had become even stronger examples of *mestizo* culture, which, of course, had been the predominant Zirosto tradition before the eruption of Parícutin.

Angahuan continued to express the highest degree of ethnic identity, but there had been substantial, if somewhat subtle changes. In 1991, the people on the streets, particularly the women, were more openly friendly. Rather than shyly hiding their faces behind somber-colored *rebozas* [shawls] as in the early 1970's, young women smiled and sometimes waved at passersby. Nearly all of the women were attired in a modified traditional dress. The younger women's skirts were in several bright colors and calf length or even just below the knee rather than long and black as in the past. Some *rebozas* were also brightly hued. Several elegant new houses, although of traditional Tarascan wood construction, were evidence that the traditional principle of "limited good" with its social sanctions against open displays of wealth may be on the decline. According to local informants and people in nearby towns, everyone in Angahuan still speaks Tarascan, and some—even children—speak no Spanish.

Conflicts Among the Towns

As noted earlier, the animosities among the kinsmen of the two Zirostos had cooled and the conflict between San Juan Nuevo and Caltzontzin was apparently resolved. All was not quiet near the lava fields, however. At the beginning of the decade of the 90s, it was Angahuan versus San Juan Nuevo as residents of the latter town sought to re-establish their claim to profits from the historic site of their community marked by the buried church. Whereas San Juan's past conflicts with the former residents of Parícutin had been over agricultural land that was regaining fertility, the clash with Angahuan centered on a tourism resource.

An effort was being mounted in San Juan Nuevo to have a road built from the new town site to the old one in the lava field. Signs posted in San Juan Nuevo announced the development of a new park in the volcanic zone. The combination of a new road and San Juan-maintained facilities would enable guides from that town to compete with those from Angahuan for volcanic-zone tourists. It also would add to the magnetism of the Lord of the Miracles shrine, and to the profit of San Juan Nuevo's citizens, because pilgrims could more easily visit the ruined church, the original home of the object of their devotion. In response, the Angahuanese claimed that they had bought the land around the church from San Juan during the eruption period, but the San Juanese denied this. Tensions had reached a peak in November, 1990, when an Angahuan man was killed in the volcanic zone and several people were injured in a confron-

tation with men from San Juan Nuevo. At the time of our visit, however, the scene was peaceful due to the intervention of outside authorities.

Prospects for the Future

As the time since the birth of Parícutin neared the half century mark, the mountain and the memories of the eruption loomed in the background as the people of the "Towns of the Volcano" faced the future. The lava flow and ash deposits had become accepted, permanent landscape features, and for people in the relocation settlements, the problems of coping with dislocation diminished as new places became home. Fewer and fewer people could remember the eruption period. Most had not yet been born, although it was still part of their heritage, even in distant Miguel Silva. There and elsewhere, young children were familiar with the stories told by their elders, and had learned through tales about the locally sanctioned strategies for dealing with change.

As the century neared its end, people of the seven towns continued to struggle with the need to adapt to changing environments of the Mexican social and economic systems. And, just as the individuals and their respective towns reacted differently to similar problems during the 28 years between the eruption and our initial study, they continued to evidence varied responses to new challenges during the subsequent 20 years.

Plant Communities

The reintroduction of plant and animal life into an area devastated by a volcanic eruption is a subject of considerable interest to botanists and zoologists. Much attention was focused on this subject following the eruptions of Krakatau (Indonesia) in 1883[98], the Valley of Ten Thousand Smokes (Alaska) in 1912[99], Jorullo Volcano (México), 75 km SE of Parícutin, in 1759-74[100], and Surtsey (Iceland) in 1963-67[101]. Botanists and zoologists similarly took advantage of the natural experiment conducted at Parícutin to document the recolonization of the devastated zone, effects of the eruption on vegetation beyond the devastated zone, and attempts to re-introduce agriculture into ash- and even lava-covered lands. Here we reprint major portions of Rees (1979), who summarized and updated the earlier works on plant successions at Parícutin[102]. This is followed by portions of earlier botanical studies by Eggler (1948 and 1963) and Dorf (1945). The section on plant communities is succeeded by a shorter section on animal communities, reprinting brief comments by Foshag and González-Reyna (1956) and an investigation of vertebrates by Burt (1961).

Effects on Natural and Agricultural Vegetation

Rees (1979)

Earlier portions of this article describing the landscape, vegetation, and land use patterns in the region are reprinted on p. 34-36.

Impact of Airborne and Water-Transported Ash on the Rural Economy (1943 to 1945)

Ashfall was greatest during the period 18 March - 9 June 1943. During this period, [termed the heavy cineritic phase by Foshag and González-Reyna (see p. 76-78)], great damage was done to buildings, croplands, and forests. As far as 5 km to the north of the Parícutin cone, large tree branches were broken, and throughout the area saplings were bent over under the burden of the ash. In the fields within 8 km of the cone, crops were killed and agriculture rendered impossible. But famine did not follow, largely because the eruption began 60 days after the end of the annual *maize* harvest, at a time when most families had already stored several months' supply of grain in their houses.

The eruption began in February and the sowing of *maize* usually takes place in March and April. On sites where *maize* seeds were planted after the eruption, germinating seedlings met with a harsh environment. In areas near the cone, ash was falling faster than *maize* could grow through it, whereas throughout the ashfall zone, undernourished seedlings were subjected to abrasion by both falling ash and ash blown across the surface by wind. *Maize* was killed where the plants were buried or where fungus diseases entered ash-bruised tissues. Attempts to plant seedlings in shallow pure ash where roots might penetrate down to the old soil failed as a result of fungus attack during the heavy ashfall. Parcels on the open fields with more than a 14-cm ash depth could not be cultivated because the wooden plow in general use at the time did not reach the old soil surface [see ash thicknesses on inside-front-cover map]. Small-scale plantings of *maize*, however, were possible on house lots where ash was removed by hand and where abrasion by windborne ash was less. In sum, heavy ashfall during the first 2 years of the eruption dissuaded most of the Tarascan farmers from planting *maize* or other crops. On the other hand, Arias-Portillo[103] reported excellent crops of wheat and barley beyond the Itzícuaro Valley [in which the new volcano lies] where only 3 cm of ash fell.

Fruit crops in areas as far away as 48 km were adversely affected by the heavy ashfalls of 1943 and 1944. Within the area where ash depth averages at least 25 cm, fruit trees were defoliated by falling ash, whereas beyond the Itzícuaro Valley (around Uruapan, 21½ km SE of the new volcano), fine ash entered avocado flowers, preventing pollination. The avocado crop loss around Uruapan was more than $300,000 U.S. by the end of 1943[104].

Ashfalls also upset the ecological balance between insects and crops. Near Los Reyes [26 km WNW of the new volcano], subtropical and tropical fruits were able to grow more successfully for several years following the heavy cineritic phase because of the temporary elimination of a destructive fruit fly by the falling ash. On the other hand, ashfall killed a beneficial insect that preyed upon a sugar-cane boring insect in the Los Reyes region. From January 1944 to May 1945, an estimated loss of 80-90% of the sugar-cane crop resulting from a plague by the cane-boring insects was reported; a total area of 1,263 ha [12.6 km²] was affected (see p. 286).

Damage to agriculture was compounded by water-transported ash. With the onset of the summer rains of 1943, the unconsolidated ash was moved by landsliding, sheetwash, and channel erosion into ash-choked streams with increased cutting power provided by the ash. Large volumes of ash and soil were removed from the upper Itzícuaro Valley westward and deposited on the flood plains near Los Reyes. These floods destroyed the irrigation system by breaking up dams and silting up canals, and laying down beds of ash over 887 ha of sugar-cane land. A total of 2,500 ha of sugar cane and rice was devastated[103]. With the incidental blocking off of half the Río Itzícuaro watershed by the San Juan lava flow of 1944, no additional sugar-cane land had since been silted over. Though more than half the ash-silted cane land was in cultivation by 1944, cane fields were still being reclaimed by 1946 (see p. 286). Where water-transported ash had filled the basins and valleys in the upper Itzícuaro watershed, ash playas were formed on many of the open fields, having an ash cover of considerable depth that prevented crop plant seedlings from tapping resources from the deeply buried soil.

Ashfall during the heavy cineritic phase caused death to many livestock. A loss of over 4,500 cattle and 500 horses was reported[103], and an undetermined number of sheep and goats died as a result of breathing volcanic ash. Animals that were initially exposed to, and later removed from, the deep-ash zone often died months later; animals thus weakened were quickly disposed of by their Tarascan owners to outside buyers at greatly reduced prices. Upon postmortem examination, it was revealed that the lungs of animals that breathed volcanic ash were congested with an ash-mucous coating that interfered with respiration. The teeth of many dead animals also showed excessive wear from grazing on ash-coated forage. The loss of cattle amounted to a disaster for the Tarascan farmer: First, it represented an inability to plow even if conditions were permissible; second, it deprived a young farmer of the means to accumulate enough capital to purchase use rights on the open fields and to set up separate housekeeping for his family.

After the end of the heavy cineritic phase (June 1943), an intermittent ashfall continued. During this period an increasing number of villagers turned to the poorest-paying of traditional forestry activities: the collecting and selling of firewood. The huge volumes of branches broken during the heavy cineritic phase were made available to local residents. However, there was the problem of transportation because of the decreased numbers of pack animals and the scarcity of forage near the volcano. Firewood collection and the sale of firewood increased in the local region until prices were driven down to near uneconomic levels. The low price of firewood rendered shipping the surplus to more distant towns unfeasible. Similarly, there was a drop in local price of charcoal. Sale beyond the immediate market towns was curtailed by existing federal forestry regulations.

The collection of pine resin, traditionally a poorly paying part-time occupation, came to a complete halt during the heavy cineritic phase. Ash fell into the collecting cups of the pine, and resin that was thus contaminated was found unacceptable by the distilleries in Uruapan.

Exploitation of the standing timber proved to be the only form of resource utilization that sustained a sizable population in areas of heavy ashfall. As the months of eruption wore on, increasing quantities of hand-hewn lumber products were made and sold illegally, both locally and to other areas of México.

. . . . .

Pre-Eruption Vegetation

The three types of forest vegetation present in the Itzícuaro Valley were all adversely affected by the Parícutin eruption: (a) the fir (Abies) forest located on Cerros de Tancítaro and the Cerros de Angahuan [the main mountain massifs just SW and NE, respectively, of the new volcano: see inside-cover maps]; (b) the mixed pine-oak forest that covered ash-derived soils and old lava surfaces on slopes and valley-flats below the fir zone; and (c) the broadleaf subtropical forest restricted to humid *barrancas*.

The Fir Forest

The fir forest in the affected zone was largely restricted to the upper slopes of Cerros de Tancítaro and Cerros de Angahuan between 2,700 and 3,040 m in elevation. Prior to the eruption the fir forest suffered only a limited interference by man; killing frosts discouraged *maize* cultivation, and distance from the villages inhibited timber exploitation. Fir forest is common at these elevations on deep, well-drained humid volcanic soils in many areas of central México. High atmospheric humidities and more than adequate rainfall encouraged a dense forest dominated by *Abies religiosa* that attained a height of 45 m.

Shrub, herb, and moss-lichen strata were present in the fir forest with the maximum heights at 5.0 m, 1.5 m, and 5.0 cm, respectively. Fewer species were present in the flora of the fir forest than in the pine-oak community found at lower elevations because of winters with extreme minima from -5.0 to -11°C[105]. Oak, pine, and other tree species had a minor role except in the transition to pine-oak forest, where two oak species, *Pinus montezumae*, and other tree species were intermixed with fir.

The Mixed Pine-Oak Forest

The subtropical mixed pine-oak forest covered most of the pre-eruption landscape below 2,700 m elevation that was not in crops or pasture. A less humid atmosphere than in the fir forest, the concentration of rainfall in the months between June and November, and droughts during the less rainy season favor pine-oak forest over fir or broadleaf subtropical forest.

The pine-oak forest adjacent to pre-eruption settlements was heavily exploited and altered. A complex patch-quilt of differing timber stands resulted from heavy and usually premature forest exploitation for lumber, charcoal, firewood, pine resin, shifting cultivation, and grazing. Most pine-oak stands on ash-derived soils were former cropping sites usually under individual usufruct [lands owned individually but available to other community members for non-damaging use]; species composition and age and size of trees usually reflected the forest occupation of the man controlling the woodlot. For example, shingle makers removed large-diameter pines, and charcoal makers removed medium-sized oaks.

Some forested sites were cleared for shifting cultivation. This altered the soils and accelerated the erosion process, resulting in impoverished and delayed forest succession. Repeated fires on many abandoned cropping sites suppressed broadleaf trees and shrubs and favored the development of even-aged pine woodlots with an underlying dense sward of grass.

Within the pine-oak forest different soil (edaphic) conditions produce four different subtypes of vegetation: Subtype 1 is found on well-drained soils [derived from pre-historic ash] of the hill slopes; Subtype 2 grows on humid ash-derived soils of the canyons and draws of cinder cones and hill slopes; Subtype 3 is found on humid moss-covered blocky lava *malpais*[12]; and Subtype 4 occurs on weathered lava flows with dry (xeric) rocky shallow soils. The description of these four subtypes is based on a study of the pine-oak forest in the Itzícuaro Valley some 8 km east of the Parícutin cone[11].

Subtype 1 is the most extensive and is found on slopes with deep well-drained ash-derived soils where *Pinus montezumae* and *P. pseudostrobus* with two *Quercus* spp. form a canopy to 30 m in height in mature stands subjected to infrequent fires. Underneath, a short-tree stratum of *Alnus jorullensis*, *Clethra mexicana*, *Arbutus xalapensis*, *Crataegus mexicana*, and others grows to a height of 10-15 m. A tall-shrub stratum to 6 m in height is present with *Arctostaphylos rupestris*, *Ceanothus coeruleus*, and others. Also present is a substratum to 3 m with *Lupinus elegans*, *Monnina xalapensis*, *Cestrum thyrsoideum*, *Arracacia atropurpurea*, *Baccharis* spp., *Solanum* spp., *Crotalaria* sp., *Salvia* spp., *Fuchsia* spp., *Rubus adenotrichos*, and others not identified. The short-tree and shrub layers increase their diversity with increase in the oak crown cover.

The herb stratum in Subtype 1 is less varied under the dense forest, where only about six grass species predominate, but becomes more varied in forest openings where can be found *Lopezia racemosa*, *Oxalis divergens*, *Geranium mexicanum*, *Cuphea* spp., *Viola* spp., *Portulaca oleracea*, *Sigesbeckia jorullensis*, and others. On old forest clearings, fields, and field edges, the herb flora become even richer with many Compositae such as *Eryngium carlinae*, *Stevia* spp., *Tagetes* spp., *Heterotheca inuliodes*, *Bidens* spp., *Cosmos* spp., *Dahlia* spp., *Galinsoga* spp., *Heterotheca* spp., *Tithonia* sp., and *Vigueria* sp. Also present are the crucifers *Eruca sativa* and *Lepidium virginicum*, several legumes including *Dalea* spp., *Solanaceae* such as *Saracha procumbens*, and also an *Amaranthus hybrid*. Among the most prominent weeds on fallow fields are *Argemone platiceras* and *Mirabilis jalapa*, and on infertile clearings *Cestrum thyrsoideum* and spiny *Solanum* sp. Many other herbaceous plants are also present.

Subtype 2 is found on humid, ash-derived soils in the canyons and draws of cinder cones and hill slopes that favor a greater development of the short-tree and shrub strata. More frequently encountered than in the nearby mesic [characterized by a moderate amount of water, neither hydric nor xeric] sites are the trees *Prunus capuli, Garrya laurifolia, Arbutus xalapensis, Clethra mexicana,* and other broadleaf trees. Shrubs likely to be present are *Satureja laevigata, Monnina xalapensis, Arctostaphylos rupestris, Fuchsia* spp., *Ceanothus coeruleus,* and *Salvia* spp., among others.

Subtype 3 vegetation grows on the humid blocky lava *malpais;* trees and shrubs grow in crevices between blocks of lava that are often entirely covered by low vegetation. The shaded lava block surfaces are commonly covered by algae, mosses, and ferns of several genera including *Pellaea, Pityrogramma, Pteridium, Adiantum, Asplenium, Dryopteris, Cystopteris,* and others. Protected sites between rocks that have a thicker mat of soil and organic matter support succulents such as *Agave* sp., *Echeveria obtusifolia, Sedum tortuosum,* and an orchid, *Bletia* sp. Small herbs include five grass species, and herbs *Lopezia racemosa, Stevia rhombifolia, Geranium mexicanum,* and several others not identified.

The dominant trees growing on the blocky *malpais* are *Pinus pseudostrobus* and two *Quercus* spp., with the former being heavily exploited for timber. The short-tree and shrub stratum is well developed and includes two very distinctive tree species found only on the blocky *malpais, Clusia salvinii* and *Balmea stormae.* Other tree and shrub species include those mentioned for Subtype 2.

Noteworthy is the mass of epiphytes growing on broadleaf trees in the blocky *malpais.* Mosses and ferns make up the bulk, but angiosperms present are two Crassulaceae, *Echeveria obtusifolia* and *Sedum tortuosum,* a single large strap-leafed bromelaid, *Tillandsia prodigiosa,* one *Peperomia* sp., two unidentified cacti, and a rich selection of orchids, including the very common *Laelia autumnalis, Cattleya citrina, Odontoglossum cervantesii, O. insleayii, Oncidium cavendishianum, O. tigrinum, Stanhopea* sp., *Erycina* sp., and others.

Subtype 4 occurs on older xeric lava flows that have weathered to a generally flat surface with thin, droughty soil and rock occasionally jutting upward. Cut over for timber, used for grazing, and sometimes used for crop production if soil depth permits, most of these sites have been subjected to severe interfer-

ence by man, so that a description of "normal" vegetation is difficult. *Pinus leiophylla* and *Quercus peduncularis* predominate, with *Pinus pseudostrobus* increasing on less rocky and less logged-out sites.

Although *Pinus leiophylla* is dominant on such xeric sites, this may be only a successional stage, since other trees are well represented as seedlings (e.g. *Crataegus mexicana, Arbutus xalapensis, Quercus crassipes*). Most sites are characterized by the openness of the canopy—actually a parkland —with much space between middle-sized (30 cm diameter at breast height: DBH) trees. Mature shrubs are infrequent and the herb stratum is rich in species as compared with densely forested areas. Epiphytes are poorly developed.

The Broadleaf Subtropical Forest

The third major vegetation type is the broadleaf subtropical forest. This forest type is restricted to a few deep *barrancas* with long, steep slopes where increased soil moisture, lower light levels, and good air drainage result in a highly equable environment favoring mesophytic trees over adjacent pines. Tropical and humid-subtropical trees, woody lianas, and shrubs (usually associated with subtropical cloud forest at much lower elevations) are present in deep canyons and especially prominent at infrequent seeps.

The dominant trees that create a shaded canopy from 15 to 25 m in height in the broadleaf subtropical forest include *Carpinus carolineana, Fraxinus uhdei, Prunus capuli, Meliosma dentata, Quercus* spp., and *Pinus pseudostrobus.* A short-tree and tall-shrub layer of 7-15 m is composed of *Tilia houghii, Clethra mexicana, Cornus disciflora, Garrya laurifolia, Symplocos pringlii, Styrax ramirezii, Ilex brandegeana, Crataegus mexicana,* the araliads *Dendropanax arboreus* and *Oreopanax echinops,* and others not identified. The low-shrub and herb strata include unusual species. Among them are a tall, coarse fern (*Woodwardia* sp.?) found near the seeps, and subtropical elements such as a large flowering solanacous shrub and a deciduous massive woody liana. Larger trees are covered with epiphytes similar to those found on broadleaf trees in the humid *malpais* environment[11].

The subtropical broadleaf forest is usually well cut over, as the wood of these broadleaf trees sells for high prices. At seep sites utilized for village water supply the forest may be found in good condition since village officials have prohibited timber cutting lest the felling disturb the water flow.

Vegetation Destruction and Recovery

The Parícutin eruption brought about drastic changes to the vegetation of the upper Itzícuaro Valley. The effects of the volcanism upon vegetation are recognizable by the following four zones. [This analysis is based on ash-fall totals in October 1946. Although the eruption continued for nearly 5½ more years, as shown in Table 23, approximately 85% of final ash-fall volume had been erupted by this date.]

1. <u>Total-kill Zone</u>: Coincident with the cinder cone and lava flows.
2. <u>Nearly Total-kill Zone</u>: Where most individuals of all size classes of all species were eliminated, including an area of fir kill on Cerros de Tancítaro where other species survived in relatively shallow ash. Sites in this zone average 1.5 m of remaining ash depth.
3. <u>First Zone of Partial Survival</u>: Characterized by tree damage and heavy kill of shrubs and herbs; sites with 0.5-1.5 m of ash deposition.
4. <u>Second Zone of Partial Survival</u>: Characterized by slight tree damage and partial survival of shrubs and herbs; sites with 0.15-0.5 m of ash deposition.

The extent of these zones can be seen in Fig. 134. The zone of total kill and that of nearly total kill are indicated. The zones of partial survival can be correlated with isopachs of ash deposition. Table 11 indicates the total amount of pre-eruption forest land, cleared land, and village sites within these zones.

Within the total-kill zone, the cinder cone obliterated everything within 600 m of the original vent. Adjacent to the cone, moving lava flows crushed and buried vegetation with a wall of cooled lava rubble. Burning of vegetation was not common; only in a few instances did incandescent lava engulf living vegetation.

Volcanic ash caused the death or decline of most natural and cultivated vegetation. Four obvious causes are suggested:

1. Complete burial of the plant
2. Partial burial restricting root access to oxygen
3. Defoliation and prolonged absence of leaves
4. Ash covering foliage surfaces, clogging stomata and also, blocking out sunlight.

Death or decline of plants may also have resulted from unrecorded acid-bearing rains, volcanic gases, or the buildup of toxic acids in ash and underlying soil.

Beyond the area of total kill, the major environmental factor determining the survival of vegetation was the depth of airborne ash (Table 12). Other factors were general response of a species to ash deposition, size class of individual plant, and site characteristics influencing stripping of ash.

Many species adapted poorly to ash deposition—for example, the moss-lichen stratum and the stratum of herbs became buried. Epiphytes on broadleaf trees perished under conditions of ashfall, partial burial, and strong sunlight as trees defoliated.

With few exceptions, most shrubs died in deeper ash. In 1945 Eggler[106] noted the survival of several shrub species growing through 40 cm to 1.3 m of ash, some growing continuously, others following injury. Included were *Baccharis pteronoides* and *Fuchsia pringlei* in ash to 50 cm, and *Cestrum terminale* in 1.3 m of ash. By the late 1950s, there was little evidence of pre-eruption shrubs surviving where over 50 cm of ash remained; however, they did survive on sites partially or entirely stripped of ash.

Two species of herbs, *Argemone platyceras* and *Mirabilis jalapa*, and three grasses, *Cynodon dactylon*, *Epicampes* sp., and *Digitaria velutina*, are commonly known to have survived 50-cm ash because of their ability to grow up through the deepening ash. Some of these draw strength from tubers; others develop adventitious roots in the ash.

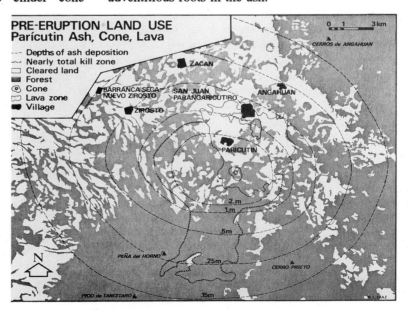

Fig. 134. Map of pre-eruption land use, Parícutin ash depths, the cone, and lava fields.

Table 11. Zones of vegetation devastation and recovery.

Zones	Total area	Forest (pre-eruption) Area	Forest (pre-eruption) Percentage	Cleared[a] (pre-eruption) Area	Cleared[a] (pre-eruption) Percentage	Villages (pre-eruption) Area	Villages (pre-eruption) Percentage
Total-kill Zone	2480	975	39.3	1374	55.4	131	5.3
Nearly Total-kill Zone	4375	3435	78.5	940	21.5	0	0
First Zone of Partial Survival	5245	3866	73.7	1379	26.3	0	0
Second Zone of Partial Survival	26,110	17,363	66.5	8695	33.3	52	0.2

[a]Cleared land = lands under cultivation, in annual fallow, in long fallow with shifting cultivation without timber.
Sources: Data computed from map of pre-eruption land use, Parícutin ash, cone, lava prepared by author. Data sources: base map and former land use from air photos taken in 1934 by Cía Mexicana Aereofoto S.A. for the Banco de Crédito Agrícola; cone and border of lava field from Segerstrom (1960:plate 1); isopachs of airborne ash to October 1946 from Segerstrom (1950:plate 1).

It might be expected that mature trees would be little affected by ash since the foliage mass would be above the ash deposits; this proved not to have been the case. Survival rates varied for each species. *Alnus* was found to have survived in 1945[106], but no individuals were seen in the ash areas in 1957. *Arbutus* seemed to have nearly died out, although Eggler[107] noted some regrowth, probably from old roots, at a site on Cerros de Tancítaro. *Abies* on the upper slopes of Tancítaro was killed, apparently by light but frequent ashfalls upon foliage; other species were scarcely affected under similar conditions. Located downwind and at a higher elevation, *Abies* possibly was intolerant of volcanic gases and acidic water vapor rising from Parícutin. This is only conjecture, however. Evaluation of the extent of *Abies* survival is difficult to assess owing to salvage lumbering of living, along with dead or dying, timber during the late 1940s.

Few trees of the broadleaf subtropical forest seem to have survived, even up to 1945. *Clethra* and *Symplocos* survived in 10 cm of ash in 1945 but were not seen later[106]. Only *Tilia* has survived on uncovered soil at sites stripped of ash[107]. Nothing is known of *Carpinus, Meliosma, Cornus, Garrya,*

Styrax, Illex, Dendropanax, and Oreopanax; defoliation during the heavy cineritic phase may have prevented the identification of ash-killed individuals.

The death or survival of pine and oak has been correlated to the basal-diameter size class of the individual tree, as well as to the depth of the ash mantle[106,107]. Among the three common species of pine, seedlings and small trees were killed owing to excessive bending and burial, whereas large, mature timber suffered from branch breakage under loads of ash. The 10-30 cm basal-diameter size class of pine was the last to succumb because of stems strong enough to resist excessive bending yet sufficiently flexible to dump part of the ash load and avoid breakage. However, almost all pine died when ash deposition exceeded 2 m, regardless of rates of removal of ash from foliage or stripping of surface ash by accelerated erosion.

The several species of oak were uniformly slower to die than the pines; basal-diameter size class survival, interestingly enough, was similar to that of pine, except that fewer oak survived on sites with ash depths over 1.5 m. Other tree species, including *Alnus, Arbutus,* and *Abies,* have not survived as well. An exception is *Crataegus*: old gnarled trees survived in abandoned gardens in San Juan Parangaricutiro in 75 cm of ashfall.

Uncovering of the soil through removal of ash stimulated the growth of vegetation. Soil creep and particularly landslides often destroyed vegetation on a steep site, but removal of ash then created a favorable environment for seedling development. Most stripping away of ash took place through channel erosion. By 1967 most steeper sites had been severely gullied and many even cleared of ash. Exposure of roots, stumps, or standing tree trunks at the old soil level during the 1940s encouraged sprouting of many shrubs and trees that were thought to have been killed but later regrew. On the steep slopes of Cuaxándaran, 5 km WNW of Parícutin volcano, complete stripping of 1.5-2.0 m ash permitted the survival of medium-sized pine and oak. On the slopes of Tiripan, 6

Table 12. Zones of thickness of ash deposition to October 1946.

Zones	Total area	Forest (pre-eruption) Area	Forest (pre-eruption) Percentage	Cleared[a] (pre-eruption) Area	Cleared[a] (pre-eruption) Percentage	Villages (pre-eruption) Area	Villages (pre-eruption) Percentage
Ash over 2.0 m	1430[b]	1035	72.4	395	27.6	0	0
Ash 2.0–1.0 m	2290	1685	73.6	605	26.4	0	0
Ash 1.0–0.5 m	4830	3009	62.3	1792	37.1	29	0.6
Ash 0.5–0.25 m	9810	6429	67.6	3015	31.7	67	0.7
Ash 0.25–0.15 m	16600	10890	65.6	5710	34.4	0	0

[a]Cleared land = lands under cultivation, in annual fallow, in long fallow with shifting cultivation without timber.
[b]Lava field excluded.
Sources: Data computed from map of pre-eruption land use, Parícotin cone and lava prepared by author. Data sources: base map and former land use from air photos taken in 1934 by Cía Mexicana Aereofoto S.A. for the Banco de Crédito Agrícola; cone and border of lava field from Segerstrom (1960:plate 1); isopachs of airborne ash to October 1946 from Segerstrom (1950:plate 1)

km NW of the new volcano, isolated individuals of *Tilia* and *Alnus* are growing back after 1 m of ash was removed by gullying. Near the [3,842 m] summit of Cerros de Tancítaro, growth of plants continued all through the eruption as ash was removed almost as fast as it fell[107]. In all cases where old soil has been exposed, plants have established themselves. By 1959 most areas of deep ashfall (1.5-3.0 m) had plants growing on uncovered soil in gullies. All of the herbs and most of the shrubs growing in the gullies were post-eruption seedlings . . . . The more common shrubs growing in 1959 were *Senecio* and *Piqueria*, followed by *Eupatorium*, *Baccharis* (all four are composites), *Ceanothus*, and *Salix*. Herbs present were *Dalea*, *Crotolaria*, *Desmodium*, *Hosackia* (all papilianaceous legumes), *Penstemon*, *Castilleja*, and *Solanum*[107]. Two species of *Buddleia* were also becoming common by 1963[108]. In 1965 Segerstrom[109] observed six species of *Eupatorium*, two *Baccharis* species, and three species of *Senecio* growing on exposed soil in gullies.

Protection by trees or other living or dead vegetation has permitted the survival of occasional shrubs, herbs, and grasses. In 1957 most live shrubs observed in deeper ash grew at the base of living or dead trees[10]. The trees offered protection against windblown ash and provided sources for moisture and nutrients.

In areas with less than 50-cm ash deposits, the rate of survival and seedling development improved. Sufficient individuals of medium-sized pine and oak survived to provide a leaf litter that protected the sites from erosion as well as supported seedling growth. Medium-sized pine, some oaks, and *tejocote* (*Crataegus mexicana*) survived at Cuezeño, a site with rolling terrain 5½ km north of the volcano. At the same location, seedlings of pine and other plants were observed in 1950; by 1959 over 6 species of trees, 7 shrubs and 17 species of herbs, 4 grasses, 3 ferns, 1 sedge, and various mosses were present[107]. Pine was well represented in all diameter-size classes. Eggler considered that as far as pine is concerned, the forest at Cuezeño had practically recovered from the effects of volcanism 14 years after the maximum ashfall had ceased.

Other forested sites with less than 50 cm of ash similarly provided a leaf mulch supporting seedlings. Vegetation succession is not uniform and the seedling composition varies considerably within short distances; in part, this reflects the survival of nearby propagule sources.

The great open fields are poor sites for plant survival and colonization. Herbs and grasses that grew

Fig. 135. Sterile ash playa enriched with animal manure supporting seedlings of *Geranium Conyza*, and a *Gramineae*, 1968.

on annual fallow land were in most cases buried and killed in 1943. Planting sites of that year had been twice plowed in preparation for seedlings and were largely devoid of vegetation. Most of the open fields became ash playas during the heavy cineritic phase and remain so today [1979]. Less erosion has taken place on the open fields because of slight gradients, and many sites have received insufficient eroded soil or organic material to sustain plant life. Scattered plants found in deep pure ash are often survivors that have grown up through the ash, such as the grasses *Cynodon dactylon* and *Digitaria velutina* and the herbs *Argemone platyceras* and *Mirabilis jalapa*.

Few seedlings have established themselves on open fields retaining a deeper ash mantle. Sterility of the ash is the main limitation, but other factors make the ash fields a difficult environment for growth of seedlings; the crust formed on ash surfaces after rainfalls makes both seed burial and seedling emergence difficult; also windblown surface ash is abrasive to seedling tissue. Despite these difficulties, a ground cover of seedlings was able to colonize open fields where the ash is shallow (under 15 cm depth), or where ash is enriched with water-transported soil or organic materials such as leaf litter, dead timber, or animal dung (Fig. 135).

In summary, vegetation in the region mantled by more than 15 cm of airborne ash has not recovered from the eruption. Only a small fraction of the tree and shrub species native to the Itzícuaro Valley have successfully survived or colonized the ash or the ash-cleared sites. An even smaller proportion of the small herb species common in fallow fields and forest openings 8 km east of the cone are present in the devastated areas. Most of the herbs and many of the shrubs present in the devastated area are plants usually found elsewhere in the region on disturbed or less fertile soils. By 1972 the vegetation of the devastated area was undergoing delayed successional stages leading to the normal species composition. The absence of seed sources, inadequate plant nutrition, and excessive grazing contribute to the delay of the succession.

Vegetation rapidly colonized the lava flows and the cone, encouraged by favorable moisture conditions. In large part, the rapid colonization was made possible because of the humid climatic condition for most of the year and a lava surface that retains moisture in vesicles, hollows, and narrow crevices. By 1950 blue green algae, crustose lichens, mosses, and ferns were reported growing on the 1944 flows[107]. (This early colonization parallels the 1883 Krakatoa eruption, where blue green algae colonized pumice 3 years after the eruption[110].) By 1960 the Parícutin lavas were supporting 33 species: 2 pines, 15 angiosperms, 12 ferns, and 4 mosses[107]. Few individuals of any species were present except for the mosses and ferns that were more abundant (Fig. 136).

Eighteen years later vegetation cover remained sparse on the lava, with most trees and shrubs

Fig. 136 - 1944 lava flow supporting moss, lichen, ferns, and two Angiosperms in 1972.

Fig. 137. *Buddleia cordata, Clethra mexicana* thriving on 1944 lava flow. Height of trees 4 m in 1978.

growing in crevices (Fig. 137). However, by 1978 three trees were frequently seen on the lava, and all three grew to 4 m: *Buddleia cordata* had become the most common and visually prominent, *Clethra mexicana* was also vigorous, and *Pinus leiophylla* was present (some individuals appeared chlorotic, possibly from nitrogen deficiency). Eggler observed that the flows of 1944 supported more plants than those of 1945 and 1950; he concluded that it was not age but the character of the crevices to collect more ash and moisture that made the 1944 flows a more favorable environment for plants. Segerstrom[109] appropriately noted that the early flows received considerable ashfall and the later flows less.

As the lava weathers and vegetation cover expands, an increasingly organic and mesic soil environment will develop. In several hundred years vegetation succession should result in a humid, blocky lava *malpais* subtype of pine-oak forest . . . .

By 1957, 5 years after the end of the eruptions, the cone rim was colonized. Lichen and two angiosperm species were found growing on coarse pyroclastic materials moistened by warm acidic fumarolic water vapor issuing from fissures (see p. 231). Fourteen species of higher plants grew on the cone rim by 1958; included were a pine and several shrubs[111]. Many of the plants were single individuals; most grew near fissures or depressions with additional moisture from fumarolic water vapor and rain channeling[107].

The limiting of plant colonization to the most favorable environments on the cone and lava makes it likely that it will be centuries before the Parícutin cone and lava surfaces weather sufficiently to support a dense plant cover similar to pre-1943 vegetation.

Recovery of Grazing Following Return of Vegetation

A partial recovery of forage following the heavy cineritic phase brought about a return of grazing animals to reclaimed and new pasturelands. Although the pastures did not initially produce as much forage as in pre-eruption times, forage conditions soon improved and, at the time, were more than adequate for the reduced number of animals grazing.

Grazing for a limited number of livestock developed on five types of sites within the ashland: (a) forested sites where leaf litter supports seedling growth; (b) eroded slopes where soil is exposed; (c) deposition areas with soil-ash mixtures; (d) croplands after harvest or in fallow; and (e) open-field croplands subjected to deposition and erosion.

Grazing is poor and unevenly distributed on the open fields because of the patchy, thin colonization of seedlings on the varying depths of the ash mantle. The open fields near Zirosto, for example, provide poor grazing on hummocks of surviving *Cynodon* grass and a sparse cover of seedlings of other species that have invaded the eroding ash beds.

Soil-ash mixtures on alluvial fans and playas support a good growth of herb and shrub seedlings, but these areas are heavily grazed and often fenced and converted to croplands open to grazing after harvest or during fallow. In general, palatable seedlings growing near settlements are heavily grazed, whereas the nonpalatable species, such as *Argemone*, are left by the grazing animals to grow to full size.

Beginning with the rains of 1943-1944, continual erosion of ash from the slopelands permitted a plant cover to develop on areas of bare soil, and on sites where ash has been mixed with soil or plant litter. Following the rains of 1943-1944, pastureland has been developing on sites near the volcano. However, forage production and animal capacity near the volcano are limited because large areas still retain an ash mantle. In addition, the 2,480 ha of lava and cone represent a permanent loss of usable land [for the foreseeable future].

The most heavily grazed sites are forested areas near villages where leaf litter supports seedling growth. On the more distant forested slopes of Cerros de Tancítaro, the light grazing after 1943 and the greater retention of soil moisture resulting from the thin mantle of remaining ash allowed for a more luxuriant herb and grass cover. Grazing capacity was further augmented by timber felling on the slopes south of the volcano between Tancítaro and Cerro Prieto. Over 800 ha were cleared through the removal of timber on the communal lands of Parícutin and Parangaricutiro during the late 1940s and early 1950s. These clearings support a dense cover of annuals and grasses that is utilized for long-term pasturage in the fir forest zone; at lower elevations they serve for pasturage before, and after *maize* cultivation.

In the late 1940s, sizable numbers of sheep were herded on the lands of Angahuan and Parícutin. Sheep were purchased in nearby Corupo [10½ km NNE of the new volcano]. Lack of funds encouraged the purchase of sheep rather than cattle. Also, sheep could get along on poorer forage than cattle. However, by 1965 the higher economic and prestige value of cattle, combined with the continuing improvement of forage as a result of increased plant cover, favored cattle grazing. People with little capital were now able to exploit forage resources on village communal lands by livestock production. In Caltzontzin [the resettlement site for Parícutin village, 27 km ESE of the volcano], for example, several individuals each owned more than 100 cattle—many more than in 1945. In Caltzontzin, most of the cattle were pastured on Parícutin communal lands on the slopes of Cerros de Tancítaro; the cattle population in 1965 was 2,500 as against 450 in 1950.

In the mid-1950s, the raising of cattle yielded income not only from the sale of cattle in villages and market towns, but also from dairy products. Traditionally, milk is consumed only by children among the Tarascans. Since the mid-1950s, milk has been converted into cheese and sold in the market towns.

Cattle owned by the villagers on communal lands of Parícutin and San Juan Parangaricutiro are generally low-grade animals and have low milk production. These cows produce on the average 4-5 liters of milk per day for a period of 2-3 months, whereas those owned by Tarascans in Cherán [38 km NE of the new volcano] yield 8-12 liters per day for more than 7 months. Low milk production is caused by inadequate watering and nutrition. No supplementary grain or forage or water is supplied by the villagers to their cattle, even during droughts that occur in March and April. On top of all these setbacks, the distances and difficulties of transportation make the sale of fresh milk impractical even today.

Despite their low milk production, the Tarascan cattle are still highly prized as an easily salable, high-return speculative investment. Nonetheless, the pri-

Recovery of Agriculture

Successful re-establishment of agriculture is closely related to conditions permitting survival, recovery, and re-establishment of native vegetation. Ash characteristics that inhibited native vegetation were detrimental to economic crops. As mentioned before, during the heavy cineritic phase, *maize* seedlings near the cone were buried; those not buried died as a result of the infertility and droughtiness of the ash beds, and from fungus attacks through bruised tissues from windblown ash. Of all the negative factors, the lack of nutrients was by far the most important.

Pure ash devoid of vegetation had only 55 ppm of nitrogen at 2 cm of depth, as compared with 350 ppm in the underlying old soil. Ash with a pine-needle litter of supporting grass had higher nitrogen values (105 ppm) at surface levels, and lower values with increasing depth until true soil was reached[107]. Farmers found that the nutrients in a thin layer of pine-needle litter plowed into pure ash were not sufficient to mature a *maize* crop.

Experiments carried out in the 1950s by agronomist Eduardo Limón[112] showed that the ash must be heavily fertilized and continually supplied with nitrogenous materials to produce a *maize* crop. Enriching ash with commercial fertilizers seemed economically feasible only if the farmer were in a position to sell the *maize* grain, plow under all the remaining plants, and reinvest the sale proceeds in purchasing fertilizer for the next year. By the end of the third year, the enriched ash should be sufficient to sustain a *maize* crop without further fertilizing, although stubble should still be plowed under for ash enrichment. The entire process would require a capital outlay before the first crop was in; it presumed, therefore, that the farmer had sufficient resources to sustain his family for almost 3 years without having to rely on income from the farmland. In reality, the average Tarascan farmer did not have the money even to pay for the first year's fertilizer.

Fertilizing pure ash allows the farmer to produce a mature *maize* crop, but the yield is not sufficient to both feed the farmer and pay for fertilizer. On the other hand, fertilizing soil-ash mixture results in a dramatic increase in productivity that could provide subsistence for the farmer, plus crop surpluses to pay for fertilizer costs. Crop experiments in 1948 by Miller showed that traditional *maize* grown in fertilized soil-ash mixture on open field cropland at Angahuan yielded 2.025 metric tons of shelled grain

per hectare when fertilized with a treatment of 40 kg N and 40 kg P_2O_5 per hectare. This is in sharp contrast with the unfertilized plots that produced only 0.633 metric tons (896 liters) per hectare[113]. Miller's data indicate that the Angahuan plots were well suited for heavy fertilizing owing to the more than adequate rainfall during the critical months of *maize* growth and ear development[113].

Crop experiments by Tarascan farmers 20 years later in nearby San Lorenzo [15 km ENE of the new volcano] showed that fertilizing soil-ash mixture yielded 2,800 kg of *maize* per hectare. The 1,700-kg increase over the usual 1,080-kg yields sold for 1,360 pesos, more than double the cost of fertilizing[11]. Unfortunately, effective use of commercial fertilizer, insecticides, and close planting did not begin to take place in the Itzícuaro Valley until as late as 1973.

In the absence of government technical support and funding for a commercial fertilization program, Limón suggested enriching the ash with the planting of two native herbs: one, *Lupinus leucophyllus*, a native legume, which failed to germinate properly in ash, and the other, *Mirabilis jalapa*, an herb with a large tuberous root, which succeeded. But *Mirabilis* was rejected by the Tarascan farmers as being a troublesome weed on *maize* lands.

The Tarascan farmers then attempted several approaches of their own: (a) the wholesale removal of ash by sluicing; (b) removal by bulldozing; (c) manual removal by digging of pits to reach old soil; (d) deep plowing by tractor; (e) furrow plowing on the ash mantle using animal traction, a wooden plow, and later a steel plow. The first four approaches met with various difficulties; the last, furrow plowing, was successful.

The sluicing away of ash by directing floodwaters across the fields, used in experiments in Angahuan during the heavy cineritic phase, resulted in deep gullying of the old soil, with high ridges of ash remaining. This technique has been little used since the mid-1940s. However, in 1978, at least one Angahuan farmer removed ash by canalizing storm runoff across a *maize* plot.

The bulldozing of the Angahuan fields by the government in 1953 initially cleared 25 ha of land but was discontinued because there were no satisfactory dumping sites for the ash spoil; ash dumped into ravines and water courses created problems downstream. The method of digging pits down to old soil and growing crops in them proved successful only on house lots. As early as 1945, *maize*, beans, and squash were produced on Angahuan house plots, but pit growing of crops was unsuited to open fields for three reasons: (a) labor and time required to dig and maintain the pits; (b) large dumping areas required to contain the ash spoil; (c) filling of pits by wind- and rain-moved ash. The deep plowing of ash to bring soil to the surface was briefly tried near Zirosto in 1947[114]. The effort was discontinued for reasons not known.

Furrow plowing, the sowing of *maize* in the old soil and soil-ash mixture, accounted for most of the productive acreage in the Itzícuaro Valley after 1945. Furrow plowing enables old soil, weeds, and crop stubble to be mixed into the ash mantle, thus providing some nitrogenous enrichment for each successive crop. The plowing of old soil into ash, however, does not guarantee the growth of *maize* evenly throughout a single field. *Maize* growth was uneven because of the differing depths of water-removed ash within a field. In many instances, plots with shallow ash produced harvested crops soon after the heavy cineritic phase, whereas adjacent plots with deeper water-removed ash did not produce their first successful crop until 1960-1962, after a series of earlier failures. In general, most fields under furrow plowing with an ash depth of less than 15 cm were cropped as early as 1945; however, they did not come up to pre-eruption productivity until the mid-1960s.

Plowing using the traditional ox-drawn wooden plow limited successful *maize* growing to sites where true soil existed within 14 cm below the ash surface. Plowing with burros further limited cropping to where soil was found within 8 cm beneath the ash. The scarcity of cattle, compounded with the high prices for horses and mules and the lack of pasturage following the heavy cineritic phase, all contributed to limiting the reclamation of land by the traditional wooden plow. The steel plow, which permits plowing to 22 cm of ash, was not in general use until the late 1940s, when forestry activities and earnings sent home by *bracero* workers made its purchase possible.

In areas of deep ash where the plow did not reach the old soil, two solutions were applied: (a) successive cropping; and (b) waiting until natural vegetation developed before applying the first plowing. With the first method, *maize* was seeded into pure ash where the lack of nutrients caused the seedlings to yellow and die; the field was then laid fallow for a year, and the procedure repeated until humus and weed growth provided sufficient nutrients to mature the *maize* plants. This, however, proved to be time-consuming, painstaking, and costly in *maize* seed, and was therefore avoided by most farmers. The second method, waiting for the return of a natural pasturage before applying the first plowing, required

no active participation on the part of the farmer and was therefore preferred.

Some former cropping sites buried under ash cannot be easily reclaimed on account of the presence of a hummocky landscape that prevents plowing. On a site near Zirosto, for example, mounds were created by windblown ash caught and retained by the presence of *Cynodan* grass; ground between mounds was then lowered by channel and wind erosion, and the irregular surface thus formed made the reclamation of the cropping site difficult.

Most former cropping sites buried under 15-25 cm of initial ash deposition are presently under cultivation, with the exception of sites buried under water-transported ash. Many fields with an initial ash deposit of 25 cm were, by 1958-1962, eroded down to a remaining ash depth of 15 cm and were supporting a pasture reclaimed for crop growing during the same period. Fertility was often low during the initial years and many *maize* crops did not mature. Fallow periods of 2 or 3 years were common, and grain production was usually less than half of that in a contemporaneous forest clearing devoid of ash.

On sites where the initial ash deposition was between 25 and 50 cm, the recovery of crop growing varies conspicuously from field to field, reflecting differences in either erosion, or enrichment of the ash with deposition of soil and organic material. By 1965, some plots were in the first years of cultivation, whereas others were still in the pasture stage. Over the years few farmers have attempted to enrich the ash by direct application of organic debris or animal fertilizer. Direct enrichment of the ash with a small handful of animal manure placed with the *maize* seed at planting time was practiced by some farmers at Angahuan in 1978 (Fig. 138). The fertilized plants are undernourished, resulting in undersized *maize* ears not satisfactory for dry grain but picked early to prepare *atole* (a corn soup). Adjacent unfertilized *maize* was stunted and failed to produce ears.

In areas where the former croplands received more than 50 cm of ash, the recovery of crop growing was limited to plots where the ash mantle had been removed, or where crops were sustained by soil and organic debris eroded from adjacent slopes. By 1978, *maize* sustained by eroded soil and organic debris grew on seven debris basin sites at the margins of the lava field. The first site cultivated was Chórotiro (at the NE edge of the lava field) in 1946; most other sites came into cultivation in the 1950s (see p. 306, 309). Generally, these sites are fertile enough to sustain cropping every other year without animal or chemical fertilizer. The *maize* growing at Chórotiro in

Fig. 138. *Maize* on an ash playa 0.5 km SW of Angahuan, 1978. Unfertilized plot at left, animal-manure enriched soil on right in third year of planting.

Juan Parangaricutiro, Parícutin, Zirosto, Angahuan) where the initial ash deposition was shallow, and where erosion of ash was accelerated. Salvage lumbering and deforestation on the slopes of Tancítaro following the heavy cineritic phase increased the availabilty of lands cleared for cropping. Almost continuous cropping of slopeland clearings has occurred since 1945, resulting, in many cases, in poor yields, shorter fallow periods, and severe erosion.

None of the pre-eruption cleared land covered by exposed lava (a total of 1,370 ha) will ever be reclaimed. Unlike most of the ash mantle, the lava surface will not be cultivable for several thousand years [but see lava reclamation efforts on p. 306, 309]. Most of the ash-covered cropland could have returned to pre-eruption productivity shortly after the heavy cineritic phase (1943-1945) if subsoil plows drawn by tractors had been used. The subsoil plow is used in older irrigation districts in other areas of México, and is capable of plowing to depths exceeding 1.8 m.

Reclamation has been speeded up recently because of changes in government policy and increased profitability in avocado production. Since 1973, government financing and technical support for reclamation of cropland has rapidly improved agriculture in Angahuan and Zirosto. The federal government has provided credit for chemical fertilizer to a group of 70 Angahuan farmers who are producing successful *maize* crops on soil-ash mixtures. The Michoacán State Forestry Commission has provided budded *membrillo* (*Cydonia oblongata*) and other fruit trees and technical aid to farmers willing to plant, protect, and care for trees planted on unreclaimed ash-covered fields where the ash is not deep. Some of the deeper ash sites are being reclaimed as the Forestry Commission encourages planting of well-developed pine seedlings provided without cost. By 1978 most pine planted on Angahuan lands appeared to be healthy and fast-growing.

A portion of the ash-covered fields of Zirosto now support avocado orchards. The federal government supervises contracts between village officials and outside private capital that leases the land and develops and operates the orchards using local labor. The villagers receive land rental income, wage income, and eventual ownership of the trees. The high

September 1978 looked healthy and grew to 2 m. Unfortunately, the Chórotiro site receives more runoff, sediment, and debris than desirable from the *arroyo* that drains a large area east of Angahuan. The runoff cut destructive swaths 4-15 m wide through the growing *maize*. Past construction of timber, rock, and brush walls have not controlled runoff at Chórotiro as successfully as at other sites. However, the proportion of crop lost to flooding is small. Productivity at Chórotiro is described as a seed-to-harvest ratio of 1:45 (approximately equivalent to 0.630 metric tons per hectare).

Slopelands that were partially cleared of deeper ash by sheet, rill, and channel erosion saw a return to crop productivity as early as the spring of 1945. For example, the upper portion of the inclined open fields adjacent to Zacán was reclaimed in the mid-1940s because the initial ash deposition of 25 cm had already been eroded to a depth that permitted the plowing of old soil into the ash.

As a result of early crop failures on most of the open fields, crop growing has greatly expanded on the slopelands after the spring of 1945. Planting of *maize* was intensified on existing permanent fields, shifting cultivation sites, and pasturelands located on the slopes of Cerros de Tancítaro and Cerros de Angahuan .... Most existing clearings were enlarged and new clearings created where sites could remain undetected by the federal forestry police. Most of these sites are located within communal forests (San profits from avocado production encouraged growers to pay the cost of creating soil-ash mixture for each tree, a heavy fertilizer program, and other development costs. Winter frosts will probably prevent the planting of avocados on the deeper ash areas of the higher elevations nearer Parícutin. Without outside subsidy, the deeper ash areas will continue to remain uncultivated until plant succession enriches the ash with sufficient nutrients to mature a *maize* crop.

Post-Eruption Forestry Activities

Prior to the eruption, timber exploitation in the upper Itzícuaro Valley had always been on a small scale, with sales aimed at the village and local market, and usually not included in official statistics. From the beginning of the eruption, during the time when normal agriculture and grazing were arrested, villagers earned cash by greatly expanding the illegal cutting of dead and dying timber. Large quantities of firewood, charcoal, shingles, and hand-hewn and hand-sawn lumber and timbers were produced up to 1944, when large-scale lumbering and commercial milling were introduced to exploit timber devastated by ash. By 1954, the excessive cutting of timber brought commercial timber production to an end.

During and following the heavy cineritic phase, firewood collection and oak charcoal production experienced an initial boom. The low prices of firewood limited its sale to local regions, but the government allowed large volumes of charcoal to be shipped to urban markets in other parts of México. Today, firewood collection for sale to market towns is a minor activity. The ample supply of milling scrapwood from lumber mills in Uruapan has led to low firewood prices, and there is a reduction in market demand for firewood because of the shift to use of petroleum fuel by major consumers in Uruapan—the bakeries and the public baths. The long-distance hauling of firewood by burros from areas near the volcano has become the exclusive occupation of old men, since it pays less than the legal minimum wage. The production of oak charcoal, aimed exclusively at market towns, has continued on a much reduced scale since the 1940s. Market demand, however, remains constant in Uruapan despite the shift to bottled gas as cooking fuel, because charcoal is still being used by older residents and impoverished immigrants. Presently, oak charcoal continues to be supplied from the forests of Angahuan and San Juan Parangaricutiro, where there is ample oak timber beyond the devastated zone.

During 1943 and 1944, an unusually large number of pine and fir shingles was produced for sale outside the devastated zone. Traditional hand-tooled lumber products such as beams and other squared timber were sold to outside buyers, usually to be milled later into small lumber. Today, a limited number of lumber products are made. Continued efforts are being made by the federal forestry officials to restrict timber exploitation to quantities consumed in each village. Timber cutting at Zacán, Zirosto, and Barranca Seca is now limited to production of lumber for village house construction. Beams, square timber, and pine shingles, produced at Angahuan, are sold locally or to buyers from more distant markets, with or without official permission.

Carpentry that uses unseasoned pine and nails to make chairs, cabinets, and panel doors was a part-time activity of some individuals during the early years of the eruption. In 1965, full-time carpenters could be found in Caltzontzin, San Juan Nuevo, and Angahuan, and part-time carpenters in Zirosto, Barranca Seca, and Zacán. Cabinetry and furniture are the only products of wood that can be sold legally beyond the village without prior government permission. Carpentry items are sold locally and to market venders in Uruapan; however, lack of knowledge of marketing and of easy access to large trucks prevents furniture from being sold to Guadalajara or México City, where prices are twice those of Uruapan.

The illegal cutting and selling of timber by villagers in 1943 and 1944 was allowed by federal forestry officials for fear of public criticism if laws against it were enforced. However, by 1944, villagers were required to apply for permits to cut timber. In this way, the first legal small-scale timber exploitation began to take place on the forest lands of Zirosto, San Juan Parangaricutiro, and Parícutin.

From 1944 to 1954, commercial lumber mills operated on forest lands of Zirosto, San Juan Parangaricutiro, Parícutin, and Angahuan. Commercial lumbering was introduced when forestry officials decided to maximize utilization of salvaged timber. The wastefulness of using high-quality large-diameter pine for traditional shingle making encouraged the government to introduce commercial milling. Contracts were awarded to the Tarascan communal mill at San Felipe [16½ km NE of the new volcano], and to non-Tarascan contractors to establish mills at Barranca Seca [New Zirosto] and Pantzingo (a hamlet located on the communal lands of San Juan Parangaricutiro), and to existing mills in Uruapan. Power sources at these mills varied from electricity to steam power to gasoline motors. Commercial lumbering increased the rate of cutting and salvaged huge volumes of damaged timber that would otherwise have decomposed and been wasted. It also permitted close federal control over timber cutting and tax payments, and provided payment for timber from communal forests to village communal funds.

In the initial phase of lumbering for the mills, hand-hewn squared timber was produced in the forest and converted into lumber at the mill. This procedure kept the villagers employed and diverted maximum income to the Tarascan laborers rather than to mill operators. However, timber squared with axes wastes too much wood in chips. Motor-driven saws are usually less wasteful. Therefore, government forestry officials decided to encourage the hand-tool production of logs and cants (short logs for boxwood) for later milling into lumber at the mills. The mills made contracts with individual villages to purchase felled timber. Contracts specified payment of the felled timber to the communal fund of each village and payment to villagers working in the logging and milling operations. Wages paid to the Tarascan woodcutter were on a piecework basis; those paid to men working in road building, timber hauling, and milling were on a fixed daily-wage basis. Income to the village communal funds, believed to have amounted to over U.S. $200,000, was held in trust by the federal government and helped to pay for resettlement—as in the case of Barranca Seca—and for general improvements, such as electricity and piped water in all the villages.

From 1944 to 1954, men from Zirosto, Miguel Silva, San Juan Nuevo, Caltzontzin, and Angahuan alternated from crop growing on their own fields to lumber operations to contract farm labor in the United States. The men of Zacán, not involved in commercial lumbering, farmed on their own reclaimed fields or migrated as harvest laborers to the United States or to other parts of México.

By 1954, most of the devastated timber had been removed. Federal forestry officials were aware that much live timber was being illegally cut on the communal lands of Zirosto; permission to cut timber was withdrawn and commercial lumbering in the Itzícuaro Valley came to an end.

Resin production, traditionally a secondary occupation for most farmers, came to a complete halt during the heavy cineritic phase because falling ash polluted the bleeding faces of the pine, as well as the collection cups. Resin production was resumed when the ashfall subsided. Ash-polluted pine was bled for resin as early as 1946 on private holdings of residents of San Juan Parangaricutiro. Production on communal lands was delayed because wages paid to resin collectors were low as compared with lumbering wages and wages paid for harvest outside the region. By the mid-1950s, the government renewed or approved new contracts with existing turpentine distilleries in Uruapan, and the acreage in pine resin production steadily increased. By the mid-1960s, more men were employed in resin collection than in any other forest activity. Most men in Zirosto, Zacán, Barranca Seca, and Angahuan supplemented their income by working approximately 6 days per month in resin collection. The majority of men possessed collection rights averaging between 200 and 500 trees; a few had rights to 1,000 or over. Each tree yielded between 3 and 5 kg of resin annually. The government further stimulated production by establishing a government-sponsored cooperative turpentine distillery in the Tarascan village of Cherán [38 km NE of the new volcano]. In 1968, the Cherán distillery paid members of its resin collection cooperative one peso per kilo, whereas privately owned distilleries were paying only 45-67 centavos per kilo.

The recovery of the pine forests and the higher price for resin account for the present success of resin activities. Unfortunately, the quest for resin income has resulted in poor management of young pine stands. Crowding and poor nutrition produce narrow crowns and small-diameter trunks—the poorest characteristics for resin production. Many of these trees are under 20 cm in diameter at breast height and show three bleeding faces. The exploitation of premature young pines will ultimately result in reduced resin yields and lowered quality of wood as a whole for use as lumber.

Pine-Oak Forest Inventory

Eggler (1948)

Willis A. Eggler (Fig. 139), a botanist from Tulane University, conducted systematic surveys of vegetation on the cone and lava flows of Parícutin and the surrounding region in 1945, 1950, and 1959-60. His work was published in a series of three articles: Eggler (1948, 1959, 1963). Most of his data were collected by laying out square plots at many different locations and characterizing all plant species in the plots for size and abundance. Eggler also measured nitrogen contents of ash samples taken in vertical profiles at many locations in an attempt to understand the role that volcanic gases and microbial activity played in supplying nitrogen to invading plants.

Eggler's work at Parícutin was summarized and updated in the preceding article by Rees (1979). Here we reproduce only two short sections from Eggler's articles: a systematic survey of pre-eruption plant communities in the pine-oak forest of the Parícutin area, and a discussion of the succession of plant species on the cone itself.

Plant Communities
Before Volcanism Began

Prior to the eruption of Parícutin volcano about 75% of the land of the region was forested (estimated from an aerial photo taken prior to February, 1943 [similar to Figs. 12 and 13]. This was generally the part too rough for agriculture. Conifers usually predominate in the forests but hardwoods are also present, except at the highest altitudes.

There are three rather distinct vegetational zones. Occupying the plateau area between cones, and the sides of cones up to about 2,750 m is a pine-oak forest. From 2,750 m to about 3,050 m fir is the dominant tree; and above 3,050 m pines are dominant, continuing to the summit of even the highest mountain, Cerros de Tancítaro [3,842 m]. There is no timber line and trees do not appear to decrease in size with increased altitude[115].

Pine-Oak Forest

This is the most important plant community from an economic standpoint as it covers the greatest area and furnishes forest products for local industry. It is variable in composition, ranging from mixed pine and hardwoods to nearly pure stands of pine or to almost pure hardwoods. Several sources of information were used in studying this community: general observations throughout the area, data on density and frequency

Fig. 139 - Willis Eggler (front left) and others eating lunch at the "Upper Casita" observatory on Cerro de Jarátiro, July 1945. Abrora, the cook, stands in the rear. Others at the table (left to right): unidentified, Frederick Pough (American Museum of Natural History), unidentified, George Bertram (Army photographer), Carl Graton (Harvard), Oliver Gish (Carnegie Institution), Ralph Alex (Sikorsky Co.).

from a mixed forest, and the ages and rates of growth of pine trees as obtained from increment cores.

General Observations

The most striking thing about this forest of lower altitudes, when first seen, is the predominance of pines over other tree species, particularly in the more level places. Two species, *Pinus leiophylla* Schl. & Cham.[116] and *P. psuedostrobus* Lindl., are about equal in importance and make up most of the pine population. A third, *P. teocote* Schl. & Cham., is of minor importance. When out-of-the-way spots are examined, such as steep sides of cones some distance from a village or road, it becomes evident that hardwoods, particularly oaks, are present and important. In many places they equal or exceed the pines in numbers. Continued observance reveals that even in areas where pines are dominant a few small hardwoods may be scattered among them and occasionally a large oak of great age is present. Eight oaks were identified from the area. These are *Quercus Fournieri* Trel., *Q. magnoliaefolia* Neé, *Q. mexicana* var. *angustifolia* H. & B., *Q. obtusata* H. & B., *Q. oligodontophylla* Trel., *Q. orbiculata* Trel., *Q. Radlkoferiana* Trel., and *Q. transmontana* Trel.

Next in importance among the trees, after Pinus and Quercus, are alder (*Alnus jorullensis* HBK.) and madroña (*Arbutus xalapensis* HBK.). In protected ravines are basswood (*Tilia Houghi* Rose), and fir (*Abies religiosa* (HBK.) Schl. & Cham.), in very small numbers. A cherry (*Prunus Capuli* Cav.),

Table 13. Density and frequency of tree species in plots on south side of a cinder cone near San Lorenzo. Angle of slope about 38°. Area, 1,400 m².

| | Less than 1* | | 1–3 | | 4–9 | | 10 or more | | Totals |
	D.	F.	D.	F.	D.	F.	D.	F.	D.
Symplocos prionophylla	2060	50%	1	7%	0	0%	0	0%	2061
Quercus magnoliaefolia	630	36	23	50	20	57	9	43	682
Taonabo Pringlei	280	43	11	29	7	14	1	7	299
Arbutus xalapensis	140	43	6	29	2	7	0	0	148
Quercus orbiculata	120	21	17	14	3	7	2	7	142
Pinus pseudostrobus	130	29	3	21	2	14	6	43	141
Pinus leiophylla	80	14	0	0	0	0	1	7	81
Alnus jorullensis	60	7	5	21	2	14	0	0	67
Quercus obtusata	0	0	20	14	7	14	0	0	27
Clethra sp.	0	0	4	7	5	14	0	0	9
									3682

Above the size-class columns: *Diameter size classes in inches*

* Values have been multiplied by 10 to compensate for the smaller area sampled.

hawthorn (*Crataegus pubescens* (HBK.) Steud.), and ash (*Fraxinus Uhdei* (Wenzig) Lingelsheim), are minor members of the community. They are more often along the margins of fields and in fence rows where they may have been planted.

Shrubs of importance in the pine-oak community are *Arctostaphylos rupestris* Rob. & Seat., *Ceanothus coeruleus* Lag., *Cestrum terminale* var. *latifolium* Francey, *Baccharis pteronoides* DC., *Buddleia parviflora* HBK., *Fuchsia Pringlei* Rob. & Seat., *Salix Hartwegii* Benth., and *Symphoricarpos microphyllus* HBK.

Statistical Studies

Forest in which Quercus [oak] is of major importance is relatively scarce and is generally confined to slopes of cones. This type of forest is dense, particularly in the shrub stratum. The south side of an old volcanic cone about 450 m high and 1½ km in diameter at the base was chosen for detailed studies of this forest type. There were no evident differences in the vegetation on different sides of this cone. The cone lay about 3.2 km east of the village of San Lorenzo and 16 km from the volcano[117]. It had been little affected by Parícutin's volcanism, beyond receiving a thin layer of ash on its surface, and seemed to be little disturbed by cutting and grazing. The angle of the slope was about 38° where the study was made. Fourteen plots, 10 m by 10 m in size, were evenly spaced through the middle two-thirds of the side of the cone. Disturbance was less there than at the base and summit. In the plots all trees an inch or over in diameter (as measured 4 feet from the ground), were counted and grouped in several size classes [these values were not converted to metric equivalents because Eggler's data were tabulated in inches and feet (Table 13)]. Trees under an inch and shrubs were tabulated in plots 2 m by 5 m; and herbs in plots 0.5

m by 2 m. The small plots were always located in the one next larger in size, in a pre-determined corner. Results of these studies are given in Tables 13 and 14. An indication of the importance of a tree species in a community is its presence in many size classes with a high density and frequency for each class. On that basis Quercus [oak], with four species collectively, occupies first place among trees; Pinus [pine] is second, and Arbutus [madroña] third. *Symplocos prionophylla* Hemsl. and *Taonabo Pringlei* Rose, though they have high densities, are small trees and only subordinate members of the community. Pinus contributes the tallest and most conspicuous members of the forest. *P. pseudostrobus* is the more important of the two species in the plots; it has the greater density and is present in all size classes. Economically it is said to be superior to *P. leiophylla*, both as a lumber tree and as a turpentine source. Trees of other species are all small and are subordinate members of the community.

Table 14. Density and frequency of shrubs and herbs on the south side of a cinder cone near San Lorenzo. Angle of slope about 38°. Values are based on an area of 140 m². Shrubs tabulated in fourteen 2 m by 5 m plots; herbs computed in fourteen plots 0.5 m by 2 m.

	Density*	Frequency
Shrubs		
Arctostaphylos rupestris	167	86%
Fuchsia michóacánensis	102	93
Coriaria thymifolia	92	36
Ceanothus coeruleus	68	50
Salvia longispicata	44	36
Russelia polyedra	41	36
Cologania biloba (Lindl.) Nichols	39	57
Xylosma flexuosum Hemsl.	8	7
Crotalaria pumila Ort.	6	21
Cestrum terminale var. *latifolium*	4	7
	571	
Herbs		
Bromus pendulinus Sessé	210	36
Stipa mucronata HBK.	190	43
Cystopteris fragilis (L.) Bernh.	150	7
Ranunculus sp.	120	21
Passiflora sp.	90	7
Trifolium amabile HBK.	70	14
Physalis subintegra Fern.	70	14
Adiantum Poiretii Wikstr.	60	7
Cynodon dactylon (L.) Pers.	50	7
Lupinus elegans HBK.	50	7
Pteridium aquilinum (L.) Kuhn	40	7
Onosmodium strigosum Don.	20	14
Cyperus flanus (Vahl.) Nees	10	7
Begonia balmsiana Ruiz	10	7
	1140	

* Multiplied by 10 in case of herbs to compensate for smaller area.

Ten species of shrubs were present, the two most important being Arctostaphylos and *Fuchsia michoacanensis* S. & M. *Coriaria thymifolia* H. & B., number three in terms of density, has a rather low frequency, 36%, which indicates it is not widespread, but grows in colonies. *Salvia longispicata* M. & G. and *Russelia polyedra* Zucc. are as well distributed as Coriaria, but each is only half as dense. It is worth noting that only three of the ten shrubs in the plots were included in the list of those considered to be important throughout the region. This may mean the other seven are confined to forests with considerable hardwood present, or it may mean that they have been killed out of other forests by the eruption. The first explanation seems more likely.

There was an unimpressive number of herb species in the plots, only 14 species, and those in small numbers. Frequency is also low in all cases. The first two places are taken by grasses and third by a fern. A heavy canopy of trees and shrubs, which overshadowed most of these plots, probably inhibited the growth of more herbaceous ground-cover.

Rate of Growth of Pines

Increment cores were taken from 65 pine trees, *Pinus pseudostrobus* and *P. leiophylla*, located in 18 different stations . . . . The trees selected were generally of moderate size, between about 5 and 12 inches in diameter. One station that furnished three trees was in the upper pine zone; all others were in the pine-oak zone.

The cores showed the annual diameter increment of the pine trees to be rather "moderate" in amount. The maximum diameter increase for any tree for a year was 24.4 mm. The minimum increase was 2.8 mm.; the average for all trees was 8.5 mm.

Revegetation of the Parícutin cone

Eggler (1963)

The final explosive activity from the crater of Parícutin cone occurred on March 4, 1952 (see p. 181), but hot gases continued to issue from many different fumarolic vents [and were continuing to do so in 1993]. Some vents were in the throat and some on the walls of the crater, but more were on the rim. Water vapor was undoubtedly the chief constituent of the emanations but NH$_4$Cl was present too. An oblique aerial photograph of Parícutin cone and crater,

taken by Fries on April 29, 1952, shows white, snow-like crusts of NH$_4$Cl on the east wall of the crater[118].

The two most striking changes in the appearance of the upper part of the cone in 1959 as compared with 1950, other than the cessation of active eruption, were (1) the presence of many plants around the rim of the crater and (2) the great amount of fissuring and slumping that had taken place. The fissures generally ran in a NE-SW direction; slumping was generally in a NW-SE direction, but some slumping went in other directions also . . . . The effect of slumping and fissuring on plant invasion has been a retarding one because of the instability of the substrate. Not only is the surface unstable but the fumarolic outlets changed and there is considerable dependence of plants on fumarolic gases.

The first report of plants on the cinder cone was made by Segerstrom[76,119], who found lichens and two kinds of vascular plants growing near the summit in February, 1957, five years after activity ceased. The vascular plants were identified as *Gnaphthalium* and *Eryngium*.

In the summer of 1958 (6½ years after activity ceased) Beaman[102] collected 14 species of vascular plants on or near the rim of the crater. His collection

Table 15. Species of plants invading Parícutin cinder cone between 1957 and 1960.

	Segerstrom 1957	Beaman 1958	Eggler 1959	Eggler 1960
I. Gymnosperms				
Pinus montezumae ?		×		
P. pseudostrobus				×
II. Angiosperm shrubs or small trees				
Baccharis glutinosa		×		
Buddleia cordata		×		
Coriaria thymifolia			×	×
Eupatorium adenochaenium (abundant)			×	×
E. mairetianum				×
E. pazcuarense		×		
Salix hartwegii			×	×
Wigandia kunthii			×	×
III. Angiosperm herbs				
Aegopogon cenchroides H. & B.		×	×	×
Aster exilis		×	×	×
Conyza coronopifolia		×	×	×
Cyperus flavus (Vahl.) Nees.				×
Erigeron scaposus DC.			×	
Gnaphthalium sp.	×			
G. attenuatum		×		
G. cansecens (abundant)			×	×
G. semiamplexicaule		×		
Muhlenbergia minutiflora (abundant)			×	×
Phytolacca icosandra				×
IV. Ferns				
Cheilanthes angustifolia				×
C. farinosa (abundant)			×	×
Pellaea ternifolia (Cav.) Link var. *ternifolia*		×		
Pityrogramma calomelanos (L.) Link		×		
P. tartarea (abundant)		×	×	×
Pteridium aquilinum		× (var. feei)	×	×
V. Moss				
Anobryum filiforme var. *mexicana*			×	×
VI. Crustose lichens	×		×	×

231

Table 16. Plants in 1.5 m x 1.5 m plots on Parícutin cinder cone in 1959 and 1960 (vascular plants expressed as density, mosses as coverage in dm²).

	I 1959	I 1960	II 1959	II 1960	III 1959	III 1960
Aegopogon cenchroides						
Cheilanthes farinosa						
Eupatorium adenochaenium	13	30				
Erigeron scaposus						
Gnaphthalium canescens	1	3	1			
Muhlenbergia minutiflora						
Phytolacca icosandra						
Pityrogramma tartarea			1	10	6	
Salix hartwegii					1	
Mosses dm²	0.4	0.4	100	0.1	56.2	

	IV 1959	IV 1960	V 1959	V 1960	VI 1959	VI 1960
Aegopogon cenchroides	1	1				
Cheilanthes farinosa	12	6				
Eupatorium adenochaenium	11	4	5	11		
Erigeron scaposus					1	
Gnaphthalium canescens		2			1	
Muhlenbergia minutiflora					5	
Phytolacca icosandra			1			
Pityrogramma tartarea	16	25	10	4	1	
Salix hartwegii						
Mosses dm²	4	6.3	3	4	2	

included 4 species of ferns, 1 pine, 1 grass, 5 composites, a *Buddleia*, and 2 unidentified species. It included *Gnaphthalium* but not *Eryngium*, the plants collected by Segerstrom.

I made several trips onto the cone in the summers of 1959 and 1960. The plants observed included 14 species of angiosperms, 1 pine, 4 ferns, and 1 species of moss. Plants known to be on the cinder cone in the years 1957 to 1960 are shown in Table 15.

Only five species of vascular plants were present in sufficient quantity in 1959 and 1960 so there was reasonable certainty of their continuance. These were, beginning with the most abundant: *Eupatorium adenochaenium*, *Pityrogramma tartarea*, *Gnaphthalium canescens*, *Muhlenbergia minutiflora* (Steud.) Swallen, and *Cheilanthes farinosa*. Others were more sparse and in some instances represented by only one plant.

The area with densest plant growth in 1959 and 1960 was a section of the north rim about 6 m wide x 15 m long, which supported ferns and *Eupatorium*, with a few willows and *Coriaria*. The plants were all under 30 cm tall. The east wall of the crater supported a relatively good growth of *Eupatorium*, ferns, willows, and grasses. The plants were even smaller, scarcely over 8 cm tall, and were several meters apart.

Plants on the cone were generally located near fumaroles, but the bottoms of fissures (trenches, usually about a meter deep) sometimes supported plants also. Moisture was apparently the critical factor. Fumaroles supplied it in most instances, but runoff from rain accumulated in the bottoms of fissures and depressions. A fumarole in a depression was the best combination.

The plant population on Parícutin has been a transient one. Beaman[102] found no *Cheilanthes* ferns in 1958; I found *C. angustifolia* in 1960, and *C. farinosa* in 1959 and 1960. Beaman found *Pellaea ternifolia* and I found none, but did find it on the 1944 flow. We both found *Pityrogramma tartarea* and *Pteridium aquilinum* on the cone. Beaman found a plant of *Pinus montezumae* and I saw a small *P. pseudostrobus*. Beaman reported no willows and I saw several; the same applies to *Phytolacca*, *Coriaria*, *Wigandia*, *Muhlenbergia*, *Cyperus*, and *Eupatorium mairetianum*.

Some of the plants that disappeared undoubtedly became part of a botanist's collection, but this applied only to those with 1 or 2 individuals present. Difficult growing conditions, especially in regard to water, must have been responsible for the disappearance of many plants.

Six 1.5 m x 1.5 m plots were laid out around the rim of the crater, and vascular plants in the plots were tabulated in 1959 and 1960. Plots III and VI are for 1959 only. In the other four, some species increased and some decreased. Table 16 shows how plants within plots were observed to change within one year's time.

Preservation of Plant Remains

Dorf (1945)

Many paleobotanical studies are conducted on plant remains (leaves, seed pods, pollen, etc.) found in volcanic ash layers and associated sediments. From these remains, scientists attempt to reconstruct vegetation communities and climate records for long-vanished landscapes buried by the eruptions. In this investigation, Erling Dorf, Professor of Paleobotany at Princeton University, attempted to provide a calibration for such studies, by comparing the preservation of plant materials in various sites of ash deposition and remobilization with the plant com-

munities in the adjacent forests. Portions of his study are reprinted below, particularly those that focus on the species-dependent nature of preservation potential.

Methods of Study

During six weeks in the Parícutin region, plant remains were studied in the following situations: (1) on the surface of the ash both within and adjacent to the forest; (2) in vertical exposures of ash along stream courses; (3) in pits dug into the ash at sites selected to illustrate various conditions of sedimentation, including subaerial, alluvial-plain, stream-channel, and lake-bottom deposition.

In each situation the buried or partially buried plant remains were recovered for study by sifting of ash layers through a coarse screen. Observations were then made on the physical state of the recovered plant remains and on the degree of correlation between the conditions inferred from the buried plants and the actual conditions in the adjacent forest.

Description of the Present Forest

The forest adjacent to Parícutin is an upland, temperate pine-oak association. There are two species of pines, two of oaks, a crab apple, a madrone, and an alder on the hills and steeper slopes. The lower stream channels are bordered by the same species of pines, oaks, and crab apple, with the addition of one species of cherry, a lancewood, and a linden. Minor elements in the vegetation include ragweed, mimosa, and smilax. The gentle slopes between the hills and stream channels were almost entirely under cultivation before the eruption.

In the forest proper the proportion of pines to oaks is approximately four to one. Both crab apples and madrones are somewhat less numerous than the oaks, with the alders still less common. Along the stream channels the oaks are most numerous, with the pine, cherry, lancewood, and linden only sparsely represented.

. . . . .

Preliminary Results

(1) True fossilization, implying induration of the ash and mineralization of wood, has hardly begun.

(2) The processes of fossilization were highly selective, so that the plants were not equally susceptible to preservation.

(a) No recognizable remains of herbs were found preserved in the ash, despite their common occurrence in the forest. This absence is attributed to their fragile nature and to their habit of not shedding their leaves.

(b) The ash preserves an excellent record of both pines and oaks. The pines were represented by prodigious numbers of needles and many cones, catkins, and branches, in much greater abundance than might have been expected from the relative abundance of pines in the living forest. In one section of subaerial ash the ratio of pine needles to all types of dicot leaves was estimated as approximately 1,000 to 1. Oak leaves were the most common type of dicot leaf encountered in the ash. In proportion to the remains of pines the buried oak leaves were less common than might have been anticipated. This is obviously due to the relatively greater output of needles per pine tree than leaves per oak. However, in proportion to other dicot leaves in the ash, the oaks were more numerous than would have been expected from the proportion of oaks in the living forest. This is interpreted as mainly the result of the tough, leathery texture of the leaves of both species of oak, in contrast to the thinner and more fragile leaves of the remaining dicots. Of the latter, including crab apple, madrone, cherry, lancewood, and linden, the ash has preserved only a meager record, considerably out of proportion to their common occurrence in the living forest.

(c) These observations are of significance to the paleobotanist, who attempts to infer the composition of a forest for which the fossils are the only record. It demands of the paleobotanist a knowledge of the physical characteristics of the species concerned and an appreciation of the processes involved in the burial and preservation of the various types of plant remains.

(3) Plant remains were well preserved only if buried close to their parent trees or shrubs.

(a) With rare exceptions the remains of pines, oaks, madrones, and alders were found well preserved in the ash only within 25-30 m of their parent trees, regardless of the sedimentary process involved in their burial . . . .

(b) The buried leaves of crab apple, cherry, linden, and lancewood were not well preserved, and often were difficult to identify, even within 3 m of their parent trees. Such leaves as were recovered and recognized were curled and twisted, and often torn and broken into shreds and fragments. Here again is a reflection of the relations between physical qualities of the leaves and their chances for preservation and subsequent identification.

(4) Subaerial ash deposits contained more abundant and better preserved plant remains than stream or lake deposits.

In subaerial deposits, plant remains were found in well defined horizons, interpreted to be seasonal. Both leaves and needles were well preserved and presumably fell gently to the site of deposition, without undergoing damaging transport by wind or water. Species proportions were inversely related to distance of parent trees from the depositional site. Not surprisingly, many plant remains in stream deposits were highly abraded and broken. Of the two classes of stream deposits studied, valley-fill deposits contained a higher proportion of undamaged specimens than did alluvial-plain deposits. Relative species abundance and physical condition again were related to distance from the parent trees. Crab apple, cherry, and linden remains were rarely identified in stream deposits. Excavations were made in the fine-grained beds of two dried crater lakes, located in cinder cones about 1½ km from Parícutin. Although plant remains were generally well preserved, they were less abundant than expected. Crab apple, which is common in the nearby forest, was extremely rare in the lake deposits.

(5) Plant remains in the subaerial deposits are the most likely to be destroyed by future erosion . . . . From a paleobotanical point of view it is unfortunate that the deposits containing the best and most numerous plant remains are also the most likely to be destroyed.

(6) The best ultimate plant preservation, if any, is likely to be in valley-fill ash deposits buried by lava.

Animal Communities

Effects on Animals

Foshag and González-Reyna (1956)

The advent of sudden and violent change in a previously placid area brought about a rapid diminution of the animal population of the region. But it appears that fright was not an important factor in this change. Such animals and birds as persisted in the region during the early and most violent period of the volcano showed no fear of and even seemed totally oblivious to the terrible events that followed each other in quick succession.

The first animals to disappear from the region were the deer and rabbits, and with them, to a large extent, went the coyotes, owing no doubt, to the disappearance of their food supplies. As long as the pine and oak trees remained alive, squirrels and jays persisted and left only when the supply of pine cones and acorns vanished. Smaller birds, like creepers, also persisted, feeding upon insects still abundant in the forest or blown in by the winds. Eventually these too left the area, except for a few occasional stray ones that passed through. The winds brought in numerous insects of various kinds, which the falling ash battered to the ground. These moths and butterflies, grasshoppers and leafhoppers, and other forms, collected in sheltered pockets or in the shallow rills in the ash, and became a constant source of food for such animals as remained. Even after 2 years of activity field mice and foxes persisted, and their tracks could be seen on the ash, even on the ash over recent lava flows. Crows were seen almost daily about the volcano and frequently alighted on the cone, during falls of ash and bombs. It was discovered that the slopes of the cone yielded an abundant supply of insects, which undoubtedly was the principal attraction for the crows.

Reptilian life was not common. A large lizard apparently found a hole in the warm lava a congenial environment, with abundant food at his door. The few snakes we observed were obviously having a hard time of it, the loose ash not being particularly suited to their manner of locomotion. Frogs died and desiccated in the ashy environment.

Particularly striking was the apparent lack of interest or fear shown by the birds and animals to even the most violent outburst of the volcano. Horses and dogs evinced no interest whatever. On one occasion the dog of one of the natives accompanied us to the summit of the cone, and while we watched events with considerable trepidation, curled up in the ash and went to sleep. The crows, previously mentioned, during their forays to the cone, showed no apparent concern for explosive bursts from the crater.

Effects on Vertebrates

Burt (1961)

Dr. William Henry Burt, Professor of Zoology at the University of Michigan, made a reconnaissance visit to the Parícutin area in July 1944, and returned in the summer of 1945 to conduct a survey of vertebrate animals within 12-18 km of the cone. The goal was to determine quantitatively the survival rates of various animals and to deduce the critical factors involved in their survival. He repeated the survey in 1947 in an effort to document changes during the intervening two years.

At this time (1944), the San Juan lava flow was still advancing. Prickly poppies, *Mirabilis, Bouvardia,* and a few other plants that were able to keep their own crowns above the ash added color to otherwise barren ash plains that formerly were corn fields. The animal life, except for man and domesticated kinds, was practically non-existent where the ash was 15 or more centimeters deep [>300 km² in area]. There were a few insects, many of which had been carried in by the wind, on which a few kinds of birds were feeding. About the only birds seen were occasional jays flying through the area, ravens, two of which flew around the cone nearly every day, and Brown Towhees. The Brown Towhee is a bird of the villages in that area—comparable to the House Sparrow and Starling except that the towhee is a native bird that has adapted to city life. In 1944, these birds were numerous along the hot advancing lava front at San Juan Parangaricutiro. They commonly alighted on the still warm lava or ran near the advancing wall. I had no means of collecting samples for food determinations, but I suspect they were subsisting chiefly on insects and a few seeds that might have been carried in by the wind. These perhaps were individuals that had inhabited San Juan Parangaricutiro. With most of the village under lava, the population was concentrated in the remaining portion and along the lava front.

Few signs of native wild mammals were seen closer than about 7 km from the cone, where the ash was about 25 cm thick. Here, with considerable effort, I was able to get two individuals of a small deer mouse (*Peromyscus maniculatus*). They were taken about 3 m apart along an old stone fence. There were mice in the Upper Casita [observatory cabin on Cerro Jarátiro, 1½ km north of the volcano], but at that time we were not certain what they were; only their tracks and sign were seen.

No reptiles were seen near San Juan Parangaricutiro, but a small amphibian (*Tomodactylus angustidigitorum*) was present along the old stone fences where the ash depth was about 45 cm. This then was the dismal picture of a considerable area around the cone after a year and five months of continuous volcanic activity.

One year later, in 1945, Dr. N. E. Hartweg and I returned . . . . Near San Juan Parangaricutiro, where there were probably less than a dozen kinds of birds the year before, we now found 32 kinds. They were mostly insectivorous or frugivorous (25 kinds). The few seed-eaters were subsisting for the most part on insects and fruits. A few of the birds were patently migrants, and some of the others, seen but once,

undoubtedly were wandering within the general area. The common birds that were seen nearly every day were hummingbirds (two kinds), flycatchers (3), swallows, jays, ravens, chickadees, curved-billed thrashers, tanagers, grosbeaks, house finches, siskins, towhees, and juncos. Brown Towhees, although still present and nesting, were less numerous than they had been a year before when the lava front was still active at San Juan Parangaricutiro.

There were fewer kinds of mammals than of birds, but in this group also there was a marked change. Deer mice (*Peromyscus maniculatus*) were now abundant along and near the lava front. Lava that a year before was red hot now served as a shelter for these mice. One even lived out in the middle of the lava stream along a horse trail. The only food available was the offal from the horses and an occasional insect or seed that might be carried in by the wind. I believe that the population of these mice was near the peak in 1945. Near the cone, at the Upper Casita, where tracks had been seen the year before, I caught one *P. maniculatus* and two females of a larger species (*P. hylocetes*). I believe I exhausted the mouse population there. The small one was a young animal that most likely was on the prowl and ended up at the only place where there was shelter and food. The other two might have been the same individuals that were there the year before. I suspect that they had been able to survive because of the shelter and food afforded them by the scientists and tourists. Both were adult females and neither showed signs of having bred. The nearest other place that this species was taken in 1945 was on Cerros de Tancítaro [SW of the new volcano], where the ash was about 15 cm deep. One tree squirrel had ventured into the pine-oak forest at the Lower Casita [observatory cabin at Cuezeño, 5½ km north of the volcano] and a cottontail lived thereabouts. The ash there was about 60 cm deep. Pocket gophers (*Cratogeomys varius*) were found south of Corupo [10½ km NNE of the volcano], but their occurrence stopped abruptly where the ash was 15 cm deep. A gray fox ranged through the area; its tracks were seen within 800 m of the cone.

The little tree toad was more numerous than before; apparently it had been able to breed, but no lizards were found closer than Angahuan.

Two years elapsed before our next visit to Parícutin (1947). Again we were to see some rather startling changes . . . . Nearly all of the familiar birds were still there. Only one of the hummingbirds (*Hylocharis leucotis*) was encountered, flycatchers were less numerous as were grosbeaks and tanagers. But a few species were added. Acorn Woodpeckers, not seen in 1945, were fairly common in 1947; one Red-Shafted Flicker and two Hairy Woodpeckers were seen in 1945; in 1947 flickers were common, but Hairy Woodpeckers were still rare.

Cliff Swallows, whose old nests on the church were evidence of former occupancy, were not there in 1944 or 1945. They had returned by 1947. A colony of 20 or 30 individuals was nesting on the church. I suspect that availabilty of mud for nest material was one of the more important factors involved in the presence or absence of Cliff Swallows. Rains had washed the ash from many of the old adobe walls in San Juan Parangaricutiro thereby making mud available. Another species that depends on mud for nest building is the American Robin. In 1945, a few robins, probably young itinerants, were seen shortly before our departure. In 1947, the American Robin was one of the most conspicuous birds of the area. No nests were found, but young birds were seen, and collected, and adults were common throughout the forest.

Other additions to our previous list, but still not common, were: Sharp-shinned Hawk, Whip-poor-will (one heard), Horned Lark, Bewick Wren, Rock Wren, Gray Silky Flycatcher, Loggerhead Shrike, House Sparrow, and Vesper Sparrow.

The composition of the mammalian fauna had changed quite noticeably in the two years that had elapsed. The small deer mice, (*Peromyscus maniculatus*), so numerous before, were still there, but apparently were fewer. The larger species (*P. hylocetes*), taken only on Cerros de Tancítaro and at the Upper Casita before, had come in and was, in places, more numerous than the smaller representative. Cottontails (*Sylvilagus*) and tree squirrels (*Sciurus*) were more numerous, but still fairly scarce. Rock squirrels (*Citellus*) had found the cooled lava to their liking and were back in San Juan Parangaricutiro in force. Attracted chiefly by the garbage pit back of the Lower Casita, and possibly by the increased natural foods, the coyote was back. There were at least two individuals that ranged near the Lower Casita. Bats of at least two kinds were flying in San Juan Parangaricutiro and along the lava front nearly every night. South of Corupo, pocket gophers (*Cratogeomys*) had advanced some 10 m closer to the cone, but still were not beyond the zone of 15 or more centimeters of ash. The Indians, also, were planting corn and beans on the Corupo plain about 800 m closer to the cone than was true in 1945. As wind and water removed the ash so they could get

their seeds down in the original soil, they followed closely with their plantings.

Some kinds of mammals that were taken previously on Cerros de Tancítaro, but which we failed to take, are *Sorex*, *Neotomodon alstoni*, *Nelsonia neotomodon goldmani*, and *Neotoma mexicana*. With the destruction of ground-living invertebrates, shrews (*Sorex*) would undoubtedly succumb. The rodents mentioned above should have survived along with *Microtus*, *Reithrodontomys*, and *Peromyscus*. Perhaps we just missed them.

One of the most startling and interesting of our 1947 discoveries, was a salamander, (*Pseudoeurycea bellii*) in what was remaining of San Juan Parangaricutiro. Dr. Hartweg found these salamanders by the hundreds in the old adobe and stone walls and beneath boards that had been left scattered about when the Indians vacated the town. None had been encountered on our previous trips. There seemed to be no possibility of ingress from adjoining areas. These salamanders must have carried over in the shelter of stone walls or within the adobe walls of the houses. They were capable of breeding without free water. One individual was found in an old stone wall across the lava stream that nearly surrounds San Juan Parangaricutiro. No others were seen except in San Juan proper. The little tree frog had also made its way into San Juan Parangaricutiro and was everywhere more numerous than it had been previously. A lizard (*Sceloporus torquatus*) had found its way from Angahuan, the nearest place previously seen, to the lava front opposite San Juan. These lizards could have followed stone walls, with occasional stretches of open ash to cross, nearly all the way from Angahuan to San Juan Parangaricutiro.

To recapitulate briefly, during the first year of activity, when the ash fall was greatest, practically all the plant life was killed for distances of 5-8 km from the cone, depending primarily on the amount of ash that fell. Ash depths of a meter or more seemed to be fatal. Most of the animal life was exterminated out to distances of 8-13 km from the cone or out to the zone where less than about 20 cm of ash fell. Some plants and animals were affected as far as 160 km distant, but these effects were slight and probably temporary.

With the lessening of the ash fall and the coming of the rains, there was relief for the plants as well as for certain animals that had been able to survive in sufficient numbers to breed when conditions again became favorable. Some of these small animals, with their natural enemies removed, built up their populations to peak proportions in short order. Still others, probably there before the holocaust, started filtering back into the area. Those affected most were the ground-nesting or ground-dwelling kinds. Although trees and other perennials that were able to keep their crowns above the ash had survived fairly close to the cone, the small plants and annuals were destroyed much farther out. With the ground cover gone and nothing left but shifting ash, there was no place for animals that could not seek refuge in the trees or in the few old stone fences that were still partly exposed.

In addition to affecting the animals adversely by making the habitat generally unsuitable for many that lived in the area, there were more subtle influences on those that were able to persist in spite of the heavy mantle of ash. One of these was the abrasive effect of the ash. The only noticeable effect on the birds was the wearing off of the tail feathers in the woodpeckers. During the time between molts, these feathers, in many instances, were down to short stubs one-half the original length. But new feathers came in and this probably had little if any effect on the life-span of the individual bird. In mammals, this abrasive effect showed up in the teeth. We have specimens of young opossums in which the last molar teeth had but recently erupted yet the pre-molars are worn nearly to the roots. An old opossum has the crowns of the teeth completely worn away and only the roots remain. Several bats have incisors and canines worn to the gums; in two, abscesses had formed beneath the teeth. Others that showed excessive wear on the teeth were *Brassariscus*, *Urocyon*, *Sciurus*, and *Sylvilagus*. Inasmuch as the survival of a wild mammal depends on the life of the dentition of that individual, it is quite evident that the normal life-span in these animals must have been shortened. This, in turn, would affect the populations adversely by cutting down on the breeding stock. The larger, slower breeding mammals would be affected most. I imagine the same effect would be seen in domestic stock and, to a lesser extent perhaps, in the Indians of the immediate area. Regardless of how careful they might have been, particularly during the dry season, ash would get into their food and the result would be shorter life of their teeth . . . .

The article concludes with a list of 94 birds and a list of 30 mammals encountered in the Parícutin area, along with Latin and common names, comments, and descriptions of individual specimens collected.

Volcanoes of the Parícutin Region Mexico

By HOWEL WILLIAMS

GEOLOGIC INVESTIGATIO[N]

GEOLOGICAL

Prepared in coope[ration]
Secretaría de la [Economía Nacional]
de México, Dir[ección de Minas y]
Petróleo, and t[he Universidad Nacional]
Autónoma de [México, Instituto de]
Geología, und[er]
Interdepartm[ental]

Erosion Studies at Parícutin, State of Michoacán, Mexico

By KENNETH SEGERSTROM

GEOLOGIC INVESTIGATIONS IN THE PARICUTIN AREA, MEXICO

[BULLET]IN 965–A

[t]he Uni[versity]
[ma de]
[under]
[ental]
[ral]

Petrology of Parícutin Volcano Mexico

By RAY E. WILCOX

GEOLOGIC INVESTIGATIONS IN THE PARÍCUTIN AREA, MEXICO

GEOLOGICAL SURVEY BULLETIN 965–C

Prepared in cooperation with the Secretaría de la Economía Nacional de
México, Dirección de Minas y Petróleo,
[and the Universida]d Nacional Autó-
[noma de México, Instituto de] Geología,

V. Geological Studies

New Mexican Volcano to Die Young

Mexico's Newest Volcano in Violent Eruption

A Few Decades Of Real Activity Expected of It

How It Started Is Described, but No One Knows What Causes Such Phenomena

By John J. O'Neill

The new volcano which sprang into existence in the State of Michoacan, in Mexico, six months ago, on the afternoon of Feb. 20, and is still going strong, is likely to have a very brief life in a geological sense, and even in terms of the historical time scale. A second volcano broke into action on June 11, about a half-mile from the point where the first one erupted, but this should be considered merely a new vent to ~~~~~ ~~~~~~ ~~~~~~~ single sub-terranean pool of ac~~~

While it is entire~ that this new fire-s~ tain will have a lon~ as those of the It~ that have a recor~ 2,000 years of acti~ assurance that it ~ spectacular perf~ the next few dec~ it will be likely ~ regular quiescén~ plete extinction.~

The region i~ erupting cone i~ in which this ~ been repeated ~ revealed by a ~ tory made by ~ Mexico City ~ and geologi~ findings in ~ "Mining and ~ cial publica~ Institute o~ lurgical En~

100

The site~

3 New Craters Found On Paricutin Volcano

Special to THE NEW YORK TIMES.

MEXICO CITY, Oct. 26—Paricutin, Mexico's latter-day volcano that surged up in a cornfield in the State of Michoacan in February, 1943, has developed three new craters, the latest of which appeared this week.

Paricutin, which caused tremendous alarm among the peasants when it appeared three and a half years ago, subsequently became one of the country's greatest tourist attractions. It is believed to have entered a phase of renewed activity.

A steady column of smoke has been coming out of the main crater, which now towers more than 3,000 feet, while continuous streams of lava have been pouring from the three infant craters on the northeast slope.

~ne at Paracutin, in State of M

A volcano, how-~ local event. The ~arth is not a mass ~ rock under pres-~en it finds a vent ~spews some of the ~gh in the air. The ~earth for 100 miles ~olid and cold—cold, ~the sense that it is ~w the melting point ~ despite a steady in-~mperature with depth.~ion in which a volcano ~there is a pool of chem-

vast amou~ world-wid~ chemical ~ suing fro~ ture of ~ starts th~ mystery ~ amined ~ hydrog~ gas, ~ chlori~ gaseo'~

Dr.~ wher~ unit~ eno'~

El Paricutín Está de Nuevo en Actividad

Le Brotaron Tres Cráteres y hay Alarma en la Región Oct. 26-46

El Paricutín está nuevamente en funesta actividad, y los habitantes del pueblo de Zirosto, Mich., tienen encima la amenaza de los "tres hijos recién nacidos" que han brotado en las faldas del monstruo.

Pequeños montículos que comienzan, a ejemplo del volcán mayor, a lanzar llamaradas y lava, que corre hacia el poniente.

La catarata de fuego aumenta en altura cinco centímetros cada 24 horas y la acompañan en su carrera 40 detonaciones por minuto.

Por el lado oeste del Paricutín reventó también una boca a 300 metros del cráter principal, cuya base tiene en la actualidad más de mil metros de diámetro.

Un redactor de EXCELSIOR, que después de asistir a la inauguración de los nuevos servicios de alumbrado que realizó en Apatzigán la Comisión Federal de Electricidad, acaba de pasar cerca del volcán, pudo ver que las reciente~ vías han lavado las tierras sem~ destruidas y ue los nativos inten-tan nuevamente labrarlas.

Por otra parte se resienten aún algunos de los daños que la erupción del Paricutín—nombre que significa "tras lomita"—han causado inclusive la destrucción de ~ ~~~~~ ~~~~ ~~ ~~í~ ~~ ~~~~~~~

Geological Setting

Mexican Volcanic Belt

Today, Parícutin volcano is just one of several thousand volcanic cones that dominate the landscape in a broad region extending roughly E-W for over 1,200 km across southern México (Fig. 140). This zone is called the Mexican Volcanic Belt (MVB), and its frequent eruptions and earthquakes result from northeastward subduction of the Cocos and Rivera Plates beneath the southern edge of North America. The MVB is part of the "Ring of Fire", a system of subduction-related volcanic arcs and associated zones of intense earthquake activity that surround the Pacific Ocean on most sides.

Eruptive activity in the MVB began at least 10 million years ago[120,121], but most older rocks have been buried by the products of eruptions during the last 2 million years, the period of time referred to as the Quaternary. A wide range of volcanic forms have emerged in the MVB during the Quaternary, including large stratovolcanoes, smaller cinder and lava cones, and huge caldera complexes where enormous volumes of magma have erupted catastrophically[122].

The MVB can be conveniently discussed in three parts. The western portion is dominated by a system of three rift zones that intersect just south of Guadalajara. A chain of relatively small strato-volcanoes, including the historically active Volcán Ceboruco[123], extends from the intersection area to the Pacific coast along a NW trend named the Tepic-Zacoalco Rift Zone[124-126]. The Chapala Rift Zone, which extends eastward from the rift intersection area, is largely filled by Lake Chapala and appears to contain few Quaternary volcanoes. The Colima Rift Zone trends southward to the Pacific coast from the intersection area, and has been the site of numerous volcanic eruptions. A southward-younging chain of stratovolcanoes grew on the floor of the Colima Rift

Zone during the Quaternary; the active Volcán Colima marks its southern end[127,128].

The central portion of the MVB, which includes Parícutin volcano, is a westward-sloping high volcanic plateau that forms a crude, E-W-trending rectangle between 19° and 20.5°N latitude and 97° and 103.5°W longitude. Its southern margin and main axis is defined by a line of three large, historically active stratovolcanoes: Colima (4,000 m), Popo-catépetl (5,452 m), and Citlaltépetl (5,675 m). Each of these large active cones marks the southern end of a N-S-trending alignment of stratovolcanoes. Many other Quaternary stratovolcanoes can be found north of the Colima--Popocatépetl-Citlaltépetl alignment. Large caldera complexes are generally found in the northern portion of the central MVB[129]. Thousands of smaller cinder and lava cones also occur within the central MVB, either scattered on the lower flanks of larger stratovolcanoes[131], or concentrated within fields[131,132]. The largest of these cinder and lava cone fields, described on the following pages, covers an area of some 40,000 km² in the states of Michoacán and Guanajuato, and has accordingly been termed the Michoacán-Guanajuato Volcanic Field (MGVF: Fig. 140). It contains over 1,000 small volcanic structures, of which more than 900 are cinder and lava cones. Among these are the only two cinder and lava cones to have erupted in México during historical times: Parícutin (1943-1952) and Jorullo (1759-1774). Throughout the central portion of the MVB the focus of volcanic activity has been migrating southward during the Quaternary. This migration is evident in the three major southward-younging chains of stratovolcanoes[127], in morphological analysis and age dating of cinder and lava cones (see p. 256-259) and shield volcanoes in the MGVF (see p. 275-277), in age dating of volcanic rocks from the central and eastern portions of the MVB[121,133], and in the fact that

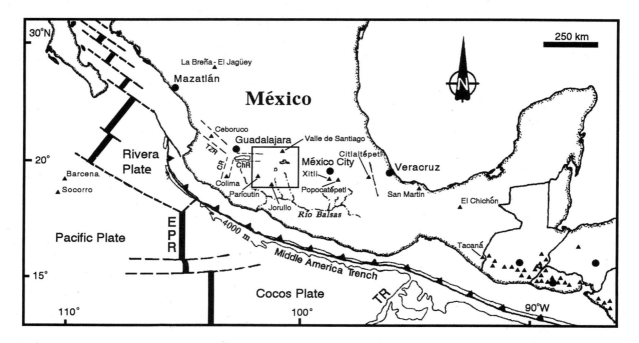

Fig. 140. Location map for southern México and principal plate tectonic features of the adjacent Pacific Ocean basin. Large dots show major cities, with those in México labelled: M - Mazatlán, G - Guadalajara, MC - México City, V - Veracruz. Triangles show volcanoes that have been active in the last 10,000 years, with those in México labelled. The three intersecting rift zones of the western Mexican Volcanic Belt are indicated by paired dashed lines: TZR - Tepic-Zacoalco Rift, ChR - Chapala Rift, CR - Colima Rift. Rectangle marks the Michoacán-Guanajuato Volcanic Field, which contains Parícutin volcano. Offshore, the Rivera, Pacific, and Cocos Plates are indicated. Thick dark lines show the segmented East Pacific Rise (EPR) oceanic spreading center. Segments are offset by transform faults (dashed). The Middle America Trench is shown by a solid line with barbs; the thin line near the MAT is the 4,000 m water depth contour, which defines the trench. The northern part of the Tehuantepec Ridge (TR) is indicated.

all historically active volcanoes in the central MVB, including Parícutin and Jorullo, lie near its southernmost margin (Fig. 140).

The low-lying eastern portion of the MVB is separated from the high volcanic plateau of the central MVB by a major N-S-trending fault zone that lies just east of Volcán Citlaltépetl. The landscape descends rapidly to the east across this fault zone until the Gulf of México is reached at Veracruz, just 130 km to the east of Citlaltépetl, the third highest peak in North America. The eastern portion of the MVB includes only two major volcanic centers, both of which produced magmas that are considerably more alkalic (richer in sodium and potassium) than magmas that typify the western and central zones. About 120 km SE from Veracruz lies the Tuxtla Volcanic Field, which contains the historically active Volcán San Martín[134]. Farther to the southeast begin the scattered volcanic centers of the Chiapanecan Arc[135]. This poorly known region includes El Chichón

volcano, which erupted explosively in 1982[136]. The Chiapanecan Arc extends to within 100 km of the Guatemala border, where Volcán Tacaná[137], which erupted in 1986, marks the beginning of the Central American Volcanic Arc.

Volcanic and seismic activity in the MVB appears to be related to subduction of the Rivera and Cocos Plates beneath the southern margin of North America along the Middle America Trench (MAT). The MAT can be identified by a narrow zone of water depths greater than 4,000 m that parallels the southern coastline of México (Fig. 140). The depth of the MAT increases systematically to the east, from barely 4,000 m at the western end to greater than 6,000 m near the Guatemala border. The axis of the MAT lies about 70 km offshore of the western and central portions of the MVB, but in the eastern zone, the coastline shifts to the north to form the Gulf of Tehuantepec, and the distance from the MAT to the coast increases to about 180 km. This shift in coastline position, and a relatively abrupt increase in depth of the MAT appear to be related to subduction of the Tehuantepec Ridge, an aseismic, former fracture zone that marks a NE-trending, major discontinuity in the subducting Cocos Plate[138].

The present-day motion between the Rivera Plate and the North American Plate has been difficult to resolve. Although earlier workers concluded that subduction of the Rivera Plate ceased in the past few million years and that the Rivera Plate then became attached to the North American Plate[139], more recent analyses of global plate motions indicate continued slow subduction of the Rivera Plate toward the NE at a rate of 2 cm/yr or less[140-142]. This slow subduction produces very few earthquakes along the trench, most of which are low magnitude, and virtually no deeper inland earthquakes, presumably because the subducting oceanic plate is very young and hot and deforms in a plastic rather than a brittle manner[124].

The present-day motion between the Cocos and North American Plates is much better understood. The Cocos Plate subducts to the NE on an azimuth that decreases eastward, from 39° near Volcán Colima to 34° near the Guatemala border[143]. Subduction velocity increases eastward along the trench from 6 cm/yr near Volcán Colima to about 7.8 cm/yr near Volcán Citlaltépetl[140,141]. In the central and eastern portions of the MVB, seismicity is limited to relatively shallow depths, with virtually no earthquakes occurring below about 100 km depth[124,141]. These earthquakes define a sloping plane that is thought to mark the position of the subducted slab. Along the central portion of the MVB the angle of subduction decreases toward the east from about 30° near Volcán Colima to perhaps as little as 20° near the Tuxtla volcanoes. The subduction angle then steepens toward the south and reaches about 40° beneath the Central American Arc[144]. The age of the subducted Cocos Plate generally increases toward the east along the central and eastern portions of the MVB.

One of the most unusual features of the central MVB subduction zone is the fact that the axis of volcanic activity is not parallel to the MAT, but diverges from it by about 20°; the Colima-Popocatépetl-Citlaltépetl alignment is oriented virtually east-west, whereas the MAT follows an approximate trend of 110°. Some studies have attributed this divergence to eastward increases in the age of the subducted Cocos Plate and its angle of descent[145], but many other studies, including several of those reprinted in the following section (Hasenaka and Carmichael, 1985; Connor, 1987, 1990), have emphasized that the locations of volcanoes are controlled by fault zones and other features in the overriding North American Plate[146-148]. The distributions of vents at both Parícutin and Jorullo volcanoes appear to reflect the local stress field of the overriding plate. Both main craters are flanked by other eruptive vents that form linear NE-SW trends, parallel to the direction of motion between the Cocos and North American Plates, and to the direction of maximum horizontal compressive stress[149].

Volcanoes of the Region

Williams (1950)

Howel Williams (Fig. 101; see p. 132 for biographical information) was a dedicated and insightful field geologist who emphasized the importance of regional stratigraphy and structures to the understanding of volcanic phenomena. His early studies were primarily focused on volcanoes in the western U.S., but his field work in the Parícutin region in 1944-45 marked a shift in this focus southward toward the volcanoes and archeology of Central America; these would dominate Williams' research until his retirement in 1966.

Williams mapped an area of about 1,550 km² centered on Parícutin volcano, an area that represents just a small fraction (<4%) of the larger Michoacán-Guanajuato Volcanic Field. His study was published as part 2 of the 4-part U.S. Geological Survey Bulletin 965 dedicated to Parícutin. Williams examined the basement geology of the Parícutin region and described the younger volcanoes in great detail, discussing their eruptive histories, relative ages, and the compositions and mineralogies of their rocks. Here we reproduce just a small portion of this major work. We have included much of the discussion of basement geology, but only a few descriptions of representative volcano types. A modified version of his geologic reconnaissance map of the larger Parícutin region (plate 8) is found on the inside back cover of this book, and should be consulted for features mentioned in this article.

Location and Topography
of Area Studied

Parícutin volcano stands in the heart of a country peopled by Tarascan Indians, in a landscape considered by many to be the most beautiful in México. Most of the region is drained westward by the Río de Itzícuaro and its tributaries, which go to feed the Río de Tepalcatepec, itself a branch of the mighty Río de Las Balsas [Fig. 140] . . . . As Graton[150] has remarked, "probably nowhere else in the world is there such a great concentration of conspicuous volcanic cones over so large an area, and nowhere are the basaltic cones more numerous than the western half of Michoacán, nor in the immediate environs of Parícutin."

. . . . .

Northward the region of coffee and banana plantations around Uruapan gives place rapidly to pine-clad hills and mountains. Within 19 km the highway climbs 600 m. Most of the cultivated valleys between the volcanoes lie above 1,950 m and below 2,400 m. Here one finds the principal settlements.

Among the volcanoes themselves, the largest and highest by far is the denuded cone forming Cerros de Tancítaro [just SW of the new volcano], the summit of which rises to 3,842 m, towering 1½ km above the encircling younger cones. Next in prominence are the twin volcanoes that make up Cerros de Angahuan [13 km NNE of Parícutin volcano], culminating in Cerro de La Purísima at an elevation of 3,292 m. Then comes the arresting peak of Cerro del Aguila [29 km NE of the new volcano], which also exceeds 3,000 m in height. Most of the host of cinder cones that crown the lava-built volcanoes and dot their flanks range from 30 to 300 m in height. Late in 1947, the top of Parícutin itself stood at an elevation of 2,775 m; the elevation of the cornfield from which it started was approximately 390 m lower [2,385 m].

Eighty percent of the region around the new volcano was forested, chiefly by pines and oak. Above 3,000 m, firs predominate. Prior to the present eruptions, half of the cultivated land was given over to corn; less important crops were wheat and beans. Apples, pears, and other fruit were plentiful. It was a countryside as pleasant as its people.

. . . . .

Zumpinito Formation

Within the area covered by this report, the oldest volcanic rocks are referred to as the Zumpinito formation from their occurrence in magnificent sections near the Zumpinito hydroelectric plant, a few kilometers south of Uruapan [21½ km SE of the new

volcano]. The formation underlies Uruapan itself and also the adjacent plain, where it is mantled by a veneer of basaltic ash blown from neighboring cinder cones. It is exposed in the gorges of the Río de Cupatitzio and its tributaries, and it forms the conspicuous Cerro de La Cruz on the outskirts of Uruapan, as well as Cerro Colorado and the Cerro de Las Ventanas to the east. The road connecting Uruapan and Apatzingán winds over a mountainous terrain carved in beds of the Zumpinito formation, and presumably the formation extends south at least as far as the valley of Apatzingán. It reappears from beneath the younger volcanoes to the west of Parícutin in the low country between San Francisco and Los Reyes [26 km WNW].

Except on Cerro de Charanda, close to Uruapan, where the beds are tilted to a high angle, the Zumpinito formation lies either horizontally or has low initial dips. No original volcanic forms are preserved; hence the erosional topography carved in the rocks of the Zumpinito formation contrasts boldly with the constructional forms built by the later volcanoes. Nor is it possible to locate any of the vents from which the lavas and the fragmental ejecta of the Zumpinito formation were expelled.

No fossil evidence has yet been found that indicates the age of the Zumpinito formation. Since, however, the formation includes at least one major disconformity and was already deeply dissected before the Tancítaro volcano began to develop, it must cover a long span of Tertiary time, and the topmost beds can hardly be younger than middle Pliocene.

. . . . .

Older Volcanoes of Post-Zumpinito Age

Williams describes in turn the older volcanoes Cerros de Tancítaro, Cerros de San Marcos, Cerro del Aguila, Cerros de Angahuan, and Cerros de los Hornos, and gives aerial photos, interpretive sketches, and cross sections. We have reproduced only the Tancítaro description. On p. 275-277 we reprint portions of Ban et al. (1992), which includes a single K-Ar date for a lava from Tancítaro of 0.55 ± 0.06 million years (Table 19, p. 276), confirming the age estimated by Williams based on the degree of erosion.

The oldest volcano of post-Zumpinito age forms the towering mass of Cerros de Tancítaro, the highest peak in the State of Michoacán. Its summit rises to an elevation of 3,842 m, providing an unparalleled view over an immense volcanic field dotted with hundreds of lesser cones.

Prior to dissection, the form of the Tancítaro volcano approximated that of a shield with slopes flattening toward the top. The visible diameter of the volcano is about 11 km; its buried extent may be twice as much, for the lower flanks are covered by the flows and fragmental ejecta of younger basaltic cones. Where the lavas of the Tancítaro volcano disappear beneath these younger rocks there is a distinct break in slope and the topography changes suddenly, narrow ridges giving place to flat-topped divides of gentler gradient.

Erosion of Tancítaro has advanced to full maturity, so that the original shield has been reduced to radiating, sharp-crested spurs separated by V-shaped canyons, some of which exceed 300 m in depth. On all sides the ridge crests descend in approximate conformity with the dips of the constituent flows. None of the original constructional surfaces remain, but some of the sharp ridges close to the foot of the mountain merge into flat-topped, wedge-shaped interfluves that coincide fairly closely with the initial flanks.

The attitudes of the flows on the upper part of the mountain indicate that the main vent or vents lay between the present summit and the conspicuous peak known as Peña del Horno, about 1½ km to the north. Probably subsidiary vents served as feeders to parasitic cones close to the summit; if not, it is difficult to account for the numerous peaks that cluster around the highest point. All signs of the main and subsidiary craters have long since disappeared.

The eruptions that built Cerros de Tancítaro were almost all of the quiet, effusive type. Some interbeds of breccia and agglomerate were observed by Ordóñez[151], but compared with the lavas they are very minor in amount. Dominantly the volcano consists of massive sheets of porphyritic andesite, some of which exceed 60 m in thickness. Apparently the flows were extremely viscous, and many, in the later stages of advance, moved by shearing rather than by laminar flow, so that highly inclined and vertical joints were developed at steep angles to the fluidal banding. True obsidians were not observed, but most of the flows are rich in interstitial glass. Some show columnar structure; others exhibit reddened, scoriaceous crusts.

A few flows of hornblende-rich andesite are present, but most of the lavas are hypersthene-augite andesites plentifully studded with large phenocrysts of feldspar. According to Ordóñez, they resemble the principal flows of Cofre de Perote, Ajusco, and Ixtaccíhuatl [large stratovolcanoes of eastern México], and they are identical with the andesites forming the coeval volcanoes of Cerros de San Marcos. They also call to mind the andesites that compose such volcanoes of the Cascade Range as Mounts Shasta, Rainier, and Hood.

Reference has already been made to the fact that previous workers considered the Tancítaro volcano to be of Pliocene or Eocene age. The latter estimate may be dismissed from consideration with the remark that no volcano of such antiquity would preserve any semblance of its original shape. However, in attempting to assign a more precise age to the volcano, there is little evidence upon which to rely. The volcano grew upon the deeply eroded surface of the Zumpinito formation, but the age of these bedrocks is still unknown. In using the degree of dissection as a criterion, it must be borne in mind that erosion has been tremendously accelerated in this region as a consequence of the explosive activity of the younger volcanoes. Every explosion of the younger cones blanketed the flanks of Tancítaro with fine ash, and during every rainy season the ejecta must have been swept into the canyons, converting the streams into muddy torrents of exceptional abrasive power. This acceleration of erosion is vividly seen·today as the new cover of ash from Parícutin is stripped from the steep hillsides during the wet summers and devastating mudflows rush down the canyons to spread their bouldery loads in huge fans far beyond the base of Cerros de Tancítaro. Coarse deposits of older lahars have built great fans around the foot of the mountain. All are mantled by deeply weathered basaltic ash, locally as much as 15 m in thickness, and in places beds of ash and flows of olivine basalt are interstratified with the bouldery debris. From this it follows that unusally rapid erosion of Tancítaro persisted throughout the growth of the encircling cones of basalt. Bearing in mind also that some of the present ridge tops almost coincide with the original slopes of the volcano and that dissection, although mature, has not proceeded far enough to expose the central feeding pipes, it can hardly be doubted that the last eruptions of Tancítaro took place either in late Pliocene or Pleistocene time.

. . . . .

Younger Volcanoes

General Statement

After the growth of the large andesitic volcanoes of Tancítaro, San Marcos, Angahuan, and Cerro del Aguila and the mixed eruptions of Cerros de Los Hornos, the centers of activity in the Parícutin region became more numerous and widespread, and the dominant lavas changed to olivine basalts and olivine-bearing basaltic andesites. Eruptions of pyroxene andesite did not come to an end; on the contrary, some of the most copious flows of andesite were discharged within the last few thousand years.

These younger volcanoes, whose symmetrical forms typify the Tarascan landscape, are so little modified by erosion that all can be assigned without hesitation to recent time. While they were active, other eruptions continued throughout the length of the Mexican Volcanic Belt [MVB] from San Andrés Tuxtla, bordering the Gulf of México, to the vicinity of Tepic, close to the Pacific coast. It was then that most of the volcanoes of the Pátzcuaro region and the basaltic cones around the valley of México and Apatzingán were formed, and it was then that the highest volcanoes of México—Popocatépetl, Citlaltépetl, Nevado de Colima, and Nevado de Toluca —which began to grow during Pleistocene or late Pliocene time, passed through maturity to their present stage of decline.

Structural Trends

Within the main east-west zone in México, the individual volcanoes show little alignment. Locally they are disposed at right angles to the belt itself. Thus Cofre de Perote lies north of Citlaltépetl, and Ixtaccíhuatl lies north of Popocatépetl. Several volcanoes in Java, though grouped in a broad east-west belt, are likewise alined perpendicular to the dominant trend.

Within the Parícutin region, most of the cones appear to be scattered haphazardly. Locally, however, a NE alignment may be detected. Thus the old andesite cones of Cerros de San Marcos and Cerro del Aguila, together with the younger cones of Cerros de Paracho and Cerros de Los Hornos, exhibit this alignment. More striking is the parallel series of youthful cinder cones including Pelón, Cumbuén, and Paracho Viejo. Indeed, if the line joining these three cones is prolonged, it passes through Parícutin volcano, through its parasite, Sapichu, and through the fissure-and-tremor zone on the opposite side of the new volcano. Other examples of the same alignment include Cutzato and its parasite, Pantzingo. The principal vent of Cerro Cojti lies NE of the minor cone on its crater rim; the vents of Cerro de Curitzerán, Cerro del Anillo, and Cerro de Sicuín are on a parallel line; the central vent of Cerro de Pario lies NE of the main vent of Cerro Prieto, just as the triple cone of Cerro del Aire lies NE of the summit vent of Cerro de La Alberca. Moreover, it may not be

fortuitous that the Jabalí and Capácuaro volcanoes, which are among the youngest in the region, are also on a NE-SW line.

. . . . .

Not a single fault scarp is to be seen in the Parícutin region. If any are present, they must be buried by accumulations of younger lava.

. . . . .

Description of Individual Volcanoes

Mesa de Zirimóndiro and Mesa de Huanárucua

At two localities, thick sheets of andesitic lava were extruded without attendant explosions of fragmental ejecta. One of these andesitic flows lies immediately north of the village of Tancítaro, forming the Mesa de Zirimóndiro, approximately 3 km long and up to 1½ km in width [22 km SW of Parícutin]. Its hummocky, cultivated top is thickly covered with yellowish basaltic ash blown from nearby cinder cones; its steep sides rise 60-75 m above the surrounding alluvial flats. Except in gullies cutting the flanks, natural outcrops of lava are scarce; fortunately a large quarry on the outskirts of Tancítaro village provides excellent exposures . . . . The entire mesa appears to be the result of a single flow of unusual viscosity; indeed, the final effusion, being unable to spread laterally, piled over the vent to form a domical mound near the northern end of the mesa.

The other mesa is that of Huanárucua [Fig. 141], extending from near the village of Angahuan to the foot of the Curitzerán volcano [7½ km NNW of Parícutin volcano]. The road linking Angahuan with San Juan Parangaricutiro and Corupo skirts its edges. Towards the south the mesa falls off abruptly in cliffs and talus slopes 75-125 m in height; toward the north it merges indefinitely into basaltic flats of Llano de Paquichu.

Huanárucua covers an area measuring 2⅔ by 2 km. The source of the flow lies close to the SE edge, where a low, elongate mound marks the accumulation of the last-erupted material . . . . The gently undulating top of the mesa is blanketed with deeply weathered basaltic ash more than 3 m thick, some of which was blown from the adjacent cone of Terutsjuata. Judging by the nature and thickness of this ash, the Huanárucua andesite is older than the flows erupted by cones of Cutzato and Tzintzungo.

. . . . .

Cerros de Curitzerán, Cerro del Anillo, and Cerro de Sicuín

The villages of San Juan Parangaricutiro and Zacán are separated by a group of wooded hills crowned by two coalescing cones known as Cerro de Curitzerán, the topmost point of which stands at an elevation of 2,533 m [8½ km north of the new volcano]. These summit cones are only slightly modified by erosion and have well-preserved craters that lie on a line trending WSW. Nearby are two smaller cones: Cerro del Anillo, at an elevation of 2,350 m, and Cerro de Sicuín, at 2,272 m. Cerro del Anillo is breached on its SW side. Taken together, the four cones are aligned approximately parallel to the main fissure zone at Parícutin.

The visible parts of the two Curitzerán cones are about 150 m high, but probably these are simply the exposed tops of much larger structures that are mainly buried by encircling lavas, for the flows from these vents form a broad pedestal up to 120 m in thickness.

Cerros de Capácuaro

This important shield volcano has been the focus of more recent detailed studies by Hasenaka and Carmichael[152]. They referred to Capácuaro as Cerro el Metate, and reported a ^{14}*C age of 4,700 ± 200 years (Table 18, p. 258), consistent with the interpretations of Williams.*

By far the most voluminous outpourings of lava within recent times are those from the vent that lies 6-8 km east of the village of Capácuaro [Figs. 142 and 143]. A large conical mound rises over the vent, but whether this is a protrusion of viscous lava or consists of fragmental ejecta is not known.

The area inundated by flows from this source approximates 150 km², and the average thickness of the lavas is not less than 60 m. Accordingly, more than 9 km³ of lava were discharged. By comparison, Parícutin erupted less than 1 km³ of lava during the first 5 years of its history. Of special note is the fact that the lavas from Capácuaro do not consist of basalt

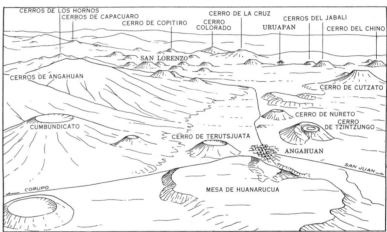

Fig. 141. Volcanoes near Angahuan, looking SE. In the foreground, on the right, the andesitic flow of Mesa de Huanárucua. Older andesitic cones of olivine basalt and basaltic andesite. In the distance the Zumpinito formation forms Cerro Colorado and Cerro de La Cruz.

or basaltic andesite like most of the recent lavas of the region but of glass-rich hypersthene andesite having a composition not markedly different from that of the andesite of Tancítaro.

Among the numerous flows of the Capácuaro volcano the largest deserves particular mention. This spread southward from the vent for about 19 km. In places its width is almost 3 km, and for most of its course it measures a 1½ km across. Not only is it exceptionally long, but the steep margins rise to heights of 75 m. Fig. 143 gives an impression of the moraine-like levees that confine the medial portions of the flow. Other massive flows spread westward to the village of Capácuaro and northward to the vicinity of Arantepacua; these also terminate in impressive blocky fronts up to 60 m in height.

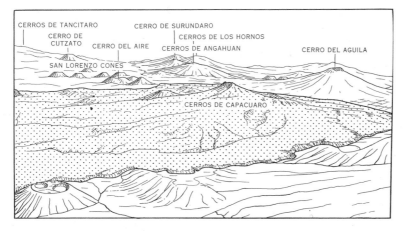

Fig. 142. Cerros de Capácuaro from the east. Area covered by the recent andesite flows of Cerros de Capácuaro is shown by stippling. Beyond lie the older andesitic volcanoes of Cerro del Aguila and Cerros de Angahuan and Cerros de Los Hornos; also the young andesite cone of Cerro de Surúndaro. View looking west.

As might be expected from their high glass content, all the flows are true block lavas. Their upper parts consist of a jumble of smooth-faced blocks, many more than 2 m across, loosely bound together by a rubble of comminuted lava chips. Downward the blocky crust grades into brecciated lava that merges in turn into massive andesite below.

Although heavily forested, the lavas are free from all but a thin, patchy cover of ash. Hence they are younger than all the cinder cones in the immediate vicinity. Their surface features are so well preserved that it seems safe to say that the flows were erupted either within the present or the preceeding millennium.

Cerro de Capatacutiro

The youthful cone of Cerro de Capatacutiro lies close to the western base of Cerro del Aguila [26 km NE of Parícutin volcano]. From the breach in the western side, several flows of basalt descended toward the México City highway. The earliest ones spread as far as Paracho Viejo [6 km north]; the later ones encircled the cone of Sicapen and flooded the valley north of the Cerros de Los Hornos.

The lavas of Capatacutiro are the least siliceous of any in the Parícutin region. They are coarse-grained

Fig. 143. Great flow of andesite from Cerros de Capácuaro, as seen from the SE. The flow is about 19 km long and locally almost 3 km wide. Note the marginal levees. In the foreground the flow is crossed by the railroad to México City. To the left (west) lies Cerro Colorado, composed of iddingsite-rich basalts, and, behind it, Cerro de La Cruz, composed mainly of andesitic lavas. Both peaks are erosional forms cut in the Zumpinito formation. The intervening valley is occupied by recent flows of olivine basalt.

olivine-augite basalts, and except for thin skins of glass they are entirely holocrystalline. In many places they exhibit crude pahoehoe forms, and their surfaces are marked by pressure ridges and collapse depressions caused by foundering of the roofs of tunnels. Here and there miniature lava tubes are still to be seen. No other lava flows within the area show these features; all other basalts and basaltic andesites are of the blocky or aa type.

The excellent state of preservation of the features just mentioned is enough to indicate that these flows are among the youngest of the Parícutin region. However, they are older than the more explosive eruptions that formed the nearby cones of Cumbuén, Pelón, and Paracho Viejo, and they are partly overridden by the lavas of the Surúndaro volcano.

. . . . .

Cerro del Jabalí Cone Cluster

In Table 18 (p. 258), Hasenaka and Carmichael (1985a) give a ^{14}C age of 3,830 ± 150 years for charcoal beneath scoriae from the northernmost vent of the Cerro del Jabalí cluster. Below, Williams describes a black, unvegetated lava flow that moved south toward Cerro del Chino [dense stippling on Fig. 144]. This flow is also obvious on Fig. 154, which shows a stereopair of air photographs for the Jabalí vents and includes the position of the charcoal sample. This youthful lava flow is probably younger than the carbon age. Williams, in fact, believed that this Jabalí lava could have erupted in historical times and was surprised to find no local legends of eruptions. Even if his supposition is not true, the unvegetated Jabalí lava is clearly one of the youngest in the volcanic field, perhaps the third youngest after the lavas of Jorullo and Parícutin.

A particularly youthful cluster of cones is to be seen a few kilometers NW of Uruapan [Fig. 144]. Surrounding it is a rugged *malpais* of lava, some of which is of such recent origin that it supports only a scant cover of vegetation. Indeed, the last flow, a tongue of black, barren lava skirted by the road between Cerro del Chino and Los Conejos (San Juan Nuevo), may well have been erupted within the last century. Marian Storm[153] records a conversation with the Tarascan Indian who cultivated the corn patch in the crater of Cerro del Chino in the following words:

When the old people of my family were little this Hill of El Chino burst open and tons of mud poured out. Then freezing cold came over all this country; the animals in corral died of it. Snow fell, but ashes covered the land as

well, shutting out the sun, and plants wilted and trees lost all their leaves. We often tell again the story of those times . . . . Look where dark, hot rivers moved down El Chino on this side and stood still in what must have been a pretty valley, to make that malpais!

If this account is interpreted in the light of geological evidence, it seems clear that the informant was mistaken in referring to an outburst of Cerro del Chino, for the lavas from that cone are covered to a great depth with weathered ash. It is far more likely that the Indian referred to the final explosions of one of the Cerros del Jabalí cones and to the black tongue of lava mentioned above, which abuts against the base of Cerro del Chino. No one seeing the Jabalí cones can doubt that they are younger than Cerro del Chino, for their slopes are still only slightly scored by erosion and the cinders that form them are scarcely decomposed. Considering the climate of the region and recalling how quickly vegetation reoccupied the country devastated by Jorullo in 1759, one cannot escape the view that several of the Jabalí cones may have erupted within the last few centuries. The surprising thing is that the people of the town of Uruapan preserve no legends concerning them.

The area covered by flows of the Jabalí cones approximates that inundated during the last 5 years by Parícutin. They poured over the SE slopes of Cerro de La Alberca from five closely spaced cones. The largest of these, Jabalí itself, rises to a height of about 110 m. Cerro de Sapien, a short distance to the east, and the southernmost cone are slightly smaller; the other two are merely low mounds of scoriae.

. . . . .

Cones and Flows Near Parícutin Volcano

Nowhere along the periphery of Cerros de Tancítaro is the cluster of cinder cones denser than in the vicinity of the new volcano [see inside-cover maps]. Although these cones vary widely in age, so that the periods of their activity overlap those of most of the "younger" volcanoes discussed in the preceding pages, they are here considered together in order to bring out more clearly the setting of Parícutin itself.

In attempting to date the cones near Parícutin on the basis of the degree of dissection, it must be borne in mind that erosion was greatly accelerated by the ash falls attending their growth. Account must also be taken of the torrential character of the rains in this region. During the wet seasons the volume of the streams increases a thousandfold. Moreover, as Segerstrom has emphasized (see p. 284), 90% of the summer rains fall in periods of no more than 30 to 60

251

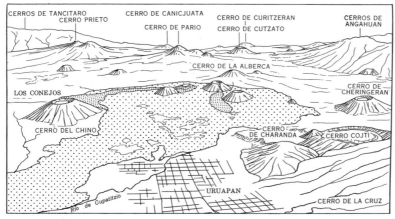

Fig. 144. Cerros del Jabalí cone cluster and its lavas, looking west over Uruapan. Older flows of the Jabalí cones are shown by light stippling; younger flows, by dense stippling. The flow that descends to Los Conejos may be less than a century old. The "Ringwall" and central lava mound of Cerro Cojti may be seen on the right [this wide crater is referred to as Costo maar by Hasenaka and Carmichael (1985a) and so labelled on Fig. 154, which is a stereo airphoto pair showing the Jabalí area]. The eroded andesitic volcanoes of Cerros de Tancítaro and Cerros de Angahuan appear in the distance; between them lie younger cones and flows of basaltic andesite.

minutes' duration. At times 5 cm of rain may fall in as many hours. As a result, loose ash is readily swept into the canyons to form torrents of great erosive power. In addition, the protective cover of vegetation is destroyed by the eruptions, and the water-soaked ash, even on gentle slopes, is subject to large-scale creep and recurrent slides. It is enough to witness the havoc caused by a single summer storm to be convinced that the deepest gullies on the oldest cones may have been excavated in a few thousand years. Many of the younger cones must have been active within the present millenium, and perhaps Loma Larga and the three Jarátiro craters ceased activity no more than a few centuries ago. Why the Tarascan

Indians have no legends concerning these eruptions is difficult to understand.

On the map [inside the front cover], the cones near Parícutin are divided into two groups, an older one comprised of cones that are deeply dissected and devoid of summit craters and a younger one in which the cones and craters are well preserved.

Older Group

Among the oldest and largest of the cones near Parícutin are the three Cerros de Zirosto [9 km WNW of the new volcano], the biggest of which is Cerro La Máscara. Long, thick flows of gray, olivine-rich basalt issued from the feet of these cones to pour down the valleys of the Río de Itzícuaro, Río de Xundan, and Río del Agua Blanca at least as far as Peribán and San Francisco. In the canyon walls of Río del Agua Blanca they rest on bouldery laharic deposits and are overlain by more than 30 m of weathered basaltic ash. Elsewhere they are likewise heavily blanketed with ash, within which several soil horizons may be recognized. Similar olivine basalts flowed down the Itzícuaro valley past Barranca Seca from the coeval cone of Tiripan.

A short distance south of Parícutin rise Cerro de Camiro and Cerro de Tzirapan, two eroded cones of approximately the same age. The crater of Cerro de Camiro has been obliterated, and the flanks are deeply cut by ravines. Lavas from the base of the cone form a pedestal no less than 240 m in thickness. Despite their large volume, however, the Camiro flows spread only a few hundred meters to the west, coming to a halt at the edge of Llano de Teruto. Northward they stretch for about 1½ km to Cerro de Nuréndiro at the margins of the Parícutin lava field. Clearly they must have been extremely viscous. No chemical analyses have been made, but the microscope shows them to be olivine-poor, hypersthene-rich lavas, and if they are not true andesites they are surely not less siliceous than basaltic andesites. Other thick, olivine-poor flows, possibly andesites, form Mesa de Cocjarao; these escaped from concealed fissures near Cátacu.

Cerro de Tzirapan consists of a principal cone and a parasite. The former rises about 180 m above the encircling flows, most of which moved to the south and east through a breach in the flank. Probably the activity of this cone began shortly after Camiro had expired.

East of Tzirapan, in the region extending from the foot of Cerro Prieto northward to Cerro de Curupichu, all the lavas are basaltic andesites. They form a series of north-trending ridges with gently sloping, hummocky tops that descend in steps at the snouts of successive flows. Presumably they issued from Jurítzicuaro and adjacent cones after the last flows of the Pario volcano but before those of Cutzato.

Not far to the north of Parícutin is a ridge of lavas capped by Cerro de Jarátiro, Cerro de Equijuata, and Cerro de Capatzun. Most of this ridge has been submerged by the lava of the new volcano. The northern end, from Cerro de Equijuata to Cerro de Capatzun, runs north for about 1½ km and is bounded by steep sides that rise between 90 and 120 m above the adjacent flats . . . . The lack of craters and scoria cones on the crest suggests that Cerro de Capatzun and Cerro de Equijuata, together with the two small peaks west of the latter, represent domical accumulations of the last-extruded viscous lava over the feeding vents.

The saddle between Cerro de Equijuata and Cerro de Jarátiro is now buried by flows from the Parícutin volcano, but as late as 1945, NE-trending ridges of oxidized and autobrecciated olivine basalt were to be seen there, separated by steep-walled, narrow depressions resembling lava gutters.

During the present survey, the Jarátiro ridge was so thickly covered by ash from Parícutin volcano that no exposures of lava were visible. At its eastern base was a perfectly preserved, almost circular crater, approximately 180 m across at the rim and about 45 m deep [see topographic map of Fig. 108 on p. 144]. In December 1944 lava from Parícutin poured over the rim and cascaded to the floor. Since then the crater has been almost completely filled. Two smaller craters, one 120 m to the south and the other 240 m to the SE, were buried by lava from Parícutin at an earlier date . . . . All three craters are much younger than the lavas of the Jarátiro ridge through which the largest was blasted; indeed, they were probably produced by the last explosions preceding the outbreak of the new volcano.

. . . . .

A short distance to the west of Parícutin are five large, eroded scoria cones: Cerro de Canicjuata, Cerro de Corucjuata, Cerro de Cuaxándaran, Cerro de Turajuata, and an unnamed cone nearby . . . . Even the smallest of these cones rises to a height of 120 m, whereas the largest, Canicjuata, is between 240 and 270 m in height. All are craterless and deeply incised by radial *barrancas*. They appear to have been formed in quick succession, Canicjuata and Corucjuata perhaps being the last to erupt. The flows from all five cones moved principally to the north and NW, and, as far as sporadic outcrops permit judgment, they all consist of olivine basalts or basaltic andesites closely resembling those now issuing from Parícutin.

Younger Group

In marked contrast to the denuded cones just enumerated are five smaller ones with craters still intact. These are Cerro del Pueblo Viejo, Loma Larga, Cerro de Huachángueran, Cerro de Cátacu, and an unnamed cone nearby [see map inside front cover]. Cerro del Pueblo Viejo is the oldest of this group, but even its activity took place long after the cones of the earlier group had become extinct. Its crater has been breached on the north side by the sapping action of a large spring; Cerro de Huachángueran and Loma Larga have been breached to a smaller extent by the headward erosion of streams. Indeed, Segerstrom observed (see p. 284) that the flanks of Loma Larga had not been appreciably gullied prior to the eruptions of Parícutin. Presumably, therefore, it was formed after all the others. Cerro de Cátacu and the neighboring cone are also very well preserved, and their shallow, saucer-like craters are hardly modified by denudation. The flows in the vicinity were not discharged from any of these cones but from a fissure at the base of Cerros de Tancítaro, a short distance west of Cerro de Cátacu. These issued in two gushes; the first sent a stream northward for about 1½ km, whereas the second, overriding the first, came to a halt a little closer to the source. Both ended with steep, blocky fronts up to 90 m in height. Their tops are covered by about a meter of weathered ash, perhaps blown from Loma Larga and Cátacu, and by some 2 m of ejecta from Parícutin. They are composed of dark, vesicular, olivine-rich basalt or basaltic andesite.

Cerro de Lópizio, approximately 3 km south of Parícutin volcano, is another youthful cone with a crater about 200 m across, girdled by a low rim. From a breach in the eastern wall a flow of olivine basalt descended to Llano de Teruto.

Had the region close to Parícutin been studied before the cover of new ash became thick, a much clearer picture might have been drawn of the sequence of events preceding the present activity. This much, however, seems clear: The first eruptions in the vicinity took place from Cerros de Zirosto and Cerro de Tiripan, and the lavas discharged were olivine-rich holocrystalline basalts. Activity then shifted to Cerro de Camiro, from which viscous flows of olivine-poor, hypersthene-rich andesites or basaltic andesites were erupted. About the same time other viscous flows of olivine-poor lava escaped from fissures to the west from Mesa de Cocjarao. A little later the double cone of Cerro de Tzirapan was formed, and perhaps the lavas of the Jarátiro-Equijuata-Capatzun ridge belong to the same period. Then the five large cones—Canicjuata, Corucjuata, Turajuata, Cuaxándaran, and an unnamed cone —developed west of Parícutin, discharging flows of basaltic andesite. A long interval of quiet ensued. Subsequently the cones of Pueblo Viejo and Huachángueran were built. Cátacu and the unnamed cone nearby erupted next, and perhaps Lópizio was active at approximately the same time. The youngest cone to develop was Loma Larga, but the final eruptions prior to the growth of Parícutin were probably those that produced the three craters close to Cerro de Jarátiro, about a 1½ km north of the new volcano. The lavas of all these younger cones are essentially similar to those now issuing from Parícutin itself.

Most of the fragmental ejecta [from Parícutin volcano] were expelled during the first 12 months. Comparison of the isopach map of the ash blanket made in May 1945 [Fig. 103 on p. 135] with that prepared in October 1946 by Segerstrom [see inside-front-cover map] shows that the amount of ash added during the intervening 18 months was extremely small. By the latter date, the volume of ash was 0.65 km³. Since then the increase has been slight. Thus far, therefore, Parícutin has repeated the history of most of the adjacent cones, its main explosive period occuring in the early stages.

At the close of the first year the main cone was already about 330 m high. During the next 4 years its height increased by only a small amount. Meanwhile, the lower part of the cone was rapidly buried by lava. Between May 1945 and June 1947, while the rim of the crater rose only 42 m, the visible height of the cone was reduced between 79 and 92 m by accumulation of flows around the base. If, as seems likely from the record of adjacent volcanoes, effusive activity continues increasingly to dominate over explosive discharge, the visible portion of the cone will be much further reduced. The present activity, therefore, suggests that the small cones that cap many of the neighboring volcanoes are not the result of weak concluding eruptions but are simply the exposed tops of large cones whose growth began at an early stage.

Michoacán-Guanajuato Volcanic Field

After the first-generation geological studies of the Parícutin area by Williams, Segerstrom, Wilcox, and Foshag and González-Reyna, all published in U.S. Geological Survey Bulletin 965, nearly 30 years were to pass before other major geological investigations were conducted, a long interval that is a tribute to the quality of the early work. The next wave of studies, which began in the mid 1980s, benefitted from many important developments in the intervening years, including the theory of plate tectonics, the U.S. space program and widely available satellite imagery, topographic maps for much of México at the scale of 1:50,000, and new types of automated analytical instruments that allowed the chemical compositions of rock samples to be determined far more rapidly and on far larger sample suites than was possible by classical methods. New maps and satellite images revealed the full spatial extent of the volcanic field into which Parícutin was born; it was found to cover some 40,000 km² in the southern part of Guanajuato state and the northern part of Michoacán state.

Toshiaki Hasenaka arrived from Japan to begin graduate studies at the University of California in 1978, 2 years before the death of Howel Williams, then an emeritus professor. For his Ph.D. dissertation Hasenaka studied the nearly 1,000 cones in the field that includes Parícutin, for which he coined the term "Michoacán-Guanajuato Volcanic Field". His dissertation considered the distribution of these cones, their ages as deduced from morphologies of the cinder cones and associated lava flows and constrained by ¹⁴C dates, and the mineralogies and chemical compositions of more than 250 rock samples from 200 volcanoes. Hasenaka published two major articles based on his dissertation, portions of which we reprint in order to better place Parícutin in the perspective of the MGVF. Along with Masao Ban and other colleagues he carried out an additional study in the MGVF, focused on the ages and distributions of shield volcanoes and parts of that work are also reprinted.

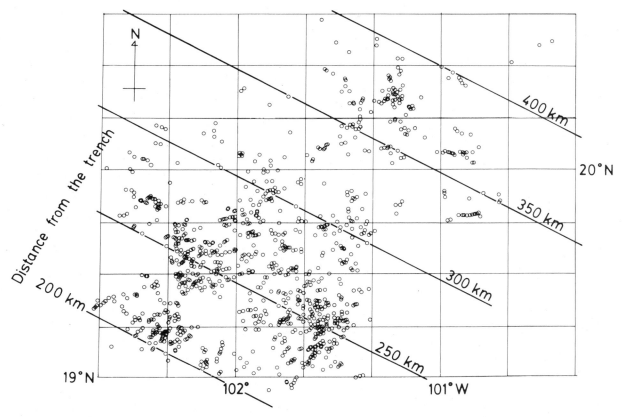

Fig. 145. Distribution of volcanoes in the Michoacán-Guanajuato Volcanic Field. Circles indicate all volcanic centers: cinder cones, lava domes, maars, tuff rings, shield volcanoes with a summit cone, or lava flows that are not associated with cones. The positions of estimated vents are used in locating the lava flows.

Age and Distribution of Cinder Cones

Hasenaka and Carmichael (1985a)

Introduction

Within the Mexican Volcanic Belt [MVB] in central México is a large concentration of cinder cones, lava cones, and central volcanoes. About 1,000 eruptive vents, mostly cinder cones, are found in the northern half of Michoacán state and the southern part of Guanajuato state. The youngest of these, Volcán Parícutin, erupted in 1943-1952; the second youngest, Volcán El Jorullo, in 1759-1774. This region, the Michoacán-Guanajuato Volcanic Field (MGVF) has an area of 40,000 km² and forms a unique part of the MVB, since it lacks the young large composite volcanoes dominant in other parts of the MVB.

The purposes of this study of the MGVF are: (1) to describe the spacing, size, and morphology of the cinder cones and their associated lavas; (2) to develop morphological age indices for cinder cones; (3) to calibrate these using radiometric ages; and (4) to estimate the eruption rate of magma in the region.

. . . . .

Distribution of Vents

A total of 1,040 volcanic vents in the MGVF were identified from topographic maps and air photographs (published by DETENAL, México City, scale 1:50,000) in conjunction with field observations. This total includes 901 cones, 43 domes, 13 young shield volcanoes with surmounting cones, 22 maars or tuff rings, and 61 lava flows with hidden vents . . . . [A table of the locations of these volcanoes with their dimensions and morphological parameters was published elsewhere[154]]. Old, highly dissected shield volcanoes and eroded hills, the nature of which is not

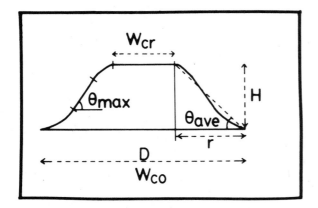

Fig. 146. Schematic diagram illustrating the parameters used to estimate cinder cone size.

easy to discern from topography, are excluded from this compilation.

Few volcanoes occur closer than 200 km to the Middle America Trench (Fig. 145). The concentration of volcanoes is greatest about 250 km from the trench, and approximately 75% of the volcanoes are found between 200 km and 300 km. Farther than 300 km, the number of volcanoes decreases; the most distant cinder cone is 440 km from the trench. A local concentration of volcanoes at 380 km corresponds to the maar cluster of Valle de Santiago.

In general, the cinder cones are randomly spaced and indicate no preferred orientation. A small number of closely associated cinder cones, however, show local alignments; these trend E-W in the northern part of the volcanic field, ENE in the middle part, and NE in the southern part near the volcanic front. In any given area, cinder cones are restricted to relatively low elevations as most cones formed either on alluvial plains or low on the flanks of eroded shield volcanoes.

The overall density of volcanoes in the MGVF is 2.5 volcanoes/100 km^2 (1,040 vents/40,000 km^2). The highest density of 11/100 km^2 is calculated for the Parícutin region (141 vents/1,250 km^2).

. . . . .

Cinder Cone Size

Morphometric parameters of cinder cones and their associated lava flows were obtained from 1:50,000 topographic maps. These parameters include cone height (H), cone basal diameter or width (W_{co}), and crater diameter or width (W_{cr}) (Fig. 146). Most of the cinder cones show a truncated cone shape, but cones that erupted on an inclined basement surface are often breached or elongated. To allow for this, W_{co} and W_{cr} are defined as the arithmetic means of the maximum

and minimum values of cone and crater widths. H is the elevation difference between the summit of the cinder cone and its base. The basal elevation is the mean of the highest and the lowest basal values. The circumferences of the crater rims and cone bases were determined where the generally equidistant topographic contours abruptly widen. Where the crater is not visible on the topographic maps, the diameter of a somewhat flatter summit was taken as the crater diameter value. From these values, the volume of a symmetrical truncated cone was calculated.

For the cones with discernable crater rims . . . median values are 90 m for the height, 800 m for the basal diameter, 230 m for the crater diameter, and 0.021 km^3 for the volume. Mean values are 100 m, 830 m, 240 m, and 0.038 km^3, respectively.

Lava Flow Volume

Volumes of lava flows whose margins were clearly observable on the air photographs (scale 1:50,000) were estimated by tracing flow margins onto topographic maps and then calculating their thickness from the contour intervals (either 20 m or 10 m). The ratio of cone to lava volume is a function of explosivity, possibly reflecting the volatile content or viscosity of magma. On the average in the MGVF, the volume of a cinder cone is roughly one-tenth that of its associated lava flow, which is the same ratio observed at Parícutin, where more precise measurements exist (see p. 312-316 and Table 23).

Geomorphological Parameters of Cinder Cone Age

One of the earliest studies of cinder cones was Colton's[155] work in the San Francisco volcanic field of Arizona, in which he classified the stages of erosion of cones and their associated lava flows. Other semi-quantitative indicators of cinder cone age include: the maximum cone slope angle[156], the ratio of cone height to cone basal diameter[156,157], the tangent of the cone slope[131], and the change of surface features of lava flows associated with cinder cones[131].

Cinder cones in the MGVF also show various stages of degradation, from which the relative ages of the cinder cones can be estimated. The youngest cones, like Parícutin, have a perfect cone shape with slope angles of 34°, the angle of repose of cinder. Their craters, whose rims are sharp and little modified by erosion, have little infilling of ash or scoriae. A large number of rills and shallow gullies have developed on the slopes of the youngest cones. The largest number of radial lineaments on the slope of Parícutin observed in air photographs, however, are not gullies but alternating bands of scoriae and lapilli [see Fig 181, p. 303]. Vegetation is sparse on Parícutin where soil is absent, but most of the surface of Volcán El Jorullo is already covered with trees only 200 years after its eruption. Under the tropical to temperate climate of the MGVF, vegetative recovery after eruption is rapid compared with the age span of cinder cones. The total annual precipitation in the MGVF is between 500 mm and 1,800 mm/year, and the mean [daily] temperature ranges between 16°C

Table 17. Geomorphological classification of lava flows.

	Flow margins	Indiv. flow units	Pressure ridges	Soil	Tree shrub cover	Cultivation	Cinder cone	Age
Hv	o	o	o	X	X	X	Paricutin El Jorullo	1943—1952 AD 1759—1774 AD
	o	o	o	X	o	X	El Jabali El Metate La Taza	3,830 y.B.P. 4,700 y.B.P. 8,430 y.B.P.
Plv₄	o	o	o	△	o	X	La Mina	17,170 y.B.P.
Plv₃	o	△	△	△	△	△	El Pueblito Las Cabras	29,000 y.B.P. >40,000 y.B.P.
Plv₂	o	X	X	o	X	o	Pelon	0.37 Ma
Plv₁	△	X	X	o	X	o		

o = feature is distinctly observed or abundant.
△ = feature is somewhat recognizable or moderately abundant.
X = feature is obscure or scarce.

weathered and oxidized ejecta than the younger cones. Craters of the older cones are filled by ash from other volcanoes and by debris eroded from the higher slopes of the craters themselves. Some of the oldest cones may be almost completely buried and have very shallow slope angles. The oldest group includes cones with flattened and rounded shapes and deeply dissected cones with breached craters.

Lava flow morphology also changes with age. Holocene lava flows display well preserved original surface features, such as flow margins, boundaries of individual flow units, pressure ridges, and levees. Lava flows lose these characteristics with time and become covered with soils that may be cultivated. In a densely populated area where almost all the useful land is cultivated, lava surfaces covered with trees and shrubs indicate the absence of arable soils and hence relative youth. The lava flows of Parícutin and El Jorullo are exceptional; they only have sparse vegetation.

The morphologic indicators of age include: (1) the ratio of cinder cone height to basal diameter (H/D); (2) maximum slope angle (θ_{max}), taken as the average of several field measurements from different directions; (3) average slope angle (θ_{ave}), which is calculated as $\tan^{-1}$ (H/r), where r is given in Fig. 146; (4) the difference between the maximum and average slope angles; (5) gully density, defined as the number of gullies determined from air photographs normalized to 90° of arc; and (6) the geomorphological classification of lava flows, as summarized in Table 17. Important measured variables are displayed in Fig. 147. These indices are relatively easily obtained from topographic maps, air photographs, or field observations.

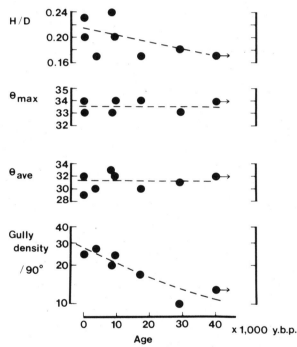

Fig. 147. Geomorphological parameters of cinder cone age plotted against ¹⁴C age. The data are from Parícutin, El Jorullo, El Jabalí, El Huanillo, La Mina, El Pueblito, Las Cabras, and El Pelón (Table 18). The data for Cerro El Metate are excluded because the cone shape is greatly modified by lava flows on the slope. Dashed lines are fitted by eye.

and 29°C[158]. The area on the plateau has a relatively cool and wet climate; in contrast, the lowland south has a relatively hot and dry climate, resulting in different erosional conditions.

Older degraded cinder cones have lower slope angles, a smaller number of gullies (which are larger and deeper), greater soil development, and more

Table 18. Dimensions and age of cinder cones.

	Cinder cone	Latitude (N)	Longitude (W)	W_{co}	W_{cr}	H	Volume	Age	Sample method
a	Volcán Parícutin	19° 29′ 33″	102° 15′ 04″	0.95	0.25	0.220	0.069	1943—1952 AD	Historical record
b	Volcán El Jorullo	18° 58′ 19″	101° 43′ 03″	1.45	0.42	0.290	0.219	1759—1774 AD	Historical record
c	Cerro El Jabali	19° 26′ 56″	102° 06′ 46″	0.93	0.38	0.160	0.057	3,830 ± 150 y.B.P.	737C charcoal [14]C
d	Cerro El Metate	19° 32′ 20″	101° 59′ 33″	0.88	0.20	0.150	0.039	4,700 ± 200 y.B.P.	761C charcoal [14]C
e	Cerro La Taza	19° 31′ 33″	101° 43′ 28″	0.70	0.18	0.170	0.029	8,430 ± 330 y.B.P.	759C charcoal [14]C
f	Hoya El Huanillo	19° 41′ 01″	101° 59′ 04″	0.95	0.35	0.190	0.068	9,180 ± 250 y.B.P.	411C3 charcoal [14]C
								9,410 ± 230 y.B.P.	411C2 charcoal [14]C
g	Volcán La Mina	19° 42′ 45″	101° 26′ 02″	1.15	0.35	0.190	0.092	17,170 ± 430 y.B.P.	622C charcoal [14]C
h	El Pueblito	19° 49′ 29″	101° 55′ 24″	1.00	0.38	0.185	0.075	29,000 ± 3,300 y.B.P.	435C charcoal [14]C
i	Cerro Las Cabras	19° 49′ 34″	101° 53′ 37″	1.18	0.55	0.195	0.120	>40,000 y. B.P.	674C charcoal [14]C
j	Cerro Pelon	19° 17′ 52″	101° 54′ 47″	0.68	0.18	0.085	0.014	0.37 ± 05 Ma	426L lava K-Ar
k	Santa Teresa	20° 29′ 50″	100° 59′ 53″	0.63	0.15	0.030	0.004	2.78 ± 07 Ma	555A scoria K-Ar

Symbols (a—k) are the same as in Fig. 1.

W_{co} = basal diameter, W_{cr} = crater diameter, H = cone height (in km).

Volume of cinder cone (in km³) is calculated as a symmetrical truncated cone, i.e.:

$$\text{Volume} = \frac{\pi H}{12} \cdot (W_{cr}^2 + W_{cr} W_{co} + W_{co}^2)$$

Cone size is measured using 1:50,000 topographic maps (DETENAL, Mexico City).

[14]C ages are obtained from the charcoal in the soil under the ash and lappili layers (analyst: Teledyne Isotopes).

Charcoal samples were collected at two different sites for Hoya El Huanillo.

K-Ar ages are obtained from the whole rock samples of lava or scoria (analyst: G. Mahood).

Radiometric Dates and Cinder Cone Ages

Radiocarbon Dates

Carbon 14 dates were obtained for 8 charcoal samples from cinder cones in the earlier stages of degradation (Table 18). The charcoal was collected from soil just beneath the ash and lapilli at distances of 500 m to 2,000 m from a cinder cone. At this distance, the continuity of the tephra from the cone is obvious. Charcoal was found at the contact of the soil and ash and up to 20 cm below it. This indicates a close temporal relationship between charcoal formation and tephra fall; thus the ^{14}C dates are used to represent the age of eruption. Most of the cones dated are relatively large and from the plateau (with a relatively cold and wet climate).

Cinder cone geomorphological parameters are plotted against the ^{14}C ages in Fig. 147. Clearly, no significant change with age occurs in the H/D ratio or the cone slope angles; both maximum and minimum values are found to remain constant within the ^{14}C span of 40,000 years. The maximum slope angle, 33° to 34°, is the initial cone slope angle and remains constant for about 40,000 years; the average slope angle shows a greater but inconsistent variation. Accordingly, the difference between maximum and average slope angles will not be meaningful. These three parameters indicate that the initial form of these cinder cones has been slow to change over a period of at least 40,000 years. During this period, major erosional processes of landsliding and gullying (see

p. 287-288)[157] have yet to modify the shape of cinder cones, which are largely comprised of permeable scoriae and lapilli.

Conversely, gully density shows a consistent change from 30/90° to 10/90° over 40,000 years, although there is some scatter of the data due to influence of vegetation, visibility of gullies, prevailing wind and weather, and cinder cone size. Smaller cones are expected to develop fewer gullies due to their smaller area and the shorter runoff distance of rainwater. Also, gullying may play a minor role in the degradation of cones under dry climate. In general, cinder cones in the lowland (relatively hot and dry climate) are rounded, show little gullying, and are similar to those of the San Francisco volcanic field in Arizona (mean annual precipitation: 490 mm [158])[155,157].

Geomorphological classification of lava flows is another useful age index for their associated cinder cones, and the surface features of lavas are correlated with radiometric dates in Table 17. The lava flows and associated cinder cones are classified into three groups: Holocene volcanoes (Hv), which are younger than 10,000 years, and the youngest two groups of Pleistocene volcanoes (Plv_4, Plv_3). Cerro Las Cabras and other similar lava flows are arbitrarily subgrouped into Plv_{2-3}, since they have surface features between Plv_2 and Plv_3.

K-Ar dates

K-Ar dates were obtained for lavas and scoriae of more-degraded cinder cones (Table 18). Cerro Pelón (0.37 ± 0.05 Ma) shows a significant difference in all

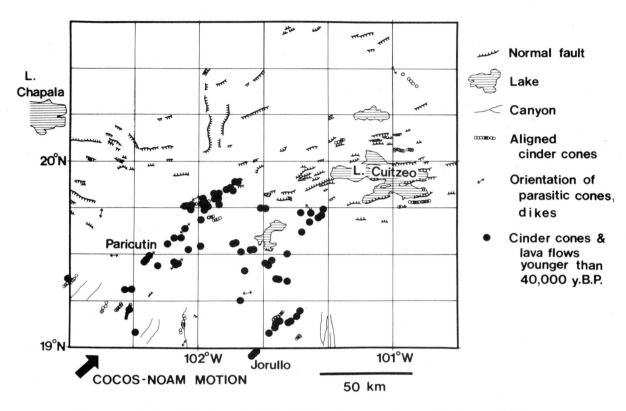

Fig. 148. Alignments of cinder cones, their vents and dikes, and normal faults in the MGVF. Large dots indicate cinder cones and lava flows younger than 40,000 years. Arrow shows the relative motion vector of the Cocos and North American Plates. Map area same as in Fig. 145 except at the eastern margin.

parameters compared to cones younger than 40,000 years; H/D ratio decreases to 0.12, maximum and average slope angles decrease to 28° and 19°, respectively. An apparent "young" value of gully density (11/90°) may be coincidentally due to a dry climate, as discussed above. The lava flows associated with this cone are classified as Plv_2 (Table 17). Note from Table 17, Plv_2 (and possibly Plv_{2-3}) lava flow morphology represents a longer time span than that of the youngest three groups. For this longer period, erosional processes became significant in changing the form of cinder cones.

The Santa Teresa cone west of Celaya, Guanajuato (2.78 ± 0.07 Ma) is probably one of the oldest in the MGVF. It has an almost flat shape, being partly buried by sediments, but is recognized as such by an open-pit quarry. Another K-Ar age is known for the San Nicholas maar near Valle de Santiago; juvenile scoriae of the maar give an age of 1.2 Ma[160].

Late Pleistocene-Recent Eruption History

The calibrated geomorphological classification of lava flows combined with the gully densities allow estimation of the relative ages of cinder cones and lava flows. The numbers of Holocene and Late-Pleistocene volcanoes (Hv, Plv_4, and Plv_3) are 16, 27, and 35, respectively; thus an estimated 78 volcanoes erupted within the last 40,000 years. These volcanoes include mostly cinder cones, but also some lavas flows not associated with cones and two shield volcanoes with summit cones. These young volcanoes are situated only in the southern part of the volcanic field, between 200 and 300 km from the Middle America Trench in an area of 15,000 km^2.

Structural Control of Eruptive Vents

Structural alignments of cinder cones and other volcanoes that have erupted within the last 40,000 years are notable (Fig. 148). One such alignment includes Parícutin and extends about 100 km farther to the NE. Another 40-km-long alignment of volcanoes, which includes El Jorullo in the south, also shows a NE direction. Although there is some scatter of cones, these alignments suggest crustal fractures along which magmas ascended. The direction of these younger cone alignments coincides with the relative motion vector of the Cocos and North America Plates (and the direction perpendicular to the minimum horizontal compressive stress) consistent with the idea that tectonic stresses control the location of magmatic conduits[149,161]. In the southern part of the field, older parasitic cones and closely associated cinder cones also show NE alignments. Additional tectonic information is difficult to obtain because the region is almost completely covered by young volcanic products.

In the northeastern part of the field, the relationship between tectonic stress and cinder cone alignments is more obvious. The area surrounding Lake Cuitzeo is characterized by east-west normal faults and parallel alignments of cinder cones. These faults may be related to the east-west-trending Chapala graben structures just west of the volcanic field.

Magma Output Rate

Multiple vents like those in the MGVF imply an absence of the long-lived shallow magma reservoirs characteristic of composite volcanoes, since on the evidence of Volcán Parícutin and Volcán El Jorullo,

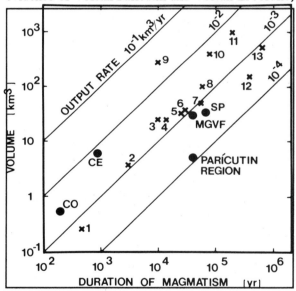

DURATION OF MAGMATISM [yr]

the vents were active less than 20 years. An exponential decrease of effusion rate at Volcán Parícutin indicates that no new magma batches were supplied during the eruption[28], and it has been suggested that the magma came from a deep reservoir[162]. If the formation of a shallow magma reservoir is prevented by a small magma supply rate, a field of cinder cones is more likely to form instead of a composite volcano[163-165].

Overall magma output rate was calculated for the MGVF for the last 40,000 years. Magma eruption

volumes (dense rock equivalent) for the Holocene and Late Pleistocene (Hv, Plv_4, Plv_3) are 9.3, 11.3, and 9.9 km^3, respectively. Thus, 30.5 km^3 of magma was discharged over 40,000 years in an area of 15,000 km^2, yielding an overall magma output rate of 0.8 $km^3/1,000$ years; this can also be represented by a rate calculated for unit length parallel to the Middle America Trench and is approximately 0.005 km^3/km per 1,000 years.

A comparison with other composite volcanoes at convergent plate boundaries is made in Fig. 149. Magma output rates of 13 composite volcanoes from Japan, USSR, and America range from 0.4 to 270 $km^3/1,000$ years[166]. In México, the output rates of Colima and Ceboruco are 2.7 $km^3/1,000$ years and 6 $km^3/1,000$ years respectively[123,127,167]. In contrast Sierra La Primavera rhyolitic complex has a relatively low magma output rate of 0.5 $km^3/1,000$ years[168-170]. The entire MGVF is among the smallest (Fig. 149).

Whether the magma discharge volume of the MGVF is equivalent to a composite volcano is difficult to estimate. Those volcanoes whose output rates were calculated for comparison have surface

Fig. 149. Magma output rates of volcanoes at convergent plate boundaries shown on a logarithmic plot of discharge volume against duration of magmatism. Diagonal lines indicate equal magma output rates. Filled circles represent the Mexican volcanoes: CO = Colima after the 1818 major ash-flow eruption[127,167]; CE = Ceboruco after the Plinian eruption of Jala Pumice (1,000 years ago)[123]; SP = Sierra La Primavera during and after the ash-flow eruption of the Tala Tuff (95,000 years ago)[166,168,169]; MGVF = Michoacán-Guanajuato Volcanic Field (this study); Crosses represent the volcanoes from other regions[166,170]: 1 = Arenal, Costa Rica; 2 = Kaimondake, Japan; 3 = Edgecumbe, USA; 4 = Sakurajima, Japan; 5 = Oshima, Japan; 6 = Asama, Japan; 7 = Fuego, Guatemala; 8 = Avachinsky, Russia; 9 = Kliuchevskoi, Russia; 10 = Fuji, Japan; 11 = Sheveluch, Russia; 12 = Hakone, Japan; 13 = Calabozos caldera, Chile. Magma output volume of the Parícutin region is also plotted.

areas less than 500 km^2 [166], whereas the last 40,000 years of activity in the MGVF covers an area of 15,000 km^2. Although the surface area of a volcano does not necessarily reflect its source, the MGVF is likely to sample a larger area of magma source region than a composite volcano, since composite volcanoes in most volcanic arcs have an average spacing closer than the dimensions of the MGVF (ca. 200 km). As an attempt to make a reasonable basis for comparison, high cone density in areas in Fig. 145 are assumed to represent a magma batch equivalent to that of a single composite volcano. For example, the Parícutin region yields a magma output rate of 0.12 km^3/1,000 years, which is about one-seventh of the entire MGVF. This value is the lowest among the reported magma output rates at convergent plate boundaries. These calculations indicate that the magma discharge rate for the MGVF is smaller than that of a single composite volcano despite the evidence of geographically extensive volcanic activity. It seems that the myriad vents of the MGVF reflect a small magma discharge rate, and probably a small supply rate to the lower crust.

Stereoscopic Aerial Photographs of Dated Cinder Cones

Photographs of volcanoes and other landforms taken from aircraft and satellites flying at high elevation provide a perspective that is of immense value to earth scientists. Many different types of photographs are used, involving different film and other sensors and different camera angles. Stereoscopic aerial photographs are probably the most widely used and informative type for field geologists. These consist of two different photographs of the same scene that are taken at slightly different camera angles. When placed side by side, and viewed in such a way that each eye focuses on the same object in a different photograph, depth can be perceived. The technique mimics the process by which humans and other animals perceive depth in everday life. The angular separation of our eyes means that when they are both focused on an object, each eye observes the object from a slightly different angle. Our brains process this information and combine the two views into a single 3-dimensional image. Most people are already familiar with stereoscopic imagery. The process of preparing and viewing stereophotographs of landscapes is identical to that used in the production of 3-dimensional Viewmaster disks for the popular children's toy. Similar techniques are used in making 3-D horror films, which are viewed through special glasses.

Stereophotographs should be viewed on a horizontal surface under good light. The observer sits in a chair and places his or her head over the photographs so that the line of sight is vertical. Some individuals can see depth in stereophotographs without special equipment by placing their eyes about 20-25 cm from the surface and training each eye to focus on the same object in a different photograph. It can be helpful to place a vertical piece of cardboard between the two images. Most people have trouble with this technique, however, and need special devices called lens stereoscopes. These have the advantage that they magnify the images, making them even clearer. The stereoscope is unfolded and placed over the photographs and adjusted for the observer's eye separation. It is positioned such that each lens is centered over the same object on a different photograph. The observer then looks through the stereoscope in the same way you would look through binoculars. Depth is significantly exaggerated in stereoscopic images, such that slopes appear to be much steeper than they really are.

Stereoscopes can be found in most university geology departments or can be purchased from outdoor equipment suppliers. They range in complexity from simple plastic versions that cost a few dollars up to professional devices costing many hundreds of dollars that use strong lenses and mirrors.

In this section we present nine pairs of stereophotographs and interpretive sketches for cinder cones of known age from the Michoacán-Guanajuato Volcanic Field (MGVF). The photos are presented in order of increasing age. The first 3 pairs are for Parícutin volcano. The next pair is for the historical volcano Jorullo, and the other five are for cones that were dated by the ^{14}C method on charcoal by Hasenaka and Carmichael, with the age data listed in Table 18. These images provide valuable documentation of the changes in cinder cones and associated lava flows with age that are discussed by Hasenaka and Carmichael (see p. 256-259). As a cinder cone ages it becomes progressively vegetated, and erosion produces networks of rills and gullies that build debris aprons at the cone base. Lava flows are buried by wind-blown ash and dust and also begin to develop soil and vegetation. These processes obscure primary features such as pressure ridges and individual flow boundaries.

Parícutin Volcano (1943-1952)

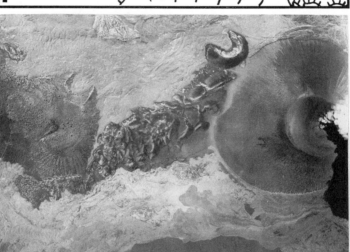

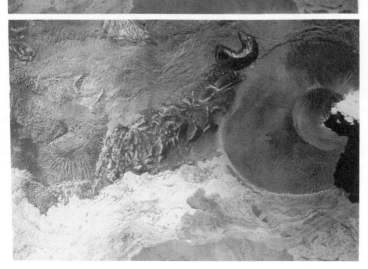

Fig. 150. Stereoscopic airphoto pair of Parícutin volcano, taken on May 26, 1945, showing the cone of Parícutin, the partially buried Sapichu vent on its NE flank, Quitzocho Ridge, and the older cones of Cerro de Jarátiro and Cerro de Canicjuata. The crater visible on the SE margin of Jarátiro began to fill with lava on Dec. 9, 1944. Ultimately the entire ridge was nearly buried by lava from Parícutin (see topographic map of Jarátiro on Fig. 108, p. 144, and small remnant visible on Fig. 152). The margins of the major lava fields are marked by hachures.

Parícutin Volcano (1943-1952)

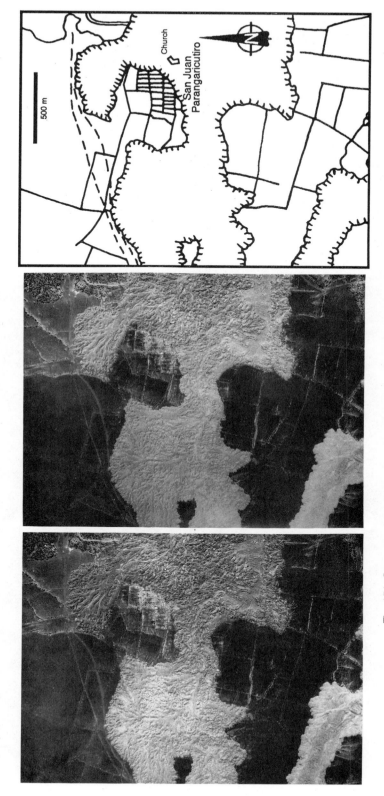

Fig. 151. Stereoscopic airphoto pair of the San Juan lava flow (January-August 1944) that partially buried the town of San Juan Parangaricutiro, taken on May 26, 1945. Hachures mark the margins of the lava field. In the western, unburied part of the town, the grid pattern of the streets is visible. The tower of the church that was surrounded by lava is also visible, about 100 m from the lava front. Other solid lines show stone fences separating farm fields. The double line shows the old unpaved road between San Juan Parangaricutiro and Angahuan to the NE. The dashed lines show new roads around the northern margin of the lava field.

263

Parícutin Volcano (1943-1952)

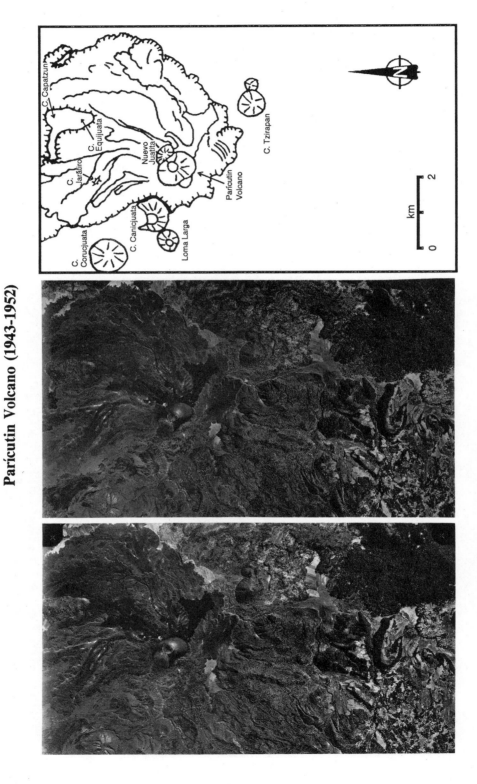

Fig. 152. Stereoscopic airphoto pair of Parícutin volcano as it appeared in the early 1970s. The NE-flank vent mound of Nuevo Juatita is labeled along with the small remaining remnant of Cerro de Jarátiro where the "Upper Casita" observatory was located. Other older volcanoes are also labeled: Cerro de Capatzun, Cerro de Equijuata, Cerro de Corucjuata, Cerro de Canicjuata, Loma Larga, and Cerro de Tzirapan. Hachures mark the margins of the lava field.

264

Jorullo Volcano (1759-1774)

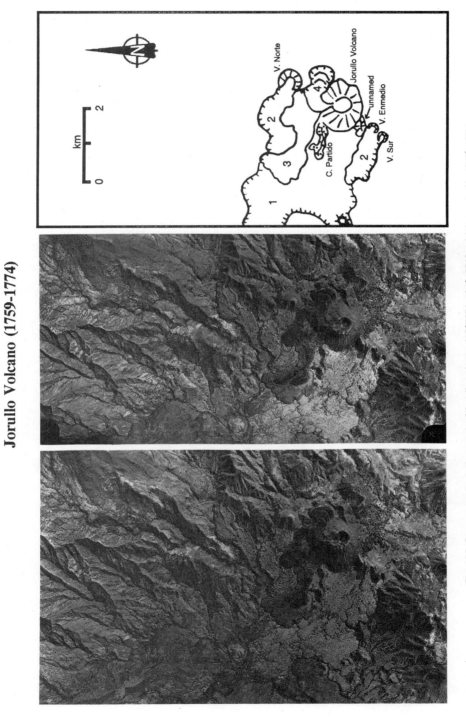

Fig. 153. Stereoscopic airphoto pair of Jorullo volcano (18°58'N, 101°43'W), which erupted in 1759-1774 (see p. 364-371). Jorullo lies 81 km SE of Parícutin volcano. The main cone of Jorullo is flanked by four aligned parasitic vents: Volcán del Norte, Unnamed, Volcán Enmedio, and Volcán del Sur. Four different stages of lava flows are indicated by numbers 1 (oldest) to 4 (youngest). Cerro Partido is an elevated ridge of volcanic basement that was surrounded by the Jorullo lavas. Hachures mark the margins of the lava field.

Cerro el Jabalí (^{14}C: 3,830 ± 150 years)

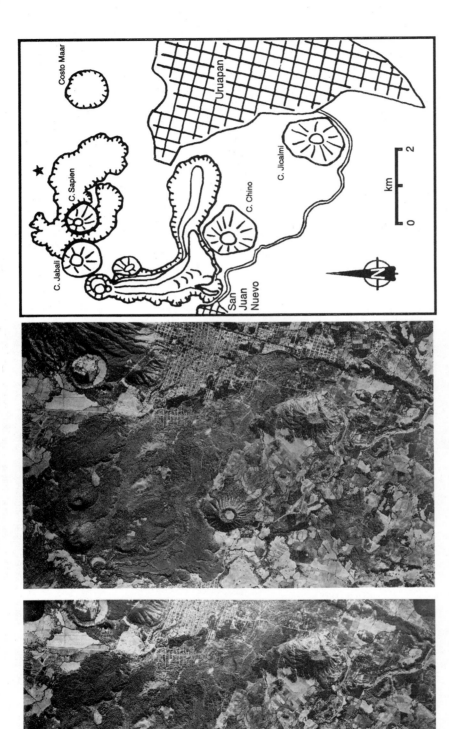

Fig. 154. Stereoscopic airphoto pair of Cerro el Jabalí volcano. Hasenaka and Carmichael (1985a) reported a ^{14}C date of 3,830 ± 150 years for charcoal collected beneath ash from Jabalí at the site marked by the star (Table 18). Cerro el Jabalí and Cerro el Sapien are two of the vents in the Jabalí cluster. Older volcanoes in the area include Costo Maar, Cerro el Chino, and Cerro el Jicalmi. Cerro el Jabalí and Cerro el Sapien have similar morphological characteristics and probably correspond to the 3,830 year old ^{14}C date. The poorly vegetated lava flow from the south side of the unnamed cone to the SW of Cerro el Jabalí may be even younger (T. Hasenaka, personal communication; see p. 251). Hachures mark the margins of all of these lava flows. Grid patterns show the major city Uruapan and the east end of the town San Juan Nuevo. The latter is the resettlement community for former residents of San Juan Parangaricutiro, which was partly buried by lava from the Paricutin eruption. Double-line shows the paved highway from Uruapan to San Juan Nuevo.

266

Hoya el Huanillo (^{14}C: 9,180 ± 250 years and 9,410 ± 230 years)

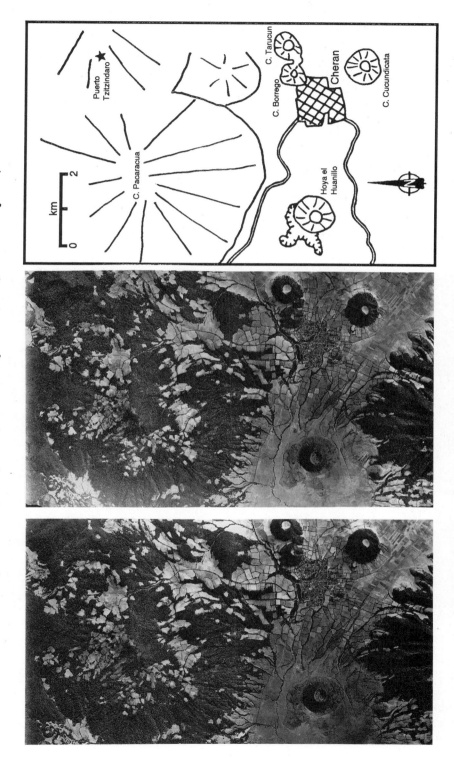

Fig. 155. Stereoscopic airphoto pair of Hoya el Huanillo (19°41'N, 101°59'W), which lies 35 km NE of Paricutin volcano. Hasenaka and Carmichael (1985a) reported ^{14}C dates of 9,180 ± 250 years and 9,410 ± 230 years for charcoal collected beneath ash from Hoya el Huanillo (Table 18). Hachures mark the margins of a small, ash-covered lava flow at the west foot of the cone. Older nearby cones with ash-filled craters: Cerro el Borrego, Cerro Tarucun, Cerro Cucundicata. To the north is the eroded stratovolcano Cerro Pacaracua, and 3½ km to the ENE is the small cinder cone Puerto Tzitzindaro (star), which erupted high on an eroded volcanic hill rather than in a low area as did Paricutin, the other cones in this image, and most cinder cones in the MGVF. The grid pattern shows the town of Cheran.

Volcán la Mina (^{14}C: 17,170 ±430 years)

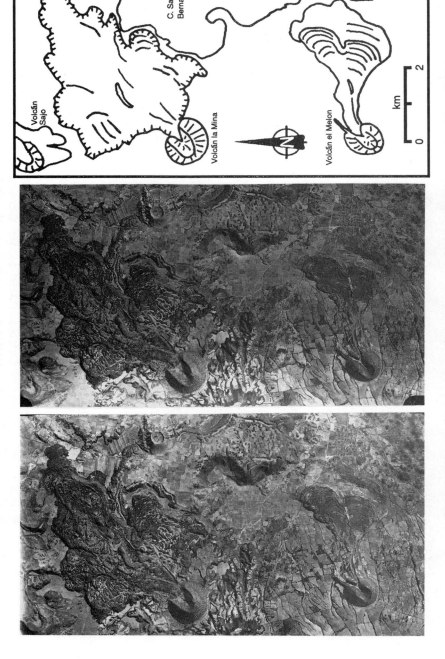

Fig. 156. Stereoscopic airphoto pair of Volcán la Mina (19°43'N, 101°26'W), which lies 89 km ENE of Paricutin volcano. Hasenaka and Carmichael (1985a) reported a ^{14}C date of 17,170 ± 430 years for charcoal collected beneath ash from Volcán la Mina (Table 18). Hachures mark the margins of its lava flow. Older nearby cinder cones and associated lava flows are Volcán Sajo and Cerro San Bernabé. As indicated by its relatively un-filled cone and the scarcity of light-colored alluvium on its lava flow, Volcán el Melon appears to be younger than Volcán la Mina. The grid pattern shows the town of Capalu.

Cerro el Pueblito (^{14}C: 29,000 ± 3,300 years)

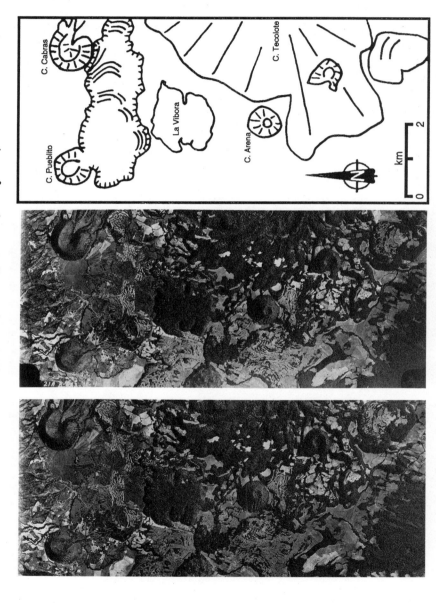

Fig. 157. Stereoscopic airphoto pair of Cerro el Pueblito (19°49'N, 101°55'W), which lies 50 km NE of Paricutín volcano. Hasenaka and Carmichael (1985a) reported a ^{14}C date of 29,000 ± 3,300 years for charcoal collected beneath ash from Cerro el Pueblito (Table 18). The lava flow from Cerro el Pueblito, whose margins are marked by hachures, was deflected slightly by the older cone of Cerro las Cabras, which was dated by ^{14}C at >40,000 years. The latter cone and its extensive lava flow are shown in Fig. 158. To the south of Cerro el Pueblito is La Víbora, a good example of a "coneless lava flow". Just to the south of La Víbora is the symmetrical cinder cone Cerro la Arena. This cone, a nearly buried vent on its SE flank, an unnamed cinder cone 2 km farther to the SE, and a "coneless lava flow" in the lower right corner of the images were all built on the SW flank of the eroded stratovolcano Cerro el Tecolote.

269

Cerro las Cabras (^{14}C: > 40,000 years)

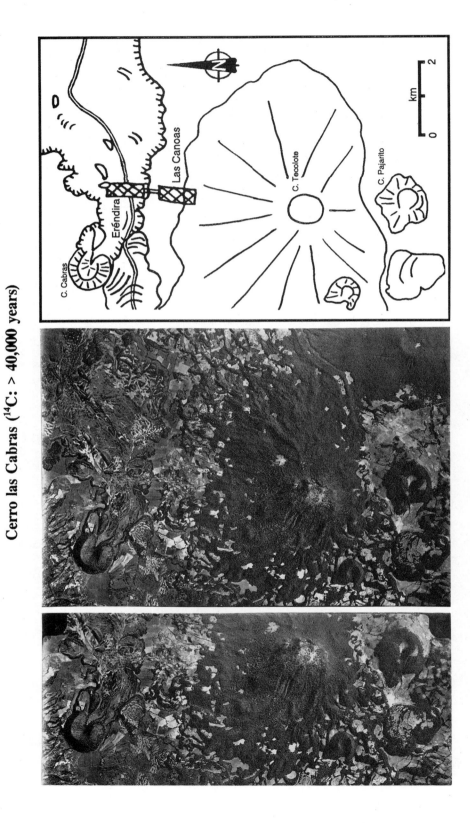

Fig. 158. Stereoscopic airphoto pair of Cerro las Cabras (19°50'N, 101°54'W), which lies 53 km NE of Parícutin volcano. Hasenaka and Carmichael (1985a) reported a ^{14}C age beyond the limit of the technique (>40,000 years) for charcoal collected beneath ash from Cerro las Cabras (Table 18). The margins of its lava flow are marked by hachures. The stratovolcano Cerro el Tecolote, with its steep upper cone, lies to the south. An unnamed cinder cone and an unnamed "coneless lava flow" (Fig. 157) are visible on its SW flank. Cinder cone Cerro el Pajarito lies just to its south. The grid patterns show the towns Eréndira and Las Canoas. The double line marks Mexican highway 15.

270

Petrology and Geochemistry of MGVF Cinder Cones

Hasenaka and Carmichael (1987)

The authors studied the mineralogy and chemical composition of specimens from nearly 200 volcanoes in the MGVF (Fig. 159). These data, in conjuction with estimated ages of eruption, are used to examine systematic variations in the nature of magma compositions with both time and distance from the Middle America trench (MAT). Furthermore, this regional analysis provides a perspective for understanding the mineralogy and composition of the suite from Parícutin volcano.

Sample Descriptions and Whole Rock Compositions

Rock types are defined by silica content: basalt <53 wt.% SiO_2, low-Si andesite 53-57% SiO_2, high-Si andesite 57-63% SiO_2, and dacite >63% SiO_2 [171]. Alkalic and non-alkalic lavas are defined by the alkali (Na_2O + K_2O) contents on an alkali vs. silica plot[172,173], and the calc-alkaline lava types are defined as non-alkalic rocks lacking iron enrichment. The majority of MGVF lavas (50-70% SiO_2) are alkali-poor types, calc-alkali, or transitional varieties (Fig. 160). These non-alkalic samples in aggregate show a typical calc-alkaline trend with slight or no iron enrichment. . . . Alkali contents vary continuously from alkalic to non-alkalic, but 21 samples (19 basalts and 2 andesites) well above the boundary between alkalic and non-alkalic rocks have characteristically high concentrations of Mg, Cr, and Ni (high-Mg type), or FeO^t (= total Fe) and TiO_2 (low-Mg type). The former is a subgroup of the high-Mg alkaline rocks, and the latter type a subgroup of low-Mg alkaline lavas. In this study, a transitional group (38 samples) of moderately alkali-rich rocks with lower concentrations of the above elements is conveniently delineated. Plagioclase and olivine are the most common phenocryst phases, and are found in all basalts, with or without augite. This mineral assemblage is also common among low-Si andesites. Augite, orthopyroxene, and hornblende phenocrysts are common in high-Si andesites and dacites. Hornblende also occurs in alkali basalts containing olivine, augite, and plagioclase phenocrysts.

. . . . .

Spatial and Temporal Variations in Magma Composition

Compositional Variations at Individual Cinder Cones

Although only one sample was analysed for most cones, more extensive sampling was conducted in a few cases to assess their compositional variation. For 42 cones from which more than two samples were collected, the following conclusions were drawn:

1. Scoriae and volcanic bombs sampled from different locations, usually the top-most scoria layer and the bottom-most layer, have compositions that are identical within (2σ) analytical error. This may just reflect the small sequence of scoriae exposed in most quarries and the low crystallinity of most samples.

2. Three lava specimens sampled from the same flow unit at varying distances from Cerro El Pueblito (Fig. 157) are nearly identical in composition and mineralogy. The compositions all fall within 1σ except for MgO, Ni, and Cr, due to the different contents of olivine and augite phenocrysts.

3. Lava samples collected from different flow units related to a single cone show variations larger than analytical error, ranging up to 5 wt.% SiO_2. Such compositional variations among lavas are also observed at Parícutin and Jorullo. The silica content of lavas changed from 55% in 1943 to 60% in 1952 at Volcán Parícutin [see Tables 26 (p. 329-330) and 31 (p. 348)]. At Volcán Jorullo, the early lavas have 52.1% SiO_2, and later ones have 54.8% SiO_2 (see p. 370). At both cones, the composition of lavas became more silicic as the eruptions proceeded (see Fig. 215 on p. 371), which is opposite to trends observed for nearly continuous eruptions at Hekla, Arenal, Fuego, and Izalco[174-177], for Kilauea[178], and for many compositionally zoned pyroclastic-flow deposits[164].

4. The largest compositional variation is found among andesitic and dacitic scoriae and lavas erupted from Cerro Las Cabras (Fig. 158): 57-70% SiO_2. Cerro El Metate (also called Cerros el Capácuaro), one of the largest shield volcanoes in the MGVF (>4 km^3), has a compositional range of 57-61% SiO_2.

Compositional Variations Among Centers of Different Volcanic Morphology

Although samples from cinder cones show a wide compositional range from 48 to 65% SiO_2, samples from shield volcanoes and thick lava flows without

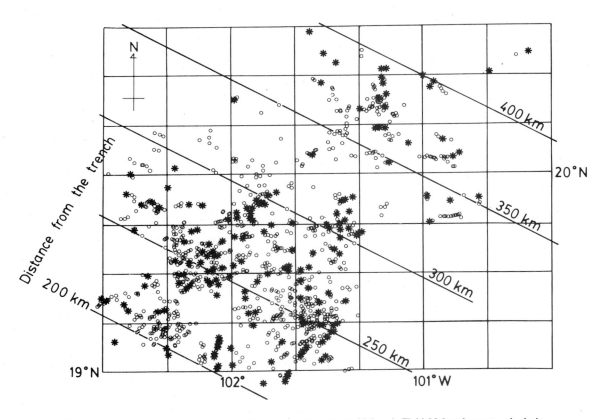

Fig. 159. Locations of volcanoes in the Michoacán-Guanajuato Volcanic Field. Volcanic centers include cinder and lava cones, lava domes, maars, tuff rings, small shield volcanoes with summit cones, and lava flows not associated with cones. Asterisks show volcanoes for which chemical data are available.

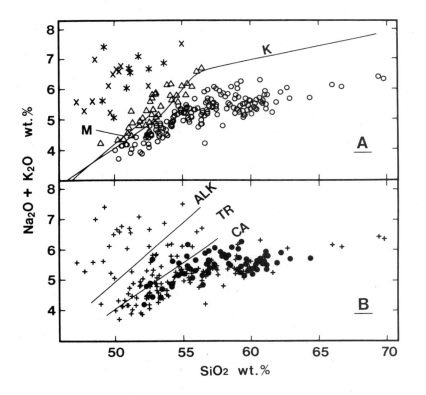

Fig. 160. Plots of $Na_2O + K_2O$ against SiO_2 for all MGVF samples.

(A) Calc-alkaline lavas (open circles), high-Mg alkaline lavas (*), low-Mg alkaline lavas (x), and transitional rocks between calc-alkaline and alkaline lavas (triangles). Boundary between alkali olivine basalts and tholeiites[173] is labelled M, and line K is the boundary between tholeiitic and high-alumina series after Kuno[172].

(B) Samples younger than 40,000 years (solid circles) and older than 40,000 years (+) are plotted. Boundaries are taken from A.

associated cones typically are more silica-rich. Shield volcanoes, some of which were coeval with cinder cones, produced voluminous lavas with SiO_2 compositions between 57 and 63% SiO_2 . . . . Ten thick lava flows whose vents are buried show silica contents between 55 and 62% . . . .

Temporal Variations of Magma Compositions

All the cinder and lava cones younger than 40,000 years are calc-alkaline with the exception of a few transitional samples. These late-Pleistocene to Recent lavas are slightly more silicic than older calc-alkaline lavas and are found only in the southern part of the MGVF, between 200 and 300 km from the trench [see Fig. 148, p. 259]. In the cinder cone field SW of México City, Holocene lavas are also reported to be more silicic than older samples[131].

Most of the alkaline rocks are found in morphologically older cones. The youngest alkaline rocks are from Cerro La Pilita, where pressure ridges of accompanying lava flows are still well-preserved. From its lava morphology and cone shape, we estimate this eruption to have occurred between 40,000 and 370,000 years ago. Thus, during the late Quaternary, coeval calc-alkaline and alkaline volcanism occurred in the MGVF, especially close to the MAT. Similar coexistence of alkaline and calc-alkaline volcanism is also found in other parts of the MVB; at the Colima Rift Zone[130,179], and near Volcán Sangangüey[180]. In both cases, volcanism is spatially related to a graben structure.

Spatial Variation of Magma Compositions

As shown in Fig. 161, both calc-alkaline and transitional lavas occur throughout the MGVF, but the high-Mg and low-Mg alkaline lavas have a restricted and distinctive distribution. High-Mg alkaline samples are always found in the southern part of the MGVF, between 200 and 270 km from the trench,

whereas the low-Mg alkaline samples . . . always occur in the northern part of the MGVF, between 350 and 400 km from the trench. Calc-alkaline samples show a similar spatial distribution of their compatible elements, as the high-Mg (>9% MgO) basalts and low-Si andesites are only found between 200 and 270 km from the trench (Figs. 161 and 162). Thus, compatible elements such as Mg, Ni, and Cr, in lavas of the same SiO_2 content, show a general decrease with distance from the trench.

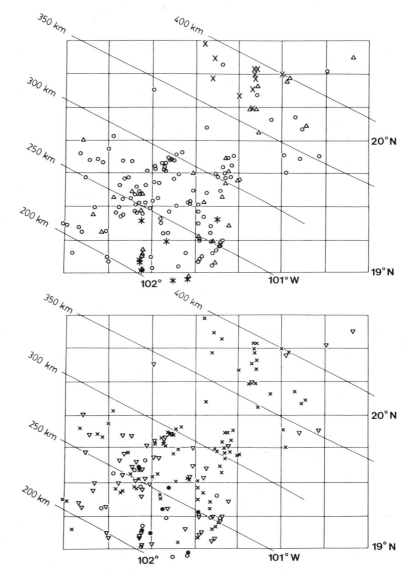

Fig. 161. Top: Locations of calc-alkaline (open circles), high-Mg alkaline (*), low-Mg alkaline (x), and transitional rocks (open triangles). The area is the same as that in Fig. 159. Bottom: Locations of high-Mg lavas. Solid circles are volcanoes with high-Mg rocks (>9 per cent MgO and mg-number >70). Open circles are volcanoes with lavas >8 per cent MgO and mg-number >68. Crosses are lavas with <5 percent MgO, and open triangles represent lavas with 5-8 per cent MgO and mg-numbers below 68.

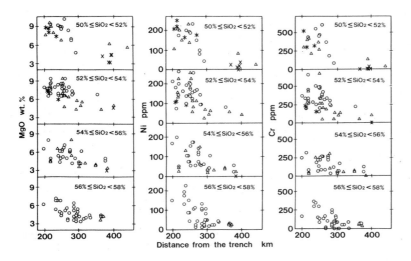

Fig. 162. Distance from the Middle America Trench and MgO, Cr, and Ni contents of the lavas. Symbols as in Fig. 163.

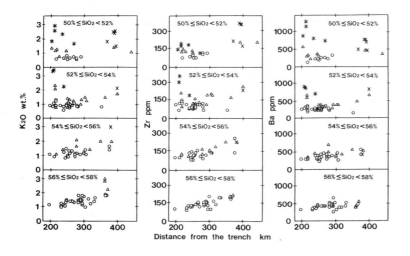

Fig. 163. The relationship between K₂O, Zr, and Ba and distance of eruptive site from the Middle America Trench, for lavas of different compositional groups. Calc-alkaline lavas (open circles), high-Mg alkaline lavas (*), low-Mg alkaline lavas (x), and transitional varieties (triangles).

about 200 km from the trench. For lavas of higher SiO_2 content, K_2O shows a better correlation with increasing distance, as has been observed in other island arcs and continental margins[181-184]. Rb, not included in the figure, shows exactly the same pattern as K_2O. Zr has a more obvious positive correlation, but the correlation between Ba (and also REEs) and distance is poorly defined even at higher SiO_2 contents (Fig. 163). Thus, positive correlations between K_2O (or Rb and Zr) and increasing distance from the trench are only observed if the high-Mg alkaline basalts are excluded.

The following two sections, not reproduced here, are titled "Petrography and Mineralogy" and "Conditions of Cinder Cone Formation". The former section summarizes mineral assemblages, mineral compositions, and derived temperatures, oxygen fugacities, and pressures calculated for magmas of the MGVF. Hasenaka and Carmichael point out that the MGVF magmas are significantly more oxidized than those erupted from mid-ocean ridge systems, a common feature of subduction-zone volcanoes. They estimate pressures of fractionation for the MGVF magmas by projecting whole-rock compositions onto ternary phase diagrams and conclude that magmas erupted in the south (i.e., Parícutin and Jorullo), closer to the trench, generally equilibrated at greater depths, near the base of the crust at about 30 km. In their interpretation, a cinder cone field develops when the magma supply rate is low. Small batches of magma rise quickly through the crust along crustal fractures or fault systems without being trapped at depth to form magma reservoirs. Thus, each volcano typically erupts only one time, and no long-lived larger volcanic systems are developed.

In contrast to MgO, K_2O contents of the volcanic rocks do not show a well-defined correlation with increasing distance from the trench. In Fig. 163, the concentrations of K_2O, Zr, and Ba are plotted against distance at 2% silica intervals. Because of the occurrence of alkali basalts in the southern part of the MGVF, the K_2O content at lower silica values has a wide variation and even shows the highest value

K-Ar Ages of Shield Volcanoes
Ban et al. (1992)

Introduction

The Michoacán-Guanajuato Volcanic Field (MGVF), with an area of 40,000 km², contains more than 1,000 small monogenetic volcanic centers including cinder cones, lava flows, maars, and lava domes. It lacks the large composite volcanoes observed in other portions of the belt. In addition to these small volcanic centers, the volcanic field contains about 300 medium-sized volcanoes, mainly shield volcanoes of about 10 km diameter. These discharged the largest volume of magma in the area. . . . In this paper we analyze the spatial and temporal variations of the volcanic activity in the MGVF based on new K-Ar ages for eight shield volcanoes and one stratovolcano as well as previously published ^{14}C ages (Table 19).

The small and medium-sized volcanic centers have similar and overlapping distribution patterns within the study area . . . . In the northern part of the volcanic field, however, medium-sized volcanoes are more frequent than small ones. Geomorphologically, the cinder cones in the north are older than those in the south [see p. 259], which suggests a SW migration of the volcanic activity. One of the purposes of the present study was to make a series of age determinations on medium-sized volcanoes at different distances from the trench in order to test the migration hypothesis for this volcano type.

Small monogenetic volcanoes are typically located between medium-sized volcanic centers, either on their lower flanks or in the surrounding alluvial plains. . . . In most cases, lava flows from cinder cones on the lower flanks of medium-sized volcanic centers are geomorphologically much younger than the volcanoes themselves. They show clearly preserved pressure ridges and flow margins, and discrete flow units can be distinguished. In contrast, the lava surfaces of the medium-sized volcanoes are deeply dissected and do not show distinct flow units. An exception is Metate shield volcano (4,700 y.b.p.), whose lava flows preserve original surface features, and encircle several older cinder cones at the foot of the volcano. Thus we can generalize that the medium-sized volcanoes predate the smaller monogenetic cones in the study area. However, at present we have insufficient age data to support and quantify this observation. The second purpose of this study, therefore, was to detemine radiometrically the differences in age between medium-sized volcanic centers and small monogenetic volcanoes occurring in the same area.

. . . . .

Shield Volcanoes of the MGVF

A variety of volcanic forms are found among the medium-sized volcanoes in the MGVF, as among the small, monogenetic volcanoes. Most of the former have a shield shape with a diameter of about 10 km, and slope angles varying between 5° and 15°. Major form types include flat shields with slightly convex slopes, shields with a summit dome or summit cinder cone, and shields with relatively steep slopes. On some shield volcanoes, primary lava flow morphologies are still partly preserved, whereas others have deep gullies cut into their slopes . . . . Shield volcanoes in the MGVF show lava flows with similar erosional stages[152]; thus, their lavas were probably discharged during a single eruptive event.

K-Ar Age Determinations

Selection of Samples

Among the nine MGVF samples selected for K-Ar dating, eight were lavas from shield volcanoes, and one was from the stratovolcano Tancítaro (Fig. 164). The locations of the summits of these volcanoes are listed in Table 19. The sampling sites were chosen so that they cover the entire area of the volcanic field; they are basically aligned in a NE-SW direction with their distances from the Middle America Trench varying from 190 km to 400 km. All the analyzed samples are calc-alkaline andesites with a limited SiO_2 range of 53 to 61 wt.% . . . . In contrast, cinder cone lavas have a wide range of composition from 47 to 70 wt.% SiO_2, and include both calc-alkaline and alkaline types [see p. 271-273]. Analyzed samples are all free from alteration with phenocryst assemblages of plagioclase ± olivine ± augite ± orthopyroxene ± hornblende in generally intersertal groundmass.

Table 19. Compilation of K-Ar and ^{14}C ages of shield volcanoes and cinder cones in the MGVF.
Volcano type: SH = shield volcano, SV = stratovolcano, C = cinder or lava cone. WR = whole rock.

Sample No.	Name of Volcanoes	Latitude(N)	Longitude(W)	Rock Type	Volcano Type	Method	Age Ma	Ref.
909	C.Paracho	19°35'21"	102°02'28"	Andesite	S.H.	K-Ar GM conc.	0.06±0.01	1
929	C.Buenavista Tomatlan	19°09'22"	102°36'31"	Andesite	S.H.	K-Ar GM conc.	0.54±0.08	1
974	C.Yahuarato	19°36'53"	101°33'06"	Andesite	S.H.	K-Ar GM conc.	0.54±0.07	1
978	Brinco del Diablo	19°56'21"	101°43'55"	Andesite	S.H.	K-Ar GM conc.	1.88±0.24	1
988	West of C.El Picacho	19°50'20"	101°58'01"	Andesite	S.H.	K-Ar GM conc.	0.17±0.03	1
995	C.Culiacán	20°20'16"	100°58'11"	Andesite	S.H.	K-Ar GM conc.	2.10±0.24	1
997	C.Grande	20°25'23"	100°52'35"	Andesite	S.H.	K-Ar GM conc.	2.27±0.27	1
999	C.Camatarán	20°10'37"	101°33'30"	Andesite	S.H.	K-Ar GM conc.	1.17±0.14	1
1023	C.Tancítaro	19°16'34"	102°24'57"	Andesite	S.V.	K-Ar GM conc.	0.53±0.06	1
—	C.El Metate	19°32'20"	101°59'33"	Andesite	S.H.	14C	0.0047±0.0002	2
—	C.Pelón	19°17'52"	101°54'47"	Basalt	C.	K-Ar WR	0.37±0.05	2
—	Santa Teresa	20°29'50"	100°59'53"	Basalt	C.	K-Ar WR	2.78±0.07	2
—	San Nicolás	20°23'17"	101°15'25"	Andesite	Maar	K-Ar WR	1.2	3
340	C.Sanambo	19°38'58"	101°26'32"	Andesite	S.H.	K-Ar WR	0.87±0.05	4
706	C.Grande La Piedad	20°18'10"	102°07'01"	Andesite	S.H.	K-Ar WR	1.60±0.10	4
881	C.Alto	19°59'18"	102°30'34"	Andesite	S.H.	K-Ar WR	2.60±0.10	4
Mex211	San Joaquin Jaripeo	19°51'00"	100°44'50"	Bas.-Andesite	S.H.	K-Ar WR	0.75±0.15	5

Cin volcano name is Cerro (= hill). Volcano type: SH = shield volcano, SV = stratovolcano, C = cinder or lava cone. WR = whole rock. GM conc. = groundmass concentrate (see text in details). Ref.: 1 = this study, 2 = Hasenaka and Carmichael (1985), 3 = Murphy and Carmichael (1984). 4 = Nixon *et al.* (1987), 5. Ferrari *et al.* (1990)

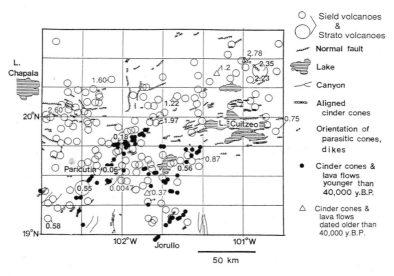

Fig. 164. Distribution of shield volcanoes and cinder cones in the MGVF and their ages. Bold numbers show K-Ar ages determined in this study (Table 19). Other numbers show K-Ar ages and ^{14}C ages from Table 18 and literature sources[121,185,186]. Alignments of cinder cones, their vents and dikes, and normal faults are taken from Fig. 148.

Analytical Results

The ages of the shield volcanoes vary from 2.27 to 0.06 Ma . . . . Fig. 164 shows both the locations and ages of shield volcanoes given in Hasenaka and Carmichael (see p. 258-259), Nixon et al.[121], and Ferrari et al.[185]. Fig. 164 also shows the locations and K-Ar ages of the San Nicolas maar dated by Murphy and Carmichael[186], the Cerro Pelón cinder cone and a cinder cone near Santa Teresa, which is nearly totally eroded, reported by Hasenaka and Carmichael (see p. 259).

Discussion

One important result of our study is the difference in age between volcanoes in the north (farther from the Middle America Trench) and those in the south (closer to the trench). All the dated volcanoes in the northern portion of the volcanic field (latitude >19°55') are older than 1 million years, whereas all the dated volcanoes in the southern portion of the volcanic field are younger than 1 million years. This relationship is observed for both shield volcanoes and small volcanic centers. Thus, from Fig. 164 we can conclude that at least in the MGVF, volcanism migrated southward about 1 million years ago. Recent volcanism is restricted to the southern part of the MGVF, as documented by Hasenaka and Carmichael's data on ^{14}C age determinations (Table 18). Fig. 165 shows the relationship between locations of these dated volcanoes and their ages. From this diagram we can see that the southward migration occurred abruptly rather than gradually at about 1 million years ago.

There are no differences between the known ages of the shield volcanoes and of small volcanic centers in the same region (Fig. 167). Both, in the south and in the north, they overlap in the same time period. It should be noted, however, that small volcanoes are among the ones with the oldest K-Ar ages in the MGVF. Cerro Pelón cinder cone (0.37 million years) in the south has lava surface morphologies of Plv$_2$ (see Table 17 on p. 257: i.e. the original surface features are obscured by erosion and soil development). A cinder cone near Santa Teresa (2.78 million years) in the north is nearly totally degraded and was only recognized because of a quarry outcrop.

Direct comparison should be made between shield lavas and cinder cone

lavas using the degree to which the original lava morphology is preserved. This may be difficult, because the original lava morphology might have been different to begin with. It was surprising to find the age of Cerro Paracho shield to be only 60,000 years, because the lava flows do not preserve such features as pressure ridges and individual lava flow units. It may be necessary to establish different criteria for calibrating ages of shield volcanoes. Also, some "shield volcanoes" may be stratovolcanes; their slopes may be covered by pyroclastic materials instead of lava flows.

Conclusions

Luhr and Carmichael[187] pointed out a general trenchward or southwestward migration of the MVB volcanism. Colima, Popocatépetl, and Citlaltépetl are all historically active composite volcanoes at the young southern limit of this volcanic chain. Cantagrel and Robin[133] also described a southward shift of magmatism since the Pliocene through K-Ar dating. Our result confirms this general trend for an area in the central sector of the MVB. In the MGVF, the area of the volcanic activity shifted about 100 km southward over the last 1 to 2 million years. The shift was not gradual, but was rather abrupt; the northern and southern parts of this volcanic field have groups of volcanoes with different ages.

The documented southward migration probably resulted from a change in motion of the underthrusting Cocos Plate. Either the subduction dip increased, or the trench position shifted seaward. At present, there are no geophysical data to support either hypothesis, because the Wadati-Benioff zone is not well defined beneath the active volcanoes of central México.

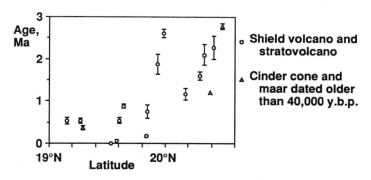

Fig. 165. Ages of shield volcanoes and cinder cones in the MGVF against their locations. Data are taken from Table 19. Vertical bars represent standard deviations of the analyses.

Structure of the Volcanic Field

Connor (1987)

For volcanic fields of the type in Michoacán-Guanajuato, which contain large numbers of small to medium-sized vents, the spatial locations of those many vents can be used to address a variety of important issues, including the stress field in the upper crust, the patterns of buried fault systems, and the likely sites of future eruptions. Charles Connor investigated the distribution and alignment of volcanic vents and fault scarps in the MGVF for his Masters thesis at Dartmouth College, and extended that work into his Ph.D. dissertation at Dartmouth with a focus on spatial clustering among the cinder cones. Connor established objective, quantitative criteria for defining a "vent", and applied various statistical techniques of alignment and cluster analysis in an effort to move beyond the subjective approaches, biased by human perception, that characterized most earlier vent-distribution studies. Portions of his two major articles on the MGVF are reprinted.

Introduction

The Michoacán-Guanajuato Volcanic Field (MGVF), in the central Mexican Volcanic Belt [MVB], covers approximately 40,000 km^2 [188] and is made up of cinder cones and a smaller number of shield volcanoes, stratovolcanoes, lava domes, and maars[189] [see p. 255-256]. These volcanoes and their associated lava flows cover Tertiary silicic volcanic rocks throughout the area. Two historically active volcanoes are located in the field, Parícutin (1943-1952) and Jorullo (1759-1774)[190].

This study describes and interprets the structural geology of the MGVF through an analysis of the distribution and alignment of volcanoes, and distribution of faults, recognized by their topographic expression. Volcanoes and topographic lineaments were mapped from 100°40'W to 103°00'W and from 19°00'N to 20°15'N by field observations and the examination of topographic maps published by the Comision de Estudios del Territorio Nacional (CETNAL). This area includes most, but not all of the volcanic field, the limits of which have yet to be defined.

To characterize the regional distribution of volcanoes, contour maps of the density of volcanoes and volcano height were made. These contour maps reveal correlations between the distribution and size of the volcanoes, and clarify several trends in volcano distribution. Alignments of volcanoes in other large volcanic fields have often been related to faults[191-195] Orientations of volcano alignments have been shown to reflect principal tectonic stresses[149,196]. Therefore, determining the relationship between faults on the periphery of the field and alignments of volcanoes within the field was a primary concern of this study.

Previous Work

Williams [see p. 245-254] described the volcanoes of the Parícutin area, in the central part of the MGVF. By observing the superposition of lava flows and comparing volcano morphologies, Williams showed that cinder cones are generally younger than stratovolcanoes in this area. He found that the young cinder cones range in composition from olivine-augite basalt to hornblende and pyroxene andesite, whereas older shield and stratovolcanoes are uniformly andesite.

Settle[194] described the distribution of 170 cinder cones in the immediate vicinity of Parícutin volcano, and characterized the field as a platform-type volcanic field, because cinder cones are widely distributed and are emplaced independent of larger volcanoes. Hasenaka and Carmichael [see p. 255] identified 1,040 volcanoes in their analysis of the distribution and morphology of volcanoes in the MGVF; they did not include extensively eroded volcanoes in their analysis. They characterized the distribution of volcanoes in the field in terms of volcano-trench distance and found that 75% of the volcanoes in the field lie between 200 and 300 km from the trench. Using the morphometric characteristics of volcanoes in the field, calibrated by ^{14}C and K-Ar dating, Hasenaka and Carmichael found 78 volcanoes less than 40,000 years old between 19°N and 20°N and 100°20'W and 102°40'W. These are mostly cinder cones. In contrast, two shield volcanoes were found to have erupted within the last 40,000 years. This corresponds to the age of monogenetic cinder cones in the Sierra Chichinautzin, south of México City[131,132].

Several authors have noted the alignment of volcanic vents and centers in the MGVF [Williams, see p. 248; Hasenaka and Carmichael, see p. 259-260]. Because of the strong scatter in the distribution of volcanoes, however, these authors did not attempt to map the alignments.

Surface expressions of faults are absent in the Parícutin area, in sharp contrast to the large number of faults found in the northern part of the field (see p. 259-260). Mooser[197] and Demant[189] mapped photo-lineaments in the central MVB. Photo-lineaments SW of the field, which trend approximately N35E, can be projected through the Parícutin area[197]. A second trend, subparallel to the Parícutin trend, passes through Jorullo volcano[198]. These trends are coincident with the convergence direction of the Cocos and North American Plates, and may be related to segmentation of the subducted Cocos Plate[199]. The distribution of cinder cones in the MGVF less than 40,000 years old further defines the N35E trend of volcanoes through the Parícutin area, and suggests a similar trend through the Jorullo area [see p. 259-260]. Hasenaka and Carmichael suggested that these trends indicate the presence of underlying crustal fractures [see p. 259].

Distribution of Volcanoes

To analyze volcano distribution, a data set[200] consisting of volcano locations and heights was compiled using topographic maps and field observa-

tions. The data set was described by statistical and graphical methods.

A total of 1894 volcanoes was identified on topographic maps (Fig. 166). Field checks were made over a 7-week period, concentrating on an area of approximately 3,000 km² around Parícutin volcano. In this area 364 volcanoes were identified on the topographic maps and an additional 16 volcanoes were identified in the the field. This difference is due to the presence of very small cinder cones, which do not have sufficient topographic expression to be seen on the quadrangle maps. Volcanoes were included regardless of their type or degree of erosion, which is frequently extensive. Cerro Paracho (19°35'25"N, 102°02'25"W), for example, has eroded to its central neck. These are included because they show additional trends.

Because of the tremendous number of volcanoes in the MGVF, volcano distribution is best shown by contouring volcano density. A contour map was constructed using a grid node spacing of 10 km and a search radius of 7.5 km (177 km² search area) about each node, which results in graphical smoothing (Fig. 167). Volcanoes are most highly concentrated in the south-central portion of the study area and are entirely absent in the west-central and SE portions (Figs. 166

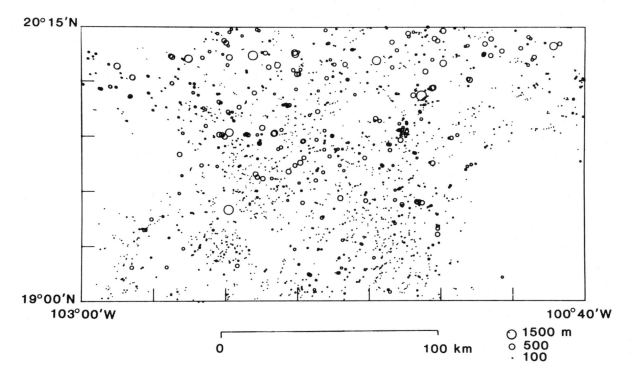

Fig. 166. Computer-generated point-pattern map of volcano distribution. Circle size is directly proportional to the measured height of the volcano. Examples of circle size for particular volcano edifice heights are shown.

and 167). The contour map suggests the NE trend in volcano concentration through the Parícutin area, noted by previous authors [see p. 248, 259]. Volcano height was measured from topographic maps by averaging the maximum and minimum height of each volcano above the surrounding terrain. A contour map of average volcano height (Fig. 168) was made with the same grid spacing and search radius used to construct the map of volcano density. This map shows a decrease in volcano height from north to south. This regional change is inverse to the change in volcano density.

. . . . .

Statistical methods were used to divide eruptive centers in the MGVF into two populations based on cone height: A for larger cones and B for smaller cones.

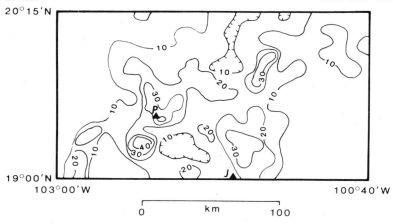

Fig. 167. Contour map of the distribution of volcanoes. Contour interval is 10 volcanoes/177 km² search area. This map, and all contour maps that follow, use a grid node spacing of 10 km and search area of 177 km². Triangles labelled P and J show Parícutin and Jorullo volcanoes, respectively.

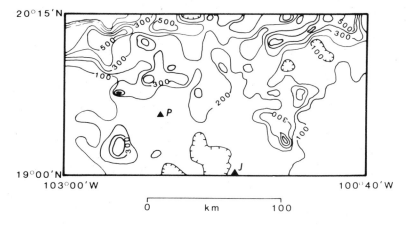

Fig. 168. Contour map of average volcano height. Contour interval is 100 m. Triangles labelled P and J show Parícutin and Jorullo volcanoes, respectively.

Distribution of Topographic and Volcanic Lineaments

Figure 169 compares the distribution of topographic lineaments to the distribution of volcanoes. These lineaments are generally scarps with greater than 40 m relief and are interpreted to be faults[189,197]. The number of observed lineaments drops off dramatically where volcano density is greater than 10 volcanoes/177 km², and particularly where the density of volcanoes less than or equal to 240 m in height is greater than 10 volcanoes/177 km².

Continuous topographic lineaments greater than 1 km in length were plotted by frequency on a Rose diagram (Fig. 170a). Lineaments oriented N50-N70E are the most abundant; these lineaments are concentrated in the NE part of the study area (Fig. 169). Scarps within this band frequently have greater than 100 m relief and form subparallel horst and graben structures, cutting Tertiary volcanics and volcaniclastics, as well as some Quaternary volcanoes [see p. 259-260][189]. Two other prominent topographic trends are oriented N50-70W and east-west. Lineaments oriented N60W are strongly concentrated in the NW part of the study area, and form a horst and graben topography. This trend is co-linear to the trend of the western MVB and the Zacoalco Graben, and parallel to the trend of volcanoes equal to or greater than 300 m in height. If these two fault zones are projected into the field, they intersect in the Parícutin area, where volcanoes are most abundant. However, there is little topographic evidence of faulting in the immediate area of Parícutin volcano [see p. 248]. East-west-trending topographic lineaments, such as those bounding the Chapala graben are abundant (Fig. 170a) and are more evenly distributed throughout the area than the N50-70W and N50-70E trends.

Alignments of volcanoes in the field were identified on a point pattern map of volcanic centers, which was filtered to include only volcanoes with nearest neighbors closer than the mean separation distance of volcanoes in the field, approximately 1,500 m. A line of

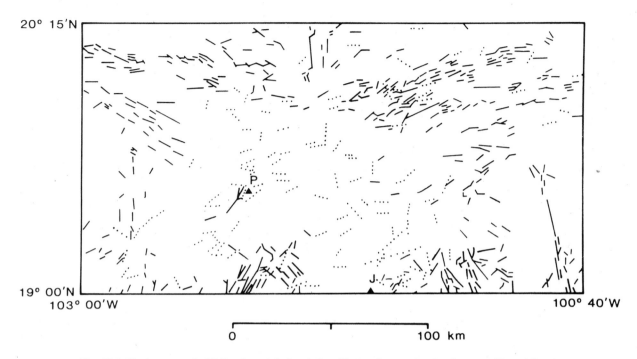

Fig. 169. Fault scarps (solid lines) and their relationship to alignments of volcanoes (dotted lines). Triangles labelled P and J show Parícutin and Jorullo volcanoes, respectively.

Fig. 170. Rose diagrams of:

(a)   orientation of topographic lineaments

(b)   orientation of aligned volcanoes. The number of volcanoes within a lineament is plotted in (b) rather than the number of lineaments. Thus a lineament of six volcanoes will have more weight than a lineament of four volcanoes.

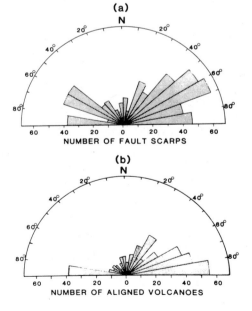

three or more volcanoes, spaced less than 1,500 m apart, was considered to be a significant lineament. By this method, 104 volcano lineaments were identified in the study area, with an average of 4.5 volcanoes per lineament.

Closely spaced volcanoes are preferentially aligned east-west (Fig. 170b). The N60E trend in fault scarps is also apparent in the orientation of aligned volcanoes. A third, but less developed volcano alignment direction is oriented N30-40E, parallel to the regional N35E trend of volcanoes. This direction of volcano alignments is generally confined to the Parícutin and Jorullo areas . . . .

Discussion

No attempt was made to classify each volcano by type, but it is clear that stratovolcanoes and shields belong to population A and cinder cones comprise population B. Stratovolcanoes and shields are generally more deeply eroded than cinder cones in the MGVF [see p. 246-248, 275-277]. The statistical difference in height between populations A and B can not be attributed to erosion, since volcanoes in A are proportionally larger than the volcanoes in B, and yet are more deeply eroded. Instead, variation between the two populations is attributed to constructional differences.

The mean height of population B volcanoes is 95 m. This corresponds well to the mean height of cinder cones in the field [100 m: see p. 256], and the mean height of cinder cones in general[132,194,201,202]. Population A has a mean height of 510 m, which is considerably less than the mean height of strato-volcanoes in continental arc settings, 1,500 m[203,204]. It is suggested that population A includes polygenetic cinder cones (cones built by more than one period of activity), as well as stratovolcanoes and shields. Although this sort of activity has not been observed directly in the MGVF, it does occur elsewhere. Cerro Negro volcano, Nicaragua (12°31'N, 86°44'W) has the morphometric characteristics of a cinder cone, yet is a small polygenetic volcano (275 m in height), having been intermittently active for over 100 years[190,205].

The distribution of topographic and volcanic lineaments in the field does not strongly reflect the N35E trend in volcano distribution, as previously suggested[132,197]. Although the intersection of the N60W and N60E fault zones may in part account for the abundance of volcanoes in the Parícutin area, the entire N35E trend cannot be attributed to this intersection.

The location and orientation of N60E-trending lineaments in the NE and the N60W-trending lineaments in the NW suggest that these are fault zones. East-west-trending faults are common and are often subsidiary to the major fault zones. Volcano alignments, which are most commonly oriented east-west, are interpreted to be associated with dilatation. This suggests that the maximum horizontal principal component of stress is oriented east-west and is not parallel to the direction of plate convergence.

Cinder Cone Clustering

Connor (1990)

Abstract

Cinder cone distributions have most often been characterized using univariate statistics. Here a new technique to volcano distribution studies, cluster analysis, is applied to cinder cone distribution in the central MVB. A total of 1,016 cinder cones are identified over an area of approximately 60,000 km^2. Application of cluster analysis reveals structure in cinder cone distribution. Using a search radius parameter of 16 km, 75% of the cinder cones within the central MVB are found within eight clusters of 45-159 cones each. These clusters are each 2,000 to 5,000 km^2 in area. Only 22 cones are found within clusters of three or fewer cinder cones, indicating that clustering is a pervasive phenomenon. Some petro-logic variation is evident among clusters; low-Mg alkaline cinder cones are found within a single cluster, 360-400 km from the trench. Application of alignment analysis techniques . . . demonstrates that cinder cone alignments have common orientations on a regional scale within three clusters, all located in the southernmost part of the Michoacán-Guanajuato Volcanic Field [MGVF] in the western portion of the study area. These alignments consist of tens of cinder cones, are 20-50 km long, and are all oriented with azimuths of 020°-040°, parallel to the direction of plate convergence. High-Mg lavas, which last fractionated at pressures in excess of 8 kilobars, are only found associated with these alignments, indicating that magma transport is significantly enhanced in these areas. Although local alignments of three to six cinder cones occur within mapped fault zones that transect the area, regional cinder cone alignment patterns, and the distribution of clusters themselves, do not appear to be affected by the presence of these fault zones.

Erosion Studies

Segerstrom (1950)

Biographical information about Kenneth Segerstrom can be found on p. 140. This report, based on fieldwork conducted in 1946-47, is Segerstrom's major study of erosion and redeposition at Parícutin. It was the first article in the classic 4-volume set on Parícutin published as U.S. Geological Survey Bulletin 965. Here we reprint significant parts of this important study. Segerstrom returned to Parícutin at later intervals and published three additional articles that updated erosional processes at the new volcano. We have also reprinted sections from two of those papers.

Introduction

The lava and ash from Parícutin, together with the heavy summer rains in the area and the winds of its long dry season, have combined to produce unusually favorable conditions for observing erosional and depositional processes in action. The lava flows have blocked drainage, the ash falls have provided a cover of nearly uniform material to be eroded, and the rain and wind have been active eroding agents. Because the terrain has been denuded of vegetation and the ash is unconsolidated, many erosive processes that are ordinarily slow have been accelerated to a degree that permits ready observation.

The purpose of the present investigation has been to study qualitatively, and wherever possible, quantitatively, the erosional processes that are taking place in the area[206]. It is hoped that the results, though derived for the most part from the detailed study of only one volcanic area (Jorullo and Ceboruco were briefly visited), can be applied in some degree to an understanding of what happened in areas where earlier eruptions occurred unobserved by man.

Several large-scale topographic maps were made to show the nature of erosion and redeposition in small areas covered by ash, and a small-scale map was made for the flood plain near Los Reyes [26 km WNW of the new volcano], where storm waters have deposited much ash on fertile farm lands. Measurements were made of the ash beds and their total thickness, and many samples of the ash were screened to determine the size distribution. Measurements were made of floods, and samples were taken of flood waters. The infiltration rate of water into ash was measured at four places, and at one place the rate was compared with the rate of infiltration into the underlying soil. Sections of pre-existing ash and soils were measured and sampled. Slope gradients were measured to determine the limits of the several types of erosion and deposition, and observations were made of blocking and other drainage changes, erosion-cycle stages, denudation and revegetation, agriculture, weather and climate, fresh ash fall, landslides and cave-ins, faulting of ash beds by moving lava, and erosion at Jorullo and Ceboruco volcanoes.

Regional Setting

Physiography and Topography
Before the Eruption

Parícutin's cone lies in an east-trending gap about 15 km wide between two high mountain masses: Cerros de Angahuan (3,292 m) to the north and the Cerros de Tancítaro (3,842 m) to the south. The altitude of the lowest part of the gap, location of the now-destroyed town of San Juan Parangaricutiro, is about 2,240 m. Parícutin broke out 5 km south of this valley, part way up the long northern slope of Cerros de Tancítaro, at an altitude of approximately 2,385 m.

In times past, isolated basins were typical of this region, but the drainage has recently been integrated and is largely tributary to the Río de Itzícuaro on the west or the Río de Cupatitzio on the east. (La

Lagunita, before it was covered by lava, was a small undrained basin about 2 km east of the new cone.) The watershed divide that separates the river systems is 6 km east of the volcano. Before the Parícutin lava field dammed part of the drainage, most of the area between the two mountain masses drained toward the west into tributaries of the Río de Itzícuaro. Both the Río de Itzícuaro and the Río de Cupatitzio are headwaters of a much larger stream, the Río de Talpalcatepec, which in turn is tributary to the Río de Las Balsas, the largest river in Mexico [Fig. 140].

. . . . .

All degrees of dissection may be seen on Parícutin's neighboring cinder cones, of which no less than 35 may be counted [within a 13 km radius]. The sides of Loma Larga [2 km west of the new volcano], except below its breached crater, were ungullied before the Parícutin eruption, whereas the flanks of Canicjuata [1 km NW], Corucjuata [3 km NW], and Cuaxándaran [5 km WNW] are deeply dissected by pre-existing *barrancas* [ravines]. All the cones except Cutzato [6 km ENE] and a few others have breached craters, which were probably formed, not by erosion, but by lava movements beneath the cones that caused parts of their flanks to move outward and the corresponding sections of crater rim to slump. Only one of the cones, Cutzato, has an easily recognized satellite cone, but some of the others may have had them too. Their bases, for the most part, probably are deeply buried by lava flows, and observations of Parícutin show that a satellite may well be buried by lava that subsequently issues from the same volcano.

The lava flows result in a cliff-and-bench topography on the long slopes that rise from San Juan Parangaricutiro toward Cerros de Tancítaro on the south and Cerros de Angahuan on the north. The height of the cliffs that rim the benches ranges from 15 to 75 m; most commonly they are 15-20 m high. The cliffs are not vertical, though steep, in general dipping about 45°. The benches have gentle slopes, usually only 2-3°, and their width varies greatly between 100 and 1,000 m. The benches and the bottom of the San Juan Parangaricutiro valley were cultivated fields before the eruption; the cliffs, cinder cones, and upper slopes of Cerros de Tancítaro and Cerros de Angahuan were heavily wooded.

. . . . .

Climate and Vegetation

Uruapan [21½ km SE of the new volcano] is the only station near the volcano where meteorological data have been recorded for any length of time, and even there observations were discontinued in 1947. The data recorded at Los Reyes [26 km WNW] are complete only for the year 1946; those at Peribán [19 km WNW] give only the rainfall for 1943. At the beginning of July 1946, I installed rain gages at Cuezeño [the observatory built by the U.S. Committee for the Study of Parícutin], 5½ km north of the volcano, and at [the "Upper Casita" observatory on Cerro de] Jarátiro, 1½ km north of the volcano. Temperatures were recorded twice a day at Cuezeño, and approximate mean daily temperatures were inferred from these readings. In October 1946, R.E. Wilcox took hourly readings, and on November 9, he began taking daily readings of maximum and minimum temperatures. At Jarátiro no temperatures were recorded.

In Tables 20 and 21 the results of precipitation measurements at Cuezeño and Jarátiro for the period July 1946 through June 1947, together with approximate mean temperatures at Cuezeño, are compared with data supplied by the Servicio Meteorológico Mexicano for Uruapan and Los Reyes.

As shown in Table 20, February, March, and April are the driest months of the year in the area, whereas June, July, August, and September are the wettest. For half the year, from December through May, the rainfall amounts to only 12-14% of the annual total. During the dry season, periods of 2-4 weeks pass between rains, and less than 24 hours after a rain the surface of the ground is usually dry. At the end of May the rainy season begins, and from then until the end of October showers fall nearly every afternoon.

At Cuezeño from July 1 to October 30, 1946, there were only 8 days without rain and only 2 occasions when the ground surface was even briefly dry. Practically all this precipitation occurred between 1:00 and 6:00 p.m. in the form of hard local showers, about 90% of the rain falling within 30-60 minutes. Nearly always the showers fell over small areas, but they were so numerous that the whole volcano area usually received a good daily wetting. Frequently, however, a heavy fall at Jarátiro was not matched by an equally heavy fall at Cuezeño, and vice versa. From July through October 1946, the most intense storms recorded at Cuezeño were the following: July 18, 46 mm in 2 hours; July 20, 32 mm in 1 hour; August 5, 18 mm in 25 minutes; September 12, 40 mm in 1 hour; September 16, 27 mm in 50 minutes.

. . . . .

As shown in the Table 21, the warmest months of the year in the area are April and May, at the end of the long dry season and immediately preceding the long summer rains. Neither the daily nor the seasonal temperature changes are great.

The prevailing upper winds are from the western quadrants during the dry season, April being the month of strongest winds, and from the eastern quadrants during the rainy season. Any variation of upper winds from this pattern is notable. During the summer, or rainy season, surface winds from the west are quite common at Cuezeño in the morning, but they shift in the afternoon. During the winter, and even more during the spring, the surface ash is almost always dry and is easily picked up by the prevailing west wind; the days dawn clear, but by 9 or 10 o'clock in the morning the freshening wind, often with no great velocity, picks up the finest grains of ash and creates a dust storm that lasts until the wind dies down again at 4 or 5 o'clock in the afternoon.

. . . . .

The following section titled "Geology" begins with a brief summary of the work of Howel Williams[207] on the basement rocks of the Parícutin area. Segerstrom them describes in detail a 29.45-m stratigraphic sequence of pre-Parícutin ashes exposed in a recent stream cut. The sequence contains at least six paleosols. These portions are not reproduced here.

Agricultural Economics

During the first year of the eruption no land was cultivated where ash was more than 10 cm thick, but since then most of the land formerly cultivated and carrying ash thicknesses between 10 and 25 cm has again been utilized. Of the area of 233 km² included within the 25-cm isopach [see inside-front-cover map], about 11 km², or 5%, was actually under cultivation at the time of the eruption. Of this 11 km², 5 km² has been covered by lava and is therefore lost to cultivation, but about 50 km² of the land covered with 25 cm or more of ash is potentially arable in the future, even though most of it was not cultivated at the time of the eruption.

Various attempts were being made in 1946 to reclaim a part of this arable land . . . . Tractors and bulldozers could push the ash from some of the land in the area, but disposal of the material removed would be a problem where the ash mantle is thick. Indeed, the problem of eventually reclaiming this land for agriculture may be one not so much of stripping as of deposition, since the areas that were cultivated before February 20, 1943, were the flats and the gentle slopes where redeposition by water, rather than erosion, is now taking place. The question is: How much admixture of pre-eruption soil is necessary for plant growth? Plowing deeper than 25 cm in an effort to accomplish admixture of old soil with the ash had not been attempted by 1947.

Damage to the sugarcane fields near Los Reyes by the Parícutin eruption has been threefold: (1) Fields were covered with ash carried down by the great 1943 floods. (2) The floods destroyed the irrigation system by breaking dams and silting up canals. (3) During 1944 a plague of cane-boring insects destroyed most of the crop, another insect that is the natural enemy of this borer having been exterminated by the ash fall.

Inundation of the flood plain near Los Reyes had occurred periodically before 1943, depositing thin beds of reddish or yellowish silt over the cane fields. Thick beds of ash laid down by the 1943 floods were

Table 20. Total monthly precipitation in Parícutin area (mm).

Station	Altitude (meters)	July	Aug.	Sept.	Oct.	Nov.	Dec.	Jan.	Feb.	Mar.	Apr.	May	June	Annual
July 1946–June 1947														
Cuezeño	2,250	288	326	327	217	51	23	67	0	2	2	103	301	[1] 1,707
Jarátiro	2,400	[2] 273	[3] 346	400	217	165	53	78	0	7	----	168	476	[4] 2,183
Los Reyes	1,300	201	194	152	69	2	0	48	----	----	----	31	182	[5]
Uruapan	1,600	216	333	274	129	10	Trace	49	[6]	[6]	[6]	[6]	[6]	[5]
Mean, July 1931–June 1940														
Uruapan	1,600	389	397	327	153	30	31	22	18	4	4	26	236	1,638

[1] Total for July 1946–June 1947.
[2] Total for 27 days.
[3] Total for 28 days.
[4] Total excludes April and 7 days in July and August.
[5] Data incomplete.
[6] Discontinued.

Table 21. Mean monthly temperature in Parícutin area[1] (°C).

Station	Altitude (meters)	July	Aug.	Sept.	Oct.	Nov.	Dec.	Jan.	Feb.	Mar.	Apr.	May	June	Annual
July 1946–June 1947														
Cuezeño [2]	2,250	17	17	16	18	15	13	13	15	17	18	18	17	16
Los Reyes	1,300	24	24	24	22	21	19	18	20	21	24	----	----	[3]
Mean, July 1931–June 1940														
Uruapan	1,600	20	20	20	20	18	17	17	18	20	21	22	21	19.5

[1] No readings taken at Jarátiro.
[2] Data are approximate.
[3] Data incomplete.

not easily plowed under. According to Juan Castañeda Díaz of the Delegación de Promoción Ejidal at Los Reyes, growers who supplied the two large sugar factories in the district reported 184,000 pesos [$38,000 in 1943 U.S. dollars] damage from silting by river-deposited ash for the period January 1943 to May 1944, with 887 hectares affected [8.9 km²].

The first large flood in 1943 destroyed all the dams on the Río de Itzícuaro: El Huatarillo, El Aguacate, and Presa de Los Limones [see Fig. 179]. None of the dams built subsequently has lasted more than 5 months; the first or second flood of the season carried away, not only several brush-and-earth diversion dams in 1944 and 1945, but the new 125,000-peso [$26,000 U.S.] Presa de Los Limones in 1946. The sugarcane fields silted over by ash-laden floods in 1943 lay between El Huatarillo and Los Limones dam sites and along the lower course of the Río de Xundan. The San Juan lava flow of 1944 blocked off half the Río de Itzícuaro watershed, and since then no more cultivated land has been silted over; the floodwaters that destroyed Presa de Los Limones were derived chiefly from the Río de Xundan. More than half the silted land had been returned to cultivation by 1944, but even in 1946 fields were still being reclaimed.

For the period January 1944 to May 1945 growers on the Los Reyes flood plain reported a loss of 80 to 90% of zafra (cut of sugarcane) because of the destruction brought about by the plague of cane-boring insects. A total of 1,263 hectares [12.6 km²] was affected, and the damage amounted to 746,000 pesos [$155,000 U.S.], whereas before 1943 the cane-boring insects destroyed an average of only 5% of each cut. Because of the importance of sugar in the Mexican economy, a Presidential decree dated August 20, 1945, allocated 1,425,000 pesos [$300,000 U.S.] from the public funds to aid the Los Reyes producers. For the next cut the loss was reduced to 15 or 20%.

. . . . .

Outside the devastated and semi-devastated area enclosed by the 25-cm isopach [see inside-front-cover map], the ash fall has been beneficial to agriculture. In the town of Corupo [10½ km NNE of the new volcano], where the original ash thickness was 10 cm and no original crops were harvested in 1943, the corn yield is said to be better now than before. Near Los Reyes [26 km WNW] the cultivation of some fruits, especially mangoes and guayabas, has been more successful since 1943 than for several years before the eruption, apparently because the falling ash killed a species of destructive fruit fly. Moreover, ash

has probably served as a mulch for much of the soil in the region.

About 4,500 head of cattle (mostly work oxen), 550 horses, and some dozens of sheep and goats died as a result of breathing ash from Parícutin. The loss in domestic animals is estimated at 1,000,000 pesos [$205,000 U.S.], according to Arias Portillo. Wild animals fled the region in the face of the destructive ash falls of 1943, but since the decline in ash-emitting activity they have been returning and domestic animals have been brought back to the devastated zone. The grazing animals browse on deciduous trees such as the crab apple, and hay and silage are brought from outside the area to feed the horses.

Effect of Eruption on Ground-Water Flow

The effect of the Parícutin eruption on local ground water appears to have been sevenfold: (1) Some of the old springs have dried up, possibly as a result of earth tremors associated with the eruption. (2) Many of the old springs have been silted up with ash. (3) Lowering of the water table by channel deepening subsequent to the eruption has caused some springs to become dry. (4) The permeability of the ash mantle, by reducing evaporation losses, has made more water available to some springs. (5) A perched water table has been formed above the contact between the permeable ash and the less permeable underlying soil and even to some extent above fine beds within the ash mantle itself. (6) Great volumes of flood water that have percolated into the Parícutin lava field are a potential supply for springs at lower levels. (7) The flood sediments redeposited on the floors of the principal *barrancas* have in places reduced the surface flow in permanent streams.

1. Since the first day of the eruption, reports of spring failure or at least a marked decrease in spring flow have been frequent, although about half the springs within a radius of 10 km from the volcano have shown no marked change in flow. Arias-Portillo[103] reports that a spring called Ojo de Teporícuaro has dried up, and it is said that some of the springs on the south side of Cerros de Tancítaro have shown such a decrease in flow since 1943 that the spring-supplied public laundry of the village of Tancítaro [25 km SW of the new volcano] can no longer be used during the dry season. Celedonio Gutiérrez states that as recently as the period July-August 1946 a large spring at Los Conejos [the resettlement village, now called San Juan Nuevo, 15 km SE of the new volcano] dried up within 6 weeks

and has since remained dry. Formerly its large volume had remained nearly constant during periods of both rain and drought. The numerous springs that emerge from beneath a lava flow in Uruapan to form the Río de Cupatitzio have continued the slow decrease in volume first noticed after 1935; in 1946 they were yielding about 87% of their earlier volume.

2. Of the springs that were destroyed after the eruption by ash silting, a few have been cleaned out; others, such as the one reported to be at the north base of Cerro de Curupichu [4 km ENE of the new volcano], still are buried by ash. Every now and then continued ash fall causes a temporary clogging of the spring-fed pipe lines that supply the towns of Angahuan and Zacán.

3. Before the eruption, Ojo de Pomacuarán, a well 2 m in diameter and 1.7 m deep, was an important source of water in the *arroyo* just west of the SW-base triangulation station [located at Cerro Cocjarao, 800 m SW of the base of the new volcano]. It is about 3 m from the channel of the *arroyo*, which has been deepened by 0.7 m since the eruption. Before 1943 the well always contained 10-15 cm of water, but it has since become dry; apparently the deeper channel has drained the water supply from the well. . . .

4. Three of the most important springs of the region, those that supply the Pantzingo sawmill and the towns of Angahuan and Zacán, are at the outlets of old craters. The flow from all these springs has increased somewhat since 1943, apparently because the ash mantle has reduced the loss by evaporation of the water that does not escape as surface runoff.

5. Where new gullies have stripped the Parícutin mantle down to the resistant surface of the underlying soil, water often trickles out from the ash exposed in the banks. Where gullies are cut not only through the ash but deeply into the weathered pre-existing material, damp zones and seeps occur along the contact. Thus the old surface produces a perched water table. The presence of still higher water tables is indicated by moist and even dripping zones at the contacts between beds of very fine ash overlain by coarse ash.

6. The four strong springs of Sipicha rise in a meadow near the *barranca* that descends from the lower end of the Parícutin lava field and passes between the towns of Zirosto and Barranca Seca. The combined flow from these springs totals about 8 m³/min and does not change appreciably with the seasons. It is said that many years ago the volume was about the same, but that for several years before the volcano erupted it was much less. A year after the birth of Parícutin, according to local inhabitants, the volume suddenly increased. It is possible that part of the lava-absorbed flood waters may find their outlet in these springs.

7. Although several streams west of the cone that had been intermittent before the eruption are now permanent, wide fluctuations in the surface flow of several permanent streams have been observed. In September 1946, for example, when it was not carrying flood waters, Barranca de Tiripan [4-5 km NW of the new volcano] was observed to carry about half the volume that it carried in February of the same year . . . . Apparently the overloaded floods had meanwhile deposited a permeable bed of sediments on the stream floor, causing much of the subsequent flow to be underground.

. . . . .

Eruptive Products

Cinder Cone

The cone has formed by successive layers of pyroclastic material and has an outer slope of 31-33°. The throat of the explosive vent is composed of coarse agglomerate, which probably occurs only around the eruptive tubes themselves. Within the base of the cone there is undoubtedly some massive lava, which probably does not extend very far up into the cone structure.

The size of the fragments deposited on the sides of the cone varies during different periods of eruption and even on different sides and at different elevations on the cone during the same period, depending partly on the size of the material being ejected, partly on the positions and inclinations of the frequently shifting explosive vents, and partly on the distribution of landslides. On October 15, 1946, for example, long narrow landslides or fans of lapilli extended almost from the top to the bottom of the west slope of the cone. The particles were round and nearly all about 2 cm in diameter, although a few scattered scoriaceous fragments up to 10 cm across were present. The fans averaged about 4 m in width, with spaces or grooves between them about 7 cm wide and 10-15 cm deep. The grooves contained many loose, irregularly shaped blocks of scoriae averaging 8 cm in length, although some were 15 cm long.

. . . . .

On the same day, a large section of the SW side of the cone had no landslides. There the surface was of unsorted material like that in the floors of the grooves farther west and north. On either side of this section were lapilli fans about 4-6 m wide, but some of the areas between them were as much as three times this width . . . . Arrangements of lapilli fans, scoria terraces, scoria cones, and surfaces of unsorted material on the sides of Parícutin are therefore as changeable as the eruptive activity. Rills and mudflows on the cone are fleeting and uncommon. They are produced when an eruption of fine material is followed immediately by a heavy rain.

. . . . .

Lava Flows

In general there is a striking contrast between the south and north borders of Parícutin's lava field. The steep slopes to the south favor the formation of narrow troughs at the edge of the lava, whereas the gentle slopes to the north result in broad lake beds.

In the steeply sloping areas to the south the following cycle of events is repeated: (1) A new lava flow leaves a V-shaped trough between its side and the adjacent hillside. (2) The trough is nearly filled by ash washed down from the hill slope. (3) A new gully forms alongside the lava and cuts through the ash down into the pre-existing soil. (4) A succeeding lava flow follows the new gully, fills it to overflowing, and, piling higher, forms a new undrained trough between it and the hillside, thus initiating a new cycle. Two factors influence the formation of these lava-side gullies: the permeability of the lava and the gradient of the trough along the lava border.

The borders of the lava flows from Parícutin are still very permeable for the most part. On September 16, 1946, during a violent storm, I saw two streams join just before reaching the border of the lava and completely disappear within it. They were each about 1 m wide and 10 cm deep, and their surface flow was at the rate of 1.7 m/sec. Despite their large volume, they entered the lava without ponding. Moreover, much larger streams were observed to enter the lava after each heavy rain, although not without being briefly impounded. The high permeability of the lava from Parícutin is temporary, however; probably the interstices are gradually being filled by the material suspended in the floods that enter the lava. At the base of Cerro de Nuréndiro, 1 km south of the volcano, the decreasing permeability of the lava is so effective in raising the water table that even in the middle of the dry season the marginal ash is boggy at the mouths of the principal gullies.

. . . . .

Although still much too permeable to stop the flow of water, the lava may slow it during floods. Ponds of storm water formed at the lava borders never last more than 2 or 3 hours except when the silt deposited in depressions makes surfaces impervious enough to hold shallow bodies of water, which gradually disappear chiefly by evaporation. Such depressions are very narrow, few are more than 100 m long, and their orientation is roughly parallel to the border of the lava.

. . . . .

In 1943 and early 1944, before the lava flows were very extensive, some ash was removed from the area by streams now blocked by lava. By filling most of the San Juan valley, lava flows from Parícutin have blocked the drainage of about 40% (nearly 100 km^2) of the terrain that is covered by ash to a depth of more than 25 cm. Fifty percent (about 60 km^2) of the terrain that is mantled by ash more than 50 cm deep is lava-blocked. (These figures include the 22 km^2 actually covered by the lava.) All this area formerly drained into the Río de Itzícuaro, which flows to the west; thus it is unlikely that the Río de Itzícuaro will again inundate Los Reyes as it did in 1943 when practically none of the tributaries in its watershed were blocked.

Ash

Physical Properties

In common with other products of the eruption, the ash from Parícutin is basaltic andesite. It consists of glass shards, pieces of vesicular and dense lava of lithoidal texture, and crystals of olivine. No marked variation in composition and mineral content of the ash, either regular or erratic, has been observed. [Although this is a defensible statement for field studies ending in March 1947, the petrologic studies by Wilcox (reprinted on p. 324-346) show that magma composition and mineralogy changed systematically throughout the life of Parícutin volcano.] Its color ranges from light greenish brown to dark gray or nearly black, the frothy particles generally being lighter-colored than the denser material. Individual particles are irregular in shape and range from fine dust to fragments several centimeters in diameter. Medium-sized particles of ash from Parícutin range from 0.15 to 0.4 mm in diameter. Ash particles of more than 4 mm in diameter, called lapilli according to the classification of pyroclastic material set up by Wentworth and Williams[208], are not uncommon, nor are particles of clay-size fineness (less than 1/256 mm)[209]. Average samples of ash not reworked by wind or water are poorly sorted; a single sample may contain particles ranging from lapilli down to clay size.

. . . . .

Distribution, Thickness, and Bedding

Most of the ash mantle was deposited during the first year of the eruption (1943), at the same time that the greater part of the cone was built. One of the heaviest ash falls occurred from March 19 to April 17, when the prevailing upper winds, as usual in the dry season, were from the west. Arnoldo Pfeiffer measured the fall on April 9 at Morelia, 125 km east of the volcano, and found it to be 112 g/m² for the 24-hour period. On the same day Ariel Hernández-Velasco[210] found the 24-hour fall at Mexico City, 320 km east of the volcano, to amount to 136 mg/m². However, very heavy falls occurred in the opposite quadrant during the entire summer or rainy season of 1943, when the prevailing winds were from the east. The map on the inside front cover shows how the curves of equal ash depth [isopachs] are elongated to the east and to the west—particularly to the west because the east winds typical of the rainy season deposited a thicker layer to the west of the volcano than was laid down to the east by the west winds of the dry season. The old cones of the region are sway-backed because of this seasonal change in deposition.

The results of ash-thickness measurements made during July, August, and September 1946 are shown on the [inside-front-cover map] . . . . The measurement at Casita Canicjuata, on the crest of a ridge nearly buried by lava [1 km NW of the new volcano], showed by far the greatest thickness of ash. In August 1946 a pit 516 cm deep was dug there, but because of cave-ins the underlying soil was not reached. In September an exceptionally heavy rain caused water to be impounded between the lava and the ridge until it overflowed and, in the one storm, cut a deep gully into the ridge crest (Fig. 171). A pit was dug in the bottom of this gully, but cave-ins again discouraged digging at a depth of only 747 cm. Subsequent storms had by October 11 deepened the gully until it exposed the pre-volcano surface and the thickness of the entire ash mantle could be measured;

Fig. 171. New barranca, or ravine, eroded into the Casita Canicjuata ridge, 1 km NW of Parícutin volcano, during a single storm.

it amounted to 1,083 cm. Finally, on October 18, a new lava flow began cascading through the cut and down the west slope of the ridge, burying the greatest thickness of Parícutin ash mantle thus far exposed (Fig. 172).

With the aid of the isopach map [inside front cover] and a few measurements of ash thickness made beyond the outer (25-cm) isopach, the volume of ash from Parícutin was roughly calculated out to the inferred 1-mm isopach, which probably passes near Guadalajara, Jalisco. In Table 22 the volumes within different isopachs are given separately. The total volume of ash erupted by Parícutin probably represents 2-3 times the volume of lava extruded in

Fig. 172. Midslope in the Casita Canicjuata barranca (Fig. 171) on the day that a new lava flow started through it.

Table 22. Volume of ash erupted by Parícutin, for areas within different isopachs.

Area	Size of area (square kilometers)	Volume of ash (cubic kilometers)[1]	Weight of ash (millions of metric tons)
Parícutin cone		0.125	[2] 300
Within 12-meter isopach	2.7	.16	[3] 400
Within 5-meter isopach	7.5	.20	[3] 500
Within 1-meter isopach	61	.30	[4] 800
Within 50-centimeter isopach	119	.34	[4] 900
Within 25-centimeter isopach	233	.38	[4] 1,000
Within 8-centimeter isopach [5] (Los Reyes)	750	.45	[4] 1,150
Within 1-centimeter isopach [5] (Jiquilpan)	6,000	.60	[4] 1,550
Within 1-millimeter isopach [5] (Guadalajara)	60,000	.65	[4] 1,700

[1] All volumes include that of the cone itself.
[2] Based on specific gravity of 2.4 and stated to nearest 50 million.
[3] Based on specific gravity of 2.5.
[4] Based on specific gravity of 2.6.
[5] Assumed to be confocal to the 25-centimeter isopach.

the form of surface flows. The volume of ash and lava together is probably slightly less than 1 km³.

. . . . .

A detailed description of a 3.91-m section of ash from a pit on Jarátiro ridge follows, along with tables and graphs of grain-size characteristics of ashes from various levels as determined from sieve analyses. These sections are not reproduced here.

Effect of Ash on Vegetation

The ash killed most of the trees and buried all the smaller plants within a radius of several kilometers from the volcano, the fine dust sealing the pores of the leaves and preventing respiration and transpiration. The ash adhered most readily to sticky surfaces, such as the needles of conifers; moreover, the weight of the ash cover broke the tree tops and branches. The resinous pines were, therefore, destroyed over a larger area than the oaks, and the more brittle, stiff old pines were killed before the limber young trees, which were arched by the ash weight but could shake off the load in a wind. According to Arias-Portillo[103], the damage in general has been directly proportional to the kind and number of "accessories" a plant possesses, such as hair, down or nap, and thorns, as well as the stickiness of the substances secreted. The least-damaged agricultural crops were wheat and barley, but regardless of the nature of the plant the destruction was complete where the ash cover was thick.

The following section, titled "Porosity and Permeability of the Ash Mantle", has not been reproduced. Segerstrom carried out field measurements of the rate of downward migration of water through ash sequences and the un-derlying soil at four locations. The data were presented in tabular and graphical form. These experiments revealed that porosity and permeability were mainly controlled by grain size and sorting of the ash layers, the arrangement of layers in a vertical sequence, and the development of fine-grained surface crusts. Fine-grained layers within an ash sequence created relatively impermeable horizons above which water perched and flowed laterally, and fine-grained surface crusts effectively "waterproofed" the deposit, promoting runoff. This section also described centimeter-scale bubble mounds on the ash surface, which formed as rising, moist air was trapped beneath the fine-grained surface crust and bulged it upwards into a small dome.

Mass Movement

Creep

Where ash-mantled slopes are steeper than 32°, which is near the angle of repose of the ash from Parícutin, the trees still standing lean downhill because of the creeping ash mantle . . . .

On hillsides, such as those on Cerro de Canicjuata [1 km NW of the new volcano], whose slopes were originally about 32° (now lessened in places to 25° or steepened to as much as 40° by landsliding and other causes), the trees stood upright before the eruption. Now they lean. The present, loose, more permeable ash mantle is creeping downhill, owing to the lack of

Fig. 173. Tilted forest on north slope of Cerro de Canicjuata, showing the effect of downslope creep of the ash blanket. About 1 km NW of the new volcano.

compaction and lubrication by water. As shown in Fig. 173, the leaning on the north slope of Cerro de Canicjuata varies with the topography from a few degrees from the vertical, as on spurs where drainage is adequate, to 90° or more in swales where poor drainage has resulted in a higher degree of saturation of the mantle with a consequent increase in the rate of creep.

Landslides

Creep is a manifestation of slow landsliding, whereas a landslide in the usual sense is the sudden descent of a large volume of material from a steep slope, leaving a concave wall at the head of the slide . . . . Landslides have stripped the entire ash mantle from large areas on *barranca* sides south of Zirosto [8½ km NW of the new volcano], and left headwalls of ash that stand a meter above the stripped surfaces. Closer to the cone, where the ash is several meters thick, landslides are controlled in part by bedding. On the north side of Cerro de Canicjuata, for example, it is common for only the top meter of material above a more resistant bed to be removed by landsliding.

That water greatly influences the landslide process can be seen, just after heavy rains, when new landslides occur in places where the toe of a slope is cut by channel erosion and where the mantle uphill from the channel is waterlogged, as indicated by mudflows that ooze from the landslide material.

The trees that remain standing on landslide slopes, even though influenced by slow creep, often serve as bastions of defense against a rapid down slip. This is shown by the presence of a cusp that joins concave headwalls on either side of a tree that has served to hold the mantle in place.

Mudflows

Mudflow development in ash from Parícutin results where a coarse-grained or comparatively well-sorted, permeable surface layer absorbs enough water to give it fluidity or lubrication, provided that: (1) fine-grained or more poorly sorted, relatively less permeable material below is unable to absorb water at the rate it falls on the surface, and (2) the slope angle is great enough to cause movement at the degree of fluidity attained by the surface layer. The flow is in narrow lobes, rather than in broad sheets.

Individual mudflows in the ash range in width from a few millimeters to 2-3 m. Fan-like groups of overlapping flows may be as much as 20 m wide; indeed, most of the alluvial fans that have formed in the area near the cone consist of mudflow material. The thickness of individual flows ranges from one-fifth to one-half the width . . . .

In fluidity, the mudflows represent an intermediate stage between creep and sheet wash. A mudflow moves down slope until its fluidity is so reduced by loss of water into the underlying permeable ash mantle that the front of the flow comes to a stop. The up-slope part of the flow behind this front continues, but owing to the progressively decreasing gradient as the material moves over the frontal lobe, successive fronts form that stop in receding waves until the movement halts completely. If the flow is relatively large, however, the material behind the stopped fronts may bypass or overrun the fore part (Fig. 174), depending largely on the supply of water available for lubrication.

. . . . .

Fig. 174. Mudflows between Cerro de Jarátiro and Parícutin volcano. The longest flow is about 50 cm wide.

Mudflow velocities vary greatly. The frontal lobe of a flow 6 cm wide was observed to travel 4 m in 6 seconds on a 11° slope [66 cm/s]. A minute later, the lobe came to a halt at a 7° slope, flowing the last 65 cm in 8 seconds [8 cm/s]. Another mudflow, 1-2 m wide, pushed its front over the last 15 m of its course in 90 seconds on a 5-7° slope [17 cm/s]. The maximum speed may be considered to approach that of water running down an equal slope.

The height of the column of relatively clear water remaining after the sediment had settled in a cylin-

Fig. 175. Angular blocks left by stepwise caving along the bank of Arroyo de Corucjuata, 2½ km NW of the new volcano. Small field case for scale.

rical flask of mudflow material, collected while flowing, varied from 5 to 19% of the total height of the sample. Samples taken from silt-laden floods in the upper part of the Río de Itzícuaro contained similar proportions of water, but the minimum water content was somewhat greater, amounting to 11% by volume. As one such flood receded, mud ridgelets 2-3 mm high and parallel to the direction of stream flow were left along the banks, together with pockets of ooze at the edges of the stream. However, the sediment-laden stream showed none of the other characteristics of mudflows, such as lobe formation, apparently because its great volume was confined and kept rapidly flowing between narrow channel walls and there was a relatively small absorption of water into the stream bed. . . .

Stream-Bank Cave-Ins

The banks of *arroyos* frequently cave because of the removal of material from their bases by flowing streams. If the stream flows at the very base of a nearly vertical or slightly overhanging bank, cutting into and undermining the base, a slice breaks off that leaves an indentation, concave toward the stream, whose walls are nearly vertical. At times, however, the central part of the slice remains standing in the form of a rectangular block . . . . Narrow segments break off on either side of such central blocks along fractures that develop normal to the direction of the stream. The central blocks may later collapse, or the cracks may be filled with water-deposited ash.

Where the base of a bank consists of an angle-of-repose slope of loose material and the stream, unable to undermine the bank directly, only carries off some of this loose material, a complete concave slice does not form. Instead, oblique tension cracks form stepwise along the top edge of the bank as if concave slices were about to form. Apparently the full concave slice cannot develop because the material at the bottom of the bank supports the central part of the slice, and only small oblique blocks break off from the leading edge of the incipient slice (Fig. 175).

Off the west bank of Arroyo de Ticuiro [5½ km NNW of the new volcano], shortly after a hard rain, arcuate slices fell for 15 minutes, one after another, along a course 200 m long. The caved slices averaged 1.2 m in length, 16 cm in thickness, and about 80 cm in height. The indentations left by these cave-ins were nearly perfect arcs, and their great number gave the bank a scalloped appearance [Fig. 176]. In some places curved cracks formed on top of the bank and outlined incipient cave-ins, some of which broke off a few minutes after the cracks formed.

Water Erosion

Raindrop Splash and Sheet Erosion

Sheet flow occurs when the rate of precipitation exceeds the coincident infiltration capacity of the mantle, and sheet erosion occurs when the excess produces an erosive force greater than the initial resistance of the mantle to erosion[211]. Initial resistance in the Parícutin mantle

Fig. 176. A series of stream-bank cave-in "scallops" on the lava-side Arroyo de Ticuiro, 5½ km NNW of the new volcano, as seen from above. Scallops average 1.2 m in length.

depends on the degree and length of slope and on particle size and compactness, which affect both the amount of ash splashed by rain impact and the amount that flows in a sheet of water. Small rock-capped pedestals left after raindrops have splashed away the ash around their bases show the degree of erosion effected by impact. During heavy rainstorms distant slopes lose their drab, gray appearance briefly and shine in the dull light like lakes or ponds because of the presence of a thin sheet of water. If the sun breaks through the clouds and strikes a place where sheet flow is occurring, the water gleams white like snow or hail. On surfaces of low slope gradient, where sheet flow is quite slow, water piles up to a depth of 5 mm or more.

According to the experimentally determined infiltration rates . . . sheet flow—given sufficient slope gradient—would start during the rainy season at Cuezeño [5½ km north of the new volcano], for example, when the rate of precipitation exceeded 16 mm in the first 10 minutes of a storm, 22 mm in the first 20 minutes, or 28 mm in the first half hour. The high degree of turbidity caused by raindrop impact, however, would reduce the permeability from the experimentally determined figures (turbidity was eliminated in the tests), so that sheet flow would actually start at a lower rate of precipitation. Sheet flow occurred on the ash at Cuezeño when approximately 10 mm of rain had fallen in the first 10 minutes of a storm, and it is possible that under special conditions an even lower rate of precipitation might produce sheet flow there.

The vegetation cover is of prime importance in reducing both the amount of splash and the intensity of sheet erosion farther down slope. By reducing raindrop impact, a protective cover also reduces turbidity and its effect on surface permeability. In the devastated zone around Parícutin, not only was all the vegetation killed, but the humus and all the biologic structures that play an important role in resistance to erosion were deeply buried (except trees, which under these conditions help to start rills).

Sheet erosion, including the antecedent effects of raindrop splashes, gives way in part to channel erosion where the slope steepens, but it continues on the interfluves [flat surfaces] between the channels all the way down to where the grade is so much reduced that deposition takes place . . . .

Rill Erosion and Mudflows

Rill-channel formation, like sheet erosion, depends on the length and steepness of a slope and the resistance of the surface to erosion. The point on a slope where rill erosion begins may become progressively higher, for some rills erode headward with each heavy rain. Where downcutting is greatest, headward retreat is most effective; hence the thickness of the easily cut ash mantle influences the distance across a crest between opposite rill heads. . . .

The rill-channel heads along the rims of craters mantled with 2-5 m of ash from Parícutin were spaced about 5/m in 1946. Each of these rill heads was an amphitheater about 7 cm wide with nearly vertical head walls about 2 cm high. At a distance of 7 m downslope from the crests of the deeply ash-mantled cones, cross grading and coalescing of the rill channels had resulted in channels ½-2 m deep, about 1 m wide, and with nearly vertical walls. The interfluves were from 1-2 m wide at this distance downslope; at distances greater than 50 m from the crests interfluve widths averaged about 3 m.

The point on a slope where rill erosion ceases and redeposition begins is not entirely related to a particular slope gradient. If the rills carry capacity loads of sediment, this point may be merely where the slope gradient decreases. Rills often dissect their own miniature fans when they carry light loads. At the bases of a large number of angle-of-repose slopes, deposition by the rills was observed in 1946 to begin at a gradient of 6-11°.

It is something of an anomaly that trees should actually initiate erosion rather than retard it, yet this happens in the Parícutin mantle where dead trunks are still standing. The rain water that runs down these trunks excavates small moats around them (Fig. 177), and the overflow initiates rill erosion if the slope gradient is sufficient to carry the water away. For example, on a long slope with a 27° gradient a dead pine 35 cm in diameter had a moat 20 cm wide around it; the overflow formed a rill channel that was 20 cm wide and 13 cm deep at a point 1 m downslope from the tree. On another slope having the same gradient a dead oak 1 m in diameter formed a rill channel 1.3 m wide and 1.5 m deep at a point 1 m downslope. Many tree moats become partly filled by material carried downslope by sheet flow and deposited against the uphill face of the trunk, and slope steepening around the edge of a moat not uncommonly causes headward retreat of the rill channel to a point far upslope from the tree.

The coarse ash on the sides of the cone and on the nearby slopes of Cerro de Canicjuata usually is too permeable to initiate surface runoff. Runoff occurs even there, however, during brief periods after the eruption of exceptionally fine ash, but the water in the rills is soon so reduced by percolation that only

Fig. 177. Rill erosion initiated in the Parícutin area by rain water running down a tree trunk.

enough remains to lubricate mass movement in the form of mudflows . . . .

On September 18, 1946, a new eruption had deposited 1.5-2 mm of fine ash over the cone. A heavy fall of rain followed, and on the south slumped block of the cone the newly deposited surface was cut by rill channels about 5 cm wide and 5 cm deep, spaced at 2-m intervals, each terminating in a small mudflow. In places the accumulation of rain water around scattered bombs and in their impact craters had much the same effect as that caused by dead trees. Rill mudflows were initiated that were larger than those resulting only from sheet flow on an undisturbed surface . . . . The usual eruption of coarse material the next day obliterated all traces of water erosion on the cone.

. . . . .

Channel Erosion

The Erosion Cycle

It is convenient, in explaining the nature of the channeling that is taking place near Parícutin, to consider the existence of a small-scale and comparatively rapid dissection cycle in the ash mantle itself. The long cycle through which the pre-existing land forms have been passing, except for the direct effect of the old topography on erosion of the ash, is best disregarded for this purpose.

The initial stage, early youth, is described above under "rill erosion" . . . . In the next stage, youth, stream piracy is common and the uniformity of the parallel drainage pattern is destroyed by complex branching. Noticeable changes in stream coalescence and bifurcation take place with each heavy rain. Except for the material removed uniformly by sheet erosion, however, the interfluves still represent the

original surface on the aerially deposited ash.

In the third stage, maturity, the interfluves on the slopes of old cones, for example, have lost their smooth constructional surface. In plan they look like oak leaves, the stems of which point uphill (Fig. 178), with observed widths varying from as much as 1.5 m to 30 cm and less. The rills formed seek constantly to spill off to one side or the other where the interfluves are narrow, tending to erode them still more deeply.

The fourth, or late mature, stage of dissection is characterized by increasingly narrow interfluves as more and more triangular facets, broad-based downhill and pointed uphill, become isolated from each other at the narrow parts of the oak-leaf pattern . . . . These facets are a miniature manifestation of the planezes described by Cotton[212].

The fifth stage, old age, is reached when the facets or planezes are removed by lateral cutting, accompanied by lowering of the sharp interfluve crests and development of wide barrancas in the ash.

The sixth or final stage might be considered the period when the last remnants of the ash mantle are being stripped from the slopes.

The rate at which these successive stages develop depends largely on: (1) the length and gradient of the slope, (2) the thickness and particle size of the ash mantle, (3) the density and distribution of the tree trunks, and (4) the rate of deposition of new ash. Because of local variations in these conditions, and because of the occasional reconstruction of some surfaces by newly deposited or redeposited ash, all the stages of dissection may be observed simultaneously in the region. The thickness of the original ash mantle is of course the most important factor in determining whether the full dissection cycle will operate at any one place. Where the ash is less than a meter thick, the channels are widened so rapidly because of the erosion resistivity of the soil floors existing before the eruption that the cycle passes directly from the stage of youth to that of old age.

Properties of Channels

In cross section the channels eroded in the ash are typically box-shaped, but the ratio of width to depth is quite variable, depending in large part on the thickness of the ash mantle. A channel is much more rapidly eroded in coarse than in fine ash, and consequently its floor is generally composed of a fine-grained bed. After a channel has been widened by lateral cutting on top of a resistant bed, the floor may be breached and a step formed that migrates rapidly up the channel. The floor then continues to be eroded down through the coarse material to the next fine-grained bed, when another period of lateral cutting begins. Theoretically this process should result in a stepped-down effect along the sides of the channel, but on fairly well-graded slopes the lateral cutting is so efficient that all the steps that may have formed above are usually removed and the walls are generally nearly vertical. Along channels of very low slope gradient, however, the stepped-down effect remains in the walls because the slower-moving flood flow has a smaller lateral cutting force.

Fig. 178. Breached crater of a youthful cone SW of Parícutin, where ash is 2.5 m thick, showing "oak-leaf" faceting of interfluves on far slope. [Although not identified, this cone is probably either Cerro del Cebo or Cerro de Huachínqueran.]

The fine beds provide support for the channel walls, as the coarse ash alone would collapse, and in many places they are etched out in miniature cliffs. Vertical channel walls more than 2-3 m high are rarely formed in the mantle of ash from Parícutin. Along deeper channels they occur generally above piles of unconsolidated debris sloping downward less steeply to the bed of the stream. Very close to the cone, where fine-grained beds are few, channel walls sloping about 45° are common and vertical walls are absent or, if present, very short-lived.

Although the ratio of width to depth in different channels is quite variable, the channels larger than rill size that are eroded entirely in ash are ordinarily about as wide as they are deep. If, however, the channel reaches the underlying soil, which is more resistant to erosion than any bed of ash, this ratio becomes quite different, although the section is still box-like . . . . At many such places no further downcutting is accomplished, and the channel becomes wider and wider until it coalesces with its nearest neighbor, resulting in the complete stripping away of the interfluve. After the channel has become several times as wide as it is deep, a narrow inner channel may be eroded into the pre-existing soil, producing a box-within-a-box profile . . . .

Ultimately the new channels become tributary to the main stream channels that were present before the eruption. About half these old channels are blocked and diverted by lava flows and therefore are filled with redeposited ash where they debouch into lava-impounded lakes, but most of the others empty into the deep, narrow gorges of the Río de Itzícuaro and its tributaries.

. . . . .

Rate of Channel Cutting

The fastest rate of channel cutting observed in the ash-covered terrain around Parícutin was in a *barranca* that cut across the Casita Canicjuata ridge [1½ km NW of the new volcano] on September 20, 1946. During a storm on that day, lava-impounded flood waters were suddenly released across the ridge and eroded a *barranca* several hundred meters long, 7-8 m wide, and as much as 5.8 m deep. On October 11 this *barranca* was 20 m wide and as much as 12.4 m deep. It had been cut, not only through the immensely thick ash mantle [1,083 cm: see p. 289], but as much as 1.6 m into the underlying soil (Fig. 171). Blocks up to 0.8 m long were washed from the Parícutin lava field and transported through the new channel as far as 175 m beyond the base of the Casita Canicjuata ridge. By October 18, when a new lava flow quickly filled the gully and effectively stopped further cutting, the width of the *barranca* had reached 30 m (Fig. 172).

The *barranca* just described was exceptional, but many other examples could be cited of relatively rapid channel cutting in the ash mantle during heavy storms. The few permanent streams present in the region have eroded into the pre-existing soils and underlying rocks, in which channel cutting is very slow compared to the rate of cutting in the new ash.

Storm Discharge and
Transportation of Sediment

The brief torrential rains that occur almost daily from June to October in the Parícutin region swell the many *arroyos* of all sizes and the few small permanent streams up to and in excess of their channel capacities. Storm waters become laden to the limit of their carrying power with easily removed ash particles and larger objects such as boulders and logs.

. . . . .

The finest stream sediments contain much higher percentages of silt-and-clay sizes than the finest ash beds sampled and . . . the coarsest stream sediments contain much lower percentages of gravel than the coarsest ash beds. [Grain-size characteristics of stream sediments from the Parícutin area are also shown graphically, but not reproduced here.] Within the area studied, channel-fill deposits contain a much greater proportion of medium-sized particles than most of the aerially deposited ash, because the finest fractions are carried downstream and out of the region.

About half the water-borne solids—virtually all those not trapped by the Parícutin lava field—are eventually carried by the westward-flowing Río de Itzícuaro through a series of narrow gorges to the broad flood plain at Los Reyes, 20 km west of the lower (NW) end of the lava field and 900 m lower in altitude [Fig. 179]. About two-thirds of the way down, the river passes through Imbarácuaro, the narrowest and deepest of all its gorges. At a place where the Imbarácuaro gorge is 22 m deep and only 6-9 m wide, a plainly seen high-water mark is 12 m above the bottom. A plane-table map was made to determine the area of the channel section up to the high-water mark, and the velocity of the permanent stream with its normal volume of water was measured by means of floating sticks. The velocity was found to be 70 m/min and the discharge 1.6 m³/sec.

The Río de Itzícuaro hydroelectric plant of the Compañía Eléctrica Morelia is near the bottom of a wider, cliff-lined gorge about 3 km below Imbarácuaro and 21 km WNW of the new volcano [Fig. 179: Planta de Itzícuaro]. The floor of the plant is 4.8 m above the bed of the river, which has an average gradient of 0.8°. Before the volcano erupted, no floods reached the floor of the plant, but on June 12, 1943, flood waters laden with ash from the new volcano were 40 cm deep inside the plant; on August 11, more than 1 m deep; and on August 29, 2.7 m deep. Estimates of flood velocity on August 29 made by plant employees varied from 15 to 24 km/hr. The lower figure, which is equivalent to about 4 m/sec—a figure certainly not too high—with an estimated

cross-section area of 240 m² gives a flood discharge of approximately 950 m³/sec, of which 80% was reported to be sediment. Following the largest flood, the turbines were not uncovered until September 5; then, on September 6, a new flood rose to a height of 1.3 m above the floor, depositing sediment that closed the plant until September 28. During the succeeding dry season, engineers straightened the river channel somewhat and made it 6 m wider for distances of 150 m both upstream and downstream, and the floods of 1944-46 did no damage to the plant.

Because no large tributaries enter the Río de Itzícuaro between Imbarácuaro and the hydroelectric plant, nearly all this flood of 950 m³/sec must have passed through the Imbarácuaro gorge, where the area of the channel section up to the high-water mark is approximately 95 m². At the time of the peak flow on August 29, 1943, the velocity of this closely confined current through the gorge must therefore have been 10 m/sec.

At the Planta de San Pedro, a hydroelectric plant of the Compañía Eléctrica Morelia on the normally spring-fed Río de Cupatitzio in Uruapan [21 km SE of the new volcano], 14 floods were recorded for 1943, 35 for 1944, 42 for 1945, and 27 for 1946. Only a very few floods in the Río de Cupatitzio occurred on the same days as floods on the Río de Itzícuaro, illustrating the characteristically local nature of the rains that fall in the region. The floods of July 3 and September 18, 1943, at Planta de San Pedro were extraordinarily large, both reaching a peak discharge of about 150 m³/sec, but the records show that only six floods reached discharges as high as 100 m³/sec in 1944, one in 1945, and one in 1946. The normal discharge of the Río de Cupatitzio used to range from 8.8 to 9 m³/sec . . . .

Transportation of Boulders and Logs

Close examination of streams that move over ash from Parícutin at normal rates of flow, when there is little suspended matter, reveals that at places where the water flows over large boulders the under edge of the comparatively clear current is dark-colored. Unsuspended particles apparently roll and bounce along the channel floor. The same effect, though on a much larger scale, is produced during flood stage, when large boulders are similarly transported. For example, a flood with a velocity of 2.4 m/sec, carrying 58% suspended solids, was seen to be moving rocks as large as 70 cm in diameter at a stream gradient of 0.8°. The rocks moved at the same speed as the largest floating logs accompanying them. The depth of the current was at least 1 m, which was

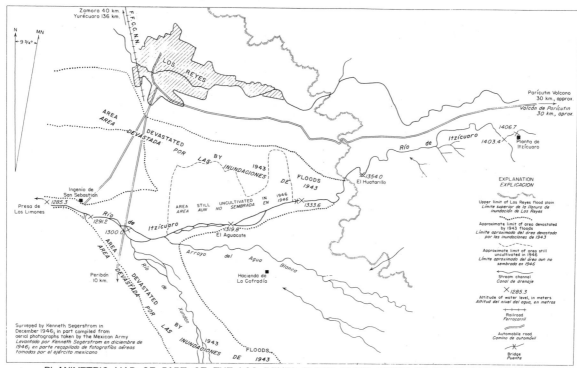

PLANIMETRIC MAP OF PART OF THE LOS REYES FLOOD PLAIN, STATE OF MICHOACAN, MEXICO
MAPA PLANIMETRICO DE UNA PARTE DE LA LLANURA DE INUNDACION DE LOS REYES, ESTADO DE MICHOACAN

Fig. 179. Planimetric map of part of the Los Reyes flood plain.

greater than the diameter of the largest boulders, yet the rocks appeared to move mostly at the surface. The specific gravity of the silt-laden flood water was found to be 1.93, and that of the boulders was probably between 2.65 and 2.95. The illusion of actually floating must have been created by the frequent saltation, or bobbing to the surface, of the boulders as they rolled and slid along the uneven channel floor.

Redeposition by Water

Water-deposited sediments may be divided into two separate groups: (1) those dropped on the slopes and stream beds as the velocity decreases, and (2) those deposited from standing water. Group 1 includes alluvial fans, flood plains (including unusually large alluvial fans), channel fills, and sheet deposits (including terraces on hillsides). Group 2 includes lake deposits of all kinds.

Alluvial Fans

Cone-shaped alluvial deposits form at the bases of all the hills in the area mantled by ash from Parícutin. The size and slope gradient of a fan depend on: (1)

the length, gradient, and number of tributaries of the gully above it; (2) the microtopography of the slope upon which the fan is built; (3) the presence of mudflows; (4) the intensity of storms; (5) the obstruction of the toe of the fan by lava or adjacent slopes; and (6) the length of time since the fan started to form. In the ash from Parícutin, channels with a gradient of 27° and a length of about 100 m build fans 5-10 m long; with a length of about 200 m, they build fans 10-20 m long. Still longer gullies have fans in proportion to their length and the number of channels tributary to them; Arroyo de Corucjuata is about 2.5 km long above its alluvial fan, which is 600 m long [and located about 4 km NW of the new volcano]. The average slope gradient of the head of a fan in the ash from Parícutin is about 7° and, for the toe, about 4.5°. Extremes are 11°, as on mudflow fans near the volcano, and 2.7°, as on the large alluvial fan at the mouth of Arroyo de Corucjuata.

Fan deposits are sorted and, except for mudflows, cross-bedded. Lapilli washed out of coarse beds are concentrated at the heads of many fans near the volcano. Gullies eroded into the underlying rock have supplied floodwaters with boulders sometimes 2 m in

297

diameter, which are deposited on the surfaces of fans built largely of ash from Parícutin . . . .

Flood Plains

The floodwaters of the Río de Itzícuaro spread out, lose their velocity, and drop their load of solids on the Los Reyes flood plain. Fig. 179 shows the part of the plain that was most affected by floods before the lava blocked the drainage at Huirambosta [5 km NW of the new volcano]. With a watershed including all the area within the 50-cm isopach [see inside-front-cover map], the Río de Itzícuaro was supplied with enormous quantities of ash in 1943, and much of the sediment carried by the floodwaters was redeposited in an area of about 4 km² between El Huatarillo, Presa de Los Limones, and the town of Los Reyes [Fig. 179]. The gradient of the river bed decreases from 1° in the gorge above El Huatarillo to 0.5° on the plain at El Aguacate.

Evidence of the large volume of ash-charged silt brought down by the Río de Itzícuaro was still visible in 1946, when about 1 km² of flood plain just north of El Aguacate was covered to an average depth of ½ m by redeposited ash from Parícutin. A maximum thickness of 1.5 m was seen in the river bank, and throughout the 4 km² area originally covered by the flood-borne ash, thicknesses of 10-20 cm were common. A stone boundary fence 60 cm high, extending for hundreds of meters across the plain, was buried to the top by ash deposited on the upstream side. If the average thickness of the ash redeposited on the Los Reyes flood plain by the Río de Itzícuaro during the 1943 floods (which have not been repeated since) was 20 cm over an area of 4 km², the total amount of material redeposited would be 800,000 m³, which is about 0.2% of the total volume of ash initially deposited over the Río de Itzícuaro drainage basin above El Huatarillo, or the equivalent of removing 3 mm of ash from the surface of this area.

Equally large quantities of ash were redeposited by the Río de Xundan, which drains a large terrain over which ash ranging in thickness from a few centimeters to ½ m had originally been deposited. Descending the NW flank of Cerros de Tancítaro, the Río de Xundan passes through the town of Peribán [19 km WNW of the new volcano] and joins the Río de Itzícuaro between El Aguacate and Presa de Los Limones [Fig. 179]. Over a distance of 8.3 km between Peribán and its mouth, where the average gradient of Río de Xundan is 1.5°, the river silted over about 4 km² of fields. The greatest concentration of large boulders dropped by this river occurs on the outskirts of Peribán, where boulders up to 2 m in diameter are not uncommon. Many of those that litter the broad area where the Río de Xundan and the Río de Itzícuaro join were brought down by the ash-laden floods of 1943; boulders 20-30 cm in diameter are common there.

Smaller flood-plain deposits cover the numerous little benches at the north base of Cerros de Tancítaro and the south base of Cerros de Angahuan, where they range in width from about 200 m to 1 km. Situated at the mouths of steeply inclined gullies, these gently sloping areas receive the heavily laden floods that are funneled out of the mountains. A great reduction in slope and a sudden release from confinement in a gorge immediately cause the torrents to drop the coarsest material, but the rest is carried across and down to lower levels . . . .

Channel Fills

Streams flowing over the easily eroded ash in the area of high relief west of the cone are quickly loaded to capacity. The sediment load is not dropped immediately, when the water reaches the gentler gradients of the Río de Itzícuaro and its principal tributaries, because the streams are confined in narrow gorges and maintain their velocity. At places of channel broadening, however, the heavily charged torrents lose substantial parts of their load as the velocity decreases and especially as the volume of the flood lessens. The resultant channel filling, followed by considerable re-excavation during the next storm, produces narrow inner channels bordered by lenses of ash as much as 5 m thick. These deposits reduce the volume of floods a channel can contain, and overflowing of the banks may occur during heavy storms.

. . . . .

Sheet Deposits

Rock fences built to separate pastures and fields in the region are usually about 1 m high by 75 cm thick. Where they cross hillsides normal to the slope, they act as check dams and impound the ash that is sheet-eroded from above. Ash has commonly piled to the tops of these fences on the uphill side, but the surface of the terraces thus formed is not horizontal and varies in slope from 2.7°, on hillsides sloping from 4.5-9°, to 4° on hillsides whose slope is about 18°. The continuity of these terraces is broken at intervals by gullies that have opened incomplete passageways through the fences.

Against the uphill sides of standing trees and large boulders, the sheet-deposited ash is well bedded in many places. Such deposits are cone-shaped and rimmed by sharp edges eroded by runoff that has passed by on either side.

Lakes Impounded by Lava

The deposits formed in lakes impounded by lava . . . are very thick on the south edge of the lava field; furthermore, the thickness increases rapidly during each rainy season. Plane-table surveys made 18 months apart in this area show that the level of the cove at the mouth of the *arroyo* 400 m south of the Cocjarao triangulation station [itself about 800 m SW of the base of the new volcano] rose 40 m (to 2,550 m above sea level) and that the level of the ash fill at the edge of the lava ½ km farther east rose 25 m (to 2,529 m). Sections through these deposits would show that the ash is interbedded with 3-4 layers of lava, each about 4 m thick, and with alluvial fans, sheet deposits, and mudflows.

North of the lava field, where the slopes are less steep and the aerially deposited ash is thinner, the lacustrine deposits increase in thickness much more slowly. Three years after the San Juan flow blocked the drainage on the north side of the San Juan valley, the edge of the lava had not yet been buried by redeposited ash except just north of Cerro de Curupichu [4 km ENE of the new volcano], where the lava thickness is unusually small (only about 3 m). At Chórotiro [5½ km NE], a pole fence 1 m high that had been built in the spring of 1946 was half buried by redeposited ash by autumn of the same year.

Since the ash mantle has been removed and some of the underlying soil has been eroded in *arroyo* channels north of the lava field, an admixture of ash and ocher-colored earlier soil characterizes the redeposited material at Chórotiro and Llano Grande [5 km north] and in other lake beds. As the water recedes, a film of transported soil is left at some places, introducing into the stratigraphic column thin zones of highly weathered material that might someday be falsely interpreted as soil horizons. Fine material, both weathered and unweathered, brought in by successive floods cannot escape as it does where the floods continue downstream; thus all the load is deposited, and the average grain size of the lacustrine deposits is finer than that of channel fills. [Plots are also presented showing grain-size characteristics of these lacustrine sediments, but not reproduced here.] An ordinary lake deposit in the Parícutin region contained 55% very fine grained sand-size material whereas a typical channel fill contained only 8%.

Lakes Impounded by Alluvial Dams

The flood-plain deposit at Llano de Teruto [4 km SSE of the new volcano] . . . has sealed off the eastern part of the plain and produced a basin. Inasmuch as the floodwaters do not drain out through permeable lava at this place, a large body of water forms and remains there for months during and following the rainy season. On September 23, 1946, this irregular body of water was 300-500 m long by 200 m wide. In the memory of the oldest inhabitants, no lake had ever formed at this place before the Parícutin eruption. If the alluvial dam at Teruto is not washed away, the sediments deposited in the lake will eventually cover an area about 1 km long by ½ km wide to the level of the dam, which was 5 m higher than the lake in 1946.

Crater Lakes

Of the 35 or more craters in an area of 85 km² around Parícutin [see inside-front-cover map], only Cutzato, Tzintzungo, and Curitzerán contain bodies of water, and those only at times. Several small craters north of Jarátiro, now buried by lava from Parícutin, formerly held water also. The shape of the area covered by water or mud flats and the position of this area with respect to the sides of the crater are significant in determining the bedding of the material being deposited.

The elliptical floor of Cutzato [6 km ENE of the new volcano] is 150-200 m wide. On July 12, 1946, the shore of an intermittent lake in this crater was 90 m out from the foot of a slope 300 m long leading to the highest point on the rim and only 30 m out from a slope 100 m long leading to a lower summit, showing that a greater volume of inclined fan deposits had originated from the longer slope . . . . A 5-m rise in the level of the lake would cover the entire crater floor with water, although such a large volume of water will probably never accumulate from runoff on such a small watershed. Nevertheless, as the horizontal lake deposits thicken and the overlapping fan deposits encroach on them from all sides, an extremely complex cross bedding is being developed.

In the crater of Tzintzungo [6 km NE], which is about 100 m wide at the bottom, water stands against the side that has a rim height of only 6 m. On July 23, 1946, the pond was crescent-shaped, for material derived from a slope beneath a summit 40 m high on the crater rim had built a fan part way across the floor. The crater is the source of the spring that emerges from the SE base of Tzintzungo and formerly supplied the town of San Juan Parangaricutiro. (Many

Fig. 180. Stone fence on Llano Grande nearly buried by wind-drifted ash from Parícutin.

of the villages in Michoacán depend on the springs of cinder cones for their water supply.)

The NE crater of Curitzerán [7½ km NNW] is about 130 m in diameter at the bottom, and the SE rim is only 1.5 m above its floor. Stripping of the ash cover on the inner crater slopes will probably cause the floor to be silted up enough to permit the water to drain out. The lowest part of the crater floor is pear-shaped, with the large end opposite the lowest saddle, the small end near the next-lowest saddle, and the indentations at the foot of two high points on the crater rim.

Water does not stand very long on the floors of these craters. In one of the Jarátiro craters [see Fig. 108], since innundated by lava, the area of a pond about 25 m wide was observed to shrink by half within 3 hours. All the other craters are much farther from Parícutin, and because the ash that was originally deposited over them was finer-grained than at Jarátiro, the lake beds in them are probably less permeable.

Wind Erosion and Redeposition

During the dry-season months (December to May), from about 10 o'clock in the morning to about 5 o'clock in the afternoon when the daily winds die down, the atmosphere is so full of ash that local visibility is at times reduced to less than 100 m. Most of the ash is picked up by winds from the western quadrant, but some is lifted by random whirlwinds or dust devils and a little by winds from the eastern quadrant.

The winnowing action of the dust devils causes enough sorting of the surface ash to leave visible tracks. In places these tracks consist of winnowed ash in zones from 20 cm to 2 m wide, but the smallest

dust devils leave only a series of discontinuous circular segments along a wavy line of winnowed surface only 1 cm wide.

. . . . .

The almost complete lack of rain from December to May, together with the strong winds that blow during these months, accounts principally for the building of ripples and dunes. Minor factors are the surficial drying of rain-soaked ash on slopes adjacent to hot lava flows and the direct deposition from an eruption of dry, new ash over the damp surface of old ash. The ripples and dunes range from a few millimeters to 2-3 m in amplitude. They have gently sloping windward faces and steep leeward slopes. Ash particles are blown up the gentle slopes and dropped over the crests.

. . . . .

Many of the largest dunes in the ash are formed as a result of, or are modified by, obstructions that cause a reduction in wind velocity and a change in its direction. Stone fences oriented across the path of the east and west winds in wide expanses of open country like that at Llano Grande [5 km north of the new volcano] are nearly buried by wind-deposited ash (Fig. 180). Little, if any, asymmetry is visible in these deposits, as they are formed by winds from both directions . . . .

Although wind direction and intensity are of great importance in initially distributing the ash erupted from the volcano, wind erosion and redeposition occur on a minor scale as compared with water erosion and redeposition. In the mountainous terrain surrounding the volcano there are no large expanses of open country where wind action is unobstructed, although the dust storms of the dry season are impressive enough to give a false impression of the extent of wind sedimentation . . . .

Stripping of Ash Mantle

The removal of new ash from the area around the volcano is taking place in four ways: (1) by landslides, (2) by the combined effects of raindrop splash and sheet erosion, (3) by channel erosion, and (4) by deflation.

The greatest volume of material removed at any one place up to 1946 was from some of the slopes at Cocjarao, about 1 km SW of the cone, where on 70-100% slopes the entire 6-m thickness of ash has descended in landslides to the border of the Parícutin lava field. Here a maximum thickness of 40 m, including some interbedded lava, accumulated from 1944 to 1946. At the head walls of old *barrancas* on the maturely dissected cones of Corucjuata [3 km NW] and Cuaxándaran [5 km WNW], where 3 m and 1.6 m, respectively, of ash from Parícutin were originally deposited, slopes with gradients of 45° have been completely stripped. The steep sides of the deep gorges south and SE of Zirosto, where slope gradients of 45° are not uncommon, have been completely stripped by landslides of an ash mantle averaging about 1 m in thickness.

Where the ash mantle was originally deposited to a depth of 25 cm or less on old cones in the vicinity, it has been completely stripped; where the mantle was thicker, the stripping by sheet erosion varied from 70% for an original thickness of 33 cm to 33% for an original thickness of 165 cm. On these cones all the ash had been stripped off in stream channels where the ash thickness was less than 165 cm; where the mantle was thicker, the channels were as much as 2 m deep. Channels on the angle-of-repose slopes of the old cones ranged in width from 0.5-1.5 m, and the interfluves between them from 1-4 m. Assuming a mean channel width of 0.75 m and an interfluve width of 2.5 m, 100% stripping in the channels alone accounted for about a 30% removal of the entire slope mantle. If the material removed from the interfluves by sheet erosion is added to that removed in the channels, the total proportion removed from areas where the original mantle was 33 cm thick amounted to 88% and, where it was 165 cm thick, about 57%.

On slopes of lower gradient and shorter length, the rate of removal is much slower. Some slopes with a gradient of 7° were nearly free from channels in 1946, although sheet erosion had removed large volumes of ash . . . . A slope that has been stripped for most of its length may still have finger-like remnants of ash mantle extending from the crest, and redeposited ash at the bottom may extend in fingers part way up the stripped slope . . . . On 1-3° slopes up to 2 km long, erosion and deposition seem to be in balance, and the 1946 mantle was about equal in thickness to the entire original mantle.

The stripping caused by deflation on the rolling plains west of Angahuan has been of some economic importance. The old soil surface exposed on the windward sides of the hills and ridges in that area was being cultivated, but the leeward slopes were still barren in 1946 because they were covered by about 25 cm of ash from Parícutin.

Accleration of Erosion on Pre-Existing Landforms

The following factors account for drainage changes and acceleration of erosion on land forms existing before the eruption: (1) Heavier loads of sediment and larger grains have correspondingly greater cutting power in old channels. (2) Killing of vegetation destroys the protective cover. (3) Some of the rill channels easily formed in ash from Parícutin may continue to erode the old surface after the ash is stripped away. (4) A sudden release of flood waters impounded by lava from Parícutin, by alluvial fans, or in old craters can remove in a few minutes all the ash and a quantity of underlying soil that would ordinarily require many years for its removal.

. . . . .

Measurements were made of 10 consecutive *barrancas* at points about 50 m up the west side of Cerro de Cutzato [6 km ENE of the new volcano], the largest of the old cinder cones in the vicinity, where about 45 cm of ash from Parícutin was originally deposited. The *barrancas* were typically V-shaped, the living vegetation on their sides had been partly thinned out by recent landslides, and their bottoms contained bare, box-shaped inner channels that had probably been eroded since the beginning of the Parícutin eruption. By measuring the depth and width of these *barrancas*, the width of the interfluves, and the dimensions of the inner channels, it was calculated that about 30% of the top 7 m of Cutzato's surface had been removed by means of the *barrancas* (ignoring sheet erosion) before the Parícutin eruption and about 0.8% more since then. If 0.8% represents the proportion removed during three rainy seasons, then 30% at the same erosion rate would represent a lapse of 112 years since this cone was formed, which is obviously an impossibly small figure but nonetheless of some significance in indicating the acceleration of erosion on Cutzato due to ash from Parícutin.

The dissection of local land forms that took place before the eruption of Parícutin must have been similarly accelerated during brief periods following each eruption of an earlier volcano.

In the channel of the Río de Itzícuaro at Zirosto [8½ km NW], only about ½ m of deepening appears to have taken place since the eruption of Parícutin. From there on downstream, the base level of the river is so controlled by successive lava crossings that most of the recent cutting appears to have been lateral rather than vertical. This is true of most of the *barrancas* tributary to this river. As a result, many of the gorges that were formerly V-shaped have had their floors widened without a corresponding widening of the distance from rim to rim and are now steeper-sided than before. The greater steepness of the sides brings about an unstable equilibrium, which thus far has not produced much landsliding but will from time to time cause slides and a widening from rim to rim of all the principal *barrancas* in the area around Zirosto.

. . . . .

Areas south and west of Parícutin that have been denuded of vegetation and lie in the path of floods that descend from Cerros de Tancítaro show greater acceleration of erosion since 1943 than the wooded slopes of Cutzato and those along the Río de Itzícuaro. A comparison of aerial photographs taken before and after the eruption reveals that several large *barrancas* now exist where there were none before. The largest of these is west of the Cocjarao triangulation station [itself 800 m SW of the base of the new volcano]. It was about 10 m deep in 1946, and the bottom 3.5 m was eroded in soil and rubbly lava that existed before the eruption. At the south base of Cerro de San Pedro [5½ km SW], a drain that was only a shallow swale before 1943 was 5 m deep and 2 m wide where it was eroded down into pre-existing soil and tuffs. Where it passes over an old lava flow, it was 2 m deep and 5 m wide.

According to Celedonio Gutiérrez, the approach to Cerros de Tancítaro from the north was formerly without obstacles. At present, however, the way is made difficult not only by several new *arroyos* but also by the post-eruption cutting of box-shaped inner channels in the old V-shaped *barrancas*. Such obstacles can be crossed only by following the channel to a lava crossing, which is always a place of widening and decreased depth. The steepness of the slopes and the enormous volume of ash being stripped from them have combined to give great force to the floods that rush down the old *barrancas* of Tancítaro and cause much landsliding of rubbly lava, which is deposited as boulders on fans hundreds of meters beyond the base of the mountain. South of the summit of Cerros de Tancítaro, the thickness of aerially deposited ash from Parícutin is not great enough to accelerate erosion to any appreciable extent.

Before 1943, the youthful cone of Loma Larga [2 km west of the new volcano] was undissected except at the breached west side. Since the eruption, 5 m of ash have been deposited over Loma Larga, and by 1946 this mantle was deeply dissected, although not yet to the underlying soil. The concentration of runoff in ash *barrancas* for some length of time will even-

tually cause deepening to the old surface and dissection of the pre-existing soil on the sides of this cone, and these scars will remain after the Parícutin mantle has been completely stripped away.

The release of flood waters impounded by lava from Parícutin has produced large-scale channel cutting into the underlying soil, tuffs, and agglomerate at the east edge of the new lava field. The process of integration of several isolated basins near Curínguaro [2½ km east] by overflow from one small basin to the next was accompanied by the cutting of *barrancas* to a depth of 5-6 m into the old soil on the bases of hills where there were no channels before 1943. Another example of this process is the carving out of the Casita Canicjuata *barranca* [Fig. 171]. A great rush of floodwaters down Arroyo de Corucjuata in 1944 formed a boulder-strewn alluvial fan as much as 6 m thick, completely blocking the course formerly followed by this stream. A new channel from 9 to 12 m deep, half of which was eroded in pre-existing material, was carved for a distance of about 1 km before the stream finally returned to its old course.

An unbreached crater of the Curitzerán cinder cones [7½ km NNW] lacked in 1946 only 1.5 m of further ash redeposition on its floor for runoff to flow over the lowest part of the rim. This will probably be accomplished by a continued stripping of the ash from the inner walls of the crater. The result will be the breaching of one side, an obvious acceleration of erosion.

Scientists from many different disciplines designed studies at Parícutin to evaluate how the effects of the eruption changed with the passage of years. As treated elsewhere in this book, such time-series studies were used to document the evolution of the human communities that were affected by the volcano and to monitor the return of vegetation, birds, and animals to the devastated area. Segerstrom also revisited the Parícutin area at later times to monitor modifications of the cinder cone, the continued erosion and redeposition of the surrounding ash blanket, and changes in the local hydrology. The preceding article (Segerstrom, 1950) was based on fieldwork conducted in 1946-47. After an absence of 10 years, Segerstrom returned to the Parícutin area in February 1957; additional work was conducted in December 1960 and June 1965. These three visits are described in Segerstrom (1960; 1961; and 1966). Here we reproduce portions of the 1960 and 1966 papers.

Segerstrom (1960)

Erosion and Redeposition of Ash

In 1957 the Parícutin area was still very active geologically, even though eruptive activity had ceased, for enormous volumes of material were being transported from higher to lower places at a rapid rate. Changes that have taken place in the ash mantle and in the local hydrological regimen are discussed below.

Mass Movement

Mass movements and flows of ash, lapilli, and scoriae have affected the appearance of the cone to a marked degree. Long narrow flows of loose lapilli extend like fingers down the sides of the cone (Fig. 181). The crater is ringed with roughly concentric fissures and faults, some of which reach the rim of the crater and some the outer slope of the cone . . . .

On February 24, 1957, the rim of the cone had prominent eastern and western summits; the western summit was 5-10 m higher than the eastern one. The crater contained two partly filled depressions, trending northeastward. These depressions were about 50 m below the SW, or lower, saddle between the two high points of the rim. Almost continuous rock slides on the inner side of the steep western summit were observed on the day of a visit to the crater. The western rim was very narrow compared with the eastern rim, and a reduction in height of the west peak to less than that of the east peak seemed imminent. By way of comparison, on April 29, 1952, 2 months after eruptive activity of the volcano had ceased, the east and west peaks were approximately equal in height, and the bottom of the crater was some 30-40 m below the two saddles[118]. The slides and resulting fluctuation in relative heights of the summits were plainly caused by subsidence of the crater.

. . . . .

Drainage Changes

Before the 1943 eruption, two intermittent streams, headwaters of the Río de Itzícuaro, drained all the area that was later covered by lava and ash [Fig. 182]. Arroyo Principal drained the area to the east and north and passed westward along the south edge of the town of San Juan Parangaricutiro. Arroyo de Parícutin drained the area to the south and passed northward along the east edge of the town of Parícutin, joining the Arroyo Principal in Huirambosta. La Lagunita, a large area of interior drainage was between the two *arroyos* NE of where Parícutin volcano later erupted. [These pre-eruption drainage patterns are shown as dotted lines on Fig. 182.]

By February 1957, in spite of the extrusion of new lava flows between 1946 and 1952, large areas north and west of the volcano that were closed basins in 1946 now drained into the west-flowing Río de Itzícuaro during flash floods. Most of the remaining area of blocked drainage south and east of the volcano, distributed between the Arroyo Principal, La Lagunita, and Arroyo de Parícutin watersheds before the eruption and into several separate undrained basins in 1946, formed a single connected system in 1957. This system drained into an ephermeral lake at Tipacua, 5 km NE of the cone, at the edge of the lava field.

The following description of the new "Arroyo Principal" encompasses the upper reaches of the stream northward around the east edge of the lava field to its undrained outlet NE of Parícutin volcano. The main headwaters of the stream are on the mountain slopes that descend eastward from the lofty peak of Cerro de Tancítaro (3,842 m). The altitude of the alluvial-fill deposit at Tipacua is about 2,310 m.

At Llano de Yahuácuaro, near the south end of Fig. 182, the small headwaters stream formerly disappeared in a sinkhole at the edge of a pre-historic but unweathered lava flow from Cerro Prieto, farther

Fig. 181. Long narrow flows of loose lapilli (light color) extending like fingers down the NW side of Parícutin cone, 5 years after the eruption ended.

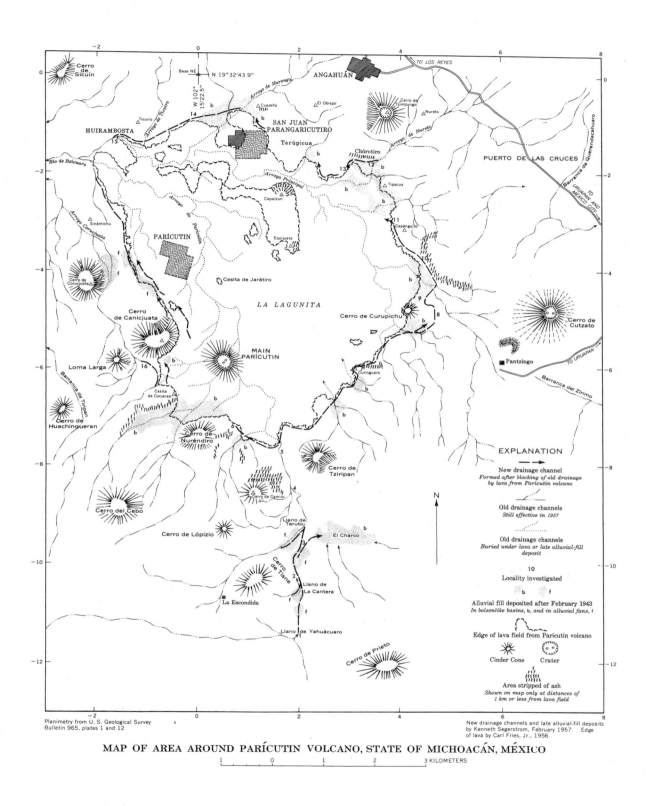

MAP OF AREA AROUND PARÍCUTIN VOLCANO, STATE OF MICHOACÁN, MÉXICO

Fig. 182. Pre- and post-eruption drainage map for the area surrounding Parícutin volcano.

to the SE. Apparently this underground outlet became choked by ash from Parícutin, so that the plain was periodically flooded. In 1954 Victor Soto, a local farmer, dug a drainage ditch 20 m long, 2 m wide, and as much as 1.3 m deep, at the north edge of the benchlike plain (loc. 1, Fig. 182). [All following location numbers are also shown on Fig. 182.] A low brush diversion dam was built across the plain to protect corn fields from flooding and to conduct flood waters to the drainage ditch. The drainage operation was so successful that in 1957 a new cut about 20 m wide and 20 m deep had been eroded in steeply sloping terrain for a distance of 350 m northward from the ditch in old ash along the west edge of the lava from Cerro Prieto.

At the mouth of this enormous cut an alluvial fan has formed in a place of sharply decreased slope gradient, near the south end of Llano de La Cantera. This fan nearly overlaps another fan farther north at the mouth of an old bedrock gully that emerges from Cerro de Tisne to the west.

Llano de La Cantera, formerly a small undrained basin on a topographic bench, was cultivated for many years before the eruption of Parícutin, but in 1943 or 1944 an ash-laden flash flood from the steep slopes of Cerro de Tisne littered the fields with logs and with boulders as much as 2 m in diameter. No cultivation has been attempted since then.

The combined arroyos from the south and west are entrenched in fresh alluvium to a depth of several meters; at the north edge of the bench, where the gradient is greater, the stream plunges into a new cut 8-12 m deep and 12 m wide in old ash (loc. 2).

Farther north the gradient is less, and the arroyo has formed another alluvial fan at the south edge of the broad Llano de Teruto. This deposit nearly overlaps another similar deposit farther north, at the mouth of a large barranca that drains the steep slopes near La Escondida, toward the SW. The plain is littered with boulders and logs. El Charco, in the eastern part of the flood plain, was an intermittent lake in 1946. The lakebed was partly covered with water every rainy season from that time until 1955 or 1956, when the alluvial dam from La Escondida was by-passed and the floods from Llano de Yahuácuaro and Llano de La Cantera began to drain northward toward the lava field from Parícutin. Corn was planted and harvested in 1956 at El Charco for the first time in 10 years.

The main arroyo increases, as it passes northward across Llano de Teruto, from 7 m in width and 1.6 m

in depth (loc. 3) to 25 m in width and 15 m in depth (loc. 4) in a distance of 1.1 km. About 1 km farther north, where the gradient is greatest, the arroyo attains a width of 50 m and a maximum depth of 35 m; most of the cut is in newly exposed ash and lava from pre-historic eruptions . . . . The gradient lessens abruptly a short distance below locality 5, and the arroyo becomes shallow; then the drainage is diverted toward the NE by the lava field from Parícutin.

At this place a tributary arroyo comes in from the west, along the south edge of the lava. The branch stream heads about 1 km away, in a low saddle at the NE base of Cerro de Nuréndiro (loc. 6). In 1957 the saddle was only 2.5 m higher than the surface of a large alluvial deposit that lies at the lower end of an extensive undrained area farther west.

The combined arroyos from Teruto and Nuréndiro flow in a single channel along and near the SE edge of the lava field for several kilometers, cutting shallowly across three former areas of deposition. Between the second and third of these areas, NE of Curínguaro, the arroyo has cut a narrow gorge in bedrock; when storm waters pass through the gorge (loc. 7) the roar of sediment-laden floods can be heard as far away as Pantzingo, 3 km to the east [Fig. 182]. However, these floods are apparently of short duration, for their roar is heard for no more than 20 minutes at Pantzingo.

Near the south base of Cerro de Curupichu, the main channel swings toward the east across a third basin-fill deposit, opposite to the former drainage direction. At locality 8, where the former watershed divide was breached during a storm in 1950, the main arroyo has cut through the ash and 2.3 m of the pre-existing soil. Several distributary channels from the south disappear before reaching the divide; hence, it is evident that only a few of the floods actually crossover to the north. Inhabitants of Pantzingo stated that the floods from the south flow beyond Curupichu only 4 or 5 times a year.

About 150 m downstream from locality 8 the arroyo channel has a box-in-box cross profile; its total width is 20 m, but only the central part, about 4 m wide, had cut into pre-existing soil by 1957, to a depth of 3.3 m. Less than 100 m steeply downstream, the channel deepens to 7 m and the deep part becomes the full width of 20 m.

At the upper edge of a basin-fill deposit on the NE side of the lava field, where the gradient is less and the stream is shallow, the NW-trending channel of the arroyo is sharply diverted to the NE and then to the

NW (locs. 9 and 10) by a low brush-and-log dam 900 m long. This primitive engineering structure was built to protect a cultivated area below the dam . . . .

At the NW end of the basin-fill area (loc. 10), a ditch 50 m long, 1 m wide, and 1.5 m deep was dug along the edge of the lava field in 1953 to provide an outlet for the diverted flood waters. The artificial channel at that place has since been eroded to a width of 4 m and a maximum depth of 3 m. About 300 m farther downstream the gully attains a width of 7-8 m and a depth of 4 m.

The *arroyo* is diverted at locality 11 from its course at the edge of the lava by a rock dam 65 m long, 1.3 m wide, and 2 m in maximum height. The diverted floods pour northwestward into a low part of the adjacent lava field, where the fill deposit being laid down in 1957 over barren rock will provide fields for future cultivation.

Before it was diverted, the *arroyo* drained into the large basin-fill area of Tipacua and Chórotiro, to the north. The older fill deposit lies along the outer edge of the lava field and extends up the tributary valleys to the east and north from which most of the sedimentary material was derived.

Cultivation of this deposit was attempted at Chórotiro as early as 1946 but was unsuccessful because of flooding from Arroyo de Nureto, which comes in from the NE. Another low brush-and-log dam was built across the mouth of Arroyo de Nureto (loc. 12) to divert flood waters westward around the upper end of the basin-fill area at Chórotiro and hence southward into the topographic low of the adjacent lava field. Another dam (loc. 13) kept the floods from following the edge of the lava field to Terúpicua.

For about 1.5 km beyond Terúpicua no drainage channel existed along the edge of the lava in 1957. A very large basin-fill area at the edge of the lava near Cuezeño, to the NW, was undrained in 1946 and was filling with sediment brought down from the NE by Arroyo de Hurengo. At some time during the decade 1947-57 the Cuezeño basin overflowed (loc. 14), and a new channel was cut along the north edge of the lava field from the place of overflow westward to Arroyo de Ticuiro, which before 1946 had also cut a channel (6 m deep in 1957) along the edge of the new lava. The *arroyo* from Hurengo and Ticuiro joins the pre-eruption Arroyo Principal at locality 15.

The lava field west of Parícutin overlaps the east base of Cerro de Canicjuata. This large cinder cone stands squarely in the way of any possible *arroyo* whose development on the west side might be comparable to that of the *arroyo* on the east side of the lava field. A major drainage change occurred during the 1947 rainy season when flood waters broke over the watershed divide at the south base of Cerro de Canicjuata [loc. 16]. Drainage that was formerly northeastward into Arroyo Principal is now diverted westward into Arroyo de Corucjuata. A large new channel, 13.5 m deep in 1957, crosses the old topographic saddle where the overflow occurred.

Stripping of the Ash Mantle

Areas of complete stripping of the ash from Parícutin to lay bare the underlying soil and rocks are shown on Fig. 182, but only at distances of 1 km or less from the edge of the lava field. At greater distances these areas are so large that their representation would obscure other details on the map. The areas shown do not include the stripped channels of *arroyos*. The degree of stripping increases rapidly outward from the lava field.

. . . . .

By 1946, the ash from Parícutin was already completely stripped at the headwalls of old *barrancas* on the maturely dissected cone of Corucjuata, [3 km NW of the new volcano] near the west edge of the lava field. This stripping was greatly aided by landsliding. Some of the stripped areas at Corucjuata had enlarged and coalesced by 1957. At that time, headwall stripping had laid bare small areas of pre-existing soil and rocks on the old, maturely dissected cone of Canicjuata and larger areas on the nearby youthful cone of Loma Larga where there were no bared areas in 1946. A relatively large area on the maturely dissected Camiro cone and another on the less dissected Tzirapan cone, both near the SE edge of the lava field, were bared during the decade 1947-57. Very steep slopes east of Equijuata and north of Capatzun, both within the large lava-free island in the north part of the lava field, were also stripped during the decade.

In general, the rate of stripping of the ash mantle seems to be decelerating. This rate was much faster from 1943 to 1946, during the first 3 years of Parícutin's activity, than during the next decade. As reclamation of the region by vegetation increases, the rate of ash stripping will further decrease, and the remaining mantle will become well enough stabilized, even on many sloping areas, for development of a new soil profile.

Redeposition of the Ash by Water

The rate of deposition notably decelerated during the decade. A crater of the Curitzerán cinder cones, NW of Angahuan and a short distance outside the area of

Fig. 182, showed no raising of its floor by redeposition of ash washed down from the inner slopes. In 1946 the crater lacked only 1.5 m of further ash redeposition on its floor for runoff to flow over the lowest part of the rim [see p. 302]. In 1957 the situation was the same. Forest growth on the crater slopes had inhibited, if not stopped, erosion and redeposition at that place.

. . . . .

Ground-Water Flow

At Terúpicua, on the north edge of the lava field, a drainage channel 2.5 m wide and 80 cm deep runs directly into a wall of lava from Parícutin . . . . The lava is extremely permeable, and provides abundant underground storage space. Although percolation of water into the lava is slower at most other places, it occurs to a marked degree on all sides of the lava field. The springs of Sipicha (outside the area of Fig. 182) rise in a meadow near the pre-existing Arroyo Principal several kilometers downstream from Huirambosta, which is at the lower end of the lava field from Parícutin. The combined discharge from these springs increased from 8 m³/min in 1946 [see p. 287] to 12.6 m³/min in 1957, probably because the effectiveness of the lava field as a recharge area was greater than before. The continued ability of prehistoric lava flows from Cerro Prieto, 6 km SE of Parícutin volcano, to absorb flood waters indicates that the lava field from Parícutin will not lose its effectiveness as an aquifer for many centuries.

A well, the Ojo de Pomacuarán, supplied San Juan Viejo, the partly repopulated and rebuilt town of San Juan Parangaricutiro, in 1957. It was said that the well of Pomacuarán, about 2 km north of the town, had three times as much water in 1957 as it had before it dried up in 1943. Reports of increased flow of other springs in the region were numerous in 1957.

On the other hand, an old spring near the north base of Cerro de Curupichu [4 km ENE of the new volcano] that had been buried by ash in 1943 and exposed by erosion after 1946 was dry in 1957. The Nuréndiro spring, near the south edge of the lava field, was flowing in 1952, but in 1957 it was buried under about 15 m of redeposited ash.

Segerstrom (1966)

Parícutin still provides an advantageous natural laboratory for studying the recovery of land devastated by lava and ash. Continued studies of this volcano and its surroundings are particularly appropriate because observations and records since the end of the eruption in 1952 have been exceptionally complete. In 1960, Parícutin and its surroundings were still strongly out of adjustment with the erosional and vegetal environment of the region[102,107,213]. By 1965, however, an approach toward stability was evident in all the devastated area: the cinder cone, the lava field with its associated ponded areas, and the surrounding ash-covered terrain . . . . This progress toward recovery is described here in the light of earlier conditions.

. . . . .

Cinder Cone

On the volcano, observations were made of the slopes and crater, of fumaroles, and of the status of vegetation. In June 1965, as in February 1957, narrow, finger-like lapilli fans extended from near the crater rim down the southern and northwestern slopes toward the base of the Parícutin cone. Those on the southern slope (Fig. 183) were similar in 1965 and 1957; on the northwestern slope, the fans extended lower in 1965 than they did in 1957. A wide area without lapilli fans existed on the southwestern and northern sides in 1957 and 1965. The persistence of fans and of fan-free areas suggests that the cone has been relatively stable in the past 8 years; in contrast, fans had been highly ephemeral when the volcano was active in 1946 [see p. 287].

An ascent of the crater on June 11, 1965, revealed little change in its various features since February 24, 1957 [see p. 303]. The rim of the cone still had an east peak and a slightly higher west peak. The lowest part of the interior, almost 40-50 m below the SW rim, was separated from a more shallow depression to the NE by a saddle about 20 m high. Large blocks of agglomerate that rested in apparently unstable positions on the north and east inner walls in 1957 had not moved much by 1965 (compare Fig. 184 top and middle), [or even by 1978: compare Fig. 184 bottom]. One difference was noted: rock slides moved almost continuously on the rubbly west inner wall on the day of the 1957 ascent, but they were not observed on the day of the 1965 ascent.

Dissection of the Parícutin cone has not yet begun, and comparison of its form and surface with those of nearby cinder cones of greater age suggests that erosion will not be apparent for at least another century. Rill erosion had not started on the sides of the cone by 1965; the pyroclastic material of the cone is still too coarse and too permeable to permit surface flow of rainwater. With the passage of time, however, as soil that is less permeable than this material accumulates, the outer slopes of Parícutin will eventually become furrowed like those of the 200-year-old Jorullo cinder cone, 81 km to the SE. Inasmuch as the inner slopes of the crater of Parícutin are comparatively coarse, it is unlikely that water erosion will be evident there even after 200 years. Such is the situation at Jorullo . . . .

Segerstrom commented about aspects of vegetation recovery in several parts of this paper. Most of these have not been reproduced in deference to more thorough studies that are presented on p. 219-223 and p. 231-232. A few of his unique insights are given below, such as his discussion of vegetation within the crater and along the rim.

Vegetation on the cone was much better established in some places in 1965 than it had been in 1960[102]; in other places little change was noted. A large area within the crater, about 20 m below the north rim, was almost completely covered with grass on June 11, 1965. Plants collected along the south rim by the author that day included a small shrub, *Pernettya mexicana* Camp, which had not been previously collected at Parícutin by Beaman[214] nor mentioned by Eggler[107]. Other signs of life seen on the rim in 1965 included an oak leaf (windborne), spiders, and moths. A few mosses, but no vascular plants, grew on the south outer slope of the cone in 1965—the only slope that was examined closely.

. . . . .

Residual heat in the lava inhibited plant growth at some places. In June 1965, hot spots still existed at the surface of flows, even near the outer edges of the lava field; they were especially evident near the Llano de Tipóracuaro [near the SW edge of the lava field]. During times of cool and humid atmospheric conditions, vapor columns rose from fumaroles in the lava. The largest and most persistent of these were on Nuevo Juatita lava-vent mound, on the NE side of the cone, and on the Puertecito and Ahuán lava-vent mounds on the SW side . . . .

Ponded Areas Associated With Lava Field

Ponded areas that border the lava field and extend into some of its lowest parts have been the first ones near the volcano to become productive again. They were formed when lava flows filled the main valley at the head of the west-flowing Río de Itzícuaro, causing the blocking of pre-existing drainage and redeposition of ash and eroded soil. The principal lava-blocked areas of deposition, called "playas" by Eggler[76,106], are the Llanos de Tipóracuaro, Curupichu,

Fig. 183. Parícutin volcano from the SW, 5 (top) and 13 years (bottom) after the eruption ended. Light-toned streaks on the cone are lapilli fans. Top, February 1957. Broken ground (middle distance) is part of lava field. Plain is lower end of Llano de Tipóracuaro, covered by litter from flash floods. Sinkhole (foreground, with man inside) disappeared before the 1965 photograph, below, was taken. Bottom, June 1965. Cornfield covers lower end of Llano de Tipóracuaro. Bushes at apparent edge of lava field, to the left, border depression through which floodwaters sink into underlying lava.

Tipacua, Chórotiro and Terúpicua, and Llano Grande [Fig. 182].

The lake-like Llano de Tipóracuaro . . . is floored with a basin-fill deposit washed in from the south and dammed by the lava field. A relatively small alluvial fan at the east end formed a low divide, about 3 m high in 1957 and 1965, and prevented drainage into a *barranca* that closely follows the eastern edge of the lava field. As recently as 1960 the northern end of the flat plain was flooded during each heavy rain. In 1965 the floodwater escaped through a depression that was 12 m across and 3½ m deep and had caving sides, into underlying lava from Parícutin (Fig. 183, bottom). A new gully from the west cut through the fill deposit to the new depression. The depression did not exist in 1957, but at that time a hole 1 m deep in a different part of the basin allowed some floodwater to filter into the lava (Fig. 183, top). This hole had disappeared by 1965. The basin fill has a large component of pre-existing soil and has been a suitable site for plants since before 1957. Because of the periodic flooding, agriculture was unsuccessful until 1962, when the subterranean drainage system became more efficient. In June 1965 a cornfield on the plain extended over an area of 2 hectares (about 5 acres) (Fig. 183, bottom).

The Llano de Curupichu lies along the *barranca* at the eastern edge of the lava field (Fig. 182). Floods that supplied most of its sediment were finally stopped in 1953 by a man-made bypass. Since then, Curupichu has been successfully cultivated.

There are two Llanos de Tipacua, on and near the NE edge of the lava field. One of them, inside the lava field, was filled as a result of man-made diversion of sediment-laden floods that bypassed Curupichu. Its fill covers a lava surface of 9 hectares (about 22 acres) with an average thickness of about 3 m. The other *llano* lies nearby but outside the lava field. Enriched by an admixture of eroded pre-existing soil, largely brought in by ash-laden floods, these two areas have been cultivated since 1959 and 1953, respectively, mostly in corn but also in beans, squash, and chilicayote. Up to 1965, the western *llano* had been invaded by water on an average of about 30 times each summer, but only 5 or 6 times by sizable flash floods. In 1965 and for several years previously, the water quickly drained away into surrounding rock of the 1944 lava flow without drowning much of the crop. Before that, an efficient drainage system had not been developed on the western *llano*, and most of the plants were killed by flooding. On the eastern *llano*, equilibrium between runoff and infiltration of water

Fig. 184. Interior of Parícutin crater from SW rim, showing progressive filling of the crater. Top, February 1957, showing two vents (lower left and middle left); middle, June 1965; bottom, early 1978.

309

Fig. 185. Parícutin volcano from the NW. Lower end of Arroyo de Canicjuata in left foreground. Top, February 1957; bottom, June 1965.

into the lava field was established much earlier, and cultivation there was profitable as early as 1957.

The Llano de Chórotiro, just north of the Llanos de Tipacua, is floored with sediment washed in chiefly from the Arroyo de Nureto, to the NE, and dammed by the lava field. In 1965 a small depression, about 1 m in diameter and 1 m deep, provided underground drainage of excess floodwater into lava near the south edge of the plain. Agriculture has been possible at Chórotiro since 1946. . . .

The relatively small Llano de Terúpicua, which was produced by lava damming of an *arroyo* from the north, has an area of about 3 hectares (about 7½ acres). A 6-cm increase in the depth of fill at the edge of the lava field was observed over the period 1957-1960, and a gully that formerly directed floodwater into the lava had been filled. A comparable increase seems to have taken place over the period 1960-65. Corn was first planted at Terúpicua in 1959 and has done well ever since.

The large Llano Grande, farther to the west, was formed chiefly by flooding from the Arroyo de Hurengo, where it was blocked by the 1944 lava flow. At some time during the period 1947-57 the basin overflowed westward toward Huirambosta. In January and February 1965, a rock dam 1½ m high and 80 m long was built at the place of overflow, and by June of that year the dam had caused considerable sedimentation upstream. Cultivation of older parts of the Llano Grande basin fill began in 1953 and progressed slowly for 7 or 8 years. In June 1965, the cultivated area was about 10 times greater than in 1960.

The springs of Sipicha, which rise in a meadow near the Río de Itzícuaro, several kilometers downstream from Huirambosta, are probably fed by ground water from the lava field of Parícutin. The flow of these springs increased more than 50% during the period 1946-57. This change was attributed to increase of effectiveness of the lava field as a recharge area [see p. 287, 307]. Surprisingly enough, by 1965 there had been a marked decline of average flow from these springs, although this decline seems not to have been accompanied by a marked lessening of mean annual rainfall.

In summary, the ponded areas dramatically illustrate recovery of the zone devastated by the volcano. Slopes along pre-existing valleys, unsuited for agriculture because of topographic relief, have been buried. In their stead, the overlying new fields, flat as a floor and enriched by flood sediment, have already become productive.

Ash-Covered Terrain
Away From the Lava Field

In 1944 . . . the ash-covered floor of the dead forest was intricately dissected with rills and gullies, even on interfluves . . . . Many of these rills and gullies were initiated by rainwater running down the tree trunks. Two decades later, the landscape just west of the lava field had a very different aspect; almost all the old tree trunks had fallen and had reached an advanced state of decay . . . .

Redeposition of ash by the wind has had two principal effects. Fields in the Zirosto area [8½ km NW of the new volcano] and toward the east, where some grass continued to grow during and since volcanic activity, had a hummocky surface in 1965. The hummocks, which are composed of thickly matted, creeping Bermuda grass, Cynodon[107], and wind-driven ash, did not exist in the region immediately before the eruption. By June 1965, however, they had grown to mounds as much as 7-8 m long and 1½ m high . . . . Another effect of aeolian action—this one in the ash-killed forest—has

been the filling of rill heads with loose ash during successive dry seasons (November to May).

. . . . .

Runoff and rill erosion on the formerly wooded ridges and slopes are now inhibited by the dead tree trunks that have fallen . . . and by the new shrubs and herbs that are springing up. This is exemplified by an area on the lower slopes of the Arroyo de Canicjuata where kill by the eruption was nearly 100% and gullying was intense (Fig. 185). The recovery here occurred without marked additional stripping of the ash mantle in 8 years.

Volume Estimates for Magma and Water

Fries (1953)

Following the end of the Parícutin eruption in 1952, the accumulated data for lava and ash eruption rates over time were synthesized by Carl Fries. This important analysis showed that both the total eruption rate and the ratio of ash to lava declined systematically during the 9 years of activity. The data of Fries have been widely quoted and used subsequent investigations including the petrologic study by McBirney et al. reprinted on p. 346-358. Based on measurements for fall times of lava blocks, Fries estimated the velocity of the exiting gas, which he assumed to be pure water, and then computed the eruption rate for water, and the magma/water eruption ratio. Only one other estimate has been made of water content for Parícutin's magma (see p. 359-363), a very important parameter that influenced both the mineralogy of the magma and its eruptive behavior. A brief biographjy of Carl Fries can be found on p. 162.

Introduction

Estimates of the weight of some of the solids erupted by Parícutin volcano have been made for short periods of its life by various geologists, but no serious attempt to estimate the weight of water vapor erupted from the crater for any particular period was made until this was done by Foshag[215]. The conclusions reached in that paper call for a more detailed analysis of the problem, as the implications arising from those conclusions are of considerable importance to geologists working with igneous rocks and ore deposits.

The earlier published figures of the weight of solids are incomplete, and most of them are based only on rough estimates of cone dimensions or lava volumes for certain periods of time rather than on direct measurement and analysis or by careful triangulation; none of them seems to take into account the full significance of the great quantities of fine ash erupted by the volcano. Sufficient data are now at hand to permit calculating with a moderate degree of accuracy the weight of solids erupted during almost any period of several months' duration in the 9-year life span of the volcano. I feel that the presentation of these data is particularly desirable at this time, for all activity ceased on March 4, 1952, and eruptions now seem unlikely to resume.

Any estimate of the weight of water vapor must necessarily be restricted to certain relatively short periods when activity in the crater is not intermittently explosive but sufficiently stable or constant to permit adequate measurement. As pointed out by Foshag[215], such a period occurred in the spring of 1945, at which time the volcano was in "average eruption" for the years 1944 and 1945. This period in the spring of 1945 will be used in the discussions that follow, for no later period when even rough measurements of water vapor could be made is known to me, and I have probably seen Parícutin at more frequent and regularly spaced intervals in its 9 years of activity than any other geologist.

. . . . .

Fries discussed the isopach map made by Segerstrom in the summer of 1946 out to ash thicknesses of 25-cm (see inside-front-cover map). Use of Segerstrom's map to calculate a total volume for the deposit as of mid-1946 is highly dependent upon the technique used to extrapolate to thinner parts of the tephra blanket. Fries discussed and criticized the assumptions made by Segerstrom in extrapolating to the 1-mm isopach, applied other assumptions to make this same extrapolation, and finally arrived at an estimate for the volume of tephra erupted as of August 1946. The problem of evaluating the volume represented by far-

flung ashes continues to plague volcanology. Various techniques for treating this problem were recently evaluated by Fierstein and Nathenson[216].

In order to arrive at estimates of tephra volumes prior to August 1946, Fries focused on five dates for which the volume of the cone was carefully measured. By making a rough estimate of the ratio of total tephra volume to cone volume, he was able to estimate the total tephra volume for these five dates.

A different technique was used to estimate tephra volumes for later time periods. From November 1946 until the end of the eruption, daily ashfall records were kept at Cuezeño Station (5½ km north of the volcano) and Jarátiro Station (1½ km north). Fries established a scaling parameter by dividing the total volume of the deposit at the end of August 1946 by the thickness of ash at Cuezeño Station at the same time. This parameter was multiplied by the thickness of new ashfall at Cuezeño during later time increments to estimate the volume of new ash for those periods.

Lava flow volumes for various time periods were based on areas covered by new lava and estimates for average lava thickness for each period. Finally, lava and tephra volumes for each time period were multiplied by estimated densities to arrive at masses of erupted material, in metric tons, as a function of time.

Summary of Volume and Weight of Pyroclastic Material and Lava

From the values given in Table 23, Parícutin appears to have erupted at least 1,310 million m^3 of pyroclastic material from the beginning of its activity up to the end of 1951, 2 months before activity ceased. This volume does not take into account the finest material erupted, which was carried by the winds beyond Segerstrom's 1-mm isopach of 1946, but it probably represents at least 90% of the total pyroclastic material erupted. Using the average weight per unit volume given in the present paper, the weight of pyroclastic material up to the end of 1951 was at least 2,227 million metric tons. The yearly volumes and weights of pyroclastic material are given in Table 23 . . . . The average daily weight in 1945 was about 690,000 metric tons.

From the values given in Table 23, Parícutin appears to have extruded about 700 million m^3 of lava from its inception to the end of 1951. This total is subject to confirmation or correction from topographic maps: one map, which is already prepared but has not yet been published, of the pre-eruption topography, and another map, for which plans are being made, of

the post-eruption topography. Based on the average weight per unit volume given in the present paper, the total weight of lava extruded was roughly 1,330 million metric tons. The weight of the average daily extrusion of lava during the year 1945 appears to have been about 510,000 metric tons.

The total weight of pyroclastic material and lava erupted at Parícutin, as shown in Table 23, amounted to 3,556 million metric tons up to the end of 1951. About 40 million metric tons of material was probably erupted in the remaining two months of the volcano's activity, making the total weight during the life span of Parícutin about 3,596 million metric tons. The average production of solids during the entire life of the volcano was, therefore, 1.1 million metric tons/day . . . . The average daily weights by year are given in the diagram in Fig. 186 [with the pyroclastic and lava weights distinguished. The pronounced decrease with time in the ratio of pyroclastic material to lava is clearly seen]. The average daily emission during 1945, the year for which the weight of water in the magma that reached the surface is calculated, was about 1.2 million metric tons.

Weight of Water Vapor Expelled Through the Crater

I first visited the crater of the volcano on May 27, 1945, and revisited it from three to six times a year until May, 1951, when explosive activity became so violent and unpredictable that trips to the crater were extremely hazardous. During the spring and summer of 1945 the eruptions were fairly constant and the emission of gases was subject to some type of rough calculation. I know of no later period in the life of the volcano when conditions were equally good for making calculations of the volume of gases emitted from the crater, and hence I will follow Foshag in using that period for the calculations.

On May 27, 1945, the crater had two separate funnel-shaped vent areas aligned in a NE-SW direction, as existed during most of the life of the volcano, except during 1949-1951, when it generally had only one vent area. The NE vent had one principal throat about 2 m in diameter, from which a continuous stream of vapors issued at high velocity; the SW vent consisted of a deep funnel with a hole in its bottom 10 m or more across, from which an enormous blast of ash- and bomb-laden vapors erupted every few hours. Foshag[215] has described this general type of activity as characteristic of the greater part of the years 1944 and 1945, although periods of stronger and weaker eruptions must have occurred from time to time; certainly the eruptions in 1944

Table. 23. Total weight and average daily weight of pyroclastic material and lava erupted at Parícutin, by years, from 1943 through 1951[a].

Year	Duration	Ash		Lava		Total weight	Average daily weight
		Volume	Weight	Volume	Weight		
	day	million cu m	million met tons	million cu m	million met tons	million met tons	thousand met tons
1943	314	601	1022	107	203	1225	3900
1944	366	280	476	122	232	708	1930
1945	365	148	252	98	186	438	1200
1946	365	103	175	87	165	340	930
1947	365	98	167	79	150	317	870
1948	366	28	48	76	144	192	520
1949	365	21	36	48	91	127	350
1950	365	16	27	40	76	103	280
1951	365	14	24	43	82	106	290
Totals and averages	3236	1309	2227	700	1329	3556	1100

[a]Calculated from values given in Tables 2, 4, and 5.

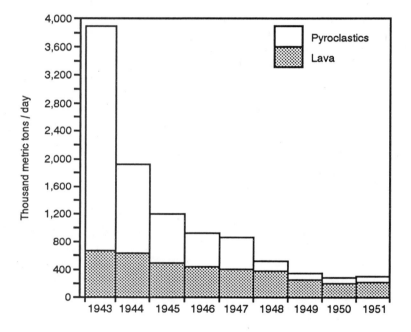

Fig. 186. Average daily weights of pyroclastic material and lava erupted at Parícutin, by years, 1943-1951.

were stronger on the average than those in 1945. Whether the volume of vapors emitted on May 27, 1945, represented an average daily volume for the year 1945 is, of course, open to question; I feel, however, that the average daily volume for that year was probably of that order and have found no other means of calculating this volume.

The only vapors issuing from the crater on May 27, 1945, that were subject to volume measurement, rushed from the 2-m throat described. Other vapors arose from different parts of the interior of the crater, and the SW vent emitted vapors with each of its long-spaced eruptions. These were not subject to measure-

ment, but in all they were certainly of minor volume compared with the main column. The lava vent emitted some water vapor, and the hot moving lava also gave off some water. However, the main column is felt to have accounted for at least 80% of the total water vapor given off to the atmosphere by the volcano on that day.

The continuous stream of vapor issuing from the main vent carried some rock and lava fragments with it, and those that rose highest required about 10 seconds to fall back to the altitude of the vent. Assuming that such pieces measured 10 cm in diameter and, being quite vesicular, had a specific gravity of 2, the terminal or greatest velocity reached on falling back to the ground may be calculated by the following equation[217]:

$$V_T = 71[a(S - \rho)/\rho]^{1/2} \qquad (1)$$

in which V_T is the terminal velocity under turbulent conditions (high speed), 71 is a constant obtained experimentally for irregular fragments of quartz, a is the radius (5 cm) of the fragment, S is the specific gravity (2.0) of the fragment, and ρ is the density (0.00092 g/cm^3) of dry air at 15°C, 2,750 m above sea level. (The value of ρ would not change significantly at the relative humidity of the air around the volcano on a clear day.) Substituting the appropriate values in this equation, we have:
$V_T = 71[5(2.0 - 0.00092)/0.00092]^{1/2} = 74$ m/sec.

The fragment would fall the distance shown in Table 24 in successive seconds from the top of its arc, reaching terminal velocity at the end of 8 seconds. The height to which the fragment was hurled was thus about 462 m above the vent.

The velocity at which the bomb left the vent may be calculated by $v = 2gs^{1/2}$, in which g is the acceleration due to gravity (9.8 m/sec^2) and s is the total distance (462 m); it is computed to be 95 m/sec. Terminal velocity does not enter into this calculation, as the initial velocity was not limited by air resistance.

The gases must have streamed past the fragment at the orifice of the vent at a velocity equal to the terminal velocity of the fragment in the gases issuing from the orifice. This terminal velocity depended upon the temperature, composition, and pressure of the gases at the orifice. Inasmuch as the walls of these gas jets in the crater were a bright red and the fragments hurled out were red or even yellowish red, the temperature of the gases at the vent must have been in the range of 600°-1,000°C. The following calculations are made for 600°, 800°, and 1,000°, although I feel that the temperature was probably nearer 800°C than the other two figures, for expansion in the throat below the orifice would have cooled the gases somewhat, but not below the temperature of the walls of the orifice. The temperature would drop exceedingly rapidly, however, the moment that the gas left the vent. The gas jet was visible immediately upon its leaving the vent, owing undoubtedly to condensation of water vapor in the form of a thin envelope around the jet. The presence of this vapor should not be interpreted to mean that the gases left the orifice at a temperature of 100°C or less.

The composition of the gases erupted through the crater is not known, for no means of sampling them could be devised because of the violence of the eruptions. The major compound was certainly water vapor, but whether this formed 80% or 99% of the total is not known. The odor of the gases indicated the presence principally of sulfur as H_2SO_4 and chlorine as HCl. CO_2 must surely have been present, and H_2S was noted on rare occasions. Probably some nitrogen and other inert gases were also expelled, and ammonium and other chlorides formed a part of the whole. For the purpose of calculation, the gases will be considered as having consisted of pure water vapor, for the molecular weight of the other minor gaseous compounds would not significantly affect the calculations of terminal velocity. Very fine ash particles were also present in the column and must have had the effect of increasing the density of the gases.

The pressure at the orifice is more difficult to determine. I assume that the pressure of the gases at the moment they left the orifice was that of the

Table. 24. Distance of fall in successive seconds.

Interval (seconds)	Distance/second (m)	Distance Fallen (m)
1	4.9	4.9
2	14.7	19.6
3	24.5	44.1
4	34.3	78.4
5	44.1	122.5
6	53.9	176.4
7	63.7	240.1
8	73.5	313.6
9	74.0	387.6
10	74.0	461.6

atmosphere at 2,750 m above sea level. If a greater pressure existed, the final values for weight of water vapor would be affected somewhat, but this effect would not be as great as one might think, because an increase in pressure would call for a greater density of water vapor and a lower velocity, which would mean that the gases would weigh more per unit volume, but that a smaller volume would leave the orifice per second.

To calculate the velocity at which the gases would stream past a 10-cm fragment held at a constant elevation at the orifice, the formula for terminal velocity is the same as that used earlier, but in this calculation, although a and S are the same, ρ is calculated for saturated water vapor at 2,750 m above sea level for the following temperatures: 600°C, ρ = 0.000161 g/cm³; 800°C, ρ = 0.000135 g/cm³; and 1,000°C, ρ = 0.000114 g/cm³.

Substitution of the appropriate values in (1) indicates that the gases streamed past the fragment at the orifice at the following velocities at the temperature given: 177 m/sec at 600°C; 193 m/sec at 800°C; and 210 m/sec at 1,000°C. The velocity was probably somewhat less, for some of the gases were denser than water vapor, and the fine ash particles must have increased the effective density.

Inasmuch as the fragment left the orifice at a velocity of 95 m/sec, this value must be added to the velocity of the gas past the fragment, giving the values: 272 m/sec at 600°C; 288 m/sec at 800°C; and 305 m/sec at 1,000°C. As the diameter of the orifice was 2 m, the volumes of the gases that would have left the vent at the above velocities were: 854 m³/sec at 600°C; 904 m³/sec at 800°C; and 958 m³/sec at 1,000°C.

According to the preceding values and the assumption that the gases were pure water vapor, the densities of the gases leaving the vent were as follows: 0.161 kg/m³ at 600°C; 0.135 kg/m³ at 800°C; and 0.114 kg/m³ at 1,000°C. The weight of the water vapor leaving the vent per second was therefore: 0.14 metric tons/sec at 600°C; 0.12 tons/sec at 800°C; and 0.11 tons/sec at 1,000°C. Consequently, the daily weight of water vapor was: 11,900 metric tons/day at 600°C; 10,500 tons/day at 800°C; and 9,400 tons/day at 1,000°C.

The weights of water vapor for the temperatures given are probably high, for the gases issuing from the vent were certainly not all water vapor; the error is probably offset somewhat, however, by the fact that the gases must have been at least a bit denser than indicated by the value used. Inasmuch as so many of the factors that enter into the calculations were not subject to direct measurement, and changes in the value of some of these factors would tend to cancel out changes in the value of other factors, I feel that the weights given above are reasonable for the temperatures given and are probably not far from reality.

Relative Weights of Water and Magma

As shown in Fig. 186 and Table 23, the total weight of lava and pyroclastic material erupted daily at Parícutin in 1945, during the period for which the weight of water emitted from the crater was calculated, amounted to an average of about 1.2 million metric tons. The weight of water vapor issuing from the crater, assuming that the temperature of expulsion was 800°C, was estimated to have amounted to some 10,500 metric tons/day. This weight probably represents at least 80% of the water issuing from the crater and the hot flows. On this assumption, the weight of water would be increased to about 13,100 metric tons/day. To this should be added the water contained in the flows after solidification, which by assay are known to average about 0.1 wt% H_2O. As the average daily lava emission in 1945 amounted to about 510,000 metric tons, some 510 tons of water were fixed daily by the lava. If this quantity is added to the weight of water from other sources, the total would amount to about 13,600 metric tons/day.

The percentage of water in the magma reaching the surface in 1945 was therefore about 1.1 wt% on average. I feel that this figure is not in error by more than a few tenths of one percent of the true water content of magma that reached the surface in that year. Inasmuch as most igneous petrologists would accept a water content of this magnitude in basaltic magmas, there is no need to postulate that the rising lava column was greatly enriched by the introduction of ground waters; the juvenile water in gaseous form and other gases could well have accounted for all the explosive activity of Parícutin, at least during 1945. If the proportion of water to total solids had been nearly constant throughout the period of activity of the volcano, the total weight of water expelled would have amounted to some 39 million metric tons—the approximate weight of a body of water about 6 km square by 1 m deep.

Temperature and Viscosity Measurements

Two instruments were used to estimate temperatures of Parícutin lavas: thermocouples and optical pyrometers. A thermocouple is a simple device consisting of two wires of dissimilar metals that are twisted together at one end and attached to a voltmeter at the other ends. That twisted junction is encased in a closed ceramic or silica-glass tube and physically inserted as far as possible into hot lava or an orifice at a fumarole or hornito. According to the "thermoelectric effect", discovered by Thomas Seebeck in 1821, when two wires of dissimilar metals are attached and one junction is heated, a current of electrons will flow in the loop. If the cold junction is broken, a potential will develop, the magnitude of which is proportional to the temperature at the other junction and measureable with a voltmeter or potentiometer. Thermocouples are the most reliable technique for measuring temperatures of lava flows (although fraught with difficulties) and of laboratory experiments. A common variety, mentioned in several of the following articles, is the chromel-alumel thermocouple. One wire is an alloy of nickel and chromium (chromel: 90% Ni - 10% Cr) and the other an alloy of nickel and aluminum (alumel: 95% Ni - 5% Al). An optical pyrometer is a hand-held device that compares the color of a glowing object against the color of a filament, whose temperature is known. Incandescent lava flows at Parícutin quickly developed dark crusts, complicating temperature measurements by optical pyrometer. Temperature measurements of Parícutin lavas were published in four different papers, pertinent parts of which are reprinted below.

Viscosity describes the ability of a fluid to resist flow. In common experience, honey has <u>high</u> viscosity and water has <u>low</u> viscosity. Lava, of course, is much more viscous than honey. The viscosity, or stiffness, of lava depends upon many factors, including its chemical composition (the lower the SiO_2 content the lower the viscosity), the abundance of crystals or gas bubbles (both increase the viscosity), and its temperature (the higher the temperature the lower the viscosity). Viscosity is measured in units called "poise", and can be calculated from measurements made at active lava flows using equations derived from laboratory experiments on other fluids. Estimates of lava-flow viscosity were made at Parícutin in two studies, the pertinent parts of which are reproduced below.

Temperature

Zies (1946)

Temperature Measurements at the Ahuán Flow

Several observers at Parícutin have noted the presence of excrescences, termed *hornitos*, near the edges of the hot lava flows. These are frequently cupola-shaped and, if not too active, are convenient orifices from which samples of gas can be taken and measurements of the temperature of the escaping gases can be made. Another type is nothing more than a large blob of congealed lava, perforated by channels. Unfortunately, none of the former type was active in December, 1944; but one of the latter was quite active, as shown by the fact that hot gases were freely emitted from all channels. It was about 1.25 m high, 1 m in diameter at the base, and was located close to the well from which the Ahuán lava was issuing [see map of Fig. 74 and photo of Fig. 95]. Several of the channels, both near the top and at the bottom of the excrescence, were probed with a 22-gauge chromel-alumel thermocouple connected to a portable potentiometer. One of the leads was insulated with unglazed porcelain tubing, especially adapted for the purpose, for a distance of about 1 m from the junction that was made by tightly twisting together the ends of the wire brightened by sandpapering. After every measurement, the junction was cut off and renewed. The element was inserted in a silica-glass jacket 1.5 m long in such a manner that the junction touched bottom. The leads were about 10 m long and were connected directly to the portable potentiometer. The cold junction was protected from extraneous sources of heat, its temperature was repeatedly taken, and the millivolt readings corrected accordingly. The entire assembly as used had been calibrated at the Geophysical Laboratory and was recalibrated on my return to Washington D.C.

. . . . .

When the channels of the lava blob were probed, it was found that the walls were so hot that a viscous plastic lava was encountered. I am indebted to Dr. Foshag for his skill in avoiding the loss of the valuable silica-glass jackets by preventing them from sticking to the walls.

Seventeen measurements were made at the *hornito*. No matter in what channels they were made, much higher temperatures were found at the bottom than at a distance of 5-10 cm from the orifice. The temperature at the latter position was about 890°C, whereas 60 cm down, the maximum temperature was 1,080°C . . . .

Temperature of the Lava

The Ahuán flow of December 1944 chilled rapidly at the surface even close to its source, but it moved freely enough to develop fractures that revealed the glowing lava. Near the source, the emission of gas raised mounds of glowing lava whose straw color and brightness enabled me to make estimates of its temperature, which based on experience in viewing hot objects in the laboratory, proved to be between 1,050° and 1,250°C. In May 1945, Fuller[218] used an optical pyrometer in an effort to measure the temperature of similar blobs of straw-colored lava and estimated it to be between 1,200° and 1,250°C. The use of this type of pyrometer is fraught with difficulties, but I believe that the value obtained by Fuller is correct.

The lava observed at the Ahuán vent was flowing freely and was building up its own levees at the side of the stream. Fruitless efforts were made to measure its temperature with the thermocouple. It quickly became obvious that the thermocouple could stand more heat than the observers' bodies, and furthermore the hot levees provided a most insecure footing. A measurement was obtained in a relatively deep (30 cm) crack in the levee. The lava was viscous and had a temperature of 1,020°C.

The next day an area was found, about 5 km north from the source of the lava, where an actively moving flow broke out of the side of one of the lobes of the main flow. The lava here was somewhat more sluggish than near the source and instead of building up levees it flowed as a mass elevated about 1¼ m above the ground. It was, however, moving actively enough so that freely flowing lava was constantly exposed. Large blocks of surface-chilled lava would form and then split open in a manner that reminded one of pulling taffy. The glowing lava revealed by this taffy-pulling motion had a bright orange, almost yellow color; it was so plastic that a Marquardt unglazed porcelain tube containing a thermoelement could be inserted to a depth of about 10 cm. These porcelain thermoelement jackets were about 30 cm long and were securely lashed to a wooden pole. This arrangement permitted one to push the jacket gently into the lava as far as its viscosity would allow. Maximum temperature was reached in about 5 minutes. The thermoelement was then withdrawn and the junction renewed. It was impossible to withdraw the porcelain jacket and hence it was necessary to use a new one for each temperature measurement. The highest temperature recorded was 1,110°C. Five measurements were made and all were close to the value just given. It should be borne in mind that this value was obtained at a position about 5 km from the source and that the lava had taken about a month to flow this far. The thermal insulation provided by the chilled protecting surface of the flow evidently must be very good indeed.

It can be readily understood that the task of making these measurements was not particularly pleasant, but it was well worth the trouble.

The taffy-pulling motion together with the recorded temperature of about 1,100°C indicated that a rise in temperature of about 100° to 150°C would produce freely flowing lava such as seen at the source. The evidence obtained with the optical pyrometer and with the thermocouple points to a value of 1,200°C as being a close approximation to the temperature of the lava as it issues from the base of the volcano. It is of interest to note that this value for the basaltic lava of Parícutin lies in the same range as that obtained by Day and Shepherd[219] and Jaggar[220] for the temperature (1,185°-1,200°C) of the basaltic lava of Kilauea and by Verhoogen[221] for the temperature (1,160°C) of the freely flowing basaltic lava of Nyamlagira [Nyamuragira] in Africa.

Temperatures of Fumaroles

All of the fumaroles investigated were located on a mound of the NE branch of the Sapichu flow. The openings were probed with the chromel-alumel thermocouple inserted in a silica-glass jacket in much the same manner as indicated above. Care had to be exercised that the leads to the potentiometer were kept off the ground, which in the vicinity of the fumaroles was usually covered with moist reaction products that could short circuit the thermoelement junction and give erroneous readings on the potentiometer. The top of the mound was made up of material cemented together by chemical reaction products and only rarely were openings found that could be probed to a greater depth than about 8 cm. The moist ground indicated that steam was present in the emanations, but with the exception of one opening at the side of the mound, no conspicuous cloud of steam was noted at any of the fumaroles. The fumes escaped quietly as a thin, blue, evidently hot haze. The one opening from which visible steam issued could be probed to a depth of 1 m, where a temperature of 105°C was obtained. All of the "blue" fumaroles exhibited much higher temperatures, varying from 350° to 640°C. The latter value was obtained at an opening located on top of the mound. In view of the fact that the orifices of these "blue" fumaroles could be probed to a depth of only about 8 cm, it seems plain that the source within the interior of the mound must be considerably hotter. These fumaroles persisted for more than a year after the emission of the flow, and their high temperature close to the surface is again evidence of the effectiveness of the thermal insulation afforded by the exterior mantle of lava. This lava was not obviously fractured but instead had been compacted by the cementing action of the products formed by interaction of the emanations, emitted at elevated temperatures, and the lava. These products, called incrustations, were collected by Dr. Foshag after the temperature measurements were made and it is hoped that they will be subjected to geochemical investigation.

Bullard (1947)

Fred Bullard kept Parícutin volcano under almost continuous observation from mid-August to late-October 1944. In this paper he gave detailed descriptions of the flow of lava from vents near the NE and SW feet of the cone, and provided a map of lava distribution from the birth of Parícutin until October 20, 1944. Because the time period and

phenomena were also covered by Foshag and González-Reyna (see p. 87-98), we have not reproduced most of this article, which nonetheless contains much important information. Here we reprint only a short paragraph on temperature measurements, followed by a brief discussion of viscosity.

The temperature of the lava was measured with a hand-model optical pyrometer. The readings were taken during the day in subdued light. The following are typical of many readings. On September 6, 1944 the lava in the cracks at the margin of the September 4 flow gave readings up to 1,021°C. Surfaces that were just beginning to crust gave readings of about 954°C. Measurements on the September 27, 1944 flow (taken the morning of September 28 and about 1½ km from the *boca*) gave readings from 943° to 954°C. Temperatures at the hottest part of the *boca* (on September 28) ranged from 1,043° to 1,057°C.

Krauskopf (1948b)

This article begins with a detailed treatment of the eruptive activity of Parícutin during the period November 1945 to February 1946. It focuses on the SW-flank vents, where lava was issuing at that time, and contains numerous sketch maps and photographs of the vents and lava flows. These sections were not included earlier in the book because the topic and time period were also covered by Krauskopf and Williams [see p. 132-136]. Here we reprint a short section on measurement of temperature and below we reprint Krauskopf's calculation of viscosity in flowing Parícutin lavas. This wide-ranging article concludes with a discussion of eruption mechanisms, which we have reprinted on p. 321-323.

Temperatures of the moving lava were measured with both an optical pyrometer and a thermocouple. [Krauskopf studied lava flows from the SW-base vents during the period November 1945 to February 1946.] The highest temperature obtained, close to one of the vents, was 1,070°C; previous workers have recorded temperatures as high as 1,100°C [Zies, above]. Temperatures downstream were only a little lower; even at the ends of flows 4-5 km from their sources temperatures of 1,000° to 1,050°C were recorded. The maintainance of temperature for such a distance is due partly to insulation by the cooled lava on top of a moving flow and partly to heat given off by the lava as it crystallizes.

Wilcox (1954)

This paragraph of temperature measurements is from Wilcox's classic study of the mineralogy and petrology of the Parícutin lavas, which is reprinted in large part on p. 324-346.

The few reliable temperature measurements that have been made on the lavas of Parícutin indicate that there has probably been a small but general decrease in temperature of successively erupted materials. In December 1944 the temperature of flowing lava 5 km from the vent was found by Zies [above] to be 1,110°C by use of a thermocouple. During November 1945 to February 1946, a series of thermocouple measurements by Krauskopf [above] gave a maximum of 1,070°C at the vent. During October and November 1946, measurements that I made with an optical pyrometer in subdued daylight gave a maximum of 1,040°C for flowing lava half a kilometer from the vent.

Viscosity of Flowing Lava

Bullard (1947)

All the lavas from Parícutin are stiff and viscous, and none of the more fluid lavas, such as are characteristic of Hawaii, are present. The lava seems to lose very little of its viscosity (or its temperature) as it flows. Even the small lateral tongues, marking the final stage of lava flow may be several kilometers from the source and must necessarily have been many days or perhaps weeks in reaching their destination. They still retain approximately the viscosity of the lava at the *boca*. Although no method of obtaining a uniform measure of viscosity was available, and descriptive terms, are not exact, the lava may be compared to taffy candy that is ready to "pull". With a long stick I was able to "pull" the molten material and mold it around the end of a stick, but it chilled and became brittle the instant it was removed from the flow.

Krauskopf (1948b)

Viscosity may be calculated from the Jeffreys formula (cited by Nichols[222]):

$$u = (g \sin A \, d^2 \, \rho)/3V$$

in which g is acceleration of gravity, A is slope, d is depth of the flow, ρ is density, and V is mean velocity with respect to depth. The faster Parícutin flows, near their vents, have maximum surface velocities of 20-40 m/min on slopes of 15-25°; the mean speeds can be taken as about half of these figures. Depths cannot be directly measured but can be estimated (1) by observing the depth to which the lava level lowers in the channel when a flow dies, and (2) by determining the rate of advance of the foot of the flow where the depth is measurable and assuming that the quantity of lava moving in all parts of the flow is the same. These methods indicate that depths in the upper parts of flows are seldom less than 1.5 m or greater than 4 m. The density of moving lava also is not determinable directly but probably lies between 1.5 and 2.5 g/cm^3. Viscosities calculated from these figures lie between 10^5 and 10^6 poises.

The validity of such calculations has been critically examined by Wentworth et al.[223], who point out the uncertainties in the measurements, the extrapolation involved in applying Jeffreys' formula, the neglected retarding effects of drag by the sides of the channel and the cooled blocks on the upper surface, and the probable variation of viscosity from point to point within the flow. They indicate that the value given by Nichols[222] for a Hawaiian flow, 4.3 x 10^4 poises, has meaning only as an order of magnitude. It seems worthy of note that values obtained for Parícutin lavas are at least one order of magnitude higher than that indicated by Nichols. The higher viscosity is probably related to the lower temperature of the Parícutin flows: 1,050°-1,070°C, opposed to an estimated 1,150°-1,200°C for the Hawaiian flow.

The viscosity of lava patently increases downstream. The very high viscosity at the lower end of a long flow is strikingly shown by the behavior of blocks of incandescent lava that break away from the moving front. When one of these blocks rolls down slowly it is indented by the cool blocks in its path and as it comes to rest adjusts its shape somewhat to its surroundings; but if it falls freely even a short distance so that it strikes another block sharply, the incandescent material shatters like a brittle solid.

In general, lava of the small, short-lived flows appears to be less viscous than that in the principal flows, whereas lava in the dome-like extrusions along fissures is more viscous.

Mechanism of Eruption

Krauskopf (1948a)

In Part III we reprinted the detailed observations of many different scientists who were involved in the task of documenting the eruption of Parícutin volcano throughout its 9 years of life. One important goal of such studies is to provide the basic data from which interpretations can be made concerning processes occurring beneath the volcano. Relatively few authors attempted this most difficult task. White[224] presented an early model to explain cyclical activity that was evident during the first year of the eruption. Here we reprint a portion of the later study by Krauskopf, who also attempted to understand the procsesses at work beneath the volcano. Krauskopf was particularly interested in the nature of sub-surface degassing, the mechanisms of lava and pyroclastic eruption, and the differences in gas composition associated with these two forms of activity: water vapor with abundant SO_2 from the summit crater and HCl-rich gas from the flanking lava vents. He appears to be the only scientist to have reported this important distinction in gas compositions with vent position.

Correlation of Different Kinds of Eruptive Activity

Flow Activity

In the area of lava *bocas* three kinds of lava movement are conspicuous: (1) long-lived flows that move for at least a week and attain lengths of at least a half a kilometer, generally welling up quietly from their *bocas*; (2) short-lived flows that are in motion for less than 2 days and attain lengths of less than 200 m, generally emerging from their *bocas* accompanied by much gas and spattering of lava; and (3) the slow movement of viscous lava out of fissures to form elongated domes and thick curved sheets. All types of lava activity at the *bocas* are accompanied by emission of gas, of which the principal odor is that of

hydrogen chloride; rough chemical tests for the sulfur gases showed no more than traces . . . .

Explosive Activity

Activity in the crater consists of the emission of gas, ash, solid lava blocks, and bombs of fluid lava. Relative and total amounts of these materials vary greatly from time to time; the manner of gas emission changes from quiet to explosive; and sound effects go through an extensive repertoire of pounding, rumbling, whistling, puffing, and complete silence. No method of collecting or analyzing gas from the crater suggested itself, but certainly the gas contains abundant water vapor, which condenses in the eruption cloud, and enough sulfur dioxide to make the crater at times uninhabitable. That sulfur is one of the gases rising through fissures in the crater is shown by abundant needles of monoclinic sulfur deposited at the mouths of the fissures.

. . . . .

Inferred Internal Structure of Area

A satisfactory hypothesis regarding the internal structure of the cone should explain the following observations:

(1) The cone, although built up almost entirely of fragmental material, is able to withstand the explosive emission of gas from a small vent. The size, shape, and position of the vent changes frequently, but even the most violent bursts of gas do not produce major changes suddenly.

(2) Emission of gas is almost entirely confined to the central vent, emission of lava to the *boca* area. The gas that accompanies the lava is negligible compared to the huge quantities that pour out of the crater. Furthermore, gas from the central vent is rich in SO_2, while that from the *bocas* is rich in HCl.

(3) The extensive inward slumping of the crater at times of quiet eruption, the slumped material evidently settling into space below occupied by fluid,

and the outward movement of a portion of the SW side of the cone, called the "slice", apparently produced by pressure of gas or liquid within, suggests that a considerable body of gas or liquid is present within the cone.

(4) At times very numerous large shapeless chunks of incandescent liquid are blown out of a small vent in the crater, suggesting that liquid lava must fill the central conduit nearly to its top.

(5) Activity at the crater is related to activity in the *boca* area in that certain major changes in one are reflected by changes in the other, but there is no appreciable correlation with respect to minor changes.

(6) Activities in adjacent *bocas* show only slight interrelationships.

(7) When two or more vents appear in the crater, their activity is usually somewhat different. Gas may shoot out of one with explosive violence, but rise in slow puffs from the other; both may show explosive activity, but with different timing; one may throw out showers of molten, incandescent fragments, while the other emits only a little fine dust. This independence of activity of closely adjacent vents has been observed at other volcanoes[225].

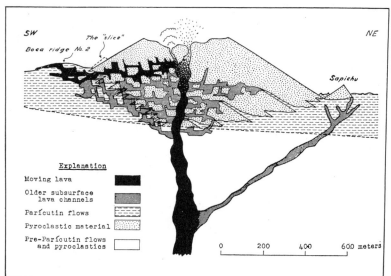

Fig. 187. Inferred vertical NE-SW section through Parícutin, December 1945.

A possible structure to account for these facts is shown in Fig. 187, a rough vertical section along a NE-SW line through Boca ridge 2 [see Fig. 105] and Sapichu. The "slice", not actually in the section, is shown by a dashed line. The floor of the volcanic structure, indicated by a dashed line, is guess work, based simply on the fact that the original surface sloped generally upward toward the SW. Because the

cone was built up of fragmental material while successive lavas inundated its base, the lower edge of the fragmental pile is shown schematically as an interfingering of ash and lava. The central conduit is approximately vertical within the cone, but its position in the basement rocks can only be guessed.

The ability of the cone to withstand violent emission of gas from a small opening suggests that the interior cannot consist wholly of loose debris. Presumably near the lava conduit or conduits the fragmental material is partly welded into a fairly solid rock. This is indicated also by observations in the throat of the crater when an exceptionally quiet eruption permits close inspection. The walls of the inner crater are made up of roughly stratified angular debris that grades downward into massive incandescent rock . . . . On the one occasion when a temperature measurement was possible, this incandescent material gave a maximum reading of 980°C, about 20° cooler than the lowest temperature recorded for the flowing lava [see p. 317-320]. Some of the solid blocks thrown out of the crater are composed of angular fragments so firmly cemented that their outlines are in part indistinct.

The welding is not complete enough, however, to give the interior of the cone great strength. New vents open in the crater at frequent intervals, showing that gas can force its way upward through new channels when old ones become clogged; and the slumping in the crater during times of quiet eruption must mean that the material of the cone can be easily cracked.

Lava, as shown on the diagram, nearly fills the central conduit and spills over into the vent area through narrow, branching fissures. Within the conduit the lava must be in continual violent agitation as gas comes out of solution and bubbles up through it. Fragments of lava splash upward as the bubbles burst, fall back, and again are carried up. The continual up-and-down motion, accompanied by the tearing apart of liquid fragments and their constant exposure to streaming gas, removes the less soluble gases (notably the sulfur gases) so that the liquid that ultimately finds its way to the lava vents contains only small amounts of the more soluble gases (notably HCl). As the boiling proceeds in the conduit, fresh lava with dissolved gas is continually supplied from below[226].

The channels connecting the conduit with the area of lava vents are shown as a network of fissures, partly radial and partly concentric around the conduit. The channels must be sufficiently narrow and winding so that temporary changes in the amount of lava supplied to the conduit or in its gas content do not immediately affect lava movement into the vents. If the connection from one lava vent to another is through similar tortuous channels, the independence in vent activity and the apparent disregard of the vents for hydrostatic equilibrium are understandable. Perhaps a similar branching and irregularity of channels may even explain the existence of two or more gas vents in the crater with different kinds of eruptive behavior . . . .

The lava channels change from time to time, probably in part because of erosion by moving lava, in part by slumping, and in part because of pressure exerted by lava and gas within the cone. But in general they remain close to the NE-SW zone of weakness that initially determined their position.

The observed slumping in the crater at times of quiet eruption may be due either to settling into an enlarged portion of the central conduit or to collapse of some of the channels that connect the conduit with the *bocas*. The slow outward movement of the "slice" is explained by the push against it of lava in fissures near the side of the cone; in early March the pressure was sufficient to break through the side of the cone and form a new flow.

This mechanism, unlike others suggested[224], assumes that lava destined for the *boca* area rises high in the central conduit and overflows, instead of branching from the main stream at depth. Assuming a branch at low levels makes it difficult to account for the separation of gas and liquid. Why should the material rising on one branch be greatly different from that in the other? Perhaps the formation of the satellite cone Sapichu, in which the eruptive activity was similar to that in the main crater [but Sapichu "showed no visible eruptive column other than the ejected bombs", see p. 99], represents a branching of the conduit at depth, but the slow welling up of lava in the *boca* requires a different explanation.

Cyclic Changes

A cyclic alternation of abundant flowing lava from the *bocas* and vigorous gas emission from the crater, similar to the alternation described by White[224] in the first year of the volcano's history, is suggested by the observations of Howel Williams in the winter and spring of 1945 [see p. 132-136]. But during the winter of 1945-46 there was little sign of such cyclic alternation. The crater's increased eruptive activity in late January and February followed by a big new lava flow from the base of the cone in March resembles the sequence of events in White's cycle, but there was no diminution in lava activity during the violent eruptive period as required by the cycle. Probably the volcano has reached a stage of activity in which White's cycle is no longer prominent—perhaps because the average gas content of the lava is now smaller, so that "boiling" takes place high in the conduit rather than at lower levels.

The only indication of cyclic repetition of events in this period of observation (1945-46) was the change in activity of the crater from moderately active to quiet and the reverse at approximately 3-week intervals between late October and late January. These alternations were unaccompanied by any significant changes in the emission of lava. They seem more plausibly explained by slight differences in the average level of lava in the conduit, or differences in its gas content, than by the periodic blowing off of gas from a magma chamber at depth.

The day-to-day behavior of the volcano, far from showing any sign of short-term periodicity, remained completely unpredictable. Intervals of quiet, periods of steady gas emission, periods of dull explosions followed one another with complete irregularity. Sometimes a single loud burst of gas would interrupt a period of quiet that otherwise endured for several hours. The form of the eruption cloud sometimes remained almost the same for days, sometimes changed from hour to hour. The 3-week periods labeled "quiet" and "moderately active" are rough generalizations only; within each period activity appropriate to the other type was not uncommon. And during the entire 4 months of observation [November 1945 to February 1946] the amount of flowing lava remained surprisingly constant.

The continual erratic minor variations in activity, combined with the virtual absence of either long-term or short-term cycles and the almost constant outflow of lava, suggest that during the winter of 1945-46 lava remained high in the conduit of the volcano but was subject to slight variations in supply from below. There is no evidence for separation of lava and gas in the magma chamber at depth, but on the contrary the great difference in the amount and kind of gas emitted from the crater and from the lava *bocas* seems good evidence that the separation takes place largely within the cone itself.

Petrologic Studies

Geologists study the chemistry and mineralogy of lavas and ash produced by volcanoes in order to understand the sub-surface processes that formed them. Parícutin's well documented and relatively short lifetime offers an excellent opportunity to investigate these processes. One well-known mechanism that changes the chemical composition of magmas is the removal of early-formed crystals. As crystals of a dense mineral settle downward and accumulate near the base of a magma reservoir, for example, the chemical composition of the overlying magma becomes depleted in elements that are enriched in that mineral. This process is known as fractional crystallization. Another important mechanism of compositional change is contamination of the magma by digestion or assimilation of its wall rocks.

In 1954, Ray Wilcox of the U.S. Geological Survey published his classic account of the petrology and mineralogy of the Parícutin rocks. He collected an extensive suite of lavas, bombs, and xenoliths (accidental inclusions of crustal rocks carried to the surface by the eruption). These samples were analyzed for their major element chemical compositions, and were studied under the microscope to determine mineral abundances, textures, and compositions. Wilcox showed that the chemical compositions and mineralogies of the magmas changed systematically during the 9 years of the eruption: early basaltic andesites had 55 wt% SiO_2 and contained the minerals olivine and plagioclase, whereas late andesites had 60% SiO_2 and contained the mineral orthopyroxene. He used graphical modeling to conclude that this compositional sequence could not have been produced simply by fractional crystallization of these minerals, but required simultaneous contamination of the Parícutin magmas by granitic crustal material, similar to that found as abundant xenoliths in the early stages of the eruption.

Wilcox's study became a classic because it was one of the first thorough demonstrations of the complex processes that operate in many natural magma systems. Almost 40 years after they were published, his conclusions still have a very "modern" ring. They were strongly reinforced by two computer-based modeling studies of his data[227,228], and in a recent study by McBirney, Taylor and Armstrong of trace element abundances and strontium and oxygen isotopic compositions in the same specimens. These samples are now housed at the Smithsonian's National Museum of Natural History. We reproduce below portions of Wilcox's account followed by parts of this later work. The chapter concludes with sections from an experimental study by Eggler to duplicate conditions of the Parícutin magma in laboratory furnaces.

Major Elements and Petrography

Wilcox (1954)

Abstract

A progressive change in composition is noted in successive ejecta of Parícutin volcano. Ejecta of 1943 are of olivine-bearing basaltic andesite containing 55 wt.% SiO_2. Succeeding ejecta are progressively more salic, until in 1952 they are orthopyroxene andesites containing over 60 wt.% SiO_2. With the exception of a sharp decrease in MgO and increase in SiO_2 in 1947, this change in composition of successive ejecta was fairly regular. The ejecta of 1943 and of the first part of 1944 are characterized by small numbers of olivine and plagioclase phenocrysts in groundmasses of plagioclase, olivine, clinopyroxene, orthopyroxene, opaque oxide, and glass. Plagioclase phenocrysts are virtually absent in ejecta after 1944. In ejecta of 1945-1952, the olivine phenocrysts carry coronas of fine-grained hypersthene; and in ejecta of late 1947, olivine phenocrysts are scarce and remain so in successive ejecta through the close of the eruption in 1952. Clinopyroxene phenocrysts occur only rarely and clinopyroxene microphenocrysts only in the ejecta of 1943-44 and in some ejecta from 1946. Orthopyroxene, which becomes more abundant and larger in size in the groundmasses of successive pre-1947 ejecta, occurs also as phenocrysts in ejecta of 1947 and later. In the individual mineral series there appears to be only a slight tendency towards more salic compositions of the minerals themselves in the later erupted materials, although the whole-rock compositions become definitely more salic. Compositions of plagioclase phenocrysts average near An_{70}, those of olivine near Fo_{80}, and those of orthopyroxene near En_{75}, as inferred from optical properties. Groundmass orthopyroxene is consistently poorer in MgO than the phenocrysts of the same specimen. The glassy mesostases of later erupted specimens have lower refractive indices than those of early erupted specimens, indicating more salic compositions.

Xenoliths of granite, quartz monzonite, dacite tuff, and other rock types are found in the ejecta of Parícutin volcano and are presumed to represent some, at least, of the types of country rock at depth. All stages of melting, inflation, and mutual solution of the mineral components of the xenoliths are seen, but there seem to be only a few easily recognized examples of intimate strewing of xenolithic material through the normal ejecta, and the visible transition zones between lava and xenolith do not usually exceed a few millimeters in width. Xenocrysts of quartz and feldspar occur sporadically in a few lava specimens that appear to be otherwise normal.

On the basis of graphical tests using the chemical and petrographic data, it is concluded that fractional crystallization alone could not have caused the observed differences between successive ejecta. A combination of fractional crystallization (involving olivine and plagioclase) and assimilation of salic country rock is shown, by use of the silica-variation diagram, to satisfy closely the chemical relationships among the lavas; and rough calculations indicate that the heat required for this process appears to be available by convection without superheat if a reasonable configuration of the magma cupola is assumed.

Introduction

The purpose of this paper will be to examine the remarkable continuity of eruptive activity and an equally remarkable progressive change in composition of successively erupted material from basaltic andesite of 55 wt.% SiO_2 in 1943 to andesite of slightly over 60 wt.% SiO_2 at the end of the eruption in 1952.

. . . . .

The present study began with a period of essentially continuous observation of the activity of Parícutin volcano from September 1946 through May 1948, and thereafter observations were confined to short monthly visits until December 1948. Specimens of the erupted material collected then, together with specimens collected by other investigators before and after the period of my field work, form the basis of the petrographic and chemical portions of this study.

. . . . .

Petrography

During the protracted eruption of Parícutin volcano, the petrographic character of successive ejecta changed from an olivine-bearing basaltic andesite to an orthopyroxene-bearing andesite, and this change was accompanied by a gradual change of whole-rock chemical compositions. In the petrographic descriptions that follow, the phenocrysts will be discussed separately from the groundmasses, which include microphenocrysts, microlites, and glassy mesostasis.

The material erupted during 1943 and early 1944 is characterized by small numbers of olivine and plagioclase phenocrysts in a groundmass composed of plagioclase, olivine, and clinopyroxene microphenocrysts (with or without orthopyroxene microphenocrysts), in a clear glass or microlite-charged mesostasis. The material erupted after the first part of 1944 is notably lacking in plagioclase phenocrysts, and until 1947 the only phenocrysts are olivine, lying in a groundmass of plagioclase, decreasing amounts of olivine and clinopyroxene microphenocrysts, and increasing amounts of orthopyroxene microphenocrysts in the glassy mesostasis. The material erupted after 1947 and until the end of 1950 is characterized by scattered orthopyroxene phenocrysts and, rarely, corroded olivine phenocrysts in a groundmass composed of plagioclase and orthopyroxene microphenocrysts and glassy mesostasis.

. . . . .

In the present study more than 125 specimens of lavas, bombs, and xenoliths from Parícutin volcano have been examined in hand specimen and in thin section. The dates of eruption of these specimens cover the period from 1943 through 1952—with unfortunate gaps during the first portion of 1946, for which specimens are not available, and during the first portion of 1948, specimens of which were lost in shipment. Optic angles and extinction angles were measured directly in thin sections on a universal stage. Refractive indices (nX') of plagioclase cleavage fragments were determined in immersion liquids with sodium light as were values of nZ for some orthopyroxene cleavage fragments. Measurements of nX, nY, and nZ for other orthopyroxenes and for olivines were made using the method of Rosenfeld[229]. Compositions of individual minerals in the Parícutin lavas have been inferred from their optical properties,

using $2V$ and nZ of orthopyroxene, refractive indices of olivine, and extinction angles $X' \wedge 010_{max}$ and $X' \wedge 010 \perp a$ for plagioclase[230].

. . . . .

The volume percentages of phenocrysts, measured by the Chayes[231] point-counting method, are given in Table 25 for all but five of the analyzed specimens and for a few additional specimens. The results are graphed according to dates of eruption in Fig. 188. Because in some specimens there is no sharp demarcation in size-frequency distribution between large and small phenocrysts, phenocrysts have been arbitrarily defined as crystals larger than 0.3 mm in longest dimension, whereas microphenocrysts are defined fined as those crystals ranging in size from 0.3 mm down to 0.03 mm, the lower limit depending somewhat on morphology. The relative abundance of microphenocrysts and microlites of plagioclase, olivine, orthopyroxene, and clinopyroxene estimated by eye in all the thin sections available, are graphed according to dates of eruption in Fig. 189. Where two or more specimens are so close in date of eruption that they could not be shown separately, the average of the results is graphed for the group of specimens of that date. In the following paragraphs the petrography will first be described for several individual specimens, then for the individual constituents through the series. This will be followed by a description of representative xenoliths and a discussion of the mutual effects between xenolith and enclosing lava.

Table 25. Volume percentages of phenocrysts, groundmass (vesicle-free), and vesicles in Parícutin lavas.

Analysis number	Specimen number	Date Erupted	Megaphenocrysts				Ground-mass	Vesicles
			Olivine	Ortho-pyrox-ene	Clino-pyrox-ene	Plagio-clase		
1	....	Feb. 22, 1943	2.2	0	0	1.1	96.7	17.7
4	11-16-1	Apr. (?) 1944	3.3	0	0	0	96.7	2.0
6	11-29-1	Nov. 1945	2.5	0	0	0	97.5	19.5
7	11-26-2	Nov.	3.6	0	0	0	96.4	17.3
8	12-7-1	Dec.	3.2	0	0	0	96.8	9.5
9	12-3-1	Dec.	3.3	0	0	0	96.7	26.6
10	12-19-1	Dec.	3.0	0	0	0	97.0	20.5
	2-7-1	Feb. 1946	4.0	0	0	0	96.0	14.5
11	W-46-27	Sept.	2.6	tr	0	0	97.4	7.3
	W-47-6	Feb. 1947	2.5	0	0	0	97.5	11.8
12	W-47-9	May	4.5	0	0	0	95.5	24.7
13	W-47-14	June	3.5	.1	0	0	96.4	15.1
14	W-47-19	Sept.	2.3	.7	0	.3	96.7	5.7
15	W-47-30	Nov.	1.8	tr	0	0	98.2	30.8
	W-47-31	Dec.	1.7	0	0	0	98.3	15.0
16	W-48-5	Aug. 1948	.9	.7	0	0	98.4	14.0
17	FP-5-49	May 1949	.2	1.4	0	0	98.4	23.5
18	FP-20-49	Dec.	.6	1.3	0	0	98.1	12.0
19	FP-20-50	Sept. 1950	0	1.2	0	.1	98.7	29.1
	FP-55-50	Dec.	.3	2.4	0	0	97.3	14.0
22	FP-16-52	Feb. 1952	.3	.7	0	.1	98.9	18.2

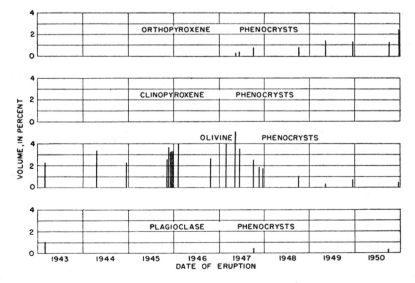

Fig. 188. Volume percentages of phenocrysts in some Parícutin ejecta, plotted according to date of eruption.

Representative Lava Specimens

Wilcox describes the petrography and optical mineralogy of ten lava samples in detail. We reproduce only four of these descriptions here, samples for which photomicrographs are shown in Fig. 190.

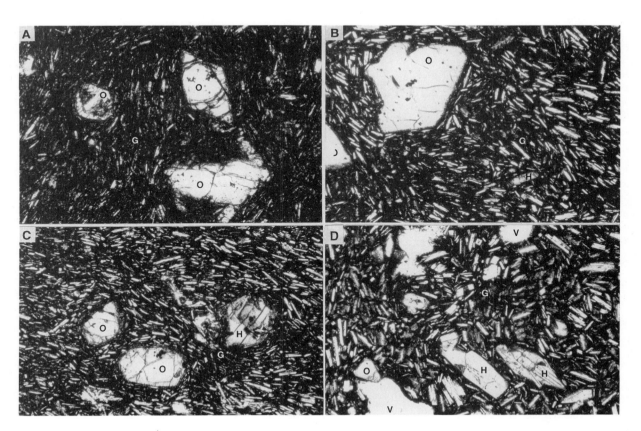

Fig. 189. Relative abundances of groundmass minerals in Parícutin ejecta, plotted according to date of eruption. Microphenocrysts are shown by solid bars, reacting olivine by circle bars, and microlites by dotted bars.

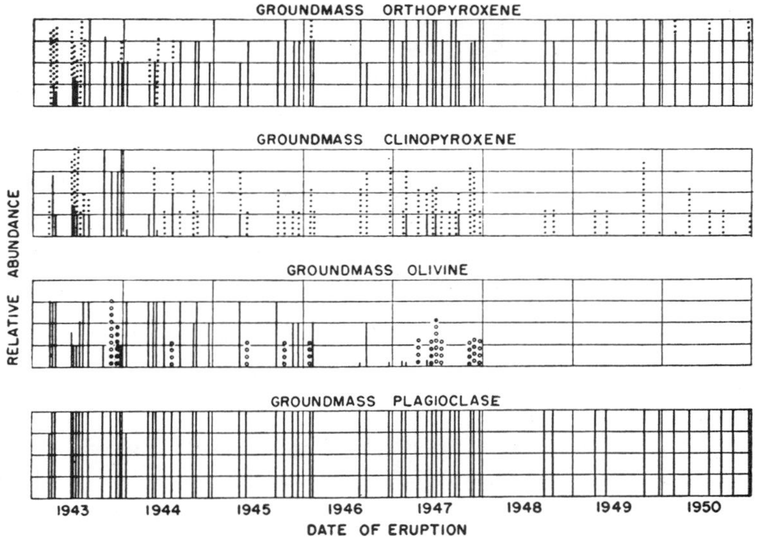

GROUNDMASS ORTHOPYROXENE

GROUNDMASS CLINOPYROXENE

GROUNDMASS OLIVINE

GROUNDMASS PLAGIOCLASE

RELATIVE ABUNDANCE

1943 1944 1945 1946 1947 1948 1949 1950

DATE OF ERUPTION

Fig. 190. Photomicrographs of four lava samples. All in plane light, 3.5 mm across. Abbreviations: G = groundmass glass with plagioclase and other microlites, H = hypersthene (orthopyroxene), O = olivine with spinel inclusions, and V = vesicles (holes). a) late-February 1943 lava 51-W-18; b) April 9, 1947 lava W-47-9; c) August 1948 lava W-48-5; d) February 25, 1952 lava FP-16-52.

327

Table 26. Analyses of lavas from Parícutin volcano.

	1	2	3	4	5	6	7	8	9	10	11
Bulk Analyses											
SiO₂	55.04	54.88	55.51	55.21	55.59	56.41	56.15	56.48	56.41	56.61	56.13
Al₂O₃	18.82	18.38	18.19	17.94	17.72	17.67	17.57	17.57	17.60	17.61	17.34
Fe₂O₃	1.92	1.31	1.63	1.60	1.33	1.39	1.80	1.63	1.67	1.45	1.74
FeO	5.69	5.97	5.38	5.96	5.99	5.40	5.08	5.18	5.18	5.35	5.42
MgO	5.68	5.57	5.31	5.37	5.60	5.66	5.68	5.56	5.62	5.64	5.58
CaO	7.17	7.40	7.19	6.98	6.99	6.89	6.95	6.95	6.90	6.89	6.99
Na₂O	3.88	3.88	3.92	3.87	4.00	3.87	3.85	3.70	3.81	3.84	3.79
K₂O	.85	.86	1.10	1.26	1.13	1.19	1.18	1.34	1.20	1.21	1.30
H₂O+	} .16 {	.13	.08	.05	.03	.04	.04	.08	.05	.05	.20
H₂O−		.05	.01	.01	.04	.03	.04	.00	.00	.03	.06
CO₂	n. d.	n. d.	n. d.	n. d.	n. d.	n. d.	n. d.	n. d.	n. d.	n. d.	.06
TiO₂	.94	.95	.97	1.08	1.05	.93	.95	.94	.93	.93	1.02
P₂O₅	.21	.29	.31	.41	.36	.30	.30	.37	.31	.30	.36
MnO	.07	.13	.12	.13	.13	.12	.12	.11	.12	.11	.12
Total	[1]100.51	99.80	99.72	99.87	99.96	99.90	99.71	99.91	99.80	100.02	100.11
Normative minerals											
Q	3.47	2.40	3.54	3.30	3.46	4.62	4.86	5.63	5.59	4.86	4.87
Or	4.99	5.56	6.67	7.77	6.62	7.22	7.23	7.77	6.69	7.23	7.80
Ab	32.40	33.01	33.52	32.44	33.82	32.45	32.49	31.39	32.04	32.46	32.04
An	31.32	30.02	28.63	27.76	26.78	27.48	27.24	27.48	27.87	27.21	26.48
Wo	1.04	2.20	2.32	1.86	2.18	2.09	2.32	1.86	1.98	2.20	2.79
En	14.16	14.00	13.28	13.38	13.91	14.19	14.20	13.88	14.13	14.10	13.93
Fs	7.37	8.58	7.26	8.04	8.26	7.52	6.60	6.86	7.02	7.52	6.88
Mt	2.77	1.86	2.32	2.32	1.85	2.09	2.55	2.32	2.33	2.09	2.56
Il	1.82	1.67	1.82	2.13	2.12	1.67	1.82	1.82	1.68	1.67	1.98
Ap	.67	.67	.67	1.01	1.00	.67	.67	1.01	.67	.67	.67
Calculated groundmass compositions											
SiO₂	55.53	--------	--------	56.12	--------	57.20	57.30	57.42	57.45	57.42	56.94
Al₂O₃	19.22	--------	--------	18.80	--------	18.34	18.53	18.39	18.46	18.36	18.02
Total Fe as FeO	7.15	--------	--------	6.92	--------	6.24	6.15	6.15	6.16	6.18	6.60
MgO	4.66	--------	--------	3.76	--------	4.41	3.94	4.01	4.02	4.18	4.34
CaO	7.29	--------	--------	7.31	--------	7.15	7.33	7.27	7.24	7.18	7.26
Na₂O	4.00	--------	--------	4.05	--------	4.02	4.06	3.87	4.00	4.01	3.93
K₂O	.88	--------	--------	1.32	--------	1.23	1.25	1.40	1.26	1.26	1.36
TiO₂	.98	--------	--------	1.13	--------	.96	1.01	.98	.97	.97	1.06
P₂O₅	.22	--------	--------	.43	--------	.31	.31	.39	.32	.31	.37
MnO	.07	--------	--------	.14	--------	.12	.12	.11	.12	.11	.12
Total	100.00	--------	--------	99.98	--------	99.98	100.00	99.99	100.00	99.98	100.00

[1] Includes 0.04 S and 0.06 BaO.

Data on specimens analysed

Analysis	Specimen	Date erupted	Collector	Analyst
1	----------------	Feb. 22, 1943	C. A. Cooper	Charles Milton (1945).
2	USNM 108058	Mar. 1943	W. H. Foshag	E. Chadbourn (Williams, 1950).
3	USNM 108073	Nov. 1943	----do	Do.
4	11-16-1	Apr. (?) 1944	K. Krauskopf	James Kerr.
5	USNM 108100	Nov. 1944	W. H. Foshag	E. Chadbourn (Williams, 1950).
6	11-29-1	Nov. 1945	K. Krauskopf	James Kerr.
7	11-26-2	Nov. 21, 1945	----do	Do.
8	12-7-1	Dec. 1945	----do	Do.
9	12-3-1	----do	----do	Do.
10	12-19-1	----do	----do	Do.
11	W-46-27	Sept. 18, 1946	J. A. Hernández V	H. Hyman.

12	13	14	15	16	17	18	19	20	21	22
Bulk Analyses—Continued										
57.05	57.63	58.13	58.39	59.09	59.41	59.77	59.93	60.24	60.38	60.07
17.27	17.50	17.59	17.78	17.55	17.30	17.29	17.31	17.30	17.27	17.28
1.42	1.38	1.27	1.87	2.04	1.57	1.21	1.23	1.19	1.10	1.37
5.21	5.12	5.20	4.51	4.27	4.78	4.95	4.95	4.59	4.66	4.39
5.64	5.16	4.55	4.03	4.03	3.81	3.72	3.55	3.55	3.59	3.73
6.94	6.77	6.72	6.75	6.46	6.36	6.28	6.21	6.14	6.16	6.16
3.71	3.71	3.79	3.86	3.92	3.71	3.74	3.73	4.01	3.89	4.00
1.23	1.38	1.41	1.30	1.50	1.67	1.67	1.72	1.66	1.69	1.67
.17	.04	.10	.11	.08	.12	.12	.10	.04	.05	.03
.02	.02	.03	.01	.03	.00	.00	.00	.04	.05	.05
.02	.01	.01	.01	.00	.02	.00	.01	.00	.00	.01
.89	.86	.84	.86	.78	.84	.83	.83	.80	.80	.81
.29	.29	.30	.30	.30	.31	.31	.30	.29	.28	.28
.12	.12	.11	.12	.11	.11	.11	.11	.10	.10	.10
99.98	99.99	100.05	99.90	100.16	100.01	100.00	99.98	99.95	100.01	99.95
Normative minerals—Continued										
6.30	7.01	7.59	9.71	10.13	10.77	10.80	11.28	10.68	11.58	10.51
7.23	8.32	8.32	7.77	8.89	10.04	10.01	10.01	10.02	10.01	10.02
31.42	31.37	32.46	32.44	32.98	31.52	31.96	31.96	34.07	32.49	34.10
26.95	26.91	26.62	27.47	25.82	25.64	25.30	25.30	24.20	25.02	24.22
2.44	2.09	2.21	1.86	1.86	1.86	1.74	1.63	1.97	1.63	1.97
14.10	12.88	11.38	10.09	10.09	9.52	9.30	8.90	8.91	9.00	9.31
7.13	6.99	7.37	5.54	5.02	6.36	6.86	6.86	6.34	6.47	5.82
2.09	2.09	1.86	2.78	3.02	2.10	1.86	1.86	1.62	1.62	1.86
1.67	1.67	1.52	1.67	1.52	1.52	1.52	1.52	1.52	1.52	1.52
.67	.67	.67	.67	.67	.67	.67	.67	.67	.67	.67
Calculated groundmass compositions—Continued										
58.37	58.65	58.91	59.10	59.44	59.71	60.16	60.16	--------	--------	--------
18.40	18.40	18.29	18.28	17.95	17.71	17.76	17.60	--------	--------	--------
5.74	5.76	5.89	5.92	5.87	5.99	5.77	5.93	--------	--------	--------
3.42	3.39	3.19	3.14	3.38	3.29	3.01	3.19	--------	--------	--------
7.40	7.11	6.98	6.94	6.61	6.51	6.46	6.32	--------	--------	--------
3.95	3.90	3.95	3.97	4.01	3.80	3.84	3.79	--------	--------	--------
1.31	1.45	1.47	1.34	1.53	1.70	1.71	1.75	--------	--------	--------
.95	.90	.88	.88	.80	.86	.85	.85	--------	--------	--------
.31	.30	.31	.31	.31	.32	.32	.31	--------	--------	--------
.13	.12	.11	.12	.11	.11	.11	.11	--------	--------	--------
99.98	99.98	99.98	100.00	100.01	100.00	99.99	100.01	--------	--------	--------

Data on specimens analysed—Continued

Analysis	Specimen	Date erupted	Collector	Analyst
12	W–47–9	Apr. 9, 1947	J. A. Hernández V.	H. HYman
13	W–47–14	June 10, 1947	C. Gutiérrez	Do.
14	W–47–19	Sept. 5, 1947	S. Shoup O.	Do.
15	W–47–30	Nov. 1947	R. E. Wilcox	Do.
16	W–48–5	Aug. 1948	do	Do.
17	FP–5–49	May 19, 1949	C. Fries, Jr	Do.
18	FP–20–49	Dec. 13, 1949	do	Do.
19	FP–20–50	Sept. 1, 1950	do	Do.
20	FP–5–51	May 1951	do	Lucile Tarrant.
21	FP–13–51	Nov. 1951	C. Gutiérrez	Do.
22	FP–16–52	Feb. 25, 1952	C. Fries, Jr	Do.

February 1943: 51-W-18

The thin section for the lava specimen of February 22, 1943 (analysis 1, Table 26), collected by G.A. Cooper and chemically analysed by Charles Milton[232], shows 2.2 vol.% euhedral olivine phenocrysts up to 0.5 mm in diameter and 1.1 vol.% plagioclase phenocrysts up to 0.4 mm in length. The hand specimen of this section was not available to the writer. An olivine phenocryst from lava erupted later in February 1943 (specimen 51-W-18 [Fig. 190a]), however, showed the following refractive indices:

nX = 1.667 ± 0.002
nY = 1.691 to 1.693 ± 0.002
nZ = 1.713 ± 0.003
Inferred composition is Fo_{82-79}.

Extinction angles $X' \wedge 010 \perp a$ of four plagioclase phenocrysts range from 39° to 36° with slight progressive normal zoning. The inferred average range of composition is An_{75-72}. Groundmass is composed of abundant microphenocrysts of plagioclase, showing slight progressive normal zoning (inferred average range An_{74-68}), many euhedral microphenocrysts, and grains of olivine (inferred composition near Fo_{70} by $2V$), and abundant microlites of orthopyroxene (?), chiefly as stubby prisms up to 0.005 mm length in a mesostasis of brown glass composing about 5 vol.% of the rock.

. . . . .

April 1947: W-47-9

Lava that issued from the NE lava vent on April 9, 1947 (Specimen W-47-9, analysis 12, Table 26) is quite vesicular and contains 4.5 vol.% olivine phenocrysts ranging up to 0.8 mm in diameter, showing corroded outlines, and carrying coronas of small orthopyroxene crystals [Fig. 190b]. . . . Refractive indices determined on cleavage fragments of olivine phenocrysts showed:

nX = 1.675
nY = 1.695
nZ = approximately 1.712
Inferred composition is about Fo_{80}.

No plagioclase phenocrysts are present. The groundmass consists of abundant plagioclase laths up to 0.25 mm in length, abundant orthopyroxene prisms up to 0.20 mm in length, a moderate number of clinopyroxene needles, scattered grains of olivine (rimmed with orthopyroxene), and dust-size, opaque oxide in a cloudy brown glass mesostasis that composes about 25 vol.% of the rock. Centers of groundmass plagioclase show $X' \wedge 010$ maximum, ranging from 35° to 38° (implying An_{60} to An_{66}) and rims range from 25° to 35° (An_{44} to An_{60}). Three groundmass crystals of orthopyroxene have optic angles (negative) $2V$ = 72° to 75° (implying En_{69} to En_{71}).

. . . . .

August 1948: W-48-5

A specimen erupted in August 1948 (specimen W-48-5, analysis 16, Table 26) is moderately vesicular and contains 0.9 vol.% of olivine phenocrysts and 0.7 vol.% (of vesicle-free rock) of orthopyroxene phenocrysts [Fig. 190c]. The olivine phenocrysts, ranging up to 0.8 mm diameter, are corroded and carry coronas of fine-grained orthopyroxene crystals. The few orthopyroxene phenocrysts occur as euhedral prisms up to 0.7 mm in length. The refractive index, nZ = 1.695 on cleavage fragments, and optic angle determination, (negative) $2V$ = 80°, for one orthopyroxene crystal imply a composition of En_{75}. The groundmass is composed of abundant orthopyroxene prisms up to 0.15 mm in length, with clinopyroxene as flanking plates on a few of them, and abundant tiny crystals and chains of opaque oxide (both adhering to and included in the orthopyroxene) and dust-like particles in the dark-brown, nearly opaque glass basis that composes about 25 vol.% of the rock. The centers of groundmass plagioclase crystals show extinction angles $X' \wedge 010_{max}$ ranging from 34° to 40° (An_{58} to An_{70}), with rims ranging down to compositions as low as An_{48}. Optic angles of six groundmass orthopyroxene crystals range from (negative) $2V$ = 65° to 68° (En_{61} to En_{65}). These exceptionally low values of En content are confirmed by the higher birefringence and stronger pleochroism observed in thin section.

. . . . .

February 25, 1952: FP-16-52

Specimen FP-16-52 (analysis 22, Table 26), from the last lava erupted, was collected at the vent a few days after lava activity had ceased on Feb. 25, 1952. It is quite vesicular and in thin section shows 0.3 vol.% olivine phenocrysts, which range up to 0.6 mm diameter and carry thin reaction rims of orthopyroxene. Also present is 0.7 vol.% euhedral orthopyroxene phenocrysts up to 0.5 mm in length and 0.1 vol.% plagioclase phenocrysts up to 0.35 mm in length [Fig. 190d]. One orthopyroxene phenocryst in the thin section had (negative) $2V$ = 79° and grains in immersion liquids showed nZ = 1.692, implying a composition about En_{75}.

Groundmass consists of abundant plagioclase microphenocrysts, generally better formed than in most earlier lavas; many orthopyroxene microphenocrysts; abundant microlites of orthopyroxene and clinopyroxene; dust-size titanomagnetite in some areas; and a brown-glass mesostasis (10-20 vol.%), which in some areas is made nearly opaque by dusty inclusions and in other areas is translucent.

The central portions of the plagioclase microphenocrysts show $X' \wedge 010_{max}$ = 33°-38° (An_{56-66}) and $X' \wedge 010 \perp a$ = 32°-36° (An_{60-70}). Refractive index on cleavage, nX' = 1.562, implies compositions about An_{65}. Zoning is normal progressive and only slightly marked, except at the extreme edges of the crystals where $X' \wedge 010 \perp a$ ranges down to as low as 30° (An_{56}) in some crystals. Orthopyroxene microphenocrysts have (negative) $2V$ = 75°-78°, implying compositions of En_{71-73}. Quite a few are intergrown or coupled with plagioclase microphenocrysts, and still others show narrow flanking plates of clinopyroxene.

Individual Constituents of Lavas

The major constituents of the successive lava ejecta of Parícutin volcano include plagioclase, olivine, orthopyroxene, clinopyroxene, opaque oxide, and glass. In this section the occurrence of each mineral as phenocrysts, microphenocrysts, and microlites will be described, with the discussion of paragenetic relations being left to a later section. Figure 188 shows the volume percentages of phenocrysts in those specimens on which modal analyses have been made (Table 25). Figure 189 shows relative abundances of microphenocrysts and microlites, estimated from all thin sections available, with no distinction being made between lavas and bombs.

Plagioclase

Phenocrysts are rare in all Parícutin ejecta except in those of 1943 and early 1944. In one thin section of March 1943 ejecta (collected by the Instituto de Geología de México), plagioclase phenocrysts up to 1 mm in length are common, as they appear to have been in several of the 1943 specimens examined by Schmitter[233]. Zoning is generally slight, and extinction angles in thin sections that I examined imply compositions of An_{68-74}. Thin rims of some crystals are progressively zoned to as low as An_{53}.

Plagioclase is present as a groundmass constituent in all the ejecta of Parícutin volcano, much in contrast to its limited occurrence as phenocrysts. Groundmass plagioclase occurs as lath- and tablet-shaped microphenocrysts, generally not more than 0.25 mm long, and microlites (length less than 0.03 mm) are not generally developed. The plagioclase microphenocrysts typically show weak, progressive normal zoning in their central portions and strong, progressive normal zoning in their narrow rims. The Rittmann zone method was used to measure the extinction angles of 10 crystal in each of 7 specimens listed in Table 27. The results in most specimens indicate a range of about 10 mol.% in apparent anorthite content from crystal to crystal. In order of dates of eruption, the average compositions for each specimen are 74, 68, 62, 63, 65, 65, and 63 mol.% anorthite. It is thus apparent that the change in average anorthite content of plagioclase microphenocrysts from 1944-52 is not great and that the trends have not been entirely consistent. It is, of course, possible that more extensive determinations might reveal a more consistent trend. The anorthite contents of the thin rims of plagioclase microphenocrysts range down to as low as An_{46} (specimen W-47-9).

Table 27. Summary of anorthite contents for central portions of plagioclase microphenocrysts. Ten crystals determined in each specimen on universal stage.

Analysis	Specimen	Date of eruption	Extinction angle		Molecular percent anorthite (after Winchell 1951) [1]	
			$X' \wedge 010_{max}$	$X' \wedge 010 \perp a$	Range	Average
1		Feb. 1943		36°-40°	70-78	74
4	11-16-2	Apr. (?) 1944		34°-37°	65-73	68
	W-47-24	Oct. 1944	34°-38°		58-66	62
12	W-47-9	May 1947	35°-38°		60-66	63
15	W-47-30	Sept. 1947	35°-40°		60-70	65
16	W-48-5	Sept 1948	34°-40°	34°	58-70	65
22	FP-16-52	Feb. 1952	33°-38°	32°-36°	56-70	63

[1] The "high-temperature" curves of Tröger (1952, p. 113) imply anorthite contents from 6 to 11 percent lower than the values listed.

Olivine

Phenocrysts of olivine are consistently present in all thin sections of specimens erupted before 1948. In specimens on which modal analyses have been made, olivine phenocrysts are present in amounts up to 4.5 vol.% (see Fig. 188), and in a few other specimens are estimated to amount to as much as 6 or 7 vol.%. In the succesive ejecta of the second half of 1947, a sudden and remarkably uniform decrease in amounts of olivine phenocrysts took place, and this finds its expression also in the sharp decrease in MgO content of the analyzed specimens (Fig. 191). Subsequent ejecta are characterized by a paucity of olivine pheno-

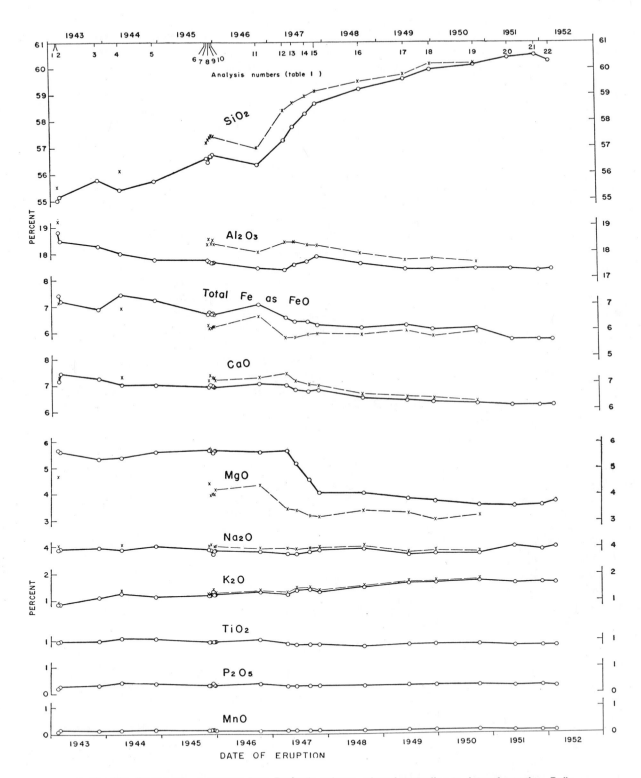

Fig. 191. Compositions of lavas from Parícutin volcano, plotted according to date of eruption. Bulk analyses (Table 26), recast with all iron as FeO and excluding volatiles are plotted as circles. Calculated groundmass compositions are plotted as crosses.

crysts. Little reaction or corrosion is shown by the olivine phenocrysts of 1943 and 1944 ejecta; in later ejecta, however, reaction rims of fine-grained orthopyroxene become more evident.

Refractive indices and inferred chemical compositions of olivine phenocrysts in several lavas of Parícutin volcano are given in Table 28. The range of composition is from Fo_{76} to Fo_{84} with the major bulk of phenocryst material judged to be of compositions between Fo_{80} and Fo_{78}. A decrease of $2V_{over\,X}$ of 2° to 3° from center to rim of some crystals implies 4-6 mol.% less Fo in the rims than in the center. The olivine phenocrysts characteristically carry tiny euhedral crystals of opaque oxide up to 0.01 mm diameter, as scattered individuals or in clusters or strings. Those I examined are opaque even in the most intense light and are presumed to be magnetite or titanomagnetite; it is noted, however, that Schmitter[233] identified spinel inclusions in olivine phenocrysts in several specimens erupted in 1943. Because of the presence of these inclusions, the bulk compositions of the olivine phenocrysts no doubt is slightly higher in iron than indicated by optical properties.

The olivine of the groundmass occurs as microphenocrysts and grains in widely varying amounts in the ejecta of 1943-46; in a few specimens the texture is seriate, and the distinction between phenocrysts and microphenocrysts (and grains) of olivine is made by using the arbitary 0.3 mm limit. The optic angle of one groundmass crystal of olivine in a lava from 1944 (Krauskopf specimen 11-23-2) is (negative) $2V = 88°$, corresponding to a theoretical composition of Fo_{74}. Excellently formed microphenocrysts of olivine are found in some of the pumices and lapilli ejected from the main vent during 1943 . . . and these show little or no reaction. Reaction rims of orthopyroxene around grains of groundmass olivine appear in some ejecta from 1943-45 and become increasingly wider in ejecta from 1946 and 1947. No groundmass olivine was found in post-1947 ejecta.

Clinopyroxene

Clinopyroxene does not occur as phenocrysts in Parícutin specimens except in rare circumstances. In the groundmasses of several of the earlier lavas and bombs of Parícutin volcano, microphenocrysts of clinopyroxene, rarely as much as 0.1 mm long, are moderately well developed. Extinction angles Z to c

Table 28. Refractive indices and inferred compositions of olivine phenocrysts in lavas of Parícutin volcano.

[~ indicates approximately]

Specimen number	Date of Eruption	nZ	nY	nX	Composition
51-W-18	Mar. 1943	1.713	1.692	1.667	Fo_{80-84}
51-W-20	May 1943	1.711	1.693	1.676	Fo_{79-81}
W-47-9	May 1947	~1.712	1.695	1.675	Fo_{79-80}
FP-20-49	Dec. 1949	~1.720	-----	1.676	Fo_{76-81}

ranging from 45° to 51° would indicate that these crystals are augitic rather than pigeonitic. Micro-phenocrysts of clinopyroxene do not occur in ejecta from 1945 and 1946, but appear again in some of the ejecta from 1947.

The most common occurrence of clinopyroxene is as microlitic prisms and needles in the glassy mesostasis of the ejecta. Clinopyroxene microlites are present in the majority of lavas erupted during 1943-47 and are spasmodically present in lavas erupted after 1947. Microlitic clinopyroxene commonly occurs also as plate-like overgrowths on the flanks of orthopyroxene microphenocrysts, sometimes extending as long swallowtails and bundles beyond the ends of the orthopyroxene crystals into the glass . . . . These flanking plates of clinopyroxene apparently lie against the (100) faces of the orthopyroxene, with coincidence of the b crystallographic axes (compare Kuno[234]). Opaque oxide adheres so thickly to the microlitic prisms of clinopyroxene in some specimens as to obscure their optical character, while the orthopyroxene of the same specimens have few if any adherent opaque oxides. Extinction angles Z to c ranging from 45° to 50° for the clinopyroxene microlites and flanking plates imply that they are augitic rather than pigeonitic.

Orthopyroxene

Phenocrysts of orthopyroxene are characteristically present in the Parícutin material erupted after 1946, but they are rarely present in earlier ejecta. In Fig. 188 it is seen that olivine gives way to orthopyroxene as the predominant phenocrysts in the later lavas and that the transition occurred mainly during 1947. Orthopyroxene phenocrysts occur generally as thick prisms up to 1.0 mm in length, rarely up to 1.4 mm, and as cruciform growths and clusters of several crystals . . . . They show weak but perceptible pleochroism, and optic angle measurements imply compositions from En_{70} to En_{80} (Table 29). Refractive index measurements for orthopyroxene phenocrysts from specimen W-48-5 (analysis 16, Table 26)

Table 29. Optic angles of orthopyroxene, with compositions inferred from curves of Winchell[230].

Specimen	Date of Eruption	Phenocrysts						Microphenocrysts				
		Number determined	Range (−) 2V	Molecular percent En			Number determined	Range (−) 2V	Molecular percent En		
				Minimum	Maximum	Average			Minimum	Maximum	Average
11-16-1	Apr. (?) 1944						2	68°–70°	65	67	66
W-47-9	May 1947						3	72°–75°	69	71	70
W-47-30	Nov. 1947						7	70°–79°	66	74	71
W-48-5	Sept. 1948	1	80°	..		75	6	65°–68°	61	65	64
W-48-9	Oct. 1948						1	68°			65
FP-20-49	Dec. 1949	5	76°–86°	72	80	75	2	75°			71
FP-20-50	Sept. 1950	5	75°–79°	71	74	73	5	69°–76°	66	72	68
FP-55-50	Dec. 1950	1	74°			70	2	68°–69°	65	66	65
FP-16-52	Feb. 1952	1	79°			74	4	75°–78°	71	73	72

showed $nZ = 1.695$, from which a composition of En_{75} is inferred.

Orthopyroxene occurs in the groundmasses of the great majority of the Parícutin lavas and bombs. In only a few of the rocks is it lacking or doubtfully present, notably those erupted during 1943. In most of 1943 and 1944 lavas, it is found as microlites and microphenocrysts of varying length and slimness from specimen to specimen, mostly too small for measurement of optic angles. In the later lavas it is found as larger prisms, and through successively erupted specimens the maximum lengths of the orthopyroxene prisms increases gradually until in 1947 the maximum exceeds 0.3 mm, the arbitrary boundary size between microphenocryst and phenocryst set here. Optic angles of orthopyroxene microphenocrysts, given in Table 29, show a range of (negative) $2V$ from 65° to 79°, from which a compositional range of En_{61} to En_{74} is inferred. There is only a slight, if any, trend towards lower En content in later ejecta, but it is apparent that the compositions of the microphenocrysts are consistently lower in En content than the phenocrysts in the corresponding specimens. In many specimens clinopyroxene overgrowths are common . . . as thin plates on the (100) faces of orthopyroxene, as described above in connection with clinopyroxene.

Opaque and Accessory Minerals

No attempt was made to distinguish between the various possible opaque minerals encountered during thin section examination except to establish that yellow metallic sulfides were not present in observable amounts or grain sizes. On the basis of the octahedral-like form of some of the better-formed crystals and on the bulk chemical analyses, it is concluded that most of these opaque crystals are magnetite or titaniferous magnetite. The opaque material occurs in several situations: as isolated, tiny, well-formed crystals up to 0.02 mm in diameter and groups included in olivine and orthopyroxene phenocrysts, as tiny crystals, clusters, and skeletal groups in the groundmass, and as minute dust-like particles distributed through the glassy mesostasis of many of the rocks. In many specimens the opaque crystals are seen to adhere individually or in clusters to the microlites and larger crystals of ferromagnesian minerals, particularly to the clinopyroxene microlites. Accessory minerals were not searched for systematically other than to determine that the great preponderance of the tiny, low-birefringent microphenocrysts were orthopyroxene rather than apatite, which, from the bulk chemical compositions, can be expected to be present in small amount.

Glass

Glass is consistently present in the suite of rocks from Parícutin. It varies in amount from a diffuse mesostasis to an appreciable portion of the groundmass. All gradations in transparency are found, from clear light-brown glass carrying scattered well-developed microphenocrysts of ferromagnesian minerals and plagioclase to nearly opaque material, which is seen under high magnification to be crowded with ferromagnesian microlites, opaque dust-like particles, and minute vesicles. There seems to be a tendency for more common occurrence of clear glass in the very early ejecta (1943-44) and in the late ejecta (1949-52) . . . .

Representative Xenoliths and Basement Rocks

Wilcox describes the petrography and optical mineralogy of eleven silica-rich xenoliths and basement samples in detail. We reproduce only four of these descriptions here, samples for which photomicrographs are shown in Fig. 192.

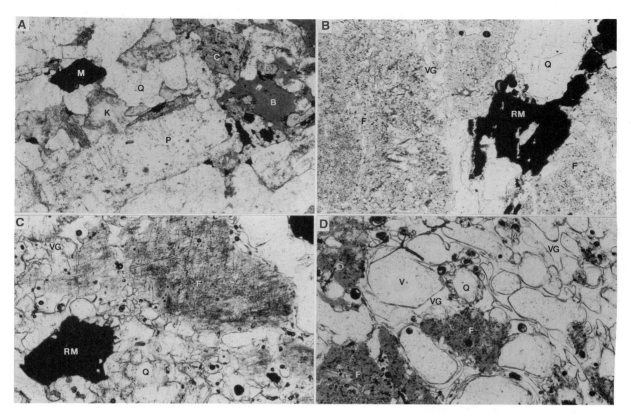

Fig. 192. Photomicrographs of a basement "granite" and three "granitic" xenoliths. All in plane light. Abbreviations: B = biotite, C = clinopyroxene, F = unspecified feldspar that is fractured and melted, with internal glass pockets, K = K-feldspar, M = magnetite or ilmenite, P = plagioclase, Q = quartz, RM = unspecified mafic mineral (pyroxene, biotite, amphibole) that has reacted upon heating to form an opaque mass, VG = vesicular glass. a) unmelted basement sample FP-20-52, 3.5 mm across; b) xenolith 51-W-1, 1.7 mm across; c) xenolith 51-W-9, 3.5 mm across; d) xenolith 51-W-8, 3.5 mm across.

Some 20 xenoliths, mostly from Parícutin bombs, have been examined in thin section. In hand specimen all of these are light colored, contrasting with the black and dark brown of the normal Parícutin material. The majority consist of highly vesicular glass through which are distributed grains of quartz, feldspar, and ferromagnesian minerals in various stages of destruction. Both plutonic and extrusive rock types appear to be represented in the specimens studied and include granite, granodiorite, quartz monzonite, and as near as could be determined, relics of dacitic and rhyolitic porphyries.

Basement Rock FP-20-52

A granodiorite (specimen FP-20-52), from what is probably the nearest outcrop area of salic plutonic rock to Parícutin volcano (30 km SE), is of interest for comparison with the Parícutin xenoliths. Its texture [Fig. 192a] is xenomorphic-granular with plagioclase

grains up to 1.5 mm in diameter composing about 35 vol.%. Progressive normal zoning is common, and some crystals range from as high as An_{70} at their centers to as low as An_{23} at their edges. The major portion appears to be between An_{30} and An_{40}. Orthoclase grains up to 1 mm in diameter compose about 25 vol.% and quartz grains up to 0.5 mm about 20 vol.%, both being generally interstitial to the plagioclase. Clinopyroxene grains up to 0.7 mm in diameter are most common of the ferromagnesian constituents and compose about 10 vol.%. Orthopyroxene, sometimes intergrown with clinopyroxene and always much altered, occurs sporadically. Biotite, amphibole (?), and opaque oxide crystals and clots compose the remainder of the rock with very minor amounts of apatite and zircon as accessories. Except for its somewhat more mafic character, the rock is similar to many of the coarse-grained Parícutin xenoliths.

Xenolith 51-W-1

One xenolith (specimen 51-W-1, analysis X-1, Table 30) erupted as the nucleus of a bomb in 1943 is only slightly altered and shows a coarse granitic texture [Fig. 192b]. It contains abundant anhedral grains of fractured and cloudy orthoclase up to 7 mm in diameter, many roughly euhedral crystals up to 3 mm in diameter of fractured and cloudy plagioclase of composition about An_5 (nX' on cleavage ranges from 1.527 to 1.529), about 20 vol.% anhedral quartz grains up to 0.4 mm in diameter, and about 15 vol.% masses of opaque material, some of which, by their outline and internal structure, must be relics of ferromagnesian minerals. Titanite, zircon, and apatite are present as accessories. The start of thermal breakdown of the rock is revealed by the thin veinlets of vesicular glass in the feldspars and along crystal contacts, by the opaque pseudomorphs of ferromagnesian minerals, and by incipient fracturing and development of streaks of tiny bubbles along fractures in quartz. Otherwise the rock is normal quartz monzonite, similar to the quartz monzonite - granodiorite suite cropping out along the edge of the plateau not far to the south of the Parícutin region.

Xenolith 51-W-9

A similar xenolith, (specimen 51-W-9, analysis X-3, Table 30), erupted during 1944 or 1945, contains about equal amounts of anhedral orthoclase grains up to 2 mm in diameter and subhedral crystals of plagioclase up to 4 mm in length [Fig. 192c]. About 20 vol.% anhedral quartz grains and 15 vol.% irregular to rectangular masses of opaque oxide, no doubt relict ferromagnesian minerals, make up the remainder of the rock. Much of the plagioclase shows both polysynthetic twins and oscillatory zoning. Predominant compositions lie between An_{25} and An_{28} (nX' on cleavage = 1.541-1.543), although some range down to An_{16} (nX' = 1.535). Both orthoclase and plagioclase are much fractured and carry many minute inclusions (both bubbles and solid material?). The feldspars are veined by vesicular glass as in specimen 51-W-1, but in addition narrow border zones of some feldspar grains are "fritted". The term "fritted" is used here to describe the minutely wrinkled or reticulate texture frequently encountered in feldspars that have been heated to high temperatures[62,235]. The intense thermal expansion apparently causes separation along the two cleavages of the feldspar and subsequent internal corrosion in these fractures to give, upon quenching, a regularly spaced reticulite of glass in which the now isolated blocks of feldspar retain their original orientations fairly closely. The process of

solution under dry conditions would consist chiefly of simple melting; in the presence of mineralizers such as water, the breakdown to liquid would be facilitated and could take place at lower temperatures. The mechanism in orthoclase above 1,170°C should also include incongruent melting to form leucite as well as liquid[236], in which case, however, the leucite could not be distinguished easily from the glass under the microscope.

Quartz grains in this specimen show marked undulatory extinction and incipient fracturing, with development of streaks of minute bubbles. The masses of opaque oxide, some rectangular in outline, show streaks and thin lenses of translucent birefringent material parallel to their long dimension that, under intense illumination, are reminiscent of cleavage in amphiboles. The translucent material is brown in reflected light. The rock is classed as a quartz monzonite near granodiorite.

. . . . .

Xenolith 51-W-8

Specimen 51-W-8 (analysis X-4, Table 30), erupted during 1944 or 1945, is composed predominantly of pumiceous glass through which are scattered fragments and relics of quartz and feldspar with some macroscopically visible streaks of darker material [Fig. 192d]. Original fractures in the rock are emphasized in the relic by their dark borders and high degree of vesiculation. The vesicular glass is clear and colorless with refractive index ranging from 1.489 to 1.493. The many irregular and cusp-shaped fragments of feldspar range in size up to 0.9 mm in diameter and show marginal fritting and numerous veinlets of vesicular glass; very few show lamellar twinning. Scattered cusp-shaped grains of quartz range up to 0.7 mm in diameter and commonly show undulatory extinction and incipient fracturing. Opaque oxide and relics of ferromagnesian minerals are rare, and the rock may originally have been granite or rhyolite tuff.

. . . . .

Transition Zones Between Lavas and Xenoliths

Of the specimens in which both lava and xenolith are present, the contacts between dark lava and light xenolith are sharply defined to the unaided eye, and obvious effects of mixing and strewing of one material in the other are absent. In thin section the gradation in color from the dark brown mesostasis of the lava to the colorless glass of the xenolith occurs across a zone usually less than a millimeter wide at most contacts [Fig. 193]. The gradation in mineral

Table 30. Analyses of xenoliths from Parícutin volcano.

Bulk Analyses					Normative minerals				
	X-1	X-2	X-3	X-4		X-1	X-2	X-3	X-4
SiO_2	70.88	71.99	71.10	75.95	Q	26.79	32.27	29.97	33.02
Al_2O_3	14.27	15.95	14.31	13.51	Or	21.75	14.43	22.22	27.82
Fe_2O_3	1.52	.68	1.43	.25	Ab	35.75	34.51	27.22	33.03
FeO	1.53	1.22	1.63	.27	An	7.53	11.38	13.33	5.28
MgO	1.17	.71	1.14	.05	C	.71	2.44	----	----
CaO	1.65	2.49	2.88	1.05	En	2.91	1.80	2.90	.10
Na_2O	4.18	4.03	3.20	3.90	Fs	2.52	1.45	1.19	.13
K_2O	3.64	2.43	3.76	4.74	Mt	.93	.93	2.09	.46
H_2O+	.11	.13	.07	.13	Il	.76	.46	.76	.15
H_2O-	.05	.02	.01	0	Ap	.34	.34	.34	----
CO_2	.02	.01	0	0					
TiO_2	.36	.21	.37	.04					
P_2O_5	.08	.09	.07	.02					
MnO	.05	.05	.05	.03					
Total	[1] 99.64	100.01	100.02	99.94					

[1] Includes 0.26S.

Data on specimens analyzed

Analysis	Specimen	Date erupted	Collector	Analyst
X-1	51-W-1	May 1943	F. H. Pough	E. Engleman.
X-2	51-W-5	1943	Inst. de Geol. de México	Do.
X-3	51-W-9	1944–45	------do	Do.
X-4	51-W-8	1944–45	------do	Do.

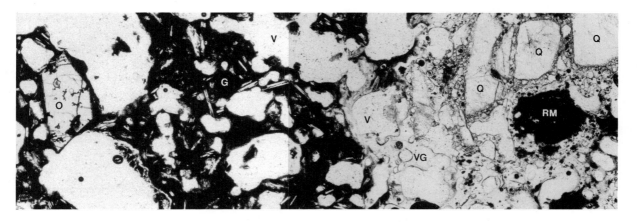

Fig. 193. Plane-light photomicrograph of lava/xenolith contact zone in sample 51-W-6, 4.5 mm across. Abbreviations: G = groundmass glass with plagioclase and other microlites, O = olivine with spinel inclusions, Q = quartz, RM = unspecified mafic mineral (pyroxene, biotite, amphibole) that has reacted upon heating to form an opaque mass, V = vesicles (holes), VG = vesicular glass.

content, however, may extend several more millimeters into the xenolith and is revealed by the growth of isolated microphenocrysts of plagioclase and ferromagnesian minerals in the otherwise normal-appearing, colorless glass of the xenolith. In the thin sections of a few of the specimens, stringers of brown glass carrying plagioclase and ferromagnesian crystals are seen to penetrate for distances of a centimeter or more into the xenolith.

A transition zone is well developed in a thin section of an "Inclusión de Marzo 1943" loaned by the Instituto de Geología de México. This xenolith is apparently of the quartz monzonite type, described above, with irregularly shaped grains of quartz and fritted orthoclase and plagioclase distributed through a matrix of colorless vesicular glass of index much lower than that of balsam. The surrounding lava contains scattered euhedral phenocrysts of olivine up to 1.5 mm in diameter and a few lath-shaped phenocrysts of plagioclase up to 0.6 mm in length in a groundmass that consists of abundant plagioclase laths, many microphenocrysts and grains of olivine, abundant prisms of orthopyroxene, and a glassy mesostasis that contains variable amounts of microlites and dusty particles. The width of gradation from brown to colorless glass in the transition zone between lava and xenolith is variable but rarely exceeds 0.8 mm. The glass of this zone not only carries fragments of xenolith crystals (quartz and feldspar), but also slender euhedral laths of plagioclase up to 0.03 mm in length and stubby euhedral crystals of olivine up to 0.01 mm in diameter. No corrosion or reaction coronas are seen on the olivine crystals, even where they occur sparsely out in the colorless glass.

. . . . .

It is noted for the normal Parícutin lavas in general that isolated quartz grains are encountered in some hand specimens and thin sections, always of irregular shape and showing evidence of reaction. Individual alkali feldspar grains are rarely found, being almost unrecognizable in hand specimen, but recognized in thin section by their fritted texture and remnants of feldspar optical characters. The greater persistence of quartz xenocrysts may be explained chiefly by their physical structure, that is, lack of cleavage or parting that would cause rapid disintegration under thermal stress.

Petrochemistry

Twenty-two chemical analyses of lavas from Parícutin volcano, selected as satisfactory from the standpoints of both quality of analysis and of definiteness of date of eruption (within 2 months), are listed in Table 26, along with calculated groundmass compositions of most specimens. Four analyses of xenoliths are given in Table 30.

. . . . .

Chemical compositions of lava specimens have been plotted against dates of eruption in Fig. 191. For purposes of this and subsequent diagrams, the ferric iron of each analysis has been recalculated as ferrous oxide and combined with the ferrous oxide actually found in order to eliminate confusion owing to the erratic but generally reciprocal relations between ferrous and ferric iron. The new value of ferrous oxide and the values of the nine other major oxides (SiO_2, TiO_2, Al_2O_3, MnO, MgO, CaO, Na_2O, K_2O, and P_2O_5) were adjusted to total 100 wt.% and were plotted as open circles on the diagram according to eruption dates of the specimens.

The resulting graph of Fig. 191 shows in a striking manner that the oxide constituents of successively erupted lavas have varied serially during the course of the eruption. SiO_2 increased from about 55 wt.% in 1943 to slightly over 60 wt.% in 1952; K_2O increased consistently if only a small amount; Na_2O remained nearly constant, while Al_2O_3, FeO^{total}, CaO, and MgO decreased. During 1947, an extra rapid increase in SiO_2 took place while Al_2O_3 also increased slightly and MgO decreased rapidly. The specimens of analyses 6-10 in Table 26 were collected by Konrad Krauskopf from lava erupted during November and December 1945 in order to determine the variation of lava composition over a short period of eruption and, in the case of analyses 8 and 9, the variation between toe and vent of the same flow. It is seen from the analyses and from Fig. 191 that the variations of analyses 6-10 are remarkably small, all being within 0.5 wt.% SiO_2 and proportionately less for the other oxide constituents. Reversals of trend are represented, however, by analyses 4 and 11, which are noticeably lower in SiO_2 and higher in iron than their immediate predecessors.

. . . . .

Calculated compositions of groundmasses, given in Table 26, are plotted as crosses on Fig. 191. In calculating the groundmass of each specimen, its phenocrysts were subtracted from the bulk analyses (total Fe as FeO, and excluding H_2O, S, CO_2, and BaO) and the residue readjusted to total 100 wt.%. In these calculations the compositions of modal phenocrysts were taken as Fo_{80} for olivine, En_{75} for orthopyroxene, and An_{70} for plagioclase. Specific gravities were taken as 3.5 for olivine, 3.4 for hypersthene, and 2.7 for plagioclase. Lacking values for the specific gravity of the individual analysed specimens, that of the bulk rocks is assumed to be 2.7.

. . . . .

Origin of Petrographic and Chemical Trends

The series of rock specimens from the protracted eruption of Parícutin volcano furnishes petrographic and chemical data that are perhaps as complete and definite in respect to time and place as have become available from any volcanic suite. In this suite, for instance, there can be no doubt that all the specimens came from the same magma chamber, that only a limited number of types of intratelluric crystals existed in the chamber, and that there were no significant interruptions of the process or processes that brought about the observed diversification of rock type. Among other things, these circumstances provide a welcome opportunity to test quantitatively whether fractional crystallization alone produced the resulting rock series—a casual postulate made so often for composite suites of other geographic areas where, because of the many possible variables of time, space, and participating minerals, the postulate can neither be supported nor refuted.

. . . . .

The chemical and petrographic differences among successively erupted materials are strikingly apparent—the more so because of their serial nature. The problem is to deduce the mechanism by which they were produced. In the discussion that follows, only two mechanisms, assimilation and fractional crystallization, are considered with respect to their individual and combined abilities to account for the observed features of the rock series. Considering only those two, I have been led to the conclusion that the

observed trends could not have been produced by fractional crystallization alone, but that they could have been produced by assimilation of granitic country rock combined with fractional crystallization of olivine and plagioclase. It is hoped that inclusion of the basic data in some detail in the previous sections will enable other workers to evaluate the possible involvement of other mechanisms or perhaps to modify or drastically revise the relative importance of the roles permitted here to assimilation and fractional crystallization.

Paragenesis of Minerals

The association of the four major crystalline constituents in the Parícutin ejecta of 1943-50 are generalized in Fig. 194 from the detailed data of Figs. 188 and 189. As noted previously, the size limit between phenocrysts and microphenocrysts has been chosen rather arbitrarily as 0.3 mm and that between

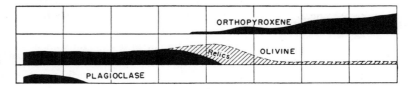

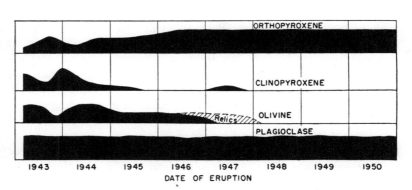

Fig. 194. Occurrence of phenocrysts (upper) and microphenocrysts (lower) in successive Parícutin ejecta from 1943 to 1950 (generalized from data of Figs. 188 and 189).

microphenocrysts and microlites (the latter not shown on Fig. 194) as 0.03 mm. The occurrence of olivine relics—crystals that are marginally converted to pyroxene—is indicated on the diagram by hatching. The overlapping of occurrence of relict and fresh olivine in the diagram is brought about not by the occurrence of both types in the same specimens but by alternation of the two types from specimen to specimen.

In most of the specimens three stages of cooling are implied by the presence of phenocrysts, microphenocrysts, and glass with microlites. Whereas the conventional assignment of these three to intratelluric, hypabyssal (conduit), and surficial cooling stages might be justified here, consideration will be given also to the possible cooling effect by admixture of foreign material in producing the microphenocryst generation while still at depth. A sharp demarcation between phenocrysts and microphenocrysts does not exist in some specimens, and here we must suppose that the change in crystallizing conditions must have been gradual. Likewise, the glassy mesostases may not have been developed in all specimens as a result of any sudden increase in the rate of cooling but simply by the inability of crystallization to keep pace with a steady cooling that had been going on for some time previously.

The degree of confidence with which one may deduce equilibrium relationships among the component minerals is, of course, not the same for the different generations. The phenocrysts may well represent minerals that were in equilibrium with the liquid and with each other. The microphenocrysts, however, are products of a more rapidly changing environment in which true equilibrium was never established, shown, for instance, by progressive zoning in the plagioclase. But, although their crystallization was no doubt forced, and somewhat removed from equilibriium, the degree of departure from equilibrium may have been roughly the same from specimen to specimen throughout the years of the continuous eruption, and one may be justified in making cautious comparisons through the series. The microlites, developed during the rapid congelation of the interstitial liquid, cannot be used to infer equilibrium relationships; and the conditions of this final congelation may have been so fortuitous from specimen to specimen that only the most general comparisons can be made between the microlites of the different members of the rock series.

In following sections, not reprinted here, Wilcox discusses in turn the phenocrysts, microphenocrysts, microlites, and glass. He emphasizes the unusual absence of plagioclase phenocrysts in most Parícutin specimens and remarks upon the similarity to "boninites" and "sanukites", volcanic rock types in which this is a characteristic feature. Wilcox also notes the general disappearance of clinopyroxene as a microphenocryst after 1945, and suggests that it may have resulted from crustal contamination.

Chemical Relationships

It can be granted at once that the Parícutin lavas had their source in a single magma chamber, and this offers an advantage not ordinarily present in an inquiry into the mode of origin of a volcanic suite. In the usual study, specimens come from various vents that had been active at widely separated intervals, thus quite probably from different chambers or from different parts of a master chamber at quite different stages of evolution. In contrast the blood relationship among members of the Parícutin suite must be very close, with proportionately less variability in the factors of time, space, and environmental conditions.

A rigorous treatment would demand that all conceivable modes of origin be examined for their possible contributions to the observed features of the chemistry of the Parícutin igneous suite. I am not prepared to give such a rigorous treatment here but rather will consider only two possible modes of origin that have already been suggested: that of fractional crystallization and that of "bodily" assimilation of country rock involving no significant differential movement of chemical constituents.

Schmitter[233] has concluded that the presence of orthopyroxene in the groundmasses of the 1943 lavas may be a result of assimilation of monzonitic country rock such as represented by the xenoliths. Although the percentage of Al_2O_3 in the Parícutin xenoliths is less than in the lavas (see Tables 26 and 30), the ratio of Al_2O_3:CaO is much higher. Thus the addition of xenolithic material to the magma may have forced the crystalization of orthopyroxene rather than clinopyroxene for much the same reasons as suggested by Bowen[236] and others in the case of assimilation of aluminous sediments. Similarly, the presence of orthopyroxene in certain lavas of Hakone volcano is attributed by Kuno[234] to assimilation of granitic wall rock, the low content of normative Wo and high content of water in which is regarded as favoring crystallization of orthopyroxene rather than clinopyroxene in contaminated magma.

Williams[237] in discussing the whole of the igneous suite of the Parícutin region, including only the lavas erupted from Parícutin volcano in 1943 and 1944, found no reason to doubt that the major control was fractional crystallization and no proof that the course of differentiation was influenced by contamination of the magma by country rock. Based on tests of the much more complete chemical and petrographic data now available, however, it is concluded here that neither assimilation nor fractional crystallization acting alone could have produced the suite of lavas of Parícutin volcano, but that assimilation and fractional crystallization acting together could have produced it. In the following discussion the ability of these two mechanisms to produce the chemical and petrographic trends will be considered first and the thermal and other requirements of the proposed mechanism second.

To test the adequacy of fractional crystallization and assimilation as factors in the production of the observed chemistry of the Parícutin lavas, the variation diagram will be the main tool. Starting with any one of the bulk analyses, which for this purpose may be presumed to represent the composition of the magma (including suspended crystals) before eruption, one may determine graphically whether removal or addition of appropriate materials could have produced the compositions of the other lavas. It should be noted that for the tests made here we are not attempting to delineate a liquid line of descent of the magma[236] but rather a "bulk line of descent". If, for instance, the graphically determined line of descent simulating fractional crystallization matches that of the plotted analyses, the conclusion would be that fractional crystallization could have been the causal mechanism—if a close match is not obtained it could not have been the sole mechanism. Similar reasoning would apply to the tests of assimilation alone and of assimilation together with fractional crystallization.

The general chemical setting of the lavas of Parícutin can be best illustrated on a small-scale silica-variation diagram, such as Fig. 195, which shows the relationships between lavas, their phenocrysts (olivine, orthopyroxene and plagioclase), and their xenolithic inclusions. The phenocryst compositions used here are olivine, Fo_{80}; orthopyroxene, En_{75}; and plagioclase An_{70}, the plagioclase being taken as somewhat more calcic than the optically determined microphenocrysts. The effects of possible departures from these assumed compositions will be considered later. The four analyses of xenoliths have been combined to give a plotted position of the "average xenolith", to be used in the following discussion as an approximate representation of the

xenolithic material. On the variation diagram at this scale, the lavas form a close-knit series in the middle silica range, whereas their olivine and plagioclase phenocrysts lie at lower silica percentages, their orthopyroxene phenocrysts within the silica range of the lavas, and their xenoliths in a much higher silica range.

As an example on Fig. 195, the simple subtraction of olivine, Fo_{80}, from the bulk analysis of no. 12 gives successive compositions lying along straight-line extentions away from the corresponding oxide constituents of the olivine. In the residuum SiO_2, Al_2O_3, CaO, Na_2O, and K_2O are seen to increase while total FeO and MgO decrease. At a given silica percentage, say that of analysis 15 (58.6 wt.% SiO_2), the content of the other oxide constituents in the residuum can be read off; and it is found that they do not even approximate the values for corresponding constituents of no. 15. The conclusion is that simple removal of olivine, Fo_{80}, alone from the magma

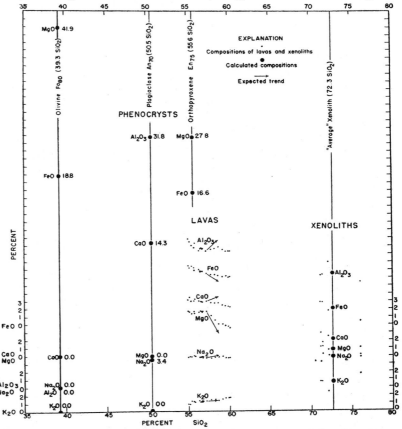

Fig. 195. Silica-variation diagram of lavas, phenocrysts, and xenoliths from Parícutin volcano. Dots represent bulk compositions of lavas and xenoliths (analyses 6-10 averaged). Values for bulk composition are counted from 0 point for each oxide at bottom of scale. Arrows from analysis 12 show trends to be expected by simple subtraction of olivine (Fo_{80}). Heads of arrows are at silica percent of analysis 15.

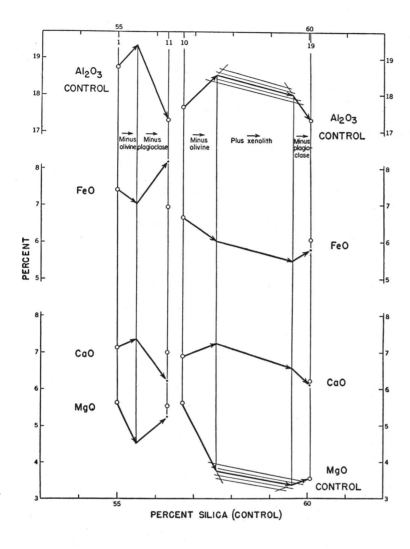

Fig. 196. Silica-variation diagram, showing graphical operations in addition and subtraction of materials from bulk compositions (represented by open circles) of lavas from Parícutin volcano. Dots opposite FeO, CaO, and MgO of no. 11 show percentages in final product subtracting olivine (Fo₈₀) and plagioclase (An₇₀) from no. 1 using SiO₂ and Al₂O₃ of no. 1 and no. 11 as controls. Dots opposite FeO and CaO of no. 19 show percentages in final product obtained by subtracting olivine, adding "average xenolith", and subtracting plagioclase from no. 19, using SiO₂, Al₂O₃, and MgO of nos. 10 and 19 as controls.

control, silica, was needed for the subtraction of a single mineral constituent, here two will be required; and for these, SiO$_2$ and Al$_2$O$_3$ have been chosen rather arbitrarily. The pair of specimens to be compared are taken as no. 1 and no. 11, and just enough olivine and plagioclase have been removed from no. 1 to attain the SiO$_2$ and Al$_2$O$_3$ percentages of no. 11. The graphical procedure is as follows: a radius is drawn from the alumina point of olivine, (outside the diagram), through the alumina point of analysis 1, and another radius is drawn from the alumina point of plagioclase through the alumina point of analysis 11. The intersection of these radii at 55.5 wt.% SiO$_2$ determines the relative proportions of olivine and plagioclase subtracted. A radius is drawn from the FeO point of olivine through the FeO point of no. 1; the radius then intersects the 55.5 wt.% SiO$_2$-vertical at 7.0 wt.% FeO. Through this point a radius is drawn from the FeO point of plagioclase and, extended, it intersects the SiO$_2$ vertical of no. 11 at 8.2 wt.% FeO, about 1.3 wt.% higher than the plotted value of FeO in no. 11. In a similar manner it is found that the test value of CaO is too low by 0.8 wt.% and that of MgO is too low by 0.3 wt.%. From the large discrepancies in both FeO and CaO it may be concluded that simultaneous subtraction of Fo$_{80}$ and An$_{70}$ does not account wholly for the major element differences in composition between no. 1 and no. 11.

The right hand portion of Fig. 196 illustrates the graphical operations in adding or subtracting three materials, here olivine, Fo$_{80}$; plagioclase, An$_{70}$; and "average xenolith". Although the constructions are more tedious than those for only two variables, the solution again is unique and essentially unaffected by the sequence in which the operations are performed. It is seen that, with three materials available for addition or subtraction, three oxide controls must be used, and for these SiO$_2$, Al$_2$O$_3$, and MgO have been chosen.

represented by analysis 12 could not have produced the magma represented by no. 15. By similar operations it can be shown that no pairs of Parícutin lavas can be related by simple addition or subtraction of olivine, Fo$_{80}$, alone, or of plagioclase, An$_{70}$, alone.

To test the effects of simultaneous addition or withdrawal of two mineral constituents, such as olivine and plagioclase, one may proceed as illustrated in the left part of Fig. 196, an enlargement of the central portion of Fig. 195. Whereas only one oxide

Using analysis 10 as the starting material and no. 19 as the end material, radii are drawn from the alumina point of olivine through the alumina point of no. 10 and from the MgO point of olivine through the MgO point of analysis 10. Similarly, radii are drawn from the alumina and MgO points of plagioclase respectively through the alumina and MgO points of analysis 19. Then a series of closely spaced radii are drawn from the alumina and MgO points of the "average xenolith", cutting the olivine and plagioclase radii. One may then choose the radii, one from xenolithic alumina and the other from xenolithic MgO, which intersect the olivine and plagioclase radii at corresponding silica percentages (here 57.6 and 59.6 wt.% SiO_2). A radius from the FeO point of olivine through the FeO point of analysis 10 cuts the 57.6 wt.% SiO_2-vertical at 6.0 wt.% FeO, and the straight line from this point towards the FeO point of the "average xenolith" cuts the 59.6 wt.% SiO_2-vertical at 5.5 wt.% FeO. A straight line from this point through the FeO point of plagioclase cuts the silica-vertical of analysis 19 at 5.8 wt.% FeO, about 0.3 wt.% lower than the actual plotted value for the FeO of analysis 19. By a similar procedure the CaO content of the graphically derived product is found to be 0.1 wt.% lower than that of analysis 19.

Here again the magnitudes of the discrepancies between graphically determined end points and their actual counterparts may be taken as the measure of the ability, from the compositional standpoint only, of the process under test to account for the derivation of the end material from the starting material or of both from a common parent. In this example the total discrepancies for the four oxides, Al_2O_3, FeO, CaO, and MgO, is 0.40 wt.%; and one may speak of an average discrepancy here of 0.10 wt.%. Another useful measure of the chemical feasibility of the graphically simulated process is the amount of divergence from the actual "trend" between starting and end materials, and in this example the divergence for the four tested oxides may be

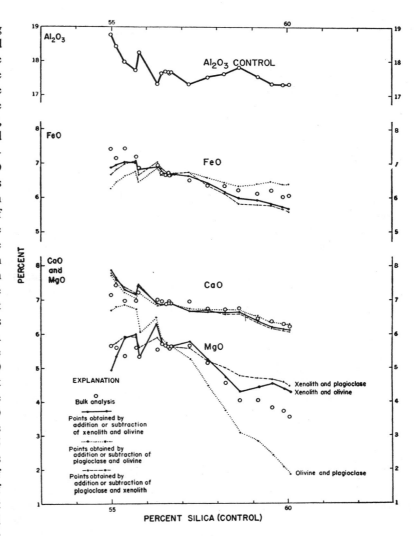

Fig. 197. Silica-variation diagram comparing actual bulk compositions of Parícutin lavas (open circles) with trends developed by graphical addition or subtraction of olivine, plagioclase, and xenolithic material from analysis 10 (Table 26), using SiO_2, Al_2O_3, and MgO as controls.

expressed as 0.03% per wt.% change of silica between analyses 10 and 19.

Figure 197 . . . shows the results of simultaneous additions or subtractions of olivine, plagioclase, and average xenolith from analysis 10. The open circles represent the plotted points of the whole-rock analyses, and the lines represent the modeled compositions. Na_2O and K_2O have been left out of the diagram . . . because the Na_2O and K_2O contents of all the materials, lavas as well as phenocrysts and xenoliths, are low and nearly in line with each other on the diagram. The discrepancies in FeO are generally less than in any of the paired variable tests [olivine, plagioclase, and xenolith tested two at a time], most of them less than 0.25 wt.% and probably approaching the combined margin of error of analysis, graphical plotting, and spurious effects. As in the case of paired variable tests, the discrepancies in CaO are generally negligible, at least for the high-silica portion. The conformance is sufficiently good to justify the conclusion that combined action of both fractional crystallization and assimilation processes—which involve olivine (Fo_{80}), plagioclase (An_{70}), and "average" xenolith—could have been the major cause of chemical differences between the lava of analysis 10 and the higher silica members of the series. From the standpoint of bulk of material involved, assimilation would appear to have been the predominant process.

Wilcox then goes on to evaluate other possible variables in a pure fractional crystallization model, including different compositions for olivine and plagioclase, and the possible involvement of orthopyroxene or titanomagnetite. These possible models are evaluated exhaustively and found unable to reproduce the trends of the Parícutin lavas.

With these tests, all the reasonable combinations that might have been involved in fractional crystallization of the Parícutin magma appear to have been considered and all appear to be infeasible, either from the standpoint of chemical requirements alone or from the standpoint of petrography and physical chemistry. The conclusion is drawn therefore that fractional crystallization could not have been the only process producing the lava suite of Parícutin volcano.

Some combination of assimilation and fractional crystallization can account for at least the chemical requirements imposed by the series. There likewise appears to be nothing in the petrographic characters of the series that would make this combination infeasible. It remains to consider whether the thermal requirements of the implied assimilation could have been met by the Parícutin magma, and this aspect will be discussed in the final section.

. . . . .

Thermal Requirements
The graphical procedure indicates that addition of 25.4 g of "average" xenolithic material and subtraction of 2.9 g of olivine (Fo_{80}) and 9.6 g of plagioclase (An_{70}) from 100 g of the groundmass material of no. 1 will give 112.9 g of material closely approximating the composition of the groundmass of

no. 19. Thus, 25.4 g of xenolithic material must be assimilated, and the heat required may conveniently be divided into two parts: that necessary to raise the temperature of the quartz monzonitic country rock to the magmatic temperature, and that necessary to convert the country rock to a liquid and incorporate it into the magma . . . .

A mechanism proposed by Holmes[238] for the upward penetration of simatic and sialic rocks by the fluxing action of magma cupolas (overhead stoping and fluxing of Daly[238]), which he applied as an explanation of the acidic-basic volcanic complexes of Scotland, appears to offer a basis for the availability of adequate heat, as well as an explanation of other observed relationships at Parícutin volcano, perhaps also of those of the whole Parícutin region. Holmes emphasized more than Daly the probability that thermal convection can furnish the great quantities of heat needed for the fluxing and stoping of the country rock at the cupola roof. Holmes[238] first supposes a deep-seated, broad basaltic magma chamber with only slight local irregularities in the roof. Thermal convection currents will tend to start under any slight arch, and once started, will tend to bring hotter magma up to the central part of the arch. Thus, the fluxing action at the apex may begin, slowly at first, but becoming more effective as the arch becomes steeper by solution and removal of the country rock at the apex.

Once under way, this process should continue to assimilate the roof rock, and the magma would dissolve out a high-arched cupola in the overlying rock, regardless of the composition of the rock.

. . . . .

It should be remarked that the slow, upward solution-penetration into the country rocks and development of the slim cupola can be accomplished by the magma even though it be crystallizing and therefore not possessing any superheat in the usually accepted sense. Thus, there is an indefinitely large amount of heat being brought by convection from the hotter main magma chamber below, and one can reason that, because of the great mass of hotter magma available in the main chamber, an entirely adequate amount of heat can be furnished to the cupola as long as the convection is effective. The heat, brought in by convection, is made available by crystallization. It is used in raising the temperature of the country rock and, where mechanically favorable, in incorporating wall rock material into the magma as liquid.

The Parícutin magma chamber, or cupola as we will now regard it, is shown in the sketch of Fig. 198 as offset from the site of the Parícutin vent on the surface. The reasons for showing it thus are indirect; and such a postulated position must, of course, be regarded as merely conjectural. In the first place, the results of the airborne magnetic survey of the region by the U.S. Geological Survey in December 1947[239] have shown a strong negative magnetic anomaly of some 200 gammas centering about a point about 3 km NNW of the volcano, and the closure of the anomaly has a radius of about 3 km. This anomaly is much larger than any other in the vicinity of the volcano and is not to be accounted for by any topographic effect. It implies that a body of a abnormally low magnetism must be located at depth below and somewhat north of the surface expression of the anomaly. It could be a boss of solid rock of low magnetism, such as granite or acid effusives, protruding upward into the generally more magnetic basaltic and andesitic surface mantle. Or it might be the thermal aureole of the Parícutin cupola, the apex of which lies not far below the base of the basaltic and andesitic mantle.

Another reason for showing the Parícutin cupola in an offset position is that such a situation might furnish the explanation for the remarkably continuous and generally steady rate of eruption at the vent during the 9 years of its life. Were a gas-charged cupola tapped at its apex, it seems reasonable to suppose that the consequent eruption would be intense but brief, probably discharging all its pent-up pressure in the space of a few months. But were a gas-charged cupola tapped on its flank, as sketched on Fig. 198, the apex portion of the cupola could continue to act for a some time as a reservoir of pressure, the rate of eruption being controlled chiefly by equilibrium between pressure and and the resistance owing to the viscosity. The surge of especially strong activity from July 1951 until final cessation in March 1952 [see p. 184], would be explainable as flushing of the upper part of the magma column with the escape of pent-up reservoir

gas when the magma surface had been forced down to the level of the offset outlet.

. . . . .

All this does not necessarily suppose that there would have been a strong concentration of solid or partially melted xenolithic material in the upper portions of the cupola. It is only necessary that the volatile material be released from the xenoliths or immediate portions of the wall rock and rise through the magma without complete resolution in the magma before reaching the apex of the cupola. In this connection, however, it seems worthwhile to examine the possible behavior and movement of the xenolithic material. The specific gravity of the xenoliths of granitic composition should be less than that of the magma, especially after having been heated to the magma tem-perature and perhaps partially inflated. It seems doubtful that even initially there would be any

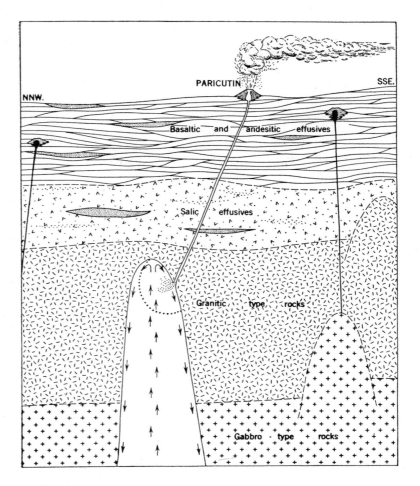

Fig. 198. Schematic cross section of Parícutin volcano and its supposed magma cupola. Arrows represent character of slow thermal convection. Area within dotted line represents cross section of approximate volume of magma erupted in 1943-52. Depth to the top of gabbroic-type rocks assumed to be about 12-15 km.

tendency for a xenolith to sink in the magma after its detachment from the wall. Rather there would be a consistent tendency to move upward in relation to the magma; and if the rate of relative upward movement were greater than the rate of the postulated downward convectional current of the peripheral zones of the magma, there would result an absolute upward migration of the xenoliths and a tendency to enrich the magma of the upper portion of the cupola in salic material.

A mechanism such as outlined above, while furnishing adequate heat and fitting into the general pattern of the behavior of Parícutin, would seem to leave the chemical and petrographic trends of the successively erupted lavas as a fortuitous relationship. It implies that the chemical differences had already existed in the magma of the cupola, only being arranged in space in such a way that the successively withdrawn samples would show the trend from femic towards salic rock that we now observe in the chronologic series of lavas at the surface. The volume of material actually erupted is such a small fraction of the supposed cupola (see Fig. 198), that, had nonhomogeneities existed in the magma, it would seem just as possible that the sequence of withdrawal could have furnished a series of lavas trending in composition in just the opposite direction, namely, from more salic towards more femic or that the trend of the first few years could be reversed later. This, of course, would be no contradiction of the general progressive development of more salic magma by the combined action of assimilation and crystal fractionation. It only illustrates that the sequence in which the successive portions of the magma were erupted was not necessarily the sequence in which they were initially formed.

The striking random scatter of young cinder cones and associated lavas over the region has been noted and implies that most of the eruptions have been short-lived and that, once interrupted, have seldom been renewed from the same vent. In contrast, the old volcanic pile of Cerros de Tancítaro must have been built by eruptions from closely spaced vents, some of which were repeatedly active. The transition may be represented by the smaller volcanic piles of the Cerros de San Marcos, Aguila, Angahuan, and Los Hornos (see p. 246-247 and inside-back-cover map), finally to the scattered short eruptions represented by the young cinder cones. Whether this type of eruption, which has continued intermittently to the present, can be regarded as a final and decadent phase of the grand cycle of eruptivity from the Michoacán magmas is, of course, a matter of conjecture.

In conclusion, it is of interest to speculate on the possible future activity of Parícutin, admitting the risk involved in predicting the behavior of any volcano. On the basis of the inferred behavior of the other young volcanoes of the area, it would seem improbable that significant renewal of activity would take place from the Parícutin vent. If the presumption of an offset outlet from the Parícutin magma cupola is well founded, renewal of activity at the Parícutin vent would seem even more improbable, although this does not rule out the possibility of future outbreaks in the area above the cupola apex.

Trace Elements and Strontium and Oxygen Isotopes

McBirney et al. (1987)

Abstract

Parícutin volcano discharged a total of 1.32 km^3 of basaltic andesite and andesite before the eruption came to an end in 1952. Until 1947, when 75% of the volume had been erupted, the lavas varied little in elemental or isotopic composition. All were basaltic andesites with 55-56 wt.% SiO_2, $\delta^{18}O$ of +6.9 to +7.0, and $^{87}Sr/^{86}Sr$ ratios close to 0.7038. Subsequent lavas were hypersthene andesites with silica contents reaching 60 wt.%, $\delta^{18}O$ values up to +7.6, and $^{87}Sr/^{86}Sr$ of 0.7040 to 0.7043. The later lavas were enriched in Ba, Rb, Li, and K_2O and depleted in MgO, Cu, Zn, Cr, Ni, Sr, and Co. The isotopic and other chemical changes, which appeared abruptly over a few months in 1947, are interpreted as the result of tapping a sharply zoned and density-stratified magma chamber. Xenoliths of partially fused felsic basement rocks in the lavas have silica contents greater than 70 wt.%, $\delta^{18}O$ of +5.6 to +9.9 and $^{87}Sr/^{86}Sr$ between 0.7043 and 0.7101. In many respects they resemble samples of basement rocks collected from nearby outcrops. Three analysed samples of the latter have silica of 65-67 wt.%, $\delta^{18}O$ of +7.7 to +8.6, and $^{87}Sr/^{86}Sr$ between 0.7047 and 0.7056.

These new data provide strong support for the original interpretations of Wilcox [see p. 340-344], who explained the chemical variations by a combination of fractional crystallization and concurrent assimilation of up to 20 wt.% continental crust. Except for a few trace elements, particularly Ba, Sr, and Zr, the chemical and isotopic compositions of the xenoliths and basement rocks that crop out nearby match the type of contaminant required to explain the late-stage lavas. Some of the discrepancies may be explained by postulating a contaminant that was older and richer in Ba, Sr, and Zr than those represented by the analysed xenoliths. Others can be attributed to chemical changes accompanying disequilibrium partial melting, contact metamorphism, and meteoric-hydrothermal alteration of the country rock. Many of the xenoliths show evidence of having been affected by such a process.

The lavas were erupted from a zoned magma chamber that had differentiated by liquid fractionation prior to the eruption. The order of appearance of the lavas can be explained in terms of withdrawal of stratified liquids of differing densities and viscosities.

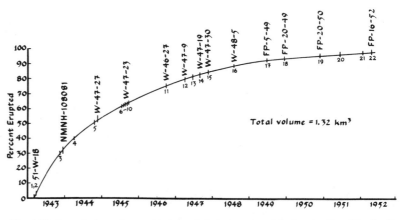

Fig. 199. Cumulative volume of lava and cinders erupted during the life of Parícutin volcano. Mass has been recalculated to volumes assuming a uniform density of 2.6 [g/cm³] (after Fries, 1953). Numbers 1 through 22 indicate original samples of Wilcox [see Table 26]. Numbers of samples used here are indicated above the curve.

Introduction

The original study of the Parícutin rocks by Wilcox [see above] utilized the optical and chemical techniques available at that time to calculate a chemical and thermal balance for the principal components of the system . . . . The quantitative nature of the mass-balance calculation, based as it was on field and petrographic evidence, seemed to offer a convincing model for the origin of andesites in general.

More recently, as studies of trace elements and isotopic ratios provided additional means of evaluating assimilation, petrologists began to question whether wholesale incorporation of crustal material was a significant factor in the origin of andesites. For example, early measurements of the strontium isotopic ratios of Parícutin rocks[240] raised doubts that assimilation had contributed materially to the observed compositional changes. It seems appropriate, therefore, to utilize these new geochemical tools to re-examine the suite of Parícutin lavas in greater detail and to reconsider the mechanisms responsible for their compositional variations.

The authors give a brief summary of Parícutin's eruptive history based on earlier reports. Although we have not reproduced this section, we have reprinted as Fig. 199 an interesting plot of the cumulative volume of magma erupted as a function of time, on which are indicated the samples investigated by both Wilcox and McBirney et al. The next section, which *summarizes the petrography of lavas and xenoliths, is likewise not reproduced.*

Major-Element Chemistry

Lavas

We have reanalysed fragments from most of Wilcox's 22 hand-specimens of lavas [see Table 26], and with the possible exception of Al_2O_3, which is slightly less abundant in some of our analyses, we find no differences between the original data and new determinations. All the major-element data given in Table 31 and Fig. 200 are taken from the original analyses with the exception of sample 108081, which is a new analysis of a sample that was generously provided by the National Museum of Natural History.

The most notable feature of the major elements is the sharp increase of SiO_2 and the corresponding decrease of MgO in the late stages of the eruption. CaO and total iron (as FeO) declined slightly, K_2O increased, and other components remained nearly constant. The most marked change occurred in early 1947, by which time about 80% of the total volume had been erupted. At that time, alumina, which declined slightly in the early stages, began to increase and continued to do so until late 1947 when 85% of the volume had been discharged; it then reversed this trend and declined until the eruption ended. Marked inflections are also found in trace-element abundances of the lavas erupted during this same interval.

The major-element variations can be related to mineralogical components by plotting the compositions on a CMAS diagram of the type devised by

Table 31. Major- and trace-element compositions of Parícutin lavas. See text and appendix for sources of samples and methods of analysis. [The analysis listed for FP-20-50 is actually the analysis for FP-5-51 from Wilcox (1954): see Table 26].

Sample no.	51-W-18	108081	W-47-27	W-47-23	W-46-27	W-47-9	W-47-30	W-48-5	FP-5-49	FP-20-49	FP-20-50	FP-16-52
Year erupted	1943	1944	1944	1945	1946	1947	1947	1948	1949	1949	1950	1952
Cumulative vol.	1%	33%	51%	64%	75%	78%	82%	85%	93%	94%	97%	100%
SiO_2	54.59	55.39	55.71	55.79	56.13	57.05	58.39	59.09	59.41	59.77	60.24	60.07
TiO_2	0.99	0.94	1.01	0.90	1.02	0.89	0.86	0.78	0.84	0.83	0.80	0.81
Al_2O_3	17.83	17.64	17.24	17.48	17.34	17.27	17.78	17.55	17.30	17.29	17.30	17.28
Fe_2O_3	2.01	2.16	2.06	1.83	1.74	1.42	1.87	2.04	1.57	1.21	1.19	1.37
FeO	5.43	5.46	5.48	5.30	5.42	5.21	4.51	4.27	4.78	4.95	4.59	4.39
MnO	0.12	0.13	0.13	0.12	0.12	0.12	0.12	0.11	0.11	0.11	0.10	0.10
MgO	5.44	5.43	5.61	5.75	5.58	5.64	4.03	4.03	3.81	3.72	3.55	3.73
CaO	7.25	7.18	6.98	6.81	6.99	6.94	6.75	6.46	6.36	6.28	6.14	6.16
Na_2O	3.95	3.98	3.99	3.81	3.79	3.71	3.86	3.92	3.71	3.74	4.01	4.00
K_2O	0.91	1.15	1.18	1.19	1.30	1.23	1.30	1.50	1.67	1.67	1.66	1.67
H_2O+	0.16	0.09	0.20	0.20	0.20	0.17	0.11	0.08	0.12	0.12	0.04	0.03
H_2O-	0.04	0.05	0.06	0.10	0.06	0.02	0.01	0.03	0.01	0.00	0.04	0.05
P_2O_5	0.27	0.35	0.33	0.30	0.36	0.29	0.30	0.30	0.31	0.31	0.29	0.28
Total	98.99	99.95	99.98	99.58	100.05	99.96	99.89	100.16	100.00	100.00	99.95	99.94
Ba	315	376	388	440	413	435	436	506	549	597	558	604
Sr	607	578	596	537	588	580	575	556	540	512	533	541
Li	12	14	16	15	16	16	19	19	20	21	20	20
Rb	14	15.4	18	13.4	15	16.8	23.2	24.6	26.3	22.2	24.6	27
Cs	nd	nd	0.22	0.37	0.36	0.54	0.52	0.60	0.53	0.55	0.63	0.66
Sc	17.33	16.6	16.45	17.02	17.12	16.19	15.03	15.05	14.45	14.41	14.41	13.76
Cr	144.7	176	155.2	170	152.7	162.4	78.5	88	75	67.8	66.5	76
Co	35	33	32	27	29.7	24.7	20.5	20.1	18.7	18.7	21.5	18.1
Ni	116	103	126	127	122	126	71	73	60	57	55	63
Cu	168	37	172	123	39	37	nd	34	34	36	37	34
Zn	140	85	230	130	80	73	75	76	76	75	76	72
Zr	116	171	174	147	167	150	160	164	175	162	174	173
Hf	2.94	3.3	3.57	3.66	3.57	3.44	3.53	3.99	3.93	3.96	4.10	3.84
Ta	0.38	nd	0.60	0.56	0.58	0.52	0.48	0.51	0.55	0.48	0.50	0.49
Th	0.94	1.42	1.62	1.54	1.69	1.51	1.49	1.76	1.74	1.77	1.87	1.91
U	nd	0.9	nd	0.70	nd	nd	nd	nd	nd	nd	nd	nd
La	13.1	16	18.1	16.9	17.6	15.6	17.0	18.6	19.1	19.6	19.5	19.6
Ce	29.6	35.7	38.9	40.4	39.6	35.9	36.5	41.4	40.5	43.0	43.4	40.9
Nd	20.6	24	24.0	25.0	21.0	13.6	nd	nd	29.0	24.0	21.0	24.6
Sm	3.8	4.5	4.6	4.2	4.4	4.0	4.1	4.2	4.2	4.5	4.4	4.3
Eu	1.32	1.39	1.41	1.36	1.44	1.27	1.34	1.45	1.34	1.33	1.35	1.29
Tb	0.67	0.62	0.69	0.72	0.72	0.61	0.64	0.68	0.65	0.68	0.67	0.64
Yb	1.79	2.2	2.06	1.88	1.84	1.73	1.73	2.09	1.96	1.95	1.72	1.78
Lu	0.28	0.29	0.31	0.31	0.31	0.28	0.28	0.29	0.28	0.31	0.29	0.28

Cawthorn and O'Hara[241] and shown here as Fig. 201. The experimentally determined field boundaries of olivine, amphibole, orthopyroxene, and plagioclase are based on rocks of other compositions. Because these boundaries are strongly affected by sodium content, water pressure, and other factors, they have been adjusted to correspond to the observed chemical trends and mineral assemblages in the Parícutin rocks.

Figure 201 reveals an inflection in the compositional trend at an early stage when 40-50% of the volume had been erupted. The change is consistent with early fractionation of olivine until the liquid reached the stability field of amphibole. Orthopyroxene would have begun to crystallize at the time of the more pronounced change in 1947, and phenocrysts of hypersthene were in fact observed to appear in the lavas at that stage.

The change that occurred later in 1947, after about 85% of the volume had been discharged, corresponds to a stage at which the phase diagram indicates the liquid would have just begun to crystallize plagioclase, and yet plagioclase is present as phenocrysts in even the earliest lavas and is seen only as microphenocrysts after about half the magma had been discharged. These differences between the observed assemblages in lavas and those predicted by the phase diagram can be reconciled, at least in part, by Eggler's experimental evidence that amphibole was stable at depth but disappeared as the magma rose to shallower levels [see p. 360-363]. Although amphi-

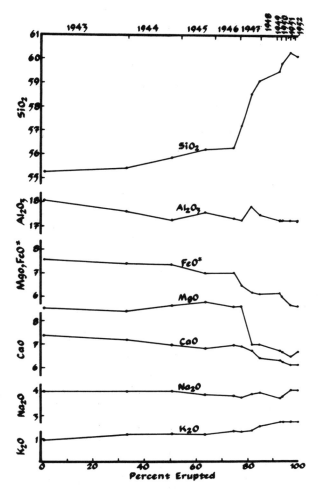

Fig. 200. Variations of major elements in Parícutin lavas plotted as a function of cumulative volume erupted.

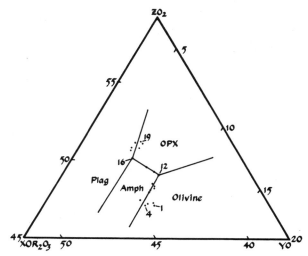

Fig. 201. CMAS diagram showing compositional variations of Parícutin lavas in relation to inferred stability fields of mineral phases determined for calc-alkaline rocks by Cawthorn and O'Hara[241]. Phase boundaries have been adjusted to fit the observed trends of Parícutin lavas. Numbers correspond to samples shown in Fig. 199. ZO_2 is essentially SiO_2 less alkalies, XOR_2O_3 is mostly CaO, Al_2O_3, and alkalies, and YO is the sum of MgO and FeO^{total}. Proportions are in mole percent. For more information on methods of plotting see Cox et al.[242].

bole has not been seen in the Parícutin rocks, it is found in the lavas of several nearby volcanoes in the Parícutin region [see p. 247, 271] . . . .

Osborne and Rawson[243] found magnetite to be a near-liquidus phase at oxygen fugacities near the Ni-NiO buffer, a water content of 2 wt.%, and total pressure between 1 and 10 kilobars [a kilobar is roughly 1,000 times the air pressure at the earth's surface; 10 kilobars is equivalent to the pressure at about 30 km depth in the earth], but phenocrysts of iron oxides are very rare in the lavas, and, as will be seen in a later section, do not seem to have affected the compositional evolution of the rocks.

The early appearance of plagioclase and absence of augite is easy to account for if it is postulated that a loss of water during ascent caused the cotectic to shift away from plagioclase toward augite[244]. The smaller size of plagioclase crystals in late-stage lavas may be due to the greater silica content of the liquid and the

slower rates of nucleation and growth of crystals that would accompany an increase in viscosity. Another factor may have been the greater concentration of water in the upper part of the reservoir.

Xenoliths and Basement Rocks

Because of the broad compositional range and differing degrees of melting of the xenoliths, it is difficult to arrive at a single composition that might be representative of the basement material incorporated into the Parícutin magma. Wilcox provided major-element analyses of four typical xenoliths [see Table 30, p. 337], and we have obtained eight new analyses for a somewhat greater range of compositions, but the effect of these additional analyses on the calculated average compositions is not great (Table 32). Three new analyses of samples of unaltered basement rocks from outcrops about 30 km from Parícutin differ somewhat from the average xenolith (Table 33), but there is no way of knowing how representative these distant outcrops are of rocks immediately under the volcano.

Three xenoliths with differing proportions of glass were analysed in bulk to see if any trend could be related to progressive melting. One of these (51-W-1) [see description on p. 336 and photomicrograph in Fig. 192b] is dense and contains only about 10%

Table 32. Major- and trace-element analyses of xenoliths.

	51-W-1	51-W-5	51-W-6	51-W-7	51-W-8	51-W-9	51-W-10	51-W-11	51-W-22	108124	108126	108132	AVE.
SiO_2	70.88	71.99	72.61	71.00	75.95	70.88	73.64	74.57	71.37	72.40	71.93	70.80	72.63
TiO_2	0.36	0.21	0.17	0.18	0.04	0.36	0.04	0.04	0.19	0.21	0.23	0.39	0.20
Al_2O_3	14.27	15.95	14.98	14.83	13.51	14.38	12.07	13.58	15.19	15.66	14.98	14.58	14.56
Fe_2O_3	1.52	0.68	0.55	0.64	0.25	1.51	0.26	0.41	0.53	0.66	0.80	0.80	0.72
FeO	1.53	1.22	1.51	1.43	0.27	1.59	0.51	0.32	1.38	1.38	1.25	1.40	1.15
MnO	0.05	0.05	0.06	0.06	0.03	0.05	0.02	0.01	0.04	0.06	0.06	0.05	0.05
MgO	1.17	0.71	0.32	0.53	0.05	1.25	3.44	0.46	0.63	0.53	0.55	1.13	0.90
CaO	1.65	2.49	2.96	3.13	1.05	2.93	4.14	1.14	2.55	3.14	2.79	3.46	2.63
Na_2O	4.18	4.03	4.75	4.13	3.90	3.32	2.41	4.15	3.99	4.80	4.67	3.36	3.99
K_2O	3.64	2.43	1.63	2.38	4.74	3.90	2.73	4.67	2.76	1.49	2.15	3.69	3.03
H_2O+	0.11	0.13	0.39	0.47	0.13	0.14	0.41	0.42	0.32	0.13	0.19	0.11	–
H_2O-	0.05	0.02	0.07	0.11	0.01	0.01	0.11	0.08	0.03	0.05	0.03	0.07	–
P_2O_5	0.08	0.09	0.16	0.19	0.02	0.06	0.06	0.01	0.32	0.21	0.27	0.08	0.13
Total	99.49	100.00	100.16	99.08	99.95	100.38	99.84	99.86	99.30	100.72	99.90	99.92	99.99
Ba	371	–	288	767	76	612	217	112	2097	289	297	508	512.2
Sr	78	–	404	452	35	186	213	44	382	547	456	167	269.5
Li	29	–	16	15	5	20	13	5.7	9	14	15	20	14.7
Rb	153	–	36	82	139	197	148	87	63	33	52	169	105.4
Cs	2.5	–	1.1	–	2.6	–	–	–	–	–	–	–	2.1
Sc	7.8	–	2.6	2.8	2.1	–	–	–	–	2.7	2.8	8.1	4.1
Ni	–	–	18	–	–	35	7.2	27	10	8.2	11	26	17.8
Cr	18	–	15	37	10	18	88	19	9	5.3	4.7	12	21.4
Co	6.5	–	2.3	–	–	4.3	tr	tr	tr	0.4	2.7	7.1	3.9
Cu	26	–	7.3	18	22	13	49	3.7	61	51	44	37	30.2
Zn	41	–	47	52	16	34	37	15	38	56	50	31	37.9
Ta	0.05	–	0.4	–	0.5	–	–	–	–	–	–	–	0.5
Zr	136	–	110	–	56	154	–	68	175	141	135	137	123.6
Hf	4.0	–	2.9	2.8	3.1	–	–	–	–	3.0	2.7	4.4	3.3
U	4.2	–	0.6	–	3.3	–	–	–	–	–	–	–	2.7
Th	21.2	–	1.7	1.7	7.2	–	–	–	–	1.7	1.6	18.2	7.6
La	14.5	–	14.7	16	3.9	–	–	–	–	13	13	20	13.6
Ce	28.6	–	28.6	27.3	11.2	–	–	–	–	25.6	26.8	40	26.9
Nd	12.2	–	–	9	7.4	–	–	–	–	10	10.1	13	10.3
Sm	3.1	–	1.8	1.9	2.1	–	–	–	–	1.8	1.9	3.5	2.3
Eu	0.59	–	0.56	0.66	–	–	–	–	–	0.52	0.49	0.60	0.57
Tb	0.39	–	0.21	0.25	0.65	–	–	–	–	0.19	0.25	0.70	0.37
Yb	1.40	–	0.84	0.86	2.56	–	–	–	–	0.94	0.94	2.06	1.37
Lu	0.31	–	0.14	0.14	0.43	–	–	–	–	0.137	0.144	0.35	0.24

glass; a second (51-W-6) is slightly vesiculated and contains about 50% glass, and the third (51-W-8) [see description on p. 336 and photomicrograph in Fig. 192d], a very frothy sample, has about 90% glass. The analyses show no discernible trend that would indicate that individual components were gained or lost during melting, but we cannot be certain that the original compositions of the xenoliths have been preserved.

We have also obtained microprobe analyses of the glassy fraction of a partly fused xenolith . . . . When compared with the bulk composition of the same rock, the glass is seen to be richer is SiO_2 and K_2O and poorer in Na_2O, MgO, and CaO. Its composition indicates that a potassium-rich mineral, probably biotite, was among the first phases to break down and that rapid melting may have caused the composition of the liquid to diverge from that expected under equilibrium conditions.

Volatile content

Estimates of the volatile contents of the magma have been uniformly low. Fries [see p. 312-316] calculated the amount of gases released in the fume cloud to be slightly more than 1 wt.% of the lava. This is much less than the estimate of Eggler [see p. 360-363], who concluded from experimental studies of phase relations that the Parícutin magma contained about 2.2 wt.% water when it was in equilibrium with its phenocrysts at a temperature of 1,110°C and more than 10 kilobars total pressure [about 30 km depth]. Water could, of course, have been exsolved during ascent of the magma and might not be represented in the fume clouds observed by Fries. Anderson[245] estimated a "before eruption" water content of about 1.5 wt.% from the compositions of glass inclusions. He also noted[246] that the Cl/K_2O ratio declined from 0.072 in glass trapped in phenocrysts to 0.05 in glass surrounding the crystals. He attributed this difference to a loss of chlorine along with about 1 wt.% water between the depth at which the phenocrysts grew and a shallower level where the magma re-equilibrated at lower pressures. His results are consistent with those of Eggler and Fries and lend support to the conclusion that the magma lost about half of its volatile content enroute to the surface . . . .

Trace elements

The lavas, xenoliths, and basement rocks have been analysed for most trace elements of petrologic interest. Zirconium, Rb, Ni, and Sr were measured by X-ray fluorescence, Ba, Sr, Rb, Co, Cr, Cu, Zn, and Li by atomic absorption or flame emission, and Sc, Hf, Ta, Th, U, Cs, and the rare-earth elements [REE] by neutron activation. These data are compiled in Tables 31-33 and are illustrated graphically in Fig. 202.

Lavas

The abundances of most trace-elements in the lavas changed only moderately as the magma evolved. A few, most notably Ba, Rb, Ni, and Cr, show a marked change around mid 1947 when about 80% of the total volume had been discharged. Except for somewhat erratic Nd values due to poor precision in the analytical determinations, little change in the chondrite-normalized curves is noticeable anywhere in the REE abundances throughout the eruptive sequence (Fig. 203); all lavas have a similar light-REE enriched pattern. The first lava of early 1943 is less enriched in the light REE (La and Ce) than are later lavas.

Xenoliths and Nearby Basement Rocks

Trace elements have a wide range of concentrations in the xenoliths and nearby basement rocks, but the concentrations of certain constituents show that the two suites are not strictly equivalent. Comparisons of the averages in Tables 32 and 33 show the basement rocks to be poorer in SiO_2, Na_2O, and Sr but richer in K_2O, Ba, Li, Rb, all transition metals, Zr, and Sr/Rb. They define a separate group on all the variation diagrams in Fig. 204.

The compositions of analysed xenoliths (Fig. 204) are scattered and for some elements fall far from the projected trend of lavas. This discrepancy is especially clear in the case of Zr, Sr, and Ba, all of which have such low abundances in the xenoliths that they are incompatible with the observed trends in the lavas. The chondrite-normalized REE patterns (Fig. 203) for the analysed xenoliths also have a wide range. The basement samples and about half of the xenoliths

Table 33. Major- and trace-element analyses of samples from exposures of basement rocks about 30 km SE of Parícutin.

	FP-20-52	FP-26-52	FP-27-52	AVE.
SiO_2	65.40	67.43	67.07	67.47
TiO_2	0.73	0.61	0.79	0.70
Al_2O_3	14.44	13.78	12.32	13.46
Fe_2O_3	2.40	1.95	1.30	1.84
FeO	3.25	2.60	3.81	3.26
MnO	0.16	0.18	0.09	0.15
MgO	2.56	1.62	2.12	2.15
CaO	5.07	3.73	4.42	4.00
Na_2O	3.40	3.20	3.31	3.30
K_2O	3.25	4.09	3.65	3.66
H_2O+	0.51	0.51	0.31	–
H_2O-	0.27	0.47	0.18	–
P_2O_5	0.14	0.11	0.08	0.07
Total	101.58	100.28	99.45	100.00
Ba	564	607	515	562
Sr	202	186	166	185
Li	28	24	28	27
Rb	123	195	170	163
Cs	4.2	–	–	4.2
Sc	18.0	11.9	14.7	14.9
Ni	18	11.6	57	28.9
Cr	49	13	35	32.3
Co	73	50	57	60
Cu	20	49	47	38.7
Zn	101	120	82	101
Zr	241	244	242	242.3
Hf	6.7	–	–	6.7
Ta	2.6	–	–	2.6
Th	11.8	11.9	14.7	12.8
U	4.5	5.0	3.9	4.5
La	19.3	20	21	20.1
Ce	37.0	40	47	41.3
Nd	28.8	16	21	21.9
Sm	4.7	4.7	5.2	4.9
Eu	0.8	0.8	0.8	0.8
Tb	0.8	0.6	0.8	0.7
Yb	2.75	2.8	3.1	2.9
Lu	0.43	0.45	0.44	0.44

have a distinct europium anomaly that is not apparent in the lavas. Most are light-REE enriched and have lower REE concentrations than the lavas, but the very frothy xenolith (51-W-8) has a flat pattern that is distinct from those of all other samples. As already noted, this specimen is also unusual in other ways.

Oxygen isotopes

Lavas

$^{18}O/^{16}O$ ratios were determined for 11 lavas and one sample of ash representing the sequence erupted from 1943 to 1952. The data are given in Table 34 and shown graphically in Fig. 205.

The first lavas to erupt have a $\delta^{18}O$ value of +6.9, typical of many basaltic andesites and andesites erupted in island-arcs and active continental margins

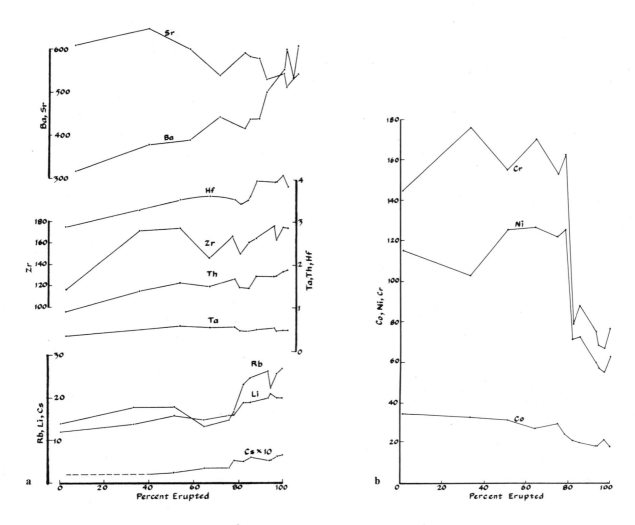

Fig. 202 a, b. Variations of trace elements in Parícutin lavas plotted against cumulative volume of magma erupted. All values are in ppm.

around the Pacific Ocean. The $\delta^{18}O$ values remained nearly constant at +6.9 to +7.1 up to 1947, but then increased abruptly to values of +7.5 to +7.7 in the later lavas. Such a change clearly indicates some type of open-system behavior such as assimilation of high-^{18}O material; it cannot be the result of simple closed-system fractional crystallization[247-251].

Xenoliths and Basement Rocks

Most of the analysed xenoliths and nearby basement rocks have $\delta^{18}O$ values of +8.2 to 9.2, distinctly greater than the values that characterize the early lavas. These values are typical of many calc-alkaline granitic rocks throughout the world, and specifically of the great Mesozoic and Cenozoic batholiths around the Pacific margins[252-254]. Thus, as far as the $^{18}O/^{16}O$ systematics are concerned, these xenoliths and base-

ment rocks represent plausible contaminants that could explain the post-1947 ^{18}O-enrichments of the lavas.

Note that most of the xenoliths in the ejecta of 1943 have very high $\delta^{18}O$ values of +9.1 to +9.9, whereas the xenoliths erupted in 1944-45 tend to be lower. One of the latter is particularly frothy and glassy and has a $\delta^{18}O$ value of +5.6, markedly lower than that of the initial Parícutin lava. The low $\delta^{18}O$ values of frothy or pumiceous xenoliths would be expected if they had high volatile contents, and the most logical interpretation of these data is that such xenoliths were altered and depleted in ^{18}O by meteoric-hydrothermal activity at the margins of the Parícutin magma chamber. The hydrous alteration minerals (chlorite, epidote, etc.) formed by this activity would have been dehydrated when the xenoliths were incorporated into the andesitic magma and the evolved water could promote melting of other phases as well.

Correlation with Major- and Trace-Element Compositions

The Parícutin lavas have a good positive correlation between $\delta^{18}O$ and the trace elements Ba, Li, Rb, and Cs, as well as a negative correlation with Sr, Sc, V, Cr, Cu, Zn, and Co (Tables 31 and 34). The $\delta^{18}O$ values of lavas show a positive correlation with SiO_2 content (Fig. 206), and the high-^{18}O 1943 xenoliths and the basement samples fall close to an extrapolation of the trend line of the Parícutin lavas, whereas the low-^{18}O xenoliths clearly do not. The low-^{18}O xenoliths have higher SiO_2 contents than the others, and in fact the xenolith population as a whole shows a good *negative* correlation between SiO_2 and $\delta^{18}O$. This trend at a high angle to the positive correlation between the lavas and high-^{18}O xenoliths suggests that the low-^{18}O xenoliths are SiO_2-rich partial melts and that the melting process was facilitated by the H_2O-rich, meteoric-hydrothermal environment at the roof of the magma chamber. Note that the lowest-^{18}O, highest-SiO_2, glass-rich xenolith (51-W-8) also has the highest K_2O content and contains by far the most radiogenic Sr ($^{87}Sr/^{86}Sr$ = 0.7101) of all the samples analysed in this study. It is also poorest in Fe, Mg, Ca, Zr, Li, Ba, Sr, Sc, Zn, La, Ce, and Nd contents of any Parícutin sample. This low-^{18}O xenolith has an atypical "flat" REE pattern (Fig. 203) and plots at extreme positions in the diagram of Fig. 204. Some of these anomalous chemical effects may be the result of hydrothermal alteration and melting.

Strontium isotopes

Strontium isotopic compositions and Rb and Sr concentrations of lavas, xenoliths, and nearby granodioritic basement rocks are reported in Table 34 and plotted in Fig. 205 . . . .

Lavas

The lavas showed no significant change in Sr isotopic composition until more than 80% of the magma had been erupted; $^{87}Sr/^{86}Sr$ remained uniform at 0.7037 to 0.7039 until 1947. Lavas of 1947 and 1952 show significant enrichment in radiogenic Sr, coincident with the increase in $\delta^{18}O$ values (Fig. 205). As the eruption progressed, the $^{87}Rb/^{86}Sr$ ratio rose only moderately (from 0.06 to 0.14) owing to a late rapid doubling of Rb content and small concurrent decrease in Sr (Fig. 202).

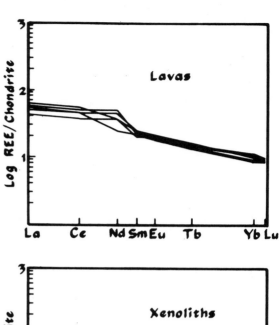

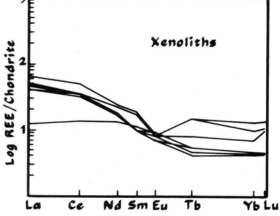

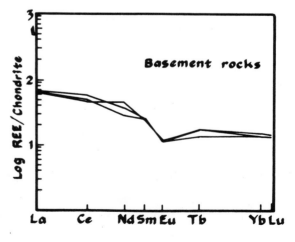

Fig. 203. Rare-earth element distribution patterns for nine selected Parícutin lavas, xenoliths, and basement rocks. Note the absence of europium anomalies in the lavas and the strong enrichment of the light rare earths. Data (from Tables 31-33) have been normalized to chondritic meteorites.

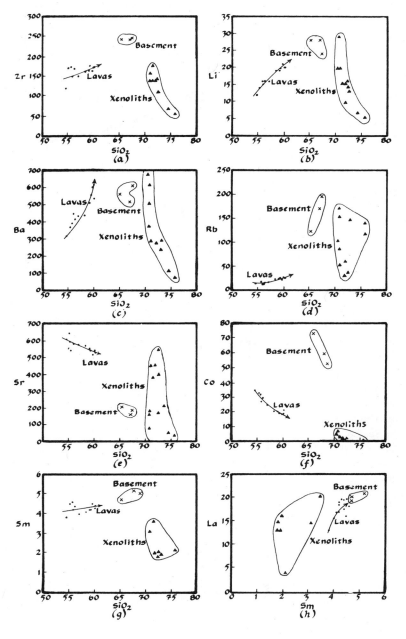

Fig. 204 a-h. Trace-element variations in lavas (*dots*) and xenoliths (*triangles*) erupted from Parícutin volcano. For comparative purposes, compositions are also shown for granitic rocks postulated to be from the basement under the volcano (*crosses*). Trends of compositional changes in the lava are indicated by *arrows* that are fitted visually through the points. In c, the values for Ba in two xenoliths are off the scale of the diagram at 767 ppm Ba, 71.0% SiO₂ and 2,097 ppm Ba, 71.4% SiO₂.

observed in volcanoes on normal to thin crust of continental margins or in island arcs[171,258] . . . .

Thus, in contrast to the Parícutin magmas, the xenoliths, Mid-Tertiary volcanic rocks, and basement samples all have more Rb, less Sr, higher Rb/Sr ratios, and, in general, more radiogenic Sr. These are accurately measured numbers, the concentrations showing close agreement with different methods and between different laboratories (Table 34), and they provide a forceful quantitative test for any contamination hypothesis.

Mass-Balance Calculations

Major Elements

Wilcox calculated the effects of fractionation of olivine and plagioclase and concurrent assimilation of "average" xenolithic material by a graphical method [see p. 340-344] that was later shown to be consistent with a mathematical solution devised by Bryan[227]. Miesch[228] used a method of vector analysis to examine variations within the same series of analyses and concluded that the compositions evolved through three stages, each of which was represented by a nearly linear compositional trend. The first could be explained by fractionation of olivine and plagioclase, the second by fractionation of Ca-poor pyroxene and plagioclase, and the third by assimilation of granitic wall rocks. The two inflections between the three trends noted by Miesch correspond closely to those shown in the CMAS diagram of Fig. 201.

Least-squares mixing calculations can be used to assess the effects of assimilating xenoliths while fractionating specific combinations of minerals. Analyses of phenocrysts and xenoliths can be used to determine whether any reasonable combination of these components might explain the variations of major- and trace-elements from one stage of differentiation to another. This has been done for each

The initial $^{87}Sr/^{86}Sr$ ratio of the main body of Parícutin magma, about 0.7038, is in the lower part of the range observed for the Mexican Volcanic Belt (0.7032 to 0.7048)[255-257] and typical of the values of the three major segments of the trends shown in Fig. 201.

The first stage has two parts, but the slight difference between them can be explained as the result of a slightly greater proportion of olivine crystallizing from the very earliest lavas. The main trend requires fractionation of plagioclase to explain the reduction in Al_2O_3 and Sr. A somewhat better fit is obtained if a small amount (about 2%) of average xenolithic material is assimilated at the same time.

· · · · ·

During the short intermediate interval in which alumina increases slightly (i.e. the middle stage of Fig. 201), the CMAS diagram indicates that amphibole and hypersthene should have been crystallizing, but a better fit is obtained by subtracting hypersthene and plagioclase and adding xenolithic material. In both the early and middle stages, the calculated results are in better agreement with the observed petrographic relations than with the inferred phase relations at elevated pressures.

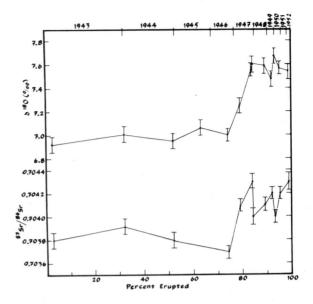

Fig. 205. Plot of $\delta^{18}O$ and $^{87}Sr/^{86}Sr$ in Parícutin lavas against cumulative percent erupted.

Table 34. Oxygen and strontium isotope ratios of Parícutin lavas, ash, xenoliths, and basement rocks.

Sample	Date erupted	$\delta^{18}O$	[a]	Rb[b]	Sr[b]	$^{87}Rb/^{86}Sr$	$^{87}Sr/^{86}Sr$
Lavas and ash							
51-W-18	Feb 1943	6.92 ± 0.09	(3)	14	607	0.067	0.7038
108081	Jan 1944	7.03 ± 0.04	(2)	15.4	578	0.077	0.7039
W-47-27	Oct 1944	6.95	(1)	18	596	0.087	0.7038
W-47-23	Sept 1945	7.06 ± 0.08	(2)	13.4	537	0.072	
W-46-27	Sept 1946	7.00 ± 0.12	(3)	15	588	0.074	0.7037
W-47-9	Apr 1947	7.25 ± 0.10	(2)	16.8	580	0.084	0.7041
Ash fall[c]	Nov 1947	7.55 ± 0.17	(2)			–	0.7043
W-47-30	Nov 1947	7.60	(1)	23.2	575	0.116	0.7040
W-48-5	Sept 1948	7.59	(1)	24.6	556	0.128	0.7041
FP-5-49	May 1949	7.48	(1)	26.3	540	0.141	0.7042
FP-20-49	Dec 1949	7.69 ± 0.06	(2)	22.2	512	0.125	0.7040
FP-20-50	Sept 1950	7.57	(1)	24.6	533	0.134	0.7042
FP-16-52	Feb 1952	7.54 ± 0.04	(2)	27	541	0.143	0.7043
Xenoliths							
51-W-1	1943	9.94 ± 0.01	(2)	153	78	5.68	0.7071
51-W-5	1943	9.44	(1)	–	–	–	0.7044
51-W-6	1943	9.11	(1)	36	404	0.26	0.7043
51-W-7[d]	1944–45	8.21	(1)	82	452	0.53	0.7047
51-W-8[d]	1944–45	5.59 ± 0.01	(2)	139	35	11.49	0.7101
51-W-9	1944–45	8.71 ± 0.00	(2)	197	186	3.07	0.7059
51-W-10[d]	1944–45	6.84	(1)	148	213	2.02	0.7054
51-W-11	1943	6.77	(1)	87	44	5.72	0.7070
51-W-22	1943	9.06 ± 0.20	(2)	63	382	0.48	0.7046
Basement rocks							
FP-20-52	–	8.57 ± 0.06	(2)	123	202	1.75	0.7047
FP-26-52	–	8.54	(1)	195	186	3.02	0.7056
FP-27-52	–	7.66	(1)	170	166	2.96	0.7056

[a] Error is average deviation from the mean; number in parentheses is number of times analysed
[b] Analyses in parts per million by X-ray fluorescence
[c] 3.5 mm ash collected 5 km north of the vent
[d] Frothy pumiceous sample

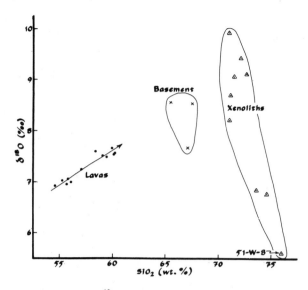

Fig. 206. Plot of δ¹⁸O vs. SiO₂ contents of lavas, basement rocks, and xenoliths. Mixing curves are approximately *straight lines* on this type of diagram, because most rocks have very similar bulk oxygen concentrations.

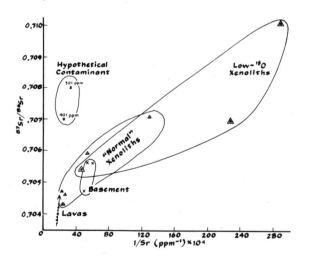

Fig. 207. Plot of ⁸⁷Sr/⁸⁶Sr vs. 1/Sr for the lavas, basement rocks, and xenoliths of Parícutin volcano. Also shown are the positions of two hypothetical contaminants (containing 401 and 301 ppm Sr) that are required by the mass-balance calculations . . . . The three low-¹⁸O xenoliths, which appear to have been hydrothermally altered, are shown as *large triangles*. Note that mixing curves are *straight lines* on this type of diagram.

The greatest compositional changes took place in the final interval represented by the last 20% of the total volume erupted. These abrupt variations can be explained almost entirely as the effect of addition of

xenoliths. A small amount of hypersthene may have crystallized but the mass-balance calculation indicates that only about 0.5 wt.% hypersthene was fractionated, an insignificant amount in terms of the reliability of the sampling and analytical data.

. . . . .

Oxygen Isotopes

The oxygen isotope data are compatible with major and trace-element mass-balance calculations. As shown in Fig. 206, the high-¹⁸O xenoliths and

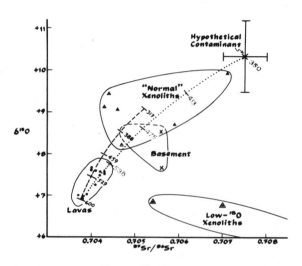

Fig. 208. Plot of δ¹⁸O vs. ⁸⁷Sr/⁸⁶Sr for lavas, xenoliths, and basement rocks. The xenoliths are subdivided into a "normal" group and a low-¹⁸O group. Also shown is the hypothetical Sr-rich contaminant with 350 ppm Sr, ⁸⁷Sr/⁸⁶Sr = 0.707 to 0.708, and δ¹⁸O = +9.5 to +11.2 required by the mass-balance calculations . . . . Two calculated mixing curves show Sr values (in ppm) at the short cross marks corresponding to 75, 50, 25, and 0% contamination of a parental magma represented by the early lavas (600 ppm Sr). The *dashed curve* is for assimilation of the average of six "normal" xenoliths (317 ppm Sr), and the *dotted curve* represents assimilation of the hypothetical contaminant.

basement plutonic rocks are both richer in ¹⁸O than the initial Parícutin magma, and they would be capable of accounting for the enrichment in ¹⁸O in the post-1947 lavas. However, a mixture of 1943 lava (δ¹⁸O = +6.9) with basement (δ¹⁸O = +8.5) would require assimilation of about 40% of the latter to produce the +7.5 to +7.7 values characteristic of the last 20% of the erupted magma. A more plausible fit is obtained by using the higher-¹⁸O xenoliths. With a xenolith of δ¹⁸O= +9.5, only about 25% contamination is required.

Strontium Isotopes

Although the analysed basement rocks and xenoliths have similar ages and compositions, they cannot be the sole contaminant responsible for the observed Sr isotopic compositions of the late-stage Parícutin lavas; a more radiogenic or more Sr-rich material is required. Figure 207 is a plot of $^{87}Sr/^{86}Sr$ versus $1/Sr$; all mixing hyperbolas define straight lines on such a diagram. Except for one low-^{18}O sample, the xenoliths and basement rocks form a nearly linear array that extrapolates toward the late-stage lavas but is distinct from the trend of the lavas themselves. The arrow indicating the effect of contamination has a much steeper slope (Fig. 207). Contamination lines calculated using typical xenoliths and basement rocks have lower slopes implying a greater increase in Rb/Sr ratio and a greater decrease in Sr content than is observed in the lavas.

Excluding the three xenoliths in Table 34 that have $\delta^{18}O$ values of +6.8 or less, the other six xenoliths form tight clusters in Figs. 206 and 207, as they do in Fig. 208 where they are designated as the "normal" group of xenoliths. The latter have a mean $\delta^{18}O$ value of +9.1, a mean Sr ratio of 0.7052, and a mean Sr content of 317 ppm. The simple dashed mixing curve in Fig. 208 indicates that about 30 to 35% assimilation of such material would be required to account for the late-stage lavas, considerably more than the 20% needed to explain most of the major and trace-element data . . . However, an overall 20% addition of the "hypothetical contaminant" with a present-day $^{87}Sr/^{86}Sr$ ratio of 0.7075, Rb content of 70 ppm, Sr content of 350 ppm, and $\delta^{18}O$ = +10.35 would yield a mixture with a Sr isotope ratio of 0.7043, 27.6 ppm Rb, 550 ppm Sr, and $\delta^{18}O$ = +7.6, very close to the latest magma (Figs. 207 and 208). Such rocks could be a combination of basement rocks, Tertiary volcanic rocks, and some other types of material, such as ancient intermediate crust with an age of about 1 Ga, seawater-altered mafic volcanic rocks, sediment derived from such material, or a variety of marine sediments, such as a Mesozoic limestone-shale mixture.

Although the high Ba and low Cr and Co contents of the contaminant implied by the plots of Fig. 204 are consistent with a sedimentary or metasedimentary character, the oxygen isotope ratios are not. Typical unmetamorphosed sedimentary rocks, particularly limestones and shales, have $\delta^{18}O$ values of +15 to +25, much too high to be compatible with the mass balance discussed in the preceding section. Igneous or metamorphic rocks with $\delta^{18}O$ values of about +9 to +13 would be more consistent with the oxygen isotope data (Fig. 208).

Mechanism of Differentiation

Certain limitations can be placed on the physical processes responsible for the variations seen in the Parícutin lavas. First, the magma must already have been compositionally zoned in its reservoir prior to the eruption; the 9-year period of activity was too short for the compositional differences to have developed by any known mechanism of differen-

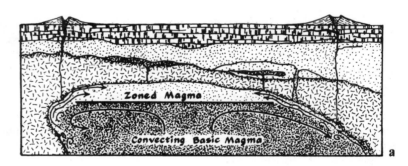

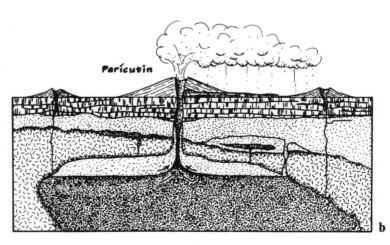

Fig. 209 a. Silica-enriched magma resulting from melting and assimilation of crustal rocks in more primitive magma is thought to have formed a bouyant boundary layer that rose and collected under the roof of the reservoir. b - Tapping of these two zones led to more rapid rise of the denser but less viscous lower magma and later eruption of the more silica-rich fraction when the rate of discharge declined.

tiation. It is more likely that the magma became zoned in a shallow reservoir before the first discharge of magma in 1943. Studies of the isotopes of radon and lead indicate that the system was probably evolving for at least 50 to 100 years prior to the eruption[259].

. . . . .

The model proposed by Wilcox to explain the evolution of the zoned magma [see p. 344-346] was based on a mechanism of convective stratification proposed by Holmes[238]. It was thought that, as the magma rose through granitic crustal rocks, its upper part became increasingly contaminated and lighter until its density was less than that of the main mass of uncontaminated magma and the two parts of the rising intrusion could no longer convect and mix as a single body. The contaminated magma would have accumulated in a separate zone overlying a much larger mass of denser, hotter magma of more primitive composition. This basic idea has been developed by more recent studies showing that the light contaminated liquid could have been fractionated and ponded under the roof as the intrusion melted its walls[260]. Nilson et al.[261] have examined the behavior of light liquids produced by crystallization or melting at the walls of a mafic intrusion and explained how a bouyant liquid could rise along the walls and accumulate in the upper levels of the reservoir. As it does so, it may back-mix with the more primitive magma, so that the liquid collected under the roof would be compositionally graded. Such a process has been shown to be capable of producing the observed volumes of zoned magma in a period on the order of decades to centuries depending on the shape and rate of cooling of the intrusion.

. . . . .

In order to explain the eruption of lavas in an order that was the reverse of what would be expected if the light differentiated magma were in the upper part of the reservoir, Wilcox proposed that the vent tapped the lower flanks of a steep-sided body and drew the magma down in such a way that the last liquid to appear was from the upper-most part of the intrusion [see p. 345-346]. Another explanation for the order of eruption can be deduced from the recent work of Blake[262], Koyaguchi[263], and Blake and Ivy[264]. The scheme depicted in the lower part of Fig. 209 requires no special geometrical relations but only a contrast in the densities and viscosities of the two parts of the

zoned magma. When magmas with differing properties rise through a channel tapping a compositionally zoned reservoir, the lower liquid tends to be drawn up and enter the central part of the conduit. If the lower liquid is less viscous, it tends to flow more rapidly and, even though it is denser and starts at a lower level, it can reach the surface before the more viscous differentiated liquid. As the rate of discharge declines, the draw-up diminishes and the lighter more viscous liquid is able to escape without entraining the lower part of the reservoir.

Conclusions

Most of the new geochemical data confirm the original interpretation of the zoned Parícutin lavas as products of extensive assimilation of felsic basement rocks by a magma with a composition of basaltic andesite represented by the earliest lavas. Improved and more detailed calculations of mass-balance relations indicate that the amount of crystal fractionation accompanying assimilation was probably less than originally estimated. Most of the heat required to assimilate felsic crustal rocks must therefore have come from a larger body of convecting mafic magma at greater depths.

The main mass of magma evolved by fractionation, first of olivine, and then hypersthene, plagioclase, and possibly amphibole. The mineral assemblages in the rocks are in general accord with the phase relations deduced experimentally by Eggler [see p. 360-363] and Cawthorn and O'Hara[241] if allowance is made for breakdown of amphibole and loss of water during ascent of the magma from the level where most of the differentiation took place.

Although the general relationships are clearly established, the exact nature and composition of the assimilated material cannot be deduced from the available samples of xenoliths and basement rocks. This may be due in part to the wide diversity of their original compositions and in part to disequilibrium partitioning of components during contact metamorphism, melting, and assimilation. The mechanism responsible for differentiation and zoning was probably one of liquid fractionation in which a contaminated magma of low density was segregated into the upper levels of a shallow chamber. The order of eruption is best explained as a result of withdrawal of liquids of differing densities and viscosities from a compositionally zoned reservoir.

Experimental Duplication of Parícutin Magma in the Laboratory

In an effort to understand the nature of magma prior to its eruption from volcanoes, scientists have devised a variety of sophisticated furnaces that allow them to recreate the high temperatures and pressures of deep magma bodies in the laboratory. Two different types of experiments were conducted on samples from Parícutin: 1) melting studies of dry samples at normal air pressure, and 2) studies at high temperature and pressure of water-bearing samples.

The first and simplest type of experiment controls only temperature. A sample of rock powder is loaded in a crucible made of gold, platinum, palladium, or alloys of these precious metals. Such metals are used because they have very high melting temperatures and do not react with the rock when it becomes molten during the experiment. The crucible is placed in a furnace, where it is heated by a resistance wire, similar to the heating element in a kitchen toaster. At very high temperatures the sample becomes completely molten. With slow progressive cooling, crystals of a particular mineral will nucleate and grow from the liquid at a specific temperature. This is referred to as the "liquidus temperature", and the mineral is referred to as the "liquidus mineral". As temperature is lowered further, a larger part of the sample will consist of crystals, and less will be liquid. Other minerals will begin to crystallize at specific lower temperatures. At the end of an experiment, the furnace is turned off and the sample is rapidly cooled, quenching the remaining liquid to form glass, which surrounds any crystals that grew prior to quenching. The manner in which an experimentalist freezes a sample in the laboratory reproduces the process by which volcanoes freeze magma to form glassy volcanic rocks by expelling them into cold water or air at the earth's surface. After this quenching, the capsule is removed from the furnace and opened. The glass and enclosed crystals can then be studied using the same microscopes and analytical instruments used to study natural rock samples.

Experiments of this sort were conducted on five samples from Parícutin by Tilley et al.[240,265], with the results shown in Table 35. The highest liquidus temperature found

was 1,227°C for olivine in sample B1, with plagioclase appearing at 1,208°C and both pyroxenes joining the assemblage at 1,145°C. These data are in general agreement with temperature measurements of up to 1,110°C made on Parícutin lavas in the field (see p. 317-320), considering that the natural lavas typically contained all four minerals, and particularly in the light of the statement by Zies (see p. 318) that the temperature of the lava as it left the vent at the base of the cone in December 1944 was probably about 1,200°C.

Far more complex are experiments that also control pressure and include water or other volatile constituents. Because pressure and volatiles can strongly affect the temperatures at which various minerals appear, only these more complex experiments can closely reproduce conditions in a natural magma body. The experiments are typically conducted on a small sample of powdered rock (20-50 milligrams) that is combined with carefully measured quantities of water or other volatile constituents and sealed inside a capsule made of precious metal. The capsule is then inserted into the furnace where it is heated by a resistance wire and pressurized using either a solid ram or high-pressure gas. Again, various minerals form at specific temperatures and pressures, and these can be studied once the sample is quenched at the end of the run. A large number of individual experiments are necessary to map out the stability fields of the different minerals on a plot of temperature versus pressure.

Below we reproduce portions of an important experimental study by Eggler concerning the phase relations of a Parícutin andesite. Eggler controlled both temperature and pressure using a device called an "internally heated pressure vessel", so named because the furnace is under pressure during the experiment. He controlled or "buffered" the state of oxidation in the experimental samples by mixing

Table 35. Results of melting experiments on the calc-alkaline lavas of Parícutin volcano.

Rock Identification	Highest Temperature of Crystallization of Major Phases	n of Glass
High-alumina basalt Bomb ejected February 20, 1943 (B1)	Ol (1227°); Pl (1208°); Opx, Cpx (1145°)	1.570
High-alumina basalt Lava of March 1944 (HAB)	Pl (1220°), Ol (1215°), Opx (1165°), Cpx (1155°)	1.553
Hypersthene andesite Lava of March 1943 (2)	Pl (1198°); Opx, Ol (1173°)	1.553
Hypersthene andesite Lava of September 1947 (14)	Pl (1203°), Opx (1178°), Ol (1170°)	1.543
Hypersthene andesite Lava of September 1950 (19)	Pl (1197°), Opx (1145°)	1.540

hydrogen gas with the argon gas used to pressurize the vessel. This buffering is important for elements, like iron, that can exist in more than one oxidation state (Fe^{2+}, Fe^{3+}). Eggler controlled the amount of water dissolved in the liquid portion of the experimental samples by mixing in with the natural rock powder carefully measured quantities of "oxalic acid", a powder that breaks down under run conditions to produce equal moles of H_2O and CO_2. One of the most important results from this study was an estimate of the water content in the natural magma of 2.2 ± 0.5 wt%.

Eggler (1972a)

Introduction

This study investigated a lava from Parícutin volcano (FP-16-52)[266] that represents one of the latest units in a well-documented series of basaltic andesites and andesites. A few runs are reported on an earlier lava (W-47-30)[267] . . . . The lavas were studied to determine the degree of water saturation to be expected in an andesitic magma in an active tectonic area.

The term "saturation" refers to the maximum amount of water that can be dissolved in the liquid part of the magma at a specific temperature and pressure. The saturation level increases strongly with increasing pressure and decreases slightly with increasing temperature. Bubbles of aqueous fluid (and other volatile components) will be present in a magma that contains more water than the saturation value, or "excess" water. Magmas that contain less than this value are said to be "undersaturated", and should contain no gas bubbles.

Pressure in this paper is given in units of "kilobars", commonly abbreviated "kb". One kilobar is essentially equivalent to 1,000 times the normal atmospheric pressure at the earth's surface. Pressure increases with depth in the shallow earth at the rate of about 1 kilobar for each 3 kilometers. The experiments of this study ranged up to pressures of 10 kilobars, or equivalent to the base of normal continental crust at a depth of 30 kilometers.

Experimental Results

Phase relations for lava FP-16-52 composition when excess H_2O was added to the charge appear in pressure-temperature projection in Fig. 210. Water-undersaturated runs have been added in Fig. 211. All the run data have been isobarically smoothed [shown schematically as lines of equal pressure ("isobaric")] to produce the various undersaturated silicate liquidi of Fig. 212. [The term "liquidi" (plural of "liquidus") is used here to describe the family of lines showing the highest temperature, for a given pressure, at which a specific mineral exists. Thus, with 2 wt.% water in the melt, plagioclase is stable only to the left of the solid line labeled "2" in Fig. 212]. Noteworthy features of these figures are: (1) Plagioclase is the liquidus phase when water contents in the liquid are less than 1.5-2.5 wt.%, depending on total pressure; when more water is present, orthopyroxene is the liquidus phase. (2) Olivine usually appears with orthopyroxene on the liquidus but quickly disappears by reaction as temperature is lowered. (3) The slope of the liquidus for a given phase becomes less positive as water content is raised. The plagioclase liquidus even becomes negative, probably because of a coupled reaction with clinopyroxene. When H_2O content in the liquid is low, clinopyroxene melts at lower temperature than plagioclase, releasing Ca into the melt. At higher H_2O contents, plagioclase melts at lower temperature than clinopyroxene in a liquid with lower Ca/Na ratio, because Ca is partitioned into clinopyroxene. Therefore the plagioclase . . . is more sodic and melts at lower temperature. (4) The crossing of orthopyroxene and plagioclase liquidi for 2 wt.% H_2O appears to be real and is probably more attributable to molar volume differences of the melting reactions than to change in plagioclase composition with pressure, or even less likely, anorthite breakdown with pressure. Dry melting data of Green and Ringwood[269] on andesite also suggest this crossing. (5) Calcium-rich clinopyroxene appears near the orthopyroxene liquidus when H_2O contents in melt are greater than 5 wt.%; no pigeonite was found. Clinopyroxene relations are complicated when hornblende is stable, because hornblende melts incongruently to liquid plus clinopyroxene[270-271]. [The term "incongruent" means that the mineral does not simply melt to form a liquid of identical composition, but rather melts to form a liquid of different composition plus another mineral.] (6) Hornblende stability may be either raised or lowered in temperature relative to the H_2O-saturated curve shown when f_{H2O} is less than $f°_{H2O}$; these reactions are discussed elsewhere[272]. [The term "f_{H2O}" stands for "fugacity of water"; "fugacity" is a thermodynamic variable very similar to "pressure". The term $f°_{H2O}$ refers to the "fugacity" of pure water.] The maximum upper temperature stability limit of hornblende is 930-950°C, well below the other silicate liquidi except for

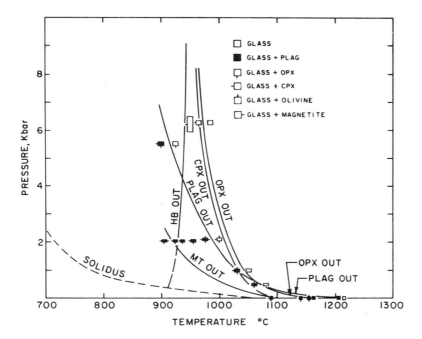

Fig. 210. Pressure-temperature projection of curves representing melting reactions in Parícutin lava FP-16-52 at H_2O-saturated conditions. Phases appearing, in order of decreasing temperature, are orthopyroxene, clinopyroxene, plagioclase, hornblende, and magnetite. All runs contained a fluid phase. Olivine was usually present with orthopyroxene on the orthopyroxene liquidus. Size of brackets indicates estimated experimental uncertainty of the run. Amphibole stability is delimited by bracketing runs shown. Solidus based on tonalite-H_2O system of Piwinskii[268]. [The term "solidus" refers to the lowest temperature at which liquid is still present. The "solidus curve" connects these points on a temperature-pressure diagram.]

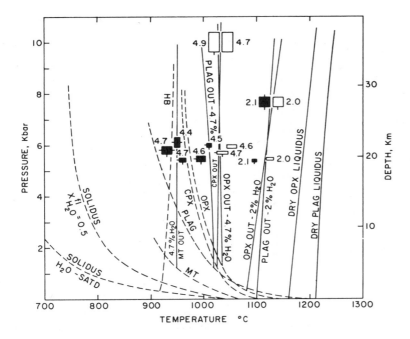

Fig. 211. Water-undersaturated melting relations in Parícutin lava FP-16-52. Run symbols same as in Fig. 210; numbers indicate wt.% H_2O in melt. All runs contained a $CO_2 + H_2O$ fluid phase. Dry liquidi are projected from data of Green and Ringwood[269]. H_2O-saturated liquidi are dashed. Solidus for X_{H_2O} in fluid = 0.5 was calculated from data of Millhollen[270].

361

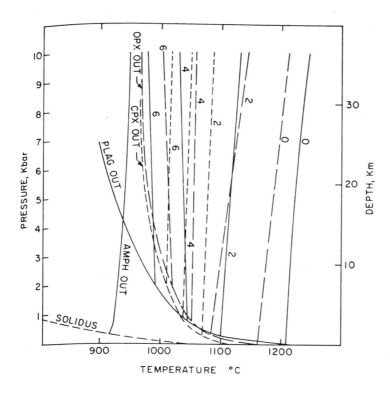

Fig. 212. Summary diagram of melting curves in lava FP-16-52. Solidus and phase-out curves at left refer to H_2O-saturated conditions. [These curves labeled "out" have the same meaning as "liquidus" curves.] Other lines are undersaturated melting curves. Numbers represent wt.% H_2O in melt; solid lines are plagioclase, long-dashed are orthopyroxene, and short-dashed are clinopyroxene liquidi. Olivine is usually present with orthopyroxene on the orthopyroxene liquidus.

H_2O-saturated conditions at pressures greater than 5 kb. (7) Magnetite appears 80-100°C below the silicate liquidus at all conditions investigated.

Some H_2O-saturated melting curves for lava W-47-30 composition appear in Fig. 213. The data show that phase relations are essentially the same as for FP-16-52 composition.

Application to Parícutin Paragenesis

Water Content of Lava

Lava FP-16-52 contains as phenocrysts 0.3 vol.% olivine, 0.7 vol.% orthopyroxene, and 0.1 vol.% plagioclase [see Table 25, p. 326]. If it is assumed that these phases were on the liquidus in about the same proportions before eruption and that total pressure was 10 kb or less when they precipitated, a direct comparison of petrographic and experimental data is possible.

. . . . .

If the natural phenocryst assemblage is a low-pressure (less than 10 kb) assemblage, we can compare the experimental data and the natural mode directly. Fig. 212 shows that plagioclase crystallizes before orthopyroxene and olivine for water contents in the melt of less than 2 wt.%. For water contents greater than about 3 wt.%, orthopyroxene crystallizes

before plagioclase, and above 3 kb, orthopyroxene is joined by clinopyroxene (Ca-rich), which is not found in the natural phenocryst assemblage. To duplicate the natural assemblage on the liquidus, therefore, a water content in the melt of 2.2 ± 0.5 wt.% is required. Because the undersaturated liquidi are steep, the temperature at which phenocrysts formed can be limited to 1,110 ± 40°C. This temperature compares favorably with a thermocouple measurement on a 1944 Parícutin flow of 1,110°C [see p. 318] and a maximum vent temperature in 1946 of 1,070°C [see p. 319].

The melt that erupted to produce lava W-47-30 probably held about the same amount of H_2O or a little more, inasmuch as the lava contains no plagioclase phenocrysts. A run containing 2.0 wt.% H_2O at 1,115°C, 7.7 kb produced glass, a small amount of orthopyroxene, and a few grains of plagioclase and olivine. Presumably, a little more H_2O would eliminate the plagioclase phenocrysts.

Interpretation of Mineral Paragenesis

There is general agreement between the petrographically determined mineral paragenesis of Parícutin lavas [see p. 325-334] and experimental phase relations. In particular, the phase relations explain the absence of clinopyroxene phenocrysts or microphenocrysts in the later lavas. For 2 wt.% H_2O in the melt, clinopyroxene crystallizes about 40°C below orthopyroxene and plagioclase and hence would be expected only in the groundmass. In fact, if the magma rose after crystallization of the phenocrysts and in the process boiled off H_2O, the melting interval between clinopyroxene and the other phases would be even greater (Fig. 212).

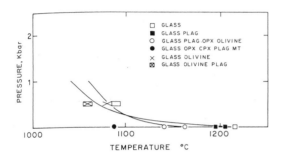

Fig. 213. Projection of curves representing melting reactions in lava W-47-30 at H_2O-saturated conditions. Run symbols indicate quenched phase assemblage. All runs contained fluid.

. . . . .

Derivation of the Parícutin Series

The experimental results show that only plagioclase, olivine, and orthopyroxene could be involved in fractional crystallization of the Parícutin series at depths of less than 30 km. These are the only phases present as phenocrysts in all lavas and in runs with the two lavas investigated. Since magnetite is not stable near the liquidus it can play no role in differentiation . . . . Petrographic examination of lavas FP-16-52 and W-47-30 in reflected light revealed no titanomagnetite phenocrysts or microphenocrysts, but only a few tiny crystals in the groundmass.

Wilcox has shown that fractionation involving plagioclase, olivine, and orthopyroxene cannot produce the Parícutin lava series [see p. 340-344]. Because compositions of phases present in experimental runs are very similar to those in the natural lavas, and the pyroxenes are not aluminous, experimentation confirms that the lava series is not a product of low-pressure fractionation.

Wilcox argued that the series could have been produced by a combination of fractional crystallization and assimilation of salic country rocks [see p. 340-344]. Mass-balance calculations confirm this possibility[227].

Comparisons with Other New Volcanoes

Parícutin is one of a small number of "new" volcanoes that have been born in historical times. Excluded from this class are those new vents that erupt on the flanks of a larger volcano and simply represent the eccentric tapping of that larger magmatic reservoir. All large volcanoes have cinder and lava cones on their flanks, born through flank-vent eruptions. Such eruptions have been relatively common throughout history, especially at highly active volcanic centers such as Etna[273]. The 1988 eruption at Navidad vent on the NE flank of the Chilean volcano Lonquimay[274], and the 1975-76 eruption on the southern flank of the Kamchatkan volcano Plosky Tolbachik[275] are good examples from subduction-related stratovolcanoes. Although the development of these flank-vent eruptions may differ little from the development of a "new" Parícutin-type volcano, they do not mark the arrival at the earth's surface of a completely new magmatic system. Admittedly, the distinction between a new volcano and a flank vent can be difficult to make, particularly in cases where the eruption occurs on the lowermost flanks of a larger cone and a direct connection to the larger magmatic plumbing system is debatable.

Bullard's[276] chapter titled "Birth of New Volcanoes" is one of the few treatments of this subject. He considers the eruptive births of continental volcanoes Parícutin, Jorullo, and Monte Nuovo (Italy), and concludes with a discussion of new island volcanoes. We encourage interested readers to consult Bullard[276] on the latter subject, but confine our treatment to continental examples of "new" volcanoes. As analogs to Parícutin we include descriptions of the births of Jorullo (1759), Monte Nuovo (1538), and Waiowa volcano (1943), born in the Goropu Mountains of Papua New Guinea in the same year as Parícutin. Another notable sequence of volcanic events began in late 1943, and even involved another cornfield; it resulted in a new mountain called Showa-Shinzan in northern Japan[277] (see Chronology of Events, p. 16-19). This dome, however, is a subsidiary feature of Usu volcano, and therefore not discussed here as a "new" volcano.

Jorullo, México (1759-1774)

Certainly the best analog to the Parícutin eruption occurred 184 years earlier and 81 km to the SE, at Jorullo volcano. Of the nearly 1,000 morphologically youthful cinder and lava cones in the Michoacán-Guanajuato Volcanic Field, Parícutin and Jorullo are the only ones to have erupted since the Spanish Conquest. Jorullo was born in a ravine in 1759. Like Parícutin, it did not form on the flank of a larger active volcano, but was a new volcano, born in a landscape dotted with other cinder and lava cones. Jorullo and Parícutin have many other things in common. In both cases a main cinder cone was flanked by NE-SW-trending lava vents that fed an extensive lava field (25 km² at Parícutin and 9 km² at Jorullo). As discussed by Wood[201], these two Mexican eruptions were both unusually long (15 years for Jorullo, 9 years for Parícutin) in comparison to all

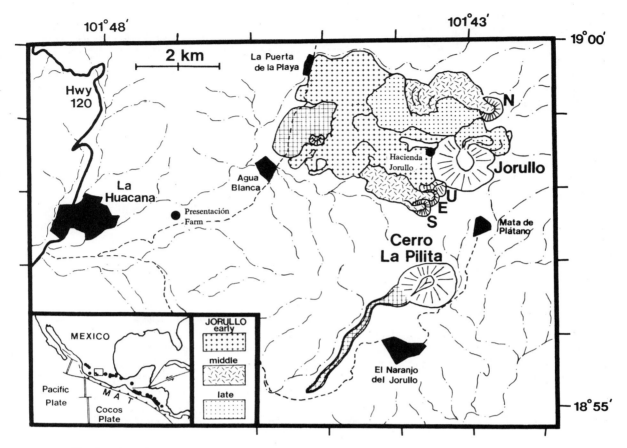

Fig. 214. Location map showing Jorullo volcano, its four parasitic cones (N = Volcán del Norte, U = unnamed, E = Volcán de Enmedio, S = Volcán del Sur), and the three stages of lava flows (see pattern key). Hacienda de Jorullo and Presentación Farm are indicated. Cross-hatched pattern shows pre-historic lava flows including that from Cerro La Pilita. Cities and villages are shown in black. Dashed lines are unpaved roads. Dot-dash lines show drainages. On inset map, small square outlines the Michoacán-Guanajuato Volcanic Field, stars show Parícutin and Jorullo, dots represent major composite volcanoes, and MAT = Middle America Trench.

other historical eruptions of cinder-and-lava cones (95% are over in 1 year or less), including that of the new volcano Monte Nuovo (7 days) described below. The eruptions of Jorullo and Parícutin both emitted 1-2 km³ of magma, which in unusual fashion, became progressively more silica-rich with time. Another similarity is that no person was directly killed by either eruption. In contrast with the intense study given to Parícutin, relatively little has been written about Jorullo[100,187,276,278-281].

We reproduce below eyewitness accounts of Jorullo's first 1½ months of activity, published by Gadow, followed by portions of Luhr and Carmichael (1985) that treat the geological setting and petrology of the eruptive products. We include a new compositional plot comparing the rock suites from Jorullo and Parícutin. Elsewhere in the book is a

stereopair of airphotographs for Jorullo (Fig. 153, p. 265), and a color photograph of the volcano from the ground (Plate 8B).

Eye-Witness Account

Gadow (1930)

This remarkable work, published posthumously, mainly concerns the return of animals and plants to the devastated district around Jorullo. In addition to that subject, however, Gadow also did an excellent job in describing the birth, evolution, and geology of the eruption, and his work has become the source book on Jorullo from which virtually all later accounts are derived. It contains an extensive appendix with translations and summaries of all *published observations on Jorullo in chronological order. From this invaluable compilation we reprint Gadow's translations of the eye-witness reports written by Sáyago, the administrator of the Hacienda de Jorullo, to the Governor of Michoacán and the Viceroy of New Spain. The two reports were written 9 and 44 days, respectively, after the volcano's birth. They were first published in 1854 by Orozco y Berra*[282].

Sáyago. Report of October 8th, 1759, transmitted on October 13th by the Governor of Michoacán to the Viceroy of New Spain.

In the district of [Ario de Rosales], José Andres de Pimentel, a resident at Pátzcuaro, possessed [two] fine properties, called the Hacienda de Jorullo and Presentación, respectively, for the production of sugar and cattle [see Fig. 214]. There and in the neighbourhood, towards the end of June in the present year of 1759 were heard and felt repeated subterranean rumblings or knocks, but without tremors, which caused the people who lived there much fear, and as these uncanny noises increased and were accompanied by slight shocks, the workmen forsook the *hacienda* to live higher up on the neighboring hills.

It is an unalterable fact that this flight did arise not so much from the horrible increases in those noises and tremors as from a vague and spreading rumour that on St. Michael's day [September 29] Jorullo would come to an end.

On the 17th of September, at 9 a.m., there was heard a formidable noise on the very spot of the Jorullo *hacienda*. This was repeated every moment and sounded like cannon discharged in the center of the earth, so that the frightened people made for the chapel, to pray, but they had to fly to the hills because the incessant earthquake burst the chapel, threw down the shingles from the roof, and did other damage.

Therefore the administrator of the farm sent to Pátzcuaro for the Jesuit Padre Isidoro Molina, to celebrate Mass, etc., in order to appease the divine ire. P. Molina arrived on the 20th and on the 21st he began with a nine-days' Mass and confessional, and all this time the tremors and noises never stopped, until the 27th for a little.

There arrived the 29th of September, the much-feared day of St. Michael, and at 3 o'clock in the morning, a quarter of a league [~1.2 km] to the SE from the farm in the ravine called Cuitinga, broke out very dark and dense steam which rose up into the sky, having been preceded by three or four very sharp tremors, and soon after the appearance of the cloud a tempestuous and horrible noise was heard and flames of fire burst out high mixed with

the cloud, which every moment became thicker and darker. When the Padre Molina, the administrator, and the other people saw this, they all, terrified, congregated in the chapel and, whilst they heard Mass, there began to rain water mixed with earth, to such an extent that when the people came out, the ground was covered with much mud and the roofs of the houses were much covered with the same; the sky was strangely dark and brown, and to the thundering reverberations was added a strong smell of sulfur.

When the administrator saw this he mounted a horse and accompanied by the *mayordomo* [see definition on p. 34] and some others, went to see the volcano; the administrator was the one who approached nearest to it, but he did not go the fourth part of the distance from the farm to the volcano, because he had to run back on account of the frantic behaviour of the horses, moreover the road was already wiped out and what with the mud, the increasing vapour, the stench of sulphur, and the darkness and noise, the farm had to be abandoned.

On this 29th day of September fell so much water, sand, and mud, that all the buildings were laid low and the farm was entirely spoiled, the damage amounting to more than 150,000 pesos, but the greatest misery was the pitiful plight of the hungry and shelterless farm-hands who had lost everything, and to see the cattle, mules and horses wandering about the hills without a twig to eat, or drowning without possibility of rescue from the inundated and sand-covered plain . . . .

During the 29th and 30th the volcano threw out masses of sand, fire, and thunder, without one minute's cessation. On the 1st of October burst forth a current of muddy water from the foot of a hill that lies on the other side of the volcano, on its southern side, and this current was so voluminous that it prevented one crossing over to the road that until this time would be used. On the same day was erupted a new outburst of sand, so hot that it set on fire whatever it fell upon; this flood of sand did not rise high, but just came to the surface and flowed downwards, following the current of the Cuitinga brook, which ran to the west. This was blocked completely; the sand, or rather the hot ashes, having run the distance of one quarter of a league [~1.2 km], and there opened one after another, three mouths, not of fire but of vapour, throwing up high sods of dirt.

On October 2nd these features increased much, especially the outburst from the volcano of fire, which extended on the 3rd as a rain of sand as far as the Presentación farm, 2 leagues [probably closer to 1½ leagues or 7.5 km WSW, see Fig. 214] to the west of the Jorullo farm, which between this day and the next, the 4th, was to a great extent inundated with soil, and it was lost entirely, the said sand having covered completely its sugar-cane fields, as the consequence of a furious earthquake that happened in the night of the 2nd.

On the 5th and 6th of October the annihilation of the Presentación was completed and the natives of the village of Guacana [La Huacana], situated about half a league [2.4 km] to the west from the Presentación farm [see Fig. 214], fled into the neighbouring hills, their priest being the last to run away; and today this priest, with his Indians and the holy images rescued by them from his church is staying at the pass called Tamacuaro.

This sudden flight was caused not so much by the continuous rain of water and sand, but by a horrible spate of the stream that comes from the Jorullo and passes between Guacana and the Presentación [see Fig. 214]. The spate was produced not only by the rain from the sky, but by springs that opened from all the hills around. Now this river is so full that it is not only fearful to look at, but having levelled its old and deep bed, its waters are overflowing now here now there, causing much destruction to the fields of sugar cane and *maize*.

It is to be feared, if the fury of the volcano increases, considering what harm it has done already in such a short time, that all the valleys of the Jorullo, the Presentación and the village of Guacana, may be turned into one big lake, as indeed they are almost already. There is first the incessant rain of sand which falls and gets mixed with the water, in addition to that which has levelled down, or filled up, the gorges and brooks, secondly the abundance of streams that all the neighbouring hills send forth, now swelling suddenly into full currents and then again suddenly running dry.

All these commotions have been witnessed and investigated by the Padre Molina, the administrator, the *mayordomos*, and all the people who had come down to rescue as much as possible of the implements, furniture, and stores of the *hacienda*, a very difficult and dangerous task amidst the everlasting earthquakes, storms, and the darkness that continued ever since St. Michael's day, and their fury may be inferred from the fact that the ashes from the volcano fell all around for more than 20 leagues [~100 km].

On the 8th of October something new happened: the volcano threw up a great lot of stones that fell down as far as half a league [2.4 km] from its mouth, and which, as we found later on, were very soft and as if over-baked, or glassy.

Until this day, the 8th of October, the houses of the *hacienda* and the chapel are still standing, because they are quite new, built upon very strong foundations with buttresses of cut stone so that they could until now withstand the impact of the rain of ashes, mud, and stones, although they are clearly cracked and are partly immersed in horribly stinking water.

The above report ends with the 8th of October; if there should happen any further news they will likewise be sent to the Governor of Michoacán. The messenger also takes a sketch or plan of the present condition and appearance of the volcano, etc.

Manuel Orozco y Berra[282] adds the following remark:

The promised sketch was really sent and is still in existence, painted black and red with little care and scarcely serving to form an approximate idea of its object. There are also instructions for the authorities to send in any further notes about the volcano, and here follows another diary of what happened:

Sáyago. Report of November 13th, 1759.

Don Manuel Román Sáyago, administrator-in-chief of the Haciendas Jorullo, Presentación, San Pedro, and dependencies, situated in the district of Ario de Rosales, in obedience to the order received from the Governor of Michoacán . . . reports as follows:

Considering as sufficient the first report, which you have already sent to his Excellency the Viceroy, I now describe what happened after the 8th of October as follows:

On Tuesday, October 9th, from 4 p.m. until the early morning of the following Wednesday alternated great noises and six sharp shocks, and on the morning of the 10th the sky for a distance of 3 leagues [14½ km] was very obscure and there fell rain and sand especially towards the NW carrying general destruction of the oak and pine forests, breaking all their branches and throwing many trees down to the ground. On this same day the sand fell as far as the Hacienda Santa Efigenia . . . about 4 leagues [19 km] from the Jorullo, right in the direction of the wind [NW]. Since this day fell moreover great masses of rocks from the cloud, some of them as large as the body of an ox, which after having been shot up like a bullet, fell around the mouth of the volcano, and the smaller pieces, thrown up higher, came down at a longer distance and in such numbers that, scattering in the cloud, they looked in the day-time like a flock of crows and in the night like a crowd of stars.

Thursday, 11th, caused the same destruction in the hills as far as the sugar plantations of Nombre de Dios and Puruarán, both 4 leagues [19 km] from Jorullo, but to the east. The globular cloud had . . . changed its direction and spent its force chiefly upon the Cucha, a range of hills between Jorullo and Puruarán. And all along from the mouth of the volcano to this hill range raged a regular battle of flashes, fire, and bombs, so that even at the copper mines of Inguaran 4 leagues [19 km] to the south of the volcano, the people were with difficulty prevented from deserting that place.

Friday, 12ᵗʰ, at 1 p.m. at a distance of 600 yards [550 m] from the main crater broke out a new mouth, extending over the whole gorge downwards to the west, and this threw into the air a new and thick cloud of steam and such a great mass of hot water that it flowed for 2 hours like a spate, whereupon the gap closed and the water ceased.

Saturday, and Sunday 14ᵗʰ, the general darkness continued to such an extent, that I was not able to go to the *hacienda*, where I had intended with a number of men to rescue the holy image of Our Lady of Guadalupe, which as tutelary Saint and Patron stood in the Chapel. With this we succeeded not until Monday, 15ᵗʰ, when the cloud had shifted to the east and away from the farm. The image was intact, thanks to its curtain, but the other pictures, etc., were destroyed by the water and the ashes. We also took down the bells from the tower; 150 people, men and women, helped to carry the sacred treasures to Cuarallo.

Tuesday, 16ᵗʰ, the volcano began to throw up sand or ashes already dry and apparently coarser; the fire was fiercer and the springs of water had run dry; the sky of the colour of straw, still discharging ashes accompanied by noise, without interruption until Saturday, 20ᵗʰ; during the whole of the following week, until Saturday 27ᵗʰ, nothing new happened except that now and then a wind arose and spread the dry ashes, which the volcano brought forth, over the whole cattle farm of San Pedro, about 4 leagues [19 km] to the SW of the Jorullo, even to Oropeo, 8 leagues [38 km] farther west and to the farm of Guadalupe farther still in the same direction. The cattle could find nothing to eat, the trees and shrubs being destroyed and the leaves covered with ashes, and nothing to drink because during all this time the water was rendered unfit by mud and sulphurous matter. The same happened at Zicuiran, Cunguripo and Guatziran, all situated towards the west at distances of 10-12 leagues [48-58 km].

At the end of this week the priest of Guacana came down with all his Indians in order to take the holy vessels, etc., out of his church, the roof of which had fallen in, and to convey them to Churumuco, some 15 leagues [72 km] to the south. I have to report, first, that until Saturday, 27ᵗʰ, the volcano did not pause one single minute spitting out its ignited matter and ashes with tempestuous noise, but it yielded no more water; secondly that the poor Indians did splendid service during the transport, although without food, and suffering much from their eyes, which became inflamed by the dust.

Sunday 28ᵗʰ, at daybreak, the cloud of the volcano was slender and ashy coloured; when it was lighted up by the sun it became white like a cotton-pod, and the noise from its mouth had changed too; every now and then it thundered like a cannon, discharging a great lot of stones without ashes; in between these eruptions it sounded like the bellows of a smithy and then again like a mortar.

And the flames shot up to such a height that they lighted up the mountains a dozen leagues [about 60 km] around. In this manner things went on until Thursday, November 1ˢᵗ, during which days we had at least the relief of being able to see the sun. But by the 2ⁿᵈ the sky had thickened again and the cloud had enlarged and returned to its old condition. No improvement took place until Wednesday, Nov. 7ᵗʰ, when Don José de Arriaga the Chaplain, and the Administrator of the Hacienda Nombre de Dios arrived on the scene in order to exorcise the volcano. This did not come off there, because a sudden fierce rumble from the crater made them run to a hill half a league [2½ km] farther, whence the monk applied the exorcism to the volcano. But on Thursday the 8ᵗʰ it was worse, and on Friday it smothered the whole valley of Urecho, 10 leagues [48 km] to the NW. The darkness was worse than ever, accompanied by furious earthquakes to which were added for the next 4 days some hurricanes with thunder, lightning, and downpours of rain all over the neighbourhood.

Today, Tuesday 13ᵗʰ, I went down (from the hills) for a new ocular inspection of Jorullo to find out whether that pitch or lava has run, about which His Excellency has asked in particular; what I have found is this, that all the old brooks of the *hacienda*, which, as I have mentioned before, now run on the top of the sandy plain, are quite thin and clear, in parts quite like crystals, as thick as a finger; they being so clear, one can see at their base a white kind of putty, something like dissolved lime, with a tint of yellow, and as thin as a sheet of blotting paper; and at the margin this stuff is transparent with the look of mother-of-pearl and fat; if one tried to take it up with the fingers, it falls to pieces or dissolves at once in the water. Therefore I could collect none of this stuff, only the grains of salt-petre which seemed to me more infected by it, if taken from the scum. Of these I am sending about one pound to you, Sr. Alcalde Mayor, which may be examined at your pleasure. I have no doubt that if these ashes be mixed with water and are allowed to settle, the said 'beton', pitch, or putty will come out. Please let His Excellency know in answer to his special question, that I neither have any knowledge of so-called lava, nor have I anyone to tell me what stuff it may be; but whatever it may be, here does not run or flow anything else.

Here ends the diary of what has hitherto been seen and observed of the never 'bien ponderado volcán', and the damage it has done, until this Tuesday, the 13ᵗʰ of

November, and in conclusion I shall only add a few remarks.

First: It did not break out on the top of some hill, as was the case with the other volcanoes that one sees in this kingdom, but it broke out in the deepest and level part of the narrow valley Cuitinga, which stands at the foot of the high hill of Cucha.

Second: The difference in the sounds that it produced since the day on which it burst, and especially when its cloud had become large and produced several storms of lightning, sparks and fiery explosions.

Third: Having belched forth such a countless mass of red hot stones so that around its mouth was formed a circular wall or ledge, which is already higher than 300 *varas* [250 m], and surpasses the others that stand on the sides of the valley, which latter it has filled up and disfigured.

Fourth: That with all this stress and ruin not one of the many unfortunate people has lost his life . . . .

All this, with the related circumstances, I, the said administrator, have seen, observed, and studied, so that I can affirm this diary to be true and nothing but the truth, as I am and have been the most immediate eye-witness of all that has been mentioned in this report, which I sign here at the Cuaralla farm, on the 13th day of November 1759. *Manuel Román Sáyago.*

Geological Setting and Petrology
Luhr and Carmichael (1985)

The Eruption of Jorullo: 1759-1774

The story of the Jorullo eruption was in a state of great confusion for many years, confusion stemming partly from the delayed publication of an eye-witness report to the Spanish Viceroy concerning the early activity, and partly from the erroneous observations of Alexander von Humboldt[280], who visited the area in 1803. Inspired by the incorrect *craters of elevation* theory of his friend von Buch[283], von Humboldt wrongly interpreted the Jorullo lava field as a large volcanic blister that rose from the ground. Gadow[100] gives an insightful account of the eruption and English translations of all important prior observations as a preface to his study of floral and faunal reclamation of the devastated area.

Prior to 1759, the area was a cultivated, west-sloping basin bounded by steeply dissected escarpments of Cenozoic intrusives, tuffs, and lavas. The area has a tropical climate and a general elevation of 600 to 800 m. Famous for its fertility, the land was known as Jorullo, or *Paradise*, in the

Tarascan Indian language. Hacienda de Jorullo was situated near Cerro Partido, which rose as an E-W-trending ridge near the basin center (Fig. 214). At the eastern end of the basin was the narrow and deep ravine of Cuitinga Creek, which followed a NE to SW course before turning west along the granite ridge forming the southern boundary of the basin.

Subterranean noises were first heard in late June of 1759, increasing to the level of cannon shots by September 17. Earthquakes badly damaged structures on the *hacienda*. On the morning of September 29, several sharp tremors were felt, and a dense dark cloud issued from the Cuitinga Creek just SE of the *hacienda*. The early part of the eruption was characterized by phreatic and phreatomagmatic activity, which blanketed the surrounding area with a sticky mud. Gadow[100] noted that despite a near absence of precipitation in the fall of 1759, large quantities of water and mud were flowing from the Jorullo area. Numerous springs became active in the surrounding hills, and streams alternated between swollen and dry. Sáyago [above] describes pulses of hot muddy water pouring from small short-lived vents. Ash falls covered the surrounding area and by October 6 the town of La Huacana, 9 km to the west (Fig. 214), was abandoned. Streams choked with ash flooded much of the valley to the west of the volcano, from La Puerta de la Playa to La Huacana. The copious outflow of water in the early stages of the eruption probably resulted from the outward migration of groundwater ahead of the rising magma body as suggested for the 1902 eruption of Mt. Pelee[284]. The first incandescent bombs were noted on October 8, and by October 14 phreatic aspects of the eruption declined in significance as it became dominantly magmatic in character. Water and mud were no longer reported as issuing from the ground. The second and final report of Sáyago was written on November 13, by which time the main cone of Jorullo had reached 250 m in height. No lava had emerged by this date, after which there is unfortunately little reliable reporting. Oral traditions refer to violent eruptions through 1764, the year of greatest activity, and lesser eruptions until 1774. A report for the new Governor in 1766 describes a scene similar to that of today [see Plate 8B], and Gadow argues that the majority of the lavas had erupted by that date, probably between 1760 and 1766.

Magma and gas issued from a NE-SW-trending line of five cinder and lava cones separated by 3 km along the course of the Cuitinga Creek (Fig. 214): the large main cone of Jorullo, a single breached cone to its NE (Volcán del Norte), and three breached cones to its

SW (unnamed, Volcán de Enmedio, Volcán del Sur). The main cone dwarfs the satellite cones in size and appears to differ from them structurally in being a composite cone of lava as well as cinder. The vents are oriented about N35E, sub-parallel to many other cinder-cone alignments in the southern Michoacán-Guanajuato Volcanic Field [see p. 248, 259-260, 280-282], including the vent alignment at Parícutin, and to the relative-motion vector for the Cocos and North American Plates[140]. This orientation is presumably perpendicular to the minimum horizontal compressive stress direction in the area[149]. Early workers identified four to six different lava flows at Jorullo[100]. Three lava stages or groups are recognized in this study: early, middle, and late (Fig. 214). At both Jorullo and Parícutin [see p. 338], the early lavas were the poorest in silica [and the most fluid]; they largely defined the final extent of the ground covered, with succeeding, more-viscous lavas generally forming thicker terraced flows upon them. The Jorullo flows consist primarily of block lava and usually have prominent levees. The early lavas issued from an unknown point, probably near the base of the main cone, and descended the gentle gradient of the basin to the west, covering 9 km^2 of the former fertile valley, an area since called *Malpais* [badlands]. Next came the middle-stage lavas, which breached the western sides of the northern and southern satellite cones. The downhill, westward flow of lava kept the western sides of these cones open, resulting in crescentic morphologies, similar in form to the Sapichu vent at Parícutin [see p. 96-103]. The late-stage lavas issued from the northern side of the main cone. Pyroclastic activity continued through the extrusion of most late-stage lavas, and all lava flows were covered by ash-fall layers. Following the end of pyroclastic activity, a small lava flow then emerged from the main cone, bringing the eruption of Jorullo to a close. This black, youngest lava flow [see Plate 8B] is still relatively unvegetated today and stands in sharp visual contrast to the subdued hues of the slightly older, but ash-covered lavas, where vegetation found an easy foothold. Since the end of the eruption, the crater has been collapsing inward along arcuate step faults, increasing both the crater diameter (400 × 500 m) and its depth (150 m)[281].

One of the most curious features of the Jorullo products is the sequence of ash layers that covers all but the youngest of the lava flows. These fine ashes form a mantling blanket of centimeter-scale layers that show only occasional cross beds, yet cover irregularities on the lava flow surfaces with slope angles up to 80°. These air-fall ashes must have been extraordinarily cohesive to be able to stick to surfaces with such steep angles. They probably were very wet when falling and upon impact they were almost instantly baked and moderately lithified by the hot underlying lavas, which still showed thousands of *hornitos* at the time of von Humboldt's visit in 1803.

The main cone of Jorullo rises some 350 m above its surroundings to an elevation of 1,220 m. It has a volume of approximately 0.20 km^3 and the smaller parasitic cones have a combined volume of 0.05 km^3. The lavas have an estimated volume of 0.50 km^3, although this figure is made uncertain by a lack of information on the depth of lava close to the vent. The volume of ash-fall deposits is unknown. By analogy with Parícutin, which produced 0.49 km^3 of magma as lavas and 0.83 km^3 of magma as tephra [see Table 23], the pyroclastic deposits of Jorullo may have represented up to 1.25 km^3 of magma. The total mass of magma erupted at Jorullo, therefore, was possibly 2 km^3.

Sample Descriptions and Whole-Rock Compositions

Interestingly, the Jorullo eruption followed the unusual pattern of the Parícutin activity in that magmas became richer in SiO_2 as time progressed. The extensive early lavas are richest in MgO, FeO^{total}, CaO, Cr, Co, and Ni, and the poorest in SiO_2, Al_2O_3, K_2O, Sr, Ba, and other incompatible elements. Various compositional criteria have been proposed to indentify primitive, mantle-derived magmas: Mg-number (100×Mg/Mg+Fe^{2+}) = 63-73[285], FeO^{total}/MgO < 1[286], and Ni = 235-400 ppm[287]. Specimen Jor-44, representative of the early Jorullo lavas, has Mg-number 73, FeO^{total}/MgO = 0.8, 260 ppm Ni, 515 ppm Cr, and less than 6 vol.% olivine phenocrysts (plus Cr-Al-Mg spinel inclusions), qualifying as a primitive magma.

Lavas from all stages at Jorullo contain olivine phenocrysts and microphenocrysts with spinel inclusions, as well as plagioclase and clinopyroxene microphenocrysts and rare phenocrysts. Late-stage basaltic andesites also contain minor orthopyroxene and hornblende. As is the case for Parícutin, granitic xenoliths are also found in many Jorullo lavas, particularly those from the middle-stage satellite cones. These xenoliths undoubtedly represent bedrock fragments similar to early Tertiary granitic rocks that crop out in the area.

The complementary nature of the Jorullo and Parícutin rock suites is apparent on Fig. 215, a plot of whole-rock SiO_2 versus K_2O. The progression from circles to triangles shows that both suites evolved to more silica-rich compositions with time. The Jorullo basalts and basaltic andesites represent a good model for the probable unerupted parental magmas to the Parícutin basaltic andesites and andesites.

Luhr and Carmichael discussed the origin of compositional trends in the Jorullo suite and showed that the abundances of major elements and many trace elements in the late-stage basaltic andesites can be modeled by closed-system fractional crystallization: the removal of early formed crystals olivine (10.8 wt.%), clinopyroxene (7.3%), and plagioclase (5.0%) from the early stage basalts. Similar simple fractionation models were rejected by Wilcox for the Parícutin suite based on graphical modeling [see p. 340-344]. The high proportion of clinopyroxene in the Jorullo model indicates that fraction-ation must have occurred at relatively high pressures, near the base of the crust. The actual mineralogy of the Jorullo lavas, however, with clinopyroxene generally absent as a phenocryst, appears to have formed at relatively low pressures. Many incompatible trace elements can not be successfully reproduced by this model, however, and may indicate selective contamination by the crust [as advocated by Wilcox at Parícutin: see p. 340-344] or other enrichment processes.

Conclusions

Jorullo (1759-1774) and Parícutin (1943-1952) are the only two historically active volcanoes in one of the largest cinder cone fields on earth. Both eruptions produced: 1) a new volcano: Jorullo rising from a ravine and Parícutin from a cornfield; 2) 1-2 km³ of magma progressing to compositions richer in SiO_2 with time; and 3) lavas containing angular xenoliths of basement granites. The products of Parícutin ranged from early basaltic andesites to late andesites, a compositional trend that is consistent with derivation by combined fractional crystallization - assimilation [see p. 340-344]. The products of Jorullo, in contrast, ranged from early primitive basalts to late basaltic andesites, a compositional trend most consistent with simple crystal fractionation of olivine + clinopyroxene + plagioclase + minor spinel at lower-crustal to upper-mantle pressures . . . .

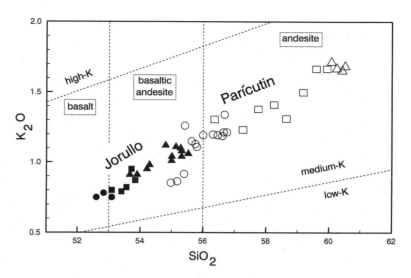

Fig. 215. Whole-rock compositions of lavas from Jorullo (solid symbols: data from Luhr and Carmichael, 1985) and Parícutin (open symbols: data from Tables 26 and 31). The suites are divided into early (*circles*), middle (*squares*), and late (*triangles*) stages. For Jorullo the designations are as described above by Luhr and Carmichael (1985). For Parícutin we have divided the samples based on year of eruption: early - 1943-45, middle - 1946-49, late - 1950-52. The boundaries separating low-K, medium-K, and high-K suites are taken from Gill[171].

Monte Nuovo, Italy (1538)

Here we reproduce Bullard's section on Monte Nuovo (New Mountain), which includes reprintings of the classic eye-witness accounts of the 1538 eruption near Naples, Italy. Additional information on this "new" volcano can be found in Rosi and Santacroce[288]. Curiously, Monte Nuovo was born on the same date as Jorullo, September 29, but 221 years earlier.

Bullard (1984)

A well-known "new" volcano of historic time was born on September 29, 1538, near Pozzuoli, a port on the Bay of Baia, about 10 km west of Naples, Italy, in the Phlegraean Fields [Fig. 216]. Named Monte Nuovo (New Mountain), it is partly on the site of Lake Lucrine, a famous resort during the time of the Roman Empire.

The Phlegraean Fields

The Phlegraean Fields contains 19 separate craters concentrated in an area of about 65 km². The craters are so closely spaced that in a number of cases they overlap, an older cone having been partly destroyed when a younger one formed. The volcanic activity in the Phlegraean Fields is older than that at Vesuvius and the area appears to have been dormant throughout

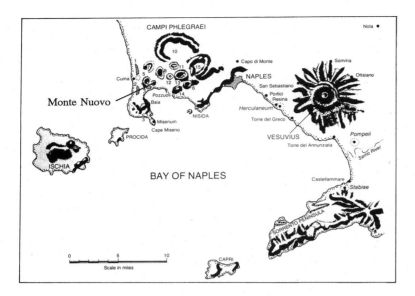

Fig. 216. Bay of Naples and surrounding area. Herculaneum, Pompeii, and Stabiae, destroyed in the A.D. 79 eruption of Vesuvius, are located on the map. Index to areas in Campi Phlegraei: (1) Lago di Licola; (2) Lago di Fusaro; (3) Mare Morto; (4) Lago Lucrino; (5) Lago Averno; (6) Lago di Agnano; (7) Monte Grillo; (8) Monte Barbaro; (9) Monte Nuovo; (10) Piano di Quarto; (11) Fossa Lupara; (12) Monte Cigliano; (13) Astroni; (14) Solfatara; (15) Pianura. After Phillips[289].

historical time with the exception of an eruption of Solfatara Volcano in 1198 and the eruption of Monte Nuovo in 1538. However, gaseous emanations from several of the craters, as well as numerous hot springs, clearly indicate that the volcanic forces are not exhausted. Several of the craters in the Phlegraean Fields contain beautiful lakes, of which Lake Avernus is perhaps the best known because of its connection with classical mythology.

Birth of the Volcano

Knowledge of the 1538 eruption of Monte Nuovo is based on four separate accounts contained in letters of eyewitnesses to the event. From these letters, parts of which are reproduced below, some helpful facts have been established.

For two years prior to the outbreak the region was disturbed by earthquakes, which reached a climax in September, 1538. On September 27 and 28 the shocks were said to have been felt almost continuously day and night. About 8:00 A.M. on September 29 a depression of the ground occurred, and from this depression water began to issue, at first cold and later tepid. Four hours later the ground was seen to swell up and open, forming a gaping fissure within which incandescent matter was visible. From this fissure numerous masses of stones, some of them "as large as an ox," with vast quantities of pumice and mud, were thrown to a great height, and these, falling upon

the sides of the opening, formed a mound. This violent ejection of material, continuing for two days and nights, by the third day had formed a cone of considerable size. Since some of the eyewitnesses at this time climbed the cone, we may assume that there was a lull in activity. When the eruptions continued the next day, many persons who had ventured onto the hill were injured, and several were killed by falling stones. Thereafter the eruptions decreased in violence, ceasing on the 7th or 8th day after the outbreak. Thus the greater bulk of Monte Nuovo was ejected during the first two days.

Monte Nuovo is a cone, rising 135 m above the shore, with a cup-shaped crater, the bottom of which is only 5.8 m above the level of the sea. It is composed entirely of ash, lapilli, and scoria, and differs in no way from the other cones in the Phlegraean Fields, except that it came into existence much later. The cone, which is about 800 m in diameter at its base, stands partly on the site of Lake Lucrine. Lake Lucrine, occupying the breached crater of an old volcano adjoining the Bay of Baia, was a favorite resort during the period of the Roman Empire, and its shores were lined with fashionable villas, among which was one belonging to Cicero. The superior flavor of the oysters obtained from the lake was another of its attractions. At that time, as today, it was separated from the Mediterranean by a narrow bar. By means of a canal the lake was accessible as a protected anchorage for the galleys of the Roman fleet. The building of Monte Nuovo largely filled Lake Lucrine, leaving only a narrow segment of the original lake.

Significance of the Eruption Record

The historical record of the birth of Monte Nuovo is of more importance than the mere story of the origin of a new volcano. During the close of the 18th century and the early part of the 19th, geologists developed a heated controversy as to the manner in which volcanic cones were formed, a dispute between supporters of Baron von Buch's *craters-of-elevation* theory, which held that volcanic cones were formed by upheaval, like a blister on the earth's surface, and supporters of the opposing idea, ably advocated by Charles Lyell, which held that the cones were the result of the accumulation of ejected material. Today it seems strange that the *craters-of-elevation* theory would have been taken seriously, but it was the widely held orthodox view of the time. The controversy was centered in Western Europe, where the science of geology developed; and since Monte Nuovo was the only "new" volcano in this region, it is quite natural that each side sought to find in the origin of Monte Nuovo evidence to support its views. As a result, the records were carefully searched for any eyewitness accounts that might throw light on the problem.

Fortunately, Sir William Hamilton, English ambassador to the Court of Naples for 36 years (1764-1800), was an ardent student of volcanoes . . . Through his efforts, two narrative accounts of the birth of Monte Nuovo by contemporary witnesses of credit were discovered and preserved. These accounts, consisting of two letters written a few months after the event, were bound in a volume, with Hamilton's translation, and presented to the British Museum. The first letter was an account by Marco Antonio delli Falconi, and the second was a report by Pietro Giacomo di Toledo. Both are quoted by Phillips[289]. Two other accounts of the eruption have been preserved. One, written immediately after the eruption by Francesco del Nero, was discovered in 1846 and published in German. An English translation[290] was published the following year.

Because of the historical interest surrounding these letters, as well as the colorful descriptions of the eruption that they afford, several excerpts are included here.

From the letter by Marco Antonio delli Falconi:

It is now two years that there have been frequent earthquakes at Pozzuoli, Naples, and the neighboring ports; on the day and in the night before . . . this eruption about 20 shocks, great and small, were felt at the above-mentioned places. The eruption made its appearance on the 29th of September, 1538; . . . it was on a Sunday, about an hour in the night; and . . . they began to see on that spot, between the hot baths . . . and Trepergule, flames of fire . . . in a short time the fire increased to such a degree that it burst open the earth at this place, and threw up so great a quantity of ashes and pumice stone mixed with water as covered the whole country; and in Naples a shower of these ashes and water fell the greater part of the night.

Next morning, which was Monday, . . . the poor inhabitants of Pozzuoli, struck with so horrible a sight, quitted their habitations . . . some with children in their arms, some with sacks full of goods; . . . others carrying quantities of birds that had fallen dead at the time the eruption began, others with fish that they had found and were to be met with in plenty upon the shore, the sea having been at that time considerably dried up . . . . The sea towards Baia had retired a considerable way, although from the quantity of ashes and broken pumice stone thrown up by the eruption it appeared almost dry. I saw likewise two springs in those lately discovered ruins . . . . Turning towards the place of the eruption, you saw mountains of smoke, part of which was very black and part very white, rising up to a great height; and in the midst of the smoke, at times, deep-colored flames burst forth with huge stones and ashes, and you heard a noise like the discharge of a number of artillery . . . . After the stones and ashes, with clouds of thick smoke, had been sent up by the impulse of the fire and windy exhalations into the middle region of the air, overcome by their own natural weight, . . . you saw them fall, . . . raining ashes with water and stones of different sizes according to the distance from the place; then by degrees with the same noise and smoke it threw out stones and ashes again, and so on in fits. This continued two days and nights, when the smoke and the force of the fire began to abate. The 4th day, which was Thursday, at 22 o'clock there was so great an eruption . . . and the quantity of ashes and stones and smoke seemed as if they would cover the whole earth and sea . . . .

Then Friday and Saturday nothing but a little smoke appeared; so many taking courage went upon the spot, and say that with the ashes and stones thrown up a mountain has been formed; . . . a thing almost incredible to those who have not seen it, that in so short a time so considerable a mountain could have been formed. On its summit there is a mouth in the form of a cup, which may be a quarter of a mile in circumference [130 m in diameter] . . . .

The Sunday following, which was the 6th of October, many people going to see this phenomenon, and having ascended half the mountain, others more, about 22 o'clock there happened so great and horrid an eruption with so great a smoke, that many of the people were stifled, some of which could never be found. I have been told that the number of the dead or lost amounted to 24...[289]

From the letter by Pietro Giacomo di Toledo:

It is now more than two years that the province of Campagna has been afflicted with earthquakes, the country about Pozzuoli much more than any other parts; but the 27th and 28th of the month of September, last, the earthquakes did not cease day or night, in the above mentioned city of Pozzuoli . . . . At last, on the 29th . . . about 2 hours in the night the earth opened near the lake and discovered a horrid mouth, from which was vomited, furiously, smoke, fire, stones, and mud composed of ashes; making at the time of its opening a noise like loud thunder. The fire that issued from the mouth went towards the walls of the unfortunate city; the smoke was partly black and partly white, . . . the stones that followed were by the devouring flames converted to pumice, the size of which (of some I say) were much larger than an ox.

The stones went about as high as a cross bow can carry, and then fell down, sometimes on the edge, sometimes in the mouth itself . . . . The mud was of the color of ashes, and at first very liquid, then by degrees less so; and in such quantity that in less than 12 hours, with the help of the above-mentioned stones, a mountain was raised of 1,000 paces height . . . .

Now this eruption lasted two days and two nights without intermission, though, it is true, not always with the same force, but more or less; when it was at its greatest height, even at Naples you heard a noise like heavy artillery when two armies are engaged. The 3rd day the eruption ceased, so that the mountain made its appearance uncovered, to the no small astonishment of everyone who saw it. On this day I went up with many people to the top of the mountain, I saw down into its mouth, which was a round concavity about 400 m in circumference [at present about 400 m in diameter] in the middle of which the stones that had fallen were boiling up, just as in a great cauldron of water that boils on the fire. The 4th day it began to throw up again, and the 7th much more, but still with less violence than on the first night. It was at this time that many people who were unfortunately on the mountain were either suddenly covered with ashes, smothered with smoke, or knocked down by stones, burnt by flame, and left dead on the spot. The smoke continues to this day, and you often see in the night time fire in the midst of it . . . .[289]

From the letter of Francesco del Nero: Del Nero mentions the drying up of the bed of the sea near Pozzuoli, which enabled the inhabitants of the town to carry away loads of fish. He then continues:

About eight o'clock in the morning of the 29th [September], the earth sank down about two *canne* [4.1 m] in that part where there is now the volcanic orifice. At noon on the same day, the earth began to swell up, so that the ground in the same place where it had sunk down was as high as Monte Ruosi . . . and about this time fire issued forth and formed the great gulf with such a force, noise, and shining light, that I, who was standing in my garden, was seized with great terror. Forty minutes afterwards, although unwell, I got upon a neighboring height, from which I saw all that took place, and by my troth, it was a splendid fire, that threw up for a long time much earth and stones . . . . Just so was it with the fiery gulf, from which there was shot up into the air, to a height which I estimate at 2.4 km, masses of earth and stones as large as an ox. They fell down near the gulf in a semi-circle of from one to three bow-shots in diameter, and in this way they filled up this part of the sea, and formed the above mentioned hill. When the earth and stones fell they were quite dry. The same fire, however, threw out at the same time, a light earth and smaller stones to a much greater height, and these fell down in a soft muddy state.[290]

Notwithstanding this overwhelming testimony in support of the *craters-of-accumulation* theory, Baron von Buch and others continued to hold to the *crater-of-elevation* explanation, even for Monte Nuovo. Lyell[291], in reviewing the problem, quotes von Buch, who in 1836 wrote, "It is an error to imagine that this hill was formed by eruption, or by ejection of pumice, scoria, and other incoherent matter; for the solid beds of upraised tuff are visible all around the crater, and it is merely the superficial covering of the cone that is made up of the ejected scoriae."

Since this natal eruption, Monte Nuovo has not renewed activity, and today, clothed with vegetation, it is indistinguishable from the prehistoric craters in the Phlegraean Fields.

Waiowa Volcano, Papua (1943-44)

Unlike the cases of Parícutin, Jorullo, and Monte Nuovo, which erupted in areas with many nearby small volcanic cones, the little-known 1943 birth of Waiowa volcano in the Goropu Mountains of Papua, occurred in a non-volcanic area. The eruption involved magma that was very rich in water, as reflected in the abundance of the water-bearing minerals hornblende and biotite in the Waiowa pumices. The release of this magmatic water resulted in an explosive eruption that produced no lava flows, and in this respect Waiowa is similar to Monte Nuovo and dissimilar to Parícutin and Jorullo. Although Waiowa ejected a relatively small amount of material, the mineralogy of its pumices recall the larger explosive eruptions of El Chichón, México, in 1982[292] and Mount Pinatubo, Philippines, in 1991[293]. We reprint portions of Baker (1946), the only detailed study of the eruption. The name Waiowa was given to the volcano after that date and is not used by Baker.

Baker (1946)

Introduction

Explosive volcanic activity has occurred since December, 1943, and is continuing spasmodically in the foothills of the Goropu Mountains, Papua, where previously no volcanic activity has been reported. Intervals between the first four recorded eruptions were 7, 23, and 5½ weeks, respectively. The Goropu Mountains lie inland from Collingwood Bay (Fig. 217), 210 km east of Port Moresby. The active vents, which are 64 km SSW of Tufi government and mission station, broke through pre-Tertiary rocks, considered to be Paleozoic or Pre-cambrian[294].

Although no volcanic activity had been reported previously from this particular locality, it is possible, since Stanley[295] has recorded hot springs and solfataric activity 105 km WNW, that minor thermal activity may also have occurred in this unexplored area. It is unlikely, however, that violent explosive phenomena of the kind dealt with herein occurred within human memory, because of the relatively close proximity of mission and government stations to the active area, from which no

previous reports of explosive vulcanicity have emanated.

Review of Eyewitness Reports

Prior to the explosive eruptions here described, columns of steam and ash from four volcanic vents were observed in October and November, 1943, and earth tremors had occurred during the previous two years, sometimes at the rate of two or three a day.

The first recorded eruption[296], that of December 27, 1943, ejected a crater-cloud of ash and steam to an estimated height of 4.5 km. An electrical storm accompanied the eruption. No tremors or noises were reported from Tufi Station in connection with this eruption. Lapilli, carbonized wood fragments, and volcanic ash landed in native gardens at Iu-ai-u (U-ai-u), a coastal village 26 km from the active vents. Fine ash and dust were thickly spread out on a 13-km radius around the vents; mud rains and sulphurous vapors were recorded. Layers of white dust covered trees some distance from the vents. Bird life and leeches had vacated the area, but larger game was still abundant. Nearer the vents the dust layers were so thick that the branches of trees were stripped off; all animal life had disappeared from the devastated region.

Ground patrols sent out by the district officer of the Australian Military Administration at Tufi noted that about 3.2 km west of the vents there occurred in the devastated area two sheer-sided depressions, 15 m deep and 30 m across, which had stony floors but were waterless. In one of these chasms occurred a still further sunken area about 24 m across and 2 m

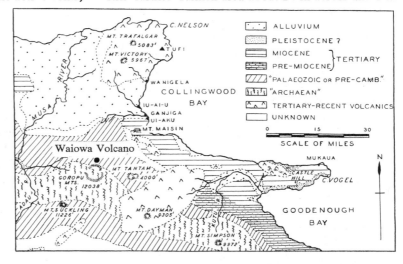

Fig. 217. Geological map of the Collingwood Bay - Goodenough Bay area, showing site of the active volcanic vents. Geology after E.R. Stanley[295].

Fig. 218. Active vents on the northern flanks of the Goropu Mountains, about 210 km east of Port Moresby, Papua. Eruption of February 14, 1944. Note craterlet on flanks of cone in foreground, and symmetrical outline of main crater.

deep. Its recent character was indicated by depths of dust greater than those occurring in the immediate neighborhood and by the uprooting of trees in the vicinity; no distinct crater could be discerned. Apparently, the disturbance had been of only sufficient strength to force dust up through the stony floor of the depressed area. Two larger, similar chasms were noted west of Wai-oa Creek, close to the area of the active vents. (Wai-oa Creek is a tributary of the drainage system, which enters the sea between Ganjiga and Ui-aku, as shown in Fig. 217). One of the chasms possessed a rim, 4 m high and 18 m long, occurring at intervals along either side of the chasm.

Mud rains, which fell during the approach of patrols to the active vents covered the ground with 5 cm of mud. On the slopes of the Goropu Mountains, only the largest trees were left standing; they had been stripped of branches, and the trunks on the northern side of the vents were pitted right up to the top. All secondary plant growth had been broken down and covered with volcanic mud. This mud had an oily appearance, and its surface reflected trees that were still standing.

In the center of the region of activity, one crater with sheer walls was estimated as 27 m across and 18 m deep. It was uncertain whether the bottom was covered with mud or solid material; sulphurous vapors were strong around this crater. Nearby were two small craters in which the only sign of activity was a slight bubbling of the mud, and below these was an area of mud about 3 acres [1.2 hectare] in extent, which emitted a white vapor. On a nearby ridge two large active craters gave off dense,

brownish-colored steam and ash; stones were being thrown up in their vents. The heights of the cones around the craters were not estimated; but from the aerial photograph (Fig. 218) it can be seen that, even at later stages of eruption, they are relatively insignificant.

Crater-clouds persisted in the volcanic area for several weeks, and at approximately 8:00 P.M. on February 13, 1944, a further, but less severe, eruption was observed from Wanigela, where an earth tremor was felt and explosions were heard coming from the vicinity of the active region. Figure 218, an aerial photograph taken on the following day from about 150-225 m above the ground, shows a phase of this eruption. No stones or debris landed in the coastal villages of Iu-ai-u, Ui-aku, or Ganjiga on this occasion, but some landed in the inland villages of Bonando and Kokoe, respectively 6½ and 11 km west from the coast and about 19 km NNE of the active vents. The area of ash and dust deposits around the vents was considerably enlarged, extending up the slopes of the Goropu Mountains and increasing the area of devastation in the tropical jungle to at least 50 km². No further vents beyond the original four were observed.

These earlier eruptions of the Goropu volcanic vents were evidently directional, as indicated by the pitting of the trunks of trees on the northern side of the vents and by the fact that lapilli were discharged to the NNE, landing at the villages of Iu-ai-u, Ui-aku, Ganjiga, Bonando, and Kokoe.

Dust from the eruption of February 13, 1944, was swept in a westerly direction by high-altitude air currents, resulting in the enveloping of the Coral Sea and Port Moresby (210 km west) in a thick pall of dust on February 14, 1944.

War-correspondent observers from a plane that flew over the vents on February 14, reported volcanic dust hanging out in thin layers from stratus clouds and stretching for kilometers out to sea and up into the mountains, where it concentrated along the valleys. The heat from one of the vents could be felt at heights of 150 m above it; at lower levels the heat was unbearable, the vapors from the crater were nauseating and had a strong sulphurous odor. What appeared like lava streams were reported passing through the brown mud around the vent, but no lava flows have yet been confirmed by ground patrols. The observed phenomena may have been hot or cold avalanches[70]. The crater appeared from the air like "an oversize bomb crater," largely masked by steam; in its center was a dull red glow, but no apparent lava stream issued from the vent itself. A great, dazzling-white pillar of steam rose some 600 m above the crater.

Later observations, made early in March, 1944, along the course of the Ui-aku Creek, south of Mount Maisin Creek (Fig. 217), indicated that the Ui-aku Creek carried unusually large volumes of water, highly charged with mud, while considerable amounts of silt with large blocks of vesicular rock had been deposited along its banks. All of the mud was being brought down by a branch of Ui-aku Creek from the area of the volcanic vents.

Numerous small, newly developed streams, which flowed at random over the surface, were also charged with silt and vesicular rock. They obviously had their origin principally in the mud rains formed by the condensation of the discharged vapors on dust particles, and probably represent the initiation of a new local drainage system in place of stretches of Wai-oa Creek, reported to have dried up in parts since the inception of volcanic activity. Dislocation of the former drainage system is also indicated nearer the center of the devastated area; the valley of a large creek that originally flowed through the flat, gradually sloping country covered with dense jungle growth is now represented by a ridge, narrow below, and widening to 800 m or so across near the craters. This ridge is cut by a creek flowing partly into Ui-aku Creek and partly into its former bed near Mount Maisin. The ridge consists of "nothing but baked earth, reddish in color and with a very loose crumb structure." It probably represents a volcanic mudflow of the type known as a *lahar* in Java[297], where the so-called mud is a mixture of water and ash containing blocks and fragments of rock of various sizes.

White vapors (principally steam), which rose through cracks 15-90 cm long in the ground around the active vents, were sufficiently hot to boil water, while stones on the surface were too hot to handle.

The vents were still pouring forth fumes at the end of April, 1944, three of them continuously and one spasmodically.

At 8:45 A.M. on July 23, 1944, there was a further explosive eruption of the Goropu craters, dust again being strewn over an extensive area, increasing the region of devastation to 75 km². All minor vents had been sealed up, and the main crater, now 460 m across, had commenced to build up its cone with greater rapidity[298]. Blocks of vesicular rock weighing up to 1 kg were found at Wo-Wo Gap, 24-32 km distant.

On August 31, 1944, dust from a later eruption fell on Port Moresby.

Petrology of the Ejected Materials

Approximately two dozen samples of lapilli and three ejected pebbles were submitted for investigation at the Melbourne University geology department. The lapilli were collected from near Iu-ai-u village, 28 km from the center of the eruption. Eight samples were employed in petrological investigations and six in chemical analysis.

The rock conforms with A. Johannsen's[299] description of a biopyribole andesite in containing four different ferromagnesian types of minerals: augite, biotite, hornblende (in two examples), and olivine . . ., set in a microcrystalline to hyaline base. The chief mineral appears as numerous, small, colorless prisms of augite in subparallel alignment. A few phenocrysts of pale-green augite show partial inversion to hornblende or to biotite; one phenocryst, altered to biotite on the outside, measured 6 x 2 x 1½ mm. Biotite, which occurs as brown elongated plates showing good alignment in the fluidal structures, consitutes the next most abundant mineral. Occasional basal plates of biotite reveal small inclusions, some of which are remnants of augite, after which the biotite crystallized; others are crystals of apatite. Hornblende is next in abundance in two of the lapilli, forming some of the larger phenocrysts (up to 3 mm long) in the rock; it is of greenish-brown color, sometimes zoned, sometimes twinned. Olivine is represented by infrequent clots, which show partial resorption and transition to biotite.

The microcrystalline to hyaline base contains abundant minute grains of ilmenite and small laths of andesine. Numerous needles of apatite and minute rounded grains of colorless garnet[300] form accessory minerals in the groundmass. The glassy matrix is grayish to colorless and varies in amount in different lapilli. The garnet is common in one of the lapilli, but scarce in others.

. . . . .

Unusual features of the rock, as disclosed by the chemical analysis, are the low total iron content, the apparent absence of Fe_2O_3 [300], the excess of K_2O over Na_2O, and the high content of MgO, which is slightly in excess of CaO.

Most andesites have lime in excess of magnesia and soda in excess of potash, whereas iron is generally more abundant. The low iron content of the Goropu lapilli indicates that the olivine and the augite are magnesia-rich varieties. The high content of MgO is a reflection of the presence of olivine crystals and also, taken in conjunction with the absence of Fe_2O_3, suggests that the biotite is a magnesia-rich variety.

The high content of MgO in the presence of a relatively high SiO$_2$ content is anomalous. This may be due to the inclusion in a moderately silica-rich magma of xenocrysts of magnesia-rich minerals, derived from the ultrabasic basement rock through which the volcano has broken in the Goropu Mountains. Alternatively, the lapilli may represent differentiation products within a cupola, from which some of the magnesia-rich xenocrysts may have sunk prior to crystallization. The fact that potash is present in excess of soda and that soda would be used up in the formation of andesine indicates that the [matrix] glass in the lapilli is potash-rich. Some of the potash is present in biotite, but it appears that, if the rock had become holocrystalline, it would have had as much orthoclase as plagioclase and would then enter into the category of the trachyandesite group of rocks. The mineralogical and chemical evidence thus indicates that the lapilli from the craters in the Goropu Mountains of Papua represent augite-biotite-hornblende-olivine-trachyandesite . . . .

Dr. Atl at Parícutin

Crausaz (1985)

Abstract

Dr. Atl (born Gerardo Murillo in 1875) was the Universal Man of México. In addition to starting the Mexican Mural Movement and launching the careers of such famous artists as Siqueiros, Rivera, and Orozco, he was a revolutionary who, with blazing guns, political intrigue, and innumerable essays, helped to forge the modern Mexican democracy. His first love was volcanoes, and for sixty years he produced an avalanche of sketches, paintings, poems, essays, and monographs devoted to that subject. The mass of paintings and two monographs constitute his main contribution to volcanology.

Between 1911 and 1914 he studied Vesuvius, Etna, and Stromboli under the European volcanologists Perret and Friedlaender. The Mexican volcano Popocatépetl was his favorite mountain. When a crew of sulfur miners awakened it by blasting the crater with dynamite, Dr. Atl prepared a monograph based on decades of personal observations, interviews, Aztec legends, early written reports, sketches, paintings, and historical photographs. He described in detail the first man-made volcanic eruption, which raged in the crater from 1919 to 1938, and formed domes similar to the ones on Mount St. Helens.

In 1943, when Parícutin erupted from a corn field, Dr. Atl raced to the site and started a seven-year study that culminated in the publication of his second scientific monograph. Although Dr. Atl was 75 at the time, his outlook was surprisingly modern. After discussing the ideas of Alfred Wegener, he declared that the forces of continental drift had formed the volcano.

At the age of 83, he sketched and painted a series of oblique landscapes from airplanes. Six years later, in 1964, while working on three murals in Cuernavaca, Dr. Atl died.

Pioneer Mexican Volcanologist

Dr. Atl was born as Jose Gerardo Francisco Murillo in the city of Guadalajara in 1875. Murillo especially disliked the romantic religious paintings of the 17th century Spanish artist Bartolome Murillo. He therefore changed his own last name to Atl, which means *water* in Aztec. Later, the famous South American poet Lugones added the title *Doctor*. Dr. Atl became a major figure in art, science, literature, revolution, philosophy, poetry, history, politics, and social science.

As an artist, Dr. Atl started both the Mexican Mural Movement and the Revolutionary Art Movement. He launched the careers of Orozco, Rivera, and Siqueiros. His impressionist paintings and sketches captured the essence of México's active volcanoes.

As a scientist, he published a monograph about the Mexican volcano Popocatépetl, and another about Parícutin. Many of his sketches and paintings realistically record the details of volcanoes and their eruptions.

As a writer he published several novels and innumerable short stories. One of the latter, *El hombre y la perla* (The man and the pearl), may have been the basis of John Steinbeck's novel *The Pearl*[301].

As a revolutionary, he persuaded the intellectuals of México City to move to the safe city of Orizaba. There he organized them into an effective propaganda machine that produced newspapers and posters. Dr. Atl is regarded as one of the fathers of the Mexican Revolution, and a father of Mexican democracy.

As a philosopher, he studied philosophy in Italy and Paris and frequently addressed the great problems of man and the universe.

As a poet he wrote, among other works, the magnificent *Las sinfonias del Popocatépetl* (The symphonies of Popocatépetl). After publication in México, it was translated into Italian and published in

Milan. While it contains little of scientific value, it captures the spirit of the wind, the forest, the rocks, the silence, the cold, and the eruptions of a great volcano.

As an historian, he published a six-volume work on the churches of México, which included photographs by the painter Frida Kahlo; as a politician, he managed to block a loan of 130 million French francs to the Mexican villain General Huerta; and as a social scientist, he published a two-volume monograph on the popular arts of México.

In later years Dr. Atl terrorized Mexican leaders with his frequent and sharp attacks in the press. By 1920 American photographer Edward Weston wrote that as they walked down Madera Avenue, every second person driving or walking "bowed or called to him"[302].

. . . . .

When the Mexican revolution began, Dr. Atl [made a second visit to Paris for a successful exposition of his Mexican volcano paintings in 1912]. Moving on to Italy, he studied volcanology at the University of Naples and learned from some of the great specialists of the time. These included Frank A Perret, an authority on Stromboli, Vesuvius, and Pelee, as well as Immannuel Friedlaender, the editor of the *Volcanological Review*. In 1921, Dr. Atl guided Friedlaender on a tour of Popocatépetl . . . . Enroute

back to México, Dr. Atl stopped in Washington to confer with President Wilson. México was in the midst of revolution, and wild rumors preceded his arrival in México City . . . . In an amusing passage, Orozco[303] describes the activities of the revolutionary:

Dr. Atl, with rifle and cartridge belt, would be off to Vera Cruz to visit Obregon on the field of battle and collect money for our whole establishment; all the while conducting a ferocious political controversy with the engineer Felix P. Palavicini and resolving a thousand problems and still having time left over in which to write editorials, and books, and even poems, without once neglecting his magnificent collection of butterflies.

With the return of peace, Dr. Atl devoted himself to painting, writing, and travel. At times he spent months on the Mexican volcanoes. The timing of the 1919 eruption of Popocatépetl was perfect. Starting in 1905, Dr. Atl had thoroughly explored the volcano, and even visited the depths of the summit crater. In 1921 he wrote in a book of poetry:

For millions of years it slept in the silence of death, for millions of years the wind lashed it, for millions of years the forces of nature have tried to destroy it. They closed its mouth, gnawed at its vertebra, they shook its formidable mass and tore its lips which in other times vibrated from thundering eloquence. But one day in its venerable old age, its entrails stirred, and from the decayed lip of the Colossus, fire shot forth again. Oh marvelous teaching of nature! Nothing is old and nothing has died: in the end of the Destruction is Life.

Fig. 219. Dr. Atl's cabin on Jarátiro ridge as seen in October 1944, half buried in ash. Quitzocho Ridge in background with north slope of Parícutin volcano to the left. The cabin was built by Celedonio Gutiérrez, who identified it in this photograph.

In February of 1943, Parícutin was born several hundred miles west of México City. When Dr. Atl disappeared shortly after the eruption, his friends were worried. He was, after all, nearly 70. They finally found him living in a shack near the base of the volcano [Fig. 219]. For months he circled it, sometimes near, sometimes far, making observations, taking notes, painting and sketching [Figs. 220 and 221]. In 1950, after consulting all the available scientific publications, he published *Como nace y crece un volcán: El Parícutin* [How a volcano is born and grows: Parícutin]. The volume was published

Fig. 220. William Foshag speaking to Dr. Atl with lava flow front from Parícutin in background. Other persons not identified. Early July, 1945.

Fig. 221. Dr. Atl painting at Parícutin volcano on August 23, 1943.

under the sponsorship of the president of México, Miguel Aleman.

. . . . .

None of the [major scientific studies of the Parícutin eruption] mention *Como nace y crece un volcan: El Parícutin* (1950), by Dr. Atl. This is unfortunate, because in many ways it is the best book on the volcano. It contains twice as many illustrations as any of the others [see sketch of Fig. 1, p. 4]. A number of these are in brilliant color, and preserve the excitement of the events as no photograph could [see Plate 7A, B, and C]. About one painting of a twisting column of glowing ash and two tornadoes, Dr. Atl wrote:

From the igneous fountain surged an enormous whirlwind of fire and other whirlwinds of ash accompanied it in a fantastic dance. The glowing column was transformed into a thick cloud, and a suffocating heat invaded the atmosphere.

Other illustrations show, in meticulous detail, the bright red ribbons of lava that flowed out of the central vent. Dr. Atl did not limit himself to strictly scientific illustrations. The book also includes a magnificent portrait of the ragged Dionisio Pulido, the man who actually witnessed the birth of Parícutin [see Fig. 3, p. 5].

Much of the text is devoted to a chronological description of the events associated with the first few years of the volcano. However, Dr. Atl was not content merely to describe events. If the first part of this book is representative of the descriptive scientist, the second part is representative of the speculative scientist, the philosopher, and the cosmologist. The main source of the volcanic heat, he wrote, could not have been from the mixing of iron and sulfur, the combustion of petroleum, or the decay of radioactive elements. He followed the suggestion of Professor Graton of Harvard that the most probable source of volcanic heat was the residual energy left over from the primitive globe[150]. To that, only a small amount of heat from radioactive decay or chemical reactions would have to be added to trigger volcanic activity.

Sunspots, he noted, were similar to volcanic eruptions. Since both were manifestations of the same

primordial fire, he suggested a cosmological definition of volcanism. It is the direct manifestation of primordial fire in celestial bodies. Had he lived, he would have been delighted by the discovery of volcanism on Io, Mars, and Venus.

In 1950, the geologists associated with Parícutin were unaware of or ignored the possible connection between continental drift (plate tectonics) and volcanism. Moreover, they never wrote about these underlying questions, although they devoted hundreds of pages to minute descriptions of the volcano's history. Dr. Atl was interested in both the details and the general principles. He embraced the theory of continental drift and began chapter one by quoting (in Spanish) from his French edition of *La génèse des continents et des océans* by Wegener. The quote reads:

One thing is certain. The same forces that produce the great folded mountains cause the displacement of the continents. Continental drift, faults and the pushing of mass, earthquakes, volcanism, the alternations of transgressions and polar migrations form, no doubt, a grand system . . .

If there could be any doubt about the enthusiasm that Dr. Atl showed for the theory of continental drift, it should be put to rest by the following quotation from his chapter "The origin of Parícutin," in which the italics are in the original:

It is possible to conclude, as a consequence, that this abundance of volcanic structures is due to innumerable fractures caused by continental drift . . .

Conclusion

Dr. Atl signed his name to 1,000 paintings, 11,000 drawings, and 1,200 copies of his book about Parícutin . . . . Today, a large book titled *Dr. Atl* graces the shelves of many Mexican book stores. In 1964, after he died, *Time* magazine noted "Last week Dr. Atl's fire finally went out at the age of 89." It was a fire that burned long and bright, and its afterglow will continue to light the worlds of art and science for years to come.

References

An extraordinary number of scientific and popular articles have been written about the Parícutin eruption in the last 50 years. The following list of 342 publications is a selected bibliography that consists mainly of articles cited in the book, but also includes several other important works. The 49 references from which we have reprinted material are in bold. Hatt (1950) gives a relatively complete bibliography for works published in the eruption's first 7 years.

Adelman, C.K.
1976   *La obra narrativa de Gerardo Murillo, Dr. Atl.* Unpublished Ph.D. dissertation, University of Illinois, Urbana, 288 p.

Allan, J.F., Carmichael, I.S.E.
1984   Lamprophyric lavas in the Colima graben, SW México. *Contributions to Mineralogy and Petrology*, 88: 203-216.

Allan, J.F., Nelson, S.A., Luhr, J.F., Carmichael, I.S.E., Wopat, M., Wallace, P.J.
1991   Pliocene-Recent rifting in SW México and associated volcanism: An exotic terrane in the making. In: J.P. Dauphin and B.A. Simoneit (editors), The Gulf and Peninsular Province of the Californias. *American Association of Petroleum Geologists Memoir*, 47: 425-445.

Anderson, A.T. Jr.
1974   Chlorine, sulfur, and water in magmas and oceans. *Bulletin of the Geological Society of America*, 85: 1485-1492.

1979   Water in some hypersthenic magmas. *Journal of Geology*, 87: 509-531.

Anderson, A.T. Jr., Clayton, R.N., Mayeda, T.
1971   Oxygen isotope geothermometry of mafic igneous rocks. *Journal of Geology*, 79: 715-729.

Arias-Portillo, P.
1945   La region devastada por el volcán de Parícutin: Mimeographed thesis. *Escuela Nacional de Agricultura*, México, 68 p.

Atl, Dr.
1950   *¿Como nace y crece un volcán?*: El Parícutin, México. Editorial Stylo, México City, 152 p.

Atwater, T.
1970   Implications of plate tectonics for the Cenozoic tectonic evolution of western North America. *Bulletin of the Geological Society of America*, 81: 3513-3536.

Backer, C.A.
1929   *The problem of Krakatoa as seen by a botanist.* Batavia, published by the author, 286 p.

Baker, G.
1946   Preliminary note on volcanic eruptions in the Goropu Mountains, southeastern Papua, during the period December, 1943, to August, 1944. *Journal of Geology*, 54: 19-31.

Ban, M., Hasanaka, T., Delgado-Granados, H., Takaoka, N.
1992   K-Ar ages of lavas from shield volcanoes in the Michoacán-Guanajuato Volcanic Field, México. *Geofísica Internacional*, 31, 4: 467-473.

Barnes, V.E., Romberg, F.
1948   Observations of relative gravity at Parícutin volcano. *Bulletin of the Geological Society of America*, 59: 1019-1026.

Beals, R.R.
1946   Cherán: A Sierra Tarascan village. *Smithsonian Institution, Washington: In-*

stitute of Social Anthropology, No. 2, 225 p.

Beals, R.R., Carrasco, P., McCorkle, T.
1944　Houses and house use of the Sierra Tarascans. *Smithsonian Institution, Washington: Institute of Social Anthropology*, No. 1, 37 p.

Beaman, J.H.
1960　Vascular plants on the cinder cone of Parícutin volcano in 1958. *Rhodora*, 62: 175-186.

1961　Vascular plants on the cinder cone of Parícutin volcano in 1960. *Rhodora*, 63: 340-344.

Ben-Avraham, Z., Nur, A.
1980　The elevation of volcanoes and their edifice heights at subduction zones. *Journal of Geophysical Research*, 85: 4325-4335.

Bernard, A., Demaiffe, D., Mattielli, N.
Punongbayan, R. S.
1991　Anhydrite-bearing pumices from Mount Pinatubo: further evidence for the existence of sulfur-rich silicic magmas. *Nature*, 354: 139-140.

Blake, S.
1981　Volcanism and the dynamics of open magma chambers. *Nature*, 289: 783-785.

Blake, S., Ivy, G.N.
1986　Density and viscosity gradients in zoned magma chambers and their influence on withdrawal dynamics. *Journal of Volcanology and Geothermal Research*, 30: 201-230.

Bloomfield, K.
1975　A late Quaternary monogenetic volcano field in central México. *Geologische Rundschau*, 64: 476-497.

Bodle, R.R.
1944　Parícutin magnetic survey. *Transactions of the American Geophysical Union*, 628-630.

Bowen, N.L.
1928　*The evolution of the igneous rocks.* Princeton University Press, Princeton. 334 p.

Brand, D.
1951　Quiroga: A Mexican municipio. *Smithsonian Institution, Washington: Institute of Social Anthropology*, No. 11, 242 p.

Bryan, W.B.
1969　Materials balance in igneous rock suites. *Carnegie Institution Washington Year Book*, 67: 241-243.

Bullard, F.M.
1947　Studies of Parícutin volcano, Michoacán, México. *Bulletin of the Geological Society of America*, 58: 433-449.

1984　*Volcanoes of the Earth.* University of Texas Press. Austin, Texas: Second revised edition. 629 p.

Burbach, G. VanNess, Frohlich, C., Pennington, W.D., Matumoto, T.
1984　Seismicity and tectonics of the subducted Cocos Plate. *Journal of Geophysical Research*, 89, B9: 7719-7735.

Burt, W.H.
1961　Some effects of Volcán Parícutin on vertebrates. *Occasional Papers of the Museum of Zoology*, Number 620, 24 p. University of Michigan Ann Arbor, Michigan.

Burton, I., Kates, R.W.
1964　The perception of natural hazards in resource management. *Journal of Natural Resources*, 3: 412-441.

Burton, I., Kates, R.W., White, G.F.
1968　*The human ecology of extreme geophysical events.* Working paper No. 1., Toronto Canada: University of Toronto, Natural Hazards Research.

1978　*The environment as hazard.* New York: Oxford University Press, 240 p.

Cantagrel, J.M., Robin, C.
1979　K-Ar dating on eastern Mexican volcanic rocks: Relations between the andesitic and alkaline provinces. *Journal of Volcanology and Geothermal Research*, 5: 99-114.

Carr, M.J., Pontier, N.K.
1981　Evolution of a young parasitic cone towards a mature central vent: Izalco and Santa Ana volcanoes in El Salvador, central America. *Journal of Volcanology and Geothermal Research*, 11: 277-292.

Carr, M.J., Stoiber, R.E., Drake, C.L.
1974　The segmented nature of some continental margins. In: C. Burke and C. L. Drake (editors), *The Geology of Conti-*

nental Margins, Springer-Verlag, New York: 105-114.

Castillo-Tejero, C.
1950   Ezequiel Ordóñez 1867-1950. *Boletin de la Asociación Mexicana de Geologos Petroleros*.

Cawthorn, R.G., O'Hara, M.J.
1976   Amphibole fractionation in calc-alkaline magma genesis. *American Journal of Science*, 276: 309-329.

Cebull, S.E., Shurbet, D.H.
1987   Mexican Volcanic Belt: an intra-plate transform? *Geofísica Internacional*, 26 (1): 1-14.

Chayes, F.
1949   A simple point counter for thin-section analysis. *American Mineralogist*, 34: 1-11.

Chesner, C.A., Rose, W.I. Jr.
1984   Geochemistry and evolution of the Fuego volcanic complex, Guatemala. *Journal of Volcanology and Geothermal Research*, 21: 25-44.

Colton, H.S.
1937   The basaltic cinder cones and lava flows of the San Francisco Mountain volcanic field. *Museum of Northern Arizona Bulletin*, 10: 1-49.

Conner, C.B.
1984   *Structure of the Michoacán Volcanic Field, México*. Unpublished M.Sc. Thesis. Dartmouth College, Hanover, NH, 189 p.

1987   **Structure of the Michoacán-Guanajuato Volcanic Field, México. *Journal of Volcanology and Geothermal Research*, 33: 191-200.**

1990   **Cinder cone clustering in the Trans-Mexican Volcanic Belt: implications for structural and petrologic models. *Journal of Geophysical Research*, 95, B12: 19395-19405.**

Cotton, C.A.
1944   *Volcanoes as landscape forms*. Whitecomb and Tombs, Christchurch, New Zealand: 416 p.

Couch, R., Woodcock, S.
1981   Gravity and structure of continental margins of southwestern México and northwestern Guatemala. *Journal of Geophysical Research*, 86: 1829-1840.

Cox, K.G., Bell, J.D., Pankhurst, R.J.
1979   *The interpretation of igneous rocks*. Allen Unwin, London: 415 p.

Crausaz, W.
1985   **Dr. Atl: Pioneer Mexican Volcanologist. *Geological Society of America Centennial Special*, 1: 251-256.**

Crisp, J.A.
1984   Rates of magma emplacement and volcanic eruption. *Journal of Volcanology and Geothermal Research*, 20: 177-211.

Criss, R.E., Taylor, H.P. Jr.
1983   An 18/16 O and D/H study of Tertiary hydrothermal systems in the southern half of the Idaho Batholith. *Bulletin of the Geological Society of America*, 94: 640-663.

Daly, R.A.
1914   *Igneous rocks and their origin*. McGraw Hill, New York: 563 p.

1933   *Igneous rocks and the depths of the earth*, McGraw Hill, New York: 598 p.

Dammerman, K.W.
1929   Krakatau's new fauna. In *Proceedings of the Fourth Pacific Science Congress* (Batavia), 83-118.

Damon, P.E., Montesinos, E.
1978   Late Cenozoic volcanism and metallogenesis over an active Benioff zone in Chiapas, México. *Arizona Geological Society Digest*, XI: 155-167.

Davis, N.Y.
1970   The role of the Russian Orthodox Church in five Pacific Eskimo villages as revealed by the earthquake. In: *The great Alaska earthquake of 1964: human ecology*. National Research Council National Academy of Sciences, Washington, D.C.

Day, A.L. and Shepherd, E.S.
1913   Water and volcanic activity. *Bulletin of the Geological Society of America*, 24: 573.

De Cserna, Z., Aranda-Goméz, J.J., Mitre-Salazar, L.M.
1988   *Mapa fotogeologico preliminar y secciones estructurales del volcán Tacaná con resumen de la historia eruptiva del volcán Tacaná, México y Guatemala*. Universidad Nacional Autonoma De México, Instituto de Geología.

De la Cruz-Martinez, V., Hernández-Zuniga, R.
1986   Geología del volcán Tacaná, *Chiapas Geotermia Revista Mexicana Geoenergia*, 2 (1): 5-21.

De la O. Carreño, A.
1943   El volcán de Parícutin en las primeras fases de su erupción. *Irrigación en México*, 24 (4): 49-80.

Demant, A.
1978   Caracteristicas del Eje Neovolcanico Transmexicano y sus problemas de interpretación. *Universidad Nacional Autonoma de México, Instituto Geologia, Revista*, 2 (2): 172-187.

1981   *The Trans-Mexican Neo-Volcanic Axis: volcanological and petrological study: Geodynamic significance.* Unpublished Ph.D. Dissertation. Universite De Droit, D'Economie et Des Sciences D'Aix-Marseille. 276 p.

DeMets, C., Stein, S.
1990   Present-day kinematics of the Rivera Plate and implications for tectonics in southwestern México. *Journal of Geophysical Research*, 95, B13: 21931-21948.

Departemento de Asuntos Agarios y Colonización. Morelia.
1973   Archives Nos. 154, 846, and 1973.

Dickenson, W.R., Hatherton, T.
1967   Andesitic volcanism and seismicity around the Pacific. *Science*, 157: 801-803.

Docters van Leeuwen, W.M.
1929   Krakatau's new flora. In *Proceedings of the Fourth Pacific Science Congress* (Batavia), 2: 56-79.

Dorf, E.
1945   Observations on the preservation of plants in the Parícutin area. *Transactions of the American Geophysical Union***, 26 (2): 257-260.**

Drabek, T.E.
1969   Social processes in disaster: Family evacuation. *Social Problems*, 16: 336-349.

Duffield, W.A., Tilling, R.I., Canul, R.
1984   Geology of El Chichón volcano, Chiapas, México. *Journal of Volcanology and Geothermal Research*, 20: 117-132.

Eggler, D.H.
1972a   Water-saturated and undersaturated melting relations in a Parícutin ande-
site and an estimate of water content in the natural magma. *Contributions to Mineralogy and Petrology*, 34: 261-271.

1972b   Amphibole stability in H_2O-undersaturated calc-alkaline melts. *Earth and Planetary Science Letters*, 15: 28-34.

Eggler, W.A.
1948   Plant communities in the vicinity of the volcano El Parícutin, México, after two and a half years of eruption. *Ecology***, 29: 415-436.**

1959   Manner of invasion of volcanic deposits by plants with further evidence from Parícutin and Jorullo. *Ecological Monographs*, 29 (2): 267-284.

1963   Plant life of Parícutin volcano, México, eight years after activity ceased. *American Midland Naturalist***, 69: 38-68.**

Eissler, H.K., McNally, K.C.
1984   Seismicity and tectonics of the Rivera Plate and implications for the 1932 Jalisco, México, earthquake. *Journal of Geophysical Research*, 89, B6: 4520- 4530.

Enciclopedia de México
1988   Ordóñez, Ezequiel. J.R. Alvarez, director, Cuidad de México: Secretaría de Educación Pública, v. 10: 6013-6014.

Ernst, A.
1908   *The new flora of the volcanic islands of Krakatoa.* Translated by A.C. Seward. Cambridge University Press, Cambridge: 74 p.

Fedotov, S.A.
1981   Magma rates in feeding conduits of different volcanic centers. *Journal of Volcanology and Geothermal Research*, 9: 379-394.

Fedotov, S.A., Balesta, S.T., Dvigalo, V.N., Razina, A.A., Flerov, G.B., Chirkov, A.M.
1991   Active volcanoes of Kamchatka. In: S. A. Fedotov and Yu. P. Masurenkov (editors), *New Tolbachik Volcanoes* Nauka Publishers, Moscow: 275-279.

Fedotov, S.A., Khrenov, A.P., Chirkov, A.M.
1976   The great 1976 fissure eruption at Tolbachik, Kamchatka, *Dokl. Akad. Nauk. SSSR.*, 228: 87-89.

Fedotov, S.A., Markhinin, Y.K.
1983   *The great Tolbachik fissure eruption.* Cambridge University Press, Cambridge.

Ferrari, L., Garduno, V.H., Pasquare, G.
1991   Geological evolution of Los Azufres Caldera, México, as a response to the

regional tectonics. *Journal of Volcanology and Geothermal Research*, 47: 129-148.

Ferriz, H., Mahood, G.A.
1986   Volcanismo riolitico en el Eje Neovolcanico Mexicano. *Geofísica Internacional*, 25: 117-156.

Fierstein, J., Nathenson, M.
1992   Another look at the calculation of fallout tephra volumes. *Bulletin of Volcanology*, 54: 156-167.

Fisher, R.V., Heiken, G.
1982   Mt. Pelee, Martinique: May 8 and 20, 1902, pyroclastic flows and surges. *Journal of Volcanology and Geothermal Research*, 13: 339-371.

Flores, T.
1945   Investigaciones geólogicas relativas al volcán Parícutin. Volcanismo y orogenia del Estado de Michoacán. In: T. Flores (editor), *El Parícutin, Estado de Michoacán*. Universidad Nacional Autónoma de México, Instituto de Geología: 3-16.

Flores-Covarrubias, L.
1945a   Investigación geofísico-sismométrica del fenómeno volcánico. In: T. Flores (editor), *El Parícutin, Estado de Michoacán*. Universidad Nacional Autónoma de México, Instituto de Geología: 23-38.

1945b   Interpretación del fenómeno volcánico a la luz de la sismología. In: T. Flores (editor), *El Parícutin, Estado de Michoacán*. Universidad Nacional Autónoma de México, Instituto de Geología: 43-58.

Foshag, W.F.
1950   The aqueous emanation from Parícutin volcano. *American Mineralogist*, 35: 749-755.

1954a   Acceptance of the Roebling Medal of the Mineralogical Society of America. *American Mineralogist*, 39: 296-299.

1954b   The life and death of a volcano. *Geographical Magazine (London)*, 17: 159-168.

Foshag, W.F., González-Reyna, J.R.
1956   **Birth and development of Parícutin volcano, México. *U. S. Geological Survey Bulletin*, 965D: 355-489.**

Foshag, W.F., Henderson, E.P.
1946   Primary sublimates at Parícutin volcano. *Transactions of the American Geophysical Union*, 27 (5): 685-686.

Foster, G.M.
1948   Empire's children: The people of Tzintzuntzan. *Smithsonian Institution, Washington: Institute of Social Anthropology*, No. 13, 369 p.

1967   *Tzintzuntzan; Mexican peasants in a changing world*. Little Brown, Boston: 372 p.

Fridriksson, S.
1975   *Surtsey: Evolution of life on a volcanic island*. John Wiley & Sons, New York: 198 p.

Fries, C. Jr.
1953   **Volumes and weights of pyroclastic material, lava, and water erupted by Parícutin volcano, Michoacán, México. *Transactions of the American Geophysical Union*, 34 (4): 603-616.**

Fries, C. Jr., Gutiérrez, C.
1950a   **Activity of Parícutin volcano from August 1, 1948 to June 30, 1949. *Transactions of the American Geophysical Union*, 31 (3): 406-418.**

1950b   **Activity of Parícutin volcano from July 1 to December 31, 1949. *Transactions of the American Geophysical Union*, 31 (5): 732-740.**

1951a   **Activity of Parícutin volcano from January 1 to June 30, 1950. *Transactions of the American Geophysical Union*. 32 (2): 212-221.**

1951b   **Activity of Parícutin volcano from July 1 to December 31, 1950. *Transactions of the American Geophysical Union*, 32 (4): 572-581.**

1952a   **Activity of Parícutin volcano from January 1 to June 30, 1951. *Transactions of the American Geophysical Union*, 33 (1): 91-100.**

1952b   **Activity of Parícutin volcano from July 1 to December 31, 1951. *Transactions of the American Geophysical Union*, 33 (5): 725-733.**

1954   **Activity of Parícutin volcano during the year 1952. *Transactions of the American Geophysical Union*, 35 (3): 486-494.**

Fries, C. Jr., Segerstrom, K., Tilling, R.I., White, D.E., and Wilcox, R.E.
1993   Movie footage of the activity of Parícutin volcano, Michoacán, México,

1945-1952. *U.S. Geological Survey Open-File Report*, 93-197-A,B: 16 p.

Fuller, R.E.
1945   A report by the United States Committee for the Study of the Parícutin Volcano. *Transactions of the American Geophysical Union*, 6,1: 131-133.
1947   The United States Committee for the Study of Parícutin Volcano. *National Research Council Annual Report*, 4 p.

Gadow, H.
1930   *Jorullo: The history of the volcano of Jorullo and the reclamation of the devastated district of animals and plants.* Cambridge University Press, London: 101 p.

Garlick, G. D.
1966   Oxygen isotope fractionation in igneous rocks. *Earth and Planetary Science Letters*, 1: 361-368.

Gill, J.B.
1981   *Orogenic andesites and plate tectonics.* Springer-Verlag, Berlin: 390 p.

González-Ferran, O., Baker, P.E., Acevedo, P.
1989   La erupción del Volcán Lonquimay 1988 y su impacto en el medio ambiente. Instituto Panamericano de Geografia e Historia, *Revista Geofísica*. 31: 39-107.

González-Reyna, J., Foshag, W.F.
1947   *The Birth of Parícutin.* Smithsonian Report for 1946, 223-224.

Graton, L.C.
1945   The genetic significance of Parícutin. *Transactions of the American Geophysical Union*, 26: 249-254.

Graves, T.D., Graves, N.B., Kobrin, M.J.
1969   Historical inferences from Guttman scales: The return of age-area magic. *Current Anthropology*, 10: 17-388.

Green, D.H.
1971   Compositions of basaltic magmas as indicators of conditions of origin: applications to oceanic volcanism. *Philosophical Transactions of the Royal Society of London*, Series A, 268: 707-725.

Green, D.H., Ringwood, A.E.
1966   Origin of calc-alkaline igneous rock suite. *Earth and Planetary Science Letters*, 1: 307-316.

Greene, M.T.
1982   *Geology in the nineteenth century—changing views of a changing world.* Cornell University Press, Ithaca, New York: 324 p.

Griggs, R.F.
1922   *The Valley of Ten Thousand Smokes, Alaska.* National Geographic Society. Washington, D.C., 340 p.
1933   The colonization of Katmai ash, A new inorganic "soil". *American Journal of Botany*, 20: 92-113.

Gutiérrez, C.
1972   **A narrative of human response to natural disaster: The eruption of Parícutin. In: Mary Lee Nolan (editor), *San Juan Nuevo Parangaricutiro: Memories of past years*. Environmental Quality Note No. 07. College Station, Texas A & M University: 78 p.**

Hardinge, H., Frankish, T.A. Taggart, A.F.
1945   *Handbook of mineral dressing, sec. 9.* Air sizing and dust collection: John Wiley & Sons, Inc.

Hasenaka, T., Carmichael, I.S.E.
1985a   **The cinder cones of Michoacán-Guanajuato, Central México: Their age, volume and distribution, and magma discharge rate. *Journal of Volcanology and Geothermal Research*, 25: 105-124.**
1985b   A compilation of location, size, and geomorphological parameters of volcanoes of the Michoacán-Guanajuato volcanic field, Central México. *Geofísica Internacional*, 24-4: 577-608.
1986   Metate and other shield volcanoes of Michoacán-Guanajuato, México. EOS, *Transactions of the American Geophysical Union*, 67: 1276.
1987   **The cinder cones of Michoacán-Guanajuato, central México: Petrology and chemistry. *Journal of Petrology*, 28 (2): 241-269.**

Hatt, R.T.
1950   *Bibliography of Parícutin volcano.* Michigan Academy of Science, 34: 227-237.

Hawkesworth, C.J.
1982   Isotope characteristics of magmas erupted along destructive plate margins. In: R.S. Thorpe (editor), *Andesites*. John Wiley & Sons, New York: 549-571.

Hernández-Velasco, J.A.
1945   Estudios de las cenizas del volcán caidas en la Ciudad de México. In: T. Flores (editor), *El Parícutin, Estado de Micho-*

acán. Universidad Nacional Autonóma de México, Instituto de Geología, 139-145.

Hewitt, K., Burton, I.
1971   *The hazardousness of a place: A regional ecology of damaging events*. University of Toronto Press, Toronto Canada.

Hildreth, W.
1981   Gradients in silicic magma chambers: Implications for lithospheric magmatism. *Journal of Geophysical Research*, 86: 10153-10192.

Hill, R., Hansen, D.A.
1962   Families in disasters. In: G.W. Baker and D.W. Chapman (editors), *Man and society in disaster*. Basic Books, New York.

Holloway, J.R., Burnham, C.W.
1972   Melting relations of basalt with equilibrium water pressure less than total pressure. *Journal of Petrology*, 13: 1-29.

Holmes, A.
1931   The problem of the association of acid and basic rocks in central complexes. *Geological Magazine*, 68: 241-255.

Horner, L.
1847   On the origin of Monte Nuovo, in a letter from an eyewitness of the eruption of 1538. *Quarterly Journal of the Geological Society of London*, 3, part 2: 19-22.

Horton, R.E.
1941   Discussion of dynamics of water erosion on land surfaces. *American Geophysical Union 22nd Annual Meeting*, part 2: 301.

Jaggar, T.A.
1917   Volcanic investigations on Kilauea, *American Journal of Science*, 44: 161-220.

Janis, I.L.
1962   Psychological effects of warnings. In: G.W. Baker and D.W. Chapman (editors), *Man and society in disaster*. Basic Books, New York.

Johannsen, A.
1937   *The intermediate rocks. A descriptive petrography of the igneous rocks*, vol. 3. University of Chicago Press, Chicago: 361 p.

Johnson, C.A., Harrison, C.G.A.
1988   Thematic mapper studies of volcanism and tectonism in central México. *Advances in Space Research, Proceedings of the twenty-seventh Planetary Meeting of COSPAR, 1988*.

Kates, R.W.
1977   Major insights: A summary and reccomendation. In: J.E. Haas, R.W. Kates, and M.J. Bowden (editors), *Reconstruction following disaster*. The MIT Press, Cambridge, Mass.: 263.

Kear, D.
1964   Volcanic alignments north and west of New Zealand's central volcanic region. *New Zealand Journal of Geology and Geophysics*, 7: 24-44.

Kendrick, T.D.
1957   *The Lisbon Earthquake*. Lipincott, Philadelphia, Pa.

Kennedy, G.C.
1946   Activity of Parícutin volcano April 12 to May 3, 1946. *Transactions of the American Geophysical Union*, 27 (3): 410-411.

Kingdon-Ward, F.
1951   Notes on the Assam earthquake. *Nature*, 167: 130-131.

Koyaguchi, T.
1985   Magma mixing in a conduit. *Journal of Volcanology and Geothermal Research*, 25: 365-369.

Kraus, E.H.
1954   Presentation of the Roebling Medal of the Mineralogical Society of America to William Frederick Foshag. *American Mineralogist*, 39: 293-295.

Krauskopf, K.B.
1948a   Mechanism of eruption at Parícutin volcano, México. *Bulletin of the Geological Society of America*, 59: 711-731.

1948b   Lava movement at Parícutin volcano, México. *Bulletin of the Geological Society of America*, 59: 1267-1283.

1962   Presentation of Arthur L. Day Medal to Konrad B. Krauskopf (response). *Geological Society of America, Proceedings for 1960*, 66-67.

1983   Acceptance speech for the V. M. Goldschmidt Medal. *Geochimica et Cosmochimica Acta*, 47: 982-983.

Krauskopf, K.B., Williams, H.
1946   The activity of Parícutin during its third year. *Transactions of the American Geophysical Union*, 27 (3): 406-410.

Kuno, H.
1950   Petrology of Hakone volcano and the adjacent areas, Japan. *Bulletin of the Geological Society of America*, 61: 957-1019.
1960   High-alumina basalt. *Journal of Petrology*, 1: 121-145.
1966   Lateral variation of basalt magma type across continental margins and island arcs. *Bulletin Volcanologique*, 29: 195-222.

Larsen, E.S., Switzer, G.
1939   An obsidian-like rock formed from the melting of a granodiorite. *American Journal of Science*, 237: 562-568.

Larson, R.L.
1972   Bathymetry, magnetic anomalies, and plate tectonic history of the mouth of the Gulf of California. *Bulletin of the Geological Society of America*, 83: 3345-3360.

Lowenstein, P.L.
1982   Problems of volcanic hazards in Papua New Guinea. *Papua New Guinea Geological Survey*, 82,7: 15-16.

Luhr, J.F., Carmicahel, I.S.E.
1980   The Colima Volcanic Complex, México: I. Post-caldera andesites from Volcán Colima. *Contributions to Mineralogy and Petrology*, 71: 343-372.
1981   The Colima Volcanic Complex, México: II. Late-Quaternary cinder cones. *Contributions to Mineralogy and Petrology*, 76: 127-147.
1982   The Colima Volcanic complex, México: III. Ash- and scoria-fall deposits from the upper slopes of Volcán Colima. *Contributions to Mineralogy and Petrology*, 80: 262-275.
1985   Jorullo Volcano, Michoacán, México (1759-1774): The earliest stages of fractionation in calc-alkaline magmas. *Contributions to Mineralogy and Petrology*, 90: 142-161.
1990   Petrological monitoring of cyclical eruptive activity at Volcán Colima, México. *Journal of Volcanology*, 42: 235-260.

Luhr, J.F., Carmichael, I.S.E., Varekamp, J.C.
1984   The 1982 eruptions of El Chichón volcano, Chiapas, México: Mineralogy and petrology of the anhydrite-bearing pumices. *Journal of Volcanology and Geothermal Research*, 23: 69-108.

Luhr, J.F., Nelson, S.A., Allan, J.F., Carmichael, I.S.E.
1985   Active rifting in southwestern México: Manifestations of an incipient eastward spreading-ridge jump. *Geology*, 13: 54-57.

Lyell, C.
1875   *Principles of Geology*. John Murray, London: 2nd volume, 12th edition.

Macdonald, G.A., Katsura, T.
1964   Chemical composition of Hawaiian lavas. *Journal of Petrology*, 5: 82-133.

Machado, F.
1974   The search for magmatic reservoirs. In: L. Civetta, P. Gasparini, G. Luongo and A. Rapolla (editors), *Physical Volcanology*, Elsevier, Amsterdam, 255-273.

Madrigal-Sanchez, X.
1964   *Contribución al conocimiento de la ecologia de los bosques de Oyamel (Abies Religiosa H. B. K.) en el Valle de México*. México, D.F.: Instituto Polytechnico Nacional. Thesis presented for the title of Biologist, Escuela Nacional de Ciencias Biologicas, 111 p.

Mahood, G.A.
1980   Geological evolution of a Pleistocene rhyolitic center: Sierra la Primavera, Jalisco, México. *Journal of Volcanology and Geothermal Research*, 8: 199-230.
1981   Chemical evolution of a Pleistocene rhyolitic center: Sierra la Primavera, Jalisco, México. *Contributions to Mineralogy and Petrology*, 77: 129-149.

Martín-Del Pozzo, A.L.
1982   Monogenetic volcanism in Sierra Chichinautzin, México. *Bulletin Volcanologique*, 45: 9-24.

Martínez-Portillo, J.
1950   Bibliografia del ingeniero don Ezequiel Ordóñez. *Boletin de la Asociación Mexicana de Geologos Petroleros*.

Masi, U., O'Neil, J.R., Kistler, R.W.
1981   Stable isotope systematics in Mesozoic granites of central and northern California and southwest Oregon. *Contributions to Mineralogy and Petrology*, 76: 116-126.

Matsuhisa, Y.
1979   Oxygen isotopic compositions of volcanic rocks from the East Japan island arcs and their bearing on petrogenesis.

Journal of Volcanology and Geothermal Research, 5: 271-296.

McBirney, A.R., Baker, B.H., Nilson, R.H.
1985   Liquid fractionation. Part I: Basic principles and experimental simulations. *Journal of Volcanology and Geothermal Research*, 24: 1-24.

McBirney, A.R., Taylor, H.P. Jr., Armstrong, R.L.
1987   **Parícutin re-examined: a classic example of crustal assimilation in calc-alkaline magma.** *Contributions to Mineralogy and Petrology*, **95: 4-20.**

McNally, K.C., Minster, J.B.
1981   Nonuniform seismic slip rates along the Middle American trench. *Journal of Geophysical Research*, 86: 4949-4959.

Melson, W.G., Saenz, R.
1984   Volume, energy, and cyclicity of eruption of Arenal volcano, Costa Rica. *Bulletin Volcanologique*, 37: 416-437.

Mendoza-Valentin, R.
1988   *Yo vi nacer un volcán: historia testigos recuerdos.* Novoa Editorial, S.A. de C.V., León, 144 p.

Miesch, A.T.
1979   Vector analysis of chemical variations in the lavas of Parícutin volcano, México. *Mathematical Geology*, 11: 345-371.

Miller, E.B., Pitner, J.B., Ricardo-Villa, J., Carlos-Romo, G.
1949   Population density of unirrigated maize and its influence upon fertilizer efficiency in central México. *Soil Science Society of America, Proceedings*, 14: 270-275.

Millhollen, G.L.
1971   Melting of nepheline syenite with H_2O and $H_2O + CO_2$, and the effect of dilution of the aqueous phase on the beginning of melting. *American Journal of Science*, 270: 244-254.

Milton, C.
1945   Notes on volcanic rocks from Parícutin, México. *Transactions of the American Geophysical Union*, 25: 618-621.

Minakami, T., Ishikawa, T., Yugi, K.
1951   The 1944 eruption of Volcano Usu in Hokkaido, Japan. *Bulletin Volcanologique*, 11: 46-157.

Minster, J.B., Jordan, T.H.
1978   Present-day plate motions. *Journal of Geophysical Research*, 83: 5331-5353.

Mohr, P.A., Wood, C.A.
1976   Volcano spacing and lithospheric attenuation in the eastern rift of Africa. *Earth and Planetary Science Letters*, 33: 126-144.

Moorbath, S., Thorpe, R.S., Gibson, I.L.
1978   Strontium isotope evidence for petrogenesis of Mexican andesites. *Nature*, 271: 437-439.

Moore, H.E.
1964   *And the winds blew.* Hogg Foundation for Mental Health, University of Texas Press, Austin, Texas.

Mooser, F.
1958   Active volcanoes of México. In: F. Mooser, H. Meyerbich, and A.R. McBirney (editors), *International Association of Volcanology, Catalogue of Active Volcanoes Part*, 6, IAVCEI, Rome, 146 p.
1969   The Mexican Volcanic Belt - Structure and development. Formation of fractures by differential crustal heating. *Pan-American Symposium on the Upper Mantle*, 2: 15-22.
1972   The Mexican Volcanic Belt: Structure and tectonics. *Geofísica Internacional*, 12: 55-70.
1975   The Mexican Volcanic Belt: Interpretations derived from fractures and form. *Transactions of the American Geophysical Union*, 56: 1066.

Morey, G.W., Bowen, N.L.
1922   The melting of potash feldspar. *American Journal of Science*, 4: 1-21.

Murata, K.J., Richter, D.H.
1966   Chemistry of the lavas of the 1959-1960 eruption of Kilauea volcano, Hawaii. *U.S. Geological Survey Professional Paper*, 537A: 1-26.

Murphy, G.P., Carmichael, I.S.E.
1984   A report on the occurrence of maars in the Michoacán-Guanajuato Volcanic Field, central México. *Geological Society of America Abstracts and Programs*, 16: 604.

Nakamura, K.
1977   Volcanoes as possible indicators of tectonic stress orientation—principles and proposal. *Journal of Volcanology and Geothermal Research*, 2: 1-16.

Nakamura, K.
1981   Two basic types of volcanoes—polygenetic and independent monogenetic groups of volcanoes, and tectonic stress. *1981 IAVCEI Symposium—Arc Volcanism*, Hakone, Tokyo, Japan: 251.

Nakamura, K., Jacob, K.H., Davies, J.N.
1977   Volcanoes as possible indicators of tectonic stress orientation—Aleutians and Alaska. *Pure Applied Geophysics*, 115: 87-112.

Nelson, S.A.
1980   Geology and petrology of Volcán Ceboruco. *Bulletin of the Geological Society of America*, 91: 2290-2431.

Nelson, S.A., Carmichael, I.S.E.
1984   Pleistocene to Recent alkaline volcanism in the region of Sangangüey volcano, Nayarit, México. *Contributions to Mineralogy and Petrology*, 85: 321-335.

Nelson, S.A., Gonzalez-Caver, E.
1992   Geology and K-Ar dating of the Tuxla Volcanic Field, Veracruz, México. *Bulletin of Volcanology*, 55: 85-96.

Nicols, R.L.
1939   Viscosity of lava. *Journal of Geology*, 47: 290-302.

Nilson, R.H., McBirney, A.R., Baker, B.H.
1985   Liquid fractionation. Part II: Fluid dynamics and quantitative implications for magmatic systems. *Journal of Volcanology and Geothermal Research*, 24: 25-54.

Nixon, G.T.
1982   The relationship between Quaternary volcanism in central México and the seismicity and structure of subducted ocean lithosphere. *Bulletin of the Geological Society of America*, 93 (6): 514-523.

Nixon, G.T., Demant, A., Armstrong, R.L., Harakal, J.L.
1987   K-Ar and geologic data bearing on the age and evolution of the Trans-Mexican Volcanic Belt. *Geofísica Internacional*, 26-1: 109-158.

Nolan, M.L.
1972   *The towns of the volcano: A study of the human consequences of the eruption of Parícutin volcano*. Unpublished Ph.D. Thesis. Department of Geography, Texas A & M University.

1973   Research on disaster and environmental hazard as viewed from the perspective of response to the eruption of the Volcano Parícutin in Michoacán, México. Texas A & M University. *Environmental Quality Note No. 14*, College Station, Texas.

1974   The reality of difference between small communities in Michoacán, México. *American Anthropologist*, 76: 47-49.

1975   The Tarascan/non-Tarascan interface. Families originating in the Sierra Tarasca: Variations in modernization. Presented at the *Seventy-fourth Annual Meeting of the American Anthropological Association*, San Francisco, Cal.

1979   Impact of Parícutin on five communities. In: P.D. Sheets and D.K. Grayson (editors), *Volcanic activity and human ecology*. Academic Press, New York: 293-338.

Ordóñez, E.
1906   *Excursion du Jorullo*. Guide des excursions du 10th Congres Geologique International, México City, 11 p.

1910   Le Pic de Tancítaro, Michoacán. *Memorias de la Sociedad Científica "Antonio Alazate"*, 30: 11-17.

1943   El Volcán de Parícutin, *Comision Impulsora y Coordinadora de la Investigación Científica, Anuario*, 241-300.

1945   El Volcán de Parícutin. *Comision Impulsora y Coordinadora de la Investigación Científica*, México.

1947   *El Volcán de Parícutin*. Editorial Fantasia, Mixcoac, D. F., 181 p.

Orozco, J.C.
1962   Orozco, an autobiography (Translated by R.C. Stevens): University of Texas Press, Austin, 171 p.

Orozco y Berra, J.
1887   Efemerides seismicas Mexicanas. *Memorias de la Sociedad Científica "Antonio Alazate"*, Tomo I: 205-541.

Orozco y Berra, M.
1854   Jorullo (Volcán de). *Diccionario de Historia y Geografía*, Tomo IV, p. 453.

Osborn, E.F., Rawson, S.A.
1980   Experimental studies of magnetite in calc-alkaline rocks. *Carnegie Institution Washington Year Book*, 79: 281-285.

Pallister, J.S., Hoblitt, R.P., Reyes, A.G.
1992   A basalt trigger for the 1991 eruptions of Pinatubo volcano. *Nature*, 356: 426-428.

Perlmuter, L.C., Monty, R.A.
1977   The importance of perceived control: Fact or fantasy. *American Scientist*, 65: 759-765.

Perret, F.A.
1912   The flashing arcs: a volcanic phenomenon. *American Journal of Science*, 34: 329-333.

1924   The Vesuvius eruption of 1906, study of a volcanic cycle. *Carnegie Institution Washington Publication*. No. 339, 151.

Phillips, J.
1869   *Vesuvius*. Clarendon Press, Oxford, 355.

Pichler, H., Weyl, R.
1976   Quaternary alkaline rocks in eastern México and Central America. *Münstersche Forshungen zur Geologie und Paläontologie*, 38: 159-178.

Piwinskii, A.J.
1968   Experimental studies of igneous rock series. Central Sierra Nevada batholith, California. *Journal of Geology*, 76: 548-570.

Poli, E., Giacomini, V.
1970   Vulkane. In: C. Kruger (editor), *Vulkane and Pflanzenleben*. Anton Schroll & Co., Vienna: 139-146.

Porter, S.C.
1972   Distribution, morphology, and size frequency of cinder cones on Mauna Kea volcano, Hawaii. *Bulletin of the Geological Society of America*, 83: 3607-3612.

Ramos, E.L.
1981   Dirección de Publicaciones Científicas, México D. F. *Geology of México*, 3, 2nd edition: 445 p.

Rees, J.D.
1961   *Changes in Tarascan settlement and economy related to the eruption of Parícutin*. Unpublished M.Sc. Thesis. Dept. of Geography, University of California, L.A.

1970   Parícutin revisited: A view of man's attempts to adapt to ecological changes resulting from volcanic catastrophe. *Geographical Forum*, 4: 7-25.

1971   *Forest utilization by Tarascan agriculturalists in Michoacán, México*: Unpublished Ph.D. Dissertation. Dept. of Geography, University of California, L.A.

1979   **Effects of the eruption of Parícutin volcano on landforms, vegetation, and human occupancy. In: P.D. Sheets and D.K. Grayson (editors), *Volcanic activity and human ecology*. Academic Press, New York: 249-292.**

Reid, M.R.
1984   Isotopic and trace element geochemistry of Parícutin volcano: Anatomy of crustal assimilation. *Proceedings of the Conference on Open Magmatic Systems*, Southern Methodist University, Institute for the Study of Earth and Man: 133- 134.

Robin, C., Camus, G., Gourgaud, A.
1991   Eruptive and magmatic cycles at Fuego de Colima volcano (México). *Journal of Volcanology and Geothermal Research*, 45: 209-225.

Robin, C., Mossand, P., Camus, G., Cantagrel, J.M. Gourgaud, A., Vincent, P.
1987   Eruptive history of the Colima Volcanic Complex (México). *Journal of Volcanology and Geothermal Research*, 31: 99-113.

Robles-Ramos, R.
1943   El volcán de Parícutin y el neo-volcanismo Mexicano. *Irrigación en México*, 24: 81-123.

Roggensack, K.
1988   *Morphology, distribution, and chemistry of shield volcanoes of the Trans-Mexican Volcanic Belt*. Unpublished M.Sc. Thesis. Dartmouth College, Hanover, N.H., 148 p.

Roobol, M.J., Smith, A.L.
1975   A comparison of the recent eruptions of Mt. Pelee, Martinique and Soufriere, St. Vincent. *Bulletin Volcanologique*, 39 (2): 1-27.

Rose, W.I. Jr, Bornhorst, T.J., Halsor, S.P., Capaul, W.A., Plumley, P.S., De La Cruz-Reyna, S., Mena, M., Mota, R.
1984   Volcán el Chichón, México: Pre-1982 S-rich eruptive activity. *Journal of Volcanology and Geothermal Research*, 23: 147- 167.

Rosenfield, J.L.
1950   Determination of all principal indices of refraction on difficultly oriented minerals

by direct measurement. *American Mineralogist*, 35: 902-905.

Rosi, M., Santacroce, R.
1984　Volcanic hazard assessment in the Phlegraean Fields: A contribution based on stratigraphic and historical data. *Bulletin Volcanologique*, 47 (2): 359-370.

Ross, C.S.
1956　Memorial of William Frederick Foshag (1894-1956). *Proceedings volume of the Geological Society of America Annual Report for 1956*: 123-126.

Ruffner, J.A.
1980　*Climates of the States, vol. 1*. Gale Research Company, Detroit, Mich.: 588 p.

Rutten, L.M.R.
1927　Voordrachten over der Geologie van Nederlandsch Oost-Indie. *Den Haag*: 149-154.

Salas, G.P.
1966　Memorial to Carl Fries, Jr. *Bulletin of the Geological Society of America*, 77 (1): P1-P3.

Sato, H.
1977　Nickel content of basaltic magmas and a measure of the degree of olivine fractionation. *Lithos*, 10: 113-120.

Scandone, R.
1979　Effusion rate and energy balance of Parícutin eruption (1943-1952), Michoacán, México. *Journal of Volcanology and Geothermal Research*, 6: 49-59.

Schaller, W.T.
1957　Memorial of William Frederick Foshag. *American Mineralogist*, 42: 249-254.

Schmitter, E.
1945　Estudio petrográfico de lavas y productos piroclásticos. Determinación de las formas cristalinas e índices de refracción de algunos de los sublimados del volcán. In: T. Flores (editor), *El Parícutin, Esatado de Michoácan*. Universidad Nacional Autónoma de México, Instituto de Geología, 111-131.

Scott, D.H., Trask, N.J.
1971　Geology of the Lunar Crater Volcanic Field, Nye County, Nevada. *U. S. Geological Survey Professional Paper*, 599-1: 22 p.

Secretaría de la Economía Nacional
1943　*Estados Unidos Mexicanos sexto censo de población, 1940. Michoacán, México D.F.*: Secretaría de la Economía Nacional, Dirección General de Estadística.

Secretaría de Hacienda y Credito Publico.
1940　*Estudios Historico-economico-fiscales sobre los estados de la republica: vol. III. Michoacán, México, D.F.*: Secretario de Hacienda y Credito Publico.

Secretaría de Industria y Comercio.
1971　*IX censo general de población, 1970. Estado de Michoacán, México.* Secretaría de Industria y Comercio, 3. Dirección General de Estadística.

Segerstrom, K.
1950　Erosion studies at Parícutin volcano, state of Michoacán, México. *U. S. Geological Survey Bulletin*, 965A: 1-164.

1960　Erosion and related phenomena at Parícutin in 1957. *Geological Survey Bulletin*, 1104-A: 1-18.

1961　Deceleration of erosion at Parícutin, México. *U. S. Geological Survey Professional Paper*, 424D: 225-227.

1966　Parícutin, 1965—Aftermath of eruption. *U. S. Geological Survey Professional Paper*, 550-C: 93-101.

Segerstrom, K., Gutiérrez, C.
1947　Activity of Parícutin volcano from May 4 to September 8, 1946. *Transactions of the American Geophysical Union*, 28 (4): 559-566.

Settle, M.
1979　The structure and emplacement of cinder cone fields. *American Journal of Science*, 279: 1089-1107.

Sharp, R.P.
1962　Presentation of Arthur L. Day Medal to Konrad B. Krauskopf. *Geological Society of America, Proceedings for 1960*, 65-66.

Shimozuru, D.
1971　A seismological approach to the prediction of volcanic eruptions. *The surveillance of volcanic activity*, UNESCO, Paris: 19-45.

Shurbet, D.H., Cebull, S.E.
1984　Tectonic interpretation of the Trans-Mexican Volcanic Belt. *Tectonophysics*, 101: 159-165.

1986　Tectonic interpretation of the Trans-Mexican Volcanic Belt: discussion and reply. *Tectonophysics*, 127: 155-160.

Simkin, T., Fiske, R.S.

1983 *Krakatau 1883: The volcanic eruption and its effects.* Smithsonian Institution Press, Washington, 464 p.

Simkin, T., Siebert, L., McClelland, L., Bridge, D., Newhall, C., Latter, J.H.

1981 *Volcanoes of the world.* Hutchinson Ross, Stroudsburg, Pa., 232 p.

Simpson, L.B.

1952 *Many Mexicos.* University of California Press, Berkeley, Cal.

Singh, S.K., Dominguez, T., Castro, R., Rodriguez, M.

1984 P waveform of large, shallow earthquakes along the Mexican subduction zone. *Bulletin of the Seismological Society of America,* 74: 2135-2156.

Sjoberg, G.

1962 Disasters and social change. In: G.W. Baker and D.W. Chapman (editors), *Man and society in disaster.* Basic Books, New York.

Smithsonian Institution, Scientific Event Alert Network (SEAN) Bulletin.

1983 *Parícutin Volcano.* 8 (4): 11.

1985 *Parícutin Volcano.* 10 (11): 9.

1986 *Parícutin Volcano.* 11 (11): 18.

1988 *Parícutin Volcano.* 13 (5): 7-8.

1989 *Parícutin Volcano.* 14 (12): 16.

Stanley, E.R.

1919 Geological expedition across the Owen Stanley Range, 1916. *Annual Report, Papua, 1917-1918.*

1923 *The Geology of Papua.* Melbourne.

Stearns, H.T., Macdonald, G.A.

1942 Geology and groundwater resources of the island of Maui, Hawaii: Territory of Hawaii. *Bulletin of the Division of Hydrography,* 7, 344 p.

Storm, M.

1945 *Enjoying Uruapan.* Editorial Bolivar, México, 778 p.

Suarez, G., Singh, S.K.

1986 Tectonic interpretation of the Trans-Mexican Volcanic Belt: discussion and reply. *Tectonophysics,* 127: 155-160.

Tatsumi, Y., Sakuyama, M., Fukuyama, H., Kushiro, I.

1983 Generation of arc basalt magmas and the thermal structure of the mantle wedge in subduction zones. *Journal Geophysical Research,* 88, B7: 5815-5825.

Taylor, H.P. Jr.

1968 The oxygen isotope geochemistry of igneous rocks. *Contributions to Mineralogy and Petrology,* 19: 1-71.

1977 Water/rock interactions and the origin of H_2O in granitic batholiths. *Journal of the Geological Society of London,* 133: 509-558.

Taylor, H.P. Jr., Silver, L.T.

1978 Oxygen isotope relationships in plutonic igneous rocks of the Peninsular Batholith, southern and Baja California. *U. S. Geological Survey Open-File Report,* 78 (701): 423-427.

Thorarinsson, S.

1954 Tephra fall from Hekla on March 29th 1947. In: T. Einarsson, G. Kjartansson, and S. Thorarinsson (editors), *The eruption of Hekla 1947/1948,* II (3), Societas Scientiarum Islandica, Reykjavik, 68 p.

Thorpe, R.S.

1977 Tectonic significance of alkaline volcanism in eastern México. *Tectonophysics,* 40: T19-T26.

Tilley, C.E., Yoder, H.S. Jr., Schairer, J.F.

1967 Melting relations of volcanic rock series. *Carnegie Institution of Washington Year Book,* 65: 260-269.

1968 Melting relations of igneous rock series. *Carnegie Institution of Washington Year Book,* 66: 450-457.

Tilling, R.I., Rubin, M., Sigurdsson, H., Carey, S., Duffield, W.A., Rose, W.I.

1984 Holocene eruptive activity of El Chichón volcano, Chiapas, México. *Science,* 224: 747-749.

Trainer, P.B., Bolin, R., Ramos, R.

1977 Reestablishing homes and jobs: Families. In: J.E. Haas, R.W. Kates, and M.J. Bowden (editors), *Reconstruction following disaster.* The MIT Press, Cambridge, Mass.

Trask, P.D.

1943 The Mexican volcano, Parícutin. *Science,* 98,2554: 501-505.

1945 El Volcán Mexicano Parícutin. In: T. Flores (editor), *El Parícutin, Estado de Michoacán.* Universidad Nacional Autónoma de México, Instituto de Geología, 103-109.

Truchan, M., Larson, R.L.
1973 Tectonic lineaments on the Cocos Plate. *Earth and Planetary Science Letters*, 17: 426-432.

Ui, T., Aramaki, S.
1978 Relationship between chemical composition of Japanese island-arc volcanic rocks and gravimetric data. *Tectonophysics*, 45: 249-259.

UNESCO
1970 *Summary of Natural Hazards: Summary report*. Godollo, Hungary.

United States Committee for the Study of Parícutin Volcano
1945a *Science*, 101 (2615): 137-138.
1945b Activity of Parícutin volcano, *Science*, 101 (2630): 530.

Verhoogen, J.
1939 New data on volcanic gases: The 1938 eruption of Nyamlagira. *American Journal of Science*, 237: 662.

Verma, S.P.
1983 Magma genesis and chamber processes at Los Humeros Caldera, México—Nd and Sr isotope data. *Nature*, 302: 52-55.

Viramonte, J.G., Ubeda, E., Martinez, M.
1971 The 1971 eruption of Cerro Negro, Nicaragua. *Smithsonian Institution Center for Short-Lived Phenomena Paper*, 28. Washington, DC: 1-28.

Von Humboldt, F.H.A.
1810 Essai sur la Nouvelle Espagne. *Journal of Natural Philosophy, Chemistry and Arts*, 25: 81-86.

Wadge, G.
1978 The storage and release of magma on Mount Etna. *Journal of Volcanology and Geothermal Research*, 2: 361-384.
1981 The variation of magma discharge during basaltic eruptions. *Journal of Volcanology and Geothermal Research*, 11: 139-168.
1982 Steady state volcanism: Evidence from eruption histories of polygenetic volcanoes. *Journal of Geophysical Research*, 87: 4035-4049.

Waitz, P.
1943 El nuevo volcán de Parícutin: *Irrigación en México*, 24 (4): 37-48.

Walker, G.P.L.
1983 Variations in the size of volcanic eruptions and their consequences. *Geological Society of America Abstracts and Programs*, 15: 713.

Washington, H.S.
1917 Persistence of vents at Stromboli. *Bulletin of the Geological Society of America*, 28: 249-278.

Watkins, N.D., Gunn, B.M., Baksi, A.K., York, D. Ade-Hall, J.
1971 Paleomagnetism, geochemistry, and potassium-argon ages of the Rio Grande de Santiago volcanics, Central México. *Bulletin of the Geological Society of America*, 82: 1955-1968.

Wentworth, C.K.
1922 A scale of grade and class terms for clastic sediments. *Journal of Geology*, 30: 377-392.

Wentworth, C.K., Carson, M.H., Finch, R.H.
1945 Discussion on the viscosity of lava. *Journal of Geology*, 53: 94-104.

Wentworth, C.K., Williams, H.
1932 The classification and terminology of the pyroclastic rocks. *National Research Council Bulletin 89, Report of the Commision on Sedimentation*, 15-53.

West, R.C.
1948 Cultural geography of the modern Tarascan area. *Smithsonian Institution, Washington: Institute of Social Anthropology*, No. 7, 77 p.

Weston, E.
1973 *The daybooks of Edward Weston, México*, N. Newhall, editor. Aperture Press, Millerton, New York, 214 p.

White, D.E.
1945 Parícutin's cyclic activity. *Transactions of the American Geophysical Union*, 25: 621-628.
1983 Introduction of Konrad B. Krauskopf for the V. M. Goldschmidt Medal 1982. *Geochimica et Cosmochimica Acta*, 47: 981-988.

White, G.D.
1974 *Natural hazards: Local, national, global*. Oxford Univ. Press, New York, 288 p.

Whitford, D.J., Bloomfield, K.
1976 Geochemistry of late Cenozoic volcanic rocks from the Nevado de Toluca area, México. *Carnegie Institution of Washington Year Book*, 75: 207-213.

Whitford, D.J., Nicholls, I.A.
1976 Potassium variation in lavas across the Sunda arc in Java and Bali. In: R.W. Johnson (editor), *Volcanism in Australasia*. Elsevier, Amsterdam: 63-75.

Wilcox, R.E.
1944 Rhyolite-basalt complex on Gardiner River, Yellowstone Park, Wyoming. *Bulletin of the Geological Society of America*, 55: 1047-1079.

Wilcox, R.E.
1947a **Activity of Parícutin volcano from September 18 to November 30, 1946.** *Transactions of the American Geophysical Union*, 28 (4): 567-572.

1947b **Activity of Parícutin volcano from December 1, 1946 to March 31, 1947.** *Transactions of the American Geophysical Union*, 28 (5): 725-731.

1948a **Activity of Parícutin volcano from April 1 to July 31, 1947.** *Transactions of the American Geophysical Union*, 29 (1): 69-74.

1948b **Activity of Parícutin volcano from December 1, 1947 to March 31, 1948.** *Transactions of the American Geophysical Union*, 29 (3): 355-360.

1954 **Petrology of Parícutin volcano, México.** *U. S. Geological Survey Bulletin*, 965C: 281-353.

Wilcox, R.E., Gutiérrez, C.
1948 Activity of Parícutin volcano from April 1 to July 31, 1948. *Transactions of the American Geophysical Union*, 29 (6): 877-881.

Wilcox, R.E., Shoup-Oropeza, S.
1948 Activity of Parícutin volcano from August 1 to November 30, 1947. *Transactions of the American Geophysical Union*, 29: 74-79.

Williams, H.
1945 Geologic setting of Parícutin volcano. *Transactions of the American Geophysical Union*, 26: 255-256.

1950 **Volcanoes of the Parícutin region.** *U.S. Geological Survey Bulletin*, 965B: 165-279.

Williams, H., McBirney, A.R.
1979 *Volcanology*. Freeman, Cooper and Co., San Francisco, Ca.: 397 p.

Winchell, A.N.
1951 *Elements of optical mineralogy: Part 2*, 4th edition. New York, 551 p.

Wolf, E.R.
1955 Types of Latin American peasantry: Preliminary discussion. *American Anthropologist*, 57: 452-469.

1959 *Sons of the shaking earth: The people of México and Guatemala—Their land, history and culture*. Phoenix Books, The University of Chicago Press, Chicago, 302 p.

Wood, C.A.
1978 Morphometric evolution of composite volcanoes. *Geophysical Research Letters*, 5: 437-439.

1980a Morphometric evolution of cinder cones. *Journal of Volcanology and Geothermal Research*, 7: 387-413.

1980b Morphometric analysis of cinder cone degradation. *Journal of Volcanology and Geothermal Research*, 8: 137-160.

Wright, J.
1981 The Rio Caliente ignimbrite: Analysis of a compound intra-plinian ignimbrite from a major late-Quaternary Mexican eruption. *Bulletin Volcanologique*, 44: 189-212.

Yoder, H.S. Jr.
1969 Calc-alkaline andesites: experimental data bearing on the origin of their assumed characteristics. In: A.R. McBirney (editor), *Proceedings of the Andesite Conference, Oregon Department of Geology and Mineral Industries Bulletin*, 65: 77-89.

Yokoyama, I.
1988 Seismic energy releases from volcanoes. *Bulletin of Volcanology*, 50: 1-13.

Yokoyama., I., Del la Cruz-Reyna, S.
1990 **Precursory earthquakes of the 1943 eruption of Parícutin volcano, Michoacán, México.** *Journal of Volcanology and Geothermal Research*, **44: 265-281.**

Young, F.W., Fujimoto, I.
1965 Social differentiation in Latin American communities. *Economic Development and Cultural Change*, 13: 344-352.

Young, M.
1954 The role of the extended family in a disaster. *Human Relations*, 7: 383-391.

Zies, E.G.
1946 **Temperature measurements at Parícutin volcano.** *Transactions of the American Geophysical Union*, **27: 178-180.**

Text Notes

Italicized entries identify our editorial notes. Normal upright text (including some italicized words) is used for original references or footnotes.

1. *Data on earthquakes in the Parícutin region during the 9-year eruption that were recorded by the Tacubaya station in México City are from an unpublished list kindly provided to us by Izumi Yokoyama.*

2. Nolan (1972)

3. Secretaria de la Economía Nacional (1943); Secretaria de Hacienda y Credito Publico (1940)

4. West (1948)

5. Beals et al. (1944)

6. Gutiérrez (1972)

7. Foster (1948)

8. Wolf (1959)

9. Foster (1967)

10. Rees (1961)

11. Rees (1971)

12. *malpais, meaning "badland", is a common Spanish term for the rugged surfaces of young lava flows with little soil or vegetation.*

13. Field reconnaissance of the affected area was conducted from October to December 1957, and brief visits paid in July 1965, December 1967, October 1972, and September 1978. Portions of the chapter have been adapted from Rees (1970), with additional information on vegetation, soils, agriculture, and forestry based on research conducted in the region in 1967-1968 (Rees, 1971), and in the devastated area in 1972.

14. *William Foshag was born at Sag Harbor, New York, on March 17, 1894. His undergraduate studies in chemistry (B.Sc. 1919) and graduate studies in mineralogy (Ph.D. 1923) were both made at the University of California.*

15. The United States Committee for the Study of Parícutin Volcano (1945a, b); Fuller (1945; 1947)

16. Kraus (1954); Foshag (1954a)

17. Ross (1956)

18. Schaller (1957)

19. *Jenaro González-Reyna was born in the town of Dos Estrellas on Nov. 14, 1905. He attended Macalester College in St. Paul Minnesota where he pursued a triple major in French, Chemistry, and Geology, receiving an A.B. degree in 1928. González-Reyna was awarded an honorary D.Sc. degree by Macalester College in 1949. Additional information about González-Reyna can be found in the Enciclopedia de México (1988).*

20. The authors [Foshag and González-Reyna] . . . prefer the spelling Cuiyútzuru, as used in the official archives of the municipio of San Juan Parangaricutiro, but for the sake of consistency have agreed to follow the spelling used in previous chapters of this bulletin [U.S. Geological Survey Bulletin 965].

21. Robles-Ramos (1943)

22. Flores-Covarrubias (1945a)

23. Flores-Covarrubias (1945b)

24. Shimozuru (1971)

25. *All observational reports by Wilcox, Gutiérrez, Fries, and colleagues, partially reprinted on p. 146-184, contained graphical plots of barometric pressure versus time.*

26. Flores (1945)

27. Trask (1945)

28. Singh et al. (1984); Scandone (1979)

29. Yokoyama (1988)

30. Orozco and Berra (1887)

31. *Foshag and González-Reyna (1956) reported that Juan Anguiano-Espinosa accompanied Jesús Martínez in approaching the vent site on February 20, 1943, and that he collected specimens and drew the sketch of Fig. 23. The earlier report of González-Reyna and Foshag (1947) includes the same discussion, but attributes these actions to Jesús Anguiano. During an interview with Jesús Martínez, conducted February 19, 1993, he told us that indeed Jesús Anguiano accompanied him and that Juan Anguiano-Espinosa did not join the group that went to the volcano. We have modified this account accordingly.*

32. *Nolan (1979) states that Dionisio Pulido died in Caltzontzin in 1949 (p. 195). The tourist book* Yo vi nacer un volcán *(1988), by Padre Rafael Mendoza-Valentin of San Juan Nuevo, however, states that Pulido died in Caltzontzin on August 30, 1954.*

33. Variously referred to by Pulido as a *cueva* (cave or grotto), *resumidero* (a hole or crevice, into which water disappears during the rainy season), or *agujero* (a hole).

34. In another account Pulido described the initial noise as a pop, as one hears upon opening a bottle of carbonated beverage.

35. De la O Carreño (1943)

36. The two bombs were later presented to us by the parish priest, Sr. José Caballero. One is now in the collection of the Instituto de Geología in México, the other in the U.S. National Museum [NMNH #109089]. The ash collected by Anguiano was presented to the Bishop of Zamora.

37. Perhaps *resacas*, or surges, like surf upon a shore, is meant.

38. This earthquake had its epicenter in the sea, near Acapulco, and was not directly related to the volcano. *See p. 52, where Yokoyama and De la Cruz-Reyna give the epicenter location and list the magnitude as 7.7*

39. *In their Table 2, Foshag and González-Reyna (1956) presented major element analyses of the two "early Parícutin bombs". Compared to analyses of 26 Parícutin lavas in Wilcox (1954) and McBirney et al. (1987)(see Tables 26 and 31), these analyses are relatively low in SiO_2, Na_2O, and K_2O, and relatively high in MgO and CaO. These differences, which were known to Foshag and González-Reyna, led them to conclude that the bombs represented fragments of older lavas that were accidentally ejected as the Parícutin magma fractured its way to the surface on February 20, 1943: (their p. 361) "Two ejected bombs recovered by Anguiano and Martínez during*

the initial outbreak at 10 p.m., February 20, 1943, were preserved by the parish priest, Sr. José Caballero, who generously presented them to us for study. The analyses in the following table show that these early ejected fragments are not bombs of Parícutin lava, but probably represent the old lavas underlying the Quitzocho-Cuiyúsuru valley. The topography suggests that these flows were derived from the ancient Cerro de Camiro cone".

40. Enciclopedia de México (1988); Castillo-Tejero (1950); Martínez-Portillo (1950)

41. Waitz (1943)

42. Perret (1912)

43. Trask (1943)

44. Unpublished notes of Ezequiel Ordóñez

45. Ordóñez (1943)

46. From notes of David Gallagher, U.S. Geological Survey

47. Ordóñez (1945)

48. From photographs by Lyn Storm

49. *On p. 192-193, Nolan (1979) cites Gutiérrez (1972) as reporting that the Turímbiro lava outbreak occurred on April 14, 1944.*

50. An uncovered open space surrounded by lava (Stearns and Macdonald, 1942).

51. *Many of the people involved in the salvage operations observed by Foshag and González-Reyna in early July (see Fig. 92 note) were probably from nearby Angahuan. Most of the residents of San Juan Parangaricutiro left the town on May 9 when the crucifix El Señor de Los Milagros was removed.*

52. Bullard (1947)

53. *Konrad Krauskopf was born in Madison, Wisconsin, on November 30, 1910, the son of a chemistry professor.*

54. Krauskopf (1948a,b)

55. Sharp (1962), Krauskopf (1962)

56. White (1983), Krauskopf (1983)

57. *Howel Williams was born on October 12, 1898, in Liverpool, England. He died in Berkeley, California, on Jan. 12, 1980.*

58. *May 5 (Cinco de Mayo) is a national holiday celebrating the defeat of the French in the 1862 Battle of Puebla).*

59. *Corrected from March 3 to April 3 in Segerstrom and Gutiérrez (1947: p. 564).*

60. *Kenneth Segerstrom was born in Denver, Colorado, on August 1, 1909. He died on October 4, 1992, just 4½ months before the 50th anniversary of Parícutin's birth.*

61. *Ray Wilcox was born on March 31, 1912, in Janesville, Wisconsin, and raised on a truck garden farm.*

62. Wilcox (1944)

63. *The August rainfall total at the Cuezeño station is reported as 277.7 mm (Table 2: Wilcox and Shoup-Oropeza, 1948), but rainfall data for these four specific days (August 11-14, 1947) are not given. It is likely, however, that this "undisturbed ash" had been rained upon and possibly leached of water-soluble components prior to collection for analysis.*

64. *The last portion of this paragraph, beginning with "...of the NE vents..." appeared as a corrigendum in Wilcox (1948b).*

65. *Carl Fries, Jr., was born on September 30, 1910, in Chicago, Illinois. His family then moved to Mazomanie, Wisconsin, where he graduated from high school in 1927.*

66. Salas (1966); Fries et al. (1993)

67. Departamento de Asuntos Agrarios y Colonización No. 846

68. Moore (1964); Drabek (1969)

69. Janis (1962)

70. Perret (1924)

71. Young (1954)

72. Hill and Hansen (1962)

73. Trainer et al. (1977)

74. Departamento de Asuntos Agrarios y Colonización No. 1973

75. Simpson (1952)

76. Eggler (1959)

77. Departamento de Asuntos Agrarios y Colonización No. 154

78. Rees (1970)

79. Graves et al. (1969)

80. The list of facilities and services was derived by means of Gutman scaling techniques applied by Young and Fujimoto (1965) to information contained in early 1940s ethnographic accounts of several small Mexican communities including the Michoacán towns of Quiroga (Brand, 1951), Cherán (Beals, 1946), and Tzintzuntzan (Foster, 1948). The second point of reference for these communities comes from 1967 data collected by Graves et al. (1969).

81. Secretaria de Industria y Comercio (1971)

82. Wolf (1955)

83. Hewitt and Burton (1971)

84. Nolan (1973)

85. UNESCO (1970)

86. Burton and Kates (1964)

87. Burton et al. (1978)

88. Burton et al. (1968)

89. White (1974)

90. Davis (1970)

91. Kendrick (1957)

92. Kingdon-Ward (1951)

93. Sjoberg (1962)

94. Kates (1977)

95. Nolan (1974)

96. Nolan (1975)

97. Perlmuter and Monty (1977)

98. Ernst (1908); Backer (1929); Docters van Leeuwen (1929); Dammerman (1929)

99. Griggs (1922, 1933)

100. Gadow (1930)

101. Fridriksson (1975)

102. Eggler (1959); Beaman (1960); Beaman (1961)

103. Arias-Portillo (1945)

104. Ordóñez (1947)

105. Madrigal-Sanchez (1964)

106. Eggler (1948)

107. Eggler (1963)

108. Eggler, written communication to Segerstrom, (October 1965)

109. Segerstrom (1966)

110. Poli and Giacomini (1970)

111. Beaman (1960)

112. Eduardo Limón (personal communication)

113. Miller et al. (1949)

114. Ray E. Wilcox (personal communication)

115. On higher mountains there may be distinct timber lines. On Popocatépetl, for example, which the writer [Eggler] visited, timber line begins very abruptly at around 12,000 feet [3,658 m]. Here also pine is the timber-line tree. There was no indication of krumholz and trees appeared erect and healthy.

116. I am indebted to Dr. Paul Standley and Dr. J.A. Steyermark of the Chicago Museum of Natural History for the identification of most of the plant species. Many of the specimens collected were unavoidably poor because of the effects of volcanism. As a consequence positive identifications, particularly of the oaks, which require the presence of good leaves, buds, and fruits, were often not possible.

117. *This location is not carefully described. Eggler probably refers to Cerro Santa Cruz, 1½ km ESE of San Lorenzo.*

118. Fries and Gutiérrez (1954)

119. Segerstrom (1960)

120. Watkins et al. (1971)

121. Nixon et al. (1987)

122. Mooser (1969); Demant (1978)

123. Nelson (1980)

124. Nixon (1982)

125. Luhr et al. (1985)

126. Allan et al. (1991)

127. Luhr and Carmichael (1980, 1990)

128. Robin et al. (1987, 1991)

129. Ferriz and Mahood (1986)

130. Luhr and Carmichael (1981)

131. Bloomfield (1975)

132. Martín del Pozzo (1982)

133. Cantagrel and Robin (1979)

134. Pichler and Weyl (1976), Thorpe (1977), Nelson and Gonzalez-Caver (1992)

135. Damon and Montesinos (1978)

136. Duffield et al. (1984), Luhr et al. (1984), Rose et al. (1984), Tilling et al. (1984)

137. De la Cruz-Martínez and Hernández-Zuniga (1986), De Cserna et al. (1988)

138. Truchan and Larson (1973), Couch and Woodcock (1981)

139. Atwater (1970), Larson (1972)

140. Minster and Jordan (1978)

141. Eissler and McNally (1984)

142. DeMets and Stein (1990)

143. McNally and Minster (1981)

144. Burbach et al. (1984)

145. Suarez and Singh (1986)

146. Mooser (1972)

147. Shurbet and Cebull (1984, 1986); Cebull and Shurbet (1987)

148. Johnson and Harrison (1988)

149. Nakamura (1977)

150. Graton (1945)

151. Ordóñez (1910)

152. Hasenaka and Carmichael (1986)

153. Storm (1945)

154. Hasenaka and Carmichael (1985b)

155. Colton (1937)

156. Scott and Trask (1971)

157. Wood (1980b)

158. Total annual precipitation and mean annual temperature maps, published by DETENAL, México City.

159. Ruffner (1980)

160. Murphy and Carmichael (1984)

161. Nakamura et al. (1977)

162. Wadge (1981)

163. Fedotov (1981)

164. Hildreth (1981)

165. Walker (1983)

166. Crisp (1984)

167. Luhr and Carmichael (1982)

168. Mahood (1980, 1981)

169. Wright (1981)

170. Wadge (1982)

171. Gill (1981)

172. Kuno (1960)

173. Macdonald and Katsura (1964)

174. Thorarinsson (1954)

175. Carr and Pontier (1981)

176. Chesner and Rose (1984)

177. Melson and Saenz (1984)

178. Murata and Richter (1966)

179. Allan and Carmichael (1984)

180. Nelson and Carmichael (1984)

181. Kuno (1966)

182. Dickenson and Hatherton (1967)

183. Whitford and Nicholls (1976)

184. Ui and Aramaki (1978)

185. Ferrari et al. (1990)

186. Murphy and Carmichael (1984)

187. Luhr and Carmichael (1985)

188. Ramos (1981)

189. Demant (1981)

190. Simkin et al. (1981)

191. Kear (1964)

192. Fedotov et al. (1976)

193. Mohr and Wood (1976)

194. Settle (1979)

195. Williams and McBirney (1979)

196. Nakamura (1981)

197. Mooser (1972)

198. Mooser (1975)

199. Carr et al. (1974)

200. Connor (1984)

201. Wood (1980a)

202. Porter (1972)

203. Wood (1978)

204. Ben-Avraham and Nur (1980)

205. Viramonte et al. (1971)

206. Two brief visits to Parícutin during the spring and summer of 1943, the first year of the volcano's activity, and triangulation assignments in its vicinity during the periods January-February 1945 and January-February 1946 provided opportunities to become acquainted with the local physiography. The period July-December 1946 was spent in the field gathering most of the data for the present report, and some additional field work was done in February and March 1947.

207. Williams (1945)

208. Wentworth and Williams (1932)

209. Wentworth (1922). Wentworth's terms, as used in the present paper, refer only to particle size and have no significance as to origin or mineralogical character of the ash.

210. Hernández-Velasco (1945)

221. Horton (1941)

212. Cotton (1944)

213. Segerstrom (1961)

214. J.H Beaman, written commun., July 1965. The collection from this area included a fern *Pityrogramma tartarea* (Cav.) Maxon, and the following herbs: *Aegopodon cenchroides* H. and B. ex. Willd., *Phytolacca icosandra* L., *Eupatorium malecolepis* Robins, *Gnaphalium semiamplexicaule* DC., and *Calamagrostis mcvaughii* Sohns?

215. Foshag (1950)

216. Fierstein and Nathenson (1992)

217. Hardinge et al. (1945)

218. Richard Fuller (personal communication)

219. Day and Shepherd (1913)

220. Jaggar (1917)

221. Verhoogen (1939)

222. Nichols (1939)

223. Wentworth et al. (1945)

224. White (1945)

225. Washington (1917)

226. In general outline this mechanism is similar to one suggested by Perret (1924) for Vesuvius.

227. Bryan (1969)

228. Miesch (1979)

229. Rosenfeld (1950)

230. Winchell (1951)

231. Chayes (1949)

232. Milton (1945)

233. Schmitter (1945)

234. Kuno (1950)

235. Larsen and Switzer (1939)

236. Morey and Bowen (1922); Bowen (1928)

237. Williams (1950)

238. Holmes (1931); Daly (1914, 1933)

239. J.R. Balsley (personal communication)

240. Tilley et al. (1968)

241. Cawthorn and O'Hara (1976)

242. Cox et al. (1979)

243. Osborne and Rawson (1980)

244. Yoder (1969)

245. Anderson (1974)

246. Anderson (1979)

247. Garlick (1966)

248. Taylor (1968)

249. Taylor (1977)

250. Matsuhisa (1979)

251. Anderson et al. (1971)

252. Taylor and Silver (1978)

253. Criss and Taylor (1983)

254. Masi et al. (1981)

255. Moorbath et al. (1978)

256. Verma (1983)

257. Whitford and Bloomfield (1976)

258. Hawkesworth (1982)

259. Reid (1984)

260. McBirney et al. (1985)

261. Nilson et al. (1985)

262. Blake (1981)

263. Koyaguchi (1985)

264. Blake and Ivy (1986)

265. Tilley et al. (1967)

266. *FP-16-52 erupted in February 1952. See whole-rock chemical analyses by Wilcox (1954) and McBirney et al. (1987) in Tables 26, 31, and 34. A point-counted mode is given in Table 25 and a photomicrograph is given in Fig. 190d.*

267. *W-47-30 erupted in November 1947. See whole-rock chemical analyses by Wilcox (1954) and McBirney et al. (1987) in Tables 26, 31, and 34. A point-counted mode is given in Table 25.*

268. Piwinskii (1968)

269. Green and Ringwood (1966)

270. Millhollen (1971)

271. Holloway and Burnham (1972)

272. Eggler (1972b)

273. Wadge (1978)

274. González-Ferrán et al. (1989)

275. Fedotov and Markhinin (1983); Fedotov et al. (1991)

276. Bullard (1984)

277. Minikami et al. (1951)

278. Ordóñez (1906)

279. Segerstrom (1950)

280. von Humboldt (1810)

281. Mooser (1958)

282. Orozco y Berra (1854)

283. Greene (1982)

284. Roobol and Smith (1975); Fisher and Heiken (1982)

285. Green (1971)

286. Tatsumi et al. (1983)

287. Sato (1977)

288. Rosi and Santacroce (1984)

289. Phillips (1869)

290. Horner (1847)

291. Lyell (1875)

292. Luhr et al. (1984)

293. Bernard et al. (1991); Pallister et al. (1992)

294. Stanley (1919)

295. Stanley (1923)

296. Lowenstein (1982) states that the first eruption actually took place on 18 September 1943.

297. Rutten (1927)

298. *Lowenstein (1982) states that after the 23 July 1944 eruption a single large crater was occupied by a 200-m-wide lake, and ". . . post-war aerial photographs show an extensive and sharply defined area surrounding this crater in which about 30 km^2 of forest had been levelled, indicating that powerful nuees ardentes must have been expelled from the crater to about 4 km NE during the final stages of the eruption . . . . A recent topographic map reveals a low-profile cone almost 150 m high, which must have resulted from strong activity in the closing stages of the eruptions."*

299. Johannsen (1937)

300. *Although garnet has been reported from some volcanic rocks, its occurrence in the Waiowa pumices is nonetheless remarkable. The reported absence of Fe$_2$O$_3$ is probably an analytical error.*

301. Adelman (1976)

302. Weston (1973)

303. Orozco (1962)

Notes on Figures, Tables, and Plates

Figures

Figures not listed here are original to this book.

Fig. 1 - Fig. 1 from Atl (1950).

Fig. 2 - Photo by Arno Brehme. Plate 39A from Foshag and González-Reyna (1956) and File No. 189-PV-89 in the U.S. National Archives.

Fig. 3 - Photo by Mary St. Albans and reprinted from Fig. 2 of Atl (1950).

Fig. 4 - Modified from Fig. 6 of Fries (1953).

Fig. 5 - Photo by Tad Nichols, July 29, 1945.

Fig. 7 - According to legend, *El Señor de Los Milagros* was acquired by Don Nicolás Moricho, founder and resident of San Juan Parangaricutiro, towards the end of the 16th century. It was given to him by a "mysterious" statue seller who would not reveal his name, place of origin, or destination. The statue seller asked nothing in return for the statue, and refused to accept any food during his stay. An Augustinian friar from the nearby town of Zirosto heard of these events and told the Moricho family to prepare a chapel for the statue, because Jesus Christ would perform miracles through it. From that time the statue was called the Lord of the Miracles. Several Indians who were asked to follow the statue seller, reported that they lost the stranger at the northern edge of town. The townspeople began to believe that the statue seller was in fact an heavenly envoy . . . .

This story was drawn from the tourist book San Juan Nuevo, Michoacán: Sus paisajes y folklore. Photo by Richard Barthelemy, no. 110-6-5, Benson Latin American Collection, University of Texas, Austin.

Fig. 8 - Photo by Richard Barthelemy, no. 521-6-3, Benson Latin American Collection, University of Texas, Austin.

Fig. 9 - Foshag Collection of the Smithsonian Archives, Box 11.

Fig. 10 - Photo by Frederick Pough.

Fig. 11 - Photo 2 - 4008, 2-L28, 116 from Defense Intelligence Agency.

Fig. 12 - Airphoto composite from National Archives, Record Group 189-PV, no. 1.

Fig. 13 - Airphoto composite, of unknown origin, loaned to us by Kenneth Segerstrom. Topographic map modified from Plate 12 in Foshag and González-Reyna (1956).

Fig. 14 - Photo by Ken Segerstrom in June 1946.

Fig. 15 - Fig. 1 from Yokoyama and De la Cruz-Reyna (1990).

Fig. 16 - Fig. 4 from Yokoyama and De la Cruz-Reyna (1990).

Fig. 17 - Modified from Fig. 5 of Yokoyama and De la Cruz-Reyna (1990).

Fig. 18 - Upper photo: Plate 16A from Foshag and González-Reyna (1956) and File No. 189-PV-3 in the U.S. National Archives. Lower photo: Plate 16B from Foshag and González-Reyna (1956) and File No. 189-PV-2 in the U.S. National Archives.

Fig. 19 - Foshag Collection of the Smithsonian Archives, Box 11.

Fig. 20 - Photo by Richard Barthelemy.

Fig. 21 - Foshag Collection of the Smithsonian Archives, Box 9.

Fig. 22 - Modified from Fig. 110 of Foshag and González-Reyna (1956).

Fig. 23 - Modified from Fig. 111 of Foshag and González-Reyna (1956).

Fig. 24 - Foshag Collection of the Smithsonian Archives, Box 9.

Fig. 25 - Photo by Salvador Ceja. Plate 17A from Foshag and González-Reyna (1956) and File No. 189-PV-4 in the U.S. National Archives.

Fig. 26 - Photo from the NE by Dr. J. Trinidad. File No. 189-PV-5 in the U.S. National Archives.

Fig. 27 - Photo by Rufus Morrow. Plate 17B from Foshag and González-Reyna (1956) and File No. 189-PV-6 in the U.S. National Archives.

Fig. 28 - Photo by Ramiro Robles-Ramos. Plate 18B from Foshag and González-Reyna (1956) and File No. 189-PV-7 in the U.S. National Archives.

Fig. 29 - Photo by Ezequiel Ordóñez. Plate 18A from Foshag and González-Reyna (1956) and File No. 189-PV-8 in the U.S. National Archives.

Fig. 30 - Photo by Ezequiel Ordóñez. File No. 189-PV-9 in the U.S. National Archives.

Fig. 31 - Photo by Ezequiel Ordóñez. File No. 189-PV-10 in the U.S. National Archives.

Fig. 32 - Photo by Rafael García. Plate 23B from Foshag and González-Reyna (1956) and File No. 189-PV-33 in the U.S. National Archives.

Fig. 33 - Photo by Instituto de Geología. Plate 19A from Foshag and González-Reyna (1956) and File No. 189-PV-17 in the U.S. National Archives.

Fig. 34 - Photo by Ezequiel Ordóñez. Plate 19B from Foshag and González-Reyna (1956) and File No. 189-PV-20 in the U.S. National Archives.

Fig. 35 - Photo by Ezequiel Ordóñez. Plate 20A from Foshag and González-Reyna (1956) and File No. 189-PV-22 in the U.S. National Archives.

Fig. 36 - Modified version of map published in Foshag and González-Reyna (1956: Plate 15).

Fig. 37 - Photo by William Foshag. Plate 20B from Foshag and González-Reyna (1956) and File No. 189-PV-25 in the U.S. National Archives.

Fig. 38 - Photo by William Foshag. Plate 21A from Foshag and González-Reyna (1956) and File No. 189-PV-26 in the U.S. National Archives.

Fig. 39 - Photo by Carl Graton. Plate 22A from Foshag and González-Reyna (1956) and File No. 189-PV-31 in the U.S. National Archives.

Fig. 40 - Photo by William Foshag. Plate 22B from Foshag and González-Reyna (1956) and File No. 189-PV-32 in the U.S. National Archives.

Fig. 41 - Photo by William Foshag. Plate 23A from Foshag and González-Reyna (1956) and File No. 189-PV-36 in the U.S. National Archives.

Fig. 42 - Fig. 112 from Foshag and González-Reyna (1956).

Fig. 43 - Fig. 113 from Foshag and González-Reyna (1956).

Fig. 44 - Photo by William Foshag. Plate 29A from Foshag and González-Reyna (1956) and File No. 189-PV-59 in the U.S. National Archives.

Fig. 45 - Photo by William Foshag. File No. 189-PV-39 in the U.S. National Archives.

Fig. 46 - Photo by William Foshag. Plate 24A from Foshag and González-Reyna (1956) and File No. 189-PV-42 in the U.S. National Archives.

Fig. 47 - Fig. 118 from Foshag and González-Reyna (1956).

Fig. 48 - Fig. 119 from Foshag and González-Reyna (1956).

Fig. 49 - Photo by Arno Brehme. Plate 25A from Foshag and González-Reyna (1956) and File No. 189-PV-44 in the U.S. National Archives.

Fig. 50 - Photo by Ezequiel Ordóñez. Plate 26A from Foshag and González-Reyna (1956) and File No. 189-PV-51 in the U.S. National Archives.

Fig. 51 - Photo by Carl Fries, Jr. Foshag Collection of the Smithsonian Archives, Box 8.

Fig. 52 - Photo by Ezequiel Ordóñez. Plate 24B from Foshag and González-Reyna (1956) and File No. 189-PV-45 in the U.S. National Archives.

Fig. 53 - Photo by Ezequiel Ordóñez. Plate 30A from Foshag and González-Reyna (1956) and File No. 189-PV-62 in the U.S. National Archives.

Fig. 54 - Fig. 120 from Foshag and González-Reyna (1956).

Fig. 55 - Photo by Ezequiel Ordóñez. Plate 29B from Foshag and González-Reyna (1956) and File No. 189-PV-61 in the U.S. National Archives.

Fig. 56 - Photo by William Foshag. Plate 42B from Foshag and González-Reyna (1956) and File No. 189-PV-112 in the U.S. National Archives.

Fig. 57 - Photo by William Foshag. Plate 28A from Foshag and González-Reyna (1956) and File No. 189-PV-48 in the U.S. National Archives.

Fig. 58 - Photo by William Foshag. Plate 26B from Foshag and González-Reyna (1956) and File No. 189-PV-49 in the U.S. National Archives.

Fig. 59 - Photo by William Foshag. Plate 27A from Foshag and González-Reyna (1956) and File No. 189-PV-53 in the U.S. National Archives.

Fig. 60 - Photo by William Foshag. Plate 27B from Foshag and González-Reyna (1956) and File No. 189-PV-54 in the U.S. National Archives.

Fig. 61 - Photo by William Foshag. Plate 28B from Foshag and González-Reyna (1956) and File No. 189-PV-55 in the U.S. National Archives.

Fig. 62 - Fig. 121 from Foshag and González-Reyna (1956).

Fig. 63 - Photo by William Foshag. Plate 30B from Foshag and González-Reyna (1956) and File No. 189-PV-63 in the U.S. National Archives.

Fig. 64 - Photo by Arno Brehme. Plate 31B from Foshag and González-Reyna (1956) and File No. 189-PV-66 in the U.S. National Archives.

Fig. 65 - Photo by Lyn Storm. Plate 32A from Foshag and González-Reyna (1956) and File No. 189-PV-67 in the U.S. National Archives.

Fig. 66 - Photo by Lyn Storm using infrared film. Plate 32B from Foshag and González-Reyna (1956) [published caption gives date of October 21, which is inconsistent with text on their p. 434] and File No. 189-PV-68 in the U.S. National Archives [this caption also gives the date as October 21].

Fig. 67 - Photo by William Foshag. Plate 33B from Foshag and González-Reyna (1956) and File No. 189-PV-74 in the U.S. National Archives.

Fig. 68 - Photo by William Foshag. Plate 33A from Foshag and González-Reyna (1956) and File No. 189-PV-71 in the U.S. National Archives.

Fig. 69 - Photo by Ezequiel Ordóñez. File No. 189-PV-73 in the U.S. National Archives.

Fig. 70 - Photo by William Foshag. Plate 43B from Foshag and González-Reyna (1956) and File No. 189-PV-113 in the U.S. National Archives.

Fig. 71 - Photo by William Foshag. Plate 35A from Foshag and González-Reyna (1956) and File No. 189-PV-76 in the U.S. National Archives.

Fig. 72 - Photo by William Foshag. Plate 35B from Foshag and González-Reyna (1956) and File No. 189-PV-77 in the U.S. National Archives.

Fig. 73 - Photo by William Foshag. Plate 34B from Foshag and González-Reyna (1956) and File No. 189-PV-75 in the U.S. National Archives.

Fig. 74 - Fig. 123 from Foshag and González-Reyna (1956).

Fig. 75 - Photo by Ezequiel Ordóñez. Plate 37B from Foshag and González-Reyna (1956) and File No. 189-PV-92 in the U.S. National Archives.

Fig. 76 - Photo by William Foshag. Plate 36B from Foshag and González-Reyna (1956) and File No. 189-PV-81 in the U.S. National Archives.

Fig. 77 - Photo by William Foshag. Plate 37A from Foshag and González-Reyna (1956) and File No. 189-PV-85 in the U.S. National Archives.

Fig. 78 - Photo by William Foshag. Plate 36A from Foshag and González-Reyna (1956) and File No. 189-PV-80 in the U.S. National Archives.

Fig. 79 - Photo by William Foshag. Plate 38A from Foshag and González-Reyna (1956) and File No. 189-PV-88 in the U.S. National Archives.

Fig. 80 - Photo by William Foshag. File No. 189-PV-94 in the U.S. National Archives.

Fig. 81 - Photo by Ward Smith. Foshag Collection of the Smithsonian Archives, Box 10.

Fig. 82 - Photo by William Foshag. Plate 40A from Foshag and González-Reyna (1956) and File No. 189-PV-97 in the U.S. National Archives.

Fig. 83 - Photo by Arno Brehme. Foshag Collection of the Smithsonian Archives, Box 8.

Fig. 84 - Photo by William Foshag. Plate 40B from Foshag and González-Reyna (1956) and File No. 189-PV-98 in the U.S. National Archives.

Fig. 85 - Photo by William Foshag. Plate 44B from Foshag and González-Reyna (1956) and File No. 189-PV-114 in the U.S. National Archives.

Fig. 86 - Photo by Otto Fisher. Plate 44A from Foshag and González-Reyna (1956) and File No. 189-PV-125 in the U.S. National Archives.

Fig. 87 - Photo by William Foshag. Plate 42A from Foshag and González-Reyna (1956) and File No. 189-PV-108 in the U.S. National Archives.

Fig. 88 - Photo by William Foshag. File No. 189-PV-99 in the U.S. National Archives.

Fig. 89 - Photo by William Foshag. Plate 41A from Foshag and González-Reyna (1956) and File No. 189-PV-100 in the U.S. National Archives.

Fig. 90 - Photo by William Foshag. File No. 189-PV-101 in the U.S. National Archives.

Fig. 91 - Photo by William Foshag. File No. 189-PV-102 in the U.S. National Archives.

Fig. 92 - Sra. Anna María Ortíz-Hernández, now a resident of San Juan Nuevo, was 17 years old and living in San Juan Parangaricutiro at the time of the evacuation. Based on the style of trousers worn by the men in this photo, she was certain that they were from the neighboring town of Angahuan, and not residents of San Juan Parangaricutiro. Photo by William Foshag. File No. 189-PV-103 in the U.S. National Archives.

Fig. 93 - Photo by Ezequiel Ordóñez. File No. 189-PV-109 in the U.S. National Archives.

Fig. 94 - Aerial photo by Frank Zierer. Plate 45B from Foshag and González-Reyna (1956) and File No. 189-PV-120 in the U.S. National Archives.

Fig. 95 - Photo by Otto Fisher. File No. 189-PV-121 in the U.S. National Archives.

Fig. 96 - Aerial photo by Otto Fisher. Plate 46A from Foshag and González-Reyna (1956) and File No. 189-PV-122 in the U.S. National Archives.

Fig. 97 - Photo by William Foshag. Plate 49A from Foshag and González-Reyna (1956) and File No. 189-PV-132 in the U.S. National Archives.

Fig. 98 - Photo by William Foshag. Plate 49B from Foshag and González-Reyna (1956) and File No. 189-PV-146 in the U.S. National Archives.

Fig. 99 - Aerial photo by William Foshag. Plate 51 from Foshag and González-Reyna (1956) and File No. 189-PV-151 in the U.S. National Archives.

Fig. 100 - Copied from original in the Parícutin museum of Celedonio Gutiérrez, San Juan Nuevo.

Fig. 101 - Foshag Collection of the Smithsonian Archives, Box 8.

Fig. 102 - Fig. 1 from Krauskopf and Williams (1946).

Fig. 103 - Fig. 2 from Krauskopf and Williams (1946).

Fig. 104 - Fig. 3 from Krauskopf and Williams (1946).

Fig. 105 - Fig. 2 from Krauskopf (1948a).

Fig. 106 - Fig. 4 from Segerstrom and Gutiérrez (1947).

Fig. 107 - Fig. 2 from Segerstrom and Gutiérrez (1947).

Fig. 108 - Fig. 3 from Segerstrom and Gutiérrez (1947).

Fig. 109 - Wilcox Collection, U.S. Geological Survey Photo Library, 313ct.

Fig. 110 - Fig. 1 from Wilcox (1947a).

Fig. 111 - Fig. 2 from Wilcox (1947a).

Fig. 112 - Fig. 3 from Wilcox (1947a).

Fig. 113 - Fig. 4 from Wilcox (1947a).

Fig. 114 - Fig. 2 from Wilcox (1947b).

Fig. 115 - Fig. 3 from Wilcox (1947b).

Fig. 116 - Fig. 2 from Wilcox (1948a).

Fig. 117 - Fig. 2 from Wilcox and Shoup-Oropeza (1948).

Fig. 118 - Fig. 2 from Wilcox (1948b).

Fig. 119 - Fig. 2 from Wilcox and Gutiérrez (1948).

Fig. 120 - Photo by Frederick Pough.

Fig. 121 - Fig. 7 from Fries and Gutiérrez (1950a).

Fig. 122 - Fig. 8 from Fries and Gutiérrez (1950a).

Fig. 123 - Fig. 6 from Fries and Gutiérrez (1950b).

Fig. 124 - Fig. 5 from Fries and Gutiérrez (1951a).

Fig. 125 - Fig. 4 from Fries and Gutiérrez (1951b).

Fig. 126 - Fig. 8 from Fries and Gutiérrez (1952a).

Fig. 127 - Fig. 6 from Fries and Gutiérrez (1952b).

Fig. 128 - Fig. 2 from Fries and Gutiérrez (1954).

Fig. 129 - Photo by Ing. Ezequiel Ordóñez. Plate 4, Figure 1 from González-Reyna and Foshag (1947).

Fig. 130 - Modified from Fig. 10.3 of Nolan (1979).

Fig. 131 - Photo by Excelsior Daily. Foshag Collection of the Smithsonian Archives, Box 11.

Fig. 132 - Modified from Fig. 10.11 of Nolan (1979).

Fig. 133 - Fig. 10.12 from Nolan (1979).

Fig. 134 - Fig. 9.2 from Rees (1979).

Fig. 135 - Fig. 9.4 from Rees (1979).

Fig. 136 - Fig. 9.5 from Rees (1979).

Fig. 137 - Fig. 9.6 from Rees (1979).

Fig. 138 - Fig. 9.8 from Rees (1979).

Fig. 139 - Photo by Tad Nichols.

Fig. 141 - Photo by the Compañia Mexicana Aerofoto, 1934. Fig. 79 from Williams (1950).

Fig. 142 - Photo by the Compañia Mexicana Aerofoto, 1934. Fig. 81 from Williams (1950).

Fig. 143 - Photo by the Compañia Mexicana Aerofoto, 1934. Fig. 82 from Williams (1950).

Fig. 144 - Photo by the Compañia Mexicana Aerofoto, 1934. Fig. 84 from Williams (1950).

Fig. 145 - Fig. 2 from Hasenaka and Carmichael (1985a).

Fig. 146 - Fig. 4 from Hasenaka and Carmichael (1985a).

Fig. 147 - Fig. 7 from Hasenaka and Carmichael (1985a).

Fig. 148 - Fig. 8 from Hasenaka and Carmichael (1985a).

Fig. 149 - Fig. 10 from Hasenaka and Carmichael (1985a).

Fig. 150 - Airphotos from Foshag Collection of the Smithsonian Archives, Box 10.

Fig. 151 - Airphotos from Foshag Collection of the Smithsonian Archives, Box 10.

Fig. 152 - Portions of 1:50,000 airphotos (#21A R-534 6-9 and 21A R-534 7-9) taken in the years 1971-75 and distributed by the Mexican map agency DETENAL.

Fig. 153 - Portions of 1:50,000 airphotos (#21A R-528 7-16 and 21A R-528 8-16) taken in the years 1971-75 and distributed by the Mexican map agency DETENAL.

Fig. 154 - Portions of 1:50,000 airphotos (#21A R-538 9-10 and 21A R-538 10-10) taken in the years 1971-75 and distributed by the Mexican map agency DETENAL.

Fig. 155 - Portions of 1:50,000 airphotos (#21A R-538 16-5 and 21A R-538 17-5) taken in the years 1971-75 and distributed by the Mexican map agency DETENAL.

Fig. 156 - Portions of 1:50,000 airphotos (#21A R-524 6-6 and 21A R-524 7-6) taken in the years 1971-75 and distributed by the Mexican map agency DETENAL.

Fig. 157 - Portions of 1:50,000 airphotos (#21A R-523 18-4 and 21A R-523 19-4) taken in the years 1971-75 and distributed by the Mexican map agency DETENAL.

Fig. 158 - Portions of 1:50,000 airphotos (#21A R-523 18-4 and 21A R-523 19-4) taken in the years 1971-75 and distributed by the Mexican map agency DETENAL.

Fig. 159 - Fig. 2 from Hasenaka and Carmichael (1987).

Fig. 160 - Fig. 3 from Hasenaka and Carmichael (1987).

Fig. 161 - Fig. 6 from Hasenaka and Carmichael (1987).

Fig. 162 - Fig. 7 from Hasenaka and Carmichael (1987).

Fig. 163 - Fig. 8 from Hasenaka and Carmichael (1987).

Fig. 164 - Fig. 2 from Ban et al. (1992).

Fig. 165 - Fig. 3 from Ban et al. (1992).

Fig. 166 - Fig. 2 from Connor (1987).

Fig. 167 - Fig. 3 from Connor (1987).

Fig. 168 - Fig. 4 from Connor (1987).

Fig. 169 - Fig. 8 from Connor (1987).

Fig. 170 - Fig. 9 from Connor (1987).

Fig. 171 - Fig. 7 from Segerstrom (1950). U.S. Geological Survey Photo Library, Segerstrom Collection, 175.

Fig. 172 - Fig. 8 from Segerstrom (1950). U.S. Geological Survey Photo Library, Segerstrom Collection, 637.

Fig. 173 - Fig. 19 from Segerstrom (1950). U.S. Geological Survey Photo Library, Segerstrom Collection, 223.

Fig. 174 - Fig. 21 from Segerstrom (1950). U.S. Geological Survey Photo Library, Segerstrom Collection, 218.

Fig. 175 - Fig. 29 from Segerstrom (1950). U.S. Geological Survey Photo Library, Segerstrom Collection, 253.

Fig. 176 - U.S. Geological Survey Photo Library, Segerstrom Collection, 132.

Fig. 177 - Fig. 39 from Segerstrom (1950). U.S. Geological Survey Photo Library, Segerstrom Collection, 151.

Fig. 178 - Fig. 41 from Segerstrom (1950). U.S. Geological Survey Photo Library, Segerstrom Collection, 84.

Fig. 179 - Plate 4 from Segerstrom (1950).

Fig. 180 - Fig. 66 from Segerstrom (1950). U.S. Geological Survey Photo Library, Segerstrom Collection, 163.

Fig. 181 - Fig. 1 from Segerstrom (1960). U.S. Geological Survey Photo Library, Segerstrom Collection, 644.

Fig. 182 - Plate 1 from Segerstrom (1960).

Fig. 183 - Fig. 2 from Segerstrom (1966). U.S. Geological Survey Photo Library, Segerstrom Collection, 533 and 534.

Fig. 184 - Top and middle photos: Fig. 3 from Segerstrom (1966) and U.S. Geological Survey Photo Library, Segerstrom Collection, 537 and 538. Bottom photo by Katia Krafft, Smithsonian Global Volcanism Program Archives, Krafft Collection, 4705.

Fig. 185 - Fig. 8 from Segerstrom (1966). U.S. Geological Survey Photo Library, Segerstrom Collection, 545 and 546.

Fig. 186 - Modified from Fig. 6 of Fries (1953).

Fig. 187 - Fig. 13 from Krauskopf (1948a).

Fig. 188 - Fig. 98 from Wilcox (1954).

Fig. 189 - Fig. 99 from Wilcox (1954).

Fig. 191 - Fig. 100 from Wilcox (1954).

Fig. 194 - Fig. 102 from Wilcox (1954).

Fig. 195 - Fig. 103 from Wilcox (1954).

Fig. 196 - Fig. 104 from Wilcox (1954).

Fig. 197 - Fig. 106 from Wilcox (1954).

Fig. 198 - Fig. 107 from Wilcox (1954).

Fig. 199 - Fig. 2 from McBirney et al. (1987).

Fig. 200 - Fig. 3 from McBirney et al. (1987).

Fig. 201 - Fig. 4 from McBirney et al. (1987).

Fig. 202 - Fig. 5 from McBirney et al. (1987).

Fig. 203 - Fig. 6 from McBirney et al. (1987).

Fig. 204 - Fig. 7 from McBirney et al. (1987).

Fig. 205 - Fig. 8 from McBirney et al. (1987).

Fig. 206 - Fig. 9 from McBirney et al. (1987).

Fig. 207 - Fig. 12 from McBirney et al. (1987).

Fig. 208 - Fig. 13 from McBirney et al. (1987).

Fig. 209 - Fig. 15 from McBirney et al. (1987).

Fig. 210 - Fig. 1 from Eggler (1972a).

Fig. 211 - Fig. 2 from Eggler (1972a).

Fig. 212 - Fig. 3 from Eggler (1972a).

Fig. 213 - Fig. 4 from Eggler (1972a).

Fig. 214 - Modified from Fig. 1 of Luhr and Carmichael (1985).

Fig. 216 - Fig. 26 from Bullard (1984).

Fig. 217 - Geology after E.R. Stanley (1923). Fig. 1 from Baker (1946).

Fig. 218 - Fig. 2 from Baker (1946).

Fig. 219 - Photo by Tad Nichols.

Fig. 220 - Foshag Collection of Smithsonian Archives, Box 8.

Fig. 221 - Photo by Navarro, and kindly loaned by Mrs. Verónica Loera y Chávez.

Tables

Table 1 - Modified from Table 1 of Wilcox (1948a).

Table 2 - Table 3 from Wilcox (1948a).

Table 3 - Table 4 from Fries and Gutiérrez (1951a).

Table 4 - Table 5 from Fries and Gutiérrez (1951a).

Table 5 - Table 4 from Fries and Gutiérrez (1952a).

Table 6 - Table 2 from Fries and Gutiérrez (1954).

Table 7 - Table 3 from Fries and Gutiérrez (1954).

Table 8 - Table 10.1 from Nolan (1979).

Table 9 - Table 10.2 from Nolan (1979).

Table 10 - Table 10.3 from Nolan (1979).

Table 11 - Table 9.2 from Rees (1979).

Table 12 - Table 9.3 from Rees (1979).

Table 13 - Table I from Eggler (1948).

Table 14 - Table II from Eggler (1948).

Table 15 - Table VII from Eggler (1963).

Table 16 - Table VIII from Eggler (1963).

Table 17 - Table 4 from Hasenaka and Carmichael (1985a).

Table 18 - Table 2 from Hasenaka and Carmichael (1985a).

Table 19 - Table 1 from Ban et al. (1992).

Table 20 - Table 1 from Segerstrom (1950).

Table 21 - Table 1 from Segerstrom (1950).

Table 22 - Table 4 from Segerstrom (1950).

Table 23 - Table 6 from Fries (1953).

Table 24 - Modified from Table 7 of Fries (1953).

Table 25 - Table 1 from Wilcox (1954).

Table 26 - Table 2 from Wilcox (1954).

Table 27 - Table 4 from Wilcox (1954).

Table 28 - Table 5 from Wilcox (1954).

Table 29 - Table 6 from Wilcox (1954).

Table 30 - Table 3 from Wilcox (1954).

Table 31 - Table 1 from McBirney et al. (1987).

Table 32 - Table 2a from McBirney et al. (1987).

Table 33 - Table 2c from McBirney et al. (1987).

Table 34 - Table 3 from McBirney et al. (1987).

Table 35 - Portion of Table 16 from Tilley et al. (1968).

Plates

Plate 1A. Photo by Instituto de Geología. From the Smithsonian's Global Volcanism Program Archives.

Plate 1B. Photo by Instituto de Geología. From the Smithsonian's Global Volcanism Program Archives.

Plate 2A. From the Smithsonian's Global Volcanism Program Archives.

Plate 2B. From the Smithsonian's Global Volcanism Program Archives. Photo probably taken on May 27, 1948.

Plate 3A. From American Museum of Natural History slide set "A Volcano is Born", 18

Plate 3B. Photo from U.S. Geological Survey Photo Library, Segerstrom Collection, 233ct.

Plate 4A. Photo from U.S. Geological Survey Photo Library, Segerstrom Collection, 164c

Plate 4B. Photo from U.S. Geological Survey Photo Library, Segerstrom Collection, 118ct.

Plate 4C. Probably taken in 1944. Photo from U.S. Geological Survey Photo Library, Wilcox Collection, 392ct.

Plate 5A. From the Smithsonian's Global Volcanism Program Archives (Howel Williams collections), 1945. Photographer and direction not known.

Plate 5B. From the Smithsonian's Global Volcanism Program Archives (Howel Williams collections). Photographer not known.

Plate 5C. Photo from U.S. Geological Survey Photo Library, Segerstrom Collection, 225ct.

Plate 6A. Photo from Smithsonian's Global Volcanism Program Archives, Krafft Collection, 4693.

Plate 6B. Taken July 8, 1947, from the NW. Photo from U.S. Geological Survey Photo Library, Wilcox Collection, 84.

Plate 6C. Photo from Smithsonian's Global Volcanism Program Archives, Krafft Collection, 4683.

Plate 7A. Fig. 71 from Atl (1950).

Plate 7B. Fig. 7 from Atl (1950).

Plate 7C. Three Mexican postage stamps featuring the work of Dr. Atl. Loaned to us by Richard Stoiber and Winston Crausaz.

Plate 8A. Photo from Smithsonian's Global Volcanism Program Archives, Krafft Collection, 4657.

Plate 8B. Photo by Jim Luhr from 4 km to the NW in February 1982.

Credits

Here we list credit information for copyrighted articles from which we have reprinted material. The majority of the book, however, was taken from public-domain articles published by the U.S. Geological Survey: Foshag and González-Reyna (1956), Segerstrom (1950, 1960, 1966), Wilcox (1954), and Williams (1950).

Atl, Dr. (1950) *¿Como nace y crece un volcán?: El Parícutin, México.* Editorial Stylo, México City, 152 p. Copyright © 1950 by Editorial Stylo.

Baker G. (1946) Preliminary note on volcanic eruptions in the Goropu Mountains, Southeastern Papua, during the period December, 1943, to August, 1944. *Journal of Geology*, 54: 19-31. Copyright © 1946 by University of Chicago Press. Reprinted with permission.

Ban M., Hasenaka T., Delgado-Granados H., and Takaoka N. (1992) K-Ar ages of lavas from shield volcanoes in the Michoacán-Guanajuato Volcanic Field, México. *Geofísica Internacional*, 31 (4): 467-473. Copyright © 1992 by Instituto de Geofísica, UNAM, México. Reprinted with permission.

Bullard F.M. (1947) Studies on Parícutin volcano, Michoacán, México. *Geological Society of America, Bulletin* 58: 433-450. Reprinted with permission of author.

Bullard F.M. (1984) *Volcanoes of the Earth.* Austin, Texas, University of Texas Press, Second revised edition, 629 p. Copyright © 1984 by the University of Texas Press. Reprinted with permission.

Burt W.H. (1961) Some effects of Volcán Parícutin on vertebrates. *Occasional Papers of the Museum of Zoology*, 620, 24 p. University of Michigan, Ann Arbor, Michigan. Reprinted with permission.

Connor C.B. (1987) Structure of the Michoacán-Guanajuato Volcanic Field, México, *Journal of Volcanology and Geothermal Research*, 33: 191-200. Copyright © 1987 by Elsevier Science Publishers, B.V. Reprinted with permission.

Connor C.B. (1990) Cinder cone clustering in the Trans-Mexican Volcanic Belt: Implications for structural and petrologic models. *Journal of Geophysical Research*, 95, B12: 19395-19405. Copyright © 1990 by the American Geophysical Union. Reprinted with permission.

Crausaz, W. (1985) Dr. Atl: Pioneer Mexican Volcanologist. *Geological Society of America Centennial Special*, 1: 251-256. Reprinted with permission of author.

Dorf, E. (1945) Observations on the preservation of plants in the Parícutin area. *Transactions of the American Geophysical Union*, 26 (2): 257-260. Copyright © 1945 by the American Geophysical Union. Reprinted with permission.

Eggler D.H. (1972a) Water-saturated and undersaturated melting relations in a Parícutin andesite and an estimate of water content in the natural magma. *Contributions to Mineralogy and Petrology*, 34: 261-271. Copyright © 1972 by Springer-Verlag. Reprinted with permission.

Eggler W.A. (1948) Plant communities in the vicinity of the volcano El Parícutin, México, after two and a half years of eruption, *Ecology*, 29: 415-436. Copyright © 1948 by Ecological Society of America. Reprinted with permission.

Eggler W.A. (1963) Plant life of Parícutin volcano, México, eight years after activity ceased. *American Midland Nat-*

uralist, 69: 38-68. Copyright © 1963 by University of Chicago Press. Reprinted with permission.

Fries C. Jr. (1953) Volumes and weights of pyroclastic material, lava, and water erupted by Parícutin volcano, Michoacán, México. *Eos, Transactions of the American Geophysical Union*, 34 (4): 603-616. Copyright © 1953 by the American Geophysical Union. Reprinted with permission.

Fries C. Jr. and Gutiérrez C. (1950a) Activity of Parícutin volcano from August 1, 1948 to June 30, 1949. *Eos, Transactions of the American Geophysical Union*, 31 (3): 406-418. Copyright © 1950 by the American Geophysical Union. Reprinted with permission.

Fries C. Jr. and Gutiérrez C. (1950b) Activity of Parícutin volcano from July 1 to December 31, 1949. *Eos, Transactions of the American Geophysical Union*, 31 (5): 732-740. Copyright © 1950 by the American Geophysical Union. Reprinted with permission.

Fries C. Jr. and Gutiérrez C. (1951a) Activity of Parícutin volcano from January 1 to June 30, 1950. *Eos, Transactions of the American Geophysical Union*, 32 (2): 212-221. Copyright © 1951 by the American Geophysical Union. Reprinted with permission.

Fries C. Jr. and Gutiérrez C. (1951b) Activity of Parícutin volcano from July 1 to December 31, 1950. *Eos, Transactions of the American Geophysical Union*, 32 (4): 572-581. Copyright © 1951 by the American Geophysical Union. Reprinted with permission.

Fries C. Jr. and Gutiérrez C. (1952a) Activity of Parícutin volcano from January 1 to June 30, 1951. *Eos, Transactions of the American Geophysical Union*, 33 (1): 91-100. Copyright © 1952 by the American Geophysical Union. Reprinted with permission.

Fries C. Jr. and Gutiérrez C. (1952b) Activity of Parícutin volcano from July 1 to December 31, 1951. *Eos, Transactions of the American Geophysical Union*, 33 (5): 725-733. Copyright © 1952 by the American Geophysical Union. Reprinted with permission.

Fries C. Jr. and Gutiérrez C. (1954) Activity of Parícutin volcano during the year 1952. *Eos, Transactions of the American Geophysical Union*, 35 (3): 486-494. Copyright © 1954 by the American Geophysical Union. Reprinted with permission.

Gadow H. (1930) *Jorullo: The history of the volcano of Jorullo and the reclamation of the devastated district of animals and plants*. London, Cambridge University Press, 101 p. Copyright © 1930 by the Cambridge University Press. Reprinted with permission.

Gutiérrez, C. (1972) A narrative of human response to natural disaster: The eruption of Parícutin. In: Mary Lee Nolan (editor), *San Juan Nuevo Parangaricutiro: Memories of past years*. Environmental Quality Note No. 7. College Station, Texas A & M University: 78 p. Copyright © 1972 by the University of Texas. Reprinted with permission.

Hasenaka T. and Carmichael I.S.E. (1985a) The cinder cones of Michoacán-Guanajuato, Central México: Their age, volume and distribution, and magma discharge rate. *Journal of Volcanology and Geothermal Research*, 25: 105-124. Copyright © 1985 by Elsevier Science Publishers, B.V. Reprinted with permission.

Hasenaka T. and Carmichael I.S.E. (1987) The cinder cones of Michoacán-Guanajuato, central México: Petrology and chemistry, *Journal of Petrology*, 28 (2): 241-269. Copyright © 1987 by Oxford University Press. Reprinted with permission.

Kennedy G.C. (1946) Activity of Parícutin volcano from April 12 to May 3, 1946. *Eos, Transactions of the American Geophysical Union*, 27 (3): 410-411. Copyright © 1946 by the American Geophysical Union. Reprinted with permission.

Krauskopf K. (1948a) Mechanism of eruption at Parícutin volcano, México. *Geological Society of America Bulletin* 59: 711-731. Reprinted with permission of author.

Krauskopf K. (1948b) Lava movement at Parícutin volcano, México. *Geological Society of America Bulletin* 59: 1267-1283. Reprinted with permission of author.

Krauskopf K. and Williams H. (1946) The activity of Parícutin during its third year. *Eos, Transactions of the American Geophysical Union*, 27 (3): 406-410. Copyright © 1946 by the American Geophysical Union. Reprinted with permission.

Luhr J.F. and Carmichael I.S.E. (1985) Jorullo Volcano, Michoacán, México (1759-1774): The earliest stages of fractionation in calc-alkaline magmas. *Contributions to*

Mineralogy and Petrology, 90: 142-161. Copyright © 1985 by Springer-Verlag. Reprinted with permission.

McBirney A.R., Taylor H.P. Jr., and Armstrong R.L. (1987) Parícutin re-examined: A classic example of crustal assimilation in calc-alkaline magma. *Contributions to Mineralogy and Petrology*, 95: 4-20. Copyright © 1987 by Springer-Verlag. Reprinted with permission.

Nolan M.L. (1979) Impact of Parícutin on five communities, in *Volcanic Activity and Human Ecology*, P.D. Sheets and D.K. Grayson, eds., 293-338. Copyright © 1979 by Academic Press, Inc. Reprinted with permission.

Ordóñez, E. (1947) *El Volcán de Parícutin*. Editorial Fantasia, Mixcoac, D.F., 181 p. Copyright © 1947 by Editorial Fantasia.

Rees J.D. (1979) Effects of the eruption of Parícutin volcano on landforms, vegetation, and human occupancy, in *Volcanic Activity and Human Ecology*, P.D. Sheets and D.K. Grayson, eds., 249-292. Copyright © 1979 by Academic Press, Inc. Reprinted with permission.

Segerstrom K. and Gutiérrez C. (1947) Activity of Parícutin volcano from May 4 to September 8, 1946. *Eos, Transactions of the American Geophysical Union*, 28 (4): 559-566. Copyright © 1947 by the American Geophysical Union. Reprinted with permission.

Wilcox R.E. (1947a) Activity of Parícutin volcano from September 18 to November 30, 1946. *Eos, Transactions of the American Geophysical Union*, 28 (4): 567-572. Copyright © 1947 by the American Geophysical Union. Reprinted with permission.

Wilcox R.E. (1947b) Activity of Parícutin volcano from December 1 1946 to March 31, 1947. *Eos, Transactions of the American Geophysical Union*, 28 (5): 725-731. Copyright © 1947 by the American Geophysical Union. Reprinted with permission.

Wilcox R.E. (1948a) Activity of Parícutin volcano from April 1 to July 31, 1947. *Eos, Transactions of the American Geophysical Union*, 29 (1): 69-74. Copyright © 1948 by the American Geophysical Union. Reprinted with permission.

Wilcox R.E. (1948b) Activity of Parícutin volcano from December 1, 1947 to March 31, 1948. *Eos, Transactions of the American Geophysical Union*, 29 (3): 355-360. Copyright © 1948 by the American Geophysical Union. Reprinted with permission.

Wilcox R.E. and Gutiérrez, C. (1948) Activity of Parícutin volcano fron April 1 to July 31, 1948. *Eos, Transactions of the American Geophysical Union*, 29 (6): 877-881. Copyright © 1948 by the American Geophysical Union. Reprinted with permission.

Wilcox R.E. and Shoup-Oropeza S. (1948) Activity of Parícutin volcano from August 1 to November 30, 1947. *Eos, Transactions of the American Geophysical Union*, 29: 74-79. Copyright © 1948 by the American Geophysical Union. Reprinted with permission.

Yokoyama I. and De la Cruz-Reyna S. (1990) Precursory earthquakes of the 1943 eruption of Parícutin volcano, Michoacán, México. *Journal of Volcanology and Geothermal Research*, 44: 265-281. Copyright © 1990 by Elsevier Science Publishers, B.V. Reprinted with permission.

Zies E.G. (1946) Temperature measurements at Parícutin volcano. *Eos, Transactions of the American Geophysical Union*, 27: 178-180. Copyright © 1946 by the American Geophysical Union. Reprinted with permission.

Index

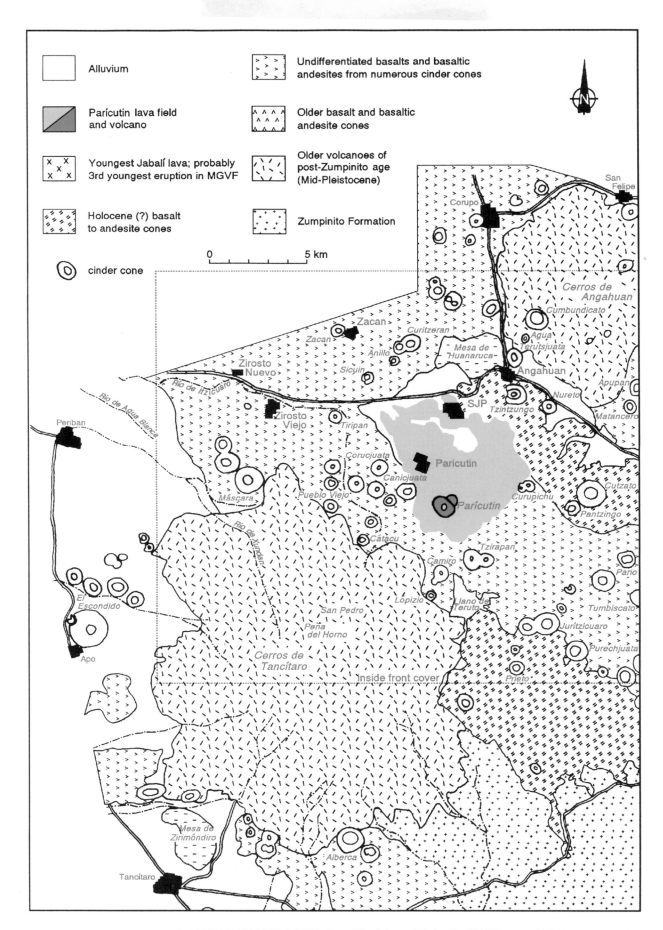

GEOLOGIC MAP OF PARICUTIN AREA (modified from Plate 8 of Williams, 1950)